CW01021161

VARIETIES OF ANOMALOUS EXPERIENCE

VARIETIES OF ANOMALOUS EXPERIENCE:
Examining the Scientific Evidence

EDITED BY

ETZEL CARDEÑA,

STEVEN JAY LYNN, &

STANLEY KRIPPNER

AMERICAN PSYCHOLOGICAL ASSOCIATION

WASHINGTON, DC

Published by
American Psychological Association
750 First Street, NE
Washington, DC 20002

Copies may be ordered from
APA Order Department
P.O. Box 92984
Washington, DC 20090-2984

In the U.K., Europe, Africa, and the Middle East, copies may be ordered from
American Psychological Association
3 Henrietta Street
Covent Garden, London
WC2E 8LU England

Typeset in Goudy by EPS Group Inc., Easton, MD

Printer: Data Reproductions Corporation, Auburn Hills, MI
Cover Designer: Anne Masters, Washington, DC
Technical/Production Editors: Rachael J. Stryker, Amy J. Clarke, and Kristine Enderle

The opinions and statements published are the responsibility of the authors, and such opinions and statements do not necessarily represent the policies of the APA.

Library of Congress Cataloging-in-Publication Data
Cardeña, Etzel.
    Varieties of anomalous experience : examining the scientific evidence /
Etzel Cardeña, Steven J. Lynn, Stanley C. Krippner.
        p.   cm.
    Includes bibliographical references and index.
    ISBN 1-55798-625-8 (alk. paper)
    1. Parapsychology.   I. Lynn, Steven Jay   II. Krippner, Stanley,
1932–   .   III. Title.
BF1031.C2455   2000
133—dc21   99-045473

British Library Cataloguing-in-Publication Data
A CIP record is available from the British Library.

Printed in the United States of America
Second Printing July 2001

To Himy, an ever-inspiring model of grace and joy. And to my wonderful companions—Blueberry and Ninnifer—who make me anomalously happy
E. C.

To Jessica, my effervescent daughter, a sparkling presence in my life
S. J. L.

To Jeanne Achterberg, Theodore X. Barber, Marcello Truzzi, and Erika Fromm, who have combined open-mindedness with scientific rigor to explore the outer limits of human capacities
S. K.

CONTENTS

CONTRIBUTORS

Jeanne Achterberg, PhD, Saybrook Graduate School, San Francisco, CA

Carlos S. Alvarado, PhD, International and Domestic Programs of the Parapsychology Foundation, New York City, NY/Centro Caribeño de Estudios Post-graduados, San Juan, PR

Stuart Appelle, PhD, Department of Psychology, State University of New York at Brockport

Richard P. Bentall, PhD, Department of Psychology, University of Manchester, Manchester, England

Howard Berenbaum, PhD, Department of Psychology, University of Illinois at Champaign–Urbana

Etzel Cardeña, PhD, Department of Psychiatry, Uniformed Services University of Health Services, Bethesda, MD

Jayne Gackenbach, PhD, Department of Psychology, Athabasca University, Athabasca, Alberta, Canada

Bruce Greyson, MD, Division of Personality Studies, University of Virginia, Charlottesville

Harvey J. Irwin, PhD, Department of Psychology, University of New England, Armidale, New South Wales, Australia

John Kerns, MA, Department of Psychology, University of Illinois at Champaign–Urbana

Stanley Krippner, PhD, Saybrook Graduate School, San Francisco, CA

Stephen LaBerge, PhD, The Lucidity Institute, Palo Alto, CA

Steven Jay Lynn, PhD, Department of Psychology, State University of New York at Binghamton

Lawrence E. Marks, PhD, John B. Pierce Laboratory, and Yale University, New Haven, CT

Antonia Mills, PhD, First Nations Studies, University of Northern British Columbia, Prince George, British Columbia, Canada

Leonard Newman, PhD, Department of Psychology, University of
  Illinois at Chicago
Ronald J. Pekala, PhD, Coatesville VA Medical Center, West Chester,
  PA
Chitra Raghavan, PhD, Department of Psychiatry, Yale University, New
  Haven, CT
Marilyn Schlitz, PhD, Institute of Noetic Sciences, Sausalito, CA
Elisabeth Targ, MD, California Pacific Medical Center,
  San Francisco
David M. Wulff, PhD, Department of Psychology, Wheaton College,
  Norton, MA

ACKNOWLEDGMENTS

We are fortunate to have had a series of enthusiastic and competent editors at APA who shepherded this book to completion: Joy Chau, acquisition editor; Adrian Harris Forman, development editor; and Rachael Stryker, production editor. Kelly Gooding did an outstanding job editing the manuscript, and Steve Hart did some excellent sleuthing to locate obscure references. Our appreciation is also extended to Arthur Hastings and Scott Lilienfeld for their thoughtful, comprehensive, and helpful reviews of the volume.

VARIETIES OF ANOMALOUS EXPERIENCE

INTRODUCTION: ANOMALOUS EXPERIENCES IN PERSPECTIVE

ETZEL CARDEÑA, STEVEN JAY LYNN, AND STANLEY KRIPPNER

Evolution . . . is a change from an indefinite, incoherent homogeneity, to a definite coherent heterogeneity. (Spencer, 1862/1991)

Tales of strange, extraordinary, and unexplained experiences and encounters with the "unknown" have long fascinated artists, scientists, and the lay audience. The period of the 19th-century European Romanticism was a time of deep interest in alterations of consciousness; such works as George Eliot's *The Lifted Veil* featured reputed parapsychological phenomena as a central part of their plot. In the 20th century, the Surrealist movement paid special attention to automatic writing and drawing, altered states of consciousness, and dreams. As evidence of more recent popular interest in anomalous phenomena, one need look no further than to the enormous international popularity of such television programs as *The Twilight Zone* or *The X-Files* during the second half of the 20th century. At the beginning of the 21st century, popular interest in such topics as near-death experiences, purported parapsychological phenomena, and mystical events has remained very strong. This can be understood, in part, because many anomalous experiences seem to hold great significance for those who have them or even for those who just vicariously partake of them.

In contrast to the public fascination with these phenomena, traditional psychology has long neglected or even derided them. Indeed, anomalous experiences are examples of what postmodernists refer to as "the other"—those phenomena that have fallen between the cracks of contemporary mainstream psychology. However, we believe that psychology has achieved enough maturity and breadth that it can take a serious look at unusual but important experiences.

Before we proceed further, it is important to clarify how we use the term *anomalous experience*. The English word *anomalous* derives from the Greek *anomalos*, meaning irregular, uneven, or unequal, in contrast to

3

homalos, which means the same or common. An anomalous experience is irregular in that it differs from common experiences, is uneven in that it is not the same as experiences that are even and ordinary. Typically, it is also unequal in that it does not draw the same attention, at least in academia, as that given to regular experiences.

We define an *anomalous experience* as an uncommon experience (e.g., synesthesia) or one that, although it may be experienced by a substantial amount of the population (e.g., experiences interpreted as telepathic), is believed to deviate from ordinary experience or from the usually accepted explanations of reality. The focus of this book is on experiences, not on testing the consensual validity of such experiences. For instance, the possibility of verified parapsychological phenomena is briefly mentioned in chapter 7 under explanatory theories, but the focus is on the experiences people have, not on the external phenomena to which they may refer, nor on "unusual people" (see, for example, Dingwall, 1962).

Although there is some overlap, we distinguish anomalous experiences from altered states of consciousness (e.g., Tart, 1969). Whereas some of the former do occur during an alteration of consciousness (e.g., near-death experiences; see Greyson, this volume, chap. 10), anomalous experiences such as synesthesia (Marks, this volume, chap. 4) may be part of the ordinary state of consciousness of the individual. We also distinguish experience from procedures such as hypnosis or meditation, which may or may not produce a major alteration in consciousness.

We also contrast *anomalous*, a term that does not have any necessary implication of psychopathology, with *abnormal*, a term that usually denotes pathology. Notwithstanding the presence of anomalous experiences in case studies of disturbed individuals, surveys of nonclinical samples have found little relationship between these experiences and psychopathology (e.g., Greeley, 1975; Spanos, Cross, Dickson, & Dubreuil, 1993). This is the case even in hallucinations, often used as a landmark of psychopathology (see Bentall, this volume, chap. 3). The relationship between psychopathology and belief systems that involve anomalous experiences is more complex because of the multidimensional structure of beliefs (Krippner & Winkler, 1996). Nonetheless, the various contributions to this volume make clear that holding such unusual beliefs as the reality of alien abduction is not an indicator per se of psychopathology (see Appelle, Lynn, & Newman, this volume, chap. 8).

Other disciplines have also used the terms *anomalous*, *anomalies*, and *anomalistic*, but only to refer to seemingly unexplainable events (i.e., a demonstrable occurrence) rather than experiences (i.e., a psychological event that may or may not be associated with a demonstrable consensual occurrence). For instance, parapsychologists often use these terms to denote an event in which there is purported access to unavailable information, such as a dream report of an airplane disaster that coincided with an actual event (e.g., Thalbourne, 1982). In an important article, the sociologist Marcello Truzzi (1971) wrote that anomalous phenomena "contradict commonsense or institutionalized (scientific or religious) knowledge"; they are "anomalous to our generally accepted cultural storehouse of truths" (p. 637). Similarly, the anthropologist Roger Wescott (1977) suggested that the word *anomalistic* be used as a prefix to the name of any discipline dealing with so-called paranormal topics. Some of these topics, for instance the possibility of the existence of Bigfoot, do not necessarily involve anomalous experiences.

INDIVIDUAL AND CULTURAL IMPORTANCE

A striking aspect of some anomalous experiences is that, even when single and transitory, they are reported to have an enormous impact on the experient. An individual may undergo a change in values after a near-death or an anomalous healing experience (see this volume, Greyson, chap. 10; Krippner & Achterberg, chap. 11), or mystics may describe experiences that will also influence many people (Wulff, this volume, chap. 12). The attribution of personal meaning to anomalous experiences has been addressed by such writers as James McClenon (1994b), who referred to them as "wondrous events" (suggesting that they stimulated the development of religious ideologies). Daniel A. Helminiak (1984) called them "extraordinary experiences" (depending on whether they further the experient's "authentic growth"), and Rhea A. White (1995) referred to them as "exceptional human experiences" (noting their transformational potential in people's lives).

To determine that an experience is uncommon or anomalous, we have to consider the cultural framework in which the evaluation of the experience occurs. Many years ago, Ruth Benedict (1934) reminded us that what is normal (or pathological) in one culture may not be so in a different one. In a similar vein, in his book *Anomalies of Personality*, the Russian psychologist Boris Bratus (1988/1990), basing his argument on statistical averages, proposed that what is anomalous in one culture may be the norm in another culture (p. 4). He used the term *anomalous* in the sense of a personality characteristic that deviates markedly from a cultural norm.

Summarizing a number of surveys conducted in the United States, MacDonald (1994) concluded that age, education, gender, race, religion, and socioeconomic status influence the likelihood of reporting various paranormal experiences, and he attributed the differences to the "shaping of individual realities" (p. 36). MacDonald conjectured that "the reality of human experience is socially constructed and is therefore subject to variation depending on the social context" (p. 36). The sociologist James McClenon's (1994a) review of the literature on altered states of consciousness and anomalous experience persuaded him that such traits as absorption, dissociation, fantasy proneness, and hypnotic susceptibility need to be considered to understand these states (see also Cardeña, 1996). McClenon considered these traits to be "normal human capacities which have not been thoroughly studied in non-clinical populations" (p. 129). The contributors to this book point out that psychology has made progress in understanding these variables and their relationship to anomalous experiences. The focus of this book is psychological, but we should not forget that neurological pathologies, such as temporal lobe abnormalities or head injuries, can give rise to unusual phenomena (Cardeña, 1997; George, 1995).

A BRIEF HISTORY

The study of anomalous experiences is currently a marginal area of concern for psychology, but it has not always been so neglected. Some of the topics covered in this book, including mystical and psi-related experiences, have figured in the history of psychodynamic psychiatry (see Ellenberger, 1970). In this Introduction, we give an overview of the psychological study of anomalous experiences, which has, at times, also included the study of anomalous events, cognitive misattributions, and related topics.

The first systematic inquiry into various anomalous experiences can be traced to the founding of the Society for Psychical Research (SPR) in London in 1882. Various notable scientists and philosophers gathered "to investigate that large body of debatable phenomena . . . without prejudice or prepossession of any kind, and in the same spirit of exact and unimpassioned inquiry which has enabled Science to solve so many problems" (Society for Psychical Research, 1882–1883, p. 2). Although the goals of the Society centered on testing claims of such purported psi phenomena as telepathy and clairvoyance (see Targ, Schlitz, & Irwin, this volume, chap. 7), it was also interested in the study of personality, dissociative phenomena, hypnosis, preconscious cognition, and related topics (Gurney, Myers, & Podmore, 1886). A few years after the founding of the SPR, a similar organization, led by William James and others, was established in the United States.

In contrast to the British and American Societies for Psychical Research, which are open to the general public, the Parapsychological Association, founded in 1957 and an affiliate of the American Association for the Advancement of Science since 1969, consists of professional members from different countries. This association is committed to looking for scientific explanations of anomalous events and experiences. (For a brief history of the scientific approach to parapsychological phenomena, see Rush, 1986.)

Within the realms of clinical and general psychology, William James (1890/1923) provided a comprehensive survey of the "Science of Mental Life, both of its phenomena and of their conditions" (p. 1). With his vast erudition and incomparable prose, James discussed anomalous phenomena in chapters dealing with more classical topics such as memory or the self. Our book follows the spirit of James's "radical empiricism," which includes the totality of human experience within the boundaries of scientific investigation. Our title, of course, pays homage to James's (1902/1958) classic volume, *The Varieties of Religious Experience*.

Besides James, F. W. H. Myers (1903/1961) attempted a bold integration of such areas as personality, sleep, and hypnosis, and other members of the scientific vanguard studied anomalous experiences. H. Sidgwick, Johnson, Myers, Podmore, and Sidgwick (1894) analyzed some 17,000 responses to the question "Have you ever . . . had a vivid impression of seeing, or being touched, or of hearing a voice; which impression, so far as you could discover, was not due to any external cause?" Affirmative answers were obtained from about 1 in 10 respondents and were categorized as sensory hallucinations (visual hallucinations were more common than auditory or tactile), ordinary sense perceptions, dreams, and what today would be considered eidetic imagery. It is striking how well the results of this study have withstood the test of time (see Bentall, this volume, chap. 3). Another landmark in the study of anomalous experiences was an inquiry into reputed psi-related phenomena, *Phantasms of the Living* (Gurney et al., 1886).

Théodore Flournoy (1901/1994), a psychology professor at the University of Geneva, wrote an in-depth case study of a medium who spoke in different voices, wrote in different handwriting styles, and used different names. Rather than positing deception or accepting the medium's claim of contact with the "spirit world," Flournoy made a case for multiple personality and produced a sophisticated interpretation of the psychodynamic foundations of the imaginary languages involved. A friend of Flournoy, Carl G. Jung (1902/1970), conducted a landmark study with another medium. Using a word-association test he had developed, Jung traced the origins of the names the medium gave him of her own "spirit guides" and of the "forces" that guide the universe. Jung terminated his work when the medium, Jung's young and enamored cousin, exhausted her flights of fancy. Later it was found that at least part of her mediumistic performances had fraudulent aspects (Ellenberger, 1970). Jung would later use his analytic psychology to explain UFO sightings and other unusual events (Jung, 1959).

The French clinical tradition at the turn of the 19th century was engaged in developing a general psychology of cognition, emotion, and experience that would be informed by abnormal conditions. For instance, Alfred Binet, mostly known to psychologists as the suffix of the Stanford–Binet IQ test, wrote an important treatise on the dissociation of identity,

On Double Consciousness (see Robinson, 1998). Another eminent French psychologist, Theodule A. Ribot, authored scientific studies on *Diseases of the Will* and *The Diseases of Personality* (see Robinson, 1998). The most lasting contributions to this area can be traced, however, to the landmark works of Pierre Janet, who researched and theorized on, among other topics, pathological and nonpathological forms of dissociation, hypnosis, memory, and the sense of time (see Van der Hart, 1998).

From the Germanic and Austrian traditions, clinicians also made important contributions to the study and conceptualization of anomalous experiences. Sigmund Freud's goal was to build a psychoanalytic theory that would "shed light upon unusual, abnormal, or pathological manifestations of the mind" (Freud, 1936/1984, p. 447), and we cannot fail to mention Karl Jaspers's undervalued *General Psychopathology* (1923/1963). Jaspers also aimed to understand abnormal and anomalous events, and his detailed descriptive analysis of experience provided an alternative to traditional psychodynamic and diagnostic classifications of psychopathology.

With regard to unusual beliefs or explanations, a student of Wilhelm Wundt, the Danish psychologist Alfred Lehmann, published a book titled *Superstition and Magic* (1898). In it, he focused on observational errors, such as the misinterpretation of optical effects, that were responsible for false belief systems. Lehmann granted that some extraordinary phenomena could not be explained away by errors of observation and would have to wait for a scientific explanation.

A few years later, the psychologist Joseph Jastrow collected a series of his essays in a book titled *Fact and Fable in Psychology* (1900). These essays provided conventional scientific explanations to anomalous beliefs. He pointed out how experience is reified, belief systems often influence interpretations of experience, and speculation takes precedence over authentication. In a later book, *Wish and Wisdom*, Jastrow (1935) posited that "wishful thinking" interferes with rationality, and he systematically applied this hypothesis to a number of anomalous experiences.

The decades-long dominance of behaviorism, launched by J. B. Watson's (1913) call to arms against the study of consciousness within psychology, explains why the more comprehensive program for psychology proposed by James and others did not progress for a number of decades. Even B. F. Skinner's less restrictive behaviorism did not study introspective reports on their own terms, but only as "verbal behaviors." The ascent of modern cognitive psychology as a dominant force in the 1950s and 1960s provided a valid framework to study mental processes (Gardner, 1985), but the study of subjective experiences, especially anomalous ones, had to wait even longer.

The first modern, systematic attempt to explain anomalous experience was *The Psychology of Anomalous Experience*, written by Canadian psychologist Graham Reed (1972, 1988). Reed studied unusual experiences from a cognitive–experiential perspective. He discussed anomalies of attention, imagery and perception, recall, recognition, experience of self, judgment and belief, qualities of consciousness, and flow of consciousness. Although a slim volume, Reed's work deserves careful attention.

Leonard Zusne and Warren H. Jones (1980, 1989) treaded a similar path to that of Jastrow in their book *Anomalistic Psychology,* the second edition of which was subtitled *A Study of Magical Thinking.* They contended that "magical thinking is wholly or partly at the root of any explanation of behavioral and experiential phenomena that violates some law of nature or suggests, without supporting evidence, the existence of principles, forces, or entities unknown to science" (Zusne & Jones, 1989, p. 13). To them, anomalous psychological phenomena are "those behaviors and experiences that seem to violate natural laws" (p. ix). Zusne and Jones (1989) presented a useful example of the relative aspect of some beliefs. When comparing bleeding from peptic ulcers and from stigmata, they wrote, "The difference between the psychophysiologically normal and the psychophysiologically anomalistic is only a matter of statistical incidence and the cultural context within which the event happens" (p. 34).

Two recent books have analyzed various forms of faulty thinking that may give rise to the belief in unusual events. Thomas Gilovich (1993) discussed cognitive (e.g., misperception and misinterpretation of random data), motivational (e.g., "seeing what we want to see"), and social (e.g., biasing effects of second-hand information) determinants of questionable beliefs in anomalous events. Theodore Schick and Lewis Vaughn (1995) discussed a number of ways in which valuable information can be ignored or misrepresented while questionable forms of evidence such as tradition or the authority of the person making a pronouncement can be overvalued. They proposed a formula in which claims need to be clearly stated, the evidence for the claims must be looked at carefully, and any alternative hypotheses must be considered and rated according to certain criteria of adequacy. To their credit, Schick and Vaughn (1995) concluded that their "considerations should not be taken as the final word on the matters investigated here" (p. 281), and they pointed out that at least one parapsychology researcher had met some of the challenges from his harshest critics (p. 231). Ray Hyman (Hyman & Honorton, 1986), a noted critic of parapsychology research, agreed that some data obtained under controlled conditions "cannot reasonably be explained by selective reporting or multiple analysis . . . (and) the final verdict awaits the outcome of future . . . experiments" (pp. 352–353).

THE PRESENT INVESTIGATION

We decided to compile this volume because we share a fascination with these phenomena, and we believe that current empirical and conceptual developments in psychology can prevent it from falling prey to either naive scrutiny or automatic rejection. Like many readers of this book, we were partly drawn to a life of science and the study of psychology by the "big" questions that some anomalous experiences pose about the nature of reality and human consciousness: What is the relationship between our conscious experience and what we call the physical world? How does healing occur? What are the boundaries between dreaming and waking life? Is there credible evidence that thoughts affect the material world or can be transferred by extrasensory means? Does consciousness persist after death? What do mystical experiences tell us about the nature of reality?

Science may not have come very far in addressing the ontological status of these questions, but readers of the book will discover that psychology has much to offer in terms of proposing appropriate ways to obtain and evaluate evidence, characterize variables associated with these phenomena, and describe and investigate anomalous experiences. In turn, some anomalous experiences may have much to offer science in terms of clarifying its current boundaries and identifying how psychology, the neurosciences, and the social sciences can join hands to explain the "dome of many-coloured glass" of life, to borrow Lord Percy Bysshe Shelley's beautiful image.

SUMMARY OF THE CHAPTERS

Part I of the book, devoted to conceptual and methodological issues, includes a chapter on the relationship among personality traits, anomalous experiences, and psychopathology, and one on the methodological opportunities and pitfalls facing the researcher of anomalous experiences.

In chapter 1, Howard Berenbaum, John Kerns, and Chitra Raghavan provide a useful model to understand peculiar sensations, experiences, and beliefs and their relation to anomalous experiences and psychopathology. Specifically, Berenbaum et al. propose that anomalous experiences can be systematically described in terms of the individual's level of awareness at the time of the experience (e.g., was the person fully conscious?) and of the ability to exert voluntary control over the onset and course of the experience. These experiences can be further classified according to the phenomenological dimensions of hedonic valence (i.e., pleasantness vs. unpleasantness), physical and metaphysical qualities (i.e., sensory focused or apparently crossing "barriers of mind, body, and space"), and any reported involvement with an individual or entity as a significant aspect of the experience.

Berenbaum et al. explore the ways in which a variety of factors, such as personality traits, trauma, and atypical patterns of brain functioning, may contribute to both psychopathology and anomalous experiences. They conclude their chapter with 10 recommendations for investigators who wish to advance the knowledge of the relationship among anomalous experiences, peculiarity, and psychopathology.

In chapter 2, Ron Pekala and Etzel Cardeña examine methodological issues in the study of altered states of consciousness and anomalous experiences. They also define and discuss the strengths and weaknesses of various methods used to study inner experience. After reviewing variables that may distort or even invalidate introspective reports (e.g., forgetting and demand characteristics), the authors describe and give examples of introspective methods (e.g., thought sampling and depth ratings) that have been fruitful in the study of normal and anomalous experience. Because reports of anomalous experiences are often accompanied by little or no corroborating physiological data or physical evidence, it is important to have a balanced evaluation of the limitations, reliability, and validity of psychological methods to study experience. The second section of the chapter is devoted to the quantitative psychophenomenological approach developed by Pekala and his colleagues (Gallagher, Kumar, & Pekala, 1994).

Although chapter 2 emphasizes research methodology, its treatment of potential threats to the validity and reliability of subjective reports should make it valuable to the clinician as well. Pekala and Cardeña also address the importance of *individual differences* in reference to who is most likely to report anomalous phenomena, and they propose specific steps to advance the study of anomalous experiences and altered states.

Part II of the book, devoted to reviews of various anomalous experiences, is grouped according to the categories described by Berenbaum et al. in the first chapter. The first section of Part II includes three sensory-focused experiences: hallucinations, synesthesia, and lucid dreaming.

Richard Bentall's chapter on hallucinations (chap. 3) provides an authoritative review of perceptlike experiences that occur in the absence of an appropriate stimulus, yet have the full force or impact of the actual corresponding perception. Although auditory and visual hallucinations are most frequently reported, any sense modality can have its corresponding hallucinatory equivalent. Some individuals adapt to recurring hallucinations, whereas others (especially individuals diagnosed with schizophrenia) have difficulty coping with them, often becoming tortured and distressed.

Of particular interest to clinicians is that large-scale surveys have identified fairly large percentages of nonclinical populations who report occasional hallucinations that are not deleterious but are even, at times, seemingly beneficial. Contrary to common belief, hallucinations are not the exclusive province of psychopathology.

In chapter 4, Lawrence Marks addresses *synesthesia*, the phenomenon in which sensory perceptions in one modality, for instance, vision, are also experienced in another modality, such as taste and hearing. In weak synesthesia, a person may describe the major and minor keys of a musical piece as bright and dark, respectively. In the case of the considerably more dramatic, phenomenologically distinct, and much rarer (fewer than 3 people per million) strong synesthesia, a musical note may stimulate a sparkling yellow color that appears very soon after the note is played and disappears slowly as the sound fades out. Strong synesthesia is vivid, intense, reliably evoked, and occurs automatically and involuntarily. Marks describes how these different kinds of synesthesia are subjectively experienced and expressed behaviorally and neurophysiologically. He also examines a number of explanations for synesthesia, including the theory that synesthetically related sensations represent the outcome of similarities in the neural coding mechanisms of different sensory systems.

In chapter 5, Stephen LaBerge and Jayne Gackenbach define *lucid dreaming* as dreaming while knowing that one is dreaming. The authors contend that this experience is clearly anomalous in comparison with the usual hallucinatory experience of nonlucid dreaming that characterizes most of our dream life. The research on the area is reviewed and different explanations for the genesis of lucid dreaming are surveyed, including information-processing models and psychophysiological perspectives.

Although lucid dreaming is a rare experience for most people, a variety of techniques have been advanced to induce it. This is a fortunate development, considering the reports that lucid dreams may have therapeutic potential in terms of nightmare management, resolving unfinished business in dealing with the death of a loved one, and in bypassing defenses and promoting personal insight.

The next section of Part II includes two types of "detachment" experiences: out-of-body and psi-related experiences.

In the out-of-body experience (OBE), people experience that their "self" or center of awareness is located outside of their physical body. According to Carlos Alvarado (chap. 6), this experience includes such features as sensations of floating, traveling to distant locations, and observing one's own physical body from outside the body. OBEs have been associated with fantasy proneness, hypnotizability, absorption, the ability to change imagery perspective, and dissociation. It is of interest that one's ability to have an OBE is correlated with one's ability to control the content of dreams or terminate them. These findings are consistent with what Alvarado terms a *psychological model* of OBE that describes this phenomenon as an imaginary or hallucinatory experience. Alvarado proposes a number of research directions and creative methodologies for inducing OBEs in the laboratory. In his concluding statement, which parallels our own stance, Alvarado proposes that future research and discourse on the topic not be "conducted solely in the context of a psychology of the exotic or the unusual, but rather in the wider context of the study of the totality of human experience."

In chapter 7, "Psi-Related Experiences," Elisabeth Targ, Marilyn Schlitz, and Harvey Irwin examine reported experiences of direct mind-to-mind communication, knowledge of distant occurrences, information about the future, and direct mental influence on the environment (collectively referred to as *psi* by parapsychological investigators). These reports have been ubiquitous throughout history, but their frequency has varied in different times and locations. Many psi-related experiences take place in dreams and other altered states of consciousness. Theoretical explanations offered include the presence of cognitive deficits or misattributions, social marginality, psychodynamic needs, as well as the possibility that experients may be reporting veridical phenomena that must be taken seriously by mainstream science. Psi-related experiences are anomalous not because they are unusual in the population—they are not—but because these reported interactions between organisms and their environments appear to contradict mainstream science's constructs of time, space, and energy.

The alien abduction experience (AAE) is a type of "corporeal movement" experience, and it is surely one of the most disturbing phenomena described in this book. As defined by Stuart Appelle, Steven Jay Lynn, and Leonard Newman in chapter 8, AAEs are characterized by subjectively real memories of being taken secretly or against one's will by apparently nonhuman entities, usually to a location interpreted as an alien spacecraft (i.e., an unidentified flying object, or UFO), and subjected to complex physical and psychological procedures. In recent years, an increasing number of reports have emphasized sexual intercourse with aliens, with some women claiming to have multiple offspring that are kept by the aliens.

The AAE is a dynamic, elaborate, and involved experience, rich in contextual detail, with considerable perceptual, psychological, cognitive, and physical concomitants. Many thousands of Americans have had an AAE, and this experience, as "nonordinary" as it appears to be, does not typically imply psychopathology. Aspects of AAEs have been explained in terms of fantasy proneness or sleep-related experiences (e.g., vivid imagery and sleep paralysis); as an attempt to escape from self-awareness through masochistic fantasy; and in terms of media influences, cultural influences, and suggestive psychotherapeutic influences that shape the memories and interpretations of the experience. In response to the claim that the AAE phenomenon does not suffer from a lack of hypotheses but from a lack of persuasive research, Appelle et al. outline methodological issues and problems that have limited research to date and make suggestions for how research and theoretical development can proceed in the future.

As a subcategory of "human transformation" experiences, chapter 9 discusses reports of past lives. Antonia Mills and Steven Jay Lynn define *past-life experiences* as the distinct impression that an individual holds of having been a different person in a previous time, and where the overlay of the past identity does not deny the current identity. The authors contrast cases that seem to arise spontaneously with cases experienced during hypnosis or following the intervention of a purported medium or psychic.

Mills and Lynn emphasize spontaneous cases of past-life experiences and evaluate explanations that include reincarnation, outright fraud, and extrasensory perception (i.e., telepathic or clairvoyant discernment of the nature of a deceased person). Another theory is that cultural forces can account for the genesis of past-life reports and their variability across disparate cultures. As in the case of alien abduction reports, fraud and chicanery can be ruled out in many, if not most, instances. The chapter concludes with a searching critique of the research base of this phenomenon and makes a number of creative suggestions for pursuing future research.

We conclude the volume with three chapters on "transcendent transformations": near-death, anomalous healing, and mystical experiences.

In chapter 10, Bruce Greyson characterizes near-death experiences (NDEs) as "profound psychological events with transcendental or mystical elements," which typically occur close to death or in situations of intense physical or emotional danger. The elements of the NDE include (a) cognitive features, including time distortion, thought acceleration, and a life review; (b) affective features of peace, joy, cosmic unity, and an encounter with light; (c) apparent extrasensory perception and an OBE; and (d) otherworldly encounters with mystical beings, visible spirits, and an uncrossable border. Although the content of the NDE may vary from person to person, the experience often permanently and dramatically alters attitudes, beliefs, and values in beneficial ways, reducing fears of death and heightening the experient's appreciation of life.

Greyson argues that NDEs cannot be explained away as culturally constructed, expectancy-driven, hallucinations; the product of medications given to dying patients; or the metabolic disturbances or brain malfunctions of a person close to death. Greyson favors a biosociological approach, based on information and systems theories, that focuses on the structure and process of the NDE rather than its content. At the same time, he does not dismiss the "survival of consciousness beyond death" hypothesis.

It would be difficult to find someone who has not at least heard about purportedly remarkable or unusual healing experiences and events. In chapter 11, Stanley Krippner and Jeanne Achterberg make an important distinction between anomalous healing *events*, defined by unusual and unexplained treatment outcomes, and anomalous healing *experiences*, the out-of-ordinary experiences associated with treatment. The chapter includes a taxonomy of various types of healing practitioners and describes their anomalous experiences and those of their patients. The authors warn of the potential clinical risks of endorsing any therapeutic practice exclusively because of a belief system or an unusual experience. They provide an account of the leading explanatory models for anomalous healing experiences and events, as well as guidelines on how to improve the systematic study of this area. They conclude that the various means that individuals have used to enhance anomalous experiences and restore health deserve our careful attention.

We end the book with what may be the most influential of all anomalous experiences: the transcendental experience of unity known as *mysticism*. The claims of mystics about having an intuitive sense of the universe that belies everyday assumptions have contributed to the origin of most religions and, directly or indirectly, touched the lives of most humans. Following a similar path to William James' (1902/1958) seminal study of religious experience, in chapter 12 David Wulff considers these potentially life-changing events. He discusses the difficulty in providing a definition of mysticism and gives various examples and useful classifications of these experiences. He also describes the various methods, including meditation and psychedelic drugs, that have been associated with mysticism. Wulff elucidates the common aftereffects of mystical experiences, along with their therapeutic potentials and clinical risks, and concludes with an overview of the various explanations of mysticism, steering away from the twin dangers of false reductionism and uncritical overacceptance.

PURPOSE OF THIS BOOK

Previous books on anomalous experiences have typically been the work of one or two authors, who had the unenviable task of covering vast and disparate bodies of literature, or they have been anthologies in which the chapters did not follow the same structure and guidelines. We decided to do something different by inviting recognized international authorities on specific anomalous experiences to contribute chapters with a common outline. This approach gave us the opportunity to cover all the issues we thought were important, and it facilitates their comparison across chapters. We also asked contributors, regardless of their own theoretical stance, to evaluate in an even-handed manner the empirical support for their and alternative explanatory models.

Another important goal for us was to cover the basic research on these experiences, while addressing topics relevant to clinicians who have to evaluate the impact of these experiences in the lives of their clients. Some chapters, such as the one on psi-related experiences, have a wider coverage of clinical issues as compared with others, for instance synesthesia, for which the clinical implications of the topic are less central. Our aim is to satisfy the reader who wants a "state of the science" account of anomalous experiences, provide useful information to the clinician, and do justice to the experiences themselves.

Our list of anomalous experiences is not comprehensive; we sought to include experiences for which there is substantial research and that are generally considered more than transient curiosities by the experient (e.g., feelings of déjà vu). An arguably important omission is a chapter on dissociative experiences not already covered here (e.g., depersonalization). We did not include such a chapter because there are recent comprehensive anthologies (e.g., Lynn & Rhue, 1994; Michelson & Ray, 1996; Powers & Krippner, 1997) and descriptions of dissociative experiences (e.g., Cardeña, 1997) that provide useful overviews and because dissociation is discussed throughout the book.

The chapters we summarized highlight a number of important reasons to study anomalous experience:

1. To paraphrase William James, psychology cannot claim to be comprehensive if it fails to account for varieties of experiences distinct from those considered normal. To fully understand the totality of human experience, we need to provide reasonable accounts of phenomena that, although unusual (e.g., strong synesthesia; see Marks, this volume, chap. 4) or apparently far-fetched (e.g., alien abduction experiences; see Appelle, Lynn, & Newman this volume, chap. 8), are an important part of the totality of human experience. Whereas Pope and Singer's (1978) complaint of a lack of study on the "stream of consciousness" has been partly addressed in recent years, a serious discussion of anomalous experiences within psychology has lagged behind.

2. As the quotation by Herbert Spencer at the beginning of the chapter implies, the current interest in evolutionary psychology should make us suspect that variety in experience, as in behavior, is to be expected. The strong normative impact of language and social conventions may deceive us into believing that we are more alike than we really are. Furthermore, to refer to James again, it is likely that at least some anomalous experiences have their "field of application and adaptation" (James, 1902/1958, p. 298). The boldest claim for a "field of application" is probably found in mysticism (see Wulff, this volume, chap. 12) in which "ordinary" experience is presumed to be severely limited. Anomalous healing experiences offer a less radical but promising example.

3. It is germane to the clinician to be able to distinguish between what is merely anomalous and what is pathological or abnormal (Stevenson, 1995). Whereas, at times, the unusual experiences of prophets and mystics have been uncritically regarded as "divine," or neurological conditions have been wrongly identified as spiritual enlightenment (see Sacks, 1995), the pendulum may have swung too far to the other side when mysticism is described as brain failure (e.g., Rose,

1976). As the many contributors to this book make clear, there is no evidence that anomalous experiences, per se, indicate psychopathology. In fact, the motivations behind similar behavior may differ among clinically distressed and nondistressed individuals (Cardeña, in press). This consistent finding highlights the importance of understanding the difference between anomalous and abnormal behavior and experience. In the future, we expect that the clinician will consult this, or a similar volume, along with the *Diagnostic and Statistical Manual of Mental Disorders* (American Psychiatric Association, 1994) to help clarify the extent to which an experience does or does not imply pathology.

4. It is possible that some anomalous experiences may developmentally precede more usual experiences, as the greater prevalence of synesthetic phenomena in childhood suggests. Deikman (1966) and Hunt (1995) suggested that an understanding of mystical experiences helps clarify the development and nature of cognition in general. Thus, a full understanding of normal cognition may require a better understanding of and differentiation from anomalous experience.

5. Anomalous phenomena can elucidate the importance, and limits, of sociocultural variables on human experience. A good example is the study by Pasricha and Stevenson (1986), who found that near-death experients from India reported that they had to return to life because a "cosmic bureaucratic" mistake had been made. In contrast, experients in the United States typically report that they are "sent back" to fulfill their responsibilities or develop their potentials. The authors explained this difference in terms of the vast influence that bureaucracy has on Indian life, while pointing out that other aspects of the NDE are remarkably similar in those two countries.

6. Some anomalous experiences suggest that ordinary ones lack aspects that may enhance our appreciation of life (e.g., synesthesia, mysticism) or have other long-lasting beneficial effects (e.g., NDEs), as James remarked some decades ago. In Western and other cultures, people will continue searching for ways to affect their states of consciousness (e.g., Siegel, 1989), and increased psychological knowledge will add valuable information to assess the actual risks and benefits of various experiences. Also, if robust evidence accumulates that some anomalous healing experiences are associated with actual improvements in health, the nature of the healing pro-

cess may need to be reexamined (see Krippner & Achterberg, this volume, chap. 11).

7. In some cases, as in psi-related experiences, the results of controlled experiments have challenged widely held tenets about the relationship between consciousness and time–space constraints. Although this evidence is more persuasive to some researchers than to others, it seems clear to us that we need to research and know a great deal more before we can claim to have a full understanding of the relation between experience and the surrounding world (Broughton, 1991). And even if all unusual experiences are eventually found to refer to ordinary events, there are still several other compelling reasons to undertake the study of anomalous experience!

The time has come for psychologists and other social and behavioral scientists to seriously consider the varieties of anomalous experience and integrate them into theory, research, and clinical practice. Our book underscores many of the challenges facing the students of these experiences. They include the need to (a) approach and study unusual, and sometimes challenging, individuals and not just the usual convenience samples; (b) develop research methods appropriate to the area of concern, rather than assume that a "one method fits all" approach will work; (c) devise appropriate models of analysis and presentation of experiences that may be unfamiliar to the audience; and (d) seek to integrate findings into the larger corpus of psychology.

Any psychology that takes the challenge of William James to build a truly comprehensive discipline will have to carefully traverse the narrow path between the abysses of uncritical acceptance and outright dismissal of anomalous experiences. Only then may we be able to understand what compelled William Butler Yeats to write in *Vacillation*:

> While on the shop and street I gazed
> My body of a sudden blazed;
> And twenty minutes more or less
> It seemed, so great my happiness
> That I was blessed and could bless.

REFERENCES

American Psychiatric Association. (1994). *Diagnostic and statistical manual of mental disorders* (4th ed.). Washington, DC: Author.

Benedict, R. (1934). *Patterns of culture*. New York: Houghton Mifflin.

Bratus, B. B. (1990). *Anomalies of personality: From the deviant to the norm* (A.

Mikheyev, S. Mikheyev, & Y. Filippov, Trans.; H. Davis, Ed.). Orlando, FL: Paul M. Deutsch Press. (Original work published 1988)

Broughton, R. (1991). *Parapsychology. The controversial science.* New York: Ballantine.

Cardeña, E. (1996). "Just floating on the sky": A comparison of shamanic and hypnotic phenomenology. In R. Quekelbherge & D. Eigner (Eds.), *6th jahrbuch für transkulturelle medizin and psychotherapie* [6th yearbook of cross-cultural medicine and psychotherapy] (pp. 367–380). Berlin: Verlag für Wissenschaft und Bildung.

Cardeña, E. (1997). The etiologies of dissociation. In S. Powers & S. Krippner (Eds.), *Broken images, broken selves* (pp. 61–87). New York: Brunner/Mazel.

Cardeña, E. (in press). "You are not your body": Commentary on the motivation for self-injury in psychiatric patients. *Psychiatry.*

Deikman, A. J. (1966). Deautomatization and the mystic experience. *Psychiatry, 29,* 324–338.

Dingwall, E. (1962). *Very peculiar people: Portrait studies in the queer, the abnormal, and the uncanny.* New Hyde Park, NY: University Books.

Ellenberger, H. F. (1970). *The discovery of the unconscious.* New York: Basic Books.

Flournoy, T. (1994). *From India to the planet Mars: A case study in multiple personality with imaginary languages.* Princeton, NJ: Princeton University Press. (Original work published 1901)

Freud, S. (1984). A disturbance of memory on the Acropolis. In A. Richards (Ed.), *Volume II. On metapsychology* (pp. 443–456). Middlesex, England: Pelican. (Original work published 1936)

Gallagher, C., Kumar, V. K., & Pekala, R. J. (1994). The Anomalous Experiences Inventory: Reliability and validity. *Journal of Parapsychology, 58,* 402–428.

Gardner, H. (1985). *The mind's new science.* New York: Basic Books.

George, L. (1995). *Alternative realities: The paranormal, the mystic and the transcendent in human experience.* New York: Facts on File.

Gilovich, T. (1993). *How we know what isn't so.* New York: Free Press.

Greeley, A. M. (1975). *The sociology of the paranormal: A reconnaissance.* Beverly Hills, CA: Sage.

Gurney, E., Myers, F. W. H., & Podmore, F. (1886). *Phantasms of the living* (2 vols.). London: Trübner.

Helminiak, D. A. (1984). Neurology, psychology, and extraordinary religious experiences. *Journal of Religion and Health, 23,* 33–46.

Hunt, H. (1995). *The nature of consciousness.* New Haven, CT: Yale University Press.

Hyman, R., & Honorton, C. (1986). A joint communique: The psi ganzfeld controversy. *Journal of Parapsychology, 50,* 351–364.

James, W. (1923). *The principles of psychology.* New York: Holt. (Original work published 1890)

James, W. (1958). *The varieties of religious experience: A study in human nature*. New York: New American Library. (Original work published 1902)

Jaspers, K. (1963). *General psychopathology* (J. Hoenig & M. Hamilton, Trans.). Manchester, UK: University Press. (Original work published 1923)

Jastrow, J. (1900). *Fact and fable in psychology*. Boston: Houghton Mifflin.

Jastrow, J. (1935). *Wish and wisdom*. New York: Appleton-Century.

Jung, C. G. (1959). *Flying saucers: A modern myth of things seen in the skies*. New York: Harcourt Brace.

Jung, C. G. (1970). On the psychology and pathology of so-called occult phenomena. In *The collected works of C. G. Jung* (Vol. 1, pp. 6–91). Princeton, NJ: Princeton University Press. (Original work published 1902)

Krippner, S., & Winkler, M. (1996). The "need to believe." In G. Stein (Ed.), *The encyclopedia of the paranormal* (pp. 441–454). Amherst, NY: Prometheus Books.

Lehmann, A. (1898). *Aberglaube and zauberei* [Superstition and magic]. Stuttgart, Germany: Enke.

Lynn, S. J., & Rhue, J. W. (Eds.). (1994). *Dissociation: Clinical, theoretical, and research perspectives*. New York: Guilford Press.

MacDonald, W. L. (1994). The popularity of paranormal experiences in the United States. *Journal of American Culture, 1*, 35–42.

McClenon, J. (1994a). Surveys of anomalous experiences: A cross-cultural analysis. *Journal of the American Society for Psychical Research, 88*, 117–135.

McClenon, J. (1994b). *Wondrous events: Foundations of religious beliefs*. Philadelphia: University of Pennsylvania Press.

Michelson, L., & Ray, W. J. (Eds.). (1996). *Handbook of dissociation*. New York: Plenum.

Myers, F. W. H. (1961). *Human personality and its survival of bodily death*. New York: University Books. (Original work published 1903)

Pasricha, S., & Stevenson, I. (1986). Near-death experiences in India. *Journal of Nervous and Mental Disease, 174*, 165–170.

Pope, K. S., & Singer, J. L. (Eds.). (1978). *The stream of consciousness*. New York: Plenum.

Powers, S., & Krippner, S. (Eds.). (1997). *Broken images, broken selves*. New York: Brunner/Mazel.

Reed, G. (1972). *The psychology of anomalous experience*. London: Hutchinson University Library.

Reed, G. (1988). *The psychology of anomalous experience* (rev. ed.). Buffalo, NY: Prometheus Books.

Robinson, D. N. (1998). Dissociation and the foundations of cognitive psychology in nineteenth century France. *Psychological Hypnosis, 7*, 15–20.

Rose, S. (1976). *The conscious brain* (rev. ed.). Middlesex, England: Penguin.

Rush, J. H. (1986). Parapsychology: A historical perspective. In H. L. Edge, R. L.

Morris, J. Palmer, & J. H. Rush (Eds.), *Foundations of parapsychology* (pp. 9–44). New York: Routledge Kegan Paul.

Sacks, O. (1995). *An anthropologist on Mars*. New York: Knopf.

Schick, T., & Vaughn, L. (1995). *How to think about weird things*. Mountain View, CA: Mayfield.

Sidgwick, H., Johnson, A., Myers, F. W. H., Podmore, F., & Sidgwick, E. (1894). Report on the census of hallucinations. *Proceedings of the Society for Psychical Research, 10*, 25–422.

Siegel, R. K. (1989). *Intoxication*. New York: Dutton.

Society for Psychical Research. (1882–1883). Objects of the society. *Proceedings of the Society for Psychical Research, 1*, 1–4.

Spanos, N. P., Cross, P. A., Dickson, K., & Dubreuil, S. C. (1993). Close encounters: An examination of UFO experiences. *Journal of Abnormal Psychology, 102*, 624–632.

Spencer, H. (1991). *Divine idea, first principles and the conditions essential to human happiness*. Albuquerque, NM: American Institute for Psychological Research. (Original work published 1902)

Stevenson, I. (1995). Six modern apparitional experiences. *Journal for Scientific Exploration, 9*, 351–366.

Tart, C. T. (Ed.). (1969). *Altered states of consciousness*. New York: Wiley.

Thalbourne, M. (1982). *A glossary of terms used in parapsychology*. London: Heinemann.

Truzzi, M. (1971). Definition and dimensions of the occult: Toward a sociological perspective. *Journal of Popular Culture, 5*, 635–646.

Van der Hart, O. (1998). Pierre Janet's major works on hysteria and hypnosis. *Psychological Hypnosis, 7*, 18–24.

Watson, J. B. (1913). Psychology as the behaviorist views it. *Psychological Review, 20*, 158–177.

Wescott, R. (1977). Paranthropology: A nativity celebration and a communion commentary. In J. K. Long (Ed.), *Extrasensory ecology: Parapsychology and anthropology* (pp. 331–346). Metuchen, NJ: Scarecrow Press.

White, R. A. (1995). Exceptional human experiences and the experiential paradigm. *ReVision, 18*, 18–25.

Zusne, L., & Jones, W. H. (1980). *Anomalistic psychology*. Hillsdale, NJ: Erlbaum.

Zusne, L., & Jones, W. H. (1989). *Anomalistic psychology: A study of magical thinking* (2nd ed.). Hillsdale, NJ: Erlbaum.

I

CONCEPTUAL AND METHODOLOGICAL CONSIDERATIONS

1

ANOMALOUS EXPERIENCES, PECULIARITY, AND PSYCHOPATHOLOGY

HOWARD BERENBAUM, JOHN KERNS,
AND CHITRA RAGHAVAN

The goal of this chapter is to explore the relations among anomalous experiences, peculiarity, and psychopathology. We begin by providing definitions of these three different phenomena. In addition, we present a cartography of anomalous experiences that focuses on dimensions that will be helpful in understanding the relationships among anomalous experiences and psychopathology. After providing definitions of psychopathology, peculiarity, and anomalous experience, we address the following two related questions: How are anomalous experiences distinguishable from peculiarity and psychopathology? and How and why might anomalous experiences be related to peculiarity and psychopathology? Finally, we provide recommendations for future research.

We thank the editors for their helpful comments on an earlier draft of this chapter.
Preparation of this chapter was supported by National Institute of Mental Health Grant
MH50531 to Howard Berenbaum.

DEFINITION OF PSYCHOPATHOLOGY

Defining psychopathology, or mental disorder, is an elusive task (e.g., Spitzer, 1997; Wakefield, 1992). Many debates over the last 30 years concern whether certain entities should be considered forms of psychopathology (e.g., late-luteal-phase dysphoric disorder and self-defeating personality disorder). These debates have highlighted the limitations of any definition to clearly demarcate what is psychopathological from what is normal. Despite the inability of researchers to agree on a single definition of psychopathology, there are several characteristics included in many definitions.

We illustrate these characteristics by presenting brief accounts of three definitions of psychopathology. According to the fourth edition of the *Diagnostic and Statistical Manual of Mental Disorders* (DSM–IV; American Psychiatric Association, 1994), *mental disorders* are conceptualized as behavioral and psychological "syndromes" that are "associated with present distress (e.g., a painful symptom) or disability (i.e., impairment in one or more important areas of functioning) or with a significantly increased risk of suffering death, pain, disability, or an important loss of freedom" (p. xxi). Furthermore, to be considered a mental disorder, the syndrome should be considered a manifestation of individual dysfunction, at least at the time of diagnosis. According to Wakefield's (1992) "harmful dysfunction" definition, mental disorders are defined as dysfunctions of natural processes that cause harm to the individual. Following Ossorio (1985), Bergner (1997) proposed that "*psychopathology* is best defined as significant restriction in the ability of an individual to engage in deliberate action and, equivalently, to participate in available social practices" (p. 246; emphasis added).

One element common to virtually all definitions of psychopathology is that they describe phenomena (reported symptoms and observed signs, including perceptions, emotions, cognitions, and behaviors) that are presumed to reflect underlying psychological processes or functions. For example, an individual with a seizure disorder that can be directly traced to limbic system lesions and who exhibits extremely intense emotional episodes coincident with seizure activity would probably not be considered as having a psychopathology because the underlying cause of the signs and symptoms is considered physical rather than psychological.

Most definitions of psychopathology also presume that reasonably stable individual causes play an important role in the development of the signs and symptoms. Subjective distress is another characteristic commonly described in many definitions of psychopathology, as is some form of functional impairment, such as the inability to work or engage in social relations. A final characteristic common to many definitions holds that the undesirable signs and symptoms either are involuntary (e.g., the person does not choose to have hallucinations) or limit the person's ability to engage in actions in which they would like to engage (e.g., social conversation).

DEFINITION OF PECULIARITY

Peculiarity is a multidimensional individual-differences variable (Berenbaum, 1996; Berenbaum & Fujita, 1994). Individuals differ in the degree to which they have peculiar sensory perceptions, have peculiar experiences, or hold peculiar beliefs. Sensory *perceptions* include auditory, visual, tactile, olfactory, gustatory, kinesthetic, pain, and equilibrium phenomena. We define *experiences* as broader than mere sensory perceptions. They may or may not include sensory perceptions, whereas all sensory perceptions that are registered in awareness are experiences. Experiences refer to the "living" of actual events or phenomena and involve the total sum of an individual's phenomenological world. *Beliefs* are the cognitive information an individual holds about the existence of a phenomenon. An individual may hold peculiar beliefs but never have peculiar experiences. Conversely, an individual may have a peculiar experience but not endorse any peculiar belief.

At the high end of the continuum, peculiar beliefs are considered delusional, and peculiar perceptions are considered hallucinations. At this end of the continuum, peculiar experiences would also be considered clinically significant; the most common example would be clinically significant dissociative experiences (see Cardeña, 1997). Although phenomena such as hallucinations and delusions are often thought of as being either present or absent, they are probably better seen as anchoring the high ends of peculiarity continua (e.g., Chapman & Chapman, 1980; Strauss, 1969).

The description of peculiarity presented above begs the question of what it is that makes a sensory perception, belief, or experience peculiar. References to phenomena at the high end of the peculiarity continuum, such as delusions and hallucinations, are not sufficient to define peculiarity for the following reason: Just as one can ask what makes a sensory perception, belief, or experience peculiar, one can ask what makes a belief delusional and what makes a sensory perception hallucinatory. With regard to sensory perceptions and beliefs, the answer seems to be their presumed veridicality, or, whether they are assumed to be an accurate reflection of reality. For example, the *DSM–IV* (American Psychiatric Association, 1994) defines a *hallucination* as "a sensory perception that has the compelling sense of reality of a true perception but that occurs without external stimulation of the relevant sensory organ" (p. 767), and it defines a *delusion* as "a false belief based on incorrect inference about external reality" (p. 765).

However, what makes an experience peculiar is not necessarily its presumed lack of veridicality (though presumed nonveridical experiences will almost always be considered peculiar), but rather the extent to which it deviates from the ordinary. For example, the experience of not remembering how one got somewhere is considered peculiar not because it is presumed to be nonveridical (i.e., the experience of not remembering how one got somewhere is accepted as accurate), but rather because such an experience deviates from the ordinary.[1] It should be pointed out, however, that not all experiences that deviate from the ordinary are considered peculiar. Winning a million-dollar lottery and winning a Nobel Prize are not ordinary experiences, but they would not be considered peculiar experiences. What is necessary for an experience to be considered peculiar is that either its genesis or physical nature is difficult to explain. For example, although winning a million-dollar lottery is not ordinary, it would generally not be difficult to explain how the experience came about; in contrast, it would probably be difficult for most people to explain why someone could not remember how he or she got somewhere.

Although we believe it is important to distinguish among sensory perceptions, beliefs, and experiences (an issue to which we return later in this chapter), we wish to point out that these distinctions are not always clear. If someone reported hearing Elvis Presley talking to her or him almost every day, would this be an example of a peculiar sensory perception, belief, or experience? The person's actual report of hearing the voice of Elvis would be a peculiar sensory perception because we presume that Elvis did not talk; thus, the perception would be (presumably) based on nonveridical sensory information. Whether the person who reported actually hearing Elvis's voice was having a peculiar experience (in addition to having a peculiar sensory perception) depends on the person's experience. According to our definition, if the person attributed meaning to hearing Elvis's voice, this would be a peculiar experience in addition to being a peculiar sensory perception. In contrast, if the person did not attribute meaning to hearing Elvis's voice (e.g., the person discounted or ignored the voice), the event would be a peculiar sensory perception but not a peculiar experience. Finally, whether the person who reported hearing Elvis has a peculiar belief depends on believing that the experience was veridical.

Although people typically equate their experiences with reality, this is not always the case. People who engage in activities associated with nonveridical sensory perceptions because of extreme conditions such as oxygen depletion (e.g., scuba diving and mountain climbing) are often

---

[1]We use the word *ordinary* according to the common dictionary definition (e.g., the following definition from *Merriam-Webster's Collegiate Dictionary Deluxe Edition* (1998): "of a kind to be expected in the normal order of events"). One implication of our use of this definition is that because what is considered ordinary will vary across time, place, and culture, so will what we define as peculiar experiences.

trained and prepared to expect and discount these perceptions. Those with Charles Bonnet Syndrome (CBS; Fernandez, Lichtshein, & Vieweg, 1997) can also distinguish between their experiences and reality. Individuals with CBS, who typically have eye disease (e.g., macular degeneration), have visual hallucinations in the context of intact sensorium, good insight, and the absence of any other signs of psychiatric disturbance. Although individuals with CBS experience visual hallucinations, they typically recognize the unreality of the visual images.

DEFINITION OF ANOMALOUS EXPERIENCE

In the Introduction to this book, Cardeña, Lynn, and Krippner define *anomalous experiences* as uncommon or irregular. They point out that anomalous experiences (e.g., psi-related experiences; see Targ, Schlitz, & Irwin, this volume, chap. 7) may be experienced by large portions of the general population but are "assumed to deviate from ordinary experiences or from the usually accepted explanations of reality." The variety of anomalous experiences that have been reported is enormous and complex. As different as each of these experiences may seem, we believe it is possible to organize and locate different anomalous experiences in a systematic fashion. An overview of our description of anomalous experiences is presented in Table 1.1.

We propose that anomalous experiences can be described using three *onset/course* dimensions and three *phenomenological* dimensions. The onset/course dimensions concern the conditions that give rise to the anomalous experience and influence its course. The first onset/course dimension in-

TABLE 1.1
Key Variations in Anomalous Experiences

Onset/Course Dimensions
    1. Level of awareness
    2. Individual volition
    3. Individual control
Phenomenological Dimensions
    1. Subjective hedonic valence
    2. Physical–metaphysical qualities
       A. Sensory-focused
       B. Barriers of mind, body, and space
          a. Detachment
          b. Corporeal movement
          c. Intrusion
          d. Human transformation
          e. Transcendent transformation
          f. Nonhuman transformation
    3. Central others

volves the individual's level of awareness at the time of the anomalous experience. For example, synesthetic experiences (see Marks, this volume, chap. 4) occur while the individual is fully aware, whereas hypnagogic images and near-death experiences (NDEs; see Greyson, this volume, chap. 10) occur during states of reduced awareness. The other two onset/course dimensions, which are strongly correlated with each other but are still distinguishable, involve individual volition and individual control.

The volition dimension concerns the degree to which the onset of the anomalous experience was voluntary. For many individuals, the onset of an anomalous experience may be involuntary, whereas some individuals may intentionally seek out or attempt to induce anomalous experiences. Some individuals, for example, intentionally ingest LSD for the purpose of having anomalous experiences. Historically, some have intentionally engaged in actions, such as fasting, that were intended to lead to what would be considered anomalous experiences (e.g., see the case of Abba Helle described in Ward and Russell 395/1980). In contrast, some anomalous experiences, such as alien abduction experiences (AAEs; see Appelle, Lynn, & Newman, this volume, chap. 8), may be entirely involuntary, at least at the fully conscious level.

The control dimension concerns the degree to which the individual is in control of the anomalous experience once it has begun. Although it is typical for individuals to be able to exert control over anomalous experiences that begin voluntarily, this is not necessarily the case. An individual may voluntarily initiate an experience of spirit possession or ingest psychoactive drugs but not have control over the experience once it begins. Just as some anomalous experiences may begin voluntarily but become uncontrolled once they begin, there are some anomalous experiences that may begin involuntarily but may be controllable later. For example, hallucinations may begin involuntarily, but the person may be able to exert some control over them once they begin by using strategies such as distraction (Slade, 1974).

Of the phenomenological dimensions, the simplest of the three is the experience's subjective hedonic valence. Some anomalous experiences, such as synesthesia, may be experienced as being very pleasant, whereas others, such as involuntary demon possession, are likely to be experienced as being very unpleasant. Each individual's anomalous experience can be placed on a bipolar pleasant–unpleasant dimension based on the individual's phenomenological experience and interpretation of pleasure.

The second phenomenological dimension refers to the physical and metaphysical qualities of the anomalous experience itself and is intended to capture the structure of the experience as reported by the participant. We have dichotomized this second phenomenological dimension into experiences that are either sensory-focused or that cross barriers of mind, body, and space. Anomalous experiences such as synesthesia and hallucinations would be considered sensory focused. Anomalous experiences such as AAEs and psychokinesis (see Targ et al., this volume, chap. 7) would fit into the category of barriers of mind, body, and space because they cross or extend traditional scientific understanding of the physical limits of mind, body, and space.

This category is further subdivided into the following: (a) *detachment*, defined by a putative travel of nonmaterial aspects of the human body (spirit, mind, soul; see Alvarado, this volume, chap. 7); (b) *corporeal movement*, which refers to the experience wherein the whole person (whose identity remains intact) is moved to another location, as in time travel and AAEs; (c) *intrusion*, defined by the experience of the corporeal body or identity being entered or taken over by another entity such as demons/spirits or somebody else's thoughts; (d) *human transformation*, or the experience of being transformed into either a different human being or the same human being at a different point in time, such as believing that one is Jesus Christ or Prophet Muhammad, or believing that one lived several centuries ago; (e) *transcendent transformation*, which refers to mind/body-transforming spiritual–religious–mystical experiences, including spiritual healing experiences, religious conversion experiences, and mystical experiences (see Wulff, this volume, chap. 12); and (f) *nonhuman transformation*, or the experience of the transformation of the human body into semi- or nonhuman forms, as when the individual experiences him- or herself as being transformed into an eagle, an android, or a werewolf.

The third and final phenomenological dimension, which we call *central others*, refers to the experient's report of contact or involvement with an individual or entity (in human or nonhuman form) who is a significant aspect of the anomalous experience. The central other is so described because were he/she/it removed from the experience, the experience would be significantly altered. For example, the report of seeing many people while flying about Illinois as an eagle would not be considered an experience with a central other. On the other hand, the report that Elvis contacted and subsequently sang "Love Me Tender" to an individual would be considered an experience with a central other (i.e., Elvis was a significant aspect of the anomalous experience and, were Elvis absent, the experience would have been significantly altered).

RELATIONSHIP BETWEEN ANOMALOUS EXPERIENCE AND PECULIARITY

As the definitions above reveal, there are important similarities between anomalous experience and peculiarity. An individual who reports anomalous experiences is likely to have high levels of peculiarity. Also, individuals with high levels of peculiarity are more likely to have anomalous experiences than are individuals with low levels of peculiarity. It is worth noting, however, that there are two important differences between anomalous experience and peculiarity. First, the construct of peculiarity is broader than that of anomalous experience. Peculiarity encompasses beliefs as well as perceptions and experiences. Second, peculiarity is an individual-differences construct, whereas anomalous experience is not. The difference between anomalous experience and peculiarity comes down to the following: Anomalous experience is something an individual has, whereas peculiarity is something an individual is.

In our view, the causal relations between anomalous experience and peculiarity are bidirectional. Having anomalous experiences contributes to an individual being judged to have high levels of peculiarity (just as enjoying a party may lead one to be judged to have high levels of extraversion). At the same time, we posit that there is something about individuals (which is tapped by the peculiarity construct) that makes some more likely than others to have anomalous experiences (just as there is something about individuals, high levels of extraversion, that makes some more likely than others to enjoy parties). Thus, that which is at the heart of the individual-differences construct of peculiarity contributes to the likelihood of having anomalous experiences (and beliefs).

RELATIONSHIP BETWEEN ANOMALOUS EXPERIENCE AND PSYCHOPATHOLOGY

As illustrated in Figure 1.1, there are four reasons why anomalous experiences may be expected to be associated with psychopathology: (a) the two overlap; (b) anomalous experience contributes to psychopathology; (c) psychopathology contributes to anomalous experience; and (d) there are "third variables" that contribute to both anomalous experience and psychopathology. In the sections that follow, we elaborate on the theoretical reasons why anomalous experience and psychopathology may be associated. However, it is necessary to point out that, on the whole, there is not good empirical support for the hypothesis that various anomalous experiences are associated with psychopathology (see, for instance, in this volume, Apelle et al., chap. 8; Greyson, chap. 10; Marks, chap. 4; and Mills & Lynn, chap. 9). One reason is that, as we point out below, anomalous experiences may sometimes contribute to positive mental health (see LaBerge & Gackenbach, chap. 5; and Wulff, chap. 12). If, as we suspect, anomalous experiences will sometimes contribute to psychopathology and also sometimes contribute to positive mental health, researchers who use dimensional measures of psychopathology will be unlikely to find that individuals who do and do not have anomalous experiences differ in their mean psychopathology scores. We recommend that researchers interested

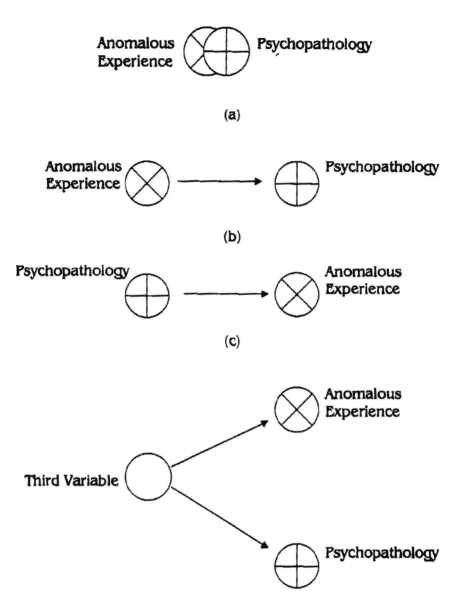

Figure 1.1. Hypothetical reasons for anomalous experience and psychopathology to be associated.

in the relationship between anomalous experience and psychopathology do more than examine mean psychopathology scores. For example, researchers can examine the proportion of individuals at either end of the psychopathology distribution who have anomalous experiences. Another reason why researchers may fail to detect an association between anomalous experiences and psychopathology is that the association is unlikely to be a simple one. As we point out below, whether anomalous experiences are associated with psychopathology most likely depends on a variety of factors, such as the type of anomalous experience, the individuals' own reaction to the anomalous experience (e.g., does it frighten them or enlighten them?), and the reactions of others (e.g., do others admire or condemn the individual who has had the anomalous experience?). Therefore, we recommend that researchers explore variables such as whether the anomalous experience confuses or clarifies the way the individual tries to make sense of the world, which may help explain the relationship between anomalous experience and psychopathology.

Overlap Between Anomalous Experience and Psychopathology

Some anomalous experiences may themselves be considered signs or symptoms of psychopathology. One factor that influences whether an anomalous experience will be considered evidence of psychopathology is the prevailing cultural beliefs and expectations. For example, hearing voices is less likely to be considered a sign of psychopathology in a culture in which this experience is considered ordinary than in a culture in which it is considered deviant. The likelihood of an anomalous experience being considered psychopathological also depends on how psychopathology is defined. However, as we noted earlier, there are several characteristics that are common to many, if not most, definitions of psychopathology. Furthermore, different anomalous experiences vary in the degree to which they match those characteristics. In fact, two of the characteristics that are common to most definitions of psychopathology can be mapped onto some of the dimensions of anomalous experience in the cartography we presented (see Table 1.1).

Subjective hedonic valence is one of the phenomenological dimensions in our proposed cartography of anomalous experiences. Anomalous experiences associated with subjective distress are more likely to be considered psychopathological than are pleasant anomalous experiences because subjective distress is common to many definitions of psychopathology. Thus, those anomalous experiences that are generally experienced as being pleasant, such as religious conversion experiences, are less likely to be considered psychopathological than are those anomalous experiences, such as AAEs, that are generally experienced as distressing.

Individual volition and individual control are two of the onset/course dimensions in our cartography of anomalous experience. Some anomalous experiences are more likely to be volitional and under the person's control than are others. Because a component of many definitions of psychopathology is that the condition is involuntary or limits the person's ability to engage in volitional behavior, those anomalous experiences that are most difficult to control are most likely to be considered psychopathological.

Functional impairment is another common characteristic of many definitions of psychopathology. Anomalous experiences, such as auditory hallucinations, that are more likely to lead to functional impairment are more likely to be considered evidence of psychopathology than are anomalous experiences, such as remembering a past life, that are less likely to lead to functional impairment. To some degree, how impairing the anomalous experience is depends on the society's response. For example, individuals who have conversations with a deity are less likely to suffer functional impairment if they are surrounded by individuals who accept (or even envy) that experience than if they are surrounded by individuals who reject that experience.

A phenomenon must be presumed to reflect underlying psychological processes or functions to be considered psychopathological. Some anomalous experiences, such as some dissociative experiences, are presumed to reflect underlying psychological processes. In contrast, other anomalous experiences, such as synesthesia, may reflect neurological rather than psychological processes. Consequently, such conditions as dissociative identity disorder are more likely to be considered psychopathological than is synesthesia (see Marks, this volume, chap. 4).

Most definitions of psychopathology hold that it is the result of reasonably stable individual causes. Some anomalous experiences, such as NDEs, are transient or occur only a limited number of times and are therefore not likely to reflect stable internal factors (see Greyson, this volume, chap. 10). Other anomalous experiences, such as hearing the voice of God while attending religious revival meetings, are likely to reflect the environment the person happens to be in and are therefore less likely to be considered to reflect internal factors. In contrast, hearing the voice of Satan throughout the day everyday for one month is likely to be considered a reflection of a reasonably stable individual factor and will be more likely to be considered a sign of psychopathology than will anomalous experiences such as NDEs.

Contribution of Anomalous Experience to Psychopathology

There are two broad ways in which anomalous experiences may contribute to psychopathology. First, the individuals' own reactions to their anomalous experiences can foster psychopathology. Numerous psychopathologists, dating back to Emil Kraepelin and Eugen Bleuler, have proposed that individuals are motivated to develop delusions as a means of coping with some psychological experiences, such as unusual perceptual experiences (Winters & Neale, 1983). Perhaps the best-developed model of anomalous experience contributing to psychopathology has been developed by Maher (1974, 1988). Maher proposed that individuals who have anomalous experiences are predisposed to develop delusions as a way to explain otherwise unexplainable—for them—anomalous experiences. For example, an individual who experiences unusual and unexplained memory losses, as seen in some forms of dissociation, may develop a delusion of thought withdrawal (the belief that another person or power is removing thoughts or ideas from the person's head or mind). As evidence for this model, Maher pointed out the high rates of delusional beliefs among individuals with undiagnosed hearing loss. Maher (1988) also pointed out that delusional beliefs are common among individuals with a variety of medical disorders and that the "delusions are much more likely to be secondary, reactive responses to some personal situation arising in connection with bodily disability, with sensory or motor features, or both, as opposed to primary disturbances of cognitive functioning arising from a predominantly motivational–conflictual basis" (p. 22).

Anomalous experiences can also contribute to psychopathology because they can bring about anxiety or depression. For instance, individuals who believe they have been abducted by an unidentified flying object, or UFO, and were tortured while on board may develop a clinically significant fear of future abductions. Similarly, individuals who believe the devil controls them and that they will be going to hell may become clinically depressed. The distress or confusion that can be elicited by anomalous experiences can also lead to psychopathology in indirect ways, such as through sleep disturbances or maladaptive coping strategies.

The reactions of others is another way in which anomalous experiences may affect psychopathology. Others' reactions to the experients' reports of anomalous experiences, such as having conversations with a supernatural being, can range from support and admiration to rejection and derision (for a discussion of how others react to reports of anomalous experiences and how such reactions vary across cultures, see Targ et al., this volume, chap. 7). Thus, the reactions of others to anomalous experiences can be anxiogenic or depressogenic; even if such reactions are not immediately distressing, the consequences of the reactions can contribute to distress and psychopathology. For example, anomalous experiences (or the reporting to others of those experiences) can lead others to prevent the individuals who had the anomalous experience from engaging in important roles. These individuals may be fired from their jobs or socially ostracized, and the inability to fulfill important roles may contribute to various forms of psychopathology, such as depressive disorder.

It should be noted that just as some anomalous experiences probably contribute to the development of psychopathology, other anomalous experiences are probably associated with positive mental health rather than with psychopathology. One reason for this is that subjective distress is often associated with psychopathology (in fact, as noted earlier, distress is often a criterion of psychopathology), yet some anomalous experiences are associated with positive emotions. Lucid dreaming is an example of an anomalous experience that is often described as pleasurable (see LaBerge &

Gackenbach, this volume, chap. 5) and that may therefore enhance well-being. Lucid dreaming might also be negatively correlated with psychopathology because it is associated with increased mental clarity and control. Increased mental clarity and control are associated with increased emotional stability (e.g., less risk for depression, Teasdale, Taylor, Cooper, Hayhurst, & Paykel, 1995; less neuroticism, Wallace & Newman, 1997). Thus, anomalous experiences associated with increased controlled processing and with reduced automatic processing (Wallace & Newman, 1997) would be expected to be associated with positive mental health. Another reason anomalous experiences may be associated with positive mental health is that they can provide the experients with a sense of meaning or purpose, or otherwise expand their spiritual lives (see this volume, Wulff, chap. 12; Targ et al., chap. 7).

Contribution of Psychopathology to Anomalous Experience

There are two types of psychopathology—substance use disorders and pathological disturbances in mood[2]—that can contribute directly to anomalous experience. For example, amphetamine intoxication and alcohol withdrawal can both cause hallucinations. Similarly, many different substances, such as cocaine, cause cognitive confusion, which might precipitate the occurrence of an anomalous experience if it induces the acceptance of contradictory information.

Pathological disturbances in mood, such as those seen in mood disorders, can also contribute to anomalous experiences. For example, individuals with major depressive disorder are prone to have mood-congruent psychotic symptoms, such as hearing voices tell them that they deserve to die or feeling that they are controlled by the devil. Individuals in the manic phase of bipolar disorder can have mood-congruent psychotic symptoms, such as believing that they are Jesus Christ.

In addition to the direct contributions of psychopathology to anomalous experience, there are two indirect ways in which psychopathology can contribute to anomalous experience. Besides being influenced by stress, some forms of psychopathology can also contribute to stress (e.g., Daley et al., 1997). Individuals with forms of psychopathology involving dysregulation of mood, such as cyclothymia and borderline personality disorder (BPD), are especially prone to creating intense and uncontrolled periods of stress. The stress that is a product of psychopathology can then contrib-

---

[2]Schizophrenia spectrum disorders (e.g., schizophrenia and schizotypal personality disorder) are also associated with anomalous experience. Because schizophrenia spectrum disorders are defined on the basis of anomalous experience, it is somewhat tautological to argue that schizophrenia spectrum disorders contribute to anomalous experience. Therefore, our discussion of psychopathology contributing to anomalous experience is limited to forms of psychopathology in which anomalous experience is not a necessary criterion.

ute to certain anomalous experiences. For example, some out-of-body experiences (OBEs) are reportedly induced by stressful incidents (Alvarado, this volume, chap. 6). Thus, heightened stress caused by psychopathology should be expected to contribute to such anomalous experiences as OBEs.

The second indirect way in which psychopathology could contribute to anomalous experiences is through disturbances in the person's identity. Some psychopathological conditions are associated with disturbances in self-concept. For example, some people with BPD have a poorly developed and contradictory self-concept. Similarly, people with narcissistic personality disorder or with bipolar disorder (in which inflated or grandiose self-esteem often accompanies elevated levels of energy and mood) might be motivated to create and maintain a highly positive self-concept, even in the face of frequently disconfirming external events. As noted earlier, changes in personal identity are a common feature of anomalous experience. People with poorly defined self-concepts, or people who are motivated to maintain clearly nonveridical self-concepts even in the face of contradictory evidence, are at increased risk of having anomalous experiences involving changes in identity. For example, someone who wants to maintain a grandiose self-concept may be inclined to entertain and accept the possibility of being contacted by alien or spirit beings, either through direct physical contact or through other means (e.g., automatic writing, when people claim to receive messages that are "channeled" through them).

Individual Differences Contributing to Both Anomalous Experience and Psychopathology

There are a variety of factors, such as personality traits, atypical patterns of brain functioning, and trauma, that can contribute to both psychopathology and anomalous experience. One personality trait that is likely to contribute to both anomalous experience and psychopathology is neuroticism or trait negative affectivity. Neuroticism can be conceptualized as a stable disposition to experience negative emotional states or, alternatively, as a stable disposition to emotional instability. Individuals who have high levels of neuroticism or trait negative affectivity are at increased risk of experiencing a broad range of psychiatric disorders, such as depressive (Clark, Watson, & Mineka, 1994), anxiety (Zinbarg & Barlow, 1995), and substance abuse (e.g., Wallace & Newman, 1997) disorders. One reason neuroticism may contribute to anomalous experiences is that neuroticism is associated with a greater likelihood of experiencing stress, which in turn increases the likelihood of anomalous experiences. A second reason neuroticism may contribute to anomalous experiences is that it is associated with increased automatic processing and reduced controlled processing (Wallace & Newman, 1997). These patterns of information processing are likely to lead individuals who are very neurotic to have diminished cognitive capacity for effortful logical thinking and less cognitive capacity to rationally analyze real-world events, thereby making them more likely to accept contradictory information that might in turn contribute to anomalous experiences.

Two related personality traits that may contribute to both psychopathology and anomalous experience are absorption and openness to experience. Absorption is the tendency to become engrossed in experience. Openness to experience is the disposition to be responsive to, and to explore, new and unconventional ideas and experiences. Some personality disorders, such as schizotypal personality disorder, have been found to be associated with high levels of openness to experience (Widiger, 1993). Several anomalous experiences, such as psi-related experiences, OBEs, NDEs, synesthesia, and mystical experiences, have also been found to be associated with absorption and openness to experience.

Individuals with high levels of absorption and openness to experience are at increased risk of having anomalous experiences because they may intentionally try to have them, or may be more likely to explore aspects of their phenomenological worlds that other people would not explore. Potentially, these explorations might develop into full-blown anomalous experiences. This assumes that some anomalous experiences might begin in only a rudimentary form (e.g., unusual sensations or feelings) but over time can be developed (either with or without intention) into full and coherent events. For example, it is possible that unusual sensations and feelings regarding one's body can be slowly molded into an OBE.

In addition to being influenced by personality traits such as neuroticism and openness to experience, anomalous experience and psychopathology may also be influenced by atypical patterns of brain functioning and arousal. For example, left temporal lobe damage might be a cause of both schizophrenia (Chua & McKenna, 1995) and hallucinations (see Bentall, this volume, chap. 3; David, 1994). Right-hemisphere dysfunction has been posited to play a causal role in schizophrenia (Cutting, 1992), and personal identity disturbances (Cutting, 1990); the right hemisphere has also been posited to play a role in anomalous experience. Atypical patterns of brain activation and arousal have been implicated in schizophrenia (e.g., Venables, 1977) as well as in lucid dreaming (see LaBerge & Gackenbach, this volume, chap. 5), synesthesia (see Marks, this volume, chap. 4), and experiences of radical personal transformation (see Wulff, this volume, chap. 12).

Intrapsychic, or endogenous, variables such as personality and brain functioning are not the only factors that can contribute to both psychopathology and anomalous experience. There are good reasons to believe that traumatic events and life circumstances can also play a role. There is abundant evidence that trauma contributes to psychopathology. For example, childhood abuse is associated with elevated levels of a variety of different forms of psychopathology (e.g., Mullen, Martin, Anderson, Romans, & Herbison, 1993), and severe traumatic experience is a specific etiological cause of posttraumatic stress disorder. There is also evidence that traumatic events contribute to dissociative experiences (e.g., Spiegel & Cardeña, 1991) and that reported childhood trauma is associated with the later occurrence of NDEs and AAEs (Ring, 1990).

Recently, in a large sample of college students, Berenbaum (1999) found that individuals who reported a history of childhood maltreatment were 10.5 times more likely than those who did not report such a history to have deviantly high scores on the Perceptual Aberration Scale (Chapman, Chapman, & Raulin, 1978), which measures uncommon visual and auditory experiences and body-image aberrations. However, the vast majority of individuals who reported a history of childhood maltreatment did not have deviantly high levels of perceptual aberration. Participants who reported a history of maltreatment and had high levels of perceptual aberration had greater nightmare distress and more night terrors than those who reported only a history of maltreatment, suggesting that high levels of perceptual aberration may be associated with incomplete emotional processing of traumatic events. In addition, among individuals with a history of maltreatment, high levels of perceptual aberration were associated with reporting feeling less emotionally safe during childhood.

Traumatic events may contribute to anomalous experiences because people have little control over them. To compensate for low actual control, people who have experienced trauma may develop unconventional beliefs that increase their perceived control over life events. In turn, these unconventional beliefs may help elicit anomalous experiences (Epstein & Meier, 1989).

FUTURE RESEARCH

We close this chapter with 10 recommendations for investigators who wish to examine when, how, and why anomalous experience will be associated with peculiarity and psychopathology.

Recommendation 1: We believe it is critical to distinguish among perceptions, experiences, and beliefs. It seems quite plausible that each of these are differentially associated with different facets of peculiarity and psychopathology.

Recommendation 2: As we noted earlier, there is not a single universally accepted definition of psychopathology. Similarly, it is not the case that there is a universally accepted set of psychopathological entities or disorders (in fact, even the *DSM* changes the number of disorders and their definitions on a regular basis). Consequently, we believe it would be best for researchers in this area to not explore relations with psychopathology as defined in a single way or with particular psychiatric disorders as defined in a single way. Instead, we recommend that researchers design their studies in such a way that they can examine how the associations between anomalous experience and psychopathology vary depending on the definition of psychopathology or psychiatric disorder used. A similar strategy has been used by schizophrenia researchers. For example, McGuffin, Farmer, Gottesman, Murray, and Reveley (1984) found that the heritability of schizophrenia varied depending on the particular definition of the disorder used.

Recommendation 3: To generate and test models of the relations among anomalous experience, peculiarity, and psychopathology, we believe investigators would be best off, whenever possible, studying multiple forms of anomalous experience, multiple forms of peculiarity, and multiple forms or aspects of psychopathology. Researchers should elucidate what forms of anomalous experience are associated with specific forms of peculiarity and with specific forms or aspects of psychopathology, instead of only determining whether a single form of anomalous experience is associated with a single form of peculiarity or psychopathology.

Recommendation 4: We recommend that investigators use a cartography of anomalous experience to explore how different types of anomalous experience are associated with peculiarity and psychopathology. Although we hope the cartography we have presented in this chapter (see Table 1.1) will be helpful, other means of organizing and categorizing anomalous experience may be just as valuable, if not more so.

Recommendation 5: We expect the relations among anomalous experience, peculiarity, and psychopathology to be complex. Therefore, we believe it would be valuable for researchers to (a) explore potential mediators and moderators of the relations among anomalous experience, peculiarity, and psychopathology and (b) explore how these phenomena may mediate or moderate the relations among each other and other variables. A moderator "is a qualitative (e.g., sex, race, class) or quantitative (e.g., level of reward) variable that affects the direction and/or strength of the relation between an independent or predictor variable and a dependent or criterion variable" (Baron & Kenny, 1986, p. 1174). In contrast, a "variable may be said to function as a mediator to the extent that it accounts for the relation between the predictor and the criterion" (Baron & Kenny, 1986, p. 1176). For instance, cultural norms may moderate the relation between anomalous experience and psychopathology, whereas anomalous experiences may mediate the relation between trauma and some forms of psychopathology.

Recommendation 6: Although anomalous experiences, peculiarity, and psychopathology can often be measured dimensionally, the underlying phenomena are not necessarily dimensional (e.g., Waller & Ross, 1997). Similarly, even when phenomena are dimensional, they may not be associated in a linear manner. Therefore, we recommend that investigators consider both taxonicity and nonlinear relations (especially threshold effects) when studying when, how, and why anomalous experience is associated with peculiarity and psychopathology. Researchers can use taxometric procedures to try to distinguish types from continua (Waller & Meehl, 1998).

Recommendation 7: Considering how interesting and potentially important the relations among anomalous experience, peculiarity, and psychopathology are, there has been surprisingly little systematic research examining them. Although we would like to encourage such research, we believe it is desirable for investigators to conduct theory-driven research rather than blindly collecting data in the absence of any theories or models of when, how, and why anomalous experience, peculiarity, and psychopathology are associated.

Recommendation 8: Although it can probably go without saying, longitudinal research is likely to be far more valuable than cross-sectional research in order to tease apart the causal relationships, if any, among anomalous experience, peculiarity, and psychopathology.

Recommendation 9: As noted by several authors in this volume, research in this area can be rather difficult. Because many anomalous phenomena are uncommon and private, it is likely to be valuable to study them using unconventional (at least by the standards of experimental psychology) research methodologies. For example, we believe that qualitative research methods and intensive case studies (especially series of case studies) may be very illuminating (Giorgi, 1970, 1986). Descriptions of several other particularly useful methods, such as diaries, thought sampling, and depth ratings, are described by Pekala and Cardeña (this volume, chap. 2).

Recommendation 10: The same experience can have very different meanings and correlates in different cultures. Therefore, our final recommendation is that researchers pay attention to cross-cultural and other contextual factors that we expect to be critical for understanding the relations among anomalous experience, peculiarity, and psychopathology.

As psychopathology researchers, we believe it is critical to study anomalous experiences because they are not infrequent and often play important roles in people's lives. We are optimistic that systematic research that follows the recommendations outlined above will lead to important breakthroughs in understanding both psychopathology and positive mental health.

REFERENCES

American Psychiatric Association. (1994). *Diagnostic and statistical manual of mental disorders* (4th ed.). Washington, DC: Author.

Baron, R. M., & Kenny, D. A. (1986). The moderator–mediator variable distinction in social psychological research: Conceptual, strategic, and statistical considerations. *Journal of Personality and Social Psychology, 51,* 1173–1182.

Berenbaum, H. (1996). Peculiarity. In C. G. Costello (Ed.), *Personality characteristics of the personality disordered* (pp. 206–241). New York: Wiley.

Berenbaum, H. (1999). Peculiarity and reported childhood maltreatment. *Psychiatry, 62,* 21–35.

Berenbaum, H., & Fujita, F. (1994). Schizophrenia and personality: Exploring the boundaries and connections between vulnerability and outcome. *Journal of Abnormal Psychology, 103,* 148–158.

Bergner, R. M. (1997). What is psychopathology? And so what? *Clinical Psychology: Science and Practice, 4,* 235–248.

Cardeña, E. (1997). The etiologies of dissociation. In S. Powers & S. Krippner (Eds.), *Broken images, broken selves* (pp. 61–87). New York: Brunner.

Chapman, L. J., & Chapman, J. P. (1980). Scales for rating psychotic and psychotic-like experiences as continua. *Schizophrenia Bulletin, 6,* 476–489.

Chapman, L. J., Chapman, J. P., & Raulin, M. J. (1978). Body-image aberration in schizophrenia. *Journal of Abnormal Psychology, 87,* 399–407.

Chua, S. E., & McKenna, P. J. (1995). Schizophrenia: A brain disease? A critical review of structural and functional cerebral abnormality. *British Journal of Psychiatry, 166,* 563–582.

Clark, L. A., Watson, D., & Mineka, S. (1994). Temperament, personality, and the mood and anxiety disorders. *Journal of Abnormal Psychology, 103,* 103–116.

Cutting, J. (1990). *The right cerebral hemisphere and psychiatric disorder.* Oxford, England: Oxford University Press.

Cutting, J. (1992). The role of right hemisphere dysfunction in psychiatric disorder. *British Journal of Psychiatry, 160,* 583–588.

Daley, S. E., Hammen, C., Burge, D., Davila, J., Paley, B., Lindberg, N., & Herzberg, D. S. (1997). Predictors of the generation of episodic stress: A longitudinal study of late adolescent women. *Journal of Abnormal Psychology, 106,* 251–259.

David, A. S. (1994). The neuropsychological origin of auditory hallucinations. In A. S. David & J. C. Cutting (Eds.), *The neuropsychology of schizophrenia* (pp. 269–313). Hove, England: Erlbaum.

Epstein, S., & Meier, P. (1989). Constructive thinking: A broad coping variable with specific components. *Journal of Personality and Social Psychology, 57,* 332–350.

Fernandez, A., Lichtshein, G., & Vieweg, V. R. (1997). The Charles Bonnet Syndrome: A review. *Journal of Nervous and Mental Disease, 185,* 195–200.

Giorgi, A. (1970). Toward phenomenologically based research in psychology. *Journal of Phenomenological Psychology, 1,* 75–98.

Giorgi, A. (1986). Status of qualitative research in the human sciences: A limited interdisciplinary and international perspective. *Methods: A Journal for Human Science, 1,* 29–62.

Maher, B. A. (1974). Delusional thinking and perceptual disorder. *Journal of Individual Psychology, 30,* 98–113.

Maher, B. A. (1988). Anomalous experience and delusional thinking: The logic of explanations. In T. F. Oltmanns & B. A. Maher (Eds.), *Delusional beliefs* (pp. 15–33). New York: Wiley.

McGuffin, P., Farmer, A. E., Gottesman, I. I., Murray, R. M., & Reveley, A. M. (1984). Twin concordance for operationally defined schizophrenia: Confirmation of familiality and heritability. *Archives of General Psychiatry, 41,* 541–545.

Merriam-Webster's Collegiate Dictionary Deluxe Edition. (1998). Springfield, MA: Merriam-Webster.

Mullen, P. E., Martin, J. L., Anderson, J. C., Romans, S. E., & Herbison, G. P. (1993). Childhood sexual abuse and mental health in adult life. *British Journal of Psychiatry, 163,* 721–732.

Ossorio, P. (1985). Pathology. In K. Davis & T. Mitchell (Eds.), *Advances in descriptive psychology* (Vol. 4, pp. 151–202). Greenwich, CT: JAI Press.

Ring, K. (1992). *The Omega Project: Near-death experiences, UFO encounters, and the mind at large.* New York: Morrow.

Slade, P. D. (1974). The external control of auditory hallucinations: An information theory analysis. *British Journal of Social and Clinical Psychology, 13,* 73–79.

Spiegel, D., & Cardeña, E. (1991). Disintegrated experience: The dissociative disorders revisited. *Journal of Abnormal Psychology, 100,* 366–378.

Spitzer, R. L. (1997). Brief comments from a psychiatric nosologist weary from his own attempts to define mental disorder: Why Ossorio's definition muddles and Wakefield's "harmful dysfunction" illuminates the issues. *Clinical Psychology: Science and Practice, 4,* 259–261.

Strauss, J. S. (1969). Hallucinations and delusions as points on continua function. *Archives of General Psychiatry, 21,* 581–586.

Teasdale, J. D., Taylor, M. J., Cooper, Z., Hayhurst, H., & Paykel, E. S. (1995). Depressive thinking: Shifts in construct accessibility or in schematic mental models. *Journal of Abnormal Psychology, 104,* 500–507.

Venables, P. H. (1977). The electrodermal physiology of schizophrenics and children at risk for schizophrenia: Controversies and developments. *Schizophrenia Bulletin, 3,* 28–48.

Wakefield, J. (1992). The concept of mental disorder: On the boundary between biological facts and social values. *American Psychologist, 47,* 373–388.

Wallace, J. F., & Newman, J. P. (1997). Neuroticism and the affective mediation of dysregulatory psychopathology. *Cognitive Therapy and Research, 21,* 135–156.

Waller, N. G., & Meehl, P. E. (1998). *Multivariate taxometric procedures.* Thousand Oaks, CA: Sage.

Waller, N. G., & Ross, C. A. (1997). The prevalence and biometric structure of pathological dissociation in the general population: Taxometric and behavior genetic findings. *Journal of Abnormal Psychology, 106,* 499–510.

Ward, B., & Russell, N. (Trans.). *The lives of the desert fathers: The historia monachorum in aegypto.* Kalamazoo, MI: Cistercian. (Original work written ca. 395)

Widiger, T. A. (1993). The *DSM–III–R* categorical personality disorder diagnoses: A critique and an alternative. *Psychological Inquiry, 4,* 75–90.

Winters, K. C., & Neale, J. M. (1983). Delusions and delusional thinking in psychotics: A review of the literature. *Clinical Psychology Review, 3,* 227–253.

Zinbarg, R. E., & Barlow, D. H. (1995). Structure of anxiety and the anxiety disorders: A hierarchical model. *Journal of Abnormal Psychology, 105,* 181–193.

2

METHODOLOGICAL ISSUES IN THE STUDY OF ALTERED STATES OF CONSCIOUSNESS AND ANOMALOUS EXPERIENCES

RONALD J. PEKALA AND ETZEL CARDEÑA

Almost 100 years ago, a grand figure in North American psychology, William James (1902/1958), wrote the following:

> Our normal waking consciousness, rational consciousness as we call it, is but one special type of consciousness, whilst all about it, parted from it by the filmiest of screens, there lie potential forms of consciousness entirely different. We may go through life without suspecting their existence; but apply the requisite stimulus, and at a touch they are there in all completeness, definite types of mentality which probably somewhere have their field of application and adaptation. No account of the universe in its totality can be final which leaves these other forms of consciousness quite disregarded. How to regard them is the question—for they are so discontinuous with ordinary consciousness. (p. 298)

At least some of the experiences addressed in this book fall within the "potential forms of consciousness entirely different" from usual experience.

The concept of altered states of consciousness is predicated on the assumption that different, alternate (Zinberg, 1977), or altered (Krippner, 1972; Ludwig, 1966/1972) states of consciousness (Pekala, 1991d; Tart, 1977) exist. These different states, in turn, may lead to different ways of knowing or experiencing the nature of reality. It is pertinent to remember James's (1902/1958) argument that although people in the ordinary waking state are certain that such a state is the purveyor of reality, an equivalent certainty ensues in other states.

Because how we know (epistemology) may determine or influence what we know (metaphysics), it is important to address basic epistemological issues. For this reason, we (a) define consciousness and its place in academic psychology; (b) focus on the limitations, reliability, and validity of introspective reports; (c) review and provide examples of various methodologies used to investigate subjective awareness, with an emphasis on a methodology developed by the first author and colleagues to quantify and statistically assess altered states of consciousness; (d) address the question of individual differences in reference to who is most likely to report anomalous phenomena; and (e) propose further lines of inquiry into the study of anomalous experience.

CONSCIOUSNESS AND ITS STUDY

The word *consciousness* comes from the Latin *conscious*, which means to "know with" or "know together" (*Webster's Seventh New Collegiate Dictionary*, 1970). Natsoulas (1989) has discussed the various senses of the term. The modern study of psychological processes started as a study of consciousness in the work of the structural psychologies of Wundt (1897) and Titchener (1898) and the functionalist psychologies of James (1890/1950) and Angell (1907).

On the European continent in the late 19th and early 20th centuries, phenomenology guided the works of Brentano (1874/1925) and Husserl (1913/1972) in philosophy and of Katz, Wertheimer, and Köhler in Gestalt psychology (Köhler, 1929/1950). The study of consciousness, however, soon faded with the rise of behaviorism (Watson, 1913) and its exclusive emphasis on observable behavior. It was not until the 1960s that the study of consciousness and its processes again became a legitimate area of psychological inquiry (Holt, 1964).

There were many reasons why the exploration of consciousness fell from grace at the beginning of the 20th century. One was that structuralists such as Titchener limited their research on consciousness to atomistic analyses of sensations, which sought to reduce complex experiences to their basic components. Another was the fact that the variations of introspective methods used in various laboratories seemed to lead to different results, without a clear way to solve these disputes. Two famous examples are the disagreements between the Titchener and Külpe laboratories concerning the number of primary sensations and whether every thought requires some type of image (Güzeldere, 1995).

According to Boring (1953), classical introspection

> went out of style after Titchener's death (1927) because it had demonstrated no functional use ... and also because it was unreliable. Laboratory atmosphere crept into the descriptions, and it was not possible to verify, from one laboratory to another, the introspective accounts of the consciousness of action, feelings, choice, and judgment. (p. 174)

Danziger (1980), however, questioned Boring's (1953) analysis and concluded that introspection "was less a victim of its intrinsic problem than a casualty of historical forces far bigger than itself" (p. 259), behaviorism foremost among them. During the decades-long dominance of behaviorism, the death-knell for the study of states of consciousness and anomalous experiences sounded stridently within academia. John Watson (1913) determined that, for behaviorism, introspection "forms no essential part of its method" (p. 158) and suggested the "elimination of states of consciousness as proper objects of investigation" (p. 177). Despite the more comprehensive behaviorist perspectives of Edward C. Tolman and a few others, for decades there was almost no inquiry into states of consciousness or anomalous experiences.

The "cognitive revolution" in psychology (Gardner, 1985) validated the possibility and importance of studying mental events, and a number of authors (e.g., Kukla, 1983; Lieberman, 1979; Richardson, 1984) argued that consciousness can be reliably and validly investigated with perceptual, psychophysiological, and phenomenological research methods. Marsh (1977), Battista (1978), and Natsoulas (e.g., 1978), among others, also paved the way toward regarding introspection, or *phenomenological observation*, as it is sometimes called (Hilgard, 1980), as an object of legitimate scientific inquiry. For instance, Singer's (1978) prolific work in the areas of daydreaming, private experience, and personality; Mandler's (1985) observations on the structure of mind and consciousness; Anderson's Adaptive Control of Thought (1983) model; Baars's (1988) global workspace theory of consciousness; Izard's (1977) differential emotions theory; and the burgeoning investigations of parallel distributed processing models of cognition (e.g., McClelland & Rumelhart, 1985) demonstrated that consciousness could be theoretically modeled and empirically investigated.

Work on the psychology of consciousness has continued with the more recent works of Baars (1997) and Rychlak (1997), among others. Professional journals directly concerned with the study of consciousness have been launched recently, including *Consciousness and Cognition* and the *Journal of Consciousness Studies*. In addition, older journals such as *Imagination, Cognition and Personality*, and the *International Journal of Clinical and Experimental Hypnosis* have discussed specific issues in consciousness.

RELIABILITY AND VALIDITY OF INTROSPECTIVE ACCESS TO CONSCIOUSNESS

Consciousness can be studied phenomenologically, by having participants introspectively report on their subjective experiences (Pekala, 1991d); psychophysiologically, by assessing changes in physiological parameters, such as electroencephalogram, or EEG, as a function of states such as dreaming (Dement, 1978) or meditation (Wallace, 1993); and socioecologically, through historical analyses of cultural consciousness (Gebser, 1986). Although theorizing about consciousness has become almost commonplace these days, it may remain fruitless unless sophisticated methodologies can adequately map states of consciousness in a reliable and valid manner.

Introspection has become an important avenue for exploring and understanding consciousness (Baars, 1997; Pekala, 1991d), but some authors consider that science is based on the premise "that knowledge should be acquired through observation" (Weiten, 1998, p. 15) of objective, "external" events as compared with subjective, "internal" experience. Because of this difference in research focus, there has been much controversy in psychology over the reliability of introspective data. Nisbett and Wilson (1977) indicated that, with regard to accessing cognitive processes, introspective access "is not sufficient to produce generally correct, or reliable reports" (p. 233). Nisbett and Wilson were partially correct when discussing the limitations of self-observations in discovering the causes of one's actions, but Smith and Miller (1978) replied that personal assessment of cognitive processes is not as inaccessible as Nisbett and Wilson had suggested. Although there may be problems with self-report data, when people are asked to describe the content (the *what*) of their subjective experience, their reports are much more accurate than when they are asked to describe the causes of those experiences (the *whys*, see Ericsson & Simon, 1980; Lieberman, 1979). Güzeldere (1995) made the relevant distinction between introspection as "the examination of one's own mental happenings" and introspection as "reasoning about the causes of one's own behaviour" (p. 38). The former type of introspection is the focus of our chapter.

In their review of the relevant literature, Singer and Kolligan (1987) stated that "reports using [self-report] questionnaires all converge in suggesting that people can generally provide reasonably valid and reliable indices of their own differential patterns of ongoing inner thought" (p. 542). Other reviews by Ericsson and Simon (1980), Klinger (1978), Lieberman (1979), and Farthing (1992) agreed that data derived through introspection can be both valid and useful, despite the misgivings of behaviorists like Rachlin (1974) and Skinner (1974, 1989).

What critics of introspective access have typically glossed over is the fact that many of the limitations of introspective reports (e.g., lying, uncertainty about the extent to which the same linguistic labels refer to the same experience) are also applicable to reports of observable data (Kukla, 1983). Indeed, determining the validity of reports of subjective experiences may be difficult, but it is not an insurmountable problem, as Richardson (1984) and others have argued. The determination of the validity of introspective data must be based on empirical investigation, rather than on philosophical predilections.

It will be useful to clarify what introspection can and cannot accomplish (see Farthing, 1992). First, as James (1890/1950) noted, most episodes in the stream of thought or awareness are not self-reflective or introspective. In fact, the frequency of reflective conscious episodes for most people is low (Langer, 1989), which is why insight meditation and similar disciplines seek to enhance the extent and control of self-reflective life. Second, introspection is not a sensory process that somehow externally "observes" the stream of thought, because introspective experiences are themselves segments of an individual's stream of thought. Third, introspection is not a report about nervous system activity, because the content of introspection refers to episodes of experience, not of physiology. Fourth, one should differentiate between an introspection, which refers to the description of a conscious event that only the experiencer can possess, and inferences drawn from behavior about the mental life of the experiencer. The methodological behaviorist school (Watson, 1913) and Wittgenstein (1953) earlier proposed that psychology could refer only to inference from behavior.

Finally, Farthing (1992) asserted that introspection does not entail direct observation of inner experience but is rather a reflection on conscious experience: "[It] is a case of reflective consciousness. It is thinking about one's conscious experience. The initial 'raw' experience is a matter of primary consciousness" (p. 46; but see Natsoulas, 1989, for a different view on the "directness" of this observation). Hence, introspection involves the description of the contents and processes of conscious experience without elaboration, inferences, or attributions; in other words, the individual "observes" the contents of his or her consciousness during the introspective period in question and describes that "raw" experience. Introspection involves reporting on the what of subjective experience, not the why or the how.

LIMITS OF INTROSPECTION

As with every other research method, introspective verbal reports present specific limitations and risks (Farthing, 1992; Richardson, 1984). We discuss these in the following sections.

Forgetting

Especially when the experience to be described occurs hours or longer before the report, it can be expected that the recall process will conform to the classical curve of forgetting described by Ebbinghaus (1885/1964) at the turn of the century. That is, unless the individual is reexposed to the material to be remembered or deliberately rehearses the information, much or most of the material will be forgotten shortly after exposure, with the gradient of forgetfulness decreasing with time. Although Ebbinghaus-like studies have been conducted with externally generated words or images, there is no a priori reason to expect that subjective experiences would produce different effects. However, mention should be made of Erdelyi's (1996) controversial finding that repeated questioning may bring about recovery of material not recalled initially. In general, data collection should occur as soon as possible after the event of interest to avoid the loss of important material. Nonetheless, some accurate recollection may be "blocked" at the time of recollection and resurface at a later point (cf. Erdelyi, 1996; Schacter, 1999).

Reconstruction Errors and Confabulation

The classical model of memory reconstruction mistakes was advanced by Bartlett (1932), who found that Western respondents followed a more typical outline when remembering a tale that did not follow the structure of a conventional Western narrative. He concluded that memories may be reconstructed to follow more closely the cultural prototype for that experience (see Appelle, Lynn, & Newman, this volume, chap. 8). More generally, Schacter (1999) concluded that knowledge, beliefs, expectations, and moods can bias the encoding and retrieval of memory (p. 193).

Besides distortions that may "normalize" a memory, in the study of anomalous experiences the researcher should also be aware of the opposite problem, namely that some respondents may reconstruct their memories to be more unusual and thus "more interesting." The researcher should consider such issues as motivation, plausibility, and internal coherence of the narrative when addressing the accuracy of memories of anomalous experiences but be careful not to dismiss the memory of an anomalous experience just because it is unusual. There is currently no infallible way to distinguish accurately recalled material, trivial memory mistakes that do not change the gist of what occurred, and outright fabrications, but this applies to memories of both "objective" and "subjective" events.

Verbal Description Difficulties

Before a discussion of the difficulties in describing anomalous experiences, it is wise to remember that even less exotic phenomena, such as describing the flavor of a particular fruit to someone who has never tasted it, resist verbal description. Even the best account of an experience cannot completely convey what the experience is really like (Nagel, 1974/1982), which is why Bertrand Russell (1917/1970) made a distinction between knowledge by description and knowledge by acquaintance. But besides this general limitation of language, some experiences seem to be especially problematic.

Mystical experiences are commonly cited as ineffable or indescribable. Attempts to put into words characteristics of the experience often involve apparent contradictions (e.g., a "brilliant darkness" or an "all encompassing void"). Thus, it is not surprising that at times the evocative language of poetry may seem a better descriptor of mystical experiences than a more analytic, denotative language (Underhill, 1911/1972). Nonetheless, these utterances and the experiences they reflect can be studied for their internal, historical, and cross-cultural consistency and have given rise to a fine distinction between types of mysticism (see Forman, 1998; Wulff, this volume, chap. 12).

Another option is to do comparative analyses of dimensions such as valence and intensity, as in the study of emotions (e.g., Frijda, 1986). This approach was taken by Clark (1983) for mental states, although with questionable success.

Distortion Through Observation and Substitution of Inferences for Observation

Kant (1781/1966) concluded that the mind could not be observed directly without distortion and thus that psychology could not aspire to be a science (Robinson, 1995). Although introspection is thought to be especially prone to this type of distortion, other research methods, with the exception of unobtrusive measures or archival research, also affect the natural progression of an individual's life. Even "innocuous" questionnaires, in asking an individual to recollect an event, are at the very least bringing a created focus onto it. The issue is not whether introspective methods affect consciousness, but whether they distort it enough to invalidate the data obtained.

Perhaps the most direct scrutiny of this issue has been undertaken with the "thinking out loud" procedure (see below). A different approach to minimize the distortion produced by introspection has been proposed by advocates of mindfulness meditation, who claim that this practice provides a more thorough and undistorted account of subjective experience than regular introspection (Varela, Thompson, & Rosch, 1991). Although it is not reasonable to assume that introspection is the only method that can affect the phenomena to which it refers, it is still wise to elucidate the extent to which an inquiry may distort the phenomenon.

Also, during introspection, individuals may confuse inferences or comments about their experiences with the experiences themselves. This problem can be reduced by clearly defining to the participants what constitutes introspection. The researcher could state that direct, immediate experience is what the person senses, feels, or thinks at the moment, whereas inferences and attributions concern explanations or comments about those experiences.

The problem of distortion through observation should be distinguished from the decision to use naïve versus proficient introspectionists. Such a decision depends on the research question, which may lead to an attempt to secure a "typical" everyday experience or to obtain more elaborate reports from trained individuals that may yield additional or clearer aspects of experience (Varela, 1996). The successful programmatic research of Siegel on the psychedelic experiences of participants trained in precise observation and verbalization exemplifies the value of providing precise descriptors when studying altered states (e.g., Siegel & West, 1975).

Censorship

Research participants, like other human beings, occasionally have bizarre or private thoughts about sexual or other matters that they may feel uncomfortable divulging to an experimenter, who is typically a stranger. The censorship of these thoughts may be inconsequential to the specific research question, but when a complete account of ideation is required, there are strategies that the researcher may use to minimize this limitation. One involves a request for complete honesty, while guaranteeing that the participants' reports will remain anonymous. When that procedure is not feasible, the experimenter may ask participants to indicate when they are censoring some event, so that an estimate of unreported material can be obtained.

Lack of Independent Verification

Perhaps the major criticism of behaviorism against the study of consciousness was the notion that whereas behavior is "public," consciousness is private and not amenable to independent verification (e.g., Watson, 1913). Methodological behaviorists were, in a way, correct in their asser-tion but fell short in their criticism. Indeed, introspective verbal reports lack direct verification by others, but so do more traditional data, such as perceptual events (e.g., a report of seeing a square on the computer screen), behavioral relations (e.g., the assumption that I am pressing a lever when I see a square on the screen, rather than randomly), and recollections or evaluations (e.g., just about any answer to a questionnaire). Paradoxically, observable data, such as social events (Ornstein, 1986) or even simple tonal stimuli (Deutsch, 1988), can have very different effects on observers, whereas internal data, such as the time it takes someone to imagine the rotation of a cube 45°, can be precisely predicted by external observers (Shepard & Cooper, 1982). As Varela (1996) stated,

> the usual opposition of first-person vs. third-person accounts is mis-leading. It makes us forget that so-called third-person, objective accounts are done by a community of concrete people who are embodied in their social and natural world as much as first-person accounts. (p. 340)

There are various procedures to independently evaluate a subjective report. They include assessing its internal consistency and its consistency with reports from comparable observers in similar contexts, the verisimilitude of the report, the reliability of the observer in other contexts, and so on. More formal methods of report validation include triangulation or cross-validation with other measures that would be expected to provide corroborating information. For instance, in the field of hypnosis, reports by highly hypnotizable individuals about suggested decreases in pain sensations are consistent with a decrease in the amplitude of related somatosensory event-related potentials (i.e., EEGs locked to the presentation of stimuli; Spiegel, Bierre, & Rootenberg, 1989).

Dissembling and Social Desirability

There is little information on the extent to which volunteers dissemble or give "socially desirable" answers during psychological experiments. Nonetheless, to assume that lying never occurs in psychological research or clinical practice would be naïve. For instance, the first author interviewed an individual who reported a near-death experience (NDE) that was incongruous with the surgeon's report of his condition at the time and with other NDE reports. The patient recanted his story after repeatedly being confronted with its various incongruities. The second author has had similar experiences in the research context.

When there is a reason to doubt the veracity of reports of anomalous experiences, the researcher can try to evaluate their internal and external consistency, the degree to which the reports can be confirmed by other indices, and the individuals' motivation to dissemble or to provide socially "appropriate" responses. More formal types of evaluation can be achieved through "lie" and "social desirability" scales (Rorer, 1990).

Demand Characteristics

Demand characteristics (Orne, 1962) can be defined as the totality of cues "within the research context that guide or bias a subject's behavior" (Heiman, 1995, p. 473). The concept of experimenter effect refers to those "subtle cues provided by the experimenter about the responses that subjects should give in a particular condition" (p. 474). Both hazards are present in other areas of psychology as well as the study of subjective experience. A classic example is the study by Orne and Scheibe (1964), in which participants were adversely affected by a "sensory deprivation study" (which actually only involved remaining alone in a room) only when the context implied that their mental condition might be negatively affected by the study. Also, some researchers may give implicit or explicit suggestions for particular answers and then reinforce such answers, thus invalidating the reports obtained (see Cardeña, 1997).

Researchers should be cognizant of the effect that implicit or explicit cues may have on the participants, which is not to say that the context should be cold and "sterile." Such a setting could, in fact, discourage a participant from revealing unusual and personal experiences. Tart (1972a) and Barabasz and Barabasz (1992) discussed these issues in greater detail and agreed that an open and collaborative setting when controlling for demand characteristics may also be optimal when studying hypnosis and states of consciousness.

Furthermore, although it has become standard practice in a research report to provide information only about the participant, there is long-standing evidence (e.g., Silverman, 1974) that demographic and other experimenter characteristics may affect the participant's response. Investigators should remember that research is a social context in which they exert influences that they should be aware of and perhaps, measure or control.

Inaccessibility Due to "State-Specific" Memory

As originally proposed by Tart (1972b) in *Science* and further developed in a later article (Tart, 1999),

> Essential science has so far been (officially) done in our ordinary state of consciousness, but my understanding of any state of consciousness is that any state has both advantages and disadvantages. There is no one state that is uniformly superior in all regards. . . . Thus if we want a complete understanding of consciousness, we must practice essential science in a variety of states of consciousness, and create and refine complementary bodies of state-specific knowledge. (p. 11)

This is a very tall order that science has yet to consider, let alone accept. Tart's (1999) theorizing, however, suggests the importance of the knowledge by acquaintance (Russell, 1917/1970) of anomalous experiences. Perhaps the best example of a program of research that has benefited enormously from the ability of the experimenter to access and control an anomalous experience is lucid dreaming (LaBerge & Gackenbach, this volume, chap. 5). On the other hand, Wulff (this volume, chap. 12) points out that researchers who may have a mystical experience could very well decide to leave traditional scientific practices altogether. In any case, it seems that Tart's ideas deserve consideration and further development.

In a more limited sense, there is evidence (e.g., Stillman, Weingartner, Wyatt, Gillin, & Eich, 1974) that information learned or remembered in a specific state of awareness may not be remembered unless accessed during a similar state to that which occurred when learning took place (i.e., "state-specific" memory). Hence, introspective access of an experience that occurs in an altered state of consciousness may not be accurately recalled unless the individual is able to reexperience a similar state. In cases in which state-dependent effects on memory are likely (see Overton, 1978), the investigator of anomalous experiences may consider evoking a similar state to that present when the experience of interest occurred. This technique may lead to a higher yield of memories, especially when there are no stronger cues available to activate the recall of the experience (Tobias, Kihlstrom, & Schacter, 1992). However, even in these circumstances, the researcher should be careful to control demand characteristics and to inform the participant that techniques such as hypnosis may overinflate the level of confidence that the individual has in his or her recollection (McConkey & Sheehan, 1995). An interesting option to enhance recall is Sheehan and McConkey's (1982/1996) Experiential Analysis Technique, in which a person who has undergone a hypnotic procedure later reviews a videotape of the same and comments on what he or she was experiencing during the procedure.

In conclusion, as with other areas of psychological research, the validity of introspective or phenomenological data finally resides "in ruling out artifacts, in replications, and ultimately, in the usefulness of data or theory for making possible other forms of prediction and, perhaps, control" (Klinger, 1978, p. 227).

METHODOLOGIES FOR STUDYING ALTERED STATES OF CONSCIOUSNESS

No understanding of anomalous experiences would be complete without considering *altered states* of consciousness (ASC). The concept of states of consciousness can be traced back to James's *The Varieties of Religious*

Experience (1902/1958). Krippner (1972), Ludwig (1966/1972), and Tart (1969) defined and popularized the terms *state of consciousness* and *altered states of consciousness*, as they are currently used today. Ludwig (1966/1972) defined an *altered state* as

> Any mental state(s), induced by various physiological, psychological, or pharmacological maneuvers or agents, which can be recognized subjectively by the individual himself [or herself] (or by an objective observer of the individual) as representing a sufficient deviation in subjective experience or psychological functioning from certain general norms for that individual during alert, waking consciousness. (p. 11)

Tart (1972a), arguably the most important theorist in ASC research, defined an *altered state of consciouness* as "a qualitative alteration in the overall pattern of mental functioning such that the experiencer feels his [or her] consciousness is radically different from the 'normal' way it functions" (p. 95).

States and ASC need to be clearly defined to determine if one particular state of consciousness is indeed altered significantly from another or from "ordinary" consciousness. Some anomalous experiences examined in this book occur mostly or completely during ASC (e.g., lucid dreaming, NDEs), whereas the nature of others (e.g., alien abduction experiences [AAEs]) is less clear. Assessment of traits such as hypnotizability, absorption, and dissociation (Cardeña, 1994; Pekala, Kumar, & Marcano, 1995) are of paramount importance to the study of anomalous experience.

The Greek etymology for "method" is *methodos*, which means "a way." The history of psychology shows a slow and, at times, arduous evolution of the empirical methods that Galileo, John Stuart Mill, and others developed (Robinson, 1995). Although the empirical method was an improvement over such epistemological approaches as authority or divine revelation, some authors have justly criticized the notion that there is a specific scientific method that can be automatically used to study any topic, without consideration of its nature or the type of question asked. Bakan (1969) coined the term *methodolatry* to denote the mindless use of methods and the sacrifice of substantive questions to methodological expediency.

With this caveat, we briefly describe some general approaches and methods that have been used to investigate subjective experience (see also Farthing, 1992), with an emphasis on the methodology developed by the first author. Bear in mind that this is not a prescriptive list, because there is no substitute for fully understanding the phenomenon being researched and the specific question being asked. It is also true that no amount of methodological sophistication can provide an intuitive "feeling for the organism" (or the phenomenon), a cardinal quality ascribed to the Nobel prize-winning geneticist Barbara McClintock.

A full consideration of the importance of culture on anomalous experience is beyond this chapter. However, we can at least state that, when studying anomalous experiences in other cultures or subcultures, one's immersion into the culture's ethnoepistemology (the group's notions of what knowledge is and how it is obtained), practices, sensory experience, and language may be necessary before that experience can be fully appreciated (Stoller, 1989). Sacks (1995) provided many examples of the necessary entry into the experiential world of individuals with various neuropathies before they can be understood, and Turnbull (1990) offered a clear example of his inability to make sense of the rituals of the Mbuti until he had an experiential taste of their "subjective mode of awareness." He was then able to discern an experience that, from his own, previously naïve, stance seemed incomprehensible.

PHENOMENOLOGICAL APPROACHES

Phenomenology is a term that refers to a philosophy, a research approach and, in a more general way, the study of experience. As a philosophy, it is a school focused on the search for the direct apprehension of reality through understanding and suspending (or "bracketing") the various assumptions and presuppositions that distort one's apprehension of "the things themselves," to use Edmund Husserl's famous dictum. Phenomenology's most influential exponents are Husserl (1913/1972) and Merleau-Ponty (1962).

Two main approaches to phenomenological methodology can be distinguished, one that emphasizes "first-person" experience and discernment and another that emphasizes a "second- and third-person" model to the study of experience. Varela (1996) illustrated a first-person "systematic exploration of . . . *the structure of human experience itself*" (p. 330). His proposed method of neurophenomenology includes steps that a phenomenological researcher has to personally undertake: attitude ("to cultivate a systematic capacity for reflexion" [p. 337] of various automatic assumptions), intimacy (a systematic cultivation of alternative forms of apprehension and intuition), description of the contents of consciousness, and sustained training in these endeavors. Clearly, this is a very different research approach than that of the usual testing of untrained participants.

Amedeo Giorgi's method (e.g., Giorgi, 1990) exemplifies a second- and third-person phenomenological approach. Giorgi suggested that researchers, at least initially, study the phenomenon of interest without theoretical assumptions, which may reveal more about their looking glasses than about the phenomenon itself. The aim of his method is to obtain a thorough description of the phenomenon, typically through detailed, open interviews to understand how a particular psychological event is experienced by the interviewees, who function more as coresearchers than as research "subjects." From the interviews, salient units of meaning are then abstracted, interpreted, and further elaborated or corroborated with the same individual and others. This process should result in an unbiased description and understanding of the phenomenon studied. By using multiple participants, the method can ascertain how generalizable a particular experience is. Giorgi also advocated using complementary methods, such as life histories and case studies, and reconsidering the value of quasi-experimental designs. As a relevant example, "deep states" of meditation were studied by Gifford-May and Thompson (1994) using this approach.

Concurrent Report Methods

In this section, we describe methods that probe for experiences or mental events as they unfold. In a sense, all reports are retrospective in that, at the very least, there is a small interval of time between the experience and its verbal or behavioral expression. Nonetheless, there is still an important difference between reports of events that just occurred and those that occurred minutes, hours, or longer ago. Concurrent reports have the advantage of not having the memory limitations of retrospective reports of events that happened some time ago. On the other hand, they may affect an ongoing experience or may not answer other valuable questions, such as what are the long-term effects of that particular event.

Thinking out loud denotes the ongoing verbal report of the contents of consciousness in a particular situation. Although Ericsson and Simon (1980) argued that thinking out loud does not affect in any meaningful way the stream of consciousness it describes, whether a specific anomalous experience of interest will be seriously affected by continuous reporting remains an empirical question. This method is particularly useful when a comprehensive (but by no means total, because of the temporal and representational limitations of language and memory), ongoing account of an anomalous experience is desirable and feasible. In cognitive psychology, thinking out loud has been used to study problem solving, among other areas (see Newell & Simon, 1972). It has been used in Ganzfeld research (Ullman, Krippner, & Vaughan, 1973; see also Targ, Schlitz, & Irwin, this volume, chap. 7), in which percipients in a context of homogeneous sensory stimulation report their stream of consciousness while attempting clairvoyance or precognitive tasks (see Radin, 1997, for a review of this research).

Event recording is a procedure in which a particular event (e.g., a thought or emotion) is defined and its every occurrence then registered by means of a counter or similar device. This procedure may be effective in gauging the frequency of a specific experiential event. Event recordings are used in therapy to evaluate, at baseline and after intervention, the incidence of a targeted event or cognition, such as obsessions (Caballo, 1991).

In the area of consciousness, Kubose (1976) used this method to evaluate thought intrusions during meditation.

Thought sampling requires that participants report what their mental activity was just before the prompt of a signaling device or pager. The signals are typically given at random times to minimize instrumentation effects such as the expectation of a page or signal at a particular time. This method can be easily used outside of the laboratory, thus enhancing its ecological validity. Because it uses repeated measures, it is also likely to provide a more representative view of the event investigated than single-testing techniques (see Epstein, 1983). However, it does not give an indication of how transient experiences may impact or be integrated into the individual's schemas of the self and the world.

Klinger (1978) offered a classic example of the thought-sampling method in his study of stream-of-consciousness among undergraduate students, and in a series of studies, Hurlburt (1990) used it to compare normal and pathological inner experience. More recently, Easterlin and Cardeña (1998/1999) used experiential sampling reports to compare the reactions to stress in samples of beginner and very experienced mindfulness meditators.

Depth ratings provide quantitative evaluations of a particular experiential dimension along a continuum. Probably the most researched variation of this method involves self-ratings of hypnotic depth (e.g., light, medium, or deep). In this case, an agreed-on numerical scale signals the individual's "depth" of hypnosis; the scale may include experiential landmarks to define specific numbers (Tart, 1979) or remain undefined (Cardeña, 1988). There is evidence that hypnotic depth ratings are significant predictors of objective and subjective responses to standardized hypnotic tests (Tart, 1979). A recent development in depth ratings involves the use of a dial to describe the participant's experience during hypnosis (McConkey, Wende, & Barnier, 1999).

Retrospective Report Methods

Most of the methods used to research anomalous experiences entail some form of retrospective reporting. In some cases, such as in AAEs and NDEs (see this volume, Appelle et al., chap. 8, and Greyson, chap. 10), this may be the only feasible approach to study the experience.

The main advantages of retrospective reports are that they will not affect an ongoing experience and may provide an account of how the person has integrated and interpreted that experience. On the other hand, these reports are more vulnerable than concurrent accounts to forgetting and other memory problems. These two problems, however, can be minimized when the report occurs shortly after the event of interest.

There are different types of retrospective report methods, among them the following.

Diaries contain longitudinal narratives of individuals' lives. Usually they are accounts of what the individual considers to be important or of particular events such as dreams. If the question of interest concerns the long-term effect of an event, such as a mystical experience, diaries can be one of the best methods available. Diaries also can be useful when the event in question, for instance, the long-term pattern of dreams, cannot be realistically studied in a laboratory setting (Hall & Van de Castle, 1966), or when investigators want to know how the person reflects about and integrates a particular experience. On the other hand, researchers should become aware that diarists can be very selective and filter out unseemly material or embellish some events, especially if they know that their diaries will be read by others.

Interviews are one of the basic staples of clinical psychology but they are rarely treated by other branches of psychology with the seriousness they deserve. Although it may not be feasible to conduct interviews with all research participants, the easiest way to find out something specific about a person's mental conflicts is usually to ask him or her about it. Most other research methods can be profitably supplemented by good interviews. For many projects, the time and energy expense of interviews are a major impediment to their use, but even short interviews should be used more often.

Interviews can be open, nondirective (as in the phenomenological approach), semistructured (with a few questions or topics that need to be addressed but that are otherwise flexible), or structured. The specific research perspective and question should dictate what approach to use. For instance, when it is important to evaluate if a particular anomalous experience occurred, say an out-of-body experience (OBE), a semistructured or structured approach may be called for (see Alvarado, this volume, chap. 6). If, on the other hand, there is concern that the questions may shape the individual's experience, a more open interview may be used (see Appelle et al., this volume, chap. 8).

Content analysis is the systematic quantitative or qualitative evaluation of previously obtained information. Such information is mostly but not exclusively verbal. The categories to be evaluated in the analysis may be syntactic (e.g., quality of verbal organization in a dream report), semantic (e.g., number of references to a theme of "unity" in a mystical experience), or both. Some examples include Hall's and van de Castle's content analyses of dreams (1966), Martindale's computer-assisted analysis of states of consciousness (1981), and discriminant analyses on autobiographical accounts of individuals reporting normal, schizophrenic, mystical, or drug-induced states (Oxman, Rosenberg, Schnurr, Tucker, & Gala, 1988).

Computer-assisted content analysis can be a valuable and time-saving strategy, but one should keep in mind that semantic nuances such as humor can be easily missed or misinterpreted by such analyses. Content analyses can help characterize a particular experience and help differentiate phenomena that are apparently related (e.g., Oxman et al., 1988). Because a word may have different meanings or interpretations in different eras and cultures or even among different individuals in the same geographic and cultural milieu, care must be taken when using this method.

Psychological tests, surveys, and questionnaires are widely used in all areas of psychology, including the study of anomalous experiences. General psychometric techniques have been of value to determine psychological characteristics of individuals who report anomalous experiences (Kumar & Pekala, in press; Pekala et al., 1995). Various ad hoc measures to study unusual states have also been developed (e.g., MacDonald, LeClair, Holland, Alter, & Friedman, 1995), although the reliability and validity of many have not been established. Tests, questionnaires, and surveys are usually economical, can be administered to many individuals at once, and permit easy comparison across studies. On the other hand, they may unduly constrain the participants' responses (Schwarz, 1999) and, in most cases, provide no information about differences in experiential content (e.g., a rating of 3 on one particular item may mean different things to different respondents). A more nomothetic use of tests is described in Wilber, Engler, and Brown (1986), who used the Rorschach and other tests to evaluate gifted meditators.

The Phenomenology of Consciousness Inventory (PCI; Pekala, 1991c) is probably the most flexible and well-documented instrument to evaluate different states of consciousness. It permits the reliable and valid measurement of various dimensions or subsystems of consciousness and allows them to be empirically quantified and statistically compared (Pekala, 1991d). It is described later in the chapter.

Case studies and life histories have a venerable tradition in clinical and developmental psychologies and neurology, but they have also proved useful in the study of anomalous experiences. Case studies refer to the systematic study of individuals or groups within a certain time frame, whereas life histories are studies that span most or all of an individual's life.

In a classic example, the Russian psychologist Luria (1968) gave a fascinating account of an individual who not only could accomplish extraordinary memory feats but who also had synesthetic experiences (see Marks, this volume, chap. 4). Although case studies cannot tell us how generalizable an experience is, they provide much more detailed information than other approaches; often indicate new or neglected areas of inquiry; and can give a sense of the complex interaction of many personal, social, and cultural variables (e.g., Erikson, 1969). For questions such as the developmental history of mystical experiences, life histories may be the most appropriate form of inquiry (see Wulff, this volume, chap. 12).

The *integration of various methods* can overcome the limitations of specific techniques. We are not proposing here only the cross-validation or triangulation of experiential and related physiological and behavioral indexes that are exemplified in the studies of lucid dreaming (see LaBerge & Gackenbach, this volume, chap. 5), and perceptual sensitivity enhancement following meditation (Brown, Forte, & Dysart, 1984). Rather, we propose integrating various methods that specifically evaluate experience. For example, Cardeña (1988, 1996; see also Wulff, this volume, chap. 12) integrated various methods in a study of the experience of hypnotic virtuosos (i.e., individuals with very high scores in standardized hypnotizability tests) asked to enter "very deep" hypnosis in three different physical conditions. In addition to using standardized tests to evaluate hypnotizability, Cardeña used depth ratings (to evaluate the participants' self-assessed hypnotic depth during the hypnotic sessions), thought sampling (to find out what the participants were experiencing during the sessions), structured questionnaires (including the PCI), retrospective reporting after the sessions, and interviews throughout the whole procedure. All of this was done within a cooperative framework in which participants were active contributors to the collection and interpretation of data. The use of various techniques enabled a comprehensive account of quantitative and qualitative variations among and between participants that could not have been obtained otherwise. For example, a questionnaire showed that the individuals' state of consciousness varied significantly across levels of hypnosis and physical activity, but thought-sampling and interviews yielded information about the content of the experience.

A PSYCHOPHENOMENOLOGICAL APPROACH

Much of the research explored in this book has relied exclusively on experiential self-reports. Because of the potential problems with unsystematic self-reports, reliable and valid techniques are needed to study anomalous experience, yet few methodologies are readily available for doing that, and fewer yet are comprehensive enough to be used across a variety of events. One approach to address these issues was developed by the first author and colleagues (e.g., Kumar & Pekala, 1988; Pekala, 1980, 1991d). It is called *psychophenomenology*, and it comprehensively evaluates, quantifies, and statistically assesses both ordinary and altered states of consciousness.

Methodology

This approach has been labeled a *psychophenomenological* approach to distinguish it from the approaches of classical introspectionism (Boring,

1953), the phenomenological psychologists (Valle & King, 1978), and the technique that Shor (1979) developed to investigate hypnotic phenomena (see also Pekala, 1991d). It is phenomenological in the sense that it seeks to describe the contents of consciousness, as do the phenomenologists and the phenomenological psychologists, but it also uses traditional psychological measurement and statistical approaches to accomplish this objective.

Whereas descriptive phenomenology seeks a "detailed description of [the phenomena of] consciousness as they appear in consciousness" (Ashworth, 1976, p. 364), psychophenomenology was designed to not only "describe, but to empirically quantify and statistically assess, the phenomena of consciousness" (Pekala, 1991d, p. 3) in a reliable and valid manner. The psychophenomenological approach usually entails retrospective phenomenological assessment of a relatively short stimulus condition to evaluate various subjective processes (e.g., imagery, cognition, and affect). Volunteers experience a short stimulus condition and then evaluate their experience retrospectively using a short self-report questionnaire.

Two self-report questionnaires are currently available in the literature. The Phenomenology of Consciousness Inventory (PCI; Pekala, 1991c) is used to map subjective experience in general, and the Dimensions of Attention Questionnaire (DAQ; Pekala, 1991a) is used to map attentional experience in particular. The PCI is a 53-item self-report inventory that maps 12 major and 14 minor dimensions of subjective experience. They include the following (subdimensions in parentheses): positive affect (joy, sexual excitement, love), negative affect (anger, sadness, fear), altered experience (body image, time sense, perception, meaning), imagery (amount, vividness), attention (direction, absorption), self-awareness, altered state of awareness, internal dialogue, rationality, volitional control, memory, and arousal. An example of a PCI item for altered state of awareness is "My state of awareness was not unusual or different from what it ordinarily is" versus "I felt in an extraordinarily unusual and nonordinary state of awareness." Each dipole of the item is separated by a 7-point Likert scale that participants use to evaluate their experience.

The DAQ measures 12 dimensions of attention: flexibility, equanimity, detachment, perspicacity (the extent to which consciousness feels spatially expanded), locus (within or outside of the body), direction (whether directed inward or outward to the environment), one-pointedness, absorption, control (passive vs. active), vigilance (the degree of scanning the environment), density (the "amount" of thoughts, feelings, etc., experienced at a given time), and simultaneity (the degree of awareness of several events at the same time). An example of a DAQ density item is "My mind was in a state of 'no thought'; I was not aware of a single thought, feeling, sensation, etc." versus "My mind was continually occupied; I was always aware of thoughts, feelings, and sensations."

Empirical Support

The PCI, the DAQ, and predecessor inventories have been found to reliably and validly map states of consciousness in a variety of contexts. These contexts include hypnosis, progressive relaxation, deep abdominal breathing (e.g., Pekala, 1991d; Pekala & Kumar, 1987), firewalking (Pekala & Ersek, 1992/1993), monotonous drumming (Maurer, Kumar, Woodside, & Pekala, 1997), and an OBE associated with a near-death event (Maitz & Pekala, 1990/1991; see this volume, Alvarado, chap. 6; Greyson, chap. 10).

The following two examples illustrate the use of the psychophenomenological approach to understand two types of anomalous experiences: one from an idiographic perspective, and one from a nomothetic perspective.

The first author published a paper with a colleague (Maitz & Pekala, 1990/1991) that attempted to quantify a veteran's report of an OBE during a NDE. The veteran's recollection of the NDE, as assessed with the PCI and the DAQ, was compared against an eyes-closed, sitting-quietly condition (baseline), a hypnosis assessment using the Stanford Scale of Hypnotic Susceptibility (Weitzenhoffer & Hilgard, 1962), and his OBE as recalled under hypnosis. Distinct differences were evident among conditions: "The OBE was experienced as more out-of-the-body, while the hypnosis conditions were experienced as occurring 'within' the body" (Maitz & Pekala, 1990/1991, p. 209). In addition, the OBE, as recollected vis-à-vis the hypnosis conditions, was associated with significantly greater perspicacity; a direction of attention that was externally focused toward the environment as opposed to inwardly toward oneself; and a decrease in attentional density (fewer thoughts passing through one's mind). The authors concluded that

> this case study appears to provide quantifiable data to support earlier claims that an OBE, in conjunction with an NDE, represents an altered state of consciousness for one particular individual. It also provides quantifiable data on the particular changes in one person's phenomenological field that occurred during an OBE, and how these changes differ from other altered states of consciousness. (Maitz & Pekala, 1990/1991, p. 211)

Firewalking, a practice in which individuals walk on recently burned and very hot coals or on extremely hot rocks or cinders, has been reported as a type of peak or *flow* experience. During flow experiences, "people are so involved in an activity that nothing else seems to matter; the experience itself is so enjoyable that people will do it even at great cost, for the sheer sake of doing it" (Csikszentmihalyi, 1990, p. 4). Several books have been written about firewalking (e.g., Danforth, 1989; Sternfield, 1992), but little in the way of empirical research on the topic has been published. It is worth reiterating that we are discussing here the subjective experience of firewalking, not the physics of the phenomenon. Whether or not successful firewalking can be explained by ordinary physical processes such as poor heat conductance of the coals or the Leidenfrost effect (a hypothesized barrier of steam between the feet and the coals), as has been discussed in the literature, was outside the scope of the studies reviewed below.

Pekala and Ersek (1992/1993) assessed "the subjective effects associated with firewalking, and compared them with the subjective effects associated with hypnosis and a baseline condition" (p. 207). In this study, 27 participants firewalked and afterward completed the PCI and the DAQ in reference to their experience, along with a questionnaire that asked if participants were "burned or blistered at all by walking over the hot embers" (p. 212). Data analyses revealed that the PCI and DAQ could discriminate those participants who were not burned or blistered from those who were. Counterintuitively, "those firewalkers who did not get burned reported less detachment, less of a feeling of being out of their bodies, and more thoughts than the firewalkers who got slightly burned" (p. 217).

The experiential nature of the firewalking experience was evaluated by comparing a different group's experience of hypnosis with a baseline sitting-quietly condition. The firewalking experience was found to be significantly different from the experience of being hypnotized; firewalking was associated with significantly more joy, absorption, one-pointedness of thought, fear, and unusual meanings than either the hypnosis or baseline condition. Whereas hypnosis is usually associated with loss of control, firewalking was found to be associated with increased control, a more aroused state and, understandably, more fear. As in the previous study, participants who blistered could be distinguished from the other firewalking participants on the basis of their DAQ scores. The data implied that different states of consciousness are associated with different types of subjective and, possibly, psychophysiological, effects.

Hillig and Holroyd (1997/1998) recently "extended and partially supported the investigation reported by Pekala and Ersek" (p. 153), suggesting that "an alteration in attention may be more important to successful firewalking than an alteration in consciousness" (p. 161).

Limitations of the Instruments and Methodology

Given the small number of items per dimension, approximately 4.5 per PCI major dimension and 3.3 per DAQ dimension, neither the PCI nor the DAQ provides very fine phenomenological discriminations. They were also not designed to provide a narrative account of the experience. The methodology for using the PCI and the DAQ involves giving the questionnaires immediately after a short stimulus condition (2 to 4 min), with volunteers retrospectively completing the inventory in reference to that time period. Because the methodology was developed in this manner to minimize inference, use of the instruments following stimuli longer than 20 min is probably suspect: "Longer time periods may involve various changes in subjective experience; hence subjects will more likely need to 'average' or infer their subjective experience over this time period" (Pekala, 1991d, p. 216). In addition, completing the instruments in reference to stimulus conditions with a considerable time delay between stimulus and response may affect the "quality" of the data obtained:

> By completing the PCI or other RPA [retrospective phenomenological assessment] instruments in reference to time periods that have to be remembered days, weeks, or months ago, the subject will probably be relying more on inference than memory. Although such inferences concerning what subjects experience are interesting in their own right . . . [they] are probably a function of both memory and inference. (Pekala, 1991d, p. 217)

Finally, the PCI and the DAQ do not include all dimensions of possible interest. Although some care was taken to be as comprehensive as possible in selecting their various items (Pekala, 1991d), the dimensions assessed are a function of the items chosen (Schwarz, 1999).

IMPORTANCE OF INDIVIDUAL-DIFFERENCES MEASURES

Some individuals report that their anomalous experiences occur only in conjunction with an ACS, whereas other individuals have anomalous experiences as part of their ordinary, not altered, state of consciousness (Tart, 1975). Their ordinary stream of consciousness may include experiences of, say, strong synesthesia (see Marks, this volume, chap. 4), which for most people would occur, if at all, only during an altered state.

In other words, individual differences may moderate or mediate anomalous experiences (see Tart, 1969, 1975). This can be illustrated by recent research on individual differences during hypnosis (e.g., Forbes & Pekala, 1996; Pekala, 1991b; Pekala & Forbes, 1997). The PCI was used to evaluate, with the use of a standardized scale, the phenomenological experience of being hypnotized. Results from this and other studies suggest that there are three types of moderately to highly hypnotizable individuals: classic highs, fantasy highs, and visualizers (Forbes & Pekala, 1996).

The *classic highs*, during hypnosis, typically report significant changes in their state of awareness and altered experiences, marked by significant decrements in volitional control, rationality, memory, and self-awareness and little in the way of internal dialogue or visual imagery. These individuals personify the classic definition of the highly hypnotizable subject (see

Brown & Fromm, 1986). As compared with the classic highs, the *fantasy highs* also experience major decrements in volitional control, rationality, memory, and self-awareness during hypnosis, yet report somewhat fewer alterations in their state of awareness or experience but exhibit enhanced visual imagery and internal dialogue. Their visual imagery appears to be spontaneously generated and independent of the hypnotist's suggestions.

Perhaps the most interesting group is the *visualizers*. Although these individuals experience very vivid visual imagery during hypnosis, they also report small decrements in volitional control, memory, or rationality and not much of an alteration in state of awareness or experience. This research suggests that the visualizers will spontaneously report vivid visual imagery when asked to sit quietly during hypnosis but will not experience other usual effects associated with hypnosis, such as loss of volitional control, decreased rationality, or marked alterations in state of awareness (Pekala, 1999; Pekala & Kumar, 1999).

No research data are yet available on the extent to which the visualizers' ordinary waking state of consciousness is an altered state in comparison with that of most individuals, but the data concerning visual imagery point in this direction. Failing to take into account this individual-differences factor when evaluating the nature of subjective experiences during hypnosis can lead to much confusion, as it did in the early days of classical introspectionism (Boring, 1953).

A different, but partly overlapping, classification of highly hypnotizable individuals has been provided recently by Barber (1999). On the basis of his previous work and that of others (e.g., Barrett, 1990; Forbes & Pekala, 1996), Barber theorized that there are three types of highly hypnotizable individuals: individuals who are fantasy prone and can vividly imagine suggested events; dissociators who report unsuggested amnesia and other dissociative experiences; and highly motivated individuals who appear to respond in a relatively conscious, goal-directed manner to suggestions. When hypnotized, these three groups appear to experience different subjective effects that are consistent with differences in personality and cognitive functioning. At least the first two groups have parallels in ritually induced alterations of consciousness in other cultures (Cardeña, 1996). Failing to take into account such differences, according to Barber (1999), has helped to fuel the controversy among different theoretical camps over the past several decades concerning the nature of hypnosis (e.g., Kihlstrom, 1997).

IS THERE A TYPE OF INDIVIDUAL MORE LIKELY TO REPORT ANOMALOUS EXPERIENCES?

Individuals who are both highly hypnotizable and highly dissociative may be particularly likely to experience and report anomalous, unusual, or paranormal experiences. Two studies (Pekala, Kumar, & Cummings, 1992; Pekala et al., 1995) examined individual differences in the reporting of anomalous or paranormal experiences as a function of hypnotizability (Hilgard, 1965) and dissociativity (Cardeña, 1994). Pekala et al. (1995) found that dissociation was the most important predictor variable of anomalous and paranormal experiences ($r = .40$) as measured by the Anomalous Experience Inventory (AEI; Kumar, Pekala, & Gallagher, 1994), whereas hypnotizability had a more modest correlation ($r = .21$). Figure 2.1 graphs the relationship between anomalous experiences as a function of both hyp-

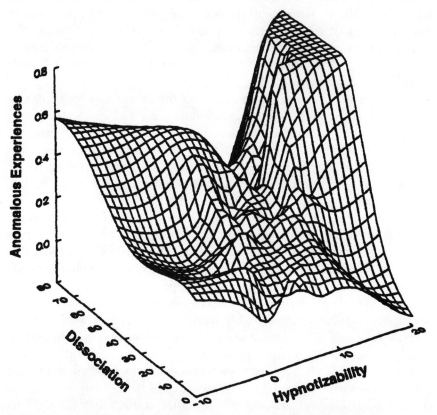

Figure 2.1. Anomalous experiences as a function of dissociation and hypnotizability. The *z*-axis, Anomalous Experiences, ranges from 0.0 to 1.0 (the higher the number, the greater the frequency of anomalous experiences). The number represents an average endorsement rate across the 29 items of this subscale, where 0 = *false* and 1 = *true*. The *x*-axis, Hypnotizability, represents participants' scores on the Harvard Group Scale of Hypnotic Susceptibility; scores range from 0 to 12; the higher the number, the more hypnotizable. The *y*-axis, Dissociation, represents participants' scores on the Dissociative Experiences Scale; scores range from 0 to 100; the higher the number, the more dissociative. From "Anomalous/Paranormal Experiences, Hypnotic Susceptibility, and Dissociation," by R. J. Pekala, V. K. Kumar, and G. Marcano, 1995, *Journal of the American Society for Psychical Research, 89*, p. 322.

notizability and dissociation. Those individuals who are both highly hyp-notizable and highly dissociative are more likely to report anomalous ex-periences. It is generally assumed that these reports correspond to an actual higher prevalence of these experiences, but this assumption has yet to be fully tested.

The AEI also has a subscale to assess *encounter*, or shamaniclike, ex-periences. This subscale includes such items as "being able to communicate with supernatural forces," "experienced other planes of existence beyond the physical," and "met an extraterrestrial." High-encounter individuals were found to be both highly hypnotizable and highly dissociative. Addi-tional analyses using the dataset of Pekala et al. (1995) indicate that highly hypnotizable individuals (the top 10% of the population) were about 6 times more likely to report such encounter experiences than nonhypnotiz-able individuals (the bottom 10% of the population). Similarly, high-dissociative types (top 10%) were about 6 times more likely to report such experiences than low-dissociative types (bottom 10%). Individuals who were both highly hypnotizable and highly dissociative were more than 25 times more likely to report such experiences than low hypnotizable/low dissociative individuals and 5 times more likely to do so than the average individual. The fact that some people are much more likely to report par-ticular types of anomalous experience suggests that personality traits and cognitive sets may partially mediate the prevalence or nature of such ex-periences.

CONCLUSIONS AND RECOMMENDATIONS

There is a major epistemological issue associated with any discussion that attempts to explain anomalous phenomena. To the extent that epis-temology precedes metaphysics (Macquarrie, 1972), what we discover to be the nature of reality will be a function of those methods, procedures, and perceptual and cognitive schemas (Baars, 1988) available to know that reality. Science has always been based on subjective experiences of scien-tists, including their perceptions, choices, and values, and the bias toward quantifiable, objective data has been a preference in, and not an intrinsic quality of, scientific inquiry (Harman, 1996). Science has been constructed, partly, on the basis of scientists' shared subjective experiences and episte-mological assumptions; thus, the difference between the objectivity of so-called objective and subjective data is one of degree rather than of kind. (This point has been made effectively by Velmans, 1993.)

The following are our recommendations to study anomalous experi-ences:

1. Because most of the anomalous experiences described in this book are based on self-reports, it is important to assess their

reliability. One way to evaluate their internal consistency is to obtain information about subjective experience with similarly worded questions, as in the PCI (Pekala, 1991d). Test–retest reliability can be measured by obtaining such information at two or three points in time. In short, great care must be taken to assure that data gathered through self-reports are internally consistent and accurate.

2. We should systematically evaluate the experiential validity of such an anomalous experience. We can attempt to determine if the self-reports of that experience are congruent with other possible ways of measuring that experience (convergent validity) but differ from the reports and correlates of a different experience (discriminant validity), how consistent they are with other reports, and so on. Measuring the psychophenomenology of the firewalking experience (in terms of both general consciousness and attention) and comparing it against the subjective experience of hypnosis, as was done by Pekala and Ersek (1992/1993), is one way of attempting to establish the nature of the experience. Simultaneously assessing the psychophysiological effects of blistering as a function of attentional changes, while attempting to validate such subjective changes vis-à-vis corroborating physical evidence, may further clarify the validity of the phenomenon in question. Whenever possible, obtaining physical validation of experiences that claim to refer to a consensual reality will be crucial to give a full explanation of these experiences. Obtaining consensual validation of the phenomenon in question by way of informant reports should be a priority when evaluating such experiences as NDEs and OBEs, where presumably independent verification of some claims can be ascertained (see this volume, Alvarado, chap. 6; Greyson, chap. 10).

3. This review has focused heavily on the use of quantitative measures to assure the reliability and validity of introspective data when attempting to understand states of consciousness associated with anomalous experiences. A systematic, quantitative approach is especially important given the unusual nature of anomalous experiences. However, we should not lose sight of the need to combine quantitative techniques with new and currently underused qualitative approaches to study anomalous experiences. We have tried to make the case that each research method has specific strengths and limitations and that a full understanding of a phenomenon will require different perspectives and methodologies.

4. Experients may need to be assessed to determine whether they are highly hypnotizable, fantasy prone, or highly dissociative. Because such individuals are much more likely than others to report imaginal experiences that may or may not have a basis in consensual reality, it is incumbent on researchers to assess these and other potential sources of individual differences. Fraud and deception among sociopathic individuals, or impression management in the broader populations, are other types of variables that should be considered, along with motivation and secondary-gain issues. Most chapters in this book also indicate the limitations of relying exclusively on convenience samples, usually undergraduate students, in which the incidence of some phenomena, such as full-fledged mystical experiences or lucid dreams, may be minimal.

5. Researchers need to realize that similar anomalous experiences may have different etiologies and mechanisms (e.g., Cardeña, in press). Until these experiences are fully understood, they need to be evaluated in their own right. For example, it may be that a given experience, as reported by different people, may sometimes be caused by outright lying, sometimes by misperceptions, and sometimes by veridical perceptions of the event in question. Thus, when evaluating 10 reports of psi-related experiences, 3 may be established to be misattributions, 3 may be frauds, and 4 may be unaccountable through these or other conventional explanations. Hence, the last may be possibly "veridical." To dismiss all 10 instances because 6 of them have been explained away is unwarranted.

6. Finally, if the ontology, or metaphysical "realness" or "being-ness" (Heidegger, 1927/1962), of the phenomenon studied is an issue of concern, great care must be taken to evaluate the experience in question. It is necessary to determine whether the experience is likely to be materially real (partaking of physical, material reality), imaginally real (partaking of mental or emotional reality), or a combination of both (Grof's 1993 proposal of a psychoid realm). Frequently, these types of beingness are not differentiated, leading to questionable conclusions. Examples of this confusion include the statement that a somatic sensation of "energy" indicates the presence of electromagnetic energy or, conversely, the conclusion that this sensation is "not real" because it is not accompanied by electromagnetic energy. (See LaBerge & Gackenbach, this

volume, chap. 5 for a related example of the a priori denial of the reality of lucid dreaming.)

Too frequently, a priori biases and philosophical tastes have taken precedence over an informed and careful consideration of the evidence concerning anomalous experiences. This stance has foreclosed scrutiny of valid perspectives that differ from that of the author(s). Instead, we prefer to follow William James (1876/1978), who concluded that the true philosopher (or methodologist, we may add) should have "the habit of always seeing an alternative" (p. 4).

REFERENCES

Anderson, J. R. (1983). *The architecture of cognition*. Cambridge, MA: Harvard University Press.

Angell, J. (1907). The province of functional psychology. *American Psychologist, 36*, 61–91.

Ashworth, P. (1976). Some notes on phenomenological approaches in psychology. *Bulletin of the British Psychological Society, 29*, 363–369.

Baars, B. J. (1988). *A cognitive theory of consciousness*. Cambridge, England: Cambridge University Press.

Baars, B. J. (1997). *In the theater of consciousness*. New York: Oxford University Press.

Bakan, D. (1969). *On method*. San Francisco: Jossey-Bass.

Barabasz, A. F., & Barabasz, M. (1992). Research designs and considerations. In E. Fromm & M. R. Nash (Eds.), *Contemporary hypnosis research* (pp. 173–200). New York: Guilford Press.

Barber, T. X. (1999). A comprehensive three-dimensional theory of hypnosis. In I. Kirsch, A. Capafons, E. Cardeña, & S. Amigó (Eds.), *Clinical hypnosis and self-regulation* (pp. 21–48). Washington, DC: American Psychological Association.

Barrett, D. (1990). Deep trance subjects: A schema of two distinct subgroups. In E. G. Kunzendorf (Ed.), *Mental imagery* (pp. 101–112). New York: Plenum.

Bartlett, F. C. (1932). *Remembering*. Cambridge, England: Cambridge University Press.

Battista, J. R. (1978). The science of consciousness. In K. S. Pope & J. L. Singer (Eds.), *The stream of consciousness* (pp. 55–90). New York: Plenum.

Boring, E. G. (1953). A history of introspection. *Psychological Bulletin, 50*, 176–189.

Brentano, F. (1925). *Psychologie vom empirischen standkpunt* [Psychology from an empirical perspective]. Leipzig, Germany: Meiner. (Original work published 1874)

Brown, D., Forte, M., & Dysart, M. (1984). Visual sensitivity and mindfulness meditation. *Perceptual and Motor Skills, 58,* 775–784.

Brown, D. P., & Fromm, E. (1986). *Hypnotherapy and hypnoanalysis.* Hillsdale, NJ: Erlbaum.

Caballo, V. E. (1991). *Manual de técnicas de terapia y modificación de conducta* [Manual of therapy and behavior modification techniques]. Madrid: Siglo Veintiuno.

Cardeña, E. (1988). The phenomenology of quiescent and physically active deep hypnosis. *International Journal of Clinical and Experimental Hypnosis, 36,* 227.

Cardeña, E. (1994). The domain of dissociation. In S. J. Lynn & J. W. Rhue (Eds.), *Dissociation: Clinical and theoretical perspectives* (pp. 15–31). New York: Guilford Press.

Cardeña, E. (1996). "Just floating on the sky": A comparison of shamanic and hypnotic phenomenology. In R. Quekelbherge & D. Eigner (Eds.), *6th jahrbuch für transkulturelle medizin und psychotherapie, 1994* [6th yearbook of cross-cultural medicine and psychotherapy, 1994] (pp. 367–380). Berlin: Verlag für Wissenchaft und Bildung.

Cardeña, E. (1997). Comments on "Monotonous percussion drumming and trance postures." *Anthropology of Consciousness, 8,* 163–167.

Cardeña, E. (in press). "You are not your body": Commentary on the motivation for self-injury in psychiatric patients. *Psychiatry.*

Clark, J. H. (1983). *A map of mental states.* London: Routledge & Kegan Paul.

Csikszentmihalyi, M. (1990). *Flow: The psychology of optimal experience.* New York: Harper Perennial.

Danforth, L. M. (1989). *Firewalking and religious healing: The Anastenaria of Greece and the American firewalking movement.* Princeton, NJ: Princeton University Press.

Danziger, K. (1980). The history of introspection reconsidered. *Journal of the History of the Behavioral Sciences, 16,* 241–262.

Dement, W. C. (1978). *Some must watch while some must sleep.* New York: Norton.

Deutsch, D. (1988). A musical paradox. *Music Perception, 3,* 275–280.

Easterlin, B. & Cardeña, E. (1998/1999). Perceived stress, cognitive and emotional differences between short- and long-term Vipassana meditators. *Imagination, Cognition and Personality, 18,* 69–82.

Ebbinghaus, H. (1964). *Memory* (H. A. Ruger & C. E. Bussenius, Trans.). New York: Dover. (Original work published 1885)

Epstein, S. (1983). A research paradigm for the study of personality and emotions. In M. M. Page (Ed.), *Personality: Current theory and research* (pp. 91–154). Lincoln: University of Nebraska Press.

Erdelyi, M. H. (1996). *The recovery of unconscious memories.* Chicago: University of Chicago Press.

Ericsson, K. A., & Simon, H. A. (1980). Verbal reports as data. *Psychological Review, 87,* 215–251.

Erikson, E. H. (1969). *Gandhi's truth*. New York: Norton.

Farthing, G. W. (1992). *The psychology of consciousness*. Englewood Cliffs, NJ: Prentice Hall.

Forbes, E. J., & Pekala, R. J. (1996). Types of hypnotically (un)susceptible individuals as a function of phenomenological experience: A partial replication. *Australian Journal of Clinical and Experimental Hypnosis, 24*, 92–109.

Forman, R. K. (1998). What does mysticism have to teach us about consciousness. *Journal of Consciousness Studies, 5*, 185–201.

Frijda, N. H. (1986). *The emotions*. Cambridge, England: Cambridge University Press.

Gardner, H. (1985). *The mind's new science: A history of the cognitive revolution*. New York: Basic Books.

Gebser, J. (1986). *The ever present origin* (N. Barstad with A. Mickunas, Trans.). Athens: Ohio University Press.

Gifford-May, D., & Thompson, N. K. (1994). "Deep states" of meditation: Phenomenological reports of experience. *Journal of Transpersonal Psychology, 26*, 117–138.

Giorgi, A. (1990). Towards an integrated approach to the study of human problems: The parameters of human science. *Saybrook Review, 8*, 111–126.

Grof, S. (1993). *The holotropic mind*. San Francisco: Harper.

Güzeldere, G. (1995). Consciousness: What it is, how to study it, what to learn from its history. *Journal of Consciousness Studies, 2*, 30–51.

Hall, C. S., & Van de Castle, R. L. (1966). *The content analysis of dreams*. New York: Appleton-Century-Croft.

Harman, W. W. (1996). Toward a science of consciousness. In S. R. Hameroff, A. W. Kaszniak, & A. C. Scott (Eds.), *Toward a science of consciousness* (pp. 743–751). Cambridge, MA: MIT Press.

Heidegger, M. (1962). *Being and time* (J. Macquarrie & E. Robinson, Trans.). New York: Harper & Row. (Original work published 1927)

Heiman, G. W. (1995). *Research methods in psychology*. Boston: Houghton Mifflin.

Hilgard, E. R. (1965). *The experience of hypnosis*. New York: Harcourt Brace Jovanovich.

Hilgard, E. R. (1980). Consciousness in contemporary psychology. *Annual Review of Psychology, 31*, 1–26.

Hillig, J. A., & Holroyd, J. (1997/1998). Consciousness, attention, and hypnoidal effects during firewalking. *Imagination, Cognition and Personality, 17*, 153–164.

Holt, R. R. (1964). Imagery: The return of the ostracized. *American Psychologist, 19*, 254–264.

Hurlburt, R. T. (1990). *Sampling normal and schizophrenic inner experience*. New York: Plenum.

Husserl, E. (1972). *Ideas: General introduction to pure phenomenology*. New York: Collier. (Original work published 1913)

Izard, C. E. (1977). *Human emotions*. New York: Plenum Press.

James, W. (1950). *The principles of psychology*. New York: Dover Press. (Original work published 1890)

James, W. (1958). *The varieties of religious experience*. New York: New American Library. (Original work published 1902)

James, W. (1978). The teaching of philosophy in our colleges. In *Essays in philosophy* (pp. 3–6). Cambridge, MA: Harvard University Press. (Original work published 1876)

Kant, I. (1966). *The critique of pure reason*. New York: Anchor Books. (Original work published 1781)

Kihlstrom, J. F. (1997). Convergence in understanding hypnosis? Perhaps, but perhaps not quite so fast. *International Journal of Clinical and Experimental Hypnosis, 45,* 324–332.

Klinger, E. (1978). Modes of normal conscious flow. In K. S. Pope & J. L. Singer (Eds.), *The stream of consciousness* (pp. 226–258). New York: Plenum.

Köhler, W. (1950). *Gestalt psychology*. New York: Liverright. (Original work published 1929)

Krippner, S. (1972). Altered states of consciousness. In J. White (Ed.), *The highest state of consciousness* (pp. 1–5). New York: Wiley.

Kubose, S. K. (1976). An experimental investigation of psychological aspects of meditation. *Psychologia, 19,* 1–10.

Kukla, A. (1983). Toward a science of experience. *Journal of Mind and Behavior, 4,* 231–246.

Kumar, V. K., & Pekala, R. J. (1988). Hypnotizability, absorption, and individual differences in phenomenological experience. *International Journal of Clinical and Experimental Hypnosis, 36,* 80–88.

Kumar, V. K., & Pekala, R. J. (in press). Relation of hypnosis-specific attitudes and behaviors to paranormal beliefs and experiences: A technical review. In J. Houran & R. Lange (Eds.), *A haunting question of perception: Scientific perspectives on hauntings and poltergeists*. Springfield, IL: Greenwood.

Kumar, V. K., Pekala, R. J., & Gallagher, C. (1994). *The Anomalous Experience Inventory (AEI)*. Unpublished manuscript, West Chester University, Pennsylvania.

Langer, E. (1989). *Mindfulness*. New York: Addison Wesley.

Lieberman, D. A. (1979). Behaviorism and the mind: A (limited) call for a return to introspection. *American Psychologist, 34,* 319–333.

Ludwig, A. H. (1972). Altered states of consciousness. In C. T. Tart (Ed.), *Altered states of consciousness* (pp. 11–24). New York: Wiley. (Original work published 1966)

Luria, A. R. (1968). *The mind of a mnemonist*. New York: Basic Books.

MacDonald, D. A., LeClair, L., Holland, C. J., Alter, A., & Friedman, H. L. (1995). A survey of measures of transpersonal constructs. *Journal of Transpersonal Psychology, 27,* 171–235.

Macquarrie, J. (1972). *Existentialism*. New York: Penguin.

Maitz, E. A., & Pekala, R. J. (1990/1991). Phenomenological quantification of an out-of-the-body experience associated with a near-death event. *Omega, 22,* 199–214.

Mandler, G. (1985). *Consciousness: An essay in cognitive psychology*. Hillsdale, NJ: Erlbaum.

Marsh, C. A. (1977). A framework for describing subjective states of consciousness. In N. E. Zinberg (Ed.), *Alternate states of consciousness* (pp. 121–144). New York: Free Press.

Martindale, C. (1981). *Cognition and consciousness*. Homewood, IL: Dorsey Press.

Maurer, R. L., Kumar, V. K., Woodside, L., & Pekala, R. J. (1997). Phenomenological experience in response to monotonous drumming and hypnotizability. *American Journal of Clinical Hypnosis, 40,* 130–145.

McClelland, J. L., & Rumelhart, D. E. (1985). Distributed memory and the representation of general and specific information. *Journal of Experimental Psychology: General, 114,* 159–188.

McConkey, K. M., & Sheehan, P. W. (1995). *Hypnosis, memory, and behavior in criminal investigation*. New York: Guilford Press.

McConkey, K. M., Wende, V., & Barnier, A. J. (1999). Measuring change in the subjective experience of hypnosis. *International Journal of Clinical and Experimental Hypnosis, 47,* 23–39.

Merleau-Ponty, M. (1962). *Phenomenology of perception* (C. Smith, Trans.). London: Routledge & Kegan Paul.

Nagel, T. (1982). What is it like to be a bat? In D. R. Hofstadter & D. C. Dennett (Eds.), *The mind's I* (pp. 391–403). New York: Bantam. (Original work published 1974)

Natsoulas, T. (1978). Consciousness. *American Psychologist, 33,* 906–914.

Natsoulas, T. (1989). An examination of four objections to self-intimating states of consciousness. *Journal of Mind and Behavior, 10,* 63–116.

Newell, A., & Simon, H. A. (1972). *Human problem solving*. Englewood Cliffs, NJ: Prentice Hall.

Nisbett, R. E., & Wilson, T. D. (1977). Telling more than we can know: Verbal reports on mental processes. *Psychological Review, 84,* 231–259.

Orne, M. T. (1962). On the social psychology of the psychological experiment: With particular reference to demand characteristics. *American Psychologist, 17,* 776–783.

Orne, M. T., & Scheibe, K. E. (1964). The contribution on non-deprivation factors in the production of sensory deprivation effects: The psychology of the panic button. *Journal of Abnormal and Social Psychology, 68,* 3–12.

Ornstein, R. (1986). *The psychology of consciousness* (Rev. ed.). New York: Penguin.

Overton, D. A. (1978). Major theories of state dependent learning. In B. T. Ho, D. W. Richards, & D. L. Chute (Eds.), *Drug discrimination and state dependent learning* (pp. 283–318). New York: Academic Press.

Oxman, T. E., Rosenberg, S. D., Schnurr, P. P., Tucker, G. J., & Gala, G. (1988). The language of altered states. *Journal of Nervous and Mental Disease, 176,* 401–408.

Pekala, R. J. (1980). *An empirical–phenomenological approach for mapping consciousness and its various "states."* Doctoral dissertation, Michigan State University, 1980. (University Microfilm No. 82–02, 489)

Pekala, R. J. (1991a). *The Dimensions of Attention Questionnaire (DAQ).* West Chester, PA: Mid Atlantic Educational Institute.

Pekala, R. J. (1991b). Hypnotic types: Evidence from a cluster analysis of phenomenal experience. *Contemporary Hypnosis, 8,* 95–104.

Pekala, R. J. (1991c). *The Phenomenology of Consciousness Inventory (PCI).* West Chester, PA: Mid Atlantic Educational Institute.

Pekala, R. J. (1991d). *Quantifying consciousness: An empirical approach.* New York: Plenum Press.

Pekala, R. J. (1999, March). *Are there different "types" of hypnotizable individuals?: Rationale, research, and clinical application.* Plenary address given at the annual meeting of the American Society of Clinical Hypnosis, Atlanta, GA.

Pekala, R. J., & Ersek, B. (1992/1993). Firewalking versus hypnosis: A preliminary study concerning consciousness, attention, and fire immunity. *Imagination, Cognition, and Personality, 12,* 207–229.

Pekala, R. J., & Forbes, E. J. (1997). Types of hypnotically (un)susceptible individuals as a function of phenomenological experience: Towards a typology of hypnotic types. *American Journal of Clinical Hypnosis, 39,* 212–224.

Pekala, R. J., & Kumar, V. K. (1987). Predicting hypnotic susceptibility via a self-report instrument: A replication. *American Journal of Clinical Hypnosis, 30,* 57–65.

Pekala, R. J., & Kumar, V. K. (1999, March). *Are there different types of trance?: Research and clinical application.* Paper presented at the annual meeting of the American Society of Clinical Hypnosis, Atlanta, GA.

Pekala, R. J., Kumar, V. K., & Cummings, J. (1992). Types of high hypnotically susceptible individuals and reported attitudes and experiences of the paranormal and the anomalous. *Journal of the American Society for Psychical Research, 86,* 135–150.

Pekala, R. J., Kumar, V. K., & Marcano, G. (1995). Anomalous/paranormal experiences, hypnotic susceptibility, and dissociation. *Journal of the American Society for Psychical Research, 89,* 313–332.

Rachlin, H. (1974). Self-control. *Behaviorism, 2,* 94–107.

Radin, D. (1997). *The conscious universe: The scientific truth of psychic phenomena.* New York: HarperEdge.

Richardson, A. (1984). *The experiential dimension of psychology.* Queensland, Australia: University of Queensland Press.

Robinson, D. N. (1995). *An intellectual history of psychology* (3rd ed.). Madison: University of Wisconsin Press.

Rorer, L. (1990). Personality assessment: A conceptual survey. In L. A. Pervin (Ed.), *Handbook of personality* (pp. 693–720). New York: Guilford Press.

Russell, B. (1970). *Mysticism and logic*. London: Allen & Unwin. (Original work published 1917)

Rychlak, J. F. (1997). *In defense of human consciousness*. Washington, DC: American Psychological Association.

Sacks, O. (1995). *An anthropologist on Mars*. New York: Knopf.

Schacter, D. (1999). The seven sins of memory. *American Psychologist, 54*, 182–203.

Schwarz, N. (1999). Self-reports: How the questions shape the answers. *American Psychologist, 54*, 93–105.

Sheehan, P. W., & McConkey, K. M. (1996). *Hypnosis and experience*. New York: Brunner/Mazel. (Original work published 1982)

Shepard, R., & Cooper, L. (1982). *Mental images and their transformations*. Cambridge, MA: MIT Press.

Shor, R. E. (1979). A phenomenological method for the measurement of variables important to an understanding of the nature of hypnosis. In E. Fromm & R. E. Shor (Eds.), *Hypnosis: Developments in research and new perspectives* (2nd ed., pp. 105–135). New York: Aldine-Atherton.

Siegel, R. K., & West, J. L. (Eds.). (1975). *Hallucination: Behavior, experience, and theory*. New York: Wiley.

Silverman, I. (1974). The experimenter: A (still) neglected stimulus object. *Canadian Psychologist, 15*, 258–270.

Singer, J. L. (1978). Experimental studies of daydreaming and the stream of consciousness. In K. S. Pope & J. L. Singer (Eds.), *The stream of consciousness: Scientific investigations into the flow of human experience* (pp. 187–225). New York: Plenum Press.

Singer, J. L., & Kolligan, J., Jr. (1987). Personality: Developments in the study of private experience. *Annual Review of Psychology, 38*, 533–574.

Skinner, B. F. (1974). *About behaviorism*. New York: Knopf.

Skinner, B. F. (1989). The origins of cognitive thought. *American Psychologist, 44*, 13–18.

Smith, E., & Miller, F. (1978). Limits on perception of cognitive processes: A reply to Nisbett and Wilson. *Psychological Review, 85*, 355–362.

Spiegel, D., Bierre, P., & Rootenberg, J. (1989). Hypnotic alteration of somatosensory perception. *American Journal of Psychiatry, 146*, 749–754.

Sternfield, J. (1992). *Firewalking: The psychology of physical immunity*. Stockbridge, MA: Berkshire House.

Stillman, R. C., Weingartner, W., Wyatt, R. J., Gillin, J. C., & Eich, J. (1974). State-dependent (dissociative) effects of marihuana on human memory. *Archives of General Psychiatry, 31*, 81–85.

Stoller, P. (1989). *The taste of ethnographic things*. Philadelphia: University of Pennsylvania Press.

Tart, C. T. (Ed.). (1969). *Altered states of consciousness*. New York: Wiley.

Tart, C. T. (1972a). Scientific foundations for the study of altered states of consciousness. *Journal of Transpersonal Psychology, 3*, 93–124.

Tart, C. T. (1972b). States of consciousness and state-specific sciences. *Science, 176*, 1203–1210.

Tart, C. T. (1975). *States of consciousness*. New York: Dutton.

Tart, C. T. (1977). Discrete states of consciousness. In P. R. Lee, R. E. Ornstein, D. Galin, A. Deikman, & C. T. Tart (Eds.), *Symposium on consciousness* (pp. 89–176). New York: Penguin.

Tart, C. T. (1979). Measuring the depth of an altered state of consciousness, with particular reference to self-report scales of hypnotic depth. In E. Fromm & R. E. Shor (Eds.), *Hypnosis: Developments in research and new perspectives* (2nd ed., pp. 567–601). New York: Aldine.

Tart, C. T. (1999). Altered states of consciousness: A thirty-year perspective. *Psychological Hypnosis, 8*, 9–14.

Titchener, E. B. (1898). The postulates of a structural psychology. *Psychological Review, 7*, 449–465.

Tobias, B. A., Kihlstrom, J. F., & Schacter, D. L. (1992). Emotion and implicit memory. In S.-A. Christianson (Ed.), *The handbook of emotion and memory* (pp. 67–92). Hillsdale, NJ: Erlbaum.

Turnbull, C. (1990). Liminality: A synthesis of subjective and objective experience. In R. Schechner & W. Appel (Eds.), *By means of performance* (pp. 50–81). Cambridge, England: Cambridge University Press.

Ullman, M., Krippner, S., & Vaughan, A. (1973). *Dream telepathy*. New York: Macmillan.

Underhill, E. (1972). *Mysticism: A study in the nature and development of man's spiritual consciousness*. New York: World Publishing. (Original work published 1911)

Valle, R. S., & King, M. (1978). An introduction to existential-phenomenological thought in psychology. In R. S. Valle & M. King (Eds.), *Existential phenomenological alternatives for psychology* (pp. 6–17). New York: Oxford University Press.

Varela, F. J. (1996). Neurophenomenology. *Journal of Consciousness Studies, 3*, 330–349.

Varela, F. J., Thompson, E., & Rosch, E. (1991). *The embodied mind*. Cambridge: University of Massachusetts Press.

Velmans, M. M. (1993). A reflexive science of consciousness. *Experimental and theoretical studies of consciousness, 174*, Chichester, England: Wiley.

Wallace, R. K. (1993). *The physiology of consciousness*. Fairfield, IA: Maharishi International University Press.

Watson, J. B. (1913). Psychology as the behaviorist views it. *Psychological Review, 20*, 158–177.

Webster's Seventh New Collegiate Dictionary. (1970). Springfield, MA: Merriam.

Weiten, W. (1998). *Psychology: Themes and variations* (4th ed.). Pacific Grove, CA: Brooks/Cole.

Weitzenhoffer, A. M., & Hilgard, E. R. (1962). *Stanford Hypnotic Susceptibility Scale, Form C.* Palo Alto, CA: Consulting Psychologists Press.

Wilber, K., Engler, J., & Brown, D. P. (1986). *Transformations of consciousness.* Boston: Shambhala.

Wittgenstein, L. (1953). *Philosophical investigations* (G. E. M. Anscombe, Trans.). New York: Macmillan.

Wundt, W. (1897). *Outlines of psychology.* New York: Gustav E. Stechart.

Zinberg, N. E. (1977). The study of consciousness states: Problems and progress. In N. E. Zinberg (Ed.), *Alternate states of consciousness* (pp. 1–36). New York: Free Press.

II

ANOMALOUS EXPERIENCES

3

HALLUCINATORY EXPERIENCES

RICHARD P. BENTALL

"Since the 1920s textbooks of general psychology have differentiated hallucinations from errors of perception by the simple expedient of locating them in separate chapters" (Sarbin & Juhasz, 1967, p. 353). This separation of phenomena that might otherwise have been thought of as connected reflects a persistent assumption that hallucinations are products of psychiatric disorder that have little to do with normal cognition. Perhaps because of this assumption, psychological research into hallucinations has not flourished until quite recently, investigators preferring instead to focus on groups of psychiatric patients defined in terms of broad diagnostic criteria for conditions such as schizophrenia or manic depression.

In the past two decades, however, there has been a change of emphasis in research on psychopathology. Investigators have now begun to focus on specific psychological phenomena—what psychologists refer to as *mental symptoms*—rather than on broad diagnoses (Bentall, 1990b; Costello, 1992; Persons, 1986). Moreover, they have attempted to explain these phenomena in terms of psychological processes known to be responsible for normal perception and reasoning. The findings from this research have shed new light on the psychological and neurophysiological processes that are responsible for hallucinations and have at the same time challenged traditional assumptions about the dividing line between mental illness and normal mental life. In this chapter I review these findings. As the majority of the recent studies have been carried out with psychiatric patients experiencing auditory hallucinations ("hearing voices"), much of the chapter focuses on this kind of experience.

DEFINITIONS

Modern concepts of hallucination date from the 18th century, during which time they were considered as independent diseases rather than symptoms of more general psychiatric conditions (Berrios, 1996). It was the French physician Jean-Etienne Esquirol (1832) who first formally distinguished between hallucinations and other disorders of perception, observing that the hallucinating person "Ascribes a body and an actuality to images that the memory recalls without the intervention of the senses" (p. 7). By the early years of the 20th century, following the development of a modern system of psychiatric classification by Emil Kraepelin and his followers in Germany, hallucinations had become regarded mainly as symptoms of schizophrenia (Sarbin & Juhasz, 1967). For Eugen Bleuler (1911/ 1950), who coined the term *schizophrenia* in preference to Kraepelin's earlier designation *dementia praecox*, hallucinations were accessory symptoms of the disorder. Kurt Schneider (1959) later advocated the view that certain types of hallucinations in the auditory modality should be regarded as "first-rank" symptoms of schizophrenia, a view that is reflected in modern diagnostic criteria such as those found in the third (1980) and later editions of the American Psychiatric Association's *Diagnostic and Statistical Manual of Mental Disorders* (DSM).

Modern definitions of hallucination draw on Esquirol's. For example, the fourth edition of the DSM (DSM–IV) defines a *hallucination* as "a sensory perception that has the compelling sense of reality of a true perception but that occurs without external stimulation of the relevant sensory organ" (American Psychiatric Association, 1994, p. 767). In an earlier review of the research literature on hallucinations, Slade and Bentall (1988) suggested a more precise definition: "Any percept-like experience which (a) occurs in the absence of an appropriate stimulus, (b) has the full force or impact of the corresponding actual (real) perception, and (c) is not amenable to the direct or voluntary control of the experiencer (p. 23). This definition has the advantage of acknowledging the role that environmental stimulation may play in eliciting hallucinations.

Some authors have attempted to distinguish between "true" hallucinations and "pseudohallucinations," so defined either because they are perceived as occurring within the body (Jaspers, 1913/1963) or because they are known to be nonveridical by the perceiver (Sedman, 1966). The DSM–IV acknowledges that

One person with auditory hallucinations may recognize that he or she is having a false sensory experience, whereas another may be convinced that the source of the stimulus has an independent physical reality. . . . Some clinicians and investigators would not include [as hallucinations] those experienced as coming from inside the head. (American Psychiatric Association, 1994, p. 767)

However, the manual goes on to argue that neither of these distinctions has any clinical utility.

METHODOLOGICAL ISSUES

The definitions above determine the presence of hallucinations entirely in terms of the private experience of the hallucinating person. Although clinical staff sometimes assert that they can determine whether a psychiatric patient is hallucinating from observations of overt behavior (e.g., by observing patients apparently distracted by imaginary voices or addressing comments to them), these claims should be treated with caution. After all, the very same behaviors may be interpreted as evidence that patients are deep in thought or emotionally aroused for other reasons.

For this reason, the only widely accepted method of deciding whether a person is experiencing hallucinations is by eliciting self-reports. Psychiatric researchers have developed a range of standardized interview schedules or rating scales for collecting data on hallucinations and other psychiatric symptoms. For example, Wing, Cooper, and Sartorius (1974) developed the Present State Examination, a structured interview schedule that allows the examiner to determine the presence of a wide range of psychiatric symptoms including both verbal and nonverbal hallucinations. Kay, Opler, and Fiszbein (1988) reported the development of the Positive and Negative Syndrome Schedule (PANSS), which allows the examiner to rate 30 psychiatric symptoms, including hallucinations, on 7-point scales of severity. The advantage of these types of instruments is that their reliability has been demonstrated. Moreover, rating scales like the PANSS have been designed specifically to be sensitive to therapeutic change and to provide data appropriate for statistical analysis as part of controlled clinical trials. The major disadvantage of these techniques is that they require interviewers to be formally trained to ensure that the scales are used appropriately. A further disadvantage is that they provide insufficient detail about hallucinations for some purposes.

To overcome this latter disadvantage, Carter, Mackinnon, Howard, Zeegers, and Copolov (1995) developed the Mental Health Research Institute Unusual Perceptions Schedule (MUPS). The schedule has been designed to assess various characteristics of auditory hallucinations, including their onset and course, number, volume, tone, and location, together with the patients' reactions to them and their use of coping strategies. Interrater reliability of the MUPS was shown to be high for individual items.

Interview schedules and rating scales do not exhaust the range of techniques that have been used to assess hallucinations. For example, clinical trials of psychological treatments often used diaries or simple self-rating scales of varying complexity to good effect (Haddock, Bentall, & Slade, 1993). Moreover, questionnaire measures of hallucinatory experiences have been shown to be reliable and useful for some purposes—for example, to identify nonpsychiatric populations whose members experience hallucinations (Bentall & Slade, 1985b).

PHENOMENOLOGY

The auditory hallucinations reported by psychiatric patients vary in form and content. They may consist of a voice speaking the individual's thoughts aloud, a voice carrying out a running commentary on the person's behavior, a collection of voices speaking about the individual in the third person, or voices issuing commands and instructions (Hamilton, 1983). Thomas (1997) argued that these different forms of auditory hallucination reflect the different social functions of speech, or "speech genres." Many of the voices described by patients appear to be negative in content (e.g., persecutory comments, criticisms of the self, and instructions to commit violent acts against the self or others), as illustrated by the case of Brian, whom I have described in more detail elsewhere (Slade & Bentall, 1988).

I saw Brian while I was working as a clinical psychologist in a secure psychiatric unit. He had been detained in the unit following a near-lethal assault on his father, with whom he had a difficult relationship. A thin, jovial man of 36 who had never been married, Brian had not responded well to medication and was eager to explore alternative ways of coping with his illness.

Brian had suffered from auditory hallucinations since his early 20s, when he had suffered a breakdown after failing to gain entry to medical school. For a while, he had attempted to pursue an alternative career in biochemistry, but feeling lonely and isolated, he had eventually dropped out. He began to develop the conviction that there was a secret conspiracy against him, and the first of many admissions to psychiatric hospitals rapidly followed. When I saw him, he was experiencing a number of voices, which he attributed to a team of parapsychologists he believed were experimenting with his mind. From the moment of waking until he went to sleep at night, the voices would sometimes shout at him, whereas at other times he was aware of only an indecipherable murmuring in the background. The repertoire was limited but highly distressing. After a relationship with a young Jewish woman failed, his voices began to tell him that there was a Jewish conspiracy to put Gentiles in concentration camps. At other times the voices would repeat "Give cancer to the crippled bastard." This last injunction became more understandable when I learned that his mother had died of cancer and observed that he had suffered crippling leg injuries after leaping from a high building in a suicide attempt.

Brian's experiences are not atypical among psychiatric patients. However, hallucinatory experiences are not always negative. Miller, O'Connor, and DePasquale (1993) interviewed a group of chronically hallucinating patients and found that many of their voices were perceived as pleasant and that the majority had incorporated their voices into their social network. Many stated that they would not like their voices to be taken away from them by treatment. Some people with positive voices lead successful lives without seeking or receiving psychiatric treatment, as the following case vignette illustrates.

Georgina was an undergraduate student who approached me after I had given a lecture on normal perception. We spoke only briefly, and so my knowledge of her experiences is necessarily limited. However, she wanted to know whether she should be worried about "hearing voices." Her inquiry led to a 15-min discussion, after which she declined my offer to meet her for a more lengthy interview. She told me that she had been hearing voices since late adolescence. The voices had first made their presence known while she was studying for her 'A' levels (British school examinations required for entry to university) and had emerged gradually from her thoughts. Georgina told me that the voices were sexless and appeared to come from a point in space somewhere to her left. She heard them approximately once or twice a week, usually in the evening when she was studying. They were comforting in tone and offered encouraging messages about her likelihood of succeeding in her career. At times she assumed that they had been sent to her by God (she was a committed Christian). At other times she preferred a more naturalistic explanation, interpreting them in terms of events happening in her brain. She said that they caused her no distress whatsoever.

Surprisingly little research has been carried out on the phenomenology of hallucinatory experiences. Aggernaes (1972b) proposed that different types of mental events including hallucinations may be distinguished by a series of *reality characteristics* or qualities: (a) sensation versus ideation; (b) behavioral relevance versus nonrelevance; (c) publicness (the experience is shared by others) versus privateness; (d) objectivity (the event is experienced in more than one modality) versus subjectivity; (e) existence (the event would have occurred without anyone to witness it) versus nonexistence; (f) independence (the event does not depend on the perceiver's mental state); and (g) involuntarity (the experience cannot be dismissed by wishing) versus voluntarity. In a study in which schizophrenia patients were interviewed about their experiences, Aggernaes (1972b) concluded that hallucinations had similar reality characteristics to general perceptions with the exception of the quality of publicness, in that most patients believe that their hallucinations were not shared by other people. In contrast, the hallucinatory experiences of LSD users were found to lack most of the positive reality characteristics of general perceptions, with the exception of sensation (Aggernaes, 1972a).

In an influential study of psychiatric patients' responses to a standardized psychiatric interview, Strauss (1969) argued that it was possible to identify reports that appeared to be intermediate between strict hallucinations and normal experiences (e.g., when an individual thinks he or she has caught a glimpse of a person through a window). On the basis of these observations, Strauss suggested that normal and abnormal mental states (he considered delusions as well as hallucinations) varied across four dimensions: (a) the strength of the individual's conviction in the objective reality of the experience, (b) the extent to which direct cultural or stimulus determinants are absent, (c) preoccupation with the experience, and (d) the implausibility of the experience.

Empirical evidence in favor of a continuum model of hallucinations has been obtained from psychometric studies, mostly conducted with nonpsychiatric populations. Beginning in the 1970s, a number of researchers in the United States (Chapman & Chapman, 1980; Chapman, Chapman, & Raulin, 1976; Chapman, Edell, & Chapman, 1980; Spitzer, Endicott, & Gibbon, 1979) and in the United Kingdom (Claridge, 1985, 1987, 1990) argued that severe mental illness, and in particular schizophrenia, should be seen as the extreme endpoint of a continuum of personality. According to this view, there are likely to be many people who show evidence of a schizotypal personality without showing the full-blown symptoms of schizophrenia. One consequence of this argument was that it led researchers to pay more attention to psychoticlike experiences in otherwise normal people. For this purpose, Chapman and Chapman (1980) developed scales for rating abnormal experiences, including hallucinations, reported in interviews on an 11-point continuum which, for example, assigned mid-scores when the individual suspected that a perceived voice was alien to the self before subsequently deciding that it was imaginary. Launay and Slade (1981) developed a 12-item questionnaire for the same purpose, which was found to have good psychometric properties and which included items varying from the unexceptional (e.g., "The sounds I hear in my daydreams are usually clear and distinct" and "No matter how much I try and concentrate on my work, unrelated thoughts always creep into my mind") to the apparently pathological (e.g., "I have been troubled by hearing voices in my head" and "On occasions I have seen a person's face in front of me when no one was in fact there").

BIOLOGICAL MARKERS

Little research has addressed the biological correlates of hallucinations. However, Toone, Cooke, and Lader (1981) reported that hallucinating schizophrenia patients had higher levels and greater fluctuations of skin conductance compared with control patients, indicating abnormal arousal. Cooklin, Sturgeon, and Leff (1983) investigated the relationship between psychophysical changes and the onset of hallucinations, using patients' self-reports of hallucinations and nonverbal indexes such as head movements and movements of the lips. In 10 patients for whom adequate data were recorded, a significant association was found between the apparent onset of hallucinations and spontaneous fluctuations in skin conductance. Although these researchers noted that such fluctuations might be concomitants of the behaviors they recorded in order to judge the onset of hallucinations, they argued that this was unlikely.

Other physiological correlates of hallucinatory experiences include activation of the speech muscles (e.g., Gould, 1948) and of various regions of the brain (McGuire, Shah, & Murray, 1993). These correlates are discussed in more detail in the later section dealing with theories of hallucination.

AFTEREFFECTS

There can be no doubt that many psychiatric patients who experience hallucinations have persisting distress and poor quality of life (Lehman, 1996), are marginalized and stigmatized by others (Barham, 1984), and have low levels of occupational and social functioning. Long-term outcome studies of patients diagnosed with schizophrenia indicate that, overall, about a third completely recover from their psychotic experiences, about a third remain disturbed and disabled throughout their adult lives, and about a third attain some kind of intermediate outcome (Bleuler, 1978; Ciompi, 1984). Poor outcome is associated with a significant economic burden to the individual and to the state (Kavanagh, 1994). However, it is important to note that these data may not be generalizable to all people who experience hallucinations, because those included in outcome studies are often formally diagnosed with a psychotic illness and inevitably experience multiple symptoms and enduring social difficulties. Studies of this sort therefore tell us very little of the natural history of hallucinations and their specific consequences for the individual.

A quite different perspective on the long-term consequences of hallucinations has been offered by a remarkable series of investigations conducted by Marius Romme and Sondra Escher (1989) in the Netherlands. Their work was heavily influenced by a patient who failed to respond to conventional psychiatric treatment but who obtained considerable comfort from reading Jaynes's (1979) theory that hallucinations were a normal part of life in Ancient Greece. Appearing on a popular Dutch television program with this patient, Romme and Escher invited people in the community who heard voices to contact them.

On the basis of an interview study with some of the 450 people who responded to the invitation, Romme and Escher (1989) argued that the process of successful adaptation to hallucinations falls into three phases. In the *startling phase*, hallucinated voices usually appear suddenly, often during a period of emotional turmoil, and often cause great anxiety, panic, and anger. During this phase, most people become confused and powerless and struggle to find ways to escape from the voices. However, after a period ranging from weeks to years, most people are able to progress into the *organization phase*, during which they actively experiment with strategies to cope with the voices. The strategies adopted vary from individual to individual and included ignoring the voices, listening and talking to positive voices, and entering into a kind of mental contract with the voices that limits their impact (e.g., deciding to listen to the voices for only a limited time every day). Finally, some people are able to move on to the *stabilization phase*, in which they are able to view the voices as a part of themselves that can have a positive influence.

Approximately two thirds of those who responded to Romme and Escher's television presentation described themselves as having difficulty coping with their voices, whereas approximately one third described themselves as coping adequately (Romme & Escher, 1989). In a comparison of questionnaire responses of the copers and the noncopers, Romme and Escher (1996) found that the copers believed themselves to be stronger than their voices, as opposed to the noncopers, who felt themselves to be weaker. Copers also experienced more positive voices and fewer negative voices than the noncopers.

Other researchers who have studied the process of coping with hallucinations have focused on the coping strategies of people who have been diagnosed as mentally ill for quite some time. Falloon and Talbot (1981) interviewed 40 outpatients diagnosed as suffering from schizophrenia and found that their coping methods included changes in behavior (e.g., undertaking an activity or engaging in social interaction), changes in physiological arousal (e.g., relaxing or exercising), and various cognitive strategies (e.g., reducing attention to voices, debating with voices, or telling voices to "go away"). Similar results have been reported by Tarrier (1987) and O'Sullivan (1994).

These observations, together with the observation that hallucinations lie on one or more continua with normal mental states, raise the question of whether hallucinations should always be regarded as pathological. There is no doubt that hallucinations often occur in the context of severe physical or psychiatric disorders. Previous reviews have noted that hallucinations are associated with a variety of medical conditions, including progressive sensory loss, fever, focal brain lesions (especially in the temporal lobe), delirium, and alcoholic states (Asaad & Shapiro, 1986; Slade & Bentall, 1988). The ability of certain drugs to elicit hallucinations in nonpsychotic individuals is well known, the most potent hallucinogen being the d-isomer of lysergic acid diethylamide (LSD), which was first synthesized by Hoffman in 1938 (Siegel & Jarvick, 1975). The hallucinogenic effects of LSD and other drugs, which appear to have specific affinity for the serotonergic nervous system, were once thought to provide a model of the processes involved in psychiatric hallucinations (Wooley & Shaw, 1954). However, the typical phenomenology of drug-induced hallucinations, which often consists of visual experiences incorporating intense colors, as well as explosive, concentric, rotational, or pulsating movements (Siegel & Jarvick, 1975), is quite different from that of hallucinations that occur in the absence of intoxication.

Even when observed in psychiatric patients, hallucinations may, on closer examination, occasionally be associated with organic pathology. Hall, Popkin, and Faillace (1978) medically examined 658 psychiatric outpatients and estimated that 9.1% had a physical disease; a substantial minority of these patients had hallucinations. Johnstone, MacMillan, and Crowe (1987) found that 15 patients out of a series of 268 who met criteria for schizophrenia had identifiable evidence of organic disorder and, of these, 10 were found to have hallucinations. In a similar survey, Cornelius, Mezzich, Fabrega, Cornelius, and Myers (1991) observed that organic hallucinations usually appeared suddenly and were often visual.

Schneider's (1959) view that hallucinations in the absence of demonstrable organic pathology should be attributed to schizophrenia is reflected in modern surveys of the symptoms experienced by psychiatric patients. A multinational study conducted by the World Health Organization (WHO) estimated that hallucinations were experienced by approximately 70% of patients who met the diagnostic criteria for schizophrenia (Sartorius, Shapiro, & Jablensky, 1974). In a subsequent WHO study of new cases of schizophrenia in 10 countries, hallucinations were also frequently recorded (Jablensky et al., 1992). Hallucinatory experiences also are frequently recorded from patients with severe affective disorders, such as manic depression (Goodwin & Jamison, 1990), and from patients diagnosed with dissociative disorders (Ross, Norton, & Wozney, 1989). In part, this attribution of hallucinations to diverse diagnostic groups reflects continuing disputes about the boundaries between different psychiatric diagnoses. (For critiques of categorical systems of psychiatric classifications such as those outlined in the various editions of the *DSM*, see Bentall, 1990b; Clark, Watson, & Reynolds, 1995.)

The first systematic attempt to determine whether hallucinations might occur in people without physical or mental illness was conducted in Great Britain at the end of the 19th century by the Society for Psychical Research (Sidgewick, 1894). In total, 7,717 men and 7,599 women were interviewed by a large team of collaborators to the project. Although no attempt was made to obtain a truly random sample, anyone with obvious signs of mental or physical illness was excluded from the study. Of the total sample, 7.8% of men and 12% of women reported at least one vivid hallucinatory experience, the most common type being a visual hallucination of a living person who was not present at the time of the experience. Hallucinations with a religious or supernatural content also were recorded, and auditory hallucinations were found to be less common than visual hallucinations. Hallucinations appeared to occur most commonly in people between 20 and 29 years of age, a period that approximately corresponds to the subsequently established high-risk period for psychotic illness.

This study was followed up by a much less extensive survey conducted by the Society more than 50 years later (D. J. West, 1948). Questionnaires were distributed to the general public by the "Mass Observation" survey organization. Many of the questionnaires either were not returned or were completed inadequately. Of the 1,519 adequate responses, 217, or 14.3%, reported a history of hallucinations. Again, visual hallucinations were more commonly reported than auditory hallucinations, and women respondents were more likely to have experienced hallucinations than men.

The first modern survey of hallucinations was conducted by McKellar (1968), who found that 125 out of 500 "normal" people questioned reported having had at least one hallucinatory experience. Posey and Losch (1983) questioned a sample of 375 college students, finding that 39% reported experiencing the Schneiderian first-rank symptom of hearing a voice out loud and that 5% reported holding conversations with their hallucinations. Subsequent surveys of students in the United Kingdom (Bentall & Slade, 1985b; Young, Bentall, Slade, & Dewey, 1986) and in the United States (Barrett & Etheridge, 1992) also revealed that a surprising proportion reported a history of hallucinatory experiences. Barrett and Etheridge (1992) established that the hallucination reports made by their students were not related to measures of social conformity or overt psychopathology. However, in a subsequent study they found evidence that students who reported hallucinations showed heightened levels of negative affect as well as heightened feelings of rejection and incompetence in social situations, as measured by a personality questionnaire (Barrett & Etheridge, 1994).

The most comprehensive survey of hallucinations in the general population to date was reported by Tien (1991). The data for this survey were collected from the Epidemiological Catchment Area (ECA) study, a large interview survey of psychiatric symptoms in a randomly selected general population sample. A total of 18,572 people were assessed, and 15,258 of these agreed to be reassessed 1 year later. The definition of hallucinations used in this study was based on that given in the third edition of the *DSM* and differs little from that given in *DSM–IV*. Tien compared the ECA data with Sidgewick's (1894) data collected nearly a century earlier, which he submitted to a reanalysis. The data from the two studies proved to be remarkably similar. Estimates of the lifetime prevalence of hallucinations in the ECA study were 13.0% at the first assessment and 11.1% at the second, figures which did not differ significantly from Sidgewick's findings. Also, as Sidgewick had found, hallucinations were reported approximately twice as often by women than by men. The main difference between the two studies concerned the age prevalence of hallucinations (the ECA data revealed that hallucinations occurred across the age spectrum but most often in elderly people) and in the prevalence of visual hallucinations, which were reported less often by Sidgewick's respondents.

Of course, it is likely that many otherwise "normal" people who report hallucinations would be classified as schizotypal by those who hold that schizophrenia represents the end of a continuum of personality characteristics. Overall, however, the finding that a substantial minority of the population experiences frank hallucinations at some point in their lives must be considered very robust. By way of comparison, estimates of the lifetime risk of schizophrenia in the general population have usually approximated 1% (Jablensky, 1995). For every person who receives a diagnosis of schizophrenia, therefore, it would appear that there are approximately 10 who experience hallucinations without receiving the diagnosis.

It would be useful to know how hallucinating people who become psychiatric patients differ from those who do not. This question was addressed in the series of studies carried out by Romme and Escher (1996) following their appearance on Dutch television. When they divided their respondents into patients (i.e., those who had sought and received psychiatric treatment) and nonpatients, they found that the nonpatients were more likely to be married and felt more able to discuss their voices with other people.

In another study, Pennings and Romme (1996) compared a small group of hallucinating patients who had been diagnosed with schizophrenia, a similar group that had been diagnosed with dissociative disorder, and a group of people who heard voices but who did not meet formal criteria for a psychiatric disorder even after being interviewed with a standardized psychiatric interview schedule (the Composite International Diagnostic Interview; Robbins, Wing, & Wittchen, 1988). Remarkably few differences were recorded for the phenomenology of the hallucinations experienced by the three groups. All three groups experienced both negative and positive voices, but the proportion of voice experiences that were positive was greater in the nonpatients. A much larger percentage of the nonpatients than the patients felt that they could control their voices or were able to refuse commands issued by their voices.

In a similar comparison of schizophrenia patients with nonpsychiatric hallucinators, Leudar, Thomas, McNally, and Glinsky (1997) found surprisingly few differences between patients and nonpatients. In both groups, the majority of the participants reported that their voices attempted to regulate everyday activities, for example, by telling them what to do or not to do and by issuing instructions about particular courses of action; the voices were rarely bizarre and were usually aligned to significant individuals in their lives.

These findings suggest that it may not be the nature of hallucinatory experiences per se that determines whether people become psychiatric patients or not, but the way in which individuals react to their experiences.

CONTEXTUAL FACTORS THAT INFLUENCE HALLUCINATIONS

Research has indicated that the experience of hallucinations can be influenced by a number of factors. The investigation of these factors has provided important clues about the psychological processes responsible for hallucinations.

Culture

The influence of culture on hallucinations was considered by Bourguignon (1970), who surveyed anthropological data collected from 488 societies worldwide and found evidence that hallucinations play a role in ritual practices in 62% of the cultures studied. In the majority, hallucinations were not induced by the ingestion of psychoactive chemicals, were positively valued, and could be understood in the context of local beliefs and practices. For example, Bourguignon noted that it is taboo for a Mohawk Indian to eat his own game and that, if he does so, he is haunted by the spirit of his kill until he has made suitable reparations. Al-Issa (1995) suggested that the positive attitude that many developing societies have toward hallucinations reflects more general metaphysical attitudes that are often quite different from those held by people in the West. On this view, Western psychiatrists' and psychologists' preoccupations with hallucinations reflect a culturally embedded materialist criterion for evaluating first-person reports that necessitates the classification of experiences as real or imaginary. In societies that hold this distinction to be less important, the possibility of misclassifying an imaginary event as real is less important.

In earlier reviews of the psychiatric literature, Al-Issa (1977, 1978) found evidence of cultural and historical differences in the kinds of hallucinations recorded by psychiatrists. Visual hallucinations were found to be much more commonly recorded in developing countries than in the developed world, an observation that was confirmed in the WHO's multinational study of new cases of psychosis (Sartorius et al., 1986). There is some evidence that a decline in the prevalence of visual hallucinations in the West has been matched by an increase in the recorded prevalence of auditory hallucinations. Hallucinatory experiences recorded in the Middle Ages were almost entirely visual (Kroll & Bachrach, 1982). Lenz (1964), by contrast, examined psychiatric records from Vienna and found that reports of visual hallucinations decreased over a 100-year period, whereas reports of auditory hallucinations increased.

The content of hallucinations also appears to be influenced by culture. Whereas hallucinatory experiences reported in the Middle Ages were almost universally religious in content (Kroll & Bachrach, 1982), those recorded by psychologists and psychiatrists today often have persecutory or technological themes. In a study of the impact of Western culture on Bantu psychiatric patients, Scott (1967) found that the type of auditory hallucinations reported changed from instructions to carry out customs in order to allay tribal guilt to accusations that signified that guilt was borne by the individual.

Environment

External stimuli and mental activities provoked by such stimuli have been shown to affect hallucinatory experiences. Although early research indicated that hallucinations could be elicited in ordinary people by periods of sensory deprivation, careful experimentation revealed that only a minority of participants reported vivid visual and auditory hallucinations in deprivation experiments and that suggestions from experimenters appeared to have played a role in these reports (Zuckerman, 1969). The role of environmental stimulation in modulating the symptoms of psychiatric patients was first studied by Harris (1959), who asked a small group of patients with schizophrenia to undergo short periods of sensory deprivation and noted little effect on their hallucinations. In a much more systematic study, Slade (1974) asked 2 patients to monitor their hallucinations while shadowing verbal information of varying complexity and found that the rate of hallucinations decreased as the complexity of the stimulus material increased.

Margo, Hemsley, and Slade (1981) carried out a similar procedure with 7 frequently hallucinating patients with schizophrenia. The nine conditions used in this investigation included no stimulation, reading aloud, listening to boring and interesting passages of text, listening to popular music, listening to regular and irregular patterns of electronic blips, listening to speech in a foreign language, sensory restriction and, finally, listening to white noise. In general, it was observed that the duration, loudness, and clarity of auditory hallucinations increased during sensory restriction and white noise but decreased while the participants were listening to meaningful stimulation or especially when they were reading aloud. These findings were almost perfectly replicated by Gallagher, Dinin, and Baker (1994).

The observation that reading aloud suppresses auditory hallucinations has also been made in clinical studies, leading some clinicians to advocate reading as a coping strategy for hallucinating patients (Erickson & Gustafson, 1968; James, 1983). Gallagher, Dinin, and Baker (1995) investigated this effect further in two experiments in which they manipulated information-processing requirements and the requirement to speak while patients monitored their voices. A card-sorting task produced a reduction in the participants' hallucinations, but this effect did not seem to be a function of the rate of information processing. The effect of card sorting was much greater when the participants were required to name the color of the card aloud, confirming that the requirement to speak had a specific inhibitory effect on auditory hallucinations.

Stress

It has been more difficult to evaluate the impact of stress on hallucinations, partly because stress itself is difficult to quantify. Although there is evidence pointing to the role of stressful life events in precipitating schizophrenia episodes, the research findings in this area have not been consistent (Bebbington, Bowen, Hirsch, & Kuipers, 1995). There is somewhat more consistent evidence that patients with a history of psychosis may be more vulnerable to future episodes if exposed to chronic stresses, in particular a hostile or overprotective family environment (Bebbington & Kuipers, 1994; Vaughn & Leff, 1976). These observations have led many theorists to propose stress–vulnerability models that explain schizophrenia breakdowns in terms of complex interactions between biological and environmental variables (Neuchterlein & Dawson, 1984; Zubin & Spring, 1977).

Case study and survey data point to the role of stress in provoking episodes of hallucination. On the basis of the interview data from a large sample of hallucinating individuals, only some of whom had received psychiatric treatment, Romme and Escher (1989) estimated that the onset of hallucinations followed some kind of stressful or traumatic experience in approximately 70% of cases. Because the sample in this study was to some degree self-selected, it is difficult to judge the extent to which this finding is generalizable. Combs (1997) asked a group of people who heard voices —some but not all of whom had a diagnosis of schizophrenia—to keep diaries of their experiences over a period of several months. In the majority of cases, hallucinations were most severe during periods of emotional distress. This was true, for example, of a socially and intellectually successful undergraduate student who heard voices but who had never sought psychiatric treatment.

Auditory and visual hallucinations are a commonly documented part of the grief reaction, with as many as 70% of recently bereaved people experiencing either illusions or hallucinations of the deceased (Grimby, 1993; Reese, 1971). Further evidence that stress may play a specific role in hallucinations has emerged from case studies of individuals exposed to extraordinary or life-threatening circumstances, such as mining accidents (Comer, Madow, & Dixon, 1967), terrorist incidents (Siegel, 1984), and military operations (Belenky, 1979; Spivak, Trottern, Mark, & Bleich, 1992). The psychophysical data collected from the hallucinating patients with schizophrenia previously referred to are also consistent with the hypothesis that the onset of hallucinations coincides with periods of stress-induced emotional arousal (Cooklin et al., 1983; Toone et al., 1981).

THEORIES

Any adequate psychological model of hallucinations must account for the impact of culture, environmental stimulation, and stress on hallucinatory experiences, as described in the preceding section. Until recently, however, theories of hallucination were constructed in relative ignorance of these factors and tended to be driven by isolated observations. For example, some authors have argued that hallucinations might be viewed as conditioned perceptual responses (Davies, Davies, & Bennett, 1982; Hefferline, Bruno, & Camp, 1973), whereas others have interpreted the effects of hallucinogenic drugs in terms of parallels with sleep or dreaming (West, 1962) or have argued that hallucinations occurred when preconscious material seeped into the conscious mind (Frith, 1979), and still others have argued that hallucinations were products of abnormal mental imagery (Horowitz, 1975). My reviews of the strengths and limitations of each of these accounts can be found in Bentall (1990a) and Slade and Bentall (1988).

MISATTRIBUTION OF INNER SPEECH

In recent years, a widespread consensus has been achieved about the nature of auditory hallucinations. According to this consensus view, auditory hallucinations occur when the individual misattributes inner speech to a source that is external or alien to the self (Bentall, 1990b; Frith, 1992; Hoffman, 1986; Thomas, 1997). The term *inner speech* refers to the internal dialogue one uses to regulate one's own behavior, for example, by commenting to oneself about what is happening or by issuing instructions to oneself about what to do. The development of inner speech in infancy was first described by the celebrated Russian psychologist Lev Vygotsky (1962) and by his student, the neuropsychologist Alexander Luria (1981). According to Vygotsky, children first learn to respond to instructions from caregivers before they begin to issue instructions to themselves, sometime during the third year of life. At this stage, children can be observed to talk out aloud to themselves, a phenomenon that Piaget (1926) mistakenly construed as evidence of infantile egocentricity. Later, the child learns to internalize inner speech, performing it silently as adults do. Even in adulthood, however, people often speak out loud to themselves, especially when alone or under stress.

It has been known for many years that inner speech in adulthood, even when silent, is accompanied by *subvocalization* or electrical activation of the speech muscles (McGuigan, 1978); indeed, this hypothesis was suggested by J. B. Watson (1924), the founder of the American behaviorist school of psychology. The first studies that demonstrated a link between inner speech and hallucinations involved electromyographic (EMG) measurements of subvocalization in hallucinating patients. Gould (1948) measured passive lip and chin EMG activity in a large group of psychiatric patients and found increased activity in 83% of hallucinating patients but only in 10% of nonhallucinating patients. Gould (1949) then demonstrated that it was possible, using a sensitive microphone to record subvocal speech from a patient who was hallucinating. This technique was later replicated by Green and Preston (1981), who showed that the content of the recorded speech matched the content of their patient's auditory hallucinations. Subsequent studies by Gould (1950) and others (Gabbard, Lazar, Hornberger, & Spiegel, 1997; Green & Kinsbourne, 1990; Inouye & Shimizu, 1970; McGuigan, 1966) established that the onset of electromyographically recorded subvocalization coincided with the onset of hallucinations and that increased electrical activity was not concurrently observable from control muscles in other parts of the body.

If auditory hallucinations are a product of inner speech, they should coincide with activation of those areas in the brain responsible for the production and perception of speech, which in most people are located in the left hemisphere. Using telemetered electrocardiogram measures, Stevens and Livermore (1982) noted a significant association between the onset of hallucinations and activation in the left temporal lobe, an area thought to be important for speech perception. More recent studies have used single-photon emission tomography (SPET) or positron emission tomography

(PET), techniques in which radioactively labeled substances are injected into the blood, allowing areas of cerebral activation to be mapped by sophisticated scanners (see Lewis and Higgins, 1996, for explanations of these and other innovations in neuroimaging). Using SPET with a small group of patients, McGuire et al. (1993) showed that auditory hallucinations were associated with activation of Broca's area (a region of the left frontal cortex responsible for speech production) and also of the left medial temporal lobe. In a subsequent study using the more sensitive PET methodology, Silbersweig et al. (1995) observed activation of the left frontal cortex but also in deeper brain structures (various subcortical nuclei and paralimbic regions). In Silbergweig et al.'s study, a single drug-free patient who experienced simultaneous visual and auditory hallucinations (of a disembodied head that talked to him) was also investigated. It was observed that the patient's hallucinations were associated with activations in both the visual association cortex and the auditory association cortex in the left hemisphere.

These physiological observations, together with the earlier EMG studies, provide strong evidence that inner speech occurs concurrently with auditory hallucinations and, therefore, that hallucinations reflect the individual's mistaken judgments about the source or location of their inner speech. Moreover, the observation that areas of the brain that are responsible for visual processing are activated during visual hallucinations suggests that hallucinations in nonauditory modalities may occur when other kinds of internal events (e.g., visual imagery) are so misattributed. In an earlier review, I pointed out that this kind of general model, which places emphasis on individuals' judgments about the source of their experiences, goes some way toward explaining the impact of the various factors known to influence hallucinations (Bentall, 1990a). To understand why this is the case, one must consider in more detail the psychological processes that might be responsible for individuals' judgments about the reality of their experiences.

SOURCE MONITORING

Most people take for granted the process of discrimination between our thoughts and images and the things we hear or see. However, there are grounds for supposing that we do not have a priori knowledge about whether perceived events are internal to ourselves and generated in our minds or are external to ourselves and generated by agencies other than the self.[1] The

---

[1] Some of these grounds are philosophical and are derived from Wittgenstein's (1953) "private language argument." Wittgenstein claimed that it would be impossible for an individual to create descriptions of events without reference to public information. One implication is that experiences do not come "pretagged" with verbal labels or descriptions such as *real* or *imaginary* (see Slade & Bentall, 1988, for a fuller account of these issues).

process of discrimination between these two kinds of events is known as *source monitoring* in the psychological literature and has been studied by Marcia Johnson and her colleagues in a series of elaborate experiments with ordinary people (Johnson & Magaro, 1987; Johnson, Hashtroudi, & Lindsay, 1993). Johnson's work, which has focused on judgments about the source of memories, has shown that human beings use a variety of cues when discriminating between memories of self-generated thoughts and memories of real events. For example, contextual information about time and location may help a person to determine whether the event "really occurred," as may sensory qualities of the memory such as vividness, detail, and complexity. People also may make use of memories of some of the cognitive operations involved. For example, people are more likely to recognize a recalled event as a self-generated thought if they recall the cognitive effort associated with generating the thought. Finally, Johnson and her colleagues argued that the coherence and plausibility of the memory trace also may influence a person's source-monitoring judgments. For example, if people recall themselves performing acts that violate natural laws or that conflict with what they know about themselves or the world, they know that what they are remembering is almost certainly a fantasy or a dream. These observations suggest that discriminating between self-generated (internal, "imaginary') events and externally generated ("real") events is best thought of as a skill and, like all skills, is likely to fail under certain circumstances.

Johnson's suggestion that source-monitoring judgments are influenced by the inherent plausibility of perceived events helps to explain the role of culture in shaping hallucinatory experiences. An individual who grows to adulthood in a society that recognizes the existence of ghosts or that values spiritual experiences is more likely to attribute reality to the image of a deceased relative than a person who reaches maturity in a materialistic, scientifically oriented society. The impact of external stimulation on hallucinations also can be understood in terms of the source-monitoring hypothesis. In conditions in which external stimulation is degraded (either by sensory restriction or by white noise), individuals are likely to adopt more liberal criteria for assuming that perceived events are real and are therefore more likely to misattribute internally generated thoughts to an external source (see below). The inhibitory effect of concurrent verbal tasks on auditory hallucinations also can be understood in terms of the hypothesis, as such tasks presumably suppress the inner speech that is misattributed to an external source. Finally, the impact of stress and emotional arousal on hallucinations can be understood if it is assumed that the cognitive operations involved in source monitoring, like other cognitive operations, are disrupted by emotional arousal. The interaction of these variables

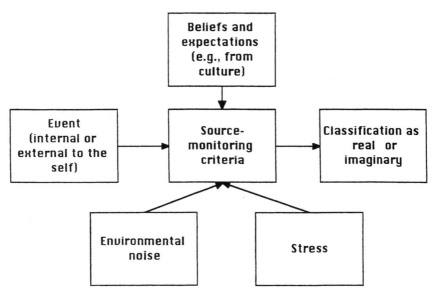

Figure 3.1. A schematic model of hallucinations, after Bentall (1990a), and Slade and Bentall (1988), showing how source-monitoring judgments are influenced by beliefs, environmental noise, and stress.

with the process of source monitoring is shown diagrammatically in Figure 3.1.[2]

Although a general account that places emphasis on defective or inaccurate source-monitoring judgments goes some way toward explaining many of the phenomena associated with hallucinations, the model does not explain why some people make more source-monitoring errors than others and are therefore more prone to hallucinations. At present, only tentative answers can be offered to this question.

Using a variety of procedures, a number of researchers have attempted to assess source-monitoring judgments in hallucinating patients and nonpatients. One of the earliest attempts to do this was reported by Heilbrun (1980), who assessed the ability of hallucinating patients and control patients (most diagnosed with schizophrenia) to recognize their own thoughts. Patients' opinions on a number of topics were tape recorded, and their verbatim remarks were later included in an individualized multiple-choice test, alongside statements that were either lexically or semantically different. The hallucinating patients were significantly poorer than control patients at recognizing their own statements. In a subsequent study, Heil-

---

[2]In an earlier account of this model (Bentall, 1990a), I argued that reinforcement also may influence the source-monitoring judgment of hallucinating patients. On this view, patients might prefer to attribute dangerous thoughts (e.g., thoughts about suicide or homicide) to an external source because this would generate less anxiety than attributing these thoughts to themselves. However, there is currently little or no evidence that hallucinations have this kind of defensive function. Moreover, as we have seen, many hallucinations have a positive content.

brun, Blum, and Haas (1983) explored the possibility that source-monitoring failures in hallucinating patients were the consequence of a deficit in the ability to spatially locate sounds. In this study, for reasons that are explained later, the patients with schizophrenia were divided into *process* (poor premorbid adjustment and insidious onset) and *reactive* (good premorbid adjustment and rapid onset) subgroups (see Heilbrun, 1996). The ability to locate sounds was judged by a test in which the participant, surrounded by screens, was required to describe the location of the experimenter's voice. It was found that the hallucinating reactive patients with schizophrenia showed poorer spatial location of sounds than the nonhallucinating control patients.

Using a different technique derived from the work of Marcia Johnson and her colleagues, Bentall, Baker, and Havers (1991) also attempted to assess hallucinating patients' ability to recognize their own thoughts. In this study, hallucinating patients with schizophrenia were compared with deluded but nonhallucinating patients with schizophrenia and with non-psychiatric control patients. Participants were asked to provide answers to simple clues (e.g., "Think of a habitat beginning with H——") and to listen to paired associates (e.g., *country–Norway*). One week later they were presented with a list of words and were asked to identify which were answers they had provided to the earlier cues (e.g., "House"), which were words that they had heard (e.g., *Norway*), and which had not appeared during the earlier stage of testing. No difference was found between the overall error scores of the hallucinating and the deluded but nonhallucinating patients. However, when types of error were examined, there was some evidence that the hallucinators were more likely to make errors in which they mistook answers to clues (i.e., items they had thought) for items they had heard. This effect was particularly evident for answers to difficult clues. The control participants in this experiment, in common with participants tested in Johnson et al.'s work (1993), showed more accurate source monitoring for difficult as opposed to easy items, indicating that recall of cognitive effort helped them to identify items as self-generated. As this effect was much less evident in the hallucinating patients, the findings could be interpreted as evidence that hallucinating patients make poor use of cognitive effort cues. Unfortunately, Seal, Crowe, and Cheung (1997) were unable to replicate these findings when they controlled for the verbal intelligence and verbal memory skills of hallucinating patients and control patients.

Clearer evidence of the role of defective source monitoring in hallucinations was found in a study by Rankin and O'Carrol (1995), who compared undergraduate students who scored high and low on the Launay–Slade questionnaire measure of disposition to hallucinations. Participants were tested with a complex paradigm, again derived from the work of Johnson, in which they were repeatedly presented with paired associates.

The number of times that the items were presented (e.g., *vehicle–car*) and tested (e.g., "Which word goes with *vehicle* . . . ?") was carefully manipulated so that, for example, some associates were presented many times but tested few times and others were presented on only a few trials but tested on many trials. After the presentation and testing of the paired associates, participants were asked to say how many times they thought they had been presented with each item. As Johnson and Magaro (1987) had previously found, participants gave inflated frequency estimates for those items on which they had been most tested, indicating that they had mistaken occasions on which they had recalled the items for occasions on which the items had been presented. This effect was most evident in participants who scored high on the Launay–Slade measure.

Morrison and Haddock (1997) argued that source-monitoring abnormalities are more likely to be detected in hallucinating patients if immediate attributions of source are measured, rather than measuring attributions based on the recall of previously presented information. One way in which this has been achieved is by signal detection theory (SDT) methodology. SDT is a mathematically based theory of perception that proposes that the detection of an external stimulus (or signal) is a function of two factors (McNichol, 1972). The first factor, perceptual sensitivity, refers to the general efficiency of the perceptual system. The second factor, response bias, refers to the individual's private criteria for deciding that a perceived event is an actual stimulus rather than internal noise. SDT provides various methodologies for independently measuring sensitivity and bias, the simplest of which involve the individual making judgments about whether a signal is present against a noisy background in a long series of trials. Judgments in these circumstances can be divided into four categories (see Figure 3.2): hits (a signal is correctly detected); misses (a signal is present but is judged to be absent); correct rejections, and false alarms (the signal is judged to be present when it is not). Various mathematical techniques are

| | **Signal detection** | | **Source monitoring** | |
	Judged Present	Judged Absent	Judged Present	Judged Absent
Stimulus Present	Hit	Miss	"It's real"	"There's nothing there"
Stimulus Absent	False alarm	Correct Rejection	Hallucination	"It's my imagination"

Figure 3.2. Relationship between choices made by participants in signal detection experiences and source-monitoring judgments. High perceptual sensitivity results in a high proportion of hits and correct rejections and few signal detection errors (misses and false alarms). Increasing bias to detect signals results in more hits and fewer misses but at the expense of an increase in false alarms (hallucinations) and a decrease in correct rejections.

available for deriving measures of sensitivity and bias from this kind of data.

Bentall and Slade (1985a) carried out two SDT experiments, one comparing patients with schizophrenia who experienced hallucinations with patients with schizophrenia who did not, and one comparing undergraduate students who scored high on the Launay–Slade scale with those who scored low on the scale. In both experiments, the hallucinating participants did not differ from the respective control participants on the measure of perceptual sensitivity but did differ on the measure of bias, indicating that they were more willing to decide that signals were present under conditions of uncertainty. This finding was later replicated by Rankin and O'Carrol (1995) in their study of student participants selected according to their scores on the Launay–Slade scale.

Morrison and Haddock (1997) reported a study in which immediate source-monitoring judgments were compared with delayed judgments of the sort made during conventional source-monitoring experiments. In a complex design, hallucinating psychotic patients, nonhallucinating psychotic patients, and control participants were asked to provide associates for words that were emotionally positive (e.g., *courage*), emotionally negative (e.g., *crazy*), or emotionally neutral (e.g., *bookcase*). Immediately after responding to each word, participants were asked to rate their responses for internality ("How much was the word that came to mind your own?"), control ("How much control did you have over the word that came to mind?"), and involuntariness ("How involuntary was your thought?"). On completion of this first phase of testing, the participants were given a conventional source-monitoring test in which they were asked to decide whether particular words had been used as cues by the experimenter or were responses they had made to cues. A significant difference was observed between the hallucinators and both the nonhallucinators and control participants for immediate source-monitoring judgments as assessed by the internality ratings, especially for the emotional items. On the delayed source-monitoring measure, there was a nonsignificant trend toward a greater number of errors by the hallucinating patients. These findings were replicated by Baker and Morrison (1998).

It is possible that the abnormal performance of hallucinating people observed in the above reviewed studies at least partially reflects the impact of beliefs and expectations on their source-monitoring judgments, rather than gross deficits in source monitoring skills. This hypothesis is consistent with clinical studies that have noted that the long-term well-being of hallucinating patients is influenced by their beliefs and attitudes (Chadwick & Birchwood, 1994; Romme & Escher, 1989). A number of experimental studies have found evidence that hallucinating patients' reports about their experiences are highly influenced by suggestions. Mintz and Alpert (1972) presented hallucinating patients and control patients with Barber and Calverley's (1964) "White Christmas" test, in which participants are asked to close their eyes and listen to a recording of the famous song of the same name, which is not played. After a suitable period, participants are asked to rate their certainty that they have heard it. Mintz and Alpert found that hallucinating patients gave higher certainty ratings than did control patients, a result that was replicated by Young, Bentall, Slade, and Dewey (1987). Haddock, Slade, and Bentall (1995) assessed the suggestibility of hallucinating patients and control patients using the verbal transformation effect, a technique in which the same nonsense word is presented repeatedly on a tape loop. Most people presented with stimuli of this sort begin to hear the word change after a short period, a phenomenon that has been of some interest to perceptual scientists (Warren, 1968). In the study by Haddock et al., participants were told that the word would change in one condition but that it would not change in a second condition. As predicted, these instructions influenced the number of verbal transformations reported, and this effect was much greater in the hallucinating patients than in the control patients.

The above studies address the psychological processes involved in accurate and deficient source monitoring. However, a complete theory of hallucinations would also identify the neuroanatomical structures responsible for these processes. Szechtman, Woody, Bowers, and Nahmias (1998) reported a PET study designed for this purpose. The participants included some individuals who were highly hypnotizable and who had been selected for their ability to hallucinate under hypnosis. Regional cerebral blood flow was measured during hearing, imagining and, in the case of the hypnotizable participants, hallucinating. A region in the right anterior cingulate (Brodmann area 32) was activated in the hypnotizable participants when they heard or hallucinated a stimulus but not when they imagined hearing it. The same conditions did not evoke the same activations in the non-hypnotizable participants. Szechtman et al. concluded that the right anterior cingulate may contain neural circuits responsible for tagging events as originating from the external world.

CLINICAL ISSUES AND RISKS

Pharmacological Treatments

Because hallucinations usually have been regarded as symptoms of mental illness, the most common form of treatment offered to people with hallucinations has been pharmacological. In the late 1940s, French naval surgeon Henri Laborit observed that the antihistamine chlorpromazine (largactil) had a tranquilizing effect on psychiatric patients, and this discovery was shortly followed by the first clinical trials of the drug with patients with schizophrenia (Shorter, 1997). Since that time, numerous controlled studies have shown that chlorpromazine and similar drugs (now collectively known as *neuroleptics*) can reduce the severity of psychotic symptoms, in particular hallucinations and delusions, and can reduce the risk of relapse for patients discharged from a hospital (Leff & Wing, 1971; Lieberman, 1993). Accompanying this development has been a vigorous search for the mode of action of the neuroleptics. The observation that the potency of these drugs correlates with their capacity to block the dopamine d-2 receptor led to the theory that schizophrenia might be caused by an abnormality of the dopamine system (Carlsson & Lindqvist, 1963). However, it is fair to say that further scientific research has not consistently supported the dopamine hypothesis, and it remains controversial (see Carlsson, 1995).

Treatment with neuroleptic medication is not without risk. A substantial proportion of patients fail to respond (Brown & Herz, 1989), and most suffer from side effects that can include Parkinsonian movement disorders (including tremors and an almost intolerable sense of subjective restlessness known as *akathisia*), cardiovascular effects (including an increased risk of sudden death), hormonal and metabolic effects (including weight gain, sexual dysfunction, and breast enlargement in men), and blood disorders (see Bentall, Day, Rogers, Healy, & Stevenson, 1996, for a review). Partly because of these side effects, tolerance of neuroleptic medication may be poor, and a substantial number of patients refuse or discontinue treatment (J. H. Green, 1988; Hoge et al., 1990). Recently, a number of "atypical" neuroleptics have appeared on the market (e.g., clozapine). These cause fewer side effects, although initial claims that they are more effective than the typical neuroleptics may have been overstated (Carpenter, Cauley, Buchanan, Breier, Tamminga, 1996). Interestingly, these drugs are not specific dopamine d-2 antagonists.

Psychological Treatments

Given the limited success of psychopharmacological interventions for patients diagnosed with schizophrenia, there has been a growing interest in psychological treatments. Although controlled trials of psychodynamic therapy for patients with schizophrenia have yielded almost entirely negative outcomes (Muesner & Berenbaum, 1990), other approaches appear to offer much more promise. A well-established treatment strategy involves targeting family members of patients with schizophrenia who have been discharged from the hospital, on the assumption that "expressed emotion" in family members increases the probability of relapse. Treatment is aimed at reducing family criticism of the patient and improving the family's ability to solve the practical problems associated with living with someone with a mental illness (see Tarrier, 1996, for a detailed account of this type of intervention). A substantial number of controlled trials have now demonstrated that this approach can reduce the probability of future hospital admissions.

More recently, attention has turned to the possibility of offering individual cognitive–behavior therapy (CBT) for specific psychotic symptoms. A large number of case studies have reported the successful CBT treatment of both delusions and hallucinations (Haddock & Slade, 1996). In an earlier review of the literature on the treatment of hallucinations, 40 case studies were identified, which fell into three main groups (Slade & Bentall, 1988). Some investigators had reported the successful use of anxiety reduction strategies such as systematic desensitization (e.g., Slade, 1972), others had used distraction strategies such as asking patients to sing to themselves or name nearby objects (Erickson & Gustafson, 1968; James, 1983). Still others had encouraged patients to monitor or focus on their hallucinated voices over a period of time (Glaister, 1985). Slade and Bentall (1988) argued that the last strategy is most likely to bring about an enduring reduction in the severity of hallucinations, as it encourages patients to integrate their voices with their selves.

Unfortunately, this prediction has not been entirely supported by further research. In a small controlled trial, focusing or distraction strategies were offered to patients who had auditory hallucinations for an average of 11 years. Therapy was provided by an experienced clinical psychologist over 20 sessions. Although there seemed to be a short-term beneficial effect of both therapies (Bentall, Haddock, & Slade, 1994; Haddock et al., 1993), no beneficial effect was discernible for either group at a 2-year follow-up (Haddock, Slade, & Bentall, 1998).

Other researchers have obtained mixed results. Nelson, Thrasher, and Barnes (1991) reported that distraction strategies were beneficial for only 1 out of 20 patients treated. However, Persaud and Marks (1995) reported the successful use of anxiety reduction with a small group of patients. Chadwick and Birchwood (1994) devised a CBT strategy that involved challenging the perceived omnipotence of hallucinated voices, predicting that this would help make the voices more bearable. It is interesting to note that all 3 patients treated by this approach reported a reduction in the frequency of their voices by the termination of therapy.

These findings can be better understood in the context of recently conducted controlled trials of CBT for patients with schizophrenia. Successful outcomes, judged in terms of symptomatic improvement, have been reported for both patients with a chronic illness (Garety, Kuipers, Fowler, Chamberlain, & Dunn, 1994; Kuipers et al., 1997; Kuipers et al., 1998; Tarrier et al. 1993; Tarrier et al., 1998; Turkington et al., 1997) and patients with an acute illness (Drury, Birchwood, Cochrane, & MacMillan, 1996) that have been treated with this approach. The success of these trials—some of which were conducted under methodologically exacting conditions

—holds great promise for the future treatment of severely ill psychiatric patients. Unfortunately, most of these studies have used composite measures of symptomatology, which make it difficult to determine the differential impact of the treatments on hallucinations as opposed to other kinds of psychotic experience. However, in their initial small-scale study, Garety et al. (1994) reported that CBT had a positive impact on delusions but not on hallucinations. In their subsequent, larger scale study, the same team reported that the experience of hallucinations was a predictor of poor outcome (Kuipers et al., 1997). These findings appear to confirm that hallucinations are less responsive to currently available psychological treatments than other kinds of psychiatric symptoms. It is important to emphasize that this conclusion holds for currently available treatments. The relative difficulty of treating hallucinations should no more deter innovation in psychotherapy research than the less-than-perfect effect of pharmacotherapy should deter research into novel drug treatments.

In the meantime, therapists should seriously consider whether it is appropriate to encourage patients to accept their hallucinatory experiences and cope with them accordingly. Indeed, the work of Romme and Escher (1989, 1996) suggests that it may not always be appropriate to offer treatment to people who have persistent hallucinatory experiences. Given the substantial iatrogenic hazards of modern psychiatric care, it may often be more helpful to encourage patients to accept their voices as an aspect of normal human variation.

FUTURE RESEARCH

There now exists a general understanding of the kinds of psychological processes that are involved in the experience of hallucinations, but much more needs to be done to identify the etiological processes involved. Overall, the findings reviewed in this chapter suggest that people who experience hallucinations are less proficient at source monitoring than those who do not. Moreover, there is some evidence that the source-monitoring judgments of those who experience hallucinations are underinfluenced by cognitive effort cues and information about spatial location and overinfluenced by prior beliefs and expectations. However, as Heilbrun (1996) pointed out, these investigations leave the developmental pathways that lead to hallucinations almost completely unexplored.

Heilbrun (1996) proposed a model in which these pathways are assumed to be different in process and reactive patients with schizophrenia. According to this model, process patients with schizophrenia react to adverse early experiences by adopting a strategy of attentional withdrawal from threatening stimuli, making them overfocused on their own autistic formulations of the external environment. Reactive patients with schizophrenia, on the other hand, become hypervigilant for threatening stimuli, which results in reduced processing capacity and poor reality testing. One difficulty with this general approach is that it makes opposite predictions about the cognitive abnormalities to be expected in the two types of hallucinating patient, with the consequence that the predictions can be difficult to test. A further difficulty is that the model does not address people who hallucinate but who do not have schizophrenia and who, according to the evidence reviewed earlier, appear to outnumber patients with schizophrenia by a factor of approximately 10 to 1. Nonetheless, Heilbrun is certainly correct in asserting that little is yet known about how hallucinations develop across the lifetime of an individual.

This chapter focused on the psychological mechanisms of hallucinations. However, if the sterile dualism that has marked much psychiatric research in the past is to be avoided in the future, studies will have to focus not only on cognitive processes but also on the physiological mechanisms that sustain those processes. The studies by McGuire et al. (1993), Silbersweig et al. (1995), and Szechtman et al. (1998) have begun this important task. The understanding of these mechanisms is likely to be enhanced by further investigations that inventively combine carefully constructed psychological measures and the new neuroimaging techniques.

REFERENCES

Aggernaes, A. (1972a). The difference between the experienced reality of hallucinations in young drug abusers and schizophrenic patients. *Acta Psychiatrica Scandinavica, 48,* 287–299.

Aggernaes, A. (1972b). The experienced reality of hallucinations and other psychological phenomena: An empirical analysis. *Acta Psychiatrica Scandinavica, 48,* 220–238.

Al-Issa, I. (1977). Social and cultural aspects of hallucinations. *Psychological Bulletin, 84,* 570–587.

Al-Issa, I. (1978). Sociocultural factors in hallucinations. *International Journal of Social Psychiatry, 24,* 167–176.

Al-Issa, I. (1995). The illusion of reality or the reality of an illusion: Hallucinations and culture. *British Journal of Psychiatry, 166,* 368–373.

American Psychiatric Association. (1980). *Diagnostic and statistical manual of mental disorders* (3rd ed.). Washington, DC: Author.

American Psychiatric Association. (1994). *Diagnostic and statistical manual of mental disorders* (4th ed.). Washington, DC: Author.

Asaad, G., & Shapiro, B. (1986). Hallucinations: Theoretical and clinical overview. *American Journal of Psychiatry, 143,* 1088–1097.

Baker, C. A., & Morrison, A. P. (1998). Cognitive processes in auditory hallucinations: Attributional biases and metacognition. *Psychological Medicine, 28,* 1199–1208.

Barber, T. X., & Calverley, D. S. (1964). An experimental study of "hypnotic" (auditory and visual) hallucinations. *Journal of Abnormal and Social Psychology, 63,* 13–20.

Barham, P. (1984). *Schizophrenia and human value.* Oxford, England: Blackwell.

Barrett, T. R., & Etheridge, J. B. (1992). Verbal hallucinations in normals: I. People who hear voices. *Applied Cognitive Psychology, 6,* 379–387.

Barrett, T. R., & Etheridge, J. B. (1994). Verbal hallucinations in normals: III. Dysfunctional personality correlates. *Personality and Individual Differences, 16,* 57–62.

Bebbington, P. E., Bowen, J., Hirsch, S. R., & Kuipers, E. A. (1995). Schizophrenia and psychosocial stresses. In S. R. Hirsch & D. R. Weinberger (Eds.), *Schizophrenia* (pp. 587–604). Oxford, England: Blackwell.

Bebbington, P. E., & Kuipers, E. (1994). The predictive utility of expressed emotion in schizophrenia. *Psychological Medicine, 24,* 707–718.

Belenky, G. L. (1979). Unusual visual experiences reported by subjects in the British Army study of sustained operations, Exercise Early Call. *Military Medicine, 144,* 695–696.

Bentall, R. P. (1990a). The illusion of reality: A review and integration of psychological research on hallucinations. *Psychological Bulletin, 107,* 82–95.

Bentall, R. P. (1990b). The syndromes and symptoms of psychosis: Or why you can't play 20 questions with the concept of schizophrenia and hope to win. In R. P. Bentall (Ed.), *Reconstructing schizophrenia* (pp. 23–60). London: Routledge.

Bentall, R. P., Baker, G. A., & Havers, S. (1991). Reality monitoring and psychotic hallucinations. *British Journal of Clinical Psychology, 30,* 213–222.

Bentall, R. P., Day, J., Rogers, A., Healy, D., & Stevenson, R. C. (1996). Side effects of neuroleptic medication: Assessment and impact on outcome of psychotic disorders. In M. Moscarelli, A. Rupp, & N. Sartorius (Eds.), *Handbook of mental health economics and health policy: Vol. 1. Schizophrenia* (pp. 133–148). London: Wiley.

Bentall, R. P., Haddock, G., & Slade, P. D. (1994). Cognitive behavior therapy for persistent auditory hallucinations: From theory to therapy. *Behavior Therapy, 25,* 51–66.

Bentall, R. P., & Slade, P. D. (1985a). Reality testing and auditory hallucinations: A signal-detection analysis. *British Journal of Clinical Psychology, 24,* 159–169.

Bentall, R. P., & Slade, P. D. (1985b). Reliability of a measure of disposition towards hallucinations. *Personality and Individual Differences, 6,* 527–529.

Berrios, G. (1996). *The history of mental symptoms: Descriptive psychopathology since the nineteenth century.* Cambridge, England: Cambridge University Press.

Bleuler, E. (1950). *Dementia praecox or the group of schizophrenias* (E. Zinkin, Trans.). New York: International Universities Press. (Original work published 1911)

Bleuler, M. (1978). *The schizophrenic disorders.* New Haven, CT: Yale University Press.

Bourguignon, E. (1970). Hallucinations and trance: An anthropologist's perspective. In W. Keup (Ed.), *Origins and mechanisms of hallucinations* (pp. 83–90). New York: Plenum.

Brown, W. A., & Herz, L. R. (1989). Response to neuroleptic drugs as a device for classifying schizophrenia. *Schizophrenia Bulletin, 15,* 123–128.

Carlsson, A. (1995). The dopamine theory revisited. In S. R. Hirsch & D. R. Weinberger (Eds.), *Schizophrenia* (pp. 379–400). Oxford, England: Blackwell.

Carlsson, A., & Lindqvist, M. (1963). Effect of chlorpromazine or haloperidol on formation of 3-methoxytyramine and normetanephrine in mouse brain. *Acta Pharmacologica et Toxicologica, 20,* 140–144.

Carpenter, W. T., Cauley, R. R., Buchanan, R. W., Breier, A., & Tamminga, C. A. (1996). Patient response and resource management: Another view of clozapine treatment of schizophrenia. *American Journal of Psychiatry, 152,* 827–832.

Carter, D. M., Mackinnon, A., Howard, S., Zeegers, T., & Copolov, D. (1995). The development and reliability of the Mental Health Research Institute Unusual Perceptions Schedule (MUPS): An instrument to record auditory hallucinatory experiences. *Schizophrenia Research, 16,* 157–165.

Chadwick, P., & Birchwood, M. (1994). The omnipotence of voices: A cognitive approach to auditory hallucinations. *British Journal of Psychiatry, 164,* 190–201.

Chapman, L. J., & Chapman, J. P. (1980). Scales for rating psychotic and psychotic-like experiences as continua. *Schizophrenia Bulletin, 6,* 477–489.

Chapman, L. J., Chapman, J. P., & Raulin, M. L. (1976). Scales for physical and social anhedonia. *Journal of Abnormal Psychology, 85,* 374–382.

Chapman, L. J., Edell, E. W., & Chapman, J. P. (1980). Physical anhedonia, perceptual aberration and psychosis proneness. *Schizophrenia Bulletin, 6,* 639–653.

Ciompi, L. (1984). Is there really a schizophrenia?: The longterm course of psychotic phenomena. *British Journal of Psychiatry, 145,* 636–640.

Claridge, G. S. (1985). *The origins of mental illness.* Oxford, England: Blackwell.

Claridge, G. S. (1987). The schizophrenias as nervous types revisited. *British Journal of Psychiatry, 151,* 735–743.

Claridge, G. S. (1990). Can a disease model of schizophrenia survive? In R. P. Bentall (Ed.), *Reconstructing schizophrenia* (pp. 157–183). London: Routledge.

Clark, L. A., Watson, D., & Reynolds, S. (1995). Diagnosis and classification of psychopathology: Challenges to the current system and future directions. *Annual Review of Psychology, 46,* 121–153.

Combs, M. (1997). *Hearing voices: Individual psychological factors.* Unpublished master's thesis, Oxford University, England.

Comer, N. L., Madow, L., & Dixon, J. J. (1967). Observations of sensory deprivation in a life-threatening situation. *American Journal of Psychiatry, 124,* 164–169.

Cooklin, R., Sturgeon, D., & Leff, J. P. (1983). The relationship between auditory hallucinations and spontaneous fluctuations of skin conductance in schizophrenia. *British Journal of Psychiatry, 142,* 47–52.

Cornelius, J. R., Mezzich, J., Fabrega, H., Cornelius, M. D., & Myers, J. (1991). Characteristics of organic hallucinosis. *Comprehensive Psychiatry, 32,* 338–344.

Costello, C. G. (1992). Research on symptoms versus research on syndromes: Arguments in favour of allocating more research time to the study of symptoms. *British Journal of Psychiatry, 160,* 304–308.

Davies, P., Davies, G. L., & Bennett, S. (1982). An effective paradigm for conditioning visual perception in human subjects. *Perception, 11,* 663–669.

Drury, V., Birchwood, M., Cochrane, R., & MacMillan, F. (1996). Cognitive therapy and recovery from acute psychosis: I. Impact on psychotic symptoms. *British Journal of Psychiatry, 169,* 593–601.

Erickson, G. D., & Gustafson, G. J. (1968). Controlling auditory hallucinations. *Hospital and Community Psychiatry, 19,* 327–329.

Esquirol, J. E. D. (1832). Sur les illusions des sens chez alienes [On the sensory illusions of the insane]. *Archives Generales de Medicine, 2,* 5–23.

Falloon, I., & Talbot, R. E. (1981). Persistent auditory hallucinations: Coping mechanisms and implications for management. *Psychological Medicine, 11,* 329–339.

Frith, C. D. (1979). Consciousness, information processing and schizophrenia. *British Journal of Psychiatry, 134,* 225–235.

Frith, C. D. (1992). *The cognitive neuropsychology of schizophrenia.* Hillsdale, NJ: Erlbaum.

Gabbard, G. O., Lazar, S. G., Hornberger, J., & Spiegel, D. (1997). The economic impact of psychotherapy: A review. *American Journal of Psychiatry, 154,* 147–155.

Gallagher, A. G., Dinin, T. G., & Baker, L. V. J. (1994). The effects of varying auditory input on schizophrenic hallucinations: A replication. *British Journal of Medical Psychology, 67,* 67–76.

Gallagher, A. G., Dinin, T. G., & Baker, L. V. J. (1995). The effects of varying information content and speaking aloud on auditory hallucinations. *British Journal of Medical Psychology, 68,* 143–155.

Garety, P. A., Kuipers, L., Fowler, D., Chamberlain, F., & Dunn, G. (1994). Cognitive behavioural therapy for drug-resistant psychosis. *British Journal of Medical Psychology, 67,* 259–271.

Glaister, B. (1985). A case study of auditory hallucinations treated by satiation. *Behaviour Research and Therapy, 23,* 213–215.

Goodwin, F. K., & Jamison, K. R. (1990). *Manic-depressive illness.* Oxford, England: Oxford University Press.

Gould, L. N. (1948). Verbal hallucinations and activity of vocal musculature. *American Journal of Psychiatry, 105,* 367–372.

Gould, L. N. (1949). Auditory hallucinations and subvocal speech. *Journal of Nervous and Mental Disease, 109,* 418–427.

Gould, L. N. (1950). Verbal hallucinations and automatic speech. *American Journal of Psychiatry, 107,* 110–119.

Green, J. H. (1988). Frequent rehospitalisation and non-compliance with treatment. *Hospital and Community Psychiatry, 39,* 963–966.

Green, M. F., & Kinsbourne, M. (1990). Subvocal activity and auditory hallucinations: Clues for behavioral treatments. *Schizophrenia Bulletin, 16,* 617–625.

Green, P., & Preston, M. (1981). Reinforcement of vocal correlates of auditory hallucinations by auditory feedback: A case study. *British Journal of Psychiatry, 139,* 204–208.

Grimby, A. (1993). Bereavement among elderly people: Grief reactions, post-bereavement hallucinations and quality of life. *Acta Psychiatrica Scandinavica, 87,* 72–80.

Haddock, G., Bentall, R. P., & Slade, P. D. (1993). Psychological treatment of chronic auditory hallucinations: Two case studies. *Behavioural and Cognitive Psychotherapy, 21,* 335–346.

Haddock, G., & Slade, P. D. (Eds.). (1996). *Cognitive–behavioural interventions with psychotic disorders.* London: Routledge.

Haddock, G., Slade, P. D., & Bentall, R. P. (1995). Auditory hallucinations and the verbal transformation effect: The role of suggestions. *Personality and Individual Differences, 19,* 301–306.

Haddock, G., Slade, P. D., & Bentall, R. P. (1998). Cognitive–behavioural treatment of auditory hallucinations: A comparison of the long-term effectiveness of two interventions. *British Journal of Medical Psychology, 71,* 339–349.

Hall, R. C., Popkin, M. K., & Faillace, L. A. (1978). Physical illness presenting as a psychiatric disease. *Archives of General Psychiatry, 35,* 1315–1320.

Hamilton, M. (Ed.). (1983). *Fish's psychopathology.* Bristol, England: Wright.

Harris, A. (1959). Sensory deprivation and schizophrenia. *Journal of Mental Science, 105,* 235–237.

Hefferline, R. F., Bruno, L. J., & Camp, J. A. (1973). Hallucinations: An experimental approach. In F. J. McGuigan & R. A. Schoonover (Eds.), *The psychophysiology of thinking: Studies of covert processes.* New York: Academic Press.

Heilbrun, A. B. (1980). Impaired recognition of self-expressed thought in patients with auditory hallucinations. *Journal of Abnormal Psychology, 89,* 728–736.

Heilbrun, A. B. (1996). Hallucinations. In C. G. Costello (Ed.), *Symptoms of schizophrenia* (pp. 59–61). New York: Wiley.

Heilbrun, A. B., Blum, N. A., & Haas, M. (1983). Cognitive vulnerability to auditory hallucinations: Preferred imagery mode and spatial location of sounds. *British Journal of Psychiatry, 143,* 294–299.

Hoffman, R. E. (1986). Verbal hallucinations and language production processes in schizophrenia. *Behavioral and Brain Sciences, 9,* 503–548.

Hoge, S. K., Appelbaum, P. S., Lawlor, T., Beck, J. C., Litman, R., Greer, A.,

Gutheil, T. G., & Kaplan, E. (1990). A prospective, multicenter study of patients' refusal of antipsychotic medication. *Archives of General Psychiatry, 47,* 949–956.

Horowitz, M. (1975). Hallucinations: An information processing approach. In R. K. Siegel & L. J. West (Eds.), *Hallucinations: Behavior, experience and theory* (pp. 163–196). New York: Wiley.

Inouye, T., & Shimizu, A. (1970). The electromyographic study of verbal hallucination. *Journal of Nervous and Mental Disease, 151,* 415–422.

Jablensky, A. (1995). Schizophrenia: The epidemiological horizon. In S. R. Hirsch & D. R. Weinberger (Eds.), *Schizophrenia* (pp. 206–252). Oxford, England: Blackwell.

Jablensky, A., Sartorius, N., Ernberg, G., Anker, M., Korten, A., Cooper, J. E., Day, R., & Bertelsen, A. (1992). Schizophrenia: Manifestations, incidence and course in different cultures. *Psychological Medicine, 20*(Suppl.), 1–97.

James, D. A. E. (1983). The experimental treatment of two cases of auditory hallucinations. *British Journal of Psychiatry, 143,* 515–516.

Jaspers, K. (1963). General psychopathology (J. Hoenig & M. W. Hamilton, Trans.). Manchester, England: Manchester University Press. (Original work published 1913)

Jaynes, J. (1979). *The origins of consciousness in the breakdown of bicameral mind.* London: Penguin.

Johnson, M. H., & Magaro, P. A. (1987). Effects of mood and severity on memory processes in depression and mania. *Psychological Bulletin, 101,* 28–40.

Johnson, M. H., Hashtroudi, S., & Lindsay, D. S. (1993). Source monitoring. *Psychological Bulletin, 114,* 3–28.

Johnstone, E. C., MacMillan, J. F., & Crowe, T. J. (1987). The occurrence of organic disease of possible or probable aetiological significance in a population of 268 cases of first episode schizophrenia. *Psychological Medicine, 17,* 371–379.

Kavanagh, S. (1994). The costs of schizophrenia. *Mental Health Research Review, 1.*

Kay, S. R., Opler, L. A., & Fiszbein, A. (1988). Reliability and validity of the Positive and Negative Syndrome Scale for schizophrenics. *Psychiatry Research, 23,* 276–286.

Kroll, J., & Bachrach, B. (1982). Visions and psychopathology in the Middle Ages. *Journal of Nervous and Mental Disease, 170,* 41–49.

Kuipers, E., Fowler, D., Garety, P., Chizholm, D., Freeman, D., Dunn, G., Bebbington, P., & Hadley, C. (1998). London–East Anglia randomised controlled trial of cognitive–behavioural therapy for psychosis: III. Follow-up and economic considerations. *British Journal of Psychiatry, 173,* 61–68.

Kuipers, E., Garety, P., Fowler, D., Dunn, G., Bebbington, P., Freeman, D., & Hadley, C. (1997). The London–East Anglia randomised controlled trial of cognitive–behaviour therapy for psychosis: I. Effects of the treatment phase. *British Journal of Psychiatry, 171,* 319–327.

Launay, G., & Slade, P. D. (1981). The measurement of hallucinatory predisposition in male and female prisoners. *Personality and Individual Differences, 2,* 221–234.

Leff, J. P., & Wing, J. K. (1971). Trial of maintenance therapy in schizophrenia. *British Medical Journal, 3,* 599–604.

Lehman, A. F. (1996). Quality of life issues and assessment among persons with schizophrenia. In M. Moscarelli, A. Rupp, & N. Sartorius (Eds.), *Handbook of mental health economics and health policy: Volume 1. Schizophrenia* (pp. 39–50). London: Wiley.

Lenz, H. L. (1964). *Verleichende psychiatrie: Ein studie uber die beziehung von kulture sociologie unf psychopathologie* [Comparative psychology: A study of the relationship between culture and psychopathology]. Vienna: Wilhelm Mandrich.

Leudar, I., Thomas, P., McNally, D., & Glinsky, A. (1997). What can voices do with words? Pragmatics of verbal hallucinations. *Psychological Medicine.*

Lewis, S., & Higgins, N. (Eds.). (1996). *Brain imaging in psychiatry.* Oxford, England: Blackwell.

Lieberman, J. A. (1993). Understanding the mechanism of action of atypical antipsychotic drugs. A review of compounds in use and development. *British Journal of Psychiatry, 163,* 7–18.

Luria, A. R. (1981). *Language and cognition.* New York: Wiley.

Margo, A., Hemsley, D. R., & Slade, P. D. (1981). The effects of varying auditory input on schizophrenic hallucinations. *British Journal of Psychiatry, 139,* 122–127.

McGuigan, F. J. (1966). Covert oral behavior and auditory hallucinations. *Psychophysiology, 3,* 73–80.

McGuigan, F. J. (1978). *Cognitive psychophysiology: Principles of covert behavior.* Englewood Cliffs, NJ: Prentice Hall.

McGuire, P. K., Shah, G. M. S., & Murray, R. M. (1993). Increased blood flow in Broca's area during auditory hallucinations. *Lancet, 342,* 703–706.

McKellar, P. (1968). *Experience and behaviour.* London: Penguin.

McNichol, D. (1972). *A primer of signal detection theory.* London: Allen & Unwin.

Miller, L. J., O'Connor, E., & DePasquale, T. (1993). Patients' attitudes to hallucinations. *American Journal of Psychiatry, 150,* 584–588.

Mintz, S., & Alpert, M. (1972). Imagery vividness, reality testing and schizophrenic hallucinations. *Journal of Abnormal and Social Psychology, 19,* 310–316.

Morrison, A. P., & Haddock, G. (1997). Cognitive factors in source monitoring and auditory hallucinations. *Psychological Medicine, 27,* 669–679.

Muesner, K. T., & Berenbaum, H. (1990). Psychodynamic treatment of schizophrenia: Is there a future? *Psychological Medicine, 20,* 253–262.

Nelson, H. E., Thrasher, S., & Barnes, T. R. E. (1991). Practical ways of alleviating auditory hallucinations. *British Medical Journal, 302,* 307.

Neuchterlein, K. H., & Dawson, M. E. (1984). A heuristic vulnerability-stress model of schizophrenic episodes. *Schizophrenia Bulletin, 10,* 300–312.

O'Sullivan, K. (1994). Dimensions of coping with auditory hallucinations. *Journal of Mental Health*, 3, 351–361.

Pennings, M., & Romme, M. (1996). Stemmen horen bij schizofrenie patienten, patienten met een dissociatieve stoornis en bij niet patienten. In M. de Hert, E. Thijs, I. Peuskens, D. Petri, & B. van Raay (Eds.), *Zin in waanzin: De wereld van schizofrenie*. Antwerp: EPO.

Persaud, R., & Marks, I. (1995). A pilot study of exposure control of chronic auditory hallucinations. *British Journal of Psychiatry*, 167, 45–50.

Persons, J. (1986). The advantages of studying psychological phenomena rather than psychiatric diagnoses. *American Psychologist*, 41, 1252–1260.

Piaget, J. (1926). *The language and thought of the child*. London: Routledge & Kegan Paul.

Posey, T. B., & Losch, M. E. (1983). Auditory hallucinations of hearing voices in 375 normal subjects. *Imagination, Cognition and Personality*, 2, 99–113.

Rankin, P., & O'Carrol, P. (1995). Reality monitoring and signal detection in individuals prone to hallucinations. *British Journal of Clinical Psychology*, 34, 517–528.

Reese, W. D. (1971). The hallucinations of widowhood. *British Medical Journal*, 210, 37–41.

Robbins, L. N., Wing, J. K., & Wittchen, H. U. (1988). The Composite International Diagnostic Interview. *Archives of General Psychiatry*, 45, 1069–1077.

Romme, M., & Escher, A. (1989). Hearing voices. *Schizophrenia Bulletin*, 15, 209–216.

Romme, M., & Escher, A. (1996). Empowering people who hear voices. In G. Haddock & P. D. Slade (Eds.), *Cognitive behavioural interventions with psychotic disorders* (pp. 137–150). London: Routledge.

Ross, C. A., Norton, G. R., & Wozney, K. (1989). Multiple personality disorder: An analysis of 236 cases. *Canadian Journal of Psychiatry*, 34, 413–418.

Sarbin, T. R., & Juhasz, J. B. (1967). The historical background of the concept of hallucination. *Journal of the History of the Behavioral Sciences*, 5, 339–358.

Sartorius, N., Jablensky, A., Korten, A., Ernberg, G., Anker, M., Cooper, J. E., & Day, R. (1986). Early manifestations and first contact incidence of schizophrenia in different cultures. *Psychological Medicine*, 16, 909–928.

Sartorius, N., Shapiro, R., & Jablensky, A. (1974). The international pilot study of schizophrenia. *Schizophrenia Bulletin*, 1, 21–25.

Schneider, K. (1959). *Clinical psychopathology*. New York: Grune & Stratton.

Scott, E. H. M. (1967). A study of the contents of delusions and hallucinations in 100 African female psychotics. *South African Medical Journal*, 4, 853–858.

Seal, M. L., Crowe, S. F., & Cheung, P. (1997). Deficits in source monitoring in subjects with auditory hallucinations may be due to differences in verbal intelligence and verbal memory. *Cognitive Neuropsychiatry*, 2, 273–290.

Sedman, G. (1966). A comparative study of pseudohallucinations, imagery and true hallucinations. *British Journal of Psychiatry*, 112, 9–17.

Shorter, E. (1997). *A history of psychiatry*. New York: Wiley.

Sidgewick, H. A. (1894). Report of the census on hallucinations. *Proceedings of the Society for Psychical Research, 26*, 259–394.

Siegel, R. K. (1984). Hostage hallucinations: Visual imagery induced by isolation and life-threatening stress. *Journal of Nervous and Mental Disease, 172*, 264–272.

Siegel, R. K., & Jarvick, M. E. (1975). Drug-induced hallucinations in animals and man. In R. K. Siegel & L. J. West (Eds.), *Hallucinations: Behavior, experience and theory* (pp. 81–162). New York: Wiley.

Silbersweig, D. A., Stern, E., Frith, C., Cahill, C., Holmes, A., Grootoonk, S., Seaward, J., McKenna, P., Chua, S. E., Schnorr, L., Jones, T., & Frackowiak, R. S. J. (1995). A functional neuroanatomy of hallucinations in schizophrenia. *Nature, 378*, 176–179.

Slade, P. D. (1972). The effects of systematic desensitization on auditory hallucinations. *Behaviour, Research and Therapy, 10*, 85–91.

Slade, P. D. (1974). The external control of auditory hallucinations: An information processing analysis. *British Journal of Social and Clinical Psychology, 13*, 73–79.

Slade, P. D., & Bentall, R. P. (1988). *Sensory deception: A scientific analysis of hallucination.* London: Croom-Helm.

Spitzer, R. L., Endicott, J., & Gibbon, M. (1979). Crossing the border into borderline personality and borderline schizophrenia. *Archives of General Psychiatry, 36*, 17–24.

Spivak, B., Trottern, S. F., Mark, M., & Bleich, A. (1992). Acute transient stress-induced hallucinations in soldiers. *British Journal of Psychiatry, 160*, 412–414.

Stevens, J. R., & Livermore, A. (1982). Telemetered EEG in schizophrenia: Spectral analysis during abnormal behaviour episodes. *Journal of Neurology, Neurosurgery and Psychiatry, 45*, 385–395.

Strauss, J. S. (1969). Hallucinations and delusions as points on continua function: Rating scale evidence. *Archives of General Psychiatry, 21*, 581–586.

Szechtman, H., Woody, E., Bowers, K. S., & Nahmias, C. (1998). Where the imaginal appears real: A positron emission tomography study of auditory hallucinations. *Proceedings of the National Academy of Sciences USA, 95*, 1956–1960.

Tarrier, N. (1987). An investigation of residual psychotic symptoms in discharged schizophrenic patients. *British Journal of Clinical Psychology, 26*, 141–143.

Tarrier, N. (1996). Family interventions and schizophrenia. In G. Haddock & P. D. Slade (Eds.), *Cognitive–behavioural interventions with psychotic disorders* (pp. 212–234). London: Routledge.

Tarrier, N., Beckett, R., Harwood, S., Baker, A., Yusupoff, L., & Ugarteburu, I. (1993). A trial of two cognitive–behavioural methods of treating drug-resistant residual psychotic symptoms in schizophrenic patients: I. Outcome. *British Journal of Psychiatry, 162*, 524–532.

Tarrier, N., Yusupoff, L., Kinner, C., McCarthy, E., Gladhill, A., Haddock, G., &

Morris, J. (1998). A randomized controlled trial of intense cognitive behaviour therapy for chronic schizophrenia. *British Medical Journal, 317*, 303–307.

Thomas, P. (1997). *The dialectics of schizophrenia.* Bristol, England: Free Association Books.

Tien, A. Y. (1991). Distribution of hallucinations in the population. *Social Psychiatry and Psychiatric Epidemiology, 26*, 287–292.

Toone, B. K., Cooke, E., & Lader, M. H. (1981). Electrodermal activity in the affective disorders and schizophrenia. *Psychological Medicine, 11*, 497–508.

Turkington, D., Sensky, T., Siddle, R., O'Carroll, M., John, C., Duddley, R., McPhilips, M., Barnes, T., Scott, J., & Kingdom, D. (1997, July). *An 18 month outcome study of cognitive–behaviour therapy versus befriending in neuroleptic resistant schizophrenia.* Paper presented at the British Association for Behavioural and Cognitive Psychotherapy Annual Conference, Canterbury, England.

Vaughn, C. E., & Leff, J. (1976). The influence of family and social factors on the course of psychiatric illness: A comparison of schizophrenic and depressed neurotic patients. *British Journal of Psychiatry, 129*, 125–137.

Vygotsky, L. S. V. (1962). *Thought and language.* Cambridge, MA: MIT Press.

Warren, R. M. (1968). Verbal transformation effect and auditory perceptual mechanisms. *Psychological Bulletin, 70*, 261–270.

Watson, J. B. (1924). *Behaviorism.* New York: Norton.

West, D. J. (1948). A mass observation questionnaire on hallucinations. *Journal of the Society for Psychical Research, 34*, 187–196.

West, L. J. (1962). A general theory of hallucinations and dreams. In L. J. West (Ed.), *Hallucinations.* New York: Grune & Stratton.

Wing, J. K., Cooper, J. E., & Sartorius, N. (1974). *The measurement and classification of psychiatric symptoms.* Cambridge, England: Cambridge University Press.

Wittgenstein, L. (1953). *Philosophical investigations.* London: Blackwell.

Wooley, D. E., & Shaw, E. (1954). A biochemical and pharmacological suggestion about certain mental disorders. *Proceedings of the National Academy of Sciences USA, 40*, 228–231.

Young, H. F., Bentall, R. P., Slade, P. D., & Dewey, M. E. (1986). Disposition towards hallucinations, gender and IQ score. *Personality and Individual Differences, 7*, 247–249.

Young, H. F., Bentall, R. P., Slade, P. D., & Dewey, M. E. (1987). The role of brief instructions and suggestibility in the elicitation of hallucinations in normal and psychiatric subjects. *Journal of Nervous and Mental Disease, 175*, 41–48.

Zubin, J., & Spring, B. (1977). Vulnerability: A new view of schizophrenia. *Journal of Abnormal Psychology, 86*, 103–126.

Zuckerman, M. (1969). Variables affecting deprivation results. In J. P. Zubek (Ed.), *Sensory deprivation: Fifteen years of research* (pp. 47–84). New York: Appleton-Century-Crofts.

4

SYNESTHESIA

LAWRENCE E. MARKS

Synesthesia refers to a curious phenomenon of perception in which sensory images or qualities of one modality, for instance, vision, find themselves transferred to another modality, such as taste or hearing. To a synesthetic perceiver, a sip of lemonade may take on a distinctive green color as well as a sour-sweet taste, or an aria sung by a soprano may take on visible form that modulates in shape, size, and tint with the pitch of each note. In synesthesia, therefore, an inducing stimulus produces, at the same time, two kinds of sensory response: the primary sensory experience that is normally associated with that stimulus and, anomalously, a secondary experience in another modality.

One of the best-known examples of synesthesia was described in detail by Luria (1968). Although Luria's patient, S., was best known for his prodigious memory, he was also synesthetic, describing sounds as having not only auditory qualities but also visual and gustatory ones.

> Presented with a tone pitched at 50 cycles per second and an amplitude of 100 decibels, S. saw a brown strip against a dark background that had red, tongue-like edges. . . . The sense of taste he experienced

Preparation of this chapter was supported by Grant DC00271-13 from the National Institute on Deafness and Other Communication Disorders.

121

was like that of sweet and sour borscht, a sensation that gripped his entire tongue. . . .

Presented with a tone pitched at 2,000 cycles per second and having an amplitude of 113 decibels, S. said: "It looks something like fireworks tinged with a pink-red hue. The strip of color feels rough and unpleasant, and it has an ugly taste—rather like that of a briny pickle. " (pp. 45–46)

To some individuals, synesthesia is part of daily living. Every voice that is heard may take on a shape, or every letter or word seen in a newspaper may take on a color. To others, however, the synesthetic experiences may be much more limited in their scope and, consequently, in their duration. Thus, to an individual who perceives synesthetic colors or shapes only when she hears music, the experience will last only as long as the inducing sound stimulus is present, perhaps a few minutes, perhaps only a few seconds.

SYNESTHESIA DESCRIBED

Although secondary qualities are exceptionally lucid and potent characteristics of phenomenal experience for some synesthetic perceivers, such as Luria's S., for others the secondary qualities may exist only as weak or vague images. More than a century ago, in 1889, the International Congress of Physiological Psychology met in Paris to discuss research findings and to consider directions that should be taken by the fledgling discipline of experimental psychology. One decision made in conjunction with that meeting was to enlist several prominent psychologists to form a committee whose charge was to standardize the terminology and advance the scientific understanding of synesthesia (see Mahling, 1926).

Weak Synesthesia

Despite the efforts at terminological standardization, synesthesia has continued to refer to a wide range of phenomena, and, as a consequence, the term has continued to be used in diverse ways and across disciplines that range from experimental psychology to neurology to literary analysis. Under the broad definition given earlier, synesthesia encompasses the tendency for many individuals to describe music written in major and minor keys as bright and dark, respectively, even if those individuals never experienced visual sensations or images while listening to Bach's "Orchestral Suite No. 1" or Beethoven's "Pathétique Sonata." Marks (1975) classified intermodal tendencies of this sort as examples of weak synesthesia. These tendencies are designated as weak because they lack the phenomenal vividness and élan so characteristic of synesthesia in its strong form.

Weak synesthesia also encompasses what has been termed *literary* or *poetic synesthesia*. Within the realm of literary criticism, synesthesia can be as much a linguistic as a perceptual phenomenon, sometimes more so, as a *façon de parler* or a figure of speech. The *Princeton Encyclopedia of Poetics* defines *synesthesia* as a "term denoting the perception, or description of the perception, of one sense modality in terms of another" (Preminger, 1974, p. 839), and the entry then goes on to note that synesthesia "occurs very widely in language and literature in an apparently universal role among civilized peoples as the metaphor of the senses" (p. 840). Examples of synesthesia in literature can be seen in documents that range from the ancient to the modern: in the 10th verse of Chapter 20 of *Exodus*, "And all the people saw the thunderings and lightnings" (*"v'khal ha-am ro-im et hakolot v'et halapedim"*); in Kipling's "dawn [that] comes up like thunder"; and in the lexical synesthesia described by the narrator of Alice Mattison's (1988) short story "The Colored Alphabet." English Romantic poetry of the 19th century is replete with synesthetic metaphors (Siebold, 1919). Although a detailed exploration of literary synesthesia exceeds the scope of this chapter, one of its goals is to illuminate the links among synesthetic metaphor (an expression commonly used to include simile as well as metaphor proper), weak perceptual synesthesia, and strong perceptual synesthesia.

Strong Synesthesia

Strong synesthesia lies at the other end of the spectrum and is considerably rarer and more dramatic. Strong synesthesia is distinctly a perceptual phenomenon that characterizes the experience of a small fraction of the population (recently estimated at 1 in 25,000 by Cytowic, 1997, who suggested nevertheless that this may be an underestimation, and to at least 1 in 2,000 by Baron-Cohen et al., 1996). To those who do perceive the world synesthetically, however, this experience can be pervasive and potent. Synesthesia is marked by phenomenal experiences in which stimuli that are normally considered appropriate to one modality not only arouse the sensory and perceptual qualities of that modality but also regularly and reliably arouse the sensory qualities of another modality. To an individual who experiences a common variety of synesthesia known as *colored hearing*, a musical note, say B-flat played above middle C, may stimulate the perception of a sparkling yellow color that appears very soon after the note is sounded and fades slowly once the note is extinguished. Or to someone who experiences lexical synesthesia, the name "Warren" may appear as a patch of dull maroon color. These kinds of synesthesia, based in psychophysical properties or lexical properties of the inducing stimulus, reflect some kind of anomalous transfer of sensory images or their attributes from one modality to another. The goals of this article are to examine how these different kinds of synesthesia express themselves phenomenologically, behaviorally, and neurophysiologically and to assess the possible underlying mechanisms. It is first and foremost the phenomenological features—the sensory and affective qualities of the experiences themselves—that distinguish strong synesthesia from weak synesthesia.

PHENOMENOLOGY

Several features characterize strong synesthesia (for reviews, see Cytowic, 1989; and Marks, 1975, 1978). Foremost are its consistency and reliability. Strong synesthesia is dependable and rigid. The same stimulus, B-flat in the example just given, will time and again arouse the same synesthetic response, the color yellow. Strong synesthetic experiences are typically described as vivid or intense. Although their strength can vary with the person's state of attention, strong synesthesia is often reported to be more like sensory experience than mental imagery. In this regard, Cytowic (1989) defined synesthetic percepts as ones that are projected externally, not perceived "in the mind's eye." Strong synesthetic responses occur automatically and unavoidably, without any willful attempt on the part of the perceiver. Sometimes, synesthetic individuals aver that the secondary sensory responses can be disruptive and annoying. Furthermore, although synesthesia can be produced by the ingestion of psychoactive drugs (e.g., Delay, Gérard, & Racamier, 1951; Simpson & McKellar, 1955; see also Cytowic, 1989), it more typically occurs naturally, as what Grossenbacher (1997) termed *constitutional synesthesia*: "the condition experienced by those individuals who report a life-long history of perceptual experience in two sense modalities under conditions where sensory stimulation and overt orienting of receptor organs are adequate for perception in only one modality" (p. 150). As Grossenbacher's definition implies, most instances of constitutional synesthesia trace back to early childhood and tend to be consistent over long periods of time. What is known about synesthesia is mostly about constitutional synesthesia.

A good example of constitutional synesthesia was found in Luria's (1968) patient S., mentioned earlier. Another example appears in the report by Cytowic and Wood (1982) of a 36-year-old man who saw geometric shapes in response to gustatory stimuli. Cytowic and Wood tested this participant's synesthesia by presenting him with taste solutions varying in proportions of sucrose and citric acid and having him match the appropriate geometric form to each taste. Although it is difficult to characterize his gustatory synesthesia by means of any simple rule, it nevertheless is clear that his behavior, defined in terms of the matches made between taste stimuli and geometric shapes, differed markedly from that of nonsynesthetic control participants.

Sensory Synesthesia

These accounts of visual hearing and geometric taste typify one class or property of synesthesia, in which the critical properties of the inducing stimulus are relatively simple physical dimensions. This makes it possible to treat the relations between inducing stimuli and secondary sensory qualities as psychophysical, by analogy to the psychophysical relations between stimuli and sensations in the primary sensory modality. Thus, the relevant or salient physical properties may be the sound frequency, the intensity, or the temporal pattern of an acoustic stimulus when the inducing stimulus is a sound; the size, shape, or spectrum of a visual stimulus when the inducing stimulus is a light; or the chemical composition of a gustatory stimulus when the inducing stimulus is a taste. The auditory system processes variations in frequency in terms of pitch, the visual system processes variations in spectrum in terms of color, and the gustatory system processes variations in stimulus composition in terms of taste quality.

Just as varying the acoustic frequency of a sound produces a corresponding variation in the phenomenal quality on the primary sensory modality, namely the sound's pitch, so in synesthetic perceivers, variation in sound frequency may produce a corresponding variation in the phenomenal quality on the secondary modality, such as visual shape or size or color. The primary neural and perceptual responses to physical properties such as sound frequency, color spectrum, or taste composition are largely hardwired into sensory systems, and differential responses to these properties can be observed soon after birth, requiring relatively little if any high-order perceptual or cognitive mediation. That these physical properties often are linked also in a direct fashion to synesthetic qualities, at least in that small fraction of the population that experiences synesthesia, implies that psychophysical synesthetic correspondences, too, may rely on hard-wired characteristics of sensorineural processing.

Perceptual Synesthesia

Often, however, the critical properties of the synesthetically inducing stimuli are much more complex, being perceptual rather than sensory. This is to say that the critical properties are susceptible to and even grounded in some kind of learning, even when and if this learning takes place early in life. Lexical synesthesia provides a good example of perceptual synesthesia. In lexical synesthesia, visually presented or acoustically presented words or individual letters of the alphabet may stimulate the perception of unique colors. Galton (1883) recounted several observations on lexical synesthesia more than a century ago.

Baron-Cohen, Wyke, and Binnie (1987) described a case of chromatic-lexical synesthesia in a 76-year-old woman for whom spoken letters, words, and numbers had their own colors. Interestingly, for her, nonsense words induced synesthetic colors that were compounded of the colors synesthetically induced by the individual letters. Thus, H was dark red, U was yellow, and K was purple, and the color of the nonsense word *HUK* was a compound of the three colors: red, yellow, and purple. The colors of real words, by way of contrast, were unique to those words themselves and unrelated to the colors of the component letters.

Analogous relations have been reported in musical synesthesia. Thus, in the synesthesia of a 7 1/2-year-old, individual musical notes had unique colors, and "chords of three or more notes [were] described as a 'jumbled mixture' of colors from the constituent notes" (Riggs & Karwoski, 1934, p. 30). In this child, colors were induced not only by individual musical notes but by entire melodies when the melodies were familiar, evidence again that some of the features of synesthetic perception result from experience. Grossenbacher (1997) suggested that the meaningfulness of the inducing stimulus is an important characteristic of strong synesthesia.

Although it may be self-evident, it is nevertheless worth noting that the lexical properties of stimuli are basically independent of their psychophysical properties. For instance, the same phoneme may take on very different loudnesses and voice pitches (sound intensity levels and fundamental frequencies), depending on the particular speaker uttering the phoneme and the context in which it is spoken; imagine, for instance, "O Sole Mio" sung by a contralto and by a baritone. Lexical and psychophysical properties are similarly independent when the stimulus is visual rather than auditory. Represented optically, the same letter of the alphabet may be written in uppercase or lowercase, may be printed or in script, and may be presented in various fonts, styles, and sizes. Thus, we may represent the 17th letter of the Roman alphabet as "q", "Q", "Q," "Q," "Q," or "**Q**." Of course, letters of the alphabet, as well as numbers and words, are cultural conventions that must be learned. In other words, the lexical properties of stimuli differ in fundamental ways from psychophysical properties. Consequently, it is conceivable that the processes underlying lexical synesthesia may differ in important ways from those underlying sensory synesthesia, a matter considered at the end of this chapter.[1]

Synesthesia may involve any of the senses, but in a disproportionate number of cases sounds are the inducing stimuli and visual sensations or images the secondary consequence. It is still not known why there should be such a nonuniform distribution of synesthesias across the different sense

---

[1] It is necessary, however, to ensure that cases of synesthesia designated as lexical do indeed rely on lexical properties of stimuli. In recounting his synesthesia, the Russian American writer Vladimir Nabokov (1949) observed that the color associated with each letter depended on neither the sight nor the sound of the letter but on the sensed motor activity or position of the vocal apparatus in producing it. Nabokov wrote "I present a fine case of 'colored hearing.' Perhaps hearing is not quite accurate, since the color sensation seems to be produced by the physiological act of my orally forming a given letter while I imagine its outline" (p. 33).

modalities. Grossenbacher (1997) suggested that hearing may be a potent inducer of synesthesia because the auditory nervous system shows a high level of neural activity, yet it is not clear why this property of the auditory system should make sounds so effective synesthetically.

Regardless of the reason, in a common variety of synesthesia called *visual hearing*, sounds serve as the inducing stimuli, evoking a mélange of visual impressions. Music, voices, and other acoustic events not only induce the primary auditory perceptions of tone quality, pitch, and loudness but also evoke secondary visual sensations or images of color, shape, and motion. The painter Wassily Kandinsky (1912) wrote extensively of interrelations among color, sound, and emotion. The composer Alexander Scriabin used his synesthesia to construct a chart of tone–color correspondences upon which he based his color–music symphony *Prometheus*, and Peacock (1985) assessed Scriabin's system based on the assignment of the color red to the key of C, yellow to D, and blue to F-sharp. In a similar vein, Bernard (1986) documented the synesthesia of the composer Olivier Messiaen and elaborated on Messiaen's system of correspondences between colors and harmonic structures. The 19th-century French author Théophile Gautier (1846) claimed to experience synesthesia as a result of ingesting hashish. Regarding the effect of hashish, Gautier wrote that, when listening to music,

> The notes quivered with such power that they pierced my breast like luminous arrows; then the musical air being played seemed to arise from within me; my fingers moved over a nonexistent keyboard; the sounds gushed out blue and red, in electric sparks. (p. 530)

Charles Baudelaire's famous sonnet "Correspondences" elaborates the ways that "odors, colors, and sounds correspond. / There are odors as fresh as children's skin, / As green as hautbois, as sweet as prairies," and Arthur Rimbaud's equally well-known "Sonnet of the Vowels" recounts the colors associated with the letters A, E, I, O, and U. Such synesthesias appear to be more common in writers, artists, and composers than in other individuals, although clear statistical evidence one way or the other is lacking.

PSYCHOPHYSICS

Although every case of synesthesia is at least somewhat idiosyncratic, the intermodal relations that are evident in synesthesia are not wholly haphazard or unpredictable. To the contrary, in many instances of both weak and strong synesthesia, and especially to the extent that the synesthesia depends on psychophysical rather than lexical properties of the stimulus, the intermodal associations are often well-organized and even rulebound. Synesthesia can consist of regular, systematic relations between or among dimensions of experience in different sense modalities, a principle first enunciated by Riggs and Karwoski (1934) and elaborated by Karwoski and Odbert (1938) and Karwoski, Odbert, and Osgood (1942).

One of the best-known and most widely acknowledged of these systematic intermodal relations is the nearly universal but correspondingly weak synesthetic connection between temperature and colors (see Marks, 1978, for a review). There is widespread agreement that certain colors, especially reds, oranges, and browns, are relatively "warm," whereas other colors, notably blues and greens, are "cool"; hence, warmth is associated with the long spectral wavelengths and coolness with short wavelengths. Although relatively few cases of synesthesia involve the strongly synesthetic perceptual induction of color by temperature (Ginsberg, 1923, and Collins, 1929, provide two examples), the weaker association of color with temperature is very common.

Furthermore, the evidence at hand suggests that weak synesthetic color–temperature relations reflect an association that is acquired through experience. Thus, it has been my observation that preadolescent children do not reliably perceive or judge the colors orange and brown to be warmer than blue and green unless the children have been explicitly taught this scheme (see also Morgan, Goodson, & Jones, 1975). That most children eventually come to make these correspondences probably stems from their experience with, say, the reds and oranges of flames and fires and perhaps the association of blue with large bodies of water. Indeed, physicists apply the term color–temperature to the change in the spectral distribution of radiation emitted by a uniform object as its temperature changes. With increasing temperature, proportionally more radiant energy is emitted at shorter as opposed to longer wavelengths, corresponding, in the visible range, to proportionally greater radiant energy in the region of green and blue than in the region of yellow and red. Thus, the physical correlation among spectrum and temperature underline a learned synesthetic association.

Within the realm of visual hearing, where sounds evoke shapes, sizes, or colors, there are several principles that describe how the secondary visual sensations or images depend psychophysically on the inducing sounds. First, many cases of visual hearing reveal a direct correspondence between the pitch of the sound and the lightness or brightness of the associated visual image: The higher the frequency of the inducing sound, and hence the higher its pitch, the greater the visual brightness or lightness. Low-frequency sounds tend to induce visual photisms with dark colors, such as brown, black, navy blue, and crimson, whereas high-frequency sounds tend to induce light or bright colors, such as white and yellow. The synesthetic relation between the pitch of the inducing sound and the brightness of the resulting photism was observed in two wide-scale studies of synesthesia from the 19th century, one conducted by Bleuler and Lehmann (1881) and the other by Flournoy (1893), and the principle was subsequently reaffirmed (see Marks, 1974, 1975, 1978; Riggs & Karwoski, 1934).

The intermodal correspondence between pitch and brightness is readily noted in the visual responses to all kinds of sound, whether noise, speech, or music. In speech, for instance, as the psychophysical property of pitch increases, synesthetic color becomes increasingly light or bright. Low vowels such as [u] (as in the French *tu*), and [o] (as in the French *mot*) invoke dark colors, whereas high vowels such as [e] (as in the French *thé*), and [i] (as in the Spanish *si*) invoke bright colors, and this tends to be true regardless of the culture or native language of the synesthetic individual (see Marks, 1975).

Two other characteristics of visual–auditory synesthesia are found in the relationship between pitch and the spatial features of size and shape (Bleuler & Lehmann, 1881; Karwoski & Odbert, 1938; Riggs & Karwoski, 1934). In synesthetic perceivers, low-pitched sounds generically produce photisms with rounded, relatively large shapes, whereas high-pitched sounds produce photisms with more angular shapes and smaller sizes. Thus, the second intermodal correspondence connects pitch with shape (angularity), and the third one connects pitch (inversely) with size. Fourth and finally, there is a connection between auditory and visual intensities, between loudness and brightness: Soft sounds invoke dim colors, loud sounds bright ones (e.g., Wheeler, 1920).

Not only does this handful of general rules characterize many of the psychophysical correspondences observed in visual–auditory synesthesia but, perhaps just as importantly, equivalent rules reveal themselves in the perceptual behavior of nonsynesthetic individuals. This is not to say that all of the intermodal correspondences observed in synesthesia find parallels in the behavior of nonsynesthetic individuals; for instance, Cytowic and Wood (1982) reported notable differences between the visual–geometric associations of their single gustatory synesthetic participants and those of nonsynesthetic control participants, and similar divergences take place in the realm of visual–auditory synesthesia as well. Nevertheless, virtually everyone, regardless of culture and age and not just synesthetic individuals, perceives the louder of two tones to resemble more closely the brighter than the dimmer of two colors, that virtually everyone perceives the higher pitched of two tones to resemble more closely the lighter than the darker of two colors, and that virtually everyone perceives the higher pitched of two tones to resemble more closely the more acute and smaller of two geometric shapes (Karwoski et al., 1942; Marks, 1974, 1975, 1978, 1989; Rader & Tellegen, 1987; Werner, 1957; Wicker, 1968).

Consider Marks's (1989) study, conducted in a test population of nonsynesthetic adults. On each trial, the participants were presented two stimuli, which might be a pair of sounds, a pair of lights, or a sound and a light. The task was to rate the relative similarity of the two stimuli to each other on a scale that ranged from extremely similar to extremely dissimilar. Sounds varied in both frequency and intensity (hence, in their pitch and loudness), whereas lights varied in luminance (hence, in their brightness). The results indicated that the participants judged as similar not only pairs of lights that were alike in brightness and pairs of sounds that were alike in pitch and in loudness, but also intermodal pairs in which the relative brightness of the light matched the loudness and the pitch of the sound.

Figure 4.1 illustrates the results. Dimensions of both auditory and visual perception, at least with respect to brightness, pitch, and loudness, collapse onto a unitary, bimodal, two-dimensional representation, in which one of the intermodal dimensions (the x-axis in Figure 4.1) corresponds to pitch/brightness and the other dimension (the y-axis) to loudness/brightness. Soft, low-pitched sounds are located at the lower left of the figure together with dim lights, whereas loud, high-pitched sounds are located at

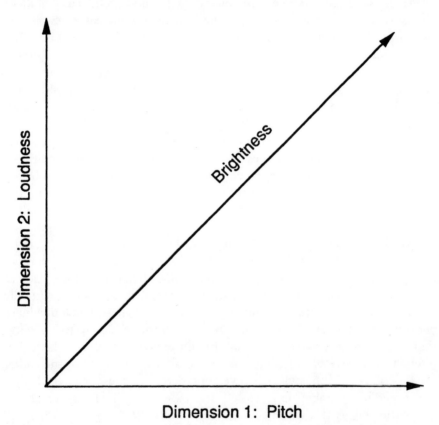

Figure 4.1. A bidimensional and bimodal spatial representation of the psychophysical relations in visual–auditory synesthesia; Low-pitched and soft sounds tend to induce dim or dark visual sensations or images (represented by locations in lower-left region of the figure), whereas high-pitched and loud sounds tend to induce bright visual sensations or images (represented by locations in the upper-right region of the figure).

the upper right of the figure together with bright lights. One feature of the results was especially interesting: The analysis of the similarity ratings, accomplished by the mathematical procedure of multidimensional scaling, showed no dimension corresponding to the difference in sensory modality. This outcome implies that, in this study at least, the difference between seeing and hearing was not salient, even to nonsynesthetic individuals.

THEORIES

The existence of both weaker and stronger forms of synesthesia suggests that they lie on a continuum of experience. Consistent with this view, Rader and Tellegen (1987) found synesthesia to be continuously distributed over the population they examined (see also Glicksohn, Salinger, & Roychman, 1992). The presence of unifying principles of cross-modal correspondence, such as that between the pitch of sounds and the lightness and brightness of colors, provides additional support. Taking this view further, it is conceivable that strong and weak synesthesia differ only quantitatively and may have common neurophysiological underpinnings. On the other hand, strong synesthesia is a relatively uncommon phenomenon and consequently may have properties that are qualitatively distinct from those of weak synesthesia. Indeed, it has long been suspected that strong synesthesia may constitute a distinct neurophysiological syndrome, although until recent years direct empirical evidence for the hypothesis was lacking.

Accounts of synesthesia couched in physiological terms trace back to the 19th century, when the earliest reports of strong synesthesia appeared, mostly in the medical literature. Perhaps the first well-documented description of synesthesia was published in a medical dissertation in 1812 by Georg Sachs (summarized by Suárez de Mendoza, 1890; Wheeler, 1920), who recounted his own synesthesia, noting in special detail the various colors that he associated with the vowels and consonants of speech and with musical notes and instruments. Prior to Sachs's study, synesthesia had received only cursory notice. For example, in a 1786 study of color harmony, Johann Hoffmann mentioned an individual who perceived vivid colors in musical notes (see Suárez de Mendoza, 1890). During the 19th century, explanations of synesthesia relied largely on hypothetical sensory pathologies. A popular theory, consistent with what was then believed to be a rigid physiological separation of the senses, proposed that synesthesia involves some kind of neural "irradiation" or "short circuit" between sensory-receptive regions of the brain (e.g., Clavière, 1898; de Rochas, 1885). Empirical evidence, however, was lacking.

Cytowic (1989, 1997) resurrected the hypothesis that synesthesia represents a distinct neurological entity, arguing in particular that strong synesthesia results from a disconnection of language areas and limbic areas in the brain and that synesthesia is related to several other phenomena such as eidetic imagery. (In this regard, Glicksohn et al., 1992, uncovered a correlation between measures of eidetic imagery and synesthesia; see also Cytowic & Wood, 1982.) Synesthesia, according to Cytowic, involves a suppression of activity in the cerebral neocortex with a concomitant increase in activity in lower neural systems, particularly the limbic system. A critical neural structure in this process is presumed to be the hippocampus. This interpretation derives largely from measures of cerebral blood flow obtained by neural imaging, taken during synesthetic episodes.

According to Cytowic's (1989) hypothesis, in synesthesia higher level cognitive processing is cut off from lower level, more primitive, sensory processing. This hypothesis appears especially compatible with the view of Maurer (1993) that synesthesia reflects, in some manner, a state of relative lack of differentiation in the nervous system.

Although Cytowic's (1989) hypothesis about the neural mechanisms underlying synesthesia is intriguing, evidence to support it remains limited. A study by Paulesu et al. (1995; see also Frith & Paulesu, 1997) seems to point in perhaps a different direction. In this study, the authors obtained positron emission tomography, or PET, scans in 6 women with spoken word–color synesthesia and 6 control participants. Presentation of a word not only led to activation of language areas of the brains of all participants but, more importantly, in participants with synesthesia led to activation of visual associative areas, including the posterior inferior temporal cortex and the parieto-occipital junctions; deactivation was noted in other areas, namely, left lingual gyrus and left insula. Presenting the word had no evident effect on lower visual areas. From these findings, Paulesu et al. inferred that word–color synesthesia may entail coactivation of regions of the cortex involved in processing language and in integrating visual features, without activating the primary visual cortex. Thus, where Cytowic proposes a subcortical mechanism as underpinning synesthesia, the findings of Paulesu et al. (see also Baron-Cohen, Harrison, Goldstein, & Wyke, 1993) implicate a high-level cortical mechanism.

Schiltz et al. (1999) used scalp electrodes to measure electrical potentials originating in the cerebral cortex; participants comprised 17 individuals with lexical-color synesthesia and 17 matched control participants. In response to lexical stimulation, the participants with synesthesia showed significantly larger positive waves in frontal and prefrontal regions as compared with control participants. Because positive electrical waves recorded at the scalp have been interpreted as reflecting cortical inhibition, these results suggest the presence of inhibitory processes in the frontal cortex during synesthetic episodes (most of the participants with synesthesia reported experiencing synesthesia during the experiment). The question is, What role, if any, does this inhibition play in inducing the synesthetic experience? Schiltz et al. suggested that frontal-lobe inhibition may produce "distractibility," with synesthesia being one consequence. The site of synesthesia itself, however, could be either subcortical or cortical.

The complexity of these findings should not be unexpected, especially when it is recognized that even strong synesthesia comes in different varieties. It is not surprising that Paulesu et al. (1995) found evidence that cortical mechanisms may underlie word–color synesthesia for, as already mentioned, the processing of lexical information itself is ipso facto cognitive, and hence the processes leading to the experience of lexically based synesthesias must rest on relatively high-level linguistic processing. Yet other types or aspects of synesthesia depend on relatively low-level psychophysical properties of sensory stimuli such as their pitch or brightness, and these types or aspects could be based in subcortical mechanisms and could take place without the involvement of high-level cognitive processing. Thus, contrary to the century-old attempt to standardize its definitions, synesthesia may designate a multiplicity of entities, entities that bear certain phenomenal and behavioral similarities but that emanate from physiologically distinct processes.

PATHOLOGY

As noted in the last section, several early theories of synesthesia were couched in physiological terms in which synesthesia was seen to reflect some sort of neuropathology or psychopathology (e.g., Bleuler, 1913), perhaps a neural "short circuit" between sensory regions in the brain (Clavière, 1898; de Rochas, 1885) or a failure of the nervous system to differentiate fully in development (Coriat, 1913). This approach, in turn, harmonized with the stance of those commentators who, in considering synesthesia from a broad cultural and literary perspective—for example, the synesthesia posed by the poet Baudelaire in his sonnet "Correspondences" and, notably, the synesthetic experiences of the antihero Des Esseintes described by Huysmans (1884) in his novel *Against the Grain*— interpreted synesthesia as a manifestation of a kind of degeneration (Nordau, 1895; cf. Babbitt, 1910). Yet the scientific evidence linking synesthesia to psychological and neural pathologies is relatively sparse and difficult to interpret.

Rader and Tellegen (1987) investigated the possible relation between synesthesia and measures of personality and cognition. Individual differences in synesthesia were not related to intelligence or, perhaps more surprisingly, to vividness of imagery (but see Glicksohn et al., 1992, who reported a connection between synesthesia and eidetic imagery). Although they did not find an association between synesthesia and psychopathology, Rader and Tellegen did find a modest relationship between vividness of synesthesia and level of absorption as measured on the Multidimensional Personality Questionnaire, in which the characteristic of absorption refers to the tendency to involve oneself greatly in perception, ideation and, especially, imaginative experiences. A connection between synesthesia and absorption also has been reported by Glicksohn et al. (1992) and Rader, Kunzendorf, and Carrabino (1996), suggesting that individuals with a disposition to absorption may be particularly disposed to synesthetic experience. In many respects, however, synesthetic perceivers are unremarkable, "normal in the conventional sense," according to Cytowic (1997, p. 19).

To be sure, occasional case studies have noted the presence of synesthesia among the symptoms of various psychological or neurological disorders. For example, Jacome and Gumnit (1979) reported the case of a man with a complex seizure disorder in which the onset of pain (without an obvious external stimulus) was associated with auditory and visual synesthesialike experiences. McKane and Hughes (1988) described two cases of women with major affective (depressive) disorders. In both patients, synesthesia appeared with the onset of their other symptoms, then disappeared, together with those symptoms, after treatment with, in one case, a monoamine oxidase inhibitor and, in the other case, with a monoamine reuptake inhibitor.

Although suggestive, it is nevertheless difficult to know how to interpret such case studies. Given a sample of individuals with constitutional synesthesia, one would expect, from simple statistical considerations, that some fraction of them would also suffer from neurological or psychopathological disorders; that is, a subset of synesthetic individuals would be expected to suffer neural or behavioral pathologies even if synesthesia and those pathologies were stochastically independent entities. This said, it seems reasonable there may be a small statistical relation between synesthesia and neural pathologies. To the extent that instances of strong synesthesia could be the phenomenal manifestation of an explicit neurophysiological syndrome, as proposed, for example, by Cytowic (1989, 1997), it would not be surprising to find that abnormal neural functioning may, in an idiosyncratic fashion, be connected with an excess number of instances of synesthesia. That ingestion of psychoactive drugs has been reported to produce episodes of synesthesia (e.g., Cytowic, 1989; Delay et al., 1951; Simpson & McKeller, 1955), presumably by their action on the central nervous system, provides indirect support for this hypothesis. Unfortunately, the low rates of occurrence of strong constitutional synesthesia impede easy statistical evaluation of this hypothesis.

INDIVIDUAL DIFFERENCES: CHILDREN AND ADULTS

Synesthesia in its strong form is a rare phenomenon, and it is not clear just what characteristics make particular individuals susceptible to it.

For instance, it has already been mentioned that synesthetic individuals seem often to be artists, musicians, or writers, although statistical evidence is lacking. One variable that clearly seems important is age. Werner (1957) argued that infancy and early childhood are marked by a lack of sensory differentiation that is reminiscent of synesthesia, and Maurer (1993) suggested that perceptual experience in early infancy may in fact be synesthetic. Consequently, it is possible that most infants are synesthetic but that their synesthesia wanes with development (Maurer, 1993; cf. Marks, 1975). Two lines of evidence can be taken to provide support for this contention or are at least consistent with the more modest view that several intersensory correspondences evident in synesthesia are intrinsic properties of perceptual processes that originate in infancy.

One line of evidence comes from developmental studies of cross-modal similarity in children. These studies indicate that several, albeit not all, of the intermodal similarities found in visual–auditory synesthesia also characterize the perceptual-matching behavior of youngsters without synesthesia. Marks, Hammeal, and Bornstein (1987) found that children as young as 4–5 years of age consistently matched the louder and higher pitched of two sounds to the brighter of two lights (even though the youngest children did not yet understand the referent to the word *pitch*). This result is consistent with the hypothesis that the correspondences between loudness and brightness and between pitch and brightness are part of the makeup of the auditory and visual systems, perhaps residing in common modes of sensory coding (a matter considered later). On the other hand, young children did not consistently match the higher pitched of two sounds to the spatially smaller of two visual stimuli; reliable and consistent behavior was not observed with the dimensions of pitch and size until about age 11, a result that is consistent with the hypothesis that the correspondence between pitch and size, unlike the correspondence between pitch and brightness or the correspondence between loudness and brightness, is not intrinsic to sensorineural processing. Instead, the correspondence between pitch and size likely derives from experience, as others have suggested (e.g., Brown, 1958; Osgood, Suci, & Tannenbaum, 1957). Like color–temperature correspondence, pitch–size correspondence may arise from observations of a correlation in the environment—in the present case, a correlation between the size or volume of an object, and hence its mass, with the object's resonance frequency. Everything else being the same, smaller objects resonate at higher frequencies than do larger objects. Both pitch–size and color–temperature correspondences could become widespread because both associations reflect links between corresponding physical properties of stimuli in the world.

The second line of evidence comes from research on infants, in which relevant findings have been reported by Wagner, Winner, Cicchetti, and Gardner (1981) and by Lewkowicz and Turkewitz (1980). Wagner et al.

used a selective-looking paradigm to show that 1-year-olds "match" tones that ascend or descend in sound frequency with arrows that point up or down in space, respectively. Perhaps even more striking, and relevant to psychophysical characteristics of synesthesia, are the results of Lewkowicz and Turkewitz, who used a habituation design, measuring cardiac deceleration as a response in 3-week-old infants. Lewkowicz and Turkewitz showed that habituation to a light of fixed luminance (brightness) transferred maximally to a sound having an intermodally corresponding level of sound intensity (loudness). That is, the infants tended to treat sounds and lights with corresponding perceptual intensities as equivalent.

Lewkowicz and Turkewitz's (1980) results imply that there is an intrinsic similarity or overlap in neonates between the auditory and visual experiences of sensory intensity. Although it is not necessary to interpret these results to mean that infants perceive their world synesthetically, precisely this hypothesis has been set forth by Maurer (1993). It is Maurer's contention that

> all of [the] evidence makes sense if one postulates that the newborn's senses are not well differentiated but are instead intermingled in a synesthetic confusion. If this is true, then for the newborn, energy from the different senses, including the kinesthetic sensations of his or her own movement, is largely if not wholly undifferentiated: the newborn perceives changes over space and time in the quantity of energy, not the sense through which it arose. (pp. 111–112)

Even if we grant that perception in early infancy is largely undifferentiated, it need not follow that such a lack of differentiation corresponds to the state of synesthesia. Lack of differentiation implies a failure to discriminate or distinguish sensory inputs delivered to different modalities. But synesthetic perceivers—for example, those with colored hearing—clearly are able to distinguish chromatic optic stimuli from acoustic stimuli. What distinguishes individuals with synesthesia from others is not necessarily a confusion of the senses but the concatenation of secondary perceptual experiences with primary experiences. In individuals with synesthesia, sound stimuli produce colors as well as qualities of tone. Even so, to the extent that sensory functioning is relatively undifferentiated at birth, there may be some connection between holistic processing of multimodal stimuli by infants and the phenomenology of synesthesia.

THEORIES LINKING WEAK AND STRONG SYNESTHESIA

As was mentioned, one prominent characteristic of strong synesthesia is its automatic, involuntary character. To strongly synesthetic perceivers, sounds may always be accompanied by visual accoutrements, the secondary visual sensations being virtually unavoidable. By way of contrast, in order to tease out analogous cross-modal correspondences in weakly synesthetic or nonsynesthetic perceivers, who may have little or no secondary sensory imagery, it is necessary to ask the latter to make direct comparisons of stimuli in different modalities. Conceivably, the resulting judgments of intermodal correspondence or similarity could be based on a relatively high-level conscious mechanism. An obvious candidate for a mechanism of conscious mediation is language: That weakly synesthetic perceivers reveal a correspondence between brightness and loudness, for instance, is hardly surprising, given that strong stimulation in both modalities may be labeled verbally as "strong" or "intense." Perhaps linguistic labels serve to mediate intermodal correspondences in individuals without synesthesia—and, conceivably, even in individuals with weak synesthetic imagery.

Evidence consistent with the hypothesis that weak synesthetic connections or associations rely at least in part on high-level cognitive processes comes from findings that individuals without synesthesia can easily reverse the polarities of their intermodal matches: The same individual may match relatively loud sounds to dark colors rather than light colors on one day, but to light colors rather than dark colors on the next (Marks, 1974). By way of contrast, the intermodal correspondences observed in strong synesthesia are marked by an automaticity and a consistency that are lacking in the intersensory matching behavior of individuals without synesthesia. One possible implication is that different mechanisms underlie weak and strong forms of synesthesia.

Granting that intermodal similarity in nonsynesthetic perceivers may be mediated by abstract cognitive mechanisms such as language, it is important nevertheless to distinguish the issue of mediating mechanism from the issue of developmental origins. Even if some intermodal correspondences are mediated through language, it need not follow that they originate in language. To the contrary, it is reasonable to hypothesize that the intermodal similarity between, for instance, pitch and brightness originates in perception itself, reflecting fundamental processes of sensory coding in the auditory and visual modalities. Once the similarity becomes available to language, however, linguistic mechanisms could then tend to dominate perceptual ones.

Support for this interpretation appears in the findings, mentioned earlier, of Marks et al. (1987), who studied the development of intermodal matching in perception and in language. Measures of the consistency of intermodal correspondences between pitch and brightness, between loudness and brightness, and between pitch and size were taken in children of various ages and in adults. Correspondences between pitch and brightness and between loudness with brightness appeared in perceptual tasks in children as young as 4 years of age, whereas the correspondence of pitch with size was evident only after age 11. In addition, Marks et al. obtained responses in a verbal task that provided measures of linguistic synesthesia or intermodal metaphor.

Figure 4.2 compares the developmental trajectories of intermodal similarity as assessed through perception and through language. In the cases of both pitch–brightness and loudness–brightness, the performance of 4-year-olds was more consistent on the perceptual task than it was on the verbal task. At age 4, the children performed essentially at chance on the verbal loudness–brightness task. This outcome is contrary to the outcome predicted by the hypothesis that intermodal similarity originates in language and is subsequently transferred to perception, but it is consistent with the hypothesis that intermodal similarity (at least, between pitch and brightness and between loudness and brightness) originates in perception per se. It is noteworthy, however, that from age 7 onward, the children's performance on the verbal loudness–brightness task exceeded their performance on the corresponding perceptual task, suggesting that verbal processes may eventually come to supplant direct perception in mediating this intermodal association. Finally, it is important to note that the correspondence between pitch and size follows a wholly different trajectory. At age

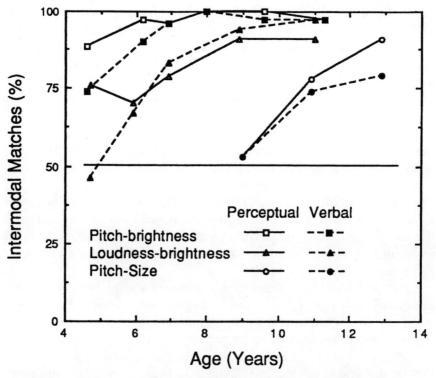

Figure 4.2. Intermodal similarity in children and adults as assessed in perception (cross-modal matching) and language (interpretation of synesthetic metaphors). In both cases, a score of 50% (horizontal line) indicates random performance. Based on data of Marks, Hammeal, and Bornstein (1987).

9, the children performed at chance on both the perceptual and verbal tasks, but at ages 11 and 13 performance exceeded chance on both tasks. This result suggests that the correspondence between auditory pitch and visual size may not be intrinsic to sensory processes or perception per se, but is consistent with the view that pitch–size association derives from experience with resonance properties of objects varying in mass (Brown, 1958; Osgood et al., 1957). Furthermore, performance at perceptual matching exceeded performance on the corresponding verbal task, implying that it is perceptual rather than linguistic experience that underlies the relationship between pitch and size.

METHODOLOGICAL ISSUES

Synesthesia consists, first and foremost, of phenomenological relations between sensory experiences on the one hand and the stimuli in the world that produce these experiences on the other hand. As a result, research on synesthesia must ultimately rely on what synesthetic individuals say about their sensations, perceptions, and feelings. Moreover, because strong synesthesia is a relatively uncommon condition, many of the studies of strong synesthesia have examined only small numbers of individuals or have reported individual case studies (for a review, see Marks, 1975). Were the reports obtained from various synesthetic individuals wholly idiosyncratic and dissimilar, scientific inquiry might not even be possible. Fortunately, as already noted, strong constitutional synesthesia does reveal a number of widely shared principles, such as consistency, long history, reliability, and automaticity. Even so, research on synesthesia has undoubtedly been impeded by both the relative rarity of the phenomenon and the lack of clear-cut and more "objective" measures of performance that might correlate with verbal reports or introspections.

In this regard, two modern lines of research point in promising directions. For example, the phenomenal properties of synesthetic experience also may make themselves known within behavioral tasks that permit more objective measures of performance, such as response times. Wollen and Ruggiero (1983) reported results obtained from a 25-year-old woman for whom both spoken and written letters produced synesthetic colors. When the woman was required to name the colors in which letters were printed, the latencies of her responses were greatly increased when the stimulus color differed from the letter's synesthetic color. This finding is analogous to the well-known Stroop effect, in which people find it difficult to name the color in which a word is printed if the word is the name of a different color (Dyer, 1973). Thus, people find it easy to name a patch of green ink as "green," but much harder to name green ink when it spells the word RED. The existence of the Stroop effect implies that the processing of perceptual information about color can be impeded by incompatibility between the color percept and an irrelevant color name. Wollen and Ruggiero's finding implies analogous effects in synesthesia: that information processing can similarly be impeded when a synesthetically induced color is incompatible with a color percept.

Another promising line of research aims to elucidate the neurological basis of synesthesia (e.g., Cytowic, 1989; Paulesu et al., 1995; Schiltz et al., 1999). Determining the physiological basis or bases of synesthesia would surely go far toward improving the scientific status of research on the topic. Nevertheless, it is important to point out that neither a behavioral nor a neurophysiological correlate of synesthesia is any more than that, a correlate. The primary and defining characteristics of synesthesia, those characteristics that must themselves ultimately be explained, are phenomenological and experiential. Consequently, an adequate neurophysiological account of synesthesia would be far-reaching, as it would have to be an account of sensory–perceptual–affective experiences per se.

Methodological issues arise also in attempts to compare experimental measures of intermodal correspondence in synesthesia with experimental measures of intermodal similarity in nonsynesthetic individuals, as there is of course an overriding difference between the two paradigms. Synesthesia, particularly strong synesthesia, is first and foremost marked by a phenomenal experience in which stimulation of one modality produces sensory qualities of another modality. Judgments of intermodal similarity do not, or at least need not, rely on such phenomenal experiences. Although cross-modal perceptual matches or judgments of intermodal correspondence in nonsynesthetic individuals do tap the conscious, phenomenal experiences of these individuals, their behavior is susceptible to the influences of nonperceptual mechanisms, especially language.

One possible way to avoid the intrusion of cognitive influences on task performance is to find measures of synesthesialike, cross-modal correspondence in experimental tasks that do not rely on conscious meditation. A direction is suggested by Wollen and Ruggiero (1983), described earlier, who found Stroop-like interference in measures of response times in a synesthetic woman. In that study, a synesthetic interaction revealed itself automatically, in an "objective" task that did not require any "subjective" report. As it turns out, several intermodal correspondences make themselves evident in an automatic fashion, even in nonsynesthetic individuals.

Bernstein and Edelstein (1971; see also Ben-Artzi & Marks, 1995, 1999; Melara & O'Brien, 1987) measured the speed of response to visual stimuli, asking their participants to respond as quickly as possible to lights that differed in their up–down position by pressing one key if the spatial location was low, another key if the location was high. At the same time, the participants heard a tone that could take on either a low or high pitch, independent of the spatial position of the light. Although the pitch of the tone was uninformative—it did not correlate in any statistical way with the spatial location of the light—the congruence relation between the pitch of the tone and the spatial location of the light on a given trial clearly affected the speed of response. When the light appeared in the high location, participants were able to respond more quickly if the tone was also high in pitch than if it was low; but when the light appeared in the low location, participants responded more quickly if the tone was also low in pitch rather than high. That is, synesthetically congruent combinations of stimuli produced better performance than did incongruent combinations of stimuli. These intermodal interactions take place spontaneously and automatically, without the perceiver being aware that she or he is "matching" stimuli in different modalities.

Note, however, that tones varying in pitch and lights varying in vertical position do share the verbal labels *low* and *high*. Consequently, Bernstein and Edelstein's (1971) findings could reflect the operation of implicit verbal mediators. That linguistic stimuli are capable of affecting response times in an analogous fashion was shown by Walker and Smith (1984) and later by Melara and Marks (1990), who obtained results comparable with those of Bernstein and Edelstein by pairing a sensory stimulus (e.g., a tone) with a verbal stimulus (e.g., a sensory word; see also Martino & Marks, 1999). Given that verbal and perceptual stimuli can interact according to their synesthetic congruence, it is conceivable that a verbal process might have mediated Bernstein and Edelstein's results, even though none of their stimuli was explicitly linguistic.

As it turns out, however, intermodal congruence can modulate speed of responding even when the stimuli are sensory (nonlinguistic) and do not share verbal labels. Melara (1989) showed that participants respond more quickly and accurately to compound visual–auditory stimuli that are cross-modally congruent than to compounds that are incongruent. Melara used tones varying in pitch (low vs. high) and surfaces varying in reflectance (white vs. black) and found that congruent stimulus compounds (low pitch + black; high pitch + white) are processed more efficiently (faster and more accurately) than incongruent compounds (low pitch + white; high pitch + black). The same principle has been shown to hold for a wide variety of intermodal relations: Wherever there are reliable and systematic synesthetic correspondences (between pitch and brightness, between loudness and brightness, and between pitch and angular shape), nonsynesthetic individuals process intermodally congruent or matching pairs of stimuli (e.g., low-pitched sounds paired with dark colors, small sizes, sharp contours; high-pitched sounds paired with bright colors, large sizes, rounded contours) more efficiently than incongruent or mismatching pairs of stimuli. The processing of intermodal stimuli compounded from dimensions, such as lightness and loudness, that show no reliable synesthetic correspondence reveals no systematic differences in efficiency of processing

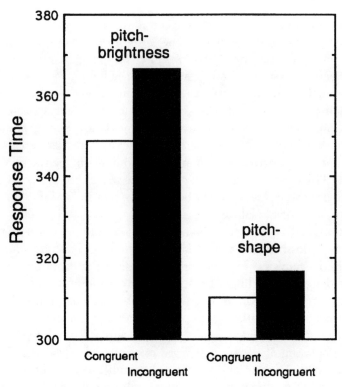

Figure 4.3. Response times to discriminate visual stimuli paired with congruent or incongruent auditory stimuli. The auditory stimuli varied in pitch (low vs. high) and visual stimuli varied in either brightness (dim vs. bright) or angularity (rounded vs. sharp). Responses to intermodally congruent pairs (low pitched + dim and high pitched + bright in the first example; low pitched + rounded and high pitched + acute in the second) are faster than responses to intermodally incongruent pairs (low pitched + bright and high pitched + dim in the first example; low pitched + acute and high pitched + rounded in the second). Derived from data of Marks (1987).

(Marks, 1987). Figure 4.3 shows how response times reflect congruence between the auditory dimension of pitch on the one hand and the visual dimensions of brightness and angularity on the other. Thus, the very same intermodal relations that are so widespread in synesthetic perception appear, automatically, in measures of stimulus identification determined under conditions that emphasize speed of responding.

CONCLUSION

To understand synesthesia in all of its varieties and manifestations, one must develop a comprehensive theory capable of explaining synesthesia's multitude of forms and contents, its variations in phenomenology, and the psychophysics involved. Undoubtedly, any viable theory will have to make reference to possible neural mechanisms underlying the phenomena.

As Marks (1978) and Cytowic (1989) pointed out, synesthesia differs markedly from those kinds of intermodal perception that are directed toward stimulus information about objects and events in the environment. After all, most perception in daily life is multimodal: As I type this chapter, I see the computer keyboard while I feel my fingers striking the keys. A colleague enters my office and I hear her voice while I watch her speaking. The multimodal integration of visual, tactual, and acoustic information differs fundamentally, however, from synesthesia, which is manifested largely through psychophysical rather than informational properties of stimuli. Those hues and tints that are synesthetically induced in a person with colored hearing or with colored taste often do not specify anything about the environment (see Marks, 1978).

Rather than reflecting common objects or events in the world, synesthetically related sensations may represent, at least in part, the outcome of similarities in neural coding mechanisms in different sensory systems. This is to say that the contents of synesthesia comprise, at least to some extent, a set of consistent and widespread alignments of sensory dimensions, and these alignments may represent the ways that the nervous system encodes various stimulus properties. According to this hypothesis, perceptual dimensions such as auditory pitch and visual brightness or auditory loudness and visual brightness correspond synesthetically because the nervous system uses similar rules to code variations along these dimensions. Thus, pitch, loudness, and brightness all seem to be encoded by temporal neural information, that is, by frequency of nerve impulses or interimpulse intervals in auditory and visual neurons (see Marks & Bornstein, 1987).

The hypothesis of common neural coding does not seek to distinguish weak from strong synesthesia as such, but applies to both. The hypothesis holds that, for example, soft sounds induce dim visual sensations in strong synesthesia or resemble dim visual sensations in weak synesthesia, whereas loud sounds induce or resemble bright visual sensations because of the way that the nervous system encodes loudness and brightness. In essence, the nervous system has a relatively small number of degrees of freedom when it comes to sensory coding; there are only a few ways that sensory attributes can be coded. Thus, the nervous system uses a time-based or frequency-based rule to encode both loudness in the auditory system and brightness in the visual system. Both loudness and brightness are encoded as relative rates of response across populations of active neurons. Low-pitched sounds also induce or resemble dim visual sensations, whereas high-pitched sounds induce or resemble bright sensations, because the auditory system relies on a temporal mechanism—the periodicity in the neural response—to encode pitch as well as loudness. The puzzling result that a single visual dimension —brightness—maps psychologically onto two auditory dimensions—pitch and loudness—thereby finds a reasonable explanation in mechanisms of sensory coding.

To be sure, this account does not explain the difference between weak and strong synesthesia per se, and in particular it does not explain why a very small number of people actually report seeing colors when they hear sounds. To understand synesthesia fully, one must also distinguish strong from weaker kinds of synesthesia. This is especially important if, as seems likely, the experiences of strong synesthesia rely on a special physiological mechanism of some sort. Conversely, evidence for a neurophysiological process that is specific to strong synesthesia would provide powerful evidence for a discontinuity between weaker and stronger forms of synesthesia.

That synesthesia may have a special neurophysiological basis does not preclude the possible role of learning. The very existence of lexical synesthesia implicates learning, given that letters of the alphabet and words of a language are learned within a particular linguistic culture. In the middle decades of the 20th century, and in particular with the advent of behaviorism, came explanations of synesthesia couched in terms of stimulus–response conditioning. Experimental studies such as those of Kelly (1934), Leuba (1940), Ellson (1941b), and Howells (1944) sought to induce synesthesia by repeatedly pairing one stimulus with another: Playing particular colors in close temporal association with particular tones resulted, after hundreds or thousands of trials, in a modest ability of the sounds to arouse color responses. Although Ellson (1941a) reported that conditioned sensations were difficult to extinguish, these sensations nevertheless appear to be very weak, quite unlike the clear, potent, vivid experiences of strong synesthesia. A study by Stevenson, Boakes, and Prescott (1998), however, provided some evidence for the formation of synesthesialike responses to odors based on associative learning, although this outcome may be specific to the olfactory sense.

It seems unlikely that associative contiguities or conjunctions can account for the phenomenology of strong synesthesia. Rizzo and Eslinger (1989) tested a 17-year-old man with colored-hearing synesthesia and found that, unlike the control participants without synesthesia, he could make strong associations between colors and musical notes after a single learning trial. This finding led Rizzo and Eslinger to suggest that synesthesia may reflect learned associations in those individuals who are disposed to learn intersensory associations with special ease. Even granting that this hypothesis might apply to a few instances of synesthesia, it leaves open an essential question: What makes it possible for certain individuals to learn intersensory associations with such ease? For even if Rizzo and Eslinger were correct, it would still remain necessary to develop a cogent account of the peculiar learning processes that lead to synesthesia (and Victor, 1989, doubted whether Rizzo and Eslinger adequately eliminated an underlying neurophysiological explanation for their findings). Such an account will most likely be neurophysiological. In this regard, technological advances in neural imaging hold special promise of identifying the neural mechanisms that underlie synesthesia and, by implication, of shedding light on the basic neural mechanisms that underlie the phenomenology of sensory perception itself.

REFERENCES

Babbitt, I. (1910). *The new Laokoon: An essay on the confusion of the arts*. Boston: Houghton Mifflin.

Baron-Cohen, S., Burt, L., Smith-Laittan, F., Harrison, J., & Bolton, P. (1996). Synaesthesia: Prevalence and familiality. *Perception, 25*, 1074–1080.

Baron-Cohen, S., Harrison, J., Goldstein, L. H., & Wyke, M. (1993). Coloured speech perception: Is synaesthesia what happens when modularity breaks down? *Perception, 22*, 419–426.

Baron-Cohen, S., Wyke, M. A., & Binnie, C. (1987). Hearing words and seeing colours: An experimental investigation of a case of synesthesia. *Perception, 16*, 761–767.

Ben-Artzi, E., & Marks, L. E. (1995). Visual–auditory interaction in speeded classification: Role of stimulus difference. *Perception & Psychophysics, 57*, 1151–1162.

Ben-Artzi, E., & Marks, L. E. (1999). Processing linguistic and perceptual dimensions of speech: Interactions in speeded classification. *Journal of Experimental Psychology: Human Perception and Performance, 25*, 579–595.

Bernard, J. W. (1986). Messiaen's synaesthesia: The correspondence between color and sound structure in his music. *Music Perception, 4*, 41–68.

Bernstein, I. H., & Edelstein, B. A. (1971). Effects of some variations in auditory input upon visual choice reaction time. *Journal of Experimental Psychology, 87*, 241–247.

Bleuler, E. (1913). Zur Theorie der Sekundärempfindungen [Toward the theory of secondary sensations]. *Zeitschrift für Psychologie, 6*, 1–39.

Bleuler, E., & Lehmann, K. (1881). *Zwangmässige Lichtempfindungen durch Schall und verwandte Erscheinungen* [Induced light sensations from sound and related phenomena]. Leipzig, Germany: Fues' Verlag.

Brown, R. (1958). *Words and things*. New York: Free Press.

Clavière, J. (1898). L'audition colorée [Colored hearing]. *L'Année Psychologique, 5*, 161–178.

Collins, M. (1929). A case of synaesthesia. *Journal of General Psychology, 2*, 12–27.

Coriat, I. H. (1913). A case of synesthesia. *Journal of Abnormal Psychology, 8*, 38–43.

Cytowic, R. E. (1989). *Synesthesia: A union of the senses*. New York: Springer-Verlag.

Cytowic, R. E. (1997). Synaesthesia: Phenomenology and neuropsychology. In S. Baron-Cohen & J. E. Harrison (Eds.), *Synaesthesia: Classic and contemporary readings* (pp. 17–39). Oxford, England: Blackwell.

Cytowic, R. E., & Wood, F. B. (1982). Synesthesia: II. Psychophysical relations in the synesthesia of geometrically shaped taste and colored hearing. *Brain and Cognition, 1,* 36–49.

Delay, J., Gérard, H.-P., & Racamier, P.-C. (1951). Les synesthésies dans l'intoxication mescalinique [Synesthesias in mescaline intoxication]. *L'Encéphale, 40,* 1–10.

de Rochas, A. (1885). L'audition colorée [Colored hearing]. *La Nature, 13* (Part 1), 306–307, 406–408; (Part 2) 274–275.

Dyer, F. N. (1973). The Stroop phenomenon and its use in the study of perceptual, cognitive, and response processes. *Memory & Cognition, 1,* 106–120.

Ellson, D. G. (1941a). Experimental extinction of an hallucination produced by sensory conditioning. *Journal of Experimental Psychology, 28,* 350–361.

Ellson, D. G. (1941b). Hallucinations produced by sensory conditioning. *Journal of Experimental Psychology, 28,* 1–20.

Flournoy, T. (1893). *Des phénomènes de synopsie* [On phenomena of synopsia]. Paris: Alcan.

Frith, C. D., & Paulesu, E. (1997). The physiological basis of synaesthesia. In S. Baron-Cohen & J. E. Harrison (Eds.), *Synaesthesia: Classic and contemporary readings* (pp. 123–147). Oxford, England: Blackwell.

Galton, F. (1883). *Inquiries into human faculty and its development*. London: Macmillan.

Gautier, T. (1846). Le club des hachichins [The hashish club]. *Revue des Deux-Mondes, 13,* 520–535.

Ginsberg, L. (1923). A case of synaesthesia. *American Journal of Psychology, 34,* 582–589.

Glicksohn, J., Salinger, O., & Roychman, A. (1992). An exploratory study of syncretic experience: Eidetics, synaesthesia and absorption. *Perception, 21,* 637–642.

Grossenbacher, P. (1997). Perception and sensory information in synaesthetic experience. In S. Baron-Cohen & J. E. Harrison (Eds.), *Synaesthesia: Classic and contemporary readings* (pp. 148–172). Oxford, England: Blackwell.

Howells, T. H. (1944). The experimental development of color–tone synesthesia. *Journal of Experimental Psychology, 34,* 87–103.

Huysmans, J.-K. (1884). *À rebours* [Against the grain]. Paris: Charpentier.

Jacome, D. E., & Gumnit, R. J. (1979). Audioalgesic and audiovisuoalgesic synesthesias: Epileptic manifestation. *Neurology, 29,* 1050–1053.

Kandinsky, W. (1912). *Über das Geistige in der Kunst, inbesondere in der Malerei* [On the spiritual in art, especially in painting]. Munich: Piper.

Karwoski, T. F., & Odbert, H. S. (1938). Color–music. *Psychological Monographs, 50*(Whole No. 222).

Karwoski, T. F., Odbert, H. S., & Osgood, C. E. (1942). Studies in synesthetic thinking: II. The role of form in visual responses to music. *Journal of General Psychology, 26,* 199–222.

Kelly, E. K. (1934). An experimental attempt to produce artificial chromaesthesia by the technique of conditioned response. *Journal of Experimental Psychology, 17,* 315–341.

Leuba, C. (1940). Images as conditioned sensations. *Journal of Experimental Psychology, 26,* 345–351.

Lewkowicz, D., & Turkewitz, G. (1980). Cross-modal equivalence in early infancy: Auditory–visual intensity matching. *Developmental Psychology, 16,* 597–607.

Luria, A. R. (1968). *The mind of a mnemonist.* New York: Basic Books.

Mahling, F. (1926). Das Problem der "Audition colorée" [The problem of "colored hearing"]. *Archiv für die Gesamte Psychologie, 57,* 165–302.

Marks, L. E. (1974). On associations of light and sound: The mediation of brightness, pitch, and loudness. *American Journal of Psychology, 87,* 173–188.

Marks, L. E. (1975). On colored-hearing synesthesia: Cross-modal translations of sensory dimensions. *Psychological Bulletin, 82,* 303–331.

Marks, L. E. (1978). *The unity of the senses: Interrelations among the modalities.* New York: Academic Press.

Marks, L. E. (1987). Auditory–visual interactions in speeded discrimination. *Journal of Experimental Psychology: Human Perception and Performance, 13,* 384–394.

Marks, L. E. (1989). On cross-modal similarity: The perceptual structure of pitch, loudness, and brightness. *Journal of Experimental Psychology: Human Perception and Performance, 15,* 586–602.

Marks, L. E., & Bornstein, M. H. (1987). Sensory similarities: Classes, characteristics, and cognitive consequences. In R. E. Haskell (Ed.), *Cognition and symbolic structures: The psychology of metaphoric transformation* (pp. 49–65). Norwood, NJ: Ablex.

Marks, L. E., Hammeal, R. J., & Bornstein, M. H. (1987). Perceiving similarity and comprehending metaphor. *Monographs of the Society for Research in Child Development, 52*(Whole No. 215).

Martino, G., & Marks, L. E. (1999). Perception and linguistic interactions in speeded classification: Tests of the semantic coding hypothesis. *Perception, 28,* 903–923.

Mattison, A. (1988). *Great wits.* New York: Morrow.

Maurer, D. (1993). Neonatal synesthesia: Implications for the processing of speech and faces. In B. de Boysson-Bardies, S. de Schoenen, P. Jusczyk, P. McNeilage, & J. Morton (Eds.), *Developmental neurocognition: Speech and face processing in the first year of life* (pp. 109–124). Dordrecht, The Netherlands: Kluwer.

McKane, J. P., & Hughes, A. M. (1988). Synaesthesia and major affective disorder. *Acta Psychiatrica Scandinavica, 77,* 493–494.

Melara, R. D. (1989). Dimensional interactions between color and pitch. *Journal of Experimental Psychology: Human Perception and Performance, 15,* 69–79.

Melara, R. D., & Marks, L. E. (1990). Processes underlying dimensional interactions: Correspondences between linguistic and nonlinguistic dimensions. *Memory & Cognition, 18,* 477–495.

Melara, R. D., & O'Brien, T. P. (1987). Interaction between synesthetically corresponding dimensions. *Journal of Experimental Psychology: General, 116,* 323–336.

Morgan, G. A., Goodson, F. E., & Jones, T. (1975). Age differences in the associations between felt temperatures and color choices. *American Journal of Psychology, 88,* 125–130.

Nabokov, V. (1949). Portrait of my mother. *New Yorker, 27*(7), 33–37.

Nordau, M. (1895). *Degeneration.* New York: Appleton.

Osgood, C. E., Suci, G. J., & Tannenbaum, P. H. (1957). *The measurement of meaning.* Urbana: University of Illinois Press.

Paulesu, E., Harrison, J., Baron-Cohen, S., Watson, J. D., Goldstein, L., Heather, J., Frackowiak, R. S., & Frith, C. D. (1995). The physiology of coloured hearing: A PET activation study of colour–word synaesthesia. *Brain, 118,* 661–676.

Peacock, K. (1985). Synesthetic perception: Alexander Scriabin's color music. *Music Perception, 2,* 483–505.

Preminger, A. (Ed.). (1974). *Princeton encyclopedia of poetics.* Princeton, NJ: Princeton University Press.

Rader, C. M., Kunzendorf, R. G., & Carrabino, C. (1996). The relation of imagery vividness, absorption, reality boundaries and synesthesia to hypnotic states and traits. In R. G. Kunzendorf, N. P. Spanos, & B. Wallace (Eds.), *Hypnosis and imagination* (pp. 99–121). Amityville, NY: Baywood.

Rader, C. M., & Tellegen, A. (1987). An investigation of synesthesia. *Journal of Personality and Social Psychology, 52,* 981–987.

Riggs, L. A., & Karwoski, T. F. (1934). Synaesthesia. *British Journal of Psychology, 25,* 29–41.

Rizzo, M., & Eslinger, P. J. (1989). Colored hearing synesthesia: An investigation of neural factors. *Neurology, 39,* 781–784.

Schiltz, K., Trocha, K., Wieringa, B. M., Emrich, H. M., Johannes, S., & Münte, T. F. (1999). Neurophysiological aspects of synesthetic experience. *Journal of Neuropsychiatry and Clinical Neuroscience, 11,* 58–65.

Siebold, E. von (1919). Synästhesien in der englischen Dichtung des 19 Jahrhunderts [Synesthesia in nineteenth century English poetry]. *Englische Studien, 53,* 1–157, 196–334.

Simpson, L., & McKellar, P. (1955). Types of synaesthesia. *Journal of Mental Science, 101,* 141–147.

Stevenson, R. J., Boakes, R. A., & Prescott, J. (1998). Changes in odor sweetness resulting from implicit learning of a simultaneous odor–sweetness association: An example of learned synesthesia. *Learning and Motivation, 29,* 113–132.

Suárez de Mendoza, F. (1890). *L'audition colorée* [Colored hearing]. Paris, France: Octave Doin.

Victor, J. D. (1989). Colored hearing synesthesia. *Neurology, 39,* 1409.

Wagner, S., Winner, E., Cicchetti, D., & Gardner, H. (1981). "Metaphorical" mapping in human infants. *Child Development, 52,* 728–731.

Walker, P., & Smith, S. (1984). Stroop interference based on the synaesthetic qualities of auditory pitch. *Perception, 13,* 75–81.

Werner, H. (1957). *Comparative psychology of mental development* (rev. ed.). New York: International Universities Press.

Wheeler, R. H. (1920). The synaesthesia of a blind subject. *University of Oregon Publications,* No. 5.

Wicker, F. W. (1968). Mapping the intersensory regions of perceptual space. *American Journal of Psychology, 81,* 178–188.

Wollen, K. A., & Ruggiero, F. T. (1983). Colored-letter synesthesia. *Journal of Mental Imagery, 72,* 83–86.

5

LUCID DREAMING

STEPHEN LaBERGE AND JAYNE GACKENBACH

I remember going to bed with mind peacefully composed and full of a quiet joy. The dream during the night that followed was at the beginning quite irrational, though perhaps more keenly followed than usual. I seemed to move smoothly through a region of space where, presently, a vivid sense of cold flowed in on me and held my attention with a strange interest.

I believe that at that moment the dream became lucid. Then suddenly, . . . all that up to now had been wrapped in confusion instantly passed away, and a new space burst forth in vivid presence and utter reality, with perception free and pin-pointed as never before; the darkness itself seemed alive. The thought that was then borne in upon me with inescapable conviction was this: "I have never been awake before." (Whiteman, 1961, p. 57)

DEFINITION

We do not ordinarily think about being awake while we are (if we indeed are awake, an assumption the lucid dream above questions). Likewise, as a rule, we are not aware of the fact that we are dreaming while we are dreaming. We ordinarily experience our dreams as if they are physical reality and only recognize them as dreams after we awaken. However, there is a significant exception to this generalization: Sometimes, while dreaming, we are explicitly aware that we are dreaming. The experience of *lucid dreaming*, as this phenomenon is termed (Van Eeden, 1913), is clearly anomalous in comparison with the usual mildly delirious experience of nonlucid dreaming. The term *lucid* is used in the psychiatric sense, indicating a condition of clear insight and correct orientation to reality in opposition to the clouded insight and deluded disorientation of the delirious.

Just as there are degrees of delirium, there are degrees of lucidity (Barrett, 1992; Kahan & LaBerge, 1994; LaBerge, 1985). In the best of cases, lucid dreamers claim to be fully in possession of their cognitive faculties while dreaming: They report being able to reason clearly, to remember the conditions of waking life, and to act (or not act) voluntarily upon reflection or in accordance with plans decided on before sleep. At the same time, they remain soundly asleep, experiencing a dream world that can seem vividly real.

The usual definition of *lucid dreaming* is simply dreaming while knowing that one is dreaming (Green, 1968; LaBerge, 1985). Some researchers (e.g., Tart, 1988; Tholey, 1988) consider this minimal criterion too broad, and they argue that the term lucid dreaming should require, in addition, correct memory for the circumstances of waking life and a degree of control over the dream. However, there are compelling reasons for preferring the simpler, minimalist definition. For example, in laboratory studies of lucid dreaming, memory for the fact that one is sleeping in the laboratory is relevant and essential for the tasks involved (LaBerge, 1990), but in other contexts, remembering where one is sleeping may be entirely irrelevant. Moreover, although dream control and dream awareness are correlated, neither requires the other (Kahan & LaBerge, 1994); there is no requirement for a fully lucid dreamer to exercise control over the dream at all. One might, for instance, choose to lucidly observe the events of the dream without interference (LaBerge, 1985). This frame of mind is similar, but not identical to, dream "witnessing" (see below; also see Alexander, 1987; Alexander, Boyer, & Orme-Johnson, 1985).

LaBerge (1985) distinguished two contrasting perspectives from which people experience their dreams and other states of consciousness: actor or observer. The actor perspective is how a person ordinarily experiences his or her dreams (and waking life)—as an actively involved participant within the dream (or waking) scene. In contrast, when a person takes the observer perspective, he or she is reflective, disengaged and, in systems theory terms, "meta" to the scene. Lucid dreaming involves a balance between detachment and participation in which both actor and observer perspectives are present simultaneously (LaBerge, 1985; Rossi, 1972). In the typical nonlucid dream, a person is identified with the actor perspective. In witnessing, whether of dreaming or nondreaming sleep, the person is identified with the detached observer (Alexander, 1987; Gackenbach, 1991a).

There are several other types of anomalous experiences similar to lucid dreaming. Most closely related is the out-of-body experience (OBE), which in some cases can be almost identical phenomenologically to lucid dreaming. However, although people having OBEs are clearly reflectively conscious that something strange is happening, they believe that they are not dreaming, in contrast to lucid dreamers (Alvarado, this volume, chap. 6; Blackmore, 1988; Irwin, 1988; LaBerge & DeGracia, in press). Nonetheless, LaBerge and colleagues have shown psychophysiological evidence for the similarities between lucid dreaming and OBE (LaBerge, Levitan, Brylowski, & Dement, 1988; Levitan, LaBerge, DeGracia, & Zimbardo, 1999).

Other related anomalous experiences include some near-death-experiences (NDEs; Greyson, this volume, chap. 10; LaBerge, 1985), some UFO abduction experiences (Gackenbach, 1991a; Appelle, Lynn, & Newman, this volume, chap. 8), some hallucinatory experiences (Bentall, this volume, chap. 3), and some mystical and meditative experiences (Gackenbach, 1991a; LaBerge, 1985; Wulff, this volume, chap. 12). Hunt (1995) argued for framing this whole set of related experiences as experiences of turning around on self or de-embedding of the self.

Under ordinary conditions, lucid dreaming is a rare experience. Although most people report having had a lucid dream at least once in their lives, only about 20% of the U.S. population reports having lucid dreams once a month or more (Snyder & Gackenbach, 1988).

As described below, lucid dreams typically occur late in the sleep cycle, nearly exclusively during REM sleep. This implies a relatively activated brain, and there is some evidence suggesting that high levels of pre-sleep activity (Garfield, 1979) or emotional arousal (Sparrow, 1976) are associated with the occurrence of lucid dreams. Meditation (Gackenbach, 1990; Hunt, 1989) and intensive psychotherapy (Rossi, 1972) may also be associated with increased rates of spontaneous lucid dreaming. Interruptions of the sleep cycle with 30–60 min of wakefulness strongly facilitates lucidity in subsequent sleep (LaBerge, Phillips, & Levitan, 1994).

Dreamers commonly become lucid when they puzzle over oddities in dream content and conclude that the explanation is that they are dreaming. Spontaneous lucidity is also frequently associated with anxiety dreams and the recognition of a dreamlike quality of the experience (Gackenbach 1988; Green, 1968). People are more likely to recognize an experience as dreamlike if they are familiar with what their dreams are like (LaBerge, 1985); this is one reason why lucid dreaming is more frequently reported by high dream recallers (Snyder & Gackenbach, 1988). Although lucid dreaming is a rare experience for most people, there is reason to believe that it is a learnable skill (LaBerge, 1980a, 1980b), and there are a variety of techniques available for inducing lucid dreams that have been summarized or reviewed by LaBerge (1985; LaBerge & Rheingold, 1990), Price and Cohen (1988), and Gackenbach (1985–1986).

As Freud (1965) noted a century ago in *The Interpretation of Dreams*, it is possible to carry a specific mental set into sleep, such as the intention to wake up at a certain hour or if the baby cries or to remember dreams. Sleep is also compatible with the intention to have lucid dreams, and several effective methods for inducing lucid dreams have been developed on the basis of this approach. Diligent practice with some of these techniques has allowed highly motivated individuals with good dream recall to become lucid at will (LaBerge, 1980a, 1980b).

Another approach to lucid dream induction is related to biofeedback. In this approach, delicate sensory stimuli are applied during REM sleep which, if incorporated into dreams, can cue dreamers to remember that they are dreaming (Hearne, 1978; LaBerge, 1980a). Various stimuli to cue lucidity have been experimented with; the most promising results so far have been with flashes of light (LaBerge & Levitan, 1995).

PHENOMENOLOGY

The realization that one is dreaming can sometimes have an extremely powerful impact on the dreamer, as illustrated by the example with which we started this chapter. The following lucid dream is similar:

> I dreamed that I was standing on the pavement outside my home. . . . I was about to enter the house when, on glancing casually at [the pavement] stones, my attention became riveted by a passing strange phenomenon, so extraordinary that I could not believe my eyes—they had seemingly all changed their position in the night, and the long sides were now parallel to the curb! Then the solution flashed upon me: though this glorious summer morning seemed as real as real could be, I was *dreaming*! With the realization of this fact, the quality of the dream changed in a manner very difficult to convey to one who has not had this experience. Instantly, the vividness of life increased a hundred-fold. Never had sea and sky and trees shone with such glamorous beauty; even the commonplace houses seemed alive and mystically beautiful. Never had I felt so absolutely well, so clear-brained, so inexpressibly *free*! The sensation was exquisite beyond words; but it lasted only a few minutes and I awoke. (Fox, 1962, pp. 32–33)

In other cases, the initiation of lucidity takes on a much calmer emotional tone, as in the following case, which also illustrates the remarkable degree of logical reasoning sometimes present in dreams:

> From the top of a rather low and unfamiliar hill, I look out across a

wide plain towards the horizon. It crosses my mind that I have no idea what time of year it is. I check the sun's position. It appears almost straight above me with its usual brightness. This is surprising, as it occurs to me that it is now autumn, and the sun was much lower only a short time ago. I think it over: the sun is now perpendicular to the equator, so here it has to appear at an angle of approximately 45 degrees. So if my shadow does not correspond to my own height, I must be dreaming. I examine it: it is about 30 centimeters long. It takes considerable effort for me to believe this almost blindingly bright landscape and all of its features to be only an illusion. (Moers-Messmer, 1938, p. 316)

Given the great variability in all types of dreams, this question can arise: On the average, how different are lucid and nonlucid dreams? Although descriptions of content differences between lucid and nonlucid dreams exist in the literature (e.g., Moers-Messmer, 1938), there are few systematic individual analyses (Gackenbach et al., 1992; Gillespie, 1988; LaBerge, 1980b). This type of content analysis gives us a detailed description of dream content but may, of course, prove uncharacteristic of the typical lucid dream (likewise, "the average lucid dream" may describe a nonexistent abstraction).

The major review of content differences between lucid and nonlucid dreams is Gackenbach's (1988), in which she evaluated the content of lucid and nonlucid dreams as measured by both self-evaluations and independent judges. The majority of data involved dreams collected either from dream diaries or from questionnaires filled out by the dreamers, with only a few content analyses on lucid dreams collected from sleep laboratories. Gackenbach concluded that, compared with nonlucid dreams, lucid dreams had, on the average, more auditory and kinesthetic sensations as well as more sense of control.

In the same review, Gackenbach (1988) reported on her study of content differences judged according to several bizarreness scales and scales based on the descriptive findings of dreamers' self-evaluations (e.g., palpable sensations, balance, and control) and also according to the Hall and Van de Castle (1966) system of content analysis. The judges' evaluations revealed few differences between lucid and nonlucid dreams. Consistent with the self-evaluations, Gackenbach found higher levels of auditory and kinesthetic dream sensations as well as dream control in lucid dreams than in nonlucid dreams. In addition, lucid dreams averaged fewer dream characters than nonlucid dreams. Gackenbach concluded that the major finding from both types of analyses was that in spite of several statistically significant content differences, lucid dreams are more similar than dissimilar to nonlucid dreams. This result should not be too surprising considering that lucid dreams and nonlucid dreams are both types of *dreams*.

Worsley (1988) pointed out that as useful as such content analyses are from groups of individuals who spontaneously experience lucidity, they fail to appreciate the subtleties of the experience undergone by the more experienced and sophisticated lucid dreamer. There are a variety of ways that this problem has been approached. LaBerge and colleagues have examined the content of lucid dreams with a sample of members of the Lucidity Institute, who are motivated and experienced enough in dreaming lucidly to offer a more comprehensive view of possible content differences between lucid and nonlucid dreams. For example, Levitan and LaBerge (1993) analyzed self-rated content scales from 699 reports provided by 52 participants. Compared with nonlucid dreams, lucid dreams had significantly higher levels of control, more positive emotions, and higher levels of visual vividness, clarity of thinking, physical activity, and changes of scene. Given the possible role of selection bias in canvassing only members of the Lucidity Institute, it is important to replicate this study with other samples to evaluate the findings' generalizability.

As a result of learning and practice, experienced lucid dreamers are likely to have lucid (and perhaps nonlucid) dreams that differ widely from the typical lucid dreams of beginners. They are also more likely to use specialized techniques for lucid dream induction, control, and stabilization (LaBerge & Rheingold, 1990). For example, to prevent premature awakening, lucid dreamers may spin their bodies until the dream restabilizes (LaBerge, 1980a; 1995).

Gackenbach and colleagues asked a group of highly experienced meditators for examples of experiences of consciousness in sleep (reported in Alexander, 1987; Gackenbach, 1991a). Based on the conceptual work of Alexander and colleagues (Alexander, Boyar, & Alexander, 1987; Alexander et al., 1985), Gackenbach and colleagues described three types of consciousness in sleep: (a) *lucid dreaming*, or dreaming while actively thinking about the fact that one is dreaming; (b) *witnessing-dreaming*, or dreaming while experiencing a quiet, peaceful, inner awareness or "wakefulness" separate from the dream; and (c) *deep sleep witnessing*, described as dreamless sleep in which one experiences a quiet, peaceful, inner state of awareness or "wakefulness." In addition to distinguishing these three varieties of consciousness in samples provided by the participants, Gackenbach et al. also examined the content of the experiences of consciousness in sleep described by the meditators and found the expected differences in feelings of separateness and dream control.

AFTEREFFECTS

In general, the aftereffects of most dreams, lucid or otherwise, appear to be relatively subtle. However, some dreams, no doubt, have changed people's lives (De Becker, 1965), and the anomalous nature of lucid dreams may give them greater potential impact.

It has been argued (Hunt, 1989; Kuiken & Sikora, 1993) that lucid and other forms of intensified dreams are more likely to affect subsequent waking feelings, judgments, and action than ordinary dreams. Insofar as lucid dreams are experienced as interesting, exciting, and relatively pleasant, mood elevations would be expected to result upon awakening (LaBerge, 1985), as observed by Levitan and LaBerge (1993) and in most of the studies reviewed by Gackenbach (1988).

There has not yet been any research on long-term effects of lucid dreaming, but research by Alexander and colleagues (Alexander, Davies, et al., 1990; Alexander, Heaton, & Chandler, 1994) suggests potential beneficial effects of long-term witnessing of dreams and sleep. In their work, high-frequency witnessing in both meditators and nonmeditators was associated with lower scores in psychopathology and in psychological, biochemical, and health-related indicators of stress. Cognitively, these experiences were found to reflect high creative thinking, absorption, field independence, and nonpropositional information processing. Repeated experiences of this form of consciousness appeared to result in enduring positive psychophysiological changes, such as lower baseline levels of spontaneous skin resistance responses, respiration rate, heart rate, and plasma lactate. Prospective, long-term studies of the salutary effects of dreams in general, and lucid dreams in particular, are a research priority to establish the causal link between lucid dreaming and its seemingly beneficial effects.

Biological Markers

It is thanks to psychophysiological methodology that lucid dreaming is accepted today as a normal, if rare, phenomenon of REM sleep. Dreams had been characterized as essentially single-minded and nonreflective (Rechtschaffen, 1978); in this context, reports of lucid dreaming were viewed with not a little suspicion. The orthodox point of view about 20 years ago might be summarized thus: (a) Lucid dreams don't happen, and (b) even if they do, they can't happen during genuine sleep.

The concept of *conscious sleep* can seem so self-contradictory and paradoxical to certain ways of thinking that some theoreticians once considered lucid dreams impossible and even absurd. Probably the most extreme example of this point of view is provided by Malcolm (1959), who argued that given the premise that being asleep means experiencing nothing whatsoever, "dreams" are not experiences during sleep at all but only the reports people tell after awakening. This concept of sleep led Malcolm to conclude that the idea that someone might reason while asleep is "meaningless" and that, moreover, "If 'I am dreaming' could express a judgement it would imply the judgement 'I am asleep,' and therefore the absurdity of the latter proves the absurdity of the former." Thus "the supposed judgement that one is dreaming" is "unintelligible" and "an inherently absurd form of words" (Malcolm, 1959, pp. 48–50).

This example shows the skeptical light in which accounts of lucid dreaming were viewed before physiological proof of the reality of lucid dreaming made philosophical arguments moot. The orthodox view in sleep and dream research assumed (until very recently) that anecdotal accounts of lucid dreams must be somehow spurious.

However, anomalous or not, people still reported experiences of lucid dreaming, thus the question Under what presumably abnormal physiological conditions do reports of "lucid" dreams occur? In the absence of empirical evidence bearing on the question, speculation largely favored two answers: either wakefulness or non-REM sleep. Most sleep researchers seemed inclined to accept Hartmann's (1975) impression that lucid dreams were "not typical parts of dreaming thought, but rather brief arousals" (p. 74; see also Berger, 1977). Schwartz and Lefebvre (1973) noted that frequent transitory arousals were common during REM sleep, and they proposed these "microawakenings" as the physiological basis for lucid dream reports. Although no one had offered any evidence for this mechanism, it seems to have been the orthodox opinion (e.g., Foulkes, 1974) up until the past few years. A similar view was expressed by Antrobus, Antrobus, and Fisher (1965), who predicted that recognition by the dreamer that he or she is dreaming would either immediately terminate the dream or continue in non-REM sleep. Likewise, Hall (1977) speculated that lucid dreams may represent "a transition from Stage-1 REM to Stage-4 mentation" (p. 312). Green (1968) seemed to have been alone in reasoning that because lucid dreams usually arise from nonlucid dreams, "we may tentatively expect to find lucid dreams occurring, as do other dreams, during the 'paradoxical' phase of sleep" (p. 128).

REM Research

Empirical evidence began to appear in the late 1970s supporting Green's (1968) speculation that lucid dreams sometimes occur during REM sleep. In a pioneering study, Ogilvie, Hunt, Sawicki, and McGowan (1978) recorded the sleep of two participants who reported lucid dreams after awakening from REM periods. However, no evidence was given that the reported lucid dreams had in fact occurred during the REM sleep immediately preceding the awakenings and reports. What was needed to unambiguously establish the physiological status of lucid dreams was some way to mark the exact time the lucid dream was taking place.

The required method was provided with a new technique involving eye movement signals, developed independently at Stanford University and Hull University. The technique was based on an earlier study (Roffwarg, Dement, Muzio, & Fischer, 1962) that found that the directions of eye

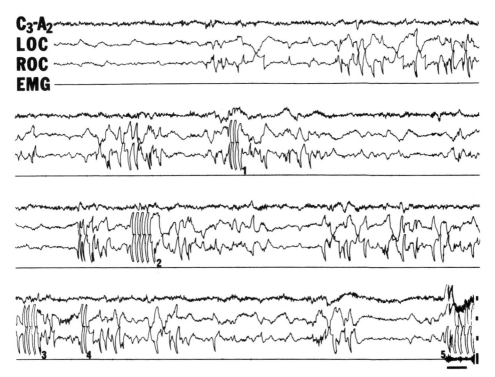

Figure 5.1. A typical dream-initiated lucid dream. Four channels of physiological data (central EEG [C_3-A_2], left (L) and right (R) eye movements [LOC and ROC], and chin muscle tone [EMG]) from the last 8 min of a 30-min REM period are shown. Upon awakening, the participant reported having made five eye movement signals (labeled 1–5 in figure). The first signal (1, LRLR) marked the onset of lucidity. Skin potential artifacts can be observed in the EEG at this point. During the following 90 s, the participant "flew about" exploring his dream world until he believed he had awakened, at which point he made the signal for awakening (2, LRLRLRLR). After another 90 s, the participant realized he was still dreaming and signaled (3) with three pairs of eye movements. Realizing that this was too many, he correctly signaled with two pairs (4). Finally, upon awakening 100 s later, he signaled appropriately (5, LRLRLRLR). (Calibrations are 50 μV and 5 s). Reprinted from "Lucid Dreaming: Psychophysiological Studies of Consciousness During REM Sleep" (p. 114), by S. LaBerge, 1990, in R. R. Bootzen, J. F. Kihlstrom, & D. L. Schacter, *Sleep and Cognition*. Washington, DC: American Psychological Association. Copyright 1990 by American Psychological Association. Reprinted with permission.

movements recorded during REM sleep sometimes exactly corresponded to the directions that participants reported they had been looking in their dreams. LaBerge (1980a) reasoned that if lucid dreamers can act volitionally, they should be able to prove it by making a prearranged eye movement signal marking the exact time they became lucid (see Figure 5.1). Using this approach, LaBerge and his colleagues at Stanford reported that claims of lucid dreams from 5 participants had been validated by eye movement signals (LaBerge, 1980a; LaBerge, Nagel, Dement, & Zarcone, 1981). All of the signals, and therefore lucid dreams, had occurred during uninterrupted REM sleep. LaBerge (1985) noted that one of the original reviewers of this study recommended rejecting the paper because he found it impossibly "difficult to imagine subjects simultaneously dreaming their dreams and signalling them to others" (p. 72).

An almost identical eye movement signaling technique was independently developed by Hearne and Worsley in England, who also found lucid dreaming exclusively during REM (Hearne, 1978). Studies in several other sleep laboratories have obtained essentially the same results (Dane, 1984; Fenwick et al., 1984; Ogilvie, Hunt, Kushniruk, & Newman, 1983), making it clear that, although perhaps paradoxical, lucid dreaming is a proven phenomenon of sleep.

The studies cited above showed that lucid dreams typically occur in REM sleep. However, REM sleep is a heterogeneous state exhibiting great physiological variability. Two distinct phases are ordinarily distinguished: periods of eye movement activity and high cortical activation (phasic REM) versus periods with few eye movements and relatively low activation (tonic REM). Several studies have shown that lucid dreams are associated with phasic REM. LaBerge, Levitan, and Dement (1986) analyzed physiological data from 76 signal-verified lucid dreams (SVLDs) of 13 participants. Physiological comparison of eye movement activity, heart rate, respiration rate, and skin potential activity for lucid versus nonlucid segments revealed that the lucid segments of the SVLD REM periods showed significantly higher levels of physiological activation than the preceding segments of nonlucid REM from the same REM periods. The study also found that REM periods in which lucid dreams occurred were more activated than those in which they did not occur. In addition, H-reflex amplitude was lower during lucid REM (Brylowski, Levitan, & LaBerge, 1989), confirming that lucid REM is a paradoxically deepened state of REM, with increased phasic activation and suppression of spinal reflexes.

Given the strong findings of autonomic activation associated with lucid dreaming, one would expect that various electroencephalograph (EEG) measures of central nervous system activation would also show activation at that time. The few studies that have compared EEG from lucid and nonlucid dreams have focused on alpha activity from one or two sites (e.g., Ogilvie et al., 1983; Ogilvie, Hunt, Tyson, Lucescu, & Jeakins, 1982) and have reached contradictory conclusions (see LaBerge, 1988, for a review). A preliminary EEG brain-mapping study (Brylowski, LaBerge, & Levitan, 1989) found the onset of lucidity to be marked by left-parietal-temporal lobe EEG activation.

Lucid dreams have been reported to occur most commonly late in the sleep cycle (Green, 1968; Van Eeden, 1913). Indeed, LaBerge et al.

(1986) found that 11 of 12 participants had more lucid dreams in the second half of their REM time than in the first half.

As discussed above, lucid dreams are reported to start either from an ongoing dream or directly from a short awakening. Accordingly, LaBerge et al. (1986) dichotomously classified SVLDs as either a wake-initiated lucid dream (WILD) or a dream-initiated lucid dream (DILD), depending on whether the reports mentioned a transient awakening in which the participant consciously perceived the external environment before reentering the dream state. Fifty-five (72%) of the SVLDs were classified as DILDs and the remaining 21 (28%) as WILDs. For all 13 participants, DILDs were more common than WILDs. As expected, in contrast to DILDs, WILDs were almost always immediately preceded by physiological indications of awakening, establishing the validity of classifying lucid dreams in this manner. See Figures 5.1 and 5.2 for illustrations of these two types of lucid dream.

Psychophysiological Relationships During REM

Lucid dreaming makes it possible to answer empirically questions that could previously be asked only theoretically. For example, how long do dreams last? LaBerge (1980a, 1985) set lucid dreamers the task of estimating a 10-s interval of time while dreaming. The dreamers marked the beginning and end of estimated dream time intervals with eye movement signals, allowing comparison of subjective dream time with objective time. In each case, the intervals of time estimated during the lucid dreams were very close in length to the actual elapsed time.

The data reported by LaBerge, Nagel, Dement, and Zarcone (1981) and LaBerge, Nagel, Taylor, et al. (1981) indicate that there is a direct and reliable relationship between gaze shift reported in lucid dreams and the direction of polygraphically recorded eye movements. The results obtained for lucid dreams (see also Dane, 1984; Fenwick et al., 1984; Hearne, 1978; Ogilvie et al., 1982) are much stronger than the generally weak correlations obtained by previous investigators. In the previous studies, to test the hypothesis that the dreamer's eyes move during the hallucinated dream gaze (e.g., Roffwarg, Dement, Muzio, & Fisher, 1962), investigators had to rely on chance occurrence of a highly recognizable eye movement pattern that could be matched to the participants' reported dream activity.

In another study, LaBerge and Dement (1982b) demonstrated that participants could voluntarily control their respiration rate during lucid dreaming. Evidence of voluntary control of other muscle groups during REM has also been found (Fenwick et al., 1984; LaBerge et al., 1981a).

Following reports of cognitive-task dependency of EEG lateralization

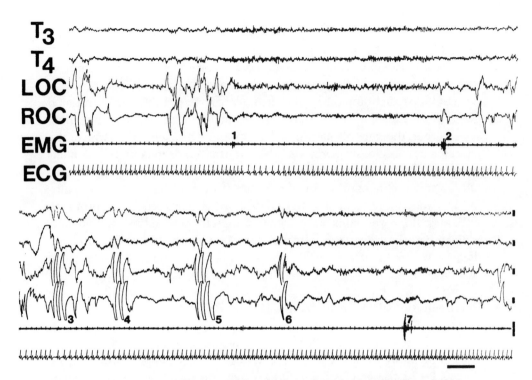

Figure 5.2. A typical lucid dream initiated from a transient awakening during REM. Six channels of physiological data (left- and right-temporal EEG [T_3 and T_4], left and right eye movements [LOC and ROC], chin muscle tone [EMG], and electrocardiogram [ECG]) from the last 3 min of a 14-min REM period are shown. The participant awoke at 1 and after 40 s returned to REM sleep at 2, and realized he was dreaming 15 s later and signaled at 3. Next he carried out the agreed-on experimental task in his lucid dream, singing between Signals 3 and 4, and counting between Signals 4 and 5. This allowed comparison of left- and right-hemisphere activation during the two tasks (LaBerge & Dement, 1982a). Note the heart rate acceleration–deceleration pattern at awakening (1) and at lucidity onset (3) and the skin potential artifacts in the EEG (particularly T_4) at lucidity onset (3). (Calibrations are 50 μV and 5 s). Reprinted from "Lucid Dreaming: Psychological Studies of Consciousness During REM Sleep" (p. 116), by S. LaBerge, 1990, in R. R. Bootzen, J. F. Kihlstrom, and D. L. Schacter, *Sleep and Cognition,* Washington, DC: American Psychological Association. Copyright 1990 by the American Psychological Association. Reprinted with permission.

in the waking state, LaBerge and Dement (1982a) recorded EEG from right and left temporal sites while participants sang and counted in their lucid dreams (see Figure 5.2). The results showed the same task-dependent lateralization in REM sleep as in the waking state: The right hemisphere was more activated than the left during singing; during counting, the reverse was true.

Sexual activity has been reported as a common theme of some lucid dreamers (Garfield, 1979; LaBerge, 1985), although content analyses of the lucid dreams of students do not seem to support the claim (Gackenbach, 1988). In a laboratory study, LaBerge, Greenleaf, and Kedzierski (1983) recorded two lucid dreamers who reported experiencing sexual arousal and orgasm in lucid dreams. The patterns of physiological activity during dream sex closely resembled those accompanying corresponding experiences in the waking state.

The psychophysiological studies summarized above all support the following view: During REM sleep, the events that we dream we experience result from patterns of brain activity that in turn produce effects on our peripheral nervous systems and bodies. These effects are to some extent modified by the specific conditions of REM sleep but are still closely similar to the effects that would occur if we were actually to experience the corresponding events while awake. This may explain in part why we are so inclined to mistake our dreams for reality: To the functional systems of neuronal activity that construct our experiential world (model), dreaming of perceiving or doing something is equivalent to actually perceiving or doing it.

INDIVIDUAL DIFFERENCES

The major review of research on individual differences related to lucid dreaming was done by Snyder and Gackenbach (1988). In it, they described and integrated the research about individuals who experience lucid dreams by presenting data derived from the study of four separable but related functional domains for which participant differences associated with lucid dreaming have been found. These functional domains are oculomotor/equilibratory, visual/imaginal, intellectual/creative, and personal/interpersonal. Snyder and Gackenbach ranked volunteers according to the prevalence and frequency of their lucidity. Such classification was accomplished through various self-report measures and is based on the assumption that lucidity ability can be measured in part by act frequency (or the number of times an activity, event, or feeling is performed or experienced), which may be related to a variety of individual differences.

Oculomotor/Equilibratory

Snyder and Gackenbach (1988) defined *oculomotor activities* as "a complex set of diverse movements subserved by cortical and subcortical structures involved in cognitive, sensoriperceptual, visuopractic, equilibratory, and affective functions" (p. 230). They observed that various aspects of balance, bodily orientation, and personal style can be said to fall in the oculomotor/equilibratory domain. Lucid dreaming ability has been experimentally related to the efficient use of one's own body as a referent during changes in spatial orientation. This is most directly illustrated in the relationship of lucidity to field independence.

Two more recent studies have examined the relationship between field independence and lucidity in sleep. Gruber, Steffen, and Vonderhaar (1995) found a relationship in the same direction as Snyder and Gackenbach (1988; i.e., field independence associated with dreaming lucidly), whereas Blagrove and Tucker (1994) did not. Methodological differences, including controlling for gender of participant, between these studies may account for their differences. The relationship between lucidity and field independence seems clear for men in all the studies but less clear for women.

Evidence to date from studies of eye movements, kinesthesia, caloric stimulation of the vestibular apparatus, and field independence indicates a possible role for the vestibular system during lucid dreaming. This role would be consistent with the known relationships between sleeping, dreaming, eye movements, the vestibular apparatus and, possibly, the rotational movements reported for lucidity (LaBerge, 1980a). This relationship has been further investigated and partially supported in a recent sleep laboratory study (Leslie & Ogilvie, 1996).

Visual/Imaginal

The second functional domain discussed by Snyder and Gackenbach (1988) is the visual/imaginal domain. Included in this domain is spontaneous waking imagery, such as hallucinations, daydreams, hypnagogic imagery, and psychic phenomena, which is typically assessed with self-report questionnaires. Induced waking imagery, which is typically induced and evaluated within a laboratory setting, is most often assessed in terms of its vividness and controllability. Snyder and Gackenbach reached several tentative conclusions based on research in this domain. In terms of the spontaneous imaginal experiences, lucid dreaming frequency appears to be positively associated with the frequency with which sleep transition hallucinations, waking hallucinations, and daydreaming are experienced. Within the domain of experiences induced in the laboratory, an enhanced vividness of imagery across several sense modalities appears to be positively related to the experience of dream lucidity. They explained that "as the visualization tasks increase in spatial complexity and/or there is less need to rely on visual field referents for successful performance, lucid dreamers become distinguishable from persons who do not dream lucidly" (Snyder & Gackenback, 1988, pp. 243–244).

Snyder and Gackenbach (1988) distinguished between visual and nonvisual imagery ability, arguing that the former is unimportant, whereas the latter, in combination with internally oriented perspectives, is important to understanding lucidity, a point also made by Hunt (1989; 1995).

Several investigators have recently used measures that appear to fall into Snyder and Gackenbach's visual/imaginal domain. The often cited link between OBEs and lucidity was replicated by Glicksohn (1989; see Alvarado, this volume, chap. 6). Wolpin, Marston, Randolph, and Clothier (1992) reported an association between the vividness of waking imagery and the frequency of lucid dreams. Reported paranormal experiences (see Targ, Schlitz, & Irwin, this volume, chap. 7) and NDEs (Green, 1995; see Greyson, this volume, chap. 10) were found to be associated with lucid frequency by Usha and Pasricha (1989). Possibly facilitating the occurrence of these anomalous experiences is the ability for high absorption in imaginal events, which Spadafora and Hunt (1990) found to be associated with dream lucidity.

Intellectual/Creative

Considering the relationship of field independence to intelligence, a relationship between intelligence and lucidity ability might be expected. However, Snyder and Gackenbach's (1988) survey of the literature found the evidence inconclusive, partly because of poor experimental designs.

In subsequent research, Gruber et al. (1995) found no dreamer type differences in intelligence, as assessed by a subscale of the Cattell 16 Personality Factor (16PF) Questionnaire. However, Cranson (1989; Cranson et al., 1991) found a relationship between performance on a choice reaction time task, thought to measure a general form of intelligence, and witnessing dreams and sleep. Although content-specific measures of intelligence may not differentiate lucidity potential, a more global measure reflecting "refinement" of the nervous system might. In the same vein, Hunt (1995) viewed dream lucidity as one of several experiences that exemplify the "deep structure of a kind of intelligence that directly reuses and reorganizes the structures of perception" (p. 28). However, further inquiry is still required.

Creativity has been positively related to field independence and thus might be expected (or not, as above) to correlate with lucidity. Snyder and Gackenbach's (1988) review concluded that the creativity findings are consistent in indicating that female lucid dreamers differ from female nonlucid dreamers in terms of ability to solve certain types of nonverbal creative tasks. The results for male dreamers indicate no differential abilities. Recently, two investigations have been conducted on creativity and lucidity, with contradictory results. Although Blagrove and Tucker (1994) found no group differences on a self-report creativity measure, Brodsky, Esquerre, and Jackson (1990–1991) found that lucid dreamers performed better at a creative problem-solving task than nonlucid dreamers. As with the creativity data summarized by Snyder and Gackenbach, performance measures may be more sensitive to group differences in lucid dreaming ability than self-report measures.

Personal/Interpersonal

If lucid dreaming ability involves multiple functional systems working in concert on an organismic level, more frequent lucid dreamers might be expected to differ from less frequent lucid dreamers along a range of personal and interpersonal dimensions. Snyder and Gackenbach (1988) found that the better-designed demographic studies have generally found no gender differences in lucid dreaming frequency, whereas studies that failed to control for dream recall found such a difference. However, gender does interact with a variety of individual difference variables, as indicated in the discussion regarding field independence.

Snyder and Gackenbach (1988) found an association of high anxiety and high lucid frequency in men, and the converse for women. However, Gruber et al. (1995) found no difference in anxiety as a function of lucid dreaming frequency for women and a significant difference for men in the opposite direction of that found by Snyder and Gackenbach. Further research is required to clarify these apparently contradictory results.

Snyder and Gackenbach also concluded that introversion was associated with lucidity ability. Gruber et al. (1995) found no difference in introversion–extroversion as measured by the 16PF second-order scales, whereas others have reported an association to introversion using the Keirsey Temperament Sorter. The latter scale conceptualizes introversion–extroversion differently than the 16PF, as a tendency to focus on the inner or outer world.

Summary

The results on individual differences are complex and often contradictory. At this point, the lack of effect sizes makes it difficult to evaluate the often conflicting results; a meta-analysis is clearly needed. Despite extensive research, it has not been possible to find individual-difference variables that predict lucid dreaming ability better than, for example, dream recall does. Most of the studies reviewed above treated dream recall merely as a confounding variable, a covariate to be removed. A question for future research is whether the proportion of lucid dreams recalled is constant for individuals low and high in dream recall. Moreover, understanding the relationship between dream recall and lucid dreaming ability is made especially difficult by the fact that lucid dreams appear to be more memorable than nonlucid dreams.

Another problem with this type of research is that lucidity frequency can vary widely within the same individual. For example, over the course of 20 years, the frequency of lucid dreaming in one of the authors (LaBerge) has varied from several lucid dreams per night to less than one per month. Thus, the same person might fall into "frequent lucid dreamer" or "nonlucid dreamer" categories at different times because of factors such as motivation and energy.

PSYCHOPATHOLOGY

There is no indication from either the individual-differences literature or the clinical literature of any relationship between psychopathology and the ability to dream lucidly. In fact, where individual-difference correlations were significant, they tended to favor an association between lucidity and mental health (Snyder & Gackenbach, 1988). For instance, Gruber et al. (1995) concluded "that frequent lucid dreamers, characterized by the unusual degree of control they often exhibit within the dream state, are also better able to manage or control various aspects of cognitive, emotional, and social functioning while awake" (p. 7). Certainly, to the extent that lucid dreaming is an early manifestation of sleep witnessing, there is ample research to show its psychological benefits. Research to date on lucid dreaming that has focused on personality has not used many scales that measure psychopathology. In a subscale of the 16PF that measures neuroticism, no group differences were found between lucid and nonlucid individuals (see Snyder & Gackenbach, 1988). At present, there is little reason to believe that dreaming lucidly is more likely to cause psychopathology than dreaming nonlucidly.

CLINICAL ISSUES

We believe that lucid dreaming has considerable potential as a psychotherapeutic tool. Over a century ago, Hervey de Saint-Denys (1859/1982) used lucidity to cure himself of a terrifying recurrent nightmare:

> One night, ... when the dream returned for the fourth time, at the moment my persecutors were about to renew their pursuit, a feeling of the truth of the situation was suddenly awakened in my mind; and the desire to combat these illusions gave me the strength to overcome my instinctive terror. Instead of fleeing, ... I resolved to contemplate with the closest attention the phantoms that I had so far only glimpsed rather than seen. ... I fixed my eyes on my principal attacker, who somewhat resembled the grinning, bristling demons which are sculpted in cathedral porticos, and as the desire to observe gained the upper hand over my emotions, I saw the following: the fantastic monster had arrived within several feet of me, whistling and cavorting in a manner

which, once it had ceased to frighten me, appeared comic. I noted the claws on one of its paws, of which there were seven, very clearly outlined. The hairs of its eyebrows, a wound it appeared to have on its shoulder and innumerable other details combined in a picture of the greatest precision. ... The attention I had concentrated on this figure had caused its companions to disappear as if by magic. The figure itself seemed to slow down in its movements, lose its clarity and take on a woolly appearance, until it changed into a kind of floating bundle of rags ... and then I awoke. [The nightmare did not recur thereafter.] (pp. 58–59)

Tholey (1988) also observed that when the dreamer courageously and openly looks at hostile dream figures, their appearance often becomes less threatening. Indeed, the great majority of people say that, more often than not, becoming lucid in a nightmare makes them feel better afterward. In a survey study of 698 college students, Levitan and LaBerge (1990) found that 81% of the 505 volunteers who reported having had both lucid dreams and nightmares claimed that becoming lucid in a nightmare usually improved the outcome. Lucidity was about seven times more likely to make nightmares better than worse.

Based on his work on lucid dreaming for personal integration, Tholey (1988) listed four advantages of lucid, as opposed to nonlucid, dreams:

1. Because of the lucidity, the dream ego is less afraid of threatening dream figures or situations. For this reason, there is less resistance to confrontation with these figures or situations.
2. Using appropriate techniques for manipulating lucid dreaming, the dream ego can get in touch with places, times, situations, or persons that are important to the dreamer.
3. Especially in dialogue with other dream figures, the dream ego is able to recognize the present personality dynamics and their etiology (diagnostic function).
4. Through appropriate activity of the dream ego, a change of personality structure is possible (therapeutic or creative function). (p. 267)

Dane (1984) described such lucid dream work as *intrapersonal* psychotherapy, in which one's own waking and dreaming consciousnesses are used therapeutically, and Sattler (personal communication, 1991) argued that this approach is in some ways preferable to traditional interpersonal psychotherapy.

Tholey (1988) researched the effect of various attitudes toward hostile dream characters, concluding that a conciliatory approach, involving engaging in dialogues with hostile dream characters, is most likely to result in a positive outcome. He found that when dreamers tried to reconcile with hostile figures, the figures often transformed from lower order into higher order creatures, or from beasts or mythological beings into humans, and that these transformations frequently allowed the dreamers to immediately understand the meaning of their dreams. Furthermore, conciliatory behavior toward threatening figures generally causes the figures to look and act in a more friendly manner. For example, Tholey himself dreamed:

> I became lucid, while being chased by a tiger, and wanted to flee. I then pulled myself back together, stood my ground, and asked, "Who are you?" The tiger was taken aback but transformed into my father and answered, "I am your father and will now tell you what you are to do!" In contrast to my earlier dreams, I did not attempt to beat him but tried to get involved in a dialogue with him. I told him that he could not order me around. I rejected his threats and insults. On the other hand, I had to admit that some of my father's criticism was justified, and I decided to change my behavior accordingly. At that moment my father became friendly, and we shook hands. I asked him if he could help me, and he encouraged me to go my own way alone. My father then seemed to slip into my own body, and I remained alone in the dream. (Tholey, 1988, p. 265)

Several clinically oriented articles have appeared since Tholey's (1988) review. Hall and Brylowski (1991) compared lucid dreaming to the Jungian conception of active imagination. They pointed out that in lucid dreaming a symbolic statement is first produced, and then, when the dream ego takes a respectful attitude toward the symbol, a transformation can occur. They explained, "Both lucid dreaming and active imagination may be used to bypass personal resistances or defenses of rationalization. As a technique in psychotherapy, lucid dreaming may be particularly useful with borderline and with obsessive–compulsive patients" (p. 35). This interesting observation could be evaluated through controlled clinical outcome research with these types of patients.

Other therapeutic discussions include the integration of lucid dreaming and hypnotherapy (Klippstein, 1986) and a redefinition of psychoanalytic topographic theory of consciousness (Wolman, 1989). Most therapists have focused on the use of dream lucidity as a tool in nightmare management, understanding, and integration (Abramovitch, 1995; Brylowski, 1990; Evers & Van de Wetering, 1993; Galvin, 1993; Holzinger, 1995). Tholey (1988) also studied the use of lucid dreaming as a means of resolving unfinished business, such as in the case of the death of a loved one (see LaBerge & Rheingold, 1990, for examples).

Although there is no indication of a relationship between lucid dreaming and psychopathology, that does not mean that there may not be risks for unstable individuals in pursuing dream lucidity, just as there are risks for unstable individuals pursuing any activity, including nonlucid dreaming, and ordinary social life. Insofar as lucid dreaming is regarded as a form of meditation (Hunt, 1995), the clinical concerns regarding the practice of meditation might be relevant to the practice of lucid dreaming.

It seems prudent that one should use the lucid dream to work through personal issues before seeking spiritual "transcendence," a point that has been repeatedly emphasized by LaBerge (1985; LaBerge & Rheingold, 1990). All too many lucid dreamers, from van Eeden (see LaBerge, 1985, p. 175) on, who have prematurely sought to transcend the self before accepting the "shadow" (i.e., the destructive or undesirable aspects of the person) have experienced demonic nightmares (see also Gackenbach et al., 1992, 1995; Kelzer, 1987). The solution we propose is to strive for self-integration before self-transcendence (LaBerge, 1985; LaBerge & Rheingold, 1990). Studies that examine the nature and sequence (e.g., self-integration before self-transcendence) of lucid dream work would help establish or disconfirm clinical observations and insights regarding the role of lucid dreaming in psychotherapy and personal growth.

THEORIES

The major psychological and psychophysiological frameworks that have emerged to explain dream lucidity are briefly delineated in this section. A more detailed review of some of these theoretical perspectives can be found in Gackenbach (1991b) and in two books by Hunt (1989, 1995).

Psychological approaches have been taken by LaBerge (1985; LaBerge & Rheingold, 1990), Blackmore (1988), and Tart (1988), all of whom viewed lucid dreaming in terms of information processing. LaBerge viewed lucidity in sleep as primarily a cognitive skill, whereas Blackmore and Tart put more emphasis on a model of self-awareness. The theoretical work of Tholey (1988, 1989), from the German Gestalt school of psychology, is conceptually similar to an information-processing view. Related to these approaches is the conceptual work of Kahan and LaBerge (1994), who treated dream lucidity as a form of metacognition.

The importance of self in conceptualizing lucid dreaming is central to the work of Moffitt and colleagues (e.g., Purcell, Moffitt, & Hoffmann, 1993). Hunt (1989) conceptualized lucidity in sleep as one form of intensified dreaming along a self-reflectiveness dimension. Gackenbach's (1991a) perspective is developmental, beginning where Purcell et al. end (i.e., lucid dreaming) and argues that lucidity is merely a bridge to post–formal operation functioning within dreaming sleep. LaBerge (1985), however, disagreed with Gackenbach's assumption that dream witnessing is necessarily a more adaptive state of consciousness than fully lucid dreaming. In his view, the ideal is not to completely detach from the dream, but to be "*in* the dream, but not *of* it" (p. 107).

Psychophysiological perspectives on lucid dreaming include the work of

LaBerge (1980a; 1990), who showed that lucidity requires a relatively highly activated brain in REM sleep. Two psychophysiological models have been proposed connecting EEG and lucidity based on the assumption of an association of lucidity to meditation. Hunt and Ogilvie (1988) and Ogilvie et al. (1982) examined the relationship of lucidity to alpha power, whereas Gackenbach (1992) emphasized EEG coherence. Travis (1994) used both indices in his "junction point" model. Snyder and Gackenbach (1988, 1991) viewed lucidity from the framework of spatial skills, especially as implicated in vestibular system functioning. Globus (1993) considered the phenomenon in terms of chaos theory and neural networks.

LaBerge and DeGracia (in press) identified three distinct factors involved in lucid dreams, OBEs, and other related states: (a) a *reference-to-state*, the metacognitive recognition that one's current state of consciousness is different from one's usual waking state; (b) a *semantic framework*, the belief system used by the individual to conceptualize the nature of the experience; and (c) a *goal-options context*, containing actions used to induce such experiences or actions exercised within such experiences. In these terms, OBEs and lucid dreams share a common reference-to-state but differ in semantic frameworks and goal-options context.

Transpersonal psychology has also incorporated dream lucidity into its theoretical perspective (Walsh & Vaughan, 1993), drawing on lucidity's historical connection to a variety of religious perspectives, especially in the Tibetan Buddhist literature (Norbu & Katz, 1992; Gyatrul, 1993). Most of the empirical work connecting consciousness in sleep to the transpersonal perspective was done by Alexander and colleagues (1987). A recent study by this group, demonstrated that in meditators who report witnessing sleep half the night or more, the EEG associated with relaxed waking could be seen superimposed on the more characteristic EEG of deep sleep (Mason, 1995; Mason, Alexander, Travis, Gackenbach, Orme-Johnson, 1995).

Many of the approaches described above have been integrated by Hunt (1995), who placed dream lucidity within a range of consciousness experiences. According to Hunt, lucid dreaming, along with a few other key experiences, bridges contemporary cognitive views of consciousness and the transpersonal perspective.

> The cross cultural commonalities in hallucinatory geometric designs (Jung's mandala images), synesthesias, out-of-body imaginal states and lucid dreaming, and the 'white light' experiences of shamans and meditators seem to indicate that such nonverbal states have a common underlying structure. (p. 28)

A key idea in Hunt's (1995) thesis is the notion of cross-modal synesthesias as presymbolic in the development of cognition and thus at the heart of the white-light—type experiences characteristic of some mystical experiences and, at times, lucidity in sleep. Hunt argued that such experiences are neither regressions to infantile narcissism nor reducible to primitive cognitive mechanisms.

METHODOLOGICAL ISSUES

Developing an appropriate methodology for the study of such phenomena as mental imagery, hallucinations, dreaming, and conscious processes in general requires solving a number of significant problems. Although subjective reports provide the most direct accounts of the contents of consciousness, they are difficult to verify objectively, and introspection is far from an unbiased, direct, or error-free process of observation.

There are several strategies available to increase our confidence in the reliability of subjective reports of lucidity (see also Pekala & Cardeña, this volume, chap. 2). First, Snyder and Gackenbach (1988) emphasized the importance of verifying that participants understand the concept of lucidity by requiring the inclusion of a recognition phrase in a sample lucid dream report (i.e., " ... and then I realized I was dreaming"). This procedure is especially important in large survey work, because in research up to 50% of volunteers have been discarded when this criterion has been used. Another empirical necessity in survey work comparing lucid to nonlucid dreamers or dreams is controlling for dream recall given the fact that high dream recall has been shown to be by far the strongest single predictor of lucid dreaming ability in untrained participants (Snyder & Gackenbach, 1988).

Another approach would be to use highly trained (and in the context of dream research, lucid) volunteers who are skillful and accurate observers of their consciousness. In addition, one can use psychophysiological methodology, because the convergent agreement of physiological measures and subjective reports provides a degree of validation to the latter (Stoyva & Kamiya, 1968).

As noted, psychophysiological methodology has been essential to the laboratory study of lucid dreaming. More broadly, the psychophysiological approach was also responsible for the explosion of dream research following the discovery of REM sleep (Aserinsky & Kleitman, 1953) and the subsequent association of REM with dreaming (Dement & Kleitman, 1957). Although the standard psychophysiological paradigm of dream research yielded fruitful results for many years (see Arkin, Antrobus, & Ellman, 1978), it possessed an important deficiency: There was no way of making certain that participants (assuming they were nonlucid) would actually dream about what the researchers were interested in studying. Presleep manipulations producing predictable and reliable effects on dream content have not been very effective (Tart, 1988). Thus, researchers could only wait and hope that eventually a dream report would turn up with what one was looking for. This was really no better than a "shot-in-the-dark" approach; for this and other reasons, some dream researchers had advocated abandoning the psychophysiological method in favor of a purely psychological approach. For example, Foulkes (1980) claimed that "psychophysiological correlation research now appears to offer such a low rate of return for effort expended as not to be a wise place for dream psychology to continue to commit much of its limited resources" (p. 249). This conclusion may well be justified, but only insofar as it refers to the psychophysiological approach as traditionally practiced, using nonlucid participants. The use of lucid dreamers overcomes the basic difficulty of the old methodology and may revitalize the psychophysiological approach to dream research.

Although eye movement signaling clearly is an important and useful methodology, it is not without its problems. For example, moving one's gaze from side to side obviously affects what one sees in the dream, sometimes disrupting the visual imagery enough to cause an awakening. Moreover, eye movement signals of any complexity are not easily executed or reliably distinguished on the polygraph record.

Other types of signals, such as finger movements monitored by the "data-glove" technology used in virtual reality devices, might be less disruptive and also capable of transmitting information more rapidly and efficiently than more conventional modes of signaling. It might be possible for lucid dreamers to communicate by means of hand gestures similar to sign language, allowing "on-the-scene" reports from the dream world.

Several researchers have used qualitative methods to study lucidity (Gackenbach et al., 1992), generally single-case studies, although quantitative methods have been applied in case studies (Gackenbach et al., 1995; Gillespie, 1988). The advantage of the qualitative approach is that it allows "sensitizing" concepts (aspects of the narrative that seem best to characterize it) to emerge from the material somewhat independent of the expectations of the investigator.

Qualitative methods also allow more sensitivity to the context in which the experience occurs. In work on the central Alberta Cree Indians (Gackenbach, 1995; Gackenbach & Kuiken, 1995; Gackenbach & Prince, 1992), lucid dream content emerged in the diary and interview materials, but it was the context, as associated with other transpersonal dream themes, that was most important to understanding them. In one series of intensive interviews with a Cree dream counselor, it became clear to Gackenbach (1992–1993) that although nominal lucidity was common, it was also superfluous to the Cree understanding of the importance of dreams. This interpretation would not have emerged in a purely quantitative inquiry, in which only the counselor's remarkable high incidence would have been noted or, perhaps, completely missed, because it took many conversations before the counselor even began to understand the language used to describe lucidity.

CONCLUSION

A parallel can be drawn (LaBerge, 1990) between the initially anomalous appearance of lucid dreaming and the state that has been called *paradoxical sleep* (i.e., REM sleep). The discovery of REM sleep, with its many anomalous characteristics (e.g., highly activated brain, autonomic nervous system variability, and muscle atonia) required the expansion of the concept of sleep. The evidence relating lucid dreaming to REM sleep reviewed above would seem to require a similar expansion of the concept of dreaming and a clarification of the concept of sleep: Lucid dreaming may well prove the most anomalous feature of paradoxical sleep.

Fenwick et al. (1984) showed that a participant was able to perceive and respond to environmental stimuli (electrical shocks) without awakening from his lucid dream. This result raises a theoretical issue: If we accept perception of the external world as the essential criterion for wakefulness (LaBerge, Nagel, Dement, & Zarcone, 1981), then we are forced to conclude that the volunteer must have been at least partially awake. On the other hand, when environmental stimuli are incorporated into dreams without producing any subjective or physiological indications of arousal, it appears reasonable to speak of the perception as having occurred during sleep.

Furthermore, it may be possible, as LaBerge (1980a) suggested, for one sense to remain functional and awake while others fall asleep. Similarly, Antrobus et al. (1965) argued that the simple question "asleep or awake?" may not have a simple answer:

> Not only do sleeping and waking shade gradually into one another but there is only limited agreement among the various physiological and subjective operations that discriminate between sleeping and waking. At any given moment, all systems of the organism are not necessarily equally asleep or awake. (pp. 398–399)

LaBerge (1990) summed up the situation as follows:

> As long as we continue to consider wakefulness and sleep as a simple dichotomy, we will lie in a Procrustean bed that is bound at times to be most uncomfortable. There must be degrees of being awake just as there are degrees of being asleep (i.e. the conventional sleep stages). Before finding our way out of this muddle, we will probably need to characterize a wider variety of states of consciousness than those few currently distinguished (e.g. "dreaming," "sleeping," "waking," and so on). (pp. 121–122)

In the context of the present chapter, the list must clearly include such anomalies of sleep as lucid dreaming, witnessing dreaming, witnessing sleep, and OBEs.

Lucid dreaming is an experience ideally situated to cast light on a range of states of consciousness, both ordinary and anomalous. Further work needs to be done in a variety of areas, including developing techniques for having and optimally making use of lucid dreams, improving the understanding of the phenomenology and neuroscience underlying the experience, and elucidating the individual differences associated with the spontaneous emergence and talent for developing lucidity.

A relatively neglected area of great interest is the relationship between the body of knowledge surveyed in this chapter and the extensive Tibetan Buddhist experiences with lucid dream yoga (Gyatrul, 1993; Norbu & Katz, 1992). As has been seen above, Western scientists have been studying lucid dreaming for little more than 20 years. In contrast, the Tibetan Buddhists have practiced a form of lucid dreaming known as "the yoga of the dream state" for more than a thousand years. Thus, Western science could clearly benefit from a study of dream yoga.

The Tibetan Buddhists' point of view reverses the order of valuation of the waking and dreaming states. Whereas Westerners consider the waking state the only reality and dreams to be unreal and unimportant, Buddhists believe the dream state to have greater potential for understanding and spiritual progress than the so-called waking state, and both states to be equally real or unreal. In addition, according to Tibetan lore, the practice of yoga provides essential preparation for the dreamlike after-death state, allowing the yogi to become illuminated at the point of death or to choose a favorable rebirth (Gyatrul, 1993).

The Tibetan dream yoga consists of four stages (Evans-Wentz, 1958): (a) comprehending the nature of the dream (i.e., that it is a dream and thus, a construction of the mind); (b) practicing the transformation of dream content until one experientially understands that all of the contents of dreaming consciousness can be changed by will and that dreams are essentially unstable; (c) realizing that the sensory experiences of waking consciousness are just as illusory as dreams and that, in a sense, "it's all a dream"; and (d) meditating on the "thatness" of the dream state, which results in union with a "clear light."

The first three stages all find parallels in the experiences of Western lucid dreamers and current constructionist psychological theories of mind. It is not yet clear to what extent the fourth stage can be studied by current scientific methodology.

Tibetan Buddhists and a number of other specialists in "inner states" (e.g., Rudolf Steiner, Sri Aurobindo, Ibn El-Arabi, to name a few; see LaBerge, 1985, for details) regard achieving continuity of consciousness among waking, dreaming, and dreamless sleep as an essential step to higher personal development. Studying conscious transitions among these three states seems an extremely promising area of investigation.

REFERENCES

Abramovitch, H. (1995). The nightmare of returning home: A case of acute onset nightmare disorder treated by lucid dreaming. *Israel Journal of Psychiatry and Related Sciences, 32,* 140–145.

Alexander, C. (1987). Dream lucidity and dream witnessing: A developmental model based on the practice of transcendental meditation. *Lucidity Letter, 6*(2), 113–124.

Alexander, C., Boyer, R., & Alexander, V. (1987). Higher states of consciousness in the Vedic psychology of Maharishi Mahesh Yogi: A theoretical introduction and research review. *Modern Science and Vedic Science, 1,* 89–126.

Alexander, C., Boyer, R., & Orme-Johnson, D. (1985). Distinguishing between transcendental consciousness and lucidity. *Lucidity Letter, 4*(2), 68–85.

Alexander, C., Davies, J. L., Dixon, C. A., Dillbeck, M. C., Oetzel, R. M., Muehlman, J. M., & Orme-Johnson, D. W. (1990). Growth of higher stages of consciousness: Maharishi's Vedic psychology of human development. In C. Alexander & E. J. Langer (Eds.), *Higher stages of human development: Perspectives on adult growth* (pp. 286–341). New York: Oxford University Press.

Alexander, C., Heaton, D. P., & Chandler, H. M. (1994). Advanced human development in the Vedic psychology of Maharishi Mahesh Yogi: Theory and research. In M. E. Miller & S. R. Cook-Greuter (Eds.), *Transcendence and mature thought in adulthood: The further reaches of adult development* (pp. 39–70). London: Rowman & Littlefield.

Antrobus, J. S., Antrobus, J. S., & Fisher, C. (1965). Discrimination of dreaming and nondreaming sleep. *Archives of General Psychiatry, 12,* 395–401.

Aserinsky, E., & Kleitman, N. (1955). Regularly occurring periods of eye motility and concomitant phenomena during sleep. *Science, 118,* 273–274.

Arkin, A. M., Antrobus, J. S., & Ellman, S. J. (1978). *The mind in sleep: Psychology and psychophysiology.* Hillsdale, NJ: Erlbaum.

Baars, B.J. (1988). *A cognitive theory of consciousness.* Cambridge, England: Cambridge University Press.

Barrett, D. (1992). Just how lucid are lucid dreams? *Dreaming: Journal of the Association for the Study of Dreams, 2,* 221–228.

Berger, R. (1977). *Psyclosis: The circularity of experience.* San Francisco: Freeman.

Blackmore, S. (1988). A theory of lucid dreams and OBEs. In J. Gackenbach & S. LaBerge (Eds.), *Conscious mind, sleeping brain* (pp. 373–387). New York:. Plenum.

Blagrove, M., & Tucker, M. (1994). Individual differences in locus of control and the reporting of lucid dreaming. *Personality and individual differences, 16,* 981–984.

Brodsky, S. L., Esquerre, J., & Jackson, R. R. (1990–1991). Dream consciousness in problem solving. *Imagination, Cognition, and Personality, 10,* 353–360.

Brylowski, A. (1990). Nightmares in crisis: Clinical applications of lucid dreaming techniques. *Psychiatric Journal of the University of Ottawa, 15*(2), 79–84.

Brylowski, A., Levitan, L., & LaBerge, S. (1989). H-reflex suppression and autonomic activation during lucid REM sleep: A case study. *Sleep, 12,* 374–378.

Cranson, R. (1989). *A Vedic perspective on intelligence.* Unpublished doctoral dissertation, Maharishi International University, Fairfield, IA.

Cranson, R. W., Orme-Johnson, D., Gackenbach, J., Dillbeck, M. C., Jones, C. H., & Alexander, C. (1991). Transcendental meditation and improved performance on intelligence-related measures: A longitudinal study. *Personality and Individual Differences, 12,* 1105–1116.

Dane, J. (1984). *An empirical evaluation of two techniques for lucid dream induction.* Unpublished doctoral dissertation, Georgia State University, Atlanta.

De Becker, R. (1965). *The understanding of dreams.* New York: Bell.

Dement, W., & Kleitman, N. (1957). Cyclic variations in EEG during sleep and their relation to eye movements, body motility, and dreaming. *Electroencephalography & clinical neurophysiology, 9,* 673–690.

Evans-Wentz, W. Y. (Ed.). (1958). *Tibetan yoga and secret doctrines.* London: Oxford University Press.

Evers, R. A., & Van de Wetering, B. J. (1993). Lucid dreams. *Tijdschrift voor Psychiatrie, 35,* 651–660.

Fenwick, P., Schatzman, M., Worsley, A., Adams, J., Stone, S., & Baker, A. (1984). Lucid dreaming: Correspondence between dreamed and actual events in one subject during REM sleep. *Biological Psychology, 18,* 243–252.

Foulkes, D. (1974). Review of Schwartz and Lefebvre (1973). *Sleep Research, 3,* 113.

Foulkes, D. (1980). Dreams and dream research. In W. Koella (Ed.), *Sleep 1980* (pp. 246–257). Basel, Switzerland: Karger.

Fox, O. (1962). *Astral projection.* New Hyde Park, NY: University Books.

Freud, S. (1965). *The interpretation of dreams.* New York: Avon Books. (Original work published 1900)

Gackenbach, J. (1985–1986). A survey of considerations for inducing conscious awareness of dreaming while dreaming. *Imagination, Cognition and Personality, 5,* 41–55.

Gackenbach, J. (1988). The psychological content of lucid versus nonlucid dreams. In J. Gackenbach & S. LaBerge (Eds.), *Conscious mind, sleeping brain: Perspectives on lucid dreaming* (pp. 181–220). New York: Plenum.

Gackenbach, J. (1990). Women and mediators as gifted lucid dreamers. In S. Krippner (Ed.), *Dreamtime and dreamwork.* Los Angeles, CA: Tarcher.

Gackenbach, J. (1991a). A developmental model of consciousness in sleep: From sleep consciousness to pure consciousness. In J. Gackenbach & A. A. Sheikh (Eds.), *Dream images: A call to mental arms* (pp. 265–308). Amityville, NY: Baywood.

Gackenbach, J. (1991b). Frameworks for understanding lucid dreaming: A review. *Dreaming, 1*, 109–128.

Gackenbach, J. (1992). Interhemispheric EEG coherence in REM sleep and meditation: The lucid dreaming connection. In J. Antrobus (Ed.), *The neuropsychology of dreaming sleep* (pp. 265–288). Hillsdale, NJ: Erlbaum.

Gackenbach, J. (1992–1993). Adaptiveness of childhood transpersonal experiences in two Cree women: A study. *Lucidity, 11*, 107–122.

Gackenbach, J. (1995). Reflections on dreamwork with central Alberta Cree: An essay on an unlikely social action vehicle. In K. Bulkeley (Ed.), *Among all these dreamers: Essays on dreaming and modern society* (pp. 51–71). Albany, NY: SUNY Press.

Gackenbach, J., Allen, N., Barth, M., Blades, M., Boorse, S., Corcoran, C., Davidson, D., Dunkle, A., Ellitt, E., Engel, L., Gordash, B., Gupta, A., Hewitt, R., Hillman, C., Hink, V., Jansen, B., Lee, B., Listener, W., Mastel, J., Morrison, K., Nelson, C., Owen, W., Robinson, D., Shouldice, J., Traeger, A., Tiller, B., Witwer, S., & Woodman, P. (1995, June). *The dream diary of a Catholic monk priest: Otherworldly origins or personal angst?* Paper presented at the 12th Annual Meeting of the Association for the Study of Dreams, New York City.

Gackenbach, J., Andrew, C., Marean, M., Massimo, L., Worth, M., Burnstad, L., Hemingson, A., Mayan, M., Zhang, X., Crump, H., Lee, C. T., Owen, M., & Percy, F. (1992, June). *From OBE to lucid to nonlucid: A qualitative dream diary analysis.* Paper presented at the 10th Annual Meeting of the Association for the Study of Dreams, University of California, Santa Cruz.

Gackenbach, J., & Kuiken, D. (1995, June). *Transpersonal and personal realizations in dreams: Native and non-native differences.* Paper presented at the 12th annual meeting of the Association for the Study of Dreams, New York.

Gackenbach, J., & Prince, W. (1992, June). *Dreams and autobiographical experiences from Alberta natives and nonnatives.* Paper presented at the 10th annual meeting of the Association for the Study of Dreams, University of California, Santa Cruz.

Galvin, F. J. (1993). The effects of lucid dream training upon the frequency and severity of nightmares. *Dissertation Abstracts International, 54*(3-B), 1665–1666.

Garfield, P. (1979). *Pathway to ecstasy.* New York: Holt, Rhinehart & Winston.

Gillespie, G. (1988). Lucid dreams in Tibetan Buddhism. In J. Gackenbach & S. LaBerge (Eds.), *Conscious mind, sleeping brain: Perspectives on lucid dreaming* (pp. 27–35). New York: Plenum.

Glicksohn, J. (1989). The structure of subjective experience: Interdependencies among the sleep–wakefulness continuum. *Journal of Mental Imagery, 13*, 99–106.

Globus, G. (1993). Connectionism and sleep. In A. Moffitt, M. Kramer, & R. Hoffman (Eds.), *The functions of dreaming* (pp. 113–138). Albany: State University of New York.

Green, C. (1968). *Lucid dreams.* London: Hamish Hamilton.

Green, J. T. (1995). Lucid dreams as one method of replicating components of the near-death experience in a laboratory setting. *Journal of Near-Death Studies, 14*(1), 49–59.

Gruber, R. E., Steffen, J. J., & Vonderhaar, S. P. (1995). Lucid dreaming, waking personality, and cognitive development. *Dreaming: Journal of the Association for the Study of Dreams, 5*(1), 1–12.

Gyatrul R. (1993). *Ancient wisdom: Nyingma teachings on dream yoga, meditation, and transformation.* (B. A. Wallace & S. Khandro, Trans.). New York: Snow Lion.

Hall, C. S., & Van de Castle, R. L. (1966). *The content analysis of dreams,* New York: Appleton-Century-Crofts.

Hall, J. A. (1977). Clinical uses of dreams. New York: Grune & Stratton.

Hall, J. A., & Brylowski, A. (1991). Lucid dreaming and active imagination: Implications for Jungian therapy. *Quadrant, 24*(1), 35–43.

Hartmann, E. (1975). Dreams and other hallucinations: An approach to the underlying mechanism. In R. K. Siegel & L. J. West (Eds.), *Hallucinations* (pp. 71–79). New York: Wiley.

Hearne, K. M. T. (1978). *Lucid dreams: An electrophysiological and psychological study.* Unpublished doctoral dissertation, University of Liverpool, Liverpool, England.

Holzinger, B. (1995, June). *Lucid dreaming as a tool in psychotherapy.* Paper presented at the 12th Annual Meeting of the Association for the Study of Dreams, New York City.

Hunt, H. T. (1989). *The multiplicity of dreams: Memory, imagination, and consciousness.* New Haven, CT: Yale University Press.

Hunt, H. T. (1995). *On the nature of consciousness: Cognitive, phenomenological, and transpersonal perspectives.* New Haven, CT: Yale University Press.

Hunt, H. T., & Ogilvie, R. D. (1988). Lucid dreams in their natural series: Phenomenological and psychophysiological findings in relation to meditative states. In J. Gackenbach & S. LaBerge (Eds.), *Conscious mind, sleeping brain* (pp. 389–417). New York: Plenum.

Irwin, H. (1988). Out-of-body experiences and dream lucidity. In J. Gackenbach & S. LaBerge (Eds.), *Conscious mind, sleeping brain* (pp. 353–371). New York: Plenum.

Kahan, T. L., & LaBerge, S. (1994). Lucid dreaming as metacognition: Implications for cognitive science. *Consciousness and Cognition, 3,* 246–264.

Kelzer, K. (1987). *The sun and the shadow: My experiment with lucid dreaming.* Virginia Beach, VA: A.R.E. Press.

Klippstein, H. (1986). Hypnotic and lucid dreams. *Hypnose und Kognition, 3*(2), 66–70.

Kuiken, D., & Sikora, S. (1993). The effects of impactful dreams on waking thoughts and feelings. In A. Moffitt, M. Kramer, & R. Hoffmann (Eds.), *The functions of dreaming* (pp. 419–476). Albany, NY: SUNY Press.

LaBerge, S. (1980a). *Lucid dreaming: An exploratory study of consciousness during sleep.* Unpublished doctoral dissertation, Stanford University, CA.

LaBerge, S. (1980b). Lucid dreaming as a learnable skill: A case study. *Perceptual and Motor Skills, 51,* 1039–1042.

LaBerge, S. (1981). Healing through lucid dreaming. *The Holmes Center Research Reporter, 5,* 2–3.

LaBerge, S. (1985). *Lucid dreaming.* Los Angeles: Tarcher.

LaBerge, S. (1988). The psychophysiology of lucid dreaming. In J. Gackenbach & S. LaBerge (Eds.), *Conscious mind, sleeping brain: Perspectives on lucid dreaming* (pp. 135–153). New York: Plenum.

LaBerge, S. (1990). Lucid dreaming: Psychophysiological studies of consciousness during REM sleep. In R. R. Bootsen, J. F. Kihlstrom, & D. L. Schacter (Eds.), *Sleep and cognition* (pp. 109–126). Washington, DC: American Psychological Association.

LaBerge, S., & DeGracia, D. J. (in press). Varieties of lucid dreaming experience. In R. G. Kunzendorf & B. Wallace (Eds.), *Individual differences in conscious experience.* Philadelphia: Benjamins.

LaBerge, S., & Dement, W. C. (1982a). Lateralization of alpha activity for dreamed singing and counting during REM sleep. *Psychophysiology, 19,* 331–332.

LaBerge, S., & Dement, W. C. (1982b). Voluntary control of respiration during REM sleep. *Sleep Research, 11,* 107.

LaBerge, S., Greenleaf, W., & Kedzierski, B. (1983). Physiological responses to dreamed sexual activity during lucid REM sleep. *Psychophysiology, 20,* 454–455.

LaBerge, S., & Levitan, L. (1995). Validity established of DreamLight cues for eliciting lucid dreaming. *Dreaming, 5,* 159–168.

LaBerge, S., Levitan, L., Brylowski, A., & Dement, W. (1988). "Out-of-body" experiences occurring during REM sleep. *Sleep Research, 17,* 115.

LaBerge, S., Levitan, L., & Dement, W. (1986). Lucid dreaming: Physiological correlates of consciousness during REM sleep. *Journal of Mind and Behavior, 7,* 251–258.

LaBerge, S., Nagel, L., Dement, W., & Zarcone, V. (1981). Lucid dreaming verified by volitional communication during REM sleep. *Perceptual and Motor Skills, 52,* 727–732.

LaBerge, S., Nagel, L., Taylor, W., Dement, W. C., & Zarcone, V., Jr. (1981). Psychophysiological correlates of the initiation of lucid dreaming. *Sleep Research, 10,* 149.

LaBerge, S., Phillips, L., & Levitan, L. (1994). An hour of wakefulness before morning naps makes lucidity more likely. *NightLight, 6*(3), 1–5.

LaBerge, S., & Rheingold, H. (1990). *Exploring the world of lucid dreaming.* New York: Ballantine.

Leslie, K. & Ogilvie, R. (1996). Vestibular dreams: Effects of rocking on dream mentation. *Dreaming: Journal of the Association for the Study of Dreams, 6*(1), 1–16.

Levitan, L., & LaBerge, S. (1990). Beyond nightmares: Lucid resourcefulness vs helpless depression. *NightLight, 2*(4), 1–6.

Levitan, L., & LaBerge, S. (1993). Day life, night life: How waking and dreaming experiences relate. *NightLight, 5*(1), 4–6.

Levitan, L., LaBerge, S., DeGracia, D. J., & Zimbardo, P. G. (1999). Out-of-body experiences, dreams, and REM sleep. *Sleep and Hypnosis, 1,* 187–197.

Malcolm, N. (1959). *Dreaming.* London: Routledge.

Mason, L. I. (1995). *Electrophysiological correlates of higher states of consciousness during sleep.* Unpublished doctoral dissertation, Maharishi International University, Fairfield, IA.

Mason, L., Alexander, C. N., Travis, F., Gackenbach, J., & Orme-Johnson, D. (1995). EEG correlates of "higher states of consciousness" during sleep. *Sleep Research, 24,* 152.

Moers-Messmer, H. von. (1938). Träume mit der gleichzeitigen erkenntnis des traumzustandes [Dreams with simultaneous cognizance of the dream state]. *Archiv für Psychologie, 102,* 291–318.

Norbu, N., & Katz, M. (1992). *Dream yoga and the practice of natural light.* New York: Snow Lion.

Ogilvie, R., Hunt, H., Kushniruk, A., & Newman, J. (1983). Lucid dreams and the arousal continuum. *Sleep Research, 12,* 182.

Ogilvie, R., Hunt, H., Sawicki, C., & McGowan, K. (1978). Searching for lucid dreams. *Sleep Research, 7,* 165.

Ogilvie, R., Hunt, H., Tyson, P. D., Lucescu, M. L., & Jeakins, D. B. (1982). Lucid dreaming and alpha activity: A preliminary report. *Perceptual and Motor Skills, 55,* 795–808.

Price, R., & Cohen D. (1988). Lucid dream induction: An empirical evaluation. In J. Gackenbach & S. LaBerge (Eds.), *Conscious mind, sleeping brain* (pp. 105–134). New York: Plenum.

Purcell, S., Moffitt, A., & Hoffmann, R. (1993). Waking, dreaming, and self-regulation. In A. Moffitt, M. Kramer, & R. Hoffmann (Eds.), *The functions of dreaming* (pp. 197–260). Albany: State University of New York Press.

Rechtschaffen, A. (1978). The single-mindedness and isolation of dreams. *Sleep, 1,* 97–109.

Roffwarg, H., Dement, W. C., Muzio, J., & Fisher, C. (1962). Dream imagery: Relationship to rapid eye movements of sleep. *Archives of General Psychiatry, 7,* 235–238.

Rossi, E. (1972). *Dreams and the growth of personality: Expanding awareness in psychotherapy.* New York: Brunner/Mazel.

Saint-Denys, H. (1982). *Dreams and how to guide them.* London: Duckworth. (Original work published 1859)

Schwartz, B. A., & Lefebvre, A. (1973). Contacts veille/P.M.O: II. Les P.M.O.

morcelees [Conjunction of waking and REM sleep: II. Fragmented REM periods]. *Revue d'Electroencephalographie et de Neurophysiologie Clinique, 3,* 165–176.

Snyder, T. J., & Gackenbach, J. (1988). Individual differences associated with lucid dreaming. In J. Gackenbach & S. LaBerge (Eds.), *Conscious mind, sleeping brain: Perspectives on lucid dreaming* (pp. 221–260). New York: Plenum.

Snyder, T. J., & Gackenbach, J. (1991). Vestibular involvement in the neurocognition of lucid dreaming. In J. Gackenbach & A. A. Sheikh (Eds.), *Dream images: A call to mental arms* (pp. 55–78). Amityville, NY: Baywood.

Spadafora, A., & Hunt, H. T. (1990, October). The multiplicity of dreams: Cognitive–affective correlates of lucid, archetypal, and nightmare dreaming. *Perceptual & Motor Skills, 71*(2), 627–644.

Stoyva, J., & Kamiya, J. (1968). Electrophysiological studies of dreaming as the prototype of a new strategy in the study of consciousness. *Psychological Review, 75,* 192–205.

Tart, C. (1988). From spontaneous event to lucidity: A review of attempts to consciously control nocturnal dreaming. In J. Gackenbach & S. LaBerge (Eds.), *Conscious mind, dreaming brain* (pp. 67–103). New York: Plenum.

Tholey, P. (1988). A model for lucidity training as a means of self-healing and psychological growth. In J. Gackenbach & S. LaBerge (Eds.), *Conscious mind, sleeping brain* (pp. 263–287). New York: Plenum.

Tholey, P. (1989). Consciousness and the ability of dream figures observed during lucid dreaming. *Perceptual & Motor Skills, 68,* 567–578.

Travis, F. T. (1994). The junction point model: A field model of waking, sleeping and dreaming, relating dream witnessing, the waking/sleeping transition, and transcendental meditation in terms of a common psychophysiological state. *Dreaming: Journal of the Association for the Study of Dreams, 4*(2), 91–104.

Usha, S., Pasricha, S. (1989, July). Claims of paranormal experiences: II. Attitudes toward psychical research and factors associated with psi and psi-related experiences. *NIMHANS Journal, 7*(2), 151–157.

Van Eeden, F. (1913). A study of dreams. *Proceedings of the Society for Psychical Research, 26,* 431–461.

Walsh, R., & Vaughan, F. (1993). Lucid dreaming: Some transpersonal implications. *Journal of Professional Psychology, 24,* 193–200.

Whiteman, J. H. M. (1961). *The mystical life.* London: Faber & Faber.

Wolman, B. B. (1989). The protoconscious. *Dynamische Psychiatrie, 22*(1–2), 22–30.

Wolpin, M., Marston, A., Randolph, C., & Clothier, A. (1992). Individual difference correlates of reported lucid dreaming frequency and control. *Journal of Mental Imagery, 16,* 231–236.

Worsley, A. (1988). Personal experience in lucid dreaming. In J. Grackenbach & S. LaBerge (Ed.), *Conscious mind, sleeping brain* (pp. 321–341). New York: Plenum.

6

OUT-OF-BODY EXPERIENCES

CARLOS S. ALVARADO

In an out-of-body experience (OBE), people feel that their "self," or center of awareness, is located outside of the physical body. The experients' reported perceptions are organized in such a way as to be consistent with this perspective and include such features as sensations of floating, traveling to distant locations, and observing the physical body from a distance. The following examples illustrate OBEs.

A 36-year-old American police officer from California wrote the following in reply to a question in one of my studies. On her first night on patrol, she pursued an armed suspect. "When I and three other officers stopped the vehicle and started getting [to] the suspect ... I was afraid. I promptly went out of my body and up into the air maybe 20 feet above the scene. I remained there, extremely calm, while I watched the entire procedure—including watching myself do exactly what I had been trained to do." Suddenly, she found herself back in her body after the suspect had been subdued.

This chapter was written with financial support from the Institut für Grenzgebiete der Psychologie und Psychohygiene (Freiburg, Germany). I am grateful to Rhea A. White for providing me with copies of numerous papers used in this chapter. Harvey J. Irwin offered many suggestions for the improvement of the chapter. Thanks are also due to Nancy L. Zingrone for editorial suggestions and for assistance with the statistical analyses reported here.

A Scottish woman wrote that, when she was 32 years old, she had an OBE while training for a marathon. "After running approximately 12–13 miles . . . I started to feel as if I wasn't looking through my eyes but from somewhere else. . . . I felt as if something was leaving my body, and although I was still running along looking at the scenery, I was looking at myself running as well. My 'soul' or whatever, was floating somewhere above my body high enough up to see the tops of the trees and the small hills.

There is some confusion in the determination of whether or not an experience counts as an OBE. Both Hart (1954) and Tart (1974) have emphasized the differences between those experiences in which the person has the somaesthetic sense of being located outside of the body (i.e., OBEs) and those other experiences in which a sense of separation from the body is not present or is unclear. In the latter sense, autoscopy, depersonalization, and other experiences reported by patients with temporal lobe epilepsy or other disorders do not qualify as OBEs. This is not to say that OBEs, which include a shifting of the sense of awareness to an exterior location, have not been reported by people who have these disorders (e.g., Brugger, Agosti, Regard, Wieser, & Landis, 1994; Green, 1968, p. 124; Steinberg, 1995). My point is rather that an experience must include the exteriorization of perceptual locus to be classified as an OBE.

Although an OBE may occur in persons who are close to death, this does not mean that this type of OBE is necessarily a near-death experience (NDE; see Greyson, this volume, chap. 10). Irwin (1985a) said, "The NDE is not simply a variety of the OBE: the former has additional facets which give it status as an experiential syndrome in its own right" (p. 12).

Descriptions of OBEs can be found in several case collections (e.g., Crookall, 1961, 1964, 1972, 1978; Green, 1968; Muldoon, 1936; Muldoon & Carrington, 1951) and in the autobiographical writings of those who claim to have the ability to induce the experience at will or who have had many spontaneous OBEs (e.g., Fox, 1939; Harary, 1978; Monroe, 1971; Muldoon & Carrington, 1929; Peterson, 1997; Vieira, 1995).

Recent writings have popularized OBEs that have occurred close to death, but they have also been reported under ordinary conditions and during illness, stress, meditation, hypnosis, and by voluntary induction. Although there is a long history of interest in and study of this phenomenon (Alvarado, 1989, 1992), it is only recently that systematic research has been conducted.

Questionnaire studies provide an estimate of how common OBEs are, although they suffer from certain methodological ambiguities that are discussed later. In the meantime, I discuss some trends in the literature, summarized in Figure 6.1.

Representative surveys of the general population have obtained a much lower prevalence of OBEs than surveys that have sampled either

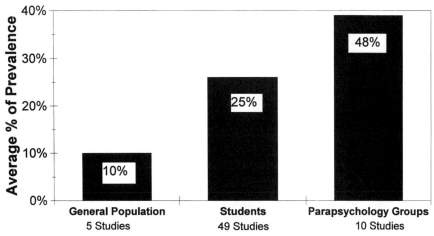

Figure 6.1. Average prevalence of out-of-body experiences in three different groups. Most of the studies used in these analyses are listed by Alvarado (1986a) and by Irwin (1985a, pp. 174–175). Additional studies include students, Alvarado and Zingrone (1997a, 1997b); Brelaz de Castro (1998); Chadha, Sahni, and Alvarado (1987); Clarke (1995); Glicksohn (1989, 1990); Irwin, 1996; McClenon, 1990; Pekala, Cumar, and Cummings (1992); Pekala, Kumar, and Marcano (1995); Severi (1995); Spanos and Moretti (1988); Stanford (1987); Tobacyk, Wells, and Miller (1998); Usha and Pasricha (1989a); Zangari and Machado (1996); and parapsychology-related groups, Alvarado and Zingrone (1999); Glicksohn (1990); Richards (1988, 1991); and Thalbourne (1994).

college students or individuals with a particular interest in parapsychological phenomena (see Targ, Schlitz, & Irwin, this volume, chap. 7). This finding is not surprising, in that many people join parapsychologically oriented interest groups primarily to share such experiences and to try to understand them. High prevalences of OBEs have also been obtained from other special samples, among them, people with schizophrenia (42%, Blackmore, 1986a), individuals highly prone to fantasy (88%, Wilson & Barber, 1983), individuals who are highly hypnotizable (Cardeña, 1988), and people who use marijuana (44%, Tart, 1971).

At this point, it is difficult to explain why student populations report more OBEs than do members of the general population. Palmer (1979a) suggested that higher use of mind-altering drugs among students may provide one answer. However, there is no evidence that the majority of college students who report OBEs experienced them while using drugs or even as a side effect of drug use. Irwin (1985a, p. 176) suggested instead that students may be better able to report OBEs, perhaps because they have greater self-observational skills, the experience occurred more recently, or they are more willing to report unusual experiences than are other individuals.

The available studies clearly show that the prevalence of multiple

OBEs is significantly higher than the prevalence of single occurrences. In a previous analysis of 19 studies, I found that, on average, 30% of respondents reported a single OBE, whereas 67% reported more than one OBE (Alvarado, 1986b). This statistically significant difference ($p < .02$) may mean that those who have had one OBE are prone to have the experience more than once, perhaps by developing the cognitive skills necessary to repeat the experience or identify it when it occurs again.

PHENOMENOLOGY

Although case studies indicate that the phenomenology of the OBE varies (Alvarado, 1984; Crookall, 1961, 1964; Gabbard & Twemlow, 1984; Giovetti, 1983; Green, 1968; Poynton, 1975; see also Alvarado, 1997), I focus here on some selected features. The analysis below of the prevalence of these specific features is based mainly on a previous literature review (Alvarado, 1986b).

During an OBE, some people have reported an awareness of separation and return to the body, whereas others just seem to see themselves out of their body or coming back into their body with no sensation of any transitions. In three studies in which respondents were asked if they had experienced sensations of leaving the body, an average of 31% reported that they had ($Mdn = 35.5$; range = 22%–36%). Many experients see their physical body from a short distance, especially from positions above their bodies; on average, 62% reported this feature ($n = 11$ studies; $Mdn = 60\%$; range = 42%–81%).

Some out-of-body (OB) experients have reported the so-called "astral cord," that is, a ropelike or stringlike connection that links the physical body to the out-of-body location (e.g., Crookall, 1964; Muldoon & Carrington, 1929). In my analysis of the literature, this feature had been reported by an average 7% of respondents ($n = 6$ studies; $Mdn = 6\%$; range 0%–20%). On close examination, the prevalence of 20% claimed by Crookall (1964) seems to be inflated, because he erroneously grouped cases with mere kinesthetic sensations he felt were consistent with such a claim with actual "cord" cases. After recategorization, only 11% of Crookall's cases actually qualify as true cord cases. This feature of the OBE, frequently claimed in the occult and popular literatures to be commonplace, is actually rare. My finding underscores the importance of systematic research into the phenomenology of the OBE.

Experients describe themselves in a variety of ways when they find themselves out of their bodies. Some experience being in another body, usually resembling their physical one ($n = 10$ studies; $M = 46\%$, $Mdn = 49\%$; range = 15%–75%). Others do not experience a body at all, describing themselves as "pure consciousness" ($n = 6$ studies; $M = 31\%$; $Mdn = $

21.5%; range = 7%–80%) or as "balls of light," "points in space," or "clouds" (*n* = 6 studies; *M* = 29%; *Mdn* = 28%; range = 13%–47%). These forms of self-perception are not necessarily distinct. Osis (1979) found that 23% of his OB experients reported that the type of "shape" experienced varied as the OBE progressed.

On average, 19% of experients (*n* = 10 studies; *Mdn* = 16.5%; range = 5%–40%) have claimed that during an OBE, they made verifiable observations. Experients generally claim that they have traveled to a particular place and have obtained information about events occurring there (Alvarado, 1983; Hart, 1954). However, there are reasons to distrust this particular prevalence figure. For example, I found that of 61 claims of OBE cases, only 3 qualified as potentially veridical when experients were asked to provide fuller descriptions (Alvarado, 1986a). This finding underscores the limitations of questionnaire data that are gathered without the addition of narrative descriptions. Some laboratory studies that are relevant to the possibility of veridical observations at locations away from the physical body are discussed later in this chapter.

A neglected area in OBE research has been the study of the variables that are related to the content (for a more detailed discussion, see Alvarado, 1997; Irwin, 1985a, pp. 81–141). Crookall (1964) claimed that the circumstances surrounding the production of an OBE affected the content of the experience, but his work has been shown to have problems of validity and reliability (Irwin, 1985a). Gabbard, Twemlow, and Jones (1981) compared OBE experience features occurring in near-death circumstances to those occurring in other circumstances. They found that the near-death OBEs had a higher prevalence of such features as hearing noises at the beginning of the experience, traveling through a tunnel, seeing the physical body, being aware of the presence of other "beings" and deceased persons, and seeing brilliant lights.

Some researchers have found a higher frequency of these types of features in the OBEs of individuals reporting multiple experiences, as compared with those reporting a single experience (Alvarado & Zingrone, 1999; Gabbard & Twemlow, 1984). In addition, recent work has found significant positive correlations between the overall number of OBE features per case and the frequency of such variables as intentionally produced OBEs, frequency of parapsychological experiences, lucid dreams, and dream recall (Alvarado & Zingrone, 1999; see LaBerge & Gackenbach, this volume, chap. 5).

Although many of the studies of OBE phenomenology have used different questionnaires, there is consistency in the type of features reported (e.g., seeing the physical body at a distance). Unfortunately, little research has been conducted as to the variables that may predict the OBE features reported.

AFTEREFFECTS

Particularly relevant to this section is the fact that most, if not all, OBE surveys include some NDE cases in which an OBE was present. Osis (1979) found that 88% of the OB experients he studied reported beneficial changes after the experience, whereas 11% reported no changes and 1% claimed to have undergone negative changes. Sixty percent of the respondents claimed improved functioning in daily life, which they related to the OBE. They reported improvement in self-rated mental health (50%) and in social relations (45%). Osis's sample comprised volunteer respondents, which may have biased his results.

In contrast, in a randomly selected sample from the electoral lists, Blackmore (1984a) found that only 10% of respondents claimed changes in their beliefs and in the quality of life as a result of their OBEs. However, a nationally representative survey conducted in Iceland found that, out of 18 OB experients interviewed, 56% claimed to have undergone positive changes in their lives, beliefs, and attitudes after the OBE (Wiedman & Haraldsson, 1980). Daily working activities were not affected in 78% of the cases, 17% reported an improvement in these activities, and only 5% felt that their working lives were negatively affected. In a study by Gabbard and Twemlow (1984, p. 23), 86% of experients reported a greater "awareness of reality" after the experience, and 78% claimed to have received lasting benefits from it.

Among the more specific transformations reported are changes in attitudes toward death and spirituality. Osis (1979) found that, after their OBEs, 73% of respondents claimed to have a new attitude about life after death, and 67% reported a reduction in their fear of death. Sixty-six percent in Gabbard and Twemlow's (1984, p. 23) sample claimed to have adopted a belief in life after death after an OBE.

Other studies have related specific phenomenological characteristics of the OBE to attitude change. Gabbard and Twemlow (1984, p. 32) found that OBEs occurring near death were associated both with more claims of life changes and with greater changes of lasting benefit than OBEs occurring during other circumstances. Gabbard and Twemlow also found that OBEs occurring in circumstances of mental calmness were more likely to be related to belief in the survival of bodily death (p. 24). In Alvarado and Zingrone (1998), the number of features reported in OBEs was the best predictor of life changes after the experience.

Irwin (1988) found no overall difference between OBE experients and nonexperients, with two exceptions: OB experients scored significantly higher on the Life Attitude Profile scales measuring positive attitudes regarding goal seeking and acceptance of death. Although there were no significant differences on the Death Perspectives Scale (DPS), those who claimed to have had OBEs under near-death circumstances scored higher on a DPS subscale measuring positive attitude when anticipating death.

The results of these studies suggest that OBEs may lead to positive attitudinal changes, but one should keep in mind that these results are from correlational studies. Therefore, it is not possible to know if the OBE brought about a change of attitudes and beliefs or if prior attitudes and beliefs in some sense induced the OBE.

PSYCHOPHYSIOLOGICAL CORRELATES

Most of the work on OBEs has been conducted with individuals who claim to be able to induce the experience at will. The first such study was conducted with Robert Monroe, a well-known OB experient. Tart (1967) reported that Monroe spent considerable time during his OBEs in "borderline states" characterized by 7–8 Hertz alpha and high amplitude theta waves, and in electroencephalographic (EEG) patterns characterizing Stage 1 sleep, with normal heart activity and few eye movements. In a later study (Tart, 1969), Monroe again showed a Stage 1 EEG pattern, theta activity, and a drop in systolic blood pressure during the first of two OBEs. The second OBE occurred after Tart observed shifts in EEG patterns between Stage 1 and Stage 2 sleep. No changes in cardiac activity were registered.

Gabbard and Twemlow (1984) also conducted studies with Monroe and reported EEG amplitude differences between the brain hemispheres. Lower EEG frequencies were recorded while Monroe was experiencing an OBE than during either of the periods before or after it. These recordings were described as ranging between 4 and 5 Hertz (Gabbard & Twemlow, 1984, p. 208) and as "being much less on the right side of his brain than on the left side" (Twemlow, 1977, p. 280). In another study with a different volunteer, Tart (1968) found that during OBEs the EEG showed an increase in 7–8 Hertz alpha activity. There were no changes in heart and galvanic skin response activity.

Osis and Mitchell (1977) measured the EEG of an OB experient, Ingo Swann, before and during his OBEs. The mean EEG amplitude during the OBE period was somewhat less than that recorded during the non-OBE period in both the right and left occipital lobes. Nonsignificant decreases in alpha activity also were reported.

A study with yet another OB experient, S. B. Harary, compared changes in psychophysiological variables from a relaxation period to an OBE period with two relaxation and two OBE periods in each session (Morris, Harary, Janis, Hartwell, & Roll, 1978). Skin potential decreased during the OBE periods, whereas respiration and heart rate increased. No significant changes were found in eye movements, plethysmographic readings, electromyography (a measure of muscle tension), or alpha frequency in the EEG. Measurements during the first and second relaxation periods and during the first and second OBE periods did not differ from each other.

Palmer (1979b) attempted to induce OBEs in participants who had never before had the experience and correlated EEG measures to questionnaire data on experiences and expectations at different times during the study. He found no significant correlations among these variables, but he did report that "the three subjects who had more than 30 percent theta in their baseline EEGs all reported rather strong OBEs" (Palmer, 1979b, p. 138).

In another study of induced OBEs conducted by Gabbard and Twemlow (1984) with a single participant, the EEG resembled a pattern of Stage 3 sleep, described as a "transitional theta-delta band [in which the participant] retains a greater degree of conscious awareness than is usual for this Stage 3 sleep state" (p. 219).

Krippner (1996) reported on a 4-night dream laboratory study with a volunteer who claimed to have occasional OBEs. In the morning after the 4th night, the participant reported having had an OBE. During that time period, the EEG record showed that his REM sleep had been interrupted by "a pattern of slow brain waves in the theta and delta frequencies" (p. 90).

McCreery and Claridge (1996b) compared volunteer student and nonclinical OB experients from whom psychophysiological data had been previously elicited with individuals who had never had an OBE. The OB experients were found to have had higher rates of right-brain hemisphere activation, higher EEG amplitude coherence between the hemispheres, and a higher rate of lability in skin conductance level than the nonexperients.

In general, the studies suggest a tendency for relaxation or low arousal states to occur during OBEs, but the results of these studies are difficult to evaluate because different measurements were taken. In addition, some of the techniques used to induce OBEs may have confounded the interpretation of psychophysiological results. Finally, few of these studies seem to have been theory driven, which would have allowed future experiments to build on previous ones in formulating testable hypotheses. Further research is needed to corroborate and extend the available data.

INDIVIDUAL DIFFERENCES

Most OBE research has focused on individual differences between experients and nonexperients as assessed by paper-and-pencil tests. Because no important differences regarding demographic variables have been found in those studies, I focus my review on psychological correlates of the OBE (see also Alvarado, 1986b, 1988; Irwin, 1985a.)

Personality Variables

The OBE has not been found to relate to extraversion, as assessed by the Differential Personality Questionnaire (DPQ; Irwin, 1980), by the Eysenck Personality Inventory (Irwin, 1985a, p. 201; McCreery & Claridge, 1995), or by the NEO Personality Inventory Revisited (Alvarado, Zingrone, & Dalton, 1996b). The traits of sensation seeking and danger seeking have been found to relate to OBEs in some studies but not in others. Using the DPQ, Gabbard and Twemlow (1984, p. 32) found lower levels of danger seeking in OB experients, although Irwin (1980) reported no significant relationship. The Risk-Taking factor of the Jackson Personality Inventory has been positively correlated with OBEs (Myers, Austrin, Grisso, & Nickeson, 1983), but Zuckerman's Sensation Seeking Scale has not (Glicksohn, 1990). Scores on excitement seeking from the Neuroticism factor of the NEO-PI-R were virtually identical for experients and nonexperients (Alvarado et al., 1996b).

Irwin (1981b) used the Edwards Personal Preference Schedule to study a variety of personality traits. Compared with the control group, an OBE group obtained lower scores in achievement and deference but higher scores on intraception (the disposition to pay attention to subjective experiences). Myers et al. (1983) found that OBEs were positively correlated with breadth of interest, innovation, responsibility, risk taking, and social participation and were negatively correlated with several aspects of personal complexity and orthodox values. They also found that OB experients were significantly more internally focused than nonexperients. Other researchers reported nonsignificant differences regarding locus of control between OB experients and nonexperients (Tobacyk, Wells, & Miller, 1998).

Spanos and Moretti (1988) found no relationship between OBEs and depressive affect. Likewise, Tobacyk and Mitchell (1987) found no differences between experients and nonexperients on such measures of adjustment as death orientation, defensive style, narcissism, self-concept, or social desirability. A hypothesized positive relationship between OBE and openness to experience has not been supported (Alvarado et al., 1996b).

Absorption, Fantasy Proneness, Hypnosis, and Dissociation

In a pioneering study using the DPQ, Irwin (1980) found a positive correlation between OBEs and the DPQ Absorption scale. Since then, several other studies have been conducted to test this relationship. Most have replicated Irwin's initial finding (Alvarado & Zingrone, 1997b [two studies]; Dalton, Zingrone, & Alvarado, 1999; Glicksohn, 1990 [two studies]; Irwin, 1981c [two studies], 1985a [three studies]; Myers et al., 1983). Four failed to replicate (Alvarado & Zingrone, 1997b [one study]; Gabbard & Twemlow, 1984, p. 32; Glicksohn, 1990 [one study]; Spanos & Moretti, 1988). (Not included here is one of Irwin's, 1985c, studies in which the Absorption scale from the DPQ was modified to measure "need for absorption.") Taken together, these studies show a moderate correlation between OBEs and absorption (Stouffer's z = 10.53, p < .001, r = .41).[1]

J. R. Hilgard's Imaginative Involvement scale correlated positively with OBE reports (Hunt, Gervais, Shearing-Johns, & Travis, 1992). In addition, fantasy proneness has been consistently and positively related to the OBE (Alvarado & Zingrone, 1994; Myers et al., 1983; Wilson & Barber, 1983). Although the data in Wilson and Barber's initial study were not analyzed statistically, I contrasted their high and low fantasy proneness group in relation to OBE prevalence, discovering significant differences between these two groups (phi = .60, p < .001).

Spanos and Moretti (1988) reported significant positive correlations between various hypnosis tests and the prevalance of OBE, and studies by Pekala and associates found higher OBE prevalence among highly hypnotizable individuals (Pekala, Kumar, & Cummings, 1992; Pekala, Kumar, & Marcano, 1995). In an experimental context, Palmer and Lieberman (1976) found that participants who reported OBEs after an induction procedure involving progressive muscular relaxation, guided instructions and a ganzfield or a uniform visual field, also obtained higher scores on Barber's Susceptibility Scale than those who did not report them.

Cardeña (1988, 1996) conducted an experimental study to investigate the phenomenology of "deep hypnosis" among individuals with very high hypnotizability. He found that spontaneous OBE-like sensations and other distortions of body image were more common in self-rated deep levels of hypnosis. These experiences were also more frequent in a state of quiescence (i.e., lying down) than while engaged in automatic or willful physical activity (i.e., pedaling a stationary bicycle or riding while a motor moved the pedals).

Richards (1991) reported significant positive correlations between the Dissociative Experiences Scale (DES) and prevalence of spontaneous and voluntary OBEs (.37 and .43, respectively) in a group of participants interested in spiritual and parapsychological phenomena. In my own studies with a colleague, we found a marginally significant (p = .06) positive correlation between dissociation and OBEs in a small group of college library employees (Zingrone & Alvarado, 1994) and a significant association in a

---

[1]This and the following analyses are frequently based on lower estimates. Consequently, they should be interpreted as a conservative approximation of overall probabilities and effect sizes. The r is based on the Fisher's z transformation (Rosenthal, 1991). Gabbard and Twemlow (1984) and Spanos and Moretti (1988) did not report p values. Consequently, I have assumed a z value of 0 for these studies.

community college student sample (Alvarado & Zingrone, 1997a). A more recent study with creative individuals also found a significant positive association between OBEs and DES scores (Dalton et al., 1999).

Imagery and Spatial Ability Variables

Although it has been thought that imagery variables correlate with the OBE, research has not demonstrated a clear relationship. Two out of six studies found a significant positive correlation between OBEs and hypnagogic (i.e., the state between being awake and falling asleep) imagery (Blackmore, 1983a; Glicksohn, 1989, 1990; McCreery & Claridge, 1996a). In regard to hypnopompic (i.e., the stage between being asleep and waking up) imagery and OBEs, only one of four studies conducted by Glicksohn (1989, 1990) found a significant, positive correlation.

Using the Vividness of Visual Imagery Questionnaire, vividness of mental imagery was negatively correlated with the OBE in one study (Irwin, 1980), positively in another (Alvarado & Zingrone, 1994), and unrelated in a third (Irwin, 1981a, 1985a, p. 268). Blackmore (1982c) found no significant differences between experients and nonexperients using the Betts' Questionnaire on Mental Imagery.

Visualizer and verbalizer coding styles did not differentiate experients from nonexperients in studies conducted by Irwin (1980, 1985a, p. 270), but McCreery (1993) found that OB experients were predominantly visualizers. Others have explored the OBE's relationship to imagery control. Blackmore (1987) reported a positive relationship between these variables when participants were asked to indicate how easily they could change their viewpoints in imaginal memory scenes. "OBErs are better than others at switching from one viewpoint to another (especially to the viewpoint above the head), [are] more proficient at producing clear and detailed images from different viewpoints, and tend to use the observer viewpoint in dream recall" (p. 64). Other studies, using the Gordon's Control of Imagery Questionnaire, did not find significant results (Blackmore, 1983b; Irwin, 1985a, p. 271). Finally, no significant relationships were found between OBEs and performance on the Necker Cube Fluctuation Test of imagery (Cook & Irwin, 1983).

OB experients were found to have better spatial abilities in a study with a device built for the research project (Cook & Irwin, 1983). Blackmore (1983b) did not obtain significant relationships between spatial abilities and OBEs using the Space Relations Test of the Differential Aptitude Test battery. Although Gackenbach (1978) found no relationship between OBEs and scores on the Embedded Figures Test, Hunt et al. (1992) did report a positive relationship.

Overall, the best predictors of the OBE seem to be some cognitive variables that are intercorrelated, namely dissociation, hypnotic susceptibility, absorption, and fantasy proneness. No consistent patterns have been found between personality variables and the OBE in the relatively small number of the studies that have been conducted.

Experiential Variables: Perceptual Distortions, Spontaneous Alterations of Consciousness, Dreams, and Parapsychological Experiences

Several findings confirm the idea that OB experients tend to experience a variety of hallucinatory and perceptual distortions. McCreery and Claridge (1995) found this to be the case when they tested OB experients on scales measuring hallucinatory experiences and perceptual aberrations (see Bentall, this volume, chap. 3). Blackmore's (1986a) findings also supported this relationship: She found distortions of body image to be more frequent among OB experients than among nonexperients in samples of students and individuals with schizophrenia. Another study found a positive relationship between the OBE and hallucinatory experiences, experiences of perceived changes in body size, and floating sensations (Blackmore, 1984a). However, the experients' awareness of somatic processes, as measured by the Body Consciousness Questionnaire, was not related to OBEs (Irwin, 1985a, pp. 279–280; Miller, Murphy, & Buss, 1981).

McCreery and Claridge's (1996a) work has also supported the importance of perceptual distortions. In their study, OB experients reported more hallucinatory experiences in response to physical and mental relaxation exercises and a higher rate of detachment from the body during a laboratory exercise than did nonexperients. More recently, two colleagues and I (Alvarado, Zingrone, & Dalton, 1996a; Dalton et al., 1999) found that OB experients, as compared with nonexperients, did not have higher rates of alterations of consciousness under conditions of laboratory-induced partial sensory deprivation. We did observe that experients had a significantly higher frequency of spontaneous loss of awareness of the surroundings and of the passage of time while engaged in tasks in daily life than did nonexperients.

Table 6.1 summarizes trends in survey studies that have assessed the relationship of the OBE to dream variables. Most of these variables, especially lucid dreams (see LaBerge & Gackenbach, this volume, chap. 5), have been consistent predictors of OBEs. In addition, Blackmore (1986b) found that persons who experienced deliberate, as compared with spontaneous, OBEs reported higher frequencies of flying dreams and the ability to control and terminate dream content.

Although OBEs have not been found to be significantly related to laboratory performance in experimental extrasensory perception (ESP) testing (Alvarado et al., 1996a; Blackmore, 1982c), they have been positively correlated with claims of spontaneous ESP experiences (Alvarado & Zingrone, 1994; Alvarado et al., 1996a; Blackmore, 1984a; Green, 1967; Hunt

TABLE 6.1
Relationships Between the Out-of-Body Experience and Dream Variables

Study	Lucid dreams	Dream recall	Vivid dreams	Flying dreams
Alvarado et al. (1996a)	ns	ns		
Blackmore (1982b)	s	s[a]		s[a]
Blackmore (1982c)				
Study 1	s	ns[a]		
Study 2	ns	ns[a]		ns[a]
Blackmore (1983a)	s[a]			ns[a]
Blackmore (1984a)	s	ns[a]	s[a]	s
Blackmore (1986b)	s			s
Drab (in Irwin, 1985b)				
Study 1	s			
Study 2	ns			
Study 3	s			
Gackenbach (1978)	s			
Glicksohn (1990)				
Study 1	s	ns		
Study 2	s	ns		
Study 3	s	ns		
Irwin (1983)	s			
Irwin (1986)	s			
Kohr (1980)	s	s	s	
Myers (1982)	ns			
Olsen (1988)		s	s	
Palmer (1979a)				
Students	ns	ns	ns	
Townspeople	s	ns	s	
Usha and Pasricha (1989b)	s	ns		
Wiedman and Haraldsson (1980)	s	ns		
Stouffer z	11.47	1.98	5.04	6.22
p	10×10^{-31}	.02	2×10^{-7}	2×10^{-10}
Mean r	.24	.05	16	.33

Note. With the exception of two of Glicksohn's (1990) studies of dream recall (1 and 3), none of the relationships are negative. s = significant; ns = nonsignificant. Missing data indicate that the relationship was not explored in the study.
[a]Analyses done with chi-squares having more than two degrees of freedom. These results have not been included in the combined analyses reported at the bottom of the table.

et al., 1992; Irwin, 1985a, p. 290; Kohr, 1980; Myers, 1982; see Targ, Schlitz, & Irwin, this volume, chap. 7). Positive relationships between the OBE and indices of a variety of parapsychological claims (Alvarado et al., 1996a; Dalton et al., 1999; Glicksohn, 1990 [two out of three studies]) and such specific purported experiences as seeing apparitions (Alvarado & Zingrone, 1994; Myers, 1982) and auras (Alvarado & Zingrone, 1994) have also been reported. Mystical experiences have been consistently but modestly related to the OBE (Blackmore, 1984a, 1986b; Hunt et al., 1992; Kohr, 1980; Myers et al., 1983; Palmer, 1979a; Wiedman & Haraldsson,

1980; Stouffer's $z = 7.21$, $p < .001$, $r = .21$), although a study by Spanos and Moretti (1988) did not support such a relationship.

Use of Drugs and Mental Disciplines

There is evidence that the frequency of OBEs is significantly higher after one's initiation into marijuana use (Tart, 1971). Some studies with student samples have found positive correlations between psychedelic drug use and OBEs (Blackmore & Harris, 1983; Myers et al., 1983; Palmer, 1979a; Usha & Pasricha, 1989b), but this relationship has not been found with nonstudent samples (Kohr, 1980; Palmer, 1979a).

With a few exceptions (Gabbard & Twemlow, 1984; Palmer, 1979a), the practice of meditation and similar disciplines generally has been positively correlated with the OBE (Alvarado et al., 1996a; Hunt et al., 1992; Kohr, 1980; Myers et al., 1983; Palmer, 1979a; Usha & Pasricha, 1989b; Stouffer's $z = 6.93$, $p < .001$; $r = .21$).

These studies imply that both spontaneous and deliberate entry into altered states are related to the OBE. These practices, in turn, may be related to absorption, hypnotic susceptibility, dissociation, perceptual distortions, and psi-experiences.

DEVELOPMENTAL VARIABLES

Initial research by Stanford (1987) uncovered significant positive correlations between OBEs while awake and reports of time spent reading or being read to during childhood, as well as between OBEs while falling asleep and reports of time spent playing with imaginary playmates. No significant relationships emerged between OBEs and spankings or deprivation during childhood. However, in a later study, Stanford (1994) failed to replicate the previous findings.

Irwin (1996) did not find a significant relationship between OBEs and measured parental support of imagination and other activities in childhood, but they found significant positive correlations between OBEs and various subscales of the Survey of Traumatic Childhood Events. They included intrafamilial sexual abuse, extrafamilial sexual abuse, extrafamilial assault, death or illness of a close friend, and isolation from friends and playmates. These findings are similar to data emerging from research on NDE experients (Irwin, 1993; Ring, 1992) and individuals with high hypnotic susceptibility (Nash, Lynn, & Givens, 1984). Stanford's (1987) initial finding and Irwin's study both deserve to be replicated, but the dearth of studies in this area make generalization of results both speculative and premature. The provocative but limited data on developmental antecedents of the OBE suggest that they deserve more attention than they have received in the past.

MEDICAL AND NEUROLOGICAL VARIABLES

Although some investigators have speculated that OBEs are related to headaches (Comfort, 1982; Lippman, 1953) and temporal-lobe epilepsy (Eastman, 1962; Persinger, 1983), virtually no research has been conducted to test these ideas. Green (1967) found that 11% of OB experients suffered migraine headaches, and Irwin (1983) reported a positive relationship between OBEs and headaches in three out of four surveys. However, when Irwin partialled out the correlation controlling for lucid dreams, he found that the relationship of OBEs to headaches was not significant. McCreery (1997, p. 267) reported a significantly higher proportion of migraines in OB experients than in nonexperients. Although Spanos and Moretti (1988) found a positive association between OBEs and psychosomatic symptoms, Gabbard and Twemlow (1984, p. 31) did not.

Penfield and Jasper (1954) were able to elicit OBE sensations by electrical stimulation of the temporal cortex. Others have suspected an association between the OBE and temporal-lobe symptomatology or epilepsy. In his examination of a handful of people diagnosed with epilepsy, McCreery (1993) found no relationship between epilepsy and OBEs. However, Kennedy, Kanthamani, and Palmer (1994) reported a significant positive correlation between items from Persinger and Makarec's (1987) Personal Philosophy Inventory, which reputedly measures temporal-lobe symptomatology, and an item asking about the occurrence of parapsychological experiences, including OBEs. Persinger (1995) found a positive correlation between epilepticlike signs, as measured by a subscale of his Personal Philosophy Inventory, and participants' reported experiences of "leaving the body" and feeling "detached" from it in the laboratory. (This relationship interacted with measures of increased global geomagnetic activity, indicating the possibility that this environmental factor influences OBE occurrence.)

Another report suggested that OBEs, like so-called autoscopic hallucinations (i.e., visual hallucinations of one's body), are related to brain hemisphericity (Brugger, Regard, & Landis, 1996). In a comparison of 13 cases of unilateral autoscopy with 27 cases of OBEs, the authors found that the majority of the autoscopic experiences occurred in the left visual field (85%), whereas most of the OBEs were perceived in the right visual field (63%), a difference that I found to be statistically significant (p = .005). Although the studies reviewed are promising, there is no strong evidence that consistently relates the OBE to medical or neurological variables.

PSYCHOPATHOLOGY

Measures of traits and symptoms related to psychosis have failed to differentiate OB experients from nonexperients (Gabbard & Twemlow, 1984; Irwin, 1980; McCreery & Claridge, 1995). McCreery (1993) found no relationship between the occurrence of OBEs and his participants' psychiatric histories. Gabbard and Twemlow (1984) concluded that "the OBE group was significantly healthier than a variety of other normative groups in the population and did not have the constellation of symptoms often equated with character disorders, such as psychosomatic disorders, alcohol and drug abuse, or stimulus seeking" (p. 32). They also argued that such phenomena as depersonalization, autoscopy, and body boundary disorders are phenomenologically different from the OB experients' range of experiences (see Twemlow, 1989). A similar analysis has been presented by Irwin (1985a). However, no one to date has conducted empirical studies that differentiate the OBE from seemingly similar phenomena in terms of phenomenology, antecedents, demographics, or other variables.

Although the link between OBEs and psychosis is not supported by most empirical evidence, an exception is the study by McCreery and Claridge (1995), in which OBEs were related to scores on several schizotypy scales (typically used to predict the onset of schizophrenia). However, the authors used Claridge's (1985, 1988) model of schizotypy in which a distinction is made between schizophrenia as a process of psychological deterioration and schizotypy as a personality trait. Hence, Claridge's model actually may be related to those psychological models of OBEs that suggest that an individual's ability to have an OBE is related to such capacities as alterations of consciousness and unusual styles of perceptual processing (Blackmore, 1984a; Irwin, 1985a; Palmer, 1978b).

In addition, McCreery and Claridge (1995) found that their OB experients scored lower on a measure of physical anhedonia (the inability to experience pleasure) than nonexperients. The authors described their OB-experients as "happy schizotypes," who are considered to be "functional despite, or perhaps even in part because of, his or her anomalous experiences" (p. 142).

In Irwin's (1980) initial study, OB experients had higher scores on the Stress Reaction Scale (related to neuroticism) of the DPQ than would be expected in the general population. However, other studies have failed to relate the OBE to such measures of psychopathology as the Anxiety and Ergic Tension factors of Cattell's 16PF Questionnaire (Gackenbach, 1978), the Anxiety scale of the Jackson Personality Inventory (Myers et al., 1983), Caine's Hysteroid Scale (Gabbard & Twemlow, 1984), the Neuroticism scale of the Eysenck Personality Inventory (Irwin, 1985a, p. 201; McCreery & Claridge, 1995; Spanos & Moretti, 1988), or the Neuroticism factor and facets of the NEO-PI-R (Alvarado et al., 1996b).

In sum, the OBE has not been related to psychopathological variables in most of the research conducted, with the possible exception of its purported relationship to schizotypy as conceptualized by Claridge (1985, 1988).

PARAPSYCHOLOGICAL RESEARCH

In a previous section, I mentioned apparently veridical perceptions during an OBE as a particular phenomenological feature of the experience. These perceptions have also been studied in the laboratory. In these tests, volunteers who claim to be capable of inducing an OBE are usually asked to travel to a nearby location and obtain information from preselected target material. They are then asked to report this information when they feel they have returned to their bodies. Some isolated positive results have been obtained (for reviews, see Alvarado, 1982a; Blackmore, 1982a).

Probably the best known of these studies is Tart's (1968) study of a woman known as "Miss Z." She was reported to have "read" a randomly selected five-digit number put on a shelf out of her reach but in the same room where she was lying in a bed with EEG electrodes connected to her head. According to Tart (1968) there was an unlikely possibility that the study's participant perceived subliminally a reflection of the number from the glass surface of a nearby clock.

Harary and Solfvin (1977) conducted a study with 6 non-experients and 2 OB experients who claimed to be able to induce the experience at will. Participants were asked to identify tape-recorded sounds played at a distance and to say if a person was present in that distant location. Only one of the "at-will" participants provided significant results on both tasks.

In a series of four studies, Palmer (Palmer, 1979b; Palmer & Lieberman, 1975, 1976; Palmer & Vassar, 1974) tested for ESP by attempting to induce OBEs in general volunteers using relaxation and sensory deprivation techniques. A later evaluation of the studies led Palmer (1978a) to conclude that those participants who had reported OBEs during the experimental induction did not achieve better ESP scores than participants who failed to report OBEs. However, there were indications of an interaction among ESP scores, a hypnagogic state, and the use of sensory deprivation procedures. Other studies on this issue failed to obtain significant results (Morris et al., 1978; Tart, 1967, 1969) or obtained them only when so many analyses were conducted that chance factors could not be ruled out (Osis, 1975).

Another line of experimental research attempts to detect anomalous physical activity at the site the OB experient is "visiting" during the OBE. I will not comment on the old studies that used photography and other means of detection because it is not clear that the participants had sensations of being located out of their bodies (see reviews by Alvarado, 1980; Blackmore, 1982a). Instead, I focus on two recent attempts to detect the OBE physically. The first used a combination of physical and biological detectors while the participant attempted to visit a distant location during an OBE (Morris et al., 1978). The measurements taken from a variety of detectors of heat, light, and other physical indexes in the visit site were not significantly related to the participant's reported OBEs. More successful were the responses of a kitten that seemed to react, at statistically significant levels, to Harary's nonphysical presence in some sessions, as measured by observations of the animal's movements and vocalizations. Other tests with the same kitten obtained good initial results, which declined in later testing. Overall, the results were not statistically significant.

In another study, researchers postulated that the detection of an OB-experient's "presence" at a distant location should correlate with his or her acquisition of information present only at that location (Osis & McCormick, 1980). The participant was asked to visit a viewing window during an OBE. The window was fitted with strain-gauge sensors that detected surrounding vibrations, a fact kept masked from the participant. As expected, during the trials in which the participant retrieved correct information (in the form of pictorial targets), higher activation levels of the sensors were obtained than in the trials in which correct information was not retrieved.

Some of these studies appear to indicate that veridical information has been acquired during an OBE in the laboratory. Unfortunately, only a handful of studies of this sort have been conducted, and the results rarely have been replicated. In addition, it is possible that the results of these studies may be explained by other processes of anomalous communication, such as ESP and psychokinesis (see Targ, Schlitz, and Irwin, this volume, chap. 7).

THEORIES

Throughout the history of OBE research, two general perspectives have guided both research and theory. On one hand, some researchers have suggested that "something" literally "goes out of the body" during an OBE. Alternatively, others see the experience as "imaginary" in nature. I refer to the former perspective as the *projection model* and to the latter as the *psychological model* (for reviews of these and other concepts, including psychophysiological speculations, see Alvarado, 1982b, 1992; Blackmore, 1982a; Irwin, 1985a).

The Projection Model

The projection model has had a long history and is traditionally associated with occult and spiritualistic systems of thought. Belief in the projection model has been maintained largely through claims by OB experients that they "see" themselves during the experience in a replica of their physical bodies and by their reports that they have "felt" sensations of "leaving" and "returning to" the body. The projection model has also been supported by alleged veridical perceptions during the OBE and by the rare reports of observers who claim to have "seen" an apparition of the OB experient at the time and place the experient later claimed to have been present (Hart, 1954, 1956; Laurentin & Mahéo, 1990). One problem with the projection model is the difficulty in attempting to test it scientifically. Projection claims are interesting, but they have not been systematically studied, and many plausible alternative explanations have been proposed (see Irwin, 1985a). Nonetheless, these ideas are still discussed in the literature in the context of the mind–body problem (Woodhouse, 1994).

The Psychological Model

The dominant model in OBE studies, by far, is the psychological one. In fact, most recent OBE research has investigated the assumptions of the psychological model in one way or another (Alvarado, 1989, 1992). There are many reasons for the domination of this model. One is the fact that contemporary psychology, as well as science at large, is hesitant to propose explanations that contradict current paradigms. But in all fairness, it should be noted that little evidence exists to support the projection model; furthermore, this model presents myriad obstacles to scientific testing. In contrast, the psychological model is far more amenable to systematic investigation. It also serves to connect the OBE anomaly to the investigative concerns of those who study a wide range of perceptual and cognitive functions.

Psychological models postulate that the OBE is an imaginary or hallucinatory experience of one sort or another (Alvarado, 1992). Palmer's (1978b) model states that OBEs are caused by an organism's reaction to its threatened identity. This reaction is initiated by the altered body image that results from radical deviations in proprioceptive input. Once the unfamiliar input is received, the individual's usual sense of identity is threatened, and this threat activates unconscious processes that attempt to restore the usual sense of identity. According to Palmer, the OBE is only one of several ways in which one's usual identity may be reestablished. Other methods may include lucid dreams at night or daytime fainting, which he contended may occur when no cognitive solution to the threat is apparent.

The OBE, then, is an attempt to prevent the jeopardy to one's identity from reaching awareness and precipitating a crisis. The hypnagogic state is considered to play an important role in this model because of the body image changes commonly reported during this state. Palmer noted that many spontaneous OBEs seem to arise in hypnagogic contexts, or in moments of extreme stress. Some scientific data exist to support Palmer's model; OBEs have occurred in the hypnagogic state in various laboratory contexts (Palmer, 1978a; Palmer & Lieberman, 1975; Palmer & Vassar, 1974). However, findings that specifically relate hypnagogic imagery to spontaneous OBEs have not been consistent. In addition, Palmer's (1978b) model is difficult to test because he postulated that these threats are typically perceived unconsciously:

> The person is unlikely to be fully aware (i.e., conscious) of the threat, or even the change of body image, as such. Indeed, the whole purpose of the OBE is to prevent the threat from reaching consciousness, where it could provoke an anxiety attack. (p. 20)

Another important psychological model has been proposed by Blackmore (1984b), who suggested that the psyche creates models of reality based on the sensory impressions it receives. However, only one such model of reality can predominate at any given time. Changes in sensory input, the effects of stress, and other factors may disrupt such stable models, making it necessary for the organism to construct another model using memory and imagination. The OBE is conceived as one such model of reality; perceptual distortions, hallucinations, lucid dreams, mystical experiences, and other alterations of consciousness may represent other models. Blackmore's notions have received some empirical support. For example, as mentioned in the section on individual differences, Blackmore (1987) found that OB experients had greater visual–spatial abilities and a greater facility to change imagery perspective than nonexperients. (Visual–spatial abilities are also linked to lucid dreaming; see LaBerge & Gackenbach, this volume, chap. 5). Blackmore considered these findings to be consistent with her model because such imagery alteration skills support the idea that the OBE is created by an active manipulation of imagery involving visual and spatial components. Blackmore also argued that deliberate induction of an OBE should require a higher demand on such skills than spontaneous experiences. This prediction found support in one of her studies, in which OB experients who claimed to be able to induce the experience at will exhibited a higher level of dream control skills than those whose OBEs had occurred spontaneously (Blackmore, 1986b). Blackmore (1993) also postulated that her model "predicts that people who habitually imagine things or dream in a bird's-eye view should be more likely to have OBEs" (p. 180).

Research relating OBEs to the observer's point of view in dreams has supported this idea (Blackmore, 1987; Irwin, 1986). Finally, Blackmore's model assumes that, as compared with nonexperients, OB experients have higher rates of both altered states of consciousness and hallucinations. My research and that of others support this (e.g., Alvarado et al., 1996a; Blackmore, 1984a; Dalton et al., 1999; McCreery & Claridge, 1995).

Another important model has been developed by Irwin (1985a, pp. 307–323). In Irwin's view, the sensation of being out of the body and other OBE features are explained by an interaction between absorption–attentional factors and the process of losing contact with bodily sensations, which Irwin called the *asomatic factor*. When attention is directed away from bodily sensations (both somatic and exteroceptive), those sensations are attenuated and the feeling of being out of the body may result.

> If the individual's information processing system becomes habituated to somaesthetic and kinesthetic stimuli (as in relaxation and repetitive, automatic motor activity) then absorption in mentation will be facilitated. Conversely, as the individual becomes increasingly absorbed in mentation, awareness of somatic processes progressively will diminish (Irwin, 1985a, p. 308)

The absorbed mentation developed in this way may give rise to the sensation of separation from the body as a result of excluding somatic input.

Irwin (1985a) argued that the sensation of disconnection from the body may be preconscious and in need of recoding or modification in order to be recognized by conscious awareness. As he explained: "Being out of touch with bodily processes inspires both the preconscious notion of the exteriorized state and the conscious mental representation of this state as a passive somaesthetic image" (Irwin, 1985a, p. 310). As this occurs, cross-modal perceptual processes, or synesthesia (see Marks, this volume, chap. 4), may define the content of the experience by changing the modality or form of the original somaesthethic image into one that, for example, arises from visual and kinesthetic perceptions. As with Blackmore's model, Irwin's ideas have received support from studies relating absorption and visual–spatial abilities to the OBE (Alvarado et al., 1996a). In addition, some evidence exists that synesthesialike items from Tellegen's Absorption scale are positively correlated with OBEs (McCreery & Claridge, 1995; Irwin, 1985a, p. 317).

McCreery (1993, 1997) and McCreery and Claridge (1995) presented some initial theoretical ideas that relate the OBE to their concept of schizotypy. They followed Claridge's (1985, 1988) model of schizotypy, in which the nervous system of schizotypes is hypothesized to lack the homeostatic mechanisms that regulate arousal. The lability in the arousal of the nervous system is considered to be related to such phenomena as OBEs and other hallucinatory experiences. The positive correlations between OBEs and a variety of schizotypy measures, related experiences, and psychophysiological processes have supported this model (McCreery & Claridge, 1995, 1996a, 1996b). It is important to note that McCreery seems to view OB experients as "adjusted" schizotypes because his model does not assume that schizotypes will necessarily become schizophrenics. Although this model has received some empirical support, it is not clear how the sensation of feeling one is out of the body can be explained by schizotypy alone.

The results of Cardeña's (1988, 1996) study with highly hypnotizable individuals, mentioned earlier, may be used to support models that posit alterations of sensory input as an underlying cause of the OBE, particularly Irwin's (1985a) model. Cardeña's study suggests that lack of physical activity or automatic physical activity may allow for a more active use of the cognitive resources necessary to construct an OBE. In any case, these results imply that other variables, such as hypnotizability level and attentional deployment, interact with amount of physical input.

What, then, is the theoretical status of OBE research? Regarding the projection model, the results of the few attempts to test for this idea are unclear at best. In addition, there is no clear theory from which to make specific predictions about this model. Systematic laboratory work needs to be conducted along the lines of the previously discussed detection studies (Morris et al., 1978; Osis & McCormick, 1980). Nonetheless, it is doubtful that this work will support the projection model, considering that in parapsychological circles such results are often explained by recourse to such nonprojection hypotheses as extrasensory perception, psychokinesis (e.g., Irwin, 1985a), or other variables.

However, several of the psychological explanations are also problematic, especially those that simply label the OBE as an example of a particular process (e.g., dissociation) or phenomenon (e.g., a hallucination) without attempting to test these ideas or relate them to other known psychological variables. It is not useful to be told simply that the OBE is "imaginary" without accompanying such pronouncements with specific testable predictions. It is encouraging to see that Palmer's, Blackmore's, Irwin's, and McCreery's models offer falsifiable predictions and attempt to systematically connect the OBE experience to other psychological processes.

Although some support has been found for the psychological models (especially those of Blackmore, Irwin, and McCreery), much more research is needed. Particularly valuable would be a series of investigations that emphasize the relationship of the OBE experience to other psychological processes. Among the variables needing additional investigation are basic constructs of body image, cognitive maps, absorption and synesthesialike processes, and the lability of the nervous system. Rigorous hypothesis testing is also needed, especially in regard to specific phenomenological features of the experience and their relationships to the main constructs of the various psychological models.

METHODOLOGICAL ISSUES

Most of the studies reviewed in this chapter depend on self-reports of introspective experiences (see Pekala & Cardeña, this volume, chap. 2). A basic problem with questionnaire studies of the OBE is that researchers can never be sure that all positive replies to a question tap the same basic experience (at least at the descriptive level) or that the experiential reports conform to even a minimal definition of the OBE (i.e., the experience of being located out of the physical body). Unfortunately, most questionnaire studies conducted to date rely on *yes* or *no* answers to questions about OBEs. No written description of the experience is requested, nor are interviews with the experients conducted. In fact, there is evidence that when researchers try to go beyond *yes* and *no* questions, the overall prevalence of OB experients decreases (Blackmore, 1986a, 1987; Irwin, 1980, 1981a; Wiedman & Haraldsson, 1980). As Palmer (1978b) argued, researchers need to pay more attention to the experient's evaluation of his or her own experience. But this does not mean that a researcher should ignore the potential confound of the inclusion of experiences that do not include the sensation of being out of the physical body or the potentially differential relationships of such experiences to psychological correlates. One hopes that this point is taken into consideration in future studies. In addition, empirically constructed OBE scales similar to those developed by NDE researchers (e.g., Greyson, 1983) are needed.

Another methodological problem is the varying construction of OBE questions and the different context in which the questions are presented. Although Blackmore (1982b) found that OBE prevalence was not affected by providing examples of OBEs to the participants, Irwin (1985a, p. 177) suggested that a respondent's willingness to acknowledge an OBE may, in fact, be influenced by the context in which the OBE question is presented. For example, the response may differ if the question is asked after other questions of a personal nature rather than after impersonal queries. The whole issue of contextual effects and demand characteristics deserves further exploration in OBE research.

As in any other area of research, the participants used in these studies must be taken into consideration when evaluating the results. Surveys have tended to overrely on samples of college students, whereas laboratory studies of OBEs have tended to rely on purportedly gifted individuals who claim to be able to induce the experience at will. These gifted individuals have usually developed specific ways of inducing the OBE experience within the context of particular belief systems. Such limited samples limit the generalizability of these studies to the population at large. The answer to these and other issues depends on future research conducted with a variety of approaches and a wider range of participants.

FUTURE RESEARCH

Comparison of OBEs With Other Phenomena

Other than analyses conducted to contrast the OBE to such psychiatric syndromes as autoscopy, depersonalization, and psychotic body boundary phenomena (Gabbard & Twemlow, 1984; Irwin, 1985a; Twemlow, 1989), there are no data on the possible differences between the OBE and these syndromes in relation to developmental factors, demographics, phenomenology, psychophysiology, and so on. In addition, recent work that relates the OBE to other states of consciousness (e.g., Gabbard & Twemlow, 1984; Glicksohn, 1989; Green & McCreery, 1994; Maitz & Pekala, 1991), including a variety of dream experiences (e.g., Palmer, 1979a), has provided useful leads that should be explored. This work will assist us in understanding the OBE in terms of its relation to other psychological experiences.

Development of Induction Techniques

Because the laboratory study of the OBE depends to a great extent on the reliable manifestation of these experiences, investigators need to focus their efforts on the development of methods to induce the phenomenon. Some promising attempts include the sensory deprivation techniques pioneered by Palmer (1978a). In one of his studies, Palmer found that participants who were given instructions to detach themselves from their bodies reported more OBEs than participants to whom no such instructions were given (Palmer & Lieberman, 1975). Irwin (1981c) explored similar methods of induction. The use of hypnotic techniques also deserves further exploration (Cardeña, 1996; Irwin, 1989; Nash, Lynn, & Stanley, 1984).

Phenomenological Studies

Although a number of researchers have studied some features of the OBE, I have argued elsewhere that more in-depth phenomenological research is needed (Alvarado, 1997), especially in regard to variables that may moderate the content of the experience. Our understanding of the experience could be much more profound if we had more reliable evidence about the relationship of OBE features to participants' previous interest in and knowledge of the phenomenon and their scores on tests of such variables as dissociation, absorption, and schizotypy.

Alternative Methodologies

Although the customary survey and experimental approaches to the study of the OBE have not been exhaustively employed, other methodologies may be useful, among them qualitative methods. The works of Green (1968), Greene (1983), and Rogo (1976) have been helpful in providing an understanding of the variety and complexity of OBE phenomenology. Similarly, we may learn a great deal from single case studies of OBEs that emphasize situational variables and psychodynamics, as exemplified by Serdahely's (1993) article about dissociation in OBEs and NDEs and Gabbard and Twemlow's (1984) clinical cases. Analysis of the content of experients' accounts may allow us to study the ways in which the experience has been integrated into their lives and identities (White, 1997). Sutherland's (1992/1995) study of NDEs serves as a model of how qualitative analysis can chart the different forms that integration of the experience can take.

Aftereffects and Meaning

With reference to clinical concerns, it is important to study the variables that moderate or mediate the aftereffects of OBEs. This research may provide insight into the factors underlying personality transformations and provide guidelines for psychologists who help OB experients adapt to life after the event. For this, the experience needs to be glimpsed from the perspective of the experients, that is, in terms of personal meaningfulness. White (1994), articulating the importance of exceptional human experiences to the process of self-exploration and personal growth, wrote,

> If one follows the ripples initiated by one's exceptional experience, it
> will eventuate in a new sense of self and a new view of reality. Once
> one engages in this process, one becomes more connected to oneself,
> to others, to other forms of life, and to the universe itself. (p. 63)

Before such a statement can be applied to OB experients, researchers need to measure the type of changes people report after the experience in more detail than has been the case so far. In addition, the assessment of these life-transforming changes may be improved by considering other measures of change than the individual's own testimony. Assessment of OBE aftereffects may draw on testimonies of spouses, family members, and friends. Investigators may act on the possibility of whether changes are related to the complexity or depth of the OBE (as done in a study by Alvarado and Zingrone, 1998) and to the circumstances of the experience's occurrence, as Irwin (1988) did in his study of near-death versus non-near-death conditions of OBE occurrence.

Parapsychological Issues

Although the parapsychological approach may be the most controversial, it is one that should not be neglected, either because of political concerns or scientific conservatism, provided the tools of science are used. Results such as those of Tart (1968), who found that his participant was able to read a randomly selected number while having an OBE, and the interaction among ESP scores, OBEs, and the hypnagogic state found by Palmer (1978a) indicate the necessity for further study. Parapsychological effects are not limited to the acquisition of information. The physical effects of the detection studies reviewed earlier (Osis & McCormick, 1980) also deserve attention, as do the rare but puzzling OBE apparitions in which others claim to have seen the experient at a distant place during the course of the OBE (Hart, 1954, 1956; Laurentin & Mahéo, 1990). Some may argue that investigating the potentially parapsychological aspects of OBEs will obscure and retard one's understanding of the experience, but the systematic study of such an anomaly as the OBE should not exclude any valid avenue of research just because it challenges the conventional paradigms of psychology.

CONCLUSION

As can be seen in this review, there is still much to be done before the OBE is understood fully. Of the work reviewed in this chapter, it seems that the best predictors of the experience are such cognitive constructs as absorption and hypnotic susceptibility as well as hallucinatory, psi, and dream experiences. They all imply a capacity for openness to experiences, especially to internally generated experiences. Such constructs tell us little about the nature of the OBE itself, however. Research needs to be expanded to understand how these variables are related to both the context in which the OBE is reported to happen and to other variables such as the aftereffects of the experience. From the clinical point of view, it is important to have a better grasp of the apparent transformative power of the OBE on attitudes and values. A close knowledge of any experience capable of producing profound life changes, as the OBE seems to do, would, in principle, help psychologists not only to counsel experients more effectively but also to learn lessons applicable to the broader area of personality and attitude change.

Another issue that is important for clinicians is the relation of OBEs to psychopathological symptoms or disorders. The research conducted to date either does not relate the OBE to pathology or presents findings that are unclear at best. Some have interpreted the relationship with schizotypy as supporting the notion that OBEs indicate a psychotic-prone personality or predict future psychotic breakdowns, but such findings themselves do not unequivocally point to pathology. The relationship of the experience to psychopathology is an area that deserves much more exploration. Research along these lines should go beyond schizotypy, studying in more detail the meaning of relationships found between OBEs and dissociative experiences, such as depersonalization.

Finally, although the evidence for parapsychological effects during OBEs is fascinating and could have important conceptual implications about the ontology of the experience, we should be aware that the situation is not so simple as to assume that a veridical perception implies that the person has left the body in a literal sense. In some cases, there may be alternative sensory explanations for the phenomenological detail of the experiences or alternative parapsychological explanations (e.g., ESP) that do not need to assume that "something" leaves the body during the experience (the projection model of OBEs). Although the evidence for parapsychological processes during the OBE is not as strong as the evidence accumulated in other areas of parapsychology, the few positive findings (and the many spontaneous cases with veridical perceptions) that do exist deserve further exploration because they have the potential to expand our understanding of consciousness as it operates during the OBE. Unfortunately, there seems to be little communication between those who have studied the parapsychological aspects of the OBE and those who have focused on the psychology of the experience. Although I think that much could be gained by bringing both camps together, pragmatically speaking we are dealing with different goals, purposes, and even world views. One group wants to show that the OBE transcends human psychology and physiology and is key to the mind–body problem, whereas the other group suggests that the OBE is part of, or at least related to, the same psychological and physiological processes that operate in a variety of human experiences. I believe this dichotomy of approach has held us back from developing a systematic research program that can actively test different models and assumptions about the experience.

Even considering the research summarized here, the fact is that, similar to many of the other phenomena discussed in this book, OBEs generally have been neglected by psychology. Consequently, little empirical knowledge exists on the subject. It is my hope that this chapter will inspire further research and that future discussions on OBEs will not have to be conducted solely in the context of a psychology of the exotic or the unusual, but in the wider context of the study of the totality of human experience.

REFERENCES

Alvarado, C. S. (1980). The physical detection of the astral body: An historical perspective. *Theta, 8*(2), 4–7.

Alvarado, C. S. (1982a). ESP during out-of-body experiences: A review of experimental studies. *Journal of Parapsychology, 46,* 209–230.

Alvarado, C. S. (1982b). Recent OBE detection studies: A review. *Theta, 10,* 35–37.

Alvarado, C. S. (1983). ESP and out-of-body experiences: A review of spontaneous studies. *Parapsychology Review, 14*(4), 11–13.

Alvarado, C. S. (1984). Phenomenological aspects of out-of-body experiences: A report of three studies. *Journal of the American Society for Psychical Research, 78,* 219–240.

Alvarado, C. S. (1986a). ESP during spontaneous out-of-body experiences: A research and methodological note. *Journal of the Society for Psychical Research, 53,* 393–397.

Alvarado, C. S. (1986b). Research on spontaneous out-of-body experiences: A review of modern developments, 1960–1984. In B. Shapin & L. Coly (Eds.), *Current trends in psi research* (pp. 140–167). New York: Parapsychology Foundation.

Alvarado, C. S. (1988). Aspectos psicológicos de las experiencias fuera del cuerpo: Revisión de estudios de casos espontneos [Psychological aspects of out-of-body experiences: A review of spontaneous case studies]. *Revista Puertorriqueña de Psicología, 5,* 31–43.

Alvarado, C. S. (1989). Trends in the study of out-of-body experiences: An overview of developments since the nineteenth century. *Journal of Scientific Exploration, 3,* 27–42.

Alvarado, C. S. (1992). The psychological approach to out-of-body experiences: A review of early and modern developments. *Journal of Psychology, 126,* 237–250.

Alvarado, C. S. (1997). Mapping the characteristics of out-of-body experiences. *Journal of the American Society for Psychical Research, 91,* 15–32.

Alvarado, C. S., & Zingrone, N. L. (1994). Individual differences in aura vision: Relationships to visual imagery and imaginative-fantasy experiences. *European Journal of Parapsychology, 10,* 1–30.

Alvarado, C. S., & Zingrone, N. L. (1997a, August). *Out-of-body experiences and dissociation.* Paper presented at the 40th Annual Convention of the Parapsychological Association, Brighton, England.

Alvarado, C. S., & Zingrone, N. L. (1997b). Relación entre la experiencia fuera del cuerpo y la absorción: Estudios con participantes puertorriqueños y norteamericanos [Relationship between out-of-body experiences and absorption: Studies with Puerto Rican and American participants]. *Revista Argentina de Psicología Paranormal, 8,* 249–261.

Alvarado, C. S., & Zingrone, N. L. (1998). La experiencia fuera del cuerpo y su

influencia sobre actitudes y creencias: El impacto de la complejidad fenomen-
ológica de la experiencia [The out-of-body experience and its influence on
attitudes and beliefs: The impact of the phenomenological complexity of the
experience]. In A. Parra (Ed.), *Tercer Encuentro Psi 1998* (pp. 6–13). Buenos
Aires, Argentina: Instituto Argentino de Psicología Paranormal.

Alvarado, C. S., & Zingrone, N. L. (1999). Out-of-body experiences among readers
of a Spanish New Age magazine. *Journal of the Society for Psychical Research,
63*, 65–85.

Alvarado, C. S., Zingrone, N. L., & Dalton, K. (1996a, August). *Out-of-body experiences, alterations of consciousness and ESP: A further analysis of the Edinburgh
Ganzfeld data.* Paper presented at the 39th Annual Convention of the Parapsychological Association, San Diego, CA.

Alvarado, C. S., Zingrone, N. L., & Dalton, K. (1996b, August). *Out-of-body
experiences, psi experiences, and the "Big Five": Relating the NEO-PI-R to the
experience claims of experimental subjects.* Paper presented at the 39th Annual
Convention of the Parapsychological Association, San Diego, CA.

Blackmore, S. J. (1982a). *Beyond the body: An investigation of out-of-the-body experiences.* London: Heinemann.

Blackmore, S. J. (1982b). Have you ever had an OBE? The wording of the question. *Journal of the Society for Psychical Research, 51*, 292–302.

Blackmore, S. J. (1982c). Out-of-the-body experiences, lucid dreams and imagery:
Two surveys. *Journal of the American Society for Psychical Research, 76*, 301–
317.

Blackmore, S. J. (1983a). Birth and the OBE: An unhelpful analogy. *Journal of the
American Society for Psychical Research, 77*, 229–238.

Blackmore, S. J. (1983b). Imagery and the OBE. In W. G. Roll, J. Beloff, &
R. A. White (Eds.), *Research in parapsychology 1982* (pp. 231–232). Metuchen, NJ: Scarecrow Press.

Blackmore, S. J. (1984a). A postal survey of OBEs and other experiences. *Journal
of the Society for Psychical Research, 52*, 225–244.

Blackmore, S. J. (1984b). A psychological theory of the out-of-body experience.
Journal of Parapsychology, 48, 201–218.

Blackmore, S. J. (1986a). Out-of-body experiences in schizophrenia: A questionnaire survey. *Journal of Nervous and Mental Disease, 174*, 615–619.

Blackmore, S. J. (1986b). Spontaneous and deliberate OBEs: A questionnaire survey. *Journal of the Society for Psychical Research, 53*, 218–224.

Blackmore, S. J. (1987). Where am I? Perspectives in imagery and the out-of-body
experience. *Journal of Mental Imagery, 11*, 53–66.

Blackmore, S. J. (1993). *Dying to live: Science and the near-death experience.* London:
Grafton.

Blackmore, S. J., & Harris, B. (1983). OBEs and perceptual distortions in
schizophrenic patients and students. In W. G. Roll, J. Beloff, & R. A. White
(Eds.), *Research in parapsychology, 1989* (pp. 232–234). Metuchen, NJ: Scarecrow Press.

Brelaz de Castro, J. F. (1998). Experiencias fuera del cuerpo: Una encuesta sobre estudiantes universitarios en Brasil [Out of body experiences: A survey of university students in Brazil]. *Revista Argentina de Psicología Paranormal*, *9*, 11–27.

Brugger, P., Agosti, R., Regard, M., Wieser, H.-G., & Landis, T. (1994). Heautoscopy, epilepsy, and suicide. *Journal of Neurology, Neurosurgery, and Psychiatry*, *57*, 838–839.

Brugger, P., Regard, M., & Landis, T. (1996). Unilaterally felt "presences": The neuropsychiatry of one's invisible Doppelgänger. *Neuropsychiatry, Neuropsychology, and Behavioral Neurology*, *9*, 114–122.

Cardeña, E. (1988, November). *The phenomenology of quiescent and physically active deep hypnosis*. Paper presented at the 39th Annual Meeting of the Society for Clinical and Experimental Hypnosis, Asheville, NC.

Cardeña, E. (1996). "Just floating on the sky": A comparison of shamanic and hypnotic phenomenology. In R. Quekelbherge & D. Eigner (Eds.), *6th Jahrbuch für Transkulturelle Medizin und Psychotherapie* [6th yearbook of cross-cultural medicine and psychotherapy] (pp. 367–380). Berlin: Verlag für Wissenschaft und Bildung.

Chadha, N. K., Sahni, V. B., & Alvarado, C. S. (1987, August). *A survey of claims of psychic phenomena with an Indian college student population*. Paper presented at the 30th Annual Convention of the Parapsychological Association, Edinburgh, Scotland.

Clarke, D. (1995). Experience and other reasons given for belief and disbelief in paranormal and religious phenomena. *Journal of the Society for Psychical Research*, *60*, 371–384.

Claridge, G. (1985). *Origins of mental illness: Temperament, deviance and disorder*. Oxford, England: Basil Blackwell.

Claridge, G. (1988). Schizotypy and schizophrenia. In P. Bebbington & P. McGuffin (Eds.), *Schizophrenia: The major issues* (pp. 187–200). Oxford, England: Heinemann Mental Health Foundation.

Comfort, A. (1982). Out-of-body experiences and migraine. *American Journal of Psychiatry*, *139*, 1379–1380.

Cook, A. M., & Irwin, H. J. (1983). Visuospatial skills and the out-of-body experience. *Journal of Parapsychology*, *47*, 23–35.

Crookall, R. (1961). *The study and practice of astral projection*. London: Aquarian Press.

Crookall, R. (1964). *More astral projections: Analyses of case histories*. London: Aquarian Press.

Crookall, R. (1972). *Case-book of astral projection 545–746*. Secaucus, NJ: University Books.

Crookall, R. (1978). *What happens when you die?* Gerrards Cross, England: Colin Smythe.

Dalton, K., Zingrone, N. L., & Alvarado, C. S. (1999, August). *Exploring out-of-body experiences, dissociation, absorption, and alteration of consciousness in the ganzfeld with a creative population.* Paper presented at the 42nd Annual Convention of the Parapsychological Association, Stanford University, Palo Alto, CA.

Eastman, M. (1962). Out-of-the-body experiences. *Proceedings of the Society for Psychical Research, 53,* 287–309.

Fox, O. (1939). *Astral projection: A record of out-of-the-body experiences.* London: Rider.

Gabbard, G. O., & Twemlow, S. W. (1984). *With the eyes of the mind: An empirical analysis of out-of-body states.* New York: Praeger Scientific.

Gabbard, G. O., Twemlow, S. W., & Jones, F. C. (1981). Do near-death experiences occur only near death? *Journal of Nervous and Mental Disease, 169,* 374–377.

Gackenbach, J. (1978). *A personality and cognitive style analysis of lucid dreaming.* Unpublished doctoral dissertation, Virginia Commonwealth University.

Giovetti, P. (1983). *Viaggi senza corpo* [Travels without the body]. Milan, Italy: Armenia.

Glicksohn, J. (1989). The structure of subjective experience: Interdependencies along the sleep–wakefulness continuum. *Journal of Mental Imagery, 13,* 99–106.

Glicksohn, J. (1990). Belief in the paranormal and subjective paranormal experience. *Personality and Individual Differences, 11,* 675–683.

Green, C. E. (1967). Ecsomatic experiences and related phenomena. *Journal of the Society for Psychical Research, 44,* 111–131.

Green, C. E. (1968). *Out-of-the-body experiences.* London: Hamish Hamilton.

Green, C. E., & McCreery, C. (1994). *Lucid dreaming: The paradox of consciousness during sleep.* New York: Routledge.

Greene, F. G. (1983). Multiple mind/body perspectives and the out-of-body experience. *Anabiosis, 3,* 39–62.

Greyson, B. (1983). The near-death experience scale: Construction, reliability and validity. *Journal of Nervous and Mental Disease, 171,* 369–375.

Harary, S. B. (1978). A personal perspective on out-of-body experiences. In D. S. Rogo (Ed.), *Mind beyond the body: The mystery of ESP projection* (pp. 260–269). Harmondsworth, England: Penguin Books.

Harary, S. B., & Solfvin, G. (1977). A study of out-of-body experiences using auditory targets. In J. D. Morris, W. G. Roll, and R. L. Morris (Eds.), *Research in parapsychology, 1976* (pp. 260–269). Metuchen, NJ: Scarecrow Press.

Hart, H. (1954). ESP projection: Spontaneous cases and the experimental method. *Journal of the American Society for Psychical Research, 48,* 121–146.

Hart, H. (1956). Six theories of apparitions. *Proceedings of the Society for Psychical Research, 50,* 153–239.

Hunt, H., Gervais, A., Shearing-Johns, S., & Travis, F. (1992). Transpersonal experiences in childhood: An exploratory empirical study of selected adult groups. *Perceptual and Motor Skills, 75,* 1135–1153.

Irwin, H. J. (1980). Out of the body down under: Some cognitive characteristics of Australian students reporting OBEs. *Journal of the Society for Psychical Research, 50,* 448–459.

Irwin, H. J. (1981a). Correspondence. *Journal of the Society for Psychical Research, 51,* 118–120.

Irwin, H. J. (1981b). The psychological function of out-of-body experiences: So who needs the out-of-body experience? *Journal of Nervous and Mental Disease, 169,* 244–248.

Irwin, H. J. (1981c). Some psychological dimensions of out-of-body experiences. *Parapsychology Review, 12*(4), 1–6.

Irwin, H. J. (1983). The association between out-of-body experiences and migraine. *Psi Research, 2*(2), 89–96.

Irwin, H. J. (1985a). *Flight of mind: A psychological study of the out-of-body experience.* Metuchen, NJ: Scarecrow Press.

Irwin, H. J. (1985b). The link between the out-of-body experience and proneness to lucid dreams: A meta-analysis. *Psi Research, 4*(2), 24–31.

Irwin, H. J. (1985c). Parapsychological phenomena and the absorption domain. *Journal of the American Society for Psychical Research, 79,* 1–11.

Irwin, H. J. (1986). Perceptual perspective of visual imagery in OBEs, dreams and reminiscence. *Journal of the Society for Psychical Research, 53,* 210–217.

Irwin, H. J. (1988). Out-of-body experiences and attitudes to life and death. *Journal of the American Society for Psychical Research, 82,* 237–251.

Irwin, H. J. (1989). Hypnotic induction of the out-of-body experience. *Australian Journal of Clinical Hypnotherapy and Hypnosis, 10,* 1–7.

Irwin, H. J. (1993). The near-death experience as a dissociative phenomenon: An empirical assessment. *Journal of Near-Death Studies, 12,* 95–103.

Irwin, H. J. (1996). Childhood antecedents of out-of-body and deja vu experiences. *Journal of the American Society for Psychical Research, 90,* 157–173.

Kennedy, J., Kanthamani, H., & Palmer, J. (1994). Psychic and spiritual experiences, health, well-being, and meaning in life. *Journal of Parapsychology, 58,* 353–383.

Kohr, R. L. (1980). A survey of psi experiences among members of a special population. *Journal of the American Society for Psychical Research, 74,* 395–411.

Krippner, S. (1996). A pilot study in ESP, dreams and purported OBEs. *Journal of the Society for Psychical Research, 61,* 88–93.

Laurentin, R., & Mahéo, P. (1990). *Bilocations de Mre Yvonne-Aime* [The bilocations of Mother Yvonne-Aime]. Paris: O.E.I.L.

Lippman, C. W. (1953). Hallucinations of physical duality in migraine. *Journal of Nervous and Mental Disease, 117,* 345–350.

Maitz, E. A., & Pekala, R. J. (1991). Phenomenological quantification of an out-of-body experience associated with a near-death event. *Omega, 22,* 199–214.

McClenon, J. (1990). Surveys of anomalous experience: A cross–cultural analysis. *Journal of American Society for Psychical Research, 88,* 117–135.

McCreery, C. (1993). *Schizotypy and out-of-the-body experiences.* Unpublished doctoral dissertation, Oxford University, Oxford, England.

McCreery, C. (1997). Hallucinations and arousability: Pointers to a theory of psychosis. In G. Claridge (Ed.), *Schizotypy: Implications for illness and health* (pp. 251–273). Oxford, England: Oxford University Press.

McCreery, C., & Claridge, G. (1995). Out-of-the-body experiences and personality. *Journal of the Society for Psychical Research, 60,* 129–148.

McCreery, C., & Claridge, G. (1996a). A study of hallucination in normal subjects: I. Self-report data. *Personality and Individual Differences, 21,* 739–747.

McCreery, C., & Claridge, G. (1996b). A study of hallucination in normal subjects: II. Electrophysiological data. *Personality and Individual Differences, 21,* 749–758.

Miller, L. C., Murphy, R., & Buss, A. H. (1981). Consciousness of body: Private and public. *Journal of Personality and Social Psychology, 41,* 397–406.

Monroe, R. (1971). *Journeys out of the body.* Garden City, NY: Doubleday.

Morris, R. L., Harary, S. B., Janis, J., Hartwell, J., & Roll, W. G. (1978). Studies of communication during out-of-body experiences. *Journal of the American Society for Psychical Research, 72,* 1–21.

Muldoon, S. J. (1936). *The case for astral projection.* Chicago: Ariel Press.

Muldoon, S. J., & Carrington, H. (1929). *The projection of the astral body.* London: Rider.

Muldoon, S. J., & Carrington, H. (1951). *The phenomena of astral projection.* London: Rider.

Myers, S. A. (1982). *Personality characteristics as related to out-of-body experiences.* Unpublished master's thesis, St. Louis University, St. Louis, MO.

Myers, S. A., Austrin, H. R., Grisso, J. T., & Nickeson, R. C. (1983). Personality characteristics as related to the out-of-body experience. *Journal of Parapsychology, 47,* 131–144.

Nash, M. R., Lynn, S. J., & Givens, D. L. (1984). Adult hypnotic susceptibility, childhood punishment, and child abuse: A brief communication. *International Journal of Clinical and Experimental Hypnosis, 32,* 6–11.

Nash, M. R., Lynn, S. J., & Stanley, S. M. (1984). The direct hypnotic suggestion of altered mind/body perception. *American Journal of Clinical Hypnosis, 27,* 95–102.

Olsen, M. (1988). The incidence of out-of-body experiences in hospitalized patients. *Journal of Near-Death Studies, 6,* 169–174.

Osis, K. (1975). Perceptual experiments on out-of-body experiences. In J. D. Morris, W. G. Roll, & R. L. Morris (Eds.), *Research in parapsychology, 1974* (pp. 53–55). Metuchen, NJ: Scarecrow Press.

Osis, K. (1979). Insider's view of the OBE: A questionnaire study. In W. G. Roll (Ed.), *Research in parapsychology 1978* (pp. 50–52). Metuchen, NJ: Scarecrow Press.

Osis, K., & McCormick, D. (1980). Kinetic effects at the ostensible location of an out-of- body projection during perceptual testing. *Journal of the American Society for Psychical Research, 74,* 319–329.

Osis, K., & Mitchell, J. L. (1977). Physiological correlates of reported out-of-body experiences. *Journal of the Society for Psychical Research, 49,* 525–536.

Palmer, J. (1978a). ESP and out-of-body experiences: An experimental approach. In D. S. Rogo (Ed.), *Mind beyond the body: The mystery of ESP projection* (pp. 193–217). Harmondsworth, England: Penguin Books.

Palmer, J. (1978b). The out-of-the body experience: A psychological theory. *Parapsychology Review, 9*(5), 19–22.

Palmer, J. (1979a). A community mail survey of psychic experiences. *Journal of the American Society for Psychical Research, 73,* 221–251.

Palmer, J. (1979b). ESP and out-of-body experiences: EEG correlates. In W. G. Roll (Ed.), *Research in parapsychology 1978* (pp. 135–138). Metuchen, NJ: Scarecrow Press.

Palmer, J., & Lieberman, R. (1975). The influence of psychological set on ESP and out-of-body experiences. *Journal of the American Society for Psychical Research, 69,* 193–213.

Palmer, J., & Lieberman, R. (1976). ESP and out-of-body experiences: A further study. In J. D. Morris, W. G. Roll, & R. L. Morris (Eds.), *Research in parapsychology 1975* (pp. 102–106). Metuchen, NJ: Scarecrow Press.

Palmer, J., & Vassar, C. (1974). ESP and out-of-the-body experiences: An exploratory study. *Journal of the American Society for Psychical Research, 68,* 257–280.

Pekala, R. J., Kumar, V. K., & Cummings, J. (1992). Types of high hypnotically susceptible individuals and reported attitudes and experiences of the paranormal and the anomalous. *Journal of the American Society for Psychical Research, 86,* 135–150.

Pekala, R. J., Kumar V. K., & Marcano, G. (1995). Anomalous/paranormal experiences, hypnotic susceptibility and dissociation. *Journal of the American Society for Psychical Research, 89,* 313–332.

Penfield, W., & Jasper, H. (1954). *Epilepsy and the functional anatomy of the human brain.* Boston: Little, Brown.

Persinger, M. A. (1983). Religious and mystical experiences as artifacts of temporal lobe function: A general hypothesis. *Perceptual and Motor Skills, 57,* 1255–1262.

Persinger, M. A. (1995). Out-of-body-like experiences are more probable in people with elevated complex partial epileptic-like signs during periods of enhanced geomagnetic activity: A nonlinear effect. *Perceptual and Motor Skills, 80,* 563–569.

Persinger, M. A., & Makarec, K. (1987). Temporal lobe signs and correlative behaviors displayed by normal populations. *Journal of General Psychology, 114,* 179–195.

Peterson, R. (1997). *Out of body experiences: How to have them and what to expect.* Charlottesville, VA: Hampton Roads.

Poynton, J. C. (1975). Results of an out-of-the-body survey. In J. C. Poynton (Ed.),

Parapsychology in South Africa (pp. 109–123). Johannesburg: South African Society for Psychical Research.

Richards, D. G. (1988, August). *Measures of subjective psi experience: Consistency, reliability, and validity.* Paper presented at the 31st Annual Convention of the Parapsychological Association, Montreal, Quebec, Canada.

Richards, D. G. (1991). A study of the correlation between subjective psychic experiences and dissociative experiences. *Dissociation, 4,* 83–91.

Ring, K. (1992). *The Omega Project: Near-death experiences, UFO encounters, and mind at large.* New York: Morrow.

Rogo, D. S. (1976). Aspects of out-of-the body experiences. *Journal of the Society for Psychical Research, 48,* 329–335.

Rosenthal, R. (1991). *Meta-analytic procedures for social research* (rev. ed.). Newbury Park, CA: Sage.

Serdahely, W. J. (1993). Near-death experiences and dissociation: Two cases. *Journal of Near-Death Studies, 12,* 85–94.

Severi, A. (1995). Indagine antropologica sulla distribuzione di alcuni stati modificati di coscienza in un campione di studenti universitari [Anthropological inquiry on the distribution of some altered stets of consciousness in a sample of college students]. *Luce e Ombra, 95,* 405–432.

Spanos, N. P., & Moretti, P. (1988). Correlates of mystical and diabolical experiences in a sample of female university students. *Journal for the Scientific Study of Religion, 27,* 106–116.

Stanford, R. G. (1987). The out-of-body experience as an imaginal journey: The developmental perspective. *Journal of Parapsychology, 51,* 137–155.

Stanford, R. G. (1994). Developmental correlates of out-of-body experiences (OBEs) in specific states of consciousness: A replication failure. *Journal of Parapsychology, 58,* 197–199.

Steinberg, M. (1995). *Handbook for the assessment of dissociation: A clinical guide.* Washington, DC: Psychiatric Press.

Sutherland, C. (1995). *Reborn in the light: Life after near-death experiences.* New York: Bantam. (Original work published 1992)

Tart, C. T. (1967). A second psychophysiological study of out-of-the body experiences in a gifted subject. *International Journal of Parapsychology, 9,* 251–258.

Tart, C. T. (1968). A psychophysiological study of out-of-the body experiences in a selected subject. *Journal of the American Society for Psychical Research, 62,* 3–27.

Tart, C. T. (1969). A further psychophysiological study of out-of-the body experiences in a gifted subject. *Proceedings of the Parapsychological Association, 6,* 43–44.

Tart, C. T. (1971). *On being stoned: A psychological study of marijuana intoxication.* Palo Alto, CA: Science and Behavior Books.

Tart, C. T. (1974). Some methodological problems in OOBE research: Comments on the symposium. In W. G. Roll, R. L. Morris, & J. D. Morris (Eds.), *Research in parapsychology 1973* (pp. 116–120). Metuchen, NJ: Scarecrow Press.

Thalbourne, M. A. (1994). The SPR Centenary Census: II. The survey of beliefs. *Journal of the Society for Psychical Research, 59*, 420–431.

Tobacyk, J. J., & Mitchell, T. P. (1987). The out-of-body experience and personality adjustment. *Journal of Nervous and Mental Disease, 175*, 367–370.

Tobacyk, J. J., Wells, D. H., & Miller, M. M. (1998). Out-of-body experience and personality functioning. *Psychological Reports, 82*, 481–482.

Twemlow, S. W. (1977). Epilogue: Personality file. In R. Monroe (Ed.), *Journeys out of the body* (pp. 275–280). Garden City, NY: Doubleday.

Twemlow, S. W. (1989). Clinical approaches to the out-of-body experience. *Journal of Near-Death Studies, 8*, 29–43.

Usha, S., & Pasricha, S. (1989a). Claims of paranormal experiences: I. A survey of psi and psi-related experiences. *NIMHANS Journal, 7*, 143–150.

Usha, S., & Pasricha, S. (1989b). Claims of paranormal experiences: II. Attitudes toward psychical research and factors associated with psi and psi-related experiences. *NIMHANS Journal, 7*, 151–157.

Vieira, W. (1995). *Projections of the consciousness: A diary of out-of-body experiences* (A. Salgado, K. de la Tour, & S. de La Tour, Trans.). Rio de Janeiro, Brazil: International Institute of Projectology.

White, R. A. (1994). *Exceptional human experience: Background papers: I*. Dix Hills, NY: Exceptional Human Experience Network.

White, R. A. (1997). Dissociation, narrative, and exceptional human experiences. In S. Krippner & S. M. Powers (Eds.), *Broken images, broken selves* (pp. 88–121). New York: Brunner/Mazel.

Wiedman, K. D., & Haraldsson, E. (1980). *Some results concerning reported OBEs in Iceland*. Unpublished manuscript.

Wilson, S. C., & Barber, T. X. (1983). The fantasy-prone personality: Implications for understanding imagery, hypnosis, and parapsychological phenomena. In A. A. Sheikh (Ed.), *Imagery: Current theory, research, and application* (pp. 340–387). New York: Wiley.

Woodhouse, M. B. (1994). Out-of-body experiences and the mind–body problem. *New Ideas in Psychology, 12*, 1–16.

Zangari, W., & Machado, F. R. (1996). Survey: Incidence and social relevance of Brazilian university students' psychic experiences. *European Journal of Parapsychology, 12*, 75–87.

Zingrone, N. L., & Alvarado, C. S. (1994, August). *Psychic and dissociative experiences: A preliminary report*. Paper presented at the 37th Annual Convention of the Parapsychological Association, Amsterdam.

7

PSI-RELATED EXPERIENCES

ELISABETH TARG, MARILYN SCHLITZ, AND HARVEY J. IRWIN

Anna Martínez moved to Los Angeles from an area outside Tepoztlán, Mexico, when she was 5 years old. She is a gentle, soft spoken, middle-aged woman with jet black hair and a rounded figure. Her life never struck her as extraordinary, just hard: an abusive father, immigration to a country where a woman of color can be invisible, and an alcoholic husband who couldn't hold a job. She often dreams of her grandmother in Mexico: "Abuelita" used to say that little Anna had "the gift," and praised her for her prescient announcements of visitors while the streets were still quiet. They used to sit for hours and talk about angels. Over the years, Anna sometimes had dreams that disturbed her and her family. In one dream, her grown daughter received a gift from a man with whom the young woman worked. Her daughter laughed when Anna told her about the dream, but 2 days later she called to say that it had come true; a man from work had given her a new scarf that he said matched her eyes. "How could you have known that he would do this, mama?," the young woman asked. Anna had no simple answer for her daughter.

Two months prior to presentation at the county hospital, Anna was

We thank Jerry Solfvin for his contributions to this chapter and Adrienne Smucker for her help in the preparation of the manuscript.

awakened by a frighteningly realistic dream. Her husband of 23 years was stepping off the curb in the downtown shopping district. In a flash, a crowd gathered around and there were sirens; he had been hit by a bus during rush hour. The dream haunted her, but she didn't dare tell her husband. Two weeks later, Anna's husband was killed by a bus not far from where he worked. Stricken by depression and guilt and fearful that she had somehow caused her husband's death by means of her "bad thoughts," the deeply religious Catholic woman abandoned her housework, stopped sleeping and eating, and kept enigmatically repeating that she "was going to be punished by God." Her daughter brought her to the emergency room.

A 2nd-year psychiatry resident evaluated the situation. He diagnosed Anna with "complicated bereavement with psychotic features." In his assessment, the bus accident was a coincidence that played into Anna's unconscious feelings about her abusive husband, and the guilt surrounding this loss had triggered depression in a woman whose history indicated a possible underlying predisposition to psychosis. The psychiatrist's focus on Anna's "reality testing" intensified Anna's anxiety and isolation. For her there was no coincidence. Her questions were different from the doctor's: How could she have known the future? Did her vision cause her husband's death? Was there something she could have done to prevent his accident, some way she could have warned him before it happened? How could she live with herself knowing that her thoughts might have killed him?

DEFINITION

Anomalous experiences like the ones reported by Anna are known as *psi-related experiences* (PREs) or *spontaneous psi*, and for over a century they have been subjected to systematic scientific scrutiny by researchers from many disciplines (see Broughton, 1991; Edge, Morris, Palmer, & Rush, 1986; Irwin, 1999; Radin, 1997). PREs include reports of apparent telepathy (direct mind-to-mind communication), clairvoyance (anomalous knowledge of distant events), precognition (knowledge of the future, as suggested by Anna's dreams), or psychokinesis (mind over matter, as illustrated by Anna's fears that her dream somehow caused the death). Note that PREs are defined in phenomenological terms; that is, it seems to the experient that some "paranormal" process is involved in these events (Irwin, 1994). When studied in a suitably controlled laboratory setting, the underlying ostensibly paranormal process, be it extrasensory or psychokinetic in nature, is termed *psi*. Thus, psi is a hypothetical construct relating to the presumed anomalous transfer of information or energy for which there is, arguably, objective evidential support (Bem & Honorton, 1994).

The focus in this chapter is on subjective reports of psi experiences rather than on attempts to differentiate the phenomenology of nonveridical and presumably veridical psi. We use the term for both phenomena to facilitate exposition. The focus of the chapter, however, carries significant limitations. Most importantly, an individual who may be having psychological reactions to a veridical psi event will necessarily have different needs than an individual who, for example, is grandiose, self-deluding, or psychotic. We therefore offer a descriptive discussion of psi experiences understanding that, without differentiating presumably veridical from nonveridical psi, we can make no generalizations concerning the etiology, sequelae, or significance of these experiences. The purpose of this chapter is therefore to acquaint the reader with a variety of experiences that are phenomenologically similar, regardless of their etiology.

An incisive understanding of Anna's experience, and others like it, is complicated by many social, cultural, psychological, and medical factors. This chapter seeks to take due account of these factors in its analysis of subjective reports of PREs. We emphasize the need and difficulty for the clinician, treating a client who has undergone these experiences, to make a diagnosis and offer appropriate treatment, usually in the context of having no means to ascertain the veridicality of the experience, let alone its paranormality. In Anna's case, for example, her experiences might have indeed been delusional, although arguably there is evidence to indicate otherwise. An extended differential diagnosis would include brief reactive psychosis, depression, dissociative disorders, posttraumatic stress disorder, schizophrenia, schizotypal personality disorder, substance abuse, and temporal-lobe epilepsy. In a psychodynamic framework, we might seek to understand Anna's experiences on the basis of the anxiety associated with her loss of and her anger toward her husband.

Perhaps Anna's view that the dreams were somehow manifestations of reality is the result of a cultural mythology that has no basis in objective fact. If so, Anna's beliefs may have been a product of her Latino heritage, which may accept that some people are capable of knowing the future, communicating with spirits, or healing others with their minds. This may not be a perspective that a Western-trained physician would endorse. Alternatively, Anna's experience may be a genuine example of psi, that is, an instance of information transfer occurring outside the currently understood perceptual–motor channels or inferential processes. In that case, Anna would be dealing with an experience that is at odds with the belief system of important sectors of the dominant North American culture, and she may find little empathy with her experience from her more acculturated family members or her physician. Each of these explanations of Anna's experience presents different challenges, treatment options, and sequelae.

PREVALENCE

Anna is not alone in her experiences of ostensible psi phenomena. Trust in apparently prescient dreams, visions, and visitations has influenced both ancient and modern human civilizations. The concept of divination is basic to not only shamanic but also Judeo-Christian traditions. As in other places, leaders in ancient Greece relied heavily on the prophetic efforts of sibyls at the Oracle of Delphi to make strategic decisions. In modern Asia, the time of escape for His Holiness, the 14th Dalai Lama, after the Chinese invasion was determined through directions from the Nechung oracle, who helped guide the spiritual and political leader of Tibet into safety in India (Gyatsu, 1991).

Reports of personal PREs such as apparent clairvoyance, telepathy, and precognition (in waking and in dream states) are common throughout the world. In the United States, for example, a 1987 survey published by the University of Chicago's National Opinion Research Center canvassed nearly 1,500 adult Americans, of whom 67% claimed to have had PREs (Greeley, 1987). In most countries where surveys have been conducted, PREs have been reported by over half the population. This level of prevalence has been found in surveys undertaken in North America (Emmons & Sobal, 1981; Greeley, 1975, 1985; McClenon, 1988, 1993; Palmer, 1979), Great Britain (Hay & Morisy, 1978), other countries in Europe (Haraldsson, 1985; Haraldsson & Houtkooper, 1991), the Middle East (Glicksohn, 1990), Brazil (Zangari & Machado, 1994), Asia (Emmons, 1982; McClenon, 1988, 1993), and Australasia (Clarke, 1995; Irwin, 1985b; Thalbourne, 1995). The most common PREs entail apparent telepathy (acknowledged by about a third, and sometimes as much as half, of the population; Haraldsson & Houtkooper, 1991) or clairvoyance (in about a fifth of the population). Reports of psychokinesis or mind-over-matter effects are much less frequent (between 5% and 10% in relative incidence; Palmer, 1979).

Survey data nevertheless indicate that the prevalence of reports of PREs does vary to some extent according to the country or culture being studied. For example, in a survey of university students in Brazil (Zangari & Machado, 1994), where Afro-Brazilian spiritism is an important cultural feature (Hess, 1992), more than 90% of those sampled reported at least one psi-related experience. Culture also plays a significant role in determining the types of experiences reported and the way in which they are reported. In many societies, PREs are frequently associated with ritual contexts that may include altered states of consciousness and strong expectations of or demands for particular outcomes (Kelly & Locke, 1981). PREs are often described within a mystical conceptual framework, as representing the intrinsic oneness of all beings and matter, or as the workings of spirits and entities from another "world" (e.g., Klimo, 1987).

The systematic study of spontaneous PREs has proceeded also through the study of numerous collections of individual case reports. The compilation of case collections began in the late 1800s (Gurney, Myers, & Podmore, 1886) and continues to the present day (Haight, 1979; Haraldsson, Gudmundsdottir, Ragnarsson, Loftsson, & Jonsson, 1977; L. E. Rhine, 1962a, 1962b, 1978). The vastness of these collections might be taken to support the view of PREs as widespread in the general population (see L. E. Rhine, 1981).

PHENOMENOLOGY

Surveys and case collections have provided a rich body of data on the phenomenological characteristics of PREs, that is, the nature of these experiences as depicted by experients themselves. The major phenomenological features of purportedly extrasensory experiences is summarized below. Considerably less information is available on the phenomenology of psychokinetic experiences; for a review of this material, the reader is referred to Irwin (1999).

For ease of exposition, and in particular to avoid repeated use of the cumbersome expression "apparent extrasensory experience," the terms *extrasensory experience* and *ESP experience* are taken to signify a spontaneous experience which, in the opinion of the experient, entailed an anomalous transfer of information.

As suggested by Anna's case, extrasensory experiences vary in their temporal context. Although the experience may seem to the experient to be in the here and now while it is taking place, subsequently it can be construed to fall into one of three temporal categories. Most ESP experiences (about 60% of the case collection of L. E. Rhine, 1981) are *contemporaneous*, that is, they relate to an event taking place concurrently in another location. Almost all of the remainder seemingly relate to future events and are termed *precognitive*. Very rarely, the experience may be *retrocognitive*, or pertain to an event in the past of which the experient claims to have previously been ignorant.

According to the analysis of cases by L. E. Rhine (1953), the ESP experience may take one of four subjective forms: intuitive impressions, hallucinations, realistic visual images, or unrealistic visual images. An intuitive impression comprises a simple, imageless impression or "hunch"; experients might say they "just knew" about some (spatially or temporally) distant event. In a hallucinatory ESP experience, the extrasensory "message" is represented as a sensory hallucination; the experient might report, for example, seeing an apparition or hearing a voice (see also Bentall, this volume, chap. 3). Realistic visual images in ESP experiences most commonly occur as dreams in which the imagery is a very detailed and relatively literal representation of the events to which they seem to refer. In unrealistic visual images, on the other hand, the imagery is of a fanciful, unreal sort. In this case, the information about the event may be dramatized or be depicted in a rather disguised, for instance symbolic, form.

The relative incidence of the four forms of subjective ESP experience is not known precisely (see Irwin, 1999). In L. E. Rhine's (1962a) sample, 26% of cases were intuitive, 9% hallucinatory, 44% realistic visual imagery, and 21% unrealistic visual imagery. The form of the experience and its temporal context are correlated. A majority of precognitive experiences occur as realistic visual images in dreams (e.g., Sannwald, 1963), whereas the intuitive form is marginally the most common among contemporaneous experiences (about a third of cases).

Extrasensory experiences usually incorporate information of only some aspects of the presumed event to which they refer. L. E. Rhine (1962a, 1962b) examined the four forms of the experience for their completeness of content, the latter being defined in gross terms as whether or not the experience conveyed the general meaning of *what* happened and to *whom*. Realistic visual images were found to have the highest level of completeness of content (91%), followed by unrealistic images (72%), intuitions (55%), and hallucinatory experiences (32%).

The content of extrasensory experiences tends to be personally significant to the experient. The experience often relates to someone emotionally close to the experient and to deaths, personal crises (illness, accident, birth, marriage), and other events of personal importance (L. E. Rhine, 1956; Sannwald, 1963; Schouten, 1981, 1982). The personal significance of the content might also vary with the form of the experience. Schouten (1981), for example, reported that the death of the referent person is more likely to be represented in waking imagery than in an imageless intuition. Similarly, tragic events are more often the subject of precognitive experiences than of contemporaneous experiences (Sannwald, 1963).

Extrasensory experiences are often depicted by experients as very compelling and meaningful. L. E. Rhine (1962a) found that in 36% of cases the experients were convinced of the truth of their experience at the time of its occurrence. This sense of conviction is most frequent in PREs involving intuitive impressions (84%) and least frequent in unrealistic visual images (19%; L. E. Rhine, 1962a; Schouten, 1981).

The circumstances surrounding spontaneous PREs have been little studied. With regard to social context, Irwin (1999) found about two thirds of experients to have been alone at the time of their experience. This is not an artifact of the occurrence of ESP experiences during sleep; Schouten (1982) reported that waking ESP experiences most often arise when the experient is alone, although this might not be the case for intuitive experiences (Schouten, 1981).

In terms of concurrent actions, 90% of Irwin's (1999) experients had been engaged in minimal physical activity such as sleeping, sitting, or standing; activity was substantial (e.g., jogging) in only 3% of cases. In the same study, experients described their mental activity at the time of the ESP experience either as minimally demanding (28%) or as not really thinking about anything in particular (50%).

AFTEREFFECTS

Although many extrasensory experiences relate to unpleasant or sad events, there has been little study of their emotional impact. In Stevenson's (1970) study of telepathic intuitive experiences, the most common emotions were anxiety and depression. In surveys of extrasensory experiences more generally, however, the most commonly reported emotions are anxiety and happiness (Irwin, 1999; Milton, 1992). The emotional impact of a PRE presumably depends on its phenomenological characteristics, such as its form and the level of conviction it inspires. If conviction in the experience is low or the content obscured by symbolism, for example, the experient might be relatively unmoved by the underlying negative tone of the content.

Another measure of the PRE's impact is whether or not it inspires the experient to tell other people about it before the facts of the alleged referent event are confirmed. In Irwin's (1999) survey, 30% had disclosed the experience before its confirmation, 53% had not because of a lack of any inclination to do so, and 17% had not because of a lack of opportunity to do so. Similar results were found in Milton's (1992) survey; some respondents had fearfully hidden the fact of their PREs ("my belief was and is that if I had talked about this experience, I should have been treated as insane or deluded . . . , my career prospects might have been seriously damaged"), whereas others eagerly shared information about the experience with their community.

The impact of PREs also might be reflected in actions taken by the experient after having them. In precognitive experiences, for example, it might be feasible to try to take evasive action, by making a deliberate attempt to avoid the outcome supposedly "predicted" by the precognitive experience. The only finding to emerge from related research is the rather tautological trend for more action if the experient can identify the person referred to in the experience (Schouten, 1981, 1982; Stevenson, 1970).

There is limited evidence that having a PRE per se induces consistent long-term psychological or physical aftereffects (Stokes, 1997, pp. 43–44). The experience may, however, affect an individual in other ways. Aftereffects may be influenced by the experients' prior education about these experiences, his or her psychological needs, ego strengths, existing social support, and the content of the individuals' own psi experience. People may construe the latter as an opening to various aspects of spiritual life, indicating the possibility of greater connectedness to nature, or they may find the experience frightening or confusing. Response to a psi-related experience, whether positive or negative, may contribute to significant changes in the experient's sense of identity and choice of life path. Longitudinal research is needed to explore these possibilities.

The interpretation and sequelae of PRE are highly culture dependent. Individuals in India or Brazil, where many consider that such experiences represent a valued talent or reflect spiritual advancement, may find themselves encouraged, lauded, or congratulated. In Brazil, for example, a large survey of college students investigating the life impact of psi-related and transcendent experiences found that 80% of respondents felt that these experiences had had a significantly positive and tangible effect on their lives. Some students even believed that the experience had saved their lives or allowed them to rescue someone else (Zangari & Machado, 1994).

In many industrial societies, however, experients may become the target of ridicule by their community, or they may be confused by the fact that what occurred to them contradicts mainstream science and medicine. Data from a clinic in the Netherlands that serves as an information clearinghouse for people with PREs offer a window into the issues for which people may seek help (Kramer, 1989). Client concerns included feeling the pains of other people, unwanted telepathic contact, precognitive dreams, or a diffuse sense of foreboding.

In the United States, there is evidence that some members of the general population are fearful of PREs. In one study, 14% of college students who reported no PREs believed that having such an experience would be detrimental (Kennedy, Kanthamani, & Palmer, 1994). In a demonstration of the fear of PREs in modern U.S. society, Tart and LaBore (1986) performed a "thought experiment." They asked participants to contemplate the possibility of having powerful "psychic" abilities and to report their reactions to this scenario. The responses were largely negative, with respondents expressing fears about whether they would be able to control the ability, of being incapacitated by overload from others' thoughts, of rejection, or of too much responsibility if such an ability became known.

A fearful response may prompt rejection of the PREs or its attribution to external factors, such as Tarot cards, tea leaves, God, or the devil. Clinical observations of reactions to these experiences include fears of being hurt or going crazy, feelings of loss of control, disorientation from one's previous understanding of the world, and bewilderment (Ehrenwald, 1977; Hastings, 1983; Lukoff & Everest, 1985; Van Dusen, 1972). Some experients (as we found in Anna's case) may feel that they are somehow responsible for causing the negative events to which the experience referred (Hastings, 1983).

Despite some individuals' anxiety about the potential negative impact of PREs, there is evidence that such experiences also may be associated with healthy and positive outcomes. For example, there is a high correlation between reports of PREs and reports of ecstatic or mystical experiences (Kennedy & Kanthamani, 1995; Palmer, 1979; see Wulff, this volume, chap. 12). The latter, in turn, are often associated with life satisfaction (Greeley, 1975), well-being, and a sense of meaning and purpose (Kennedy et al., 1994).

PREs, at least in Western societies, challenge the world view of many individuals. They may be construed as frightening or as creating the sense of an expanded awareness and connection to the world. Subsequent adjustment presumably will depend largely on the meaning that the person attributes to the experience.

INDIVIDUAL DIFFERENCES

Research on predisposition to PREs has evaluated differences between nonexperients and experients. There is also a substantial body of empirical data on the correlates of successful performance on presumably veridical psi-type tasks in the laboratory. The relevance of the latter data to a predisposition toward spontaneous everyday PREs, however, is equivocal. Some findings on the correlates of laboratory performance are contrary to those of spontaneous experiences. For these reasons, the literature on success in experimental psi-type tasks will not be addressed here (see Irwin, 1999, for a review). Our focus is a predisposition to PREs in everyday life.

Reporting of personal PREs is intrinsically linked to a belief in the paranormal. Several surveys have found at least a moderate correlation between the reported incidence of PREs and the intensity of belief in the reality of psi (Clarke, 1995; Glicksohn, 1990; Haight, 1979; Irwin, 1985c; Lawrence, Edwards, Barraclough, Church, & Hetherington, 1995; Mc-Clenon, 1982; Murphy & Lester, 1976; Sheils & Berg, 1977). Similarly, psi-related experients tend to endorse the importance of experimentally investigating the reality of psi (Palmer, 1979).

Although personal experience is often cited by the experients as their principal reason for their belief in the paranormal (Clarke, 1995), the issue of the causal direction of the relationship between belief and experience nevertheless looms as a "chicken-and-egg" problem. Personal experience might inspire and reinforce a belief in psi, or paranormal belief might prompt some people to construe their anomalous experiences in terms of the concept of psi. Both of these processes are likely to occur (Irwin, 1985b), but results of structural equation modeling imply that the effect of experience on belief might be the predominant one (Lawrence et al., 1995). That is, paranormal belief might not represent as crucial a predisposition to PRE as might have been expected.

Another possible predisposition to PREs may be the experient's dissociative tendencies. Surveys show that experients tend to score high on measures of dissociation and closely related constructs. Richards (1991), Ross and Joshi (1992), and Zingrone and Alvarado (1994) reported a positive association between dissociative tendencies and reports of PREs. According to Pekala, Kumar, and Marcano (1995), both dissociation (a mental state characterized by detachment from aspects of the self or the environment) and susceptibility to hypnosis are correlates of PREs. People who are highly hypnotizable and fantasy prone report a high frequency of such experiences (Myers & Austrin, 1985; Wilson & Barber, 1983). Similarly, Myers and Austrin (1985), Nadon and Kihlstrom (1987), and Glicksohn (1990) have established a relationship between the occurrence of PREs and psychological absorption (the capacity for total attentional involvement).

Collectively, these findings might be interpreted as suggesting that a capacity to enter altered states of consciousness is a factor in the predisposition to PREs. Certainly a state of high absorption or dissociation is a common context for PREs (Honorton, 1977). At the same time, there also seems to be a motivational component to this association. Psi-related experients tend to have a strong interest in psychologically absorbing experiences (Irwin, 1985b); for example, experients often recall and analyze their dreams (Haraldsson et al., 1977; Palmer, 1979). The predisposition to PREs, therefore, may encompass both an interest in and a tendency toward dissociation and fantasy.

Other cognitive processes have also been linked to a disposition to have PREs. People with a low formal educational background are more likely to report such experiences, at least in some countries (Haraldsson, 1985; Haraldsson & Houtkooper, 1991; Palmer, 1979). This association, however, seems to reflect not so much the experient's intelligence as other social or cultural factors governing the willingness to acknowledge PREs (Irwin, 1994a). Cognitive style might also affect the form taken by the experience. Irwin (1979) found that habitual visualizers tend to have ESP experiences involving mental imagery, whereas verbalizers are more inclined to have intuitive ESP experiences.

In terms of the more fundamental factors of personality, however, there is little to indicate that experients have a distinctive personality profile. There are occasional reports of an association between PREs and such factors as neuroticism, extraversion, and openness to experience (Alvarado, Zingrone, & Dalton, 1996; Sandford, 1979). However, there are many reports that do not find such associations (e.g., Alvarado et al., 1996; Greiner, 1964; Haight, 1979).

The effect of gender on PREs is unclear. Women certainly predominate in case collections, but this trend might well be a consequence of their greater willingness to participate in research rather than of a greater proneness to these experiences. The form of the experience may vary with gender. According to Haraldsson et al. (1977), in Iceland extrasensory dreams are more commonly reported by women than by men, although this pattern is not uniformly evident in all countries (Haraldsson, 1985; Haraldsson & Houtkooper, 1991). Telepathic experiences also are reported more commonly by women (Haraldsson & Houtkooper, 1991). With regard to marital status, spontaneous PREs are reported more often by separated, divorced, or widowed people than by married people (Haraldsson & Houtkooper, 1991; Palmer, 1979).

The nature of any predisposition to PREs therefore is not known in much detail, and the available data invariably have been gathered after the PRE; no studies have used a prospective design. It is unclear, therefore, that the data attest to a genuine predisposition to have PREs as distinct from a mere willingness or ability to disclose such experiences.

PSYCHOPATHOLOGY

Partial evidence for the involvement of psychopathology in some PREs has been found in efforts to establish a consistent biological or neurological marker of these events. Neppe (1983), for example, pointed out the similarity of many PREs to symptoms of temporal-lobe epilepsy. Furthermore, he identified a subgroup of individuals without epilepsy who experience at least three types of phenomena, including flowery olfactory hallucinations, déjà vu, and dissociation, that the experient may attribute to a paranormal process such as psi. Persinger (1984) and colleagues (Persinger & De Sano, 1986; Persinger & Valliant, 1985) have also reported correlations between temporal-lobe signs and PREs in nonclinical populations. Attributing all spontaneous PREs to subclinical temporal-lobe dysfunction, however, remains far from demonstrated. In addition, the types of experiences identified by Neppe are very specific and for the most part do not involve the experience of information transfer typically associated with psi phenomena.

Reports of PREs may arise in a variety of clinical contexts. A patient may report a single experience and perceive it only as a curiosity or, as Eisenbud (1970) suggested, may see it as a signpost directing attention to personal psychological issues. Alternatively, a patient may report many PREs that have varying degrees of apparent veridicality. Patients with dissociative tendencies, actively pursuing guided imagery or hypnosis, may report confusing experiences in which they feel they are receiving information from outside sources but that may in fact represent intense imaginary events. Other patients either may experience a combination of psychotic symptoms (e.g., delusions or hallucinations) and presumably veridical psi-experience, or may experience psychosis alone that they mistake for the occurrence of psi. PREs frequently do occur in the context of major psychiatric disorders, and it can be very difficult to determine which experiences are nonpathological and which represent impaired reality testing.

In all cases, the primary goal of the clinician should be to direct the patient away from overidentifying with the PRE and to focus on stabilizing basic coping skills and emotional tone. Within the Western medical model, however, reports of PREs are usually presumed to be linked to mental illness and emotional instability. This creates a difficulty for the clinician attempting to make a differential diagnosis in the context of a PRE. The diagnostic criteria for several psychotic, personality, and dissociative disorders contain items that are similar to those endorsed by people reporting spontaneous PREs.

The similarity between symptoms of schizotypal personality disorder and characteristics of PREs is marked. Of the nine diagnostic criteria for schizotypal personality disorder specified in the fourth edition of the *Diagnostic and Statistical Manual of Mental Disorders* (DSM–IV; American Psychiatric Association, 1994), several resemble possible forms of PREs. These include ideas of reference (interpretation of casual events as having particular personal meaning), odd beliefs or magical thinking (e.g., "belief in clairvoyance, telepathy, or 'sixth sense'"; p. 645), and unusual perceptual experiences (e.g., hearing a voice). In addition, it has been asserted that some of the social factors considered in the diagnosis of schizotypal personality disorder, including isolation, suspiciousness, or anxiety, could potentially be sequelae of poorly integrated PREs (Neppe, 1989; Thalbourne, 1995), and there is empirical evidence that people with schizotypal personality disorder are inclined to endorse paranormal beliefs (Thalbourne, 1985; Williams & Irwin, 1991).

The other diagnostic group that shows a high phenomenological overlap with PREs comprises people who have diagnosed psychotic disorders, including bipolar disorder, brief reactive psychosis, and schizophrenia. Such individuals frequently report feeling that they are receiving "telepathic messages" (American Psychiatric Association, 1994) and often are greatly distressed by this experience. Accounts of purported mind reading or precognition by individuals with psychotic disorders often differ from PREs reported by the nonclinical population. Individuals with psychotic disorders may "hear" voices communicating information, and their experiences are more detailed than is usually the case among healthy experients. In addition, individuals in psychotic states are less likely to recognize the unacceptability or strangeness of their reports than people who are not psychotic. For example, an individual in a psychotic state may report that he or she can hear perfectly the complex conversations in some distant location between his unfaithful spouse and her lover. Neppe (1984) proposed a category termed *subjective paranormal experience psychosis* to describe individuals who have a long history, starting in childhood, of PREs that then deteriorate into frank psychosis. He described the turning point as an increase in "self-reference ideation" (p. 8). Patients start having experiences not about others but about themselves, "producing enormous distress, because of the dysphoric nature of experiences such as beliefs that they may die" (Neppe, 1989, p. 152). The healthy psi experient may be at risk for developing a delusional or paranoid interpretation of his or her experience in the context of poor social support or lack of education about the nature of these experiences.

It is evident, therefore, that PREs can occur in the context of psychopathology and, indeed, that such experiences can be deeply rooted in a delusional system. It should not be presumed, however, that this association can be extrapolated to the nonclinical population so as to constitute a generalization about experients as a whole. For this reason, we now consider the relationship between PRE and mental health with particular reference to nonpsychiatric experients.

Some research suggests that psi-related experients may actually be more healthy than nonexperients. PREs have been associated with positive affect (Greeley, 1975; Haraldsson & Houtkooper, 1991) and with having a sense of meaning in life (Kennedy & Kanthamani, 1995; Kennedy et al., 1994). However, differences in psychological well-being between experients and nonexperients have not always been corroborated (Haraldsson & Houtkooper, 1991).

A less direct way to address this issue is to examine the mental health of paranormal believers. Given that the population of paranormal believers subsumes that of psi-related experients, the mental health correlates of paranormal belief might be taken as at least suggestive for the psychological status of experients. Although believers in psi are not generally inclined to be socially withdrawn (Lester, Thinschmidt, & Trautman, 1987; Thalbourne & Haraldsson, 1980), they may have a sense of social alienation and a lack of social concern (Tobacyk, 1983, 1985); they may also seem slightly narcissistic (Tobacyk & Mitchell, 1987) and more interested in the world of their own subjective experience than in the needs of other people (Irwin, 1993; Schlitz & Honorton, 1992). Of particular interest is the fact that some psi believers appear to need a sense of control over their lives and world: They may have fantasies of unlimited power and success (Tobacyk & Mitchell, 1987) and a desire for control over other people. This need for control has been associated with reports of trauma during childhood (Irwin, 1992) and is sometimes expressed in the form of magical thinking (Thalbourne, 1985; Tobacyk & Wilkinson, 1990; Williams & Irwin, 1991), which could be the basis of some psi believers' schizotypal presentation. Generally, however, the mental health of psi believers is sound: Their psychological adjustment is satisfactory, and they do not typically present with depression, anxiety, sleep disturbance, or somatic symptoms indicative of psychological dysfunction (Irwin, 1991, 1995; Tobacyk, 1982).

THERAPEUTIC POTENTIALS

The potential role of PREs in psychotherapy has been discussed intermittently since the inception of modern psychiatry. In early essays, Freud (1922a, 1922b) described what he felt might be telepathic and clairvoyant perceptions by patients that appeared to highlight emotionally important repressed material. Eisenbud (1970) wrote extensively about the possible role of psi between patient and analyst, emphasizing its significance in the transference–countertransference relationship. Typical examples from his, and our own, experience include cases in which a new patient has a dream in which he or she "sees" the therapist the night before the first therapy session. We have also observed instances in which the therapist may experience his or her own dream content as a premonition of unexpected new material from the patient. Such PREs may lead to improved bonding between patient and therapist, whether or not they are ever mentioned in the therapy. Eisenbud postulated that apparent telepathic dreams or experiences between therapist and patient may occur when fear, embarrassment, or anger prohibits direct communication between the two and that acknowledgment of these occurrences may facilitate progress in therapy. There has been no controlled research to test these conjectures, and they do not constitute an argument for or against veridical psi. Rather, they describe how the psi-related experience may function in a therapeutic relationship.

In addition to the importance of recognizing and correctly understanding and interpreting a PRE in the context of the patient's life, there are a variety of ways that these experiences and related interventions can be used in a therapeutic context. Harary (1992) conjectured that psi is a form of self-expression, evidence of healthy proximity to nature, and an opportunity to enhance communication with self, others, and the environment. It has been proposed that individuals may be taught to enhance "psi sensitivity" through relaxation and awareness exercises. Such exercises are used in therapeutic settings with the goal of enhancing group intimacy and helping individuals become more sensitive to their environment. Investigators have yet to examine the ontological reality or efficacy of these proposals through systematic research.

In cultural groups in which belief in psi is prevalent, therapists and other practitioners may attempt to use psi to diagnose or treat a variety of ailments (Benor, 1991). This is done, for example, in various parts of Latin America, where many illnesses are thought to be related to paranormal interference, imbalance, or oversensitivity. Spiritistic clinics have been set up where practitioners attempt to perceive the root cause of mental, spiritual, or physical problems and treat them through psychic communication with the "unconscious" of the patient (Hess, 1991).

CLINICAL ISSUES AND RISK

By now it should be clear that the clinical evaluation of PREs is especially complex. There is nevertheless some evidence that clinicians' appreciation of this issue is increasing (Grof & Grof, 1985; White, 1995). Furthermore, some mental health professionals are showing an interest in the therapeutic practices of alternative healers and spiritists (Koss, 1987; Schouten, 1997). The task for the clinician is, as always, to help the patient to become functional and satisfied within his or her world. This requires skill at differentiating between psychological patterns concomitant with healthy and transformational PRE and those forms of psychopathology, including fear or confusion, associated with these experiences.

Overreliance on reported PREs to diagnose schizotypal personality disorder or schizophrenia, for example, carries the substantial clinical risk of stigmatizing, alienating, or even erroneously medicating an individual. The risk of such misdiagnosis may be particularly high in circumstances in which patients are struggling to integrate PREs in the absence of guidance or reliable information. Some individuals claim that they had avoided or left the mental health system because they correctly recognized that many counselors and psychotherapists are not well informed about the phenomenology of PREs (Burg, 1975; Harary, 1992) and Hastings (1983) claimed that such individuals may become socially marginalized or seek inadequate or even self-destructive solutions to confusion or emotional distress. However, there is inadequate evidence to determine if these individuals have been poorly served by the mental health system or are simply part of a disturbed patient population.

It is essential to identify and address negative stereotypes and to find out the emotional content and significance of the PRE in the individual patient's life. It is more important, for example, to assess how an individual interprets and responds to an apparent psi experience than to engage in efforts to evaluate whether the experience did entail some paranormal process such as psi. Having the opportunity to discuss and assimilate PREs will reassure the patient that he or she is not alone in having such experiences, which are not necessarily a sign of mental illness. Reduction of anxiety, especially in dissociative patients, may have profound clinical implications. Wickramasekera (1989), for example, reported significant resolution of chronic resistant somatization disorder in patients given the opportunity to discuss and reframe their PREs.

Some authors (Harary, 1992; Hastings, 1983) have suggested beginning the intervention with patient education aimed at depathologizing the experience. This education helps the patient to avoid narrowing his or her self-concept by overidentifying with the label *psychic* or developing a grandiose or narcissistic self-concept based on this experience. It also helps to minimize the disorientation of individuals who may feel "different" from all other people or believe that they are the only ones who know that the world operates according to principles of which others are not aware.

Harary (1992) emphasized the clinical importance of helping experients differentiate themselves from stereotypes of "cultists, aliens, . . . and otherwise atypical or deviant individuals" (p. 202) portrayed as "psychic" in the Western popular media. He suggested that individuals reporting psi may be at risk of being taken advantage of by cults, which may provide the only environment that supports and accepts their experience.

Education also helps avoid a fear reaction in which people think they are "going crazy," are "possessed," or should change substantially their lives or world views based on psi experiences. Individuals with high baseline anxiety may be prone, for example, to draw unsupported conclusions from their PREs and develop delusions as the only way to integrate them. On the other hand, individuals who make their experience the new focus of their lives may create social isolation or stigmatization by proselytizing about their abilities to others. Patients can be told that paranormal phenomena have been investigated in the research laboratory, that some scientists believe the experimental evidence supports the reality of psi, but that, in any event, PREs are generally fairly limited in the amount of usable information they produce. References to books of spontaneous case collections, such as those by L. E. Rhine (1981), are useful for individuals who need help in integrating their experiences. In any case, the focus of the therapeutic discussion should be determined by the immediate needs and ego strengths of the patients. They can be told that these events sometimes emerge at times of particular upset, but that the experiences can be fostered and potentially represent a creative outlet for inner exploration and can lead to enhanced awareness of the world around them. On the other hand, psychotherapists must take care not to reinforce paranoid delusions (e.g., Ehrenwald, 1977, p. 137), irrational and "magical thinking" (e.g., Krippner & Winkler, 1996), or dysfunctional "personal myths" (e.g., Feinstein, Krippner, & Granger, 1988).

Patients are occasionally concerned that an apparently precognitive dream may actually have caused a negative event; this was the concern that Anna experienced in relation to her husband's death. Sometimes they believe that they could have used information from a premonition to prevent a negative event (Hastings, 1983). The psychodynamic underpinnings of such concerns are certainly relevant, but it is also appropriate to inform concerned individuals that there is no evidence that people can cause a negative event by dreaming about it. In addition, it is important to recognize that PREs often contain a mixture of ostensibly reality-based and imaginal elements (L. E. Rhine, 1956; Schlitz & Honorton, 1992; Stowell, 1997; Ullman, 1975). This is true despite the fact that individuals often describe their experiences as particularly vivid or lifelike (Stowell, 1997). It is extremely important to approach PREs from a balanced, supportive perspective.

THEORIES

Although experients may have a strong conviction in the existence of the paranormal, this is not necessarily the case for the professional who provides their treatment. Of course, a major issue in discussing psychological issues relevant to psi beliefs and PREs is that there is not a consensus in the scientific community as to whether such experiences represent anomalous information transfer or are entirely due to various forms of misinterpretation and self-delusion. Each of these positions could lead a professional to a different course of therapeutic action.

For more than a century, researchers have collected data to support both sides of the psi debate. Indeed, a substantial number of experimental studies have been conducted to investigate the *psi hypothesis* that psi phenomena are valid. In evaluating this experimental literature, some scientists have pointed out that sensory leakage, incomplete reporting of data, or participant or experimenter fraud could have led to erroneous conclusions of support for the psi hypothesis (Alcock, 1987; Blackmore, 1980; Hansel, 1987; Hansen, 1990; Hyman, 1985). There have also been numerous experiments that failed to find evidence of anomalous information transfer (Beloff, 1985; Blackmore, 1985; Wiseman & Smith, 1994). On the other hand, several scientists have argued that there is a substantial database to support the psi hypothesis (Bem & Honorton, 1994; J. B. Rhine, 1950; Targ & Puthoff, 1974; Targ, Puthoff, & May, 1977; Utts, 1995).

Although not free of controversy, one way to evaluate the associated database is to perform a meta-analysis, or summary evaluation, of the experimental data (Krippner et al., 1993; Utts, 1991). This statistical technique pools large numbers of studies, using stringent inclusion criteria to remove flawed or poorly controlled experiments. The data are then reanalyzed as a whole, in an attempt to evaluate the generalizability of the findings and the size of any underlying effect. Several meta-analyses have been done in the field of psi research (Bem & Honorton, 1994; Child, 1985; Hyman & Honorton, 1986; Rosenthal, 1986; Schlitz & Braud, 1997; Watt, 1994), all of which strongly suggest that research findings supportive of the psi hypothesis cannot be explained through such mechanisms as sensory leakage, randomization problems, or the "file-drawer effect." For example, Child's (1985) meta-analysis of dream–ESP studies yielded robust data supporting the proposition that psi effects could be deliberately programmed into night-time dream reports. For scores based on judgments by outside judges, working separately and unaware of target correspondences, the probability that the significant results obtained could be explained by chance was $p < .000002$.

In 1999, Milton and Wiseman updated the meta-analysis published 5 years earlier by Bem and Honorton (1994). Contrary to the earlier report, they did not find a statistical effect for any anomalous process of information transfer. However, Milton (in Carpenter, 1999) acknowledged that if the Ganzfeld studies conducted since her and Wiseman's analysis had been added to the analysis, the psi effect would again reach statistical significance. Bem (in Carpenter, 1999) pointed out that even in the Milton and Wiseman meta-analysis of 30 studies, 6 showed significant effects, which is more than could be explained by chance.

Meta-analytical techniques thereby can be extremely useful in focusing attention on a whole body of research and in counteracting the tendency to isolate individual studies from their broader research context. In relation to the investigation of the psi hypothesis, these techniques also allow researchers to objectively address skeptical claims that psi experiments are not replicable or are rare instances of extrachance findings selected from an enormous set of unreported statistically null results. In short, meta-analysis can serve both to clarify and to resolve sources of uncertainty. In conducting a sound meta-analysis, researchers must take care to avoid biased selection of studies, to provide for a fully independent coding of the procedural characteristics of each study, and to ensure that the number of studies in the final sample is sufficient to guarantee the power of the analysis.

Some of these potential problems have been the focus of criticisms of meta-analysis; for example, Slavin (1984, p. 12) argued that a "meta-analysis is no better than the studies that went into it." In addition, Irwin (1999) admitted that meta-analysis is regarded as a relatively controversial statistical technique because different judges ascribe different flaws to the same experiment (p. 74), a criticism echoed by Hyman (1985).

Another potential limitation in all meta-analyses concerns the file-drawer effect, the hypothesis that although the meta-analysis may have included all published studies, many negative studies may have gone unreported and, thus, not be included in the analysis. It is possible to calculate how many unreported studies would be required to nullify the results of a meta-analysis. Radin (1997) calculated that for the psi Ganzfeld (a condition in which participants are exposed to homogeneous visual and auditory stimulation and physical relaxation) studies, 423 unreported negative file-drawer experiments would be required to cancel out the published findings—a 15:1 ratio of unreported (and negative) to reported studies. A survey by Blackmore (1980) uncovered 19 unpublished Ganzfeld studies, 7 of which had significant positive results. On the basis of these analyses, Hyman and Honorton (1986) concluded that the file-drawer effect could not account for the positive results of the Ganzfeld meta-analyses.

Another point of debate has centered on the issue of randomization. Extensive review by a panel of 18 expert statisticians and psychologists found no evidence that randomization problems affected the outcome of the meta-analyses for psi (Utts, 1991).

The nature of the psi debate reveals important sociological dimensions of truth construction in science; any reading of the evidence for or against the psi hypothesis must take into consideration the assumptions and biases of the researchers doing the evaluation (Hess, 1992). Paradigm wars notwithstanding, the issues inherent in the psi debate clearly are of major importance in the clinical analysis of PREs.

Brief mention may be made of commentators who accept the evidence for the psi hypothesis and who have proceeded to theorize about the role of psi in psychological adjustment. Some have suggested that psi capacities may serve an ego-integrating and adaptive function for psychologically impaired individuals (Twemlow, Hendren, Gabbard, Jones, & Norris, 1982; Ullman, 1975). PREs are postulated by these authors to provide such patients with helpful information about their social, physical, and intrapsychic environment and enhance interpersonal bonding and rapport (Servadio, 1953). Regardless of their validity, these speculations do point to opportunities for the constructive use of PREs in the course of therapy. The discerning counselor or psychotherapist will treat reports of PREs with caution, knowing that some of these accounts may be an effort—either conscious or subconscious—to engage the therapist's attention, sympathy, and support in relation to quite a different problem.

Theories of PREs also have been proposed by commentators who are skeptical of the existence of psi, although strictly speaking these theories are independent of the psi hypothesis rather than alternatives to it. These theories usually are formulated in terms of paranormal belief (Irwin, 1993) but can equally be taken to address the origins and functions of PREs. In very broad terms, there are four basic conceptual approaches to PREs that do not presume the reality of psi.

Under the *social marginality hypothesis*, experients are depicted as members of socially marginal groups who unwittingly construe their anomalous experiences in terms of psi as some sort of compensation for their marginal status (Bainbridge, 1978; Wuthnow, 1976). Thus, people may feel that despite their low social rank, their PREs distinguish them as individuals who are "special" or, at least, not worthless. Socialization processes operating in specific subcultures may serve to foster such reactions. Although some demographic correlates (e.g., the high proportion of divorced and separated experients) of PREs might be interpreted to support the hypothesis, failure to identify birth order, political convictions, religiosity, and income as correlates of PREs (Palmer, 1979) indicates the lack of general validity of this hypothesis. More importantly, the social marginality hypothesis is not consistent with survey findings that a majority, or 67%, of Americans have reported psi experiences (Greeley, 1987).

The *world view hypothesis* proposes that PREs spring from a view of one's world characterized by a highly introspective and esoteric perspective on humanity, life, and the world at large (e.g., Alcock, 1987), one in which magical thinking is a dominant epistemology (Zusne & Jones, 1989) and in which inexperience with empirical data (Diaconis & Mosteller, 1996) is pervasive. Schwartz and Russek (1997) described eight "world hypotheses," the seventh of which they termed the *creative unfolding* model, spiritual and mystical in nature. From this perspective, things in nature do not occur by chance, rather they are "given the chance" to occur; this hypothesis gives "a conceptual home" to "the power of mind," spiritual healing, and prayer (pp. 15–17). Schwartz and Russek added that many scientists have operated from this hypothesis (for instance, Newton's vision of the Divine) or have at least been influenced by it (as in Einstein's conviction that "God does not play dice with the Universe" [p. 17]). The world view hypothesis has the merit of highlighting the cultural context of these experiences, because what is considered paranormal in one culture or subculture may fall into the normal spectrum in another setting (e.g., Harary, 1992; Krippner & Winkler, 1996).

For example, the concept of a spiritual body, of discarnate spirits, of channeling, and of reincarnation all characterize the world views of various spiritistic groups in Brazil (Hess, 1991; Krippner, 1987). The range of beliefs and attitudes among psi-related experients is generally consistent with the world view hypothesis. Matlock's (1990) comprehensive, cross-cultural survey demonstrated that case studies of past life reports reflect that culture's beliefs about reincarnation (p. 235; see also Mills & Lynn, this volume, chap. 9). Although helpful in many ways, the world view hypothesis begs the fundamental issue of whether or not the world view of psi-related experients is veridical.

Proponents of the *cognitive deficits hypothesis* suggest that belief in psi phenomena represents a tendency toward misattributions in which experients tend to seek and perceive patterns in random data or to selectively attend to and recall "hits" rather than "misses" (e.g., Alcock, 1981). Confirmatory bias reinforces these misattributions and prevents self-corrective cognitive strategies from facilitating appropriate reality monitoring and reality testing (e.g, Blackmore, 1996). Schumaker (1987), for example, pointed out that self-deception assists many people in coping with complex and challenging life dilemmas. Chinn and Brewer (1992) used the term *entrenched beliefs* in their discussion of members of their student sample who segregate what they learn in science class from their previous conceptions. However, there is no clear-cut evidence that psi-related experients are deficient in intelligence or critical thinking ability (Irwin, 1993; Krippner & Winkler, 1996). Furthermore, a body of research using the Paranormal Belief Scale (Tobacyk, 1983) demonstrates that there are several subsets of "believers" in psi phenomena, some of whom have test scores supporting the cognitive deficit hypothesis whereas other subsets do not. In one study, only two of the seven dimensions of the scale correlated positively with a measure of critical inference (Tobacyk, 1988), and the research data demonstrating the multidimensional nature of this scale indicate that "psi belief" is not a single, unified trait (Krippner & Winkler, 1996). Further development of measures that examine a variety of response biases in relation to diverse psi phenomena would advance research in this area. Indeed, cognitive biases should be routinely examined in studies that investigate the nature and veridicality of anomalous experiences.

Another approach to PREs construes them to serve significant psychodynamic needs of the individual. Some parapsychologists have constructed experiments to test this *psychodynamic functions hypothesis* (e.g., Stanford, 1990), assuming that when the organism has a certain need, it scans the environment using psi for information relevant to that need. Therapists who operate under the psychodynamic functions hypothesis explore the social and psychological factors served by the PRE, rather than its ontological reality (e.g., Eisenbud, 1970; Hastings, 1983). In the meantime, most psi proponents and debunkers would agree with Marks's (1986) observation that

> Mental set provides the framework within which we organize new experience. Human cognition is not a simple coping process but entails a constructive striving or "effort after meaning." What we experience is often more a confirmation of belief than a matter of plain fact. (p. 122)

as well as Beyerstein's (1996) emphasis on "the motivations, knowledge, expectations, mood, and personality" (p. 796) in understanding anomalous reports.

A different perspective proposes that the experient is psychologically deviant, often "pathological" in some respects (e.g., Grey, 1994, p. 288; Kitaigorodsky, 1972). As noted earlier in this chapter, the *DSM–IV* includes PREs as symptoms of several types of dysfunction, most notably schizotypal personality disorder (American Psychiatric Association, 1994, p. 645). Most proponents of psi phenomena would agree that a subset of experients are severely dysfunctional but that the "pathological" label does not characterize the majority of experients. Irwin (1992, 1993) provided evidence that PREs may be facilitated, at least in part, by experients' need to enhance their sense of control over a seemingly uncontrollable world, irrespective of the veridicality of their experiences.

We are open to the possibility of the existence of psi. Although acknowledging that scientific controversy continues on this issue, we work under the assumption that some people's personal PREs reflect psychopathology, cognitive errors, or cultural attributions, whereas other experiences may involve veridical psi without psychopathological elements. Within this conceptual framework, we believe we are best able to explore the therapeutic potential of PREs and to move away from a rigidly pathological perspective in our evaluation of a client's presentation.

METHODOLOGICAL ISSUES

The principal research techniques for the study of spontaneous PREs are surveys and the compilation of case collections (Stokes, 1997). The use of these techniques has generated a substantial database and a reasonably coherent empirical literature.

Some important methodological limitations of these research techniques nevertheless should be acknowledged. The representativeness of data obtained through them is doubtful (see Krippner, 1987). In submitting a case report to a researcher, experients may be likely to select the most evidentially impressive and anomalous experience they can recall. Conversely, experients may mistakenly assume that a relatively mundane or unconvincing PRE would be of little interest to a researcher. The range of experiences represented in case collections and surveys therefore may be biased to an unknown degree.

Care should also be taken when interpreting the evidential use of published case collections. Some case collections include reports from several historical periods (e.g., Gurney et al., 1886) and, given that the prevalence of paranormal beliefs can vary over time (Randall, 1990), the researcher needs to be cautious in deciding whether to collate the entire collection for statistical analysis. Furthermore, it may be appropriate to investigate the extent to which editorial factors have influenced the content of published case collections. In some case collections for out-of-body experiences, for example, a lack of editorial objectivity and consistency is apparent (see Alvarado, this volume, chap. 6; Hyman, 1977; Irwin, 1985a).

One advantage of surveys is that respondents' attention can be focused on the specific issue of interest to the researcher. The population of which the data are representative can also be defined more precisely than for case collections. Most importantly, unlike case collections, a survey can solicit data from nonexperients, thereby providing a valuable baseline against which the data of psi-related experients can be assessed. Unlike case collections, however, surveys do not allow researchers to screen for experiences with "ostensible validity." Instances strongly suggestive of a misattribution of the experience to paranormal processes (Irwin, 1999; Stowell, 1997), for example, cannot be identified for exclusion or for consideration separately from the rest of the sample. The impossibility of screening survey participants' experiences necessarily raises some doubts about the validity of prevalence and other data generated by survey techniques.

Even with a case collection, however, the researcher has limited ability to evaluate a PRE. There is no way to ensure that each case report is a depiction of a real experience, let alone ensure that the report is accurate. Apart from the problem of misattribution, some individuals' desires for prestige, influence over others, and financial gain may motivate them to falsely claim "psychic abilities" (Hastings, 1992). Conversely, political repression, fear of stigmatization or derision, and self-doubt may cause other people to "sanitize" their reports of PREs toward a culturally more conservative representation. Because the extent of the impact of these factors is unknown, data on PREs, particularly in regard to apparent cross-cultural differences, should be regarded with some caution.

Perhaps the major methodological weakness of surveys and case collections alike is their retrospective nature (but see Pekala & Cardeña, this volume, chap. 2). Both of these techniques require the experient to describe an experience that occurred some time in the past. The accounts of PREs obtained through these methods therefore are subject to the fallibility of human memory. Thus, in response to the researcher's requests for information, the experients' recollections are not simply "revived" but are reconstructed, often after extensive integration with associated beliefs and prevailing cultural values. Retrospective accounts of PREs, therefore, are likely to be imprecise representations of the original experience, marked to an unknown degree by omissions, embellishments, and other distortions.

Researchers can take some steps to reduce the impact of recollective inaccuracy. First, a population can be chosen in which these problems of recall might be expected to be minimal. College or university students, for example, are one such population: Students are young enough for their experience not to be too distant in the past; they are intelligent, articulate, and sufficiently mature to provide a perceptive account of their experience; their memory skills are likely to be above average; and their beliefs might not be so inflexible as to compromise their recall of details of the experience. Second, the survey can be conducted with a sizable sample in the hope that individual inaccuracies will stand as background "noise" from which phenomenological consistencies can be distinguished. Third, the investigator can be alert to the problem of biased formulation of questionnaire items and its potential effects on participants' responses. Fourth, checks on the consistency of response may be incorporated into survey instruments. Ultimately, however, some degree of recollective inaccuracy must be assumed as an inherent component of the study of spontaneous PREs.

A broader methodological issue that arises in the contemporary study of PRE concerns the multidimensionality of the experiences. As established principally through the research efforts of L. E. Rhine (1953, 1978, 1981), PREs vary substantially in their phenomenological characteristics. Their respective origins, functions, and sequelae also may vary. Many past empirical studies nevertheless investigated correlates of extrasensory experiences, for example, without making any distinctions among phenomenological types and facets of the experiences. Although this research strategy was defensible in the seminal work in this field, there is an increasing need for future studies to take more extensive account of the multidimensionality of PREs.

Past study of the theories of PRE and paranormal belief has tended to be dominated by researchers who are skeptical of the psi hypothesis; most parapsychologists, on the other hand, have been more interested in the pursuit of "hard" data from experimental psi tasks conducted under laboratory conditions. Although the skeptical perspective is a scientifically respectable one, its predominance in the study of spontaneous PREs may have some unintentional effects on the research. First, an investigator with a perceptibly skeptical attitude may discourage participants from being completely frank about their experiences and beliefs, thereby compromising the data (Layton & Turnbull, 1975). Second, the skeptical perspective seems to have unwittingly directed much of the research toward the selection of variables that might demonstrate the extent to which experients and paranormal believers are deficient in cognitive and other psychological functioning. Although the findings of such research may be valid when considered in isolation, the picture evoked by the collective database could be distorted by a predominance of "negative" correlates. We certainly do not wish to discourage further empirical investigation of psi-related experients' possible cognitive deficiencies, for example, but such research needs to be balanced by studies of experients' capacity for creativity, empathy, and other "positive" qualities (Krippner, 1962–1963).

At the same time, our review of the correlates of PRE has noted the presence of cultural factors that may prompt some respondents to exaggerate their experience or to fraudulently claim to have had an experience when they have not (Hastings, 1992). In future studies, the inclusion of a "lie scale" and other indexes of distorted response styles may prove valuable.

One must nevertheless remember that PREs are defined here phenomenologically: It is experients who believe psi was involved in their experience and for whom the most important aspect is the meaning of the experience in their life. It then falls to the behavioral scientist to ascertain the factors upon which the experient's construction is founded.

CONCLUSION

Regardless of the validity of the psi hypothesis, the fact remains that many people do report having PREs. The task of behavioral science is not to dismiss these experiences out of hand but to investigate in a scientific fashion their origins and functions. In an applied context, it must be appreciated that although many of these events are little else than a source of curiosity for experients, other experiences may cause them some concern. By way of a conclusion, we offer this summary of suggestions for assessing PREs and helping patients in a clinical setting.

- Assess how the patient interprets the experience rather than trying to determine whether it actually entailed paranormal processes.
- Identify the patient's positive and negative preconceptions and stereotypes about psi.
- Educate the patient about psi in general, with a focus on the fact that PREs are generally not very reliable sources of information (even though some scientists have reported data obtained under laboratory conditions that are consistent with the psi hypothesis).
- Focus on the meaning of the experience in the patient's life, exploring it as you would dream imagery.
- Ask the patient about other recent major stressors or life events, and conduct a thorough psychological interview to evaluate reality testing, perception, and cognitive abilities in spheres other than those involving the psi-related report.
- Normalize the experience when appropriate.

In the final analysis, the job of the clinician is to support and strengthen individuals without judgment—helping them to develop life satisfaction and achieve their full human potential.

REFERENCES

Alcock, J. E. (1981). *Parapsychology: Science or magic? A psychological perspective.* Elmsford, NY: Pergamon Press.

Alcock, J. E. (1987). Parapsychology: Science of the anomalous or search for the soul? *Behavioral and Brain Sciences, 10,* 553–643.

Alvarado, C. S., Zingrone, N. L., & Dalton, K. (1996, August). *Out-of-body experiences, psi experiences, and the "Big Five": Relating the NEO-PI-R to the experience claims of experimental subjects.* Paper presented at the 39th Annual Convention of the Parapsychological Association, San Diego, CA.

American Psychiatric Association. (1994). *Diagnostic and statistical manual of mental disorders* (4th ed.). Washington, DC: Author.

Bainbridge, W. S. (1978). Chariots of the gullible. *Skeptical Inquirer, 3*(2), 33–48.

Beloff, J. (1985). Research strategies for dealing with unstable phenomena. In B. Shapin & L. Coly (Eds.), *The repeatability problem in parapsychology: Proceedings of an international conference* (pp. 1–21). New York: Parapsychology Foundation.

Bem, D. J., & Honorton, C. (1994). Does psi exist? Replicable evidence for an anomalous process of information transfer. *Psychological Bulletin, 115,* 4–18.

Benor, D. (1991). *Healing research: Holistic energy medicine and spirituality. Vol. 1: Research in healing.* Oxfordshire, UK: Helix Press.

Beyerstein, B. L. (1996). Visions and hallucinations. In G. Stein (Ed.), *The encyclopedia of the paranormal* (pp. 789–797). Amherst, NY: Prometheus.

Blackmore, S. (1980). The extent of selective reporting of ESP Ganzfeld Studies. *European Journal of Parapsychology, 3,* 213–219.

Blackmore, S. J. (1985). Unrepeatability: Parapsychology's only finding. In B. Shapin & L. Coly (Eds.), *The repeatability problem in parapsychology: Proceedings of an international conference* (pp. 183–206). New York: Parapsychology Foundation.

Blackmore, S. (1996). Out-of-body experiences. In G. Stein (Ed.), *The encyclopedia of the paranormal* (pp. 471–483). Amherst, NY: Prometheus.

Broughton, R. S. (1991). *Parapsychology: The controversial science.* New York: Ballantine Books.

Burg, B. (1975, September). The puzzle of the psychic patient. *Human Behavior,* pp. 25–29.

Carpenter, S. (1999, July 21). ESP findings send controversial message. *Science News, 156,* 70

Child, I. L. (1985). Psychology and anomalous observations: The question of ESP in dreams. *American Psychologist, 40,* 1219–1230.

Chinn, C. C., & Brewer, W. F. (1992). The role of anomalous data in knowledge acquisition: A theoretical framework and implications for science instruction. *Review of Educational Research, 63,* 1–49.

Clarke, D. (1995). Experience and other reasons given for belief and disbelief in paranormal and religious phenomena. *Journal of the Society for Psychical Research, 60,* 371–384.

Diaconis, P., & Mosteller, F. (1996). Coincidences. In G. Stein (Ed.), *The encyclopedia of the paranormal* (pp. 160–168). Amherst, NY: Prometheus.

Edge, H. L., Morris, R. L., Palmer, J., & Rush, J. H. (1986). *Foundations of parapsychology: Exploring the boundaries of human capability.* Boston: Routledge & Kegan Paul.

Ehrenwald, J. (1977). Therapeutic applications. In S. Krippner (Ed.), *Advances in parapsychological research: Vol. 1. Psychokinesis* (pp. 133–148). New York: Plenum Press.

Eisenbud, J. (1970). *Psi and psychoanalysis*. New York: Grune & Stratton.

Emmons, C. F. (1982). *Chinese ghosts and ESP: A study of paranormal beliefs and experiences*. Metuchen, NJ: Scarecrow Press.

Emmons, C. F., & Sobal, J. (1981). Paranormal beliefs: Testing the marginality hypothesis. *Sociological Focus, 14,* 49–56.

Feinstein, D., Krippner, S., & Granger, D. (1988). Mythmaking and human development. *Journal of Humanistic Psychology, 28,* 23–50.

Freud, S. (1922a). Dreams and the occult. In S. Freud (Ed.), *New introductory lectures on psychoanalysis* (pp. 31–56). New York: Norton.

Freud, S. (1922b). Dreams and telepathy. *Imago, 8,* 1–22.

Glicksohn, J. (1990). Belief in the paranormal and subjective paranormal experience. *Personality and Individual Differences, 11,* 675–683.

Greeley, A. M. (1975). *The sociology of the paranormal: A reconnaissance*. Beverly Hills, CA: Sage.

Greeley, A. M. (1985). Hallucinations among the widowed. *Sociology and American Social Research, 13,* 3–8.

Greeley, A. M. (1987). Mysticism goes mainstream. *American Health, 6*(1), 47–49.

Greiner, R. P. (1964). An investigation into the personality traits of people with so-called spontaneous paranormal phenomena [Abstract]. *Journal of Parapsychology, 28,* 284.

Grey, W. (1994, Spring). Philosophy and the paranormal: Part 2. Skepticism, miracles, and knowledge. *Skeptical Inquirer,* pp. 288–294.

Grof, S., & Grof, C. (1985). Spiritual emergency: Part II. *Vital Signs, 5,* 1–30.

Gurney, E., Myers, F. W. H., & Podmore, F. (1886). *Phantasms of the living* (Vols. 1–2). London: Trübner.

Gyatsu, T. (1991). *Freedom in exile: The autobiography of the Dalai Lama*. New York: HarperCollins.

Haight, J. (1979). Spontaneous psi cases: A survey and preliminary study of ESP, attitude, and personality relationships. *Journal of Parapsychology, 43,* 179–204.

Hansel, C. E. M. (1987). Experimental evidence for paranormal phenomena. *Behavioral and Brain Sciences, 10,* 590–592.

Hansen, G. P. (1990). Deception by subjects in psi research. *Journal of the American Society for Psychical Research, 84,* 25–80.

Haraldsson, E. (1985). Representative national surveys of psychic phenomena: Iceland, Great Britain, Sweden, USA and Gallup's multinational survey. *Journal of the Society for Psychical Research, 53,* 145–158.

Haraldsson, E., Gudmundsdottir, A., Ragnarsson, A., Loftsson, J., & Jonsson, S. (1977). National survey of psychical experiences and attitudes towards the paranormal in Iceland. In J. D. Morris, W. G. Roll, & R. L. Morris (Eds.), *Research in parapsychology 1976* (pp. 182–186). Metuchen, NJ: Scarecrow Press.

Haraldsson, E., & Houtkooper, J. M. (1991). Psychic experiences in the Multinational Human Values Study: Who reports them? *Journal of the American Society for Psychical Research, 85,* 145–165.

Harary, K. (1992). Spontaneous psi in mass mythology, media and Western culture. In B. Shapin & L. Coly (Eds.), *Spontaneous psi, depth psychology and parapsychology: Proceedings of an international conference* (pp. 200–219). New York: Parapsychology Foundation.

Hastings, A. (1983). A counseling approach to parapsychological experience. *Journal of Transpersonal Psychology, 15,* 143–167.

Hastings, A. (1992). Psi and the dynamics of motivation. In B. Shapin & L. Coly (Eds.), *Spontaneous psi, depth psychology and parapsychology: Proceedings of an international conference* (pp. 100–118). New York: Parapsychology Foundation.

Hay, D., & Morisy, A. (1978). Reports of ecstatic, paranormal, or religious experience in Great Britain and the United States—A comparison of trends. *Journal for the Scientific Study of Religion, 17,* 255–268.

Hess, D. J. (1991). *Spirits and scientists: Ideology, spiritism, and Brazilian culture.* University Park: Pennsylvania State University Press.

Hess, D. J. (1992). *Science in the new age: The paranormal, its defenders and debunkers, and American culture.* Madison: University of Wisconsin Press.

Honorton, C. (1977). Psi and internal attention states. In B. B. Wolman (Ed.), *Handbook of parapsychology* (pp. 435–472). New York: Van Nostrand Reinhold.

Hyman, R. (1977, Spring/Summer). Cold reading: How to convince strangers that you know all about them. *Zetetic* (now *Skeptical Inquirer*), 18–37.

Hyman, R. (1985). The Ganzfeld psi experiment: A critical appraisal. *Journal of Parapsychology, 49,* 3–49.

Hyman, R., & Honorton, C. (1986). A joint communiqué: The psi Ganzfeld controversy. *Journal of Parapsychology, 50,* 351–364.

Irwin, H. J. (1979). Coding preferences and the form of spontaneous extrasensory experiences. *Journal of Parapsychology, 43,* 205–220.

Irwin, H. J. (1985a). *Flight of mind: A psychological study of the out-of-body experience.* Metuchen, NJ: Scarecrow Press.

Irwin, H. J. (1985b). Parapsychological phenomena and the absorption domain. *Journal of the American Society for Psychical Research, 79,* 1–11.

Irwin, H. J. (1985c). A study of the measurement and the correlates of paranormal belief. *Journal of the American Society for Psychical Research, 79,* 301–326.

Irwin, H. J. (1991). A study of paranormal belief, psychological adjustment, and fantasy proneness. *Journal of the American Society for Psychical Research, 85,* 317–331.

Irwin, H. J. (1992). Origins and functions of paranormal belief: The role of childhood trauma and interpersonal control. *Journal of the American Society for Psychical Research, 86,* 199–208.

Irwin, H. J. (1993). Belief in the paranormal: A review of the empirical literature. *Journal of the American Society for Psychical Research, 87*, 1–39.

Irwin, H. J. (1994). The phenomenology of parapsychological experiences. In S. Krippner (Ed.), *Advances in parapsychological research* (Vol. 7, pp. 10–76). Jefferson, NC: McFarland.

Irwin, H. J. (1995). Las creencias paranormales y las funciones emocionales [Paranormal belief and emotional functioning]. *Revista Argentina de Psicología Paranormal, 6*, 69–76.

Irwin, H. J. (1999). *An introduction to parapsychology.* (3rd ed.). Jefferson, NC: McFarland.

Kelly, E. F., & Locke, R. G. (1981). Altered states of consciousness and psi: An historical survey and research prospectus. *Parapsychological Monographs* (Whole No. 18).

Kennedy, J. E., & Kanthamani, H. (1995). Association between anomalous experiences and artistic creativity and spirituality. *Journal of the American Society for Psychical Research, 89*, 333–343.

Kennedy, J. E., Kanthamani, H., & Palmer, J. (1994). Psychic and spiritual experiences, health, well-being, and meaning in life. *Journal of Parapsychology, 58*, 353–383.

Kitaigorodsky, A. (1972). *Not believable, not fact.* Moscow: Molodaya gvardiya.

Klimo, J. (1987). *Channeling: Investigations on receiving information from paranormal sources.* Los Angeles: Tarcher.

Koss, J. D. (1987). Expectations and outcomes for patients given mental health care or spiritist healing in Puerto Rico. *American Journal of Psychiatry, 144*, 56–61.

Kramer, W. H. (1989). Recent experiences with psi counseling in Holland. In L. Coly & J. D. S. McMahon (Eds.), *Psi and clinical practice: Proceedings of an international conference* (pp. 124–144). New York: Parapsychology Foundation.

Krippner, S. (1962–1963). Creativity and psychic phenomena. *Indian Journal of Parapsychology, 4*, 1–20.

Krippner, S. (1987). Cross-cultural approaches to multiple personality disorder: Practices in Brazilian spiritism. *Ethos, 15*, 273–295.

Krippner, S., Braud, W., Child, I. L., Palmer, J., Rao, K. R., Schlitz, M., White, R. A., & Utts, J. (1993). Demonstration research and meta-analysis in parapsychology. *Journal of Parapsychology, 57*, 275–286.

Krippner, S., & Winkler, M. (1996). The "need to believe." In G. Stein (Ed.), *The encyclopedia of the paranormal* (pp. 441–454). Amherst, NY: Prometheus Books.

Lawrence, T., Edwards, C., Barraclough, N., Church, S., & Hetherington, F. (1995). Modelling childhood causes of paranormal belief and experience: Childhood trauma and childhood fantasy. *Personality and Individual Differences, 19*, 209–215.

Layton, B. D., & Turnbull, B. (1975). Belief, evaluation, and performance on an ESP task. *Journal of Experimental Social Psychology, 11*, 166–179.

Lester, D., Thinschmidt, J. S., & Trautman, L. A. (1987). Paranormal belief and Jungian dimensions of personality. *Psychological Reports, 61,* 182.

Lukoff, D., & Everest, H. C. (1985). The myths of mental illness. *Journal of Transpersonal Psychology, 17,* 123–153.

Marks, D. F. (1986). Investigating the paranormal. *Nature, 320,* 119–124.

Matlock, J. G. (1990). Past life memory case studies. In S. Krippner (Ed.), *Advances in parapsychological research* (Vol. 6, pp. 184–267). Jefferson, NC: McFarland.

McClenon, J. (1982). A survey of elite scientists: Their attitudes towards ESP and parapsychology. *Journal of Parapsychology, 46,* 127–152.

McClenon, J. (1988). A survey of Chinese anomalous experiences and comparison with Western representative national samples. *Journal of the Scientific Study of Religion, 27,* 421–426.

McClenon, J. (1993). Surveys of anomalous experience in Chinese, Japanese, and American samples. *Sociology of Religion, 54,* 295–302.

Milton, J. (1992). Effects of "paranormal" experiences on people's lives: An unusual survey of spontaneous cases. *Journal of the Society for Psychical Research, 58,* 314–323.

Milton, J., & Wiseman, R. (1999). Does psi exist? Lack of replication of an anomalous process of information transfer. *Psychological Bulletin, 125,* 387–391

Murphy, K., & Lester, D. (1976). A search for correlates of belief in ESP. *Psychological Reports, 38,* 82.

Myers, S. A., & Austrin, H. R. (1985). Distal eidetic technology: Further characteristics of the fantasy-prone personality. *Journal of Mental Imagery, 9(3),* 57–66.

Nadon, R., & Kihlstrom, J. F. (1987). Hypnosis, psi, and the psychology of anomalous experience. *Behavioral and Brain Sciences, 10,* 597–599.

Neppe, V. M. (1983). Temporal lobe symptomatology in subjective paranormal experients. *Journal of the American Society for Psychical Research, 77,* 1–29.

Neppe, V. M. (1984). Subjective paranormal experience psychosis. *Parapsychology Review, 15(2),* 7–9.

Neppe, V. M. (1989). Clinical psychiatry, psychopharmacology, and anomalous experience. In L. Coly & J. D. S. McMahon (Eds.), *Psi and clinical practice: Proceedings of an international conference* (pp. 145–162). New York: Parapsychology Foundation.

Palmer, J. (1979). A community mail survey of psychic experiences. *Journal of the American Society for Psychical Research, 73,* 221–251.

Pekala, R. J., Kumar, V. K., & Marcano, G. (1995). Anomalous/paranormal experiences, hypnotic susceptibility, and dissociation. *Journal of the American Society for Psychical Research, 89,* 313–332.

Persinger, M. A. (1984). Propensity to report paranormal experiences is correlated with temporal lobe signs. *Perceptual and Motor Skills, 59,* 583–586.

Persinger, M. A., & De Sano, C. F. (1986). Temporal lobe signs: Positive correlations with imaginings and hypnotic induction profiles. *Psychological Reports,* *58,* 347–350.

Persinger, M. A., & Valliant, P. M. (1985). Temporal lobe signs and reports of subjective paranormal experiences in a normal population: A replication. *Perceptual and Motor Skills, 60,* 903–909.

Radin, D. (1997). *The conscious universe: The scientific truth of psychic phenomena.* San Francisco: HarperEdge.

Randall, T. M. (1990). Belief in the paranormal declines: 1977–1987. *Psychological Reports, 66,* 1347–1351.

Rhine, J. B. (1950). Psi phenomena and psychiatry. *Proceedings of the Royal Society of Medicine, 42,* 804–814.

Rhine, L. E. (1953). Subjective forms of spontaneous psi experiences. *Journal of Parapsychology, 17,* 77–114.

Rhine, L. E. (1956). Hallucinatory psi experiences: I. An introductory survey. *Journal of Parapsychology, 20,* 233–256.

Rhine, L. E. (1962a). Psychological processes in ESP experiences. Part I. Waking experiences. *Journal of Parapsychology, 26,* 88–111.

Rhine, L. E. (1962b). Psychological processes in ESP experiences. Part II. Dreams. *Journal of Parapsychology, 26,* 172–199.

Rhine, L. E. (1978). The psi process in spontaneous cases. *Journal of Parapsychology, 42,* 20–32.

Rhine, L. E. (1981). *The invisible picture: A study of psychic experiences.* Jefferson, NC: McFarland.

Richards, D. G. (1991). A study of the correlation between subjective psychic experiences and dissociative experiences. *Dissociation, 4,* 83–91.

Rosenthal, R. (1986). Meta-analytic procedures and the nature of replication: The Ganzfeld debate. *Journal of Parapsychology, 50,* 315–336.

Ross, C. A., & Joshi, S. (1992). Paranormal experiences in the general population. *Journal of Nervous and Mental Disease, 180,* 357–361.

Sandford, J. (1979). Personality and paranormal experience: The relationship between social adjustment, extroversion, neuroticism, and the report of psychic phenomena [Abstract]. *Journal of Parapsychology, 43,* 54–55.

Sannwald, G. (1963). On the psychology of spontaneous paranormal phenomena. *International Journal of Parapsychology, 5,* 274–292.

Schlitz, M. J., & Braud, W. G. (1997). Distant intentionality and healing: Assessing the evidence. *Alternative Therapies, 3*(6), 62–73.

Schlitz, M. J., & Honorton, C. (1992). Ganzfeld psi performance within an artistically gifted population. *Journal of the American Society for Psychical Research, 86,* 83–98.

Schouten, S. A. (1981). Analysing spontaneous cases: A replication based on the Sannwald collection. *European Journal of Parapsychology, 4,* 9–48.

Schouten, S. A. (1982). Analysing spontaneous cases: A replication based on the Rhine collection. *European Journal of Parapsychology, 4,* 113–158.

Schouten, S. A. (1997). Psychic healing and complementary medicine. In S. Krippner (Ed.), *Advances in parapsychological research* (Vol. 8, pp. 126–210). Jefferson, NC: McFarland.

Schumaker, J. F. (1987). Mental health, belief deficit compensation, and paranormal beliefs. *Journal of Psychology, 121,* 451–457.

Schwartz, G. E., & Russek, L. G. (1997). The challenge of one medicine: Theories of health and eight "world hypotheses." *Advances: The Journal of Mind-Body Health, 13,* 7–23.

Servadio, E. (1953). Psychoanalysis and telepathy. In G. Devereux (Ed.), *Psychoanalysis and the occult* (pp. 210–220). New York: International Universities Press.

Sheils, D., & Berg, P. (1977). A research note on sociological variables related to belief in psychic phenomena. *Wisconsin Sociologist, 14,* 24–31.

Slavin, R. E. (1984). Meta-analysis in education: How has it been used? *Educational Researcher, 13*(8), 6–15.

Stanford, R. G. (1990). An experimentally testable model for spontaneous psi events: A review of related evidence and concepts from parapsychology and other sciences. In S. Krippner (Ed.), *Advances in parapsychological research* (Vol. 6, pp. 54–167). Jefferson, NC: McFarland.

Stevenson, I. (1970). *Telepathic impressions: A review and report of thirty-five new cases.* Charlottesville: University Press of Virginia.

Stokes, D. M. (1997). Spontaneous psi phenomena. In S. Krippner (Ed.), *Advances in parapsychological research* (Vol. 8, pp. 6–87). Jefferson, NC: McFarland.

Stowell, M. S. (1997). Precognitive dreams: A phenomenological study. Part II. Discussion. *Journal of the American Society for Psychical Research, 91,* 255–304.

Targ, R., & Puthoff, H. E. (1974). Information transmission under conditions of sensory shielding. *Nature, 252,* 602–607.

Targ, R., Puthoff, H. E., & May, E. C. (1977). State of the art in remote viewing studies at SRI. *Proceedings of the IEEE 1977 International Conference on Cybernetics and Society, 7,* 519–529.

Tart, C. T., & LaBore, C. M. (1986). Attitudes toward strongly functioning psi: A preliminary survey. *Journal of the American Society for Psychical Research, 80,* 163–173.

Thalbourne, M. A. (1985). Are believers in psi more prone to schizophrenia? In R. A. White & J. Solfvin (Eds.), *Research in parapsychology 1984* (pp. 85–88). Metuchen, NJ: Scarecrow Press.

Thalbourne, M. A. (1995). Further studies of the measurement and correlates of belief in the paranormal. *Journal of the American Society for Psychical Research, 89,* 233–247.

Thalbourne, M. A., & Haraldsson, E. (1980). Personality characteristics of sheep and goats. *Personality and Individual Differences, 1,* 180–185.

Tobacyk, J. [J.] (1982). Paranormal belief and trait anxiety. *Psychological Reports, 51,* 861–862.

Tobacyk, J. [J.] (1983). Paranormal beliefs, interpersonal trust, and social interest. *Psychological Reports, 53,* 229–230.

Tobacyk, J. J. (1985). Paranormal beliefs, alienation and anomie in college students. *Psychological Reports, 57,* 844–846.

Tobacyk, J. J. (1988). *A revised Paranormal Belief Scale.* Ruston: Louisiana State University.

Tobacyk, J. J., & Mitchell, T. E. (1987). Out-of-body experience status as a moderator of effects of narcissism on paranormal beliefs. *Psychological Reports, 60,* 440–442.

Tobacyk, J. J., & Wilkinson, L. V. (1990). Magical thinking and paranormal beliefs [Special Issue]. *Journal of Social Behavior and Personality, 5,* 255–264.

Twemlow, S. W., Hendren, R. L., Gabbard, G. O., Jones, F. C., & Norris, P. A. (1982). Ego integrating function of psi states. *Journal of Psychiatric Treatment and Evaluation, 4,* 41–49.

Ullman, M. (1975). Parapsychology and psychiatry. In A. M. Freedman, H. I. Kaplan, & B. J. Sadock (Eds.), *Comprehensive textbook of psychiatry* (2nd ed., pp. 2552–2561). Baltimore: Williams & Wilkins.

Utts, J. (1991). Replication and meta-analysis in parapsychology. *Statistical Science, 6,* 363–378.

Utts, J. (1995). An assessment of the evidence for psychic functioning. *Journal of Parapsychology, 59,* 289–320.

Van Dusen, W. (1972). *The natural depth in man.* New York: Harper & Row.

Watt, C. (1994). Meta-analysis of DMT-ESP studies and an experimental investigation of perceptual defense/vigilance and extrasensory perception. In E. W. Cook & D. L. Delanoy (Eds.), *Research in parapsychology 1991* (pp. 64–68). Metuchen, NJ: Scarecrow Press.

White, R. A. (1995). EHE counseling: II. An ongoing annotated bibliography. *EHE News, 2,* 26–30.

Wickramasekera, I. (1989). Risk factors for parapsychological verbal reports, hypnotizability and somatic complaints. In B. Shapin & L. Coly (Eds.), *Parapsychology and human nature: Proceedings of an international conference* (pp. 19–35). New York: Parapsychology Foundation.

Williams, L. M., & Irwin, H. J. (1991). A study of paranormal belief, magical ideation as an index of schizotypy, and cognitive style. *Personality and Individual Differences, 12,* 1339–1348.

Wilson, S. C., & Barber, T. X. (1983). The fantasy-prone personality: Implications for understanding imagery, hypnosis, and parapsychological phenomena. In A. A. Sheikh (Ed.), *Imagery: Current theory, research, and application* (pp. 340–387). New York: Wiley.

Wiseman, R., & Smith, M. D. (1994, August). *A further look at the detection of unseen gaze.* Paper presented at the 37th Annual Convention of the Parapsychological Association, Amsterdam.

Wuthnow, R. (1976). Astrology and marginality. *Journal for the Scientific Study of Religion, 15,* 157–168.

Zangari, W., & Machado, F. R. (1994, August). *Incidence and social relevance of Brazilian university students' psychic experiences.* Paper presented at the 37th Annual Convention of the Parapsychological Association, Amsterdam.

Zingrone, N. L., & Alvarado, C. S. (1994, August). *Psychic and dissociative experiences: A preliminary report.* Paper presented at the 37th Annual Convention of the Parapsychological Association, Amsterdam.

Zusne, L., & Jones, W. H. (1989). *Anomalistic psychology: A study of extraordinary phenomena of behavior and experience* (2nd ed.). Hillsdale, NJ: Erlbaum.

8

ALIEN ABDUCTION EXPERIENCES

STUART APPELLE, STEVEN JAY LYNN, AND LEONARD NEWMAN

Elisabeth Barnes (a pseudonym) is quiet, retired, and 60 years of age; she lives alone in a small but comfortable A-frame home near Castleton, Vermont. Elisabeth is a deeply private person, is a good cook, and describes herself as an "arts-and-craftsy" person. One evening, on a small road she drove as a short-cut to her home, she recalls noticing a bright light in the sky. At first she thought it was a meteorite. When the light looked like a "dime on its side," Elisabeth felt very tired, pulled off the road, and fell asleep. She awoke some time later and, after she arrived at her home and watched her favorite television program, she realized she had experienced two hours of "missing time" she could not account for. She also complained of coughing and a strange itching feeling all over her body. About a week later, Elisabeth saw a television program about an elderly woman who was abducted by aliens. The woman was hypnotized by government agents to recall the experience. Ms. Barnes immediately identified with the woman in the program who experienced a puzzling episode of "missing time" in conjunction with her abduction. Her curiosity piqued, Ms. Barnes spoke with several of her friends and followed their suggestion to contact a lay-hypnotist in her community. The hypnotist immediately agreed to use hypnosis to help Elisabeth recover memories of what she surmised was her possible abduction by aliens.

During hypnosis, a story emerged in which Elisabeth was levitated and transported to a spacecraft by small and efficient gray aliens who were devoid of affect and who examined her with a variety of advanced, highly technological medical instruments, the likes of which she had never seen before. Elisabeth also reported that she recovered memories during the session of her car moving at impossible speeds, of being surrounded by a brilliant light as she was lifted into the air and then confronted by "emaciated" aliens who subjected her to a medical examination. The examination included removing various body parts that were examined from all angles and replaced with intricate surgical procedures. After the medical proceedings, she reported being levitated and floated back to her car.

Hypnosis also evoked a report that she had been abducted and examined on two prior occasions and that she had been taken on a "soul journey" to the aliens' home world where she heard ethereal music and felt at total peace with the universe. After these events, she had been telepathically commanded to forget what had occurred; hence, she was amnestic for what had purportedly transpired until hypnosis was used to recover her memories.

One of Elisabeth's family friends was a psychiatrist who provided a prosaic account of what occurred. He explained that her unusual experiences were a product of hypnagogic hallucinations (i.e., images and sensations sometimes experienced in the state between being awake and asleep) that occurred while she was driving and trying to stay awake. He explained that her interpretation of the experience as being associated with aliens was entirely consistent with her long-standing belief in alien visitations to the earth and was further elaborated and solidified by suggestive hypnotic procedures to conform to a UFO abduction scenario. The psychiatrist also pointed out that Elisabeth had long suffered terrible allergies and that her coughing and itching might have resulted from her driving by a field near her home that was rife with ragweed. Although Ms. Barnes listened attentively to the alternative explanations offered, she nevertheless continued to "trust her feelings" and steadfastly maintained, to her close friends at least, that she had repeatedly encountered alien life forms.

Elisabeth's account includes many features of alien abduction experiences (AAEs). Indeed, AAEs are characterized by subjectively real memories of being taken secretly and/or against one's will by apparently non-human entities, usually to a location interpreted as an alien spacecraft (i.e., a UFO), where individuals are subjected to complex physical and psychological procedures. Such experiences can occur as isolated events but more commonly are recalled as repeated episodes over several years. AAEs can appear in ordinary conscious experience as intact or partial recollections (sometimes long after the experience was remembered as having occurred) but often emerge (or are enhanced) only after aggressive retrieval techniques such as hypnotic regression.

DEFINITION

Although there is no universal agreement regarding what contextual or experiential features are necessary or sufficient to define the AAE (Gotlib, Appelle, Rodeghier, & Flamburis, 1994), a number of descriptions have been proposed. Bullard (1987), basing his analysis on a sample of 270 abduction reports, described the most common features of AAEs as capture (being caught and taken aboard a UFO) and examination (being subjected by the UFO abductors to physical, mental, or spiritual examinations). Other elements present in some abduction reports include conference (communication with the abductors), tour (guided examination of the UFO), otherworldly journey (transport to another place on earth or an unearthly environment), theophany (receipt of religious or spiritual messages), return (egress from the UFO and return to earth), and aftermath (postabduction experience effects).

On the basis of hundreds of AAEs he investigated, Jacobs (1992) categorized their content into primary, secondary and ancillary events involving physical activities (the removal from earthly surroundings to an alien craft or environment, the taking of tissue samples, and the insertion of implants), mental activities (telepathic manipulation, psychological testing, and information exchange), and reproductive procedures (egg/sperm collection, embryo implantation, fetus removal, actual or simulated sexual activity, and presentation of human–alien hybrid babies). Hopkins, Jacobs, and Westrum (1992) noted that the experience is also associated with waking up paralyzed, with a sense of a strange figure or figures present, with "missing time" (unaccounted-for periods in conscious memory), with seeing strange balls of light in one's room, and with the presence or sudden appearance of puzzling scars on the body. Newman and Baumeister (1996a) noted that in recent years an increasing number of reports have emphasized sexual intercourse with aliens, with some women claiming to have multiple offspring (kept by the aliens) that resulted from these acts (Jacobs, 1992, 1998). If nothing else, these descriptions illustrate that the AAE is a dynamic, elaborate, and involved experience, rich in contextual detail, with considerable perceptual, psychological, cognitive, and physical concomitants.

PREVALENCE

It is impossible to provide a firm estimate of the number of people who believe they have been abducted by aliens, but the number of reported AAEs is not small. Many abductees may be reluctant to disclose their perceptions of encounters with aliens for fear of being disbelieved and possibly ridiculed or stigmatized. Nevertheless, when Bullard (1994) surveyed 13 investigators of UFO-related phenomena, he found that even this small number of researchers had a total of 1,700 separate abduction reports in their files. Whitley Strieber (author of the 1987 best-selling book *Communion*, a detailed account of a series of purported abductions) asserted he received "nearly a quarter of a million letters claiming (alien) contact, with more than thirty thousand of them offering detailed descriptions of the encounters" (1998, p. 86). Even more startling is Jacobs's (1992) suggestion that 15 million Americans may have had such experiences. His estimate, however, was based on a simple extrapolation from a survey of students at one university.

Other writers have asserted that self-reports of abductions cannot form the basis of an accurate assessment of the extent of the phenomenon, because, in their opinion, most abduction experients have had their memories for the experience tampered with by their alien captors. Hopkins et al. (1992) thus included multiple indirect questions in a national survey conducted by the Roper organization designed to estimate the number of abduction experients in the United States (e.g., respondents were asked whether they recalled ever "waking up paralyzed with a sense of a strange person or presence or something else in the room"). On the basis of the survey data, Hopkins et al. concluded that 3.7 million Americans had been abducted as of 1992. Klass (1993) estimated that if their estimate were correct, then 340 Americans have been abducted every day since 1961, a number that he regarded as implausibly high.

Even if the numbers are much lower than some of these estimates, it is clear that many thousands of Americans believe they have been abducted by aliens. Indeed, the number of reported AAEs is sufficiently large to have attracted considerable attention from the media and the entertainment industry in general. It has also attracted attention from the scientific community, including, among other things, a conference dedicated to the subject at the Massachusetts Institute of Technology (see Pritchard, Pritchard, Mack, Kasey, & Yapp, 1994) and a focus issue of the journal *Psychological Inquiry* (Vol. 7, No. 2, 1996).

AFTEREFFECTS

Bullard (1987, 1994) cataloged the physical and psychological conditions reported as aftermaths of the AAE. The following statistics are based on his 1987 analyses of 270 abduction reports and are supported by his more recent (Bullard, 1994) survey of AAE investigators. Bullard cautioned that these statistics may underrepresent the actual effects in that systematic attention to aftereffects is rare, few investigators bother to record or report them, and long-term follow-up is uncommon. Mindful of these limitations, the following descriptions provide insight into the range and frequency of the physical and psychological conditions that are reported to follow AAEs.

Bullard's (1987, 1994) analyses revealed a number of physical conditions reported as immediate consequences of an AAE. These include the following: injuries—cuts, bruises, scrapes, puncture wounds (11 cases); eye and vision problems—burning, inflamed or bloodshot eyes, watering, irritation, conjunctivitis, sensitivity to light, pupil dilation, impaired or blurred vision (22 cases); skin burns and irritation—"sunburn" or redness of skin, blisters, itchiness, rash (23 cases); gastrointestinal distress—nausea, diarrhea, constipation, gastric pain (13 cases); equilibrium and coordination problems—balance, disorientation, fainting (14 cases); and thirst and dehydration (12 cases). Intermediate and long-term physical aftereffects include 13 instances in which the experient claims to have been healed of some preexisting ailment, 5 instances of weight loss, and 9 cases of recurring conditions such as skin or balance problems that immediately followed the initial AAE.

Among the psychological aftereffects reported by Bullard (1987, 1994), fear, anticipation, anxiety, and recurring nightmares were common. These and similar characteristics have been described as consistent with posttraumatic stress disorder (Laibow & Laue, 1993; Powers, 1994a; J. Wilson, 1990).

Paranormal experiences (e.g., seeing apparitions or events interpreted as apparent telepathy) and personality changes are also widely reported. These accounts have attracted the attention of Ring (1992), who found that abduction experients share these outcomes with individuals who have had a near-death experience (see Greyson, this volume, chap. 10). This fact, Ring posited, reflects a common propensity for and common consequence of "extraordinary encounters" (p. 13).

BIOLOGICAL MARKERS

Except for multiple abduction cases (in which more than one person claims to have been involved in an abduction), there exist almost no instances in which an individual has been observed during the time period when he or she reported that the AAE had occurred. Thus, the condition of an abduction experient at the time of an AAE is unknown, and speculation about the physiological concomitants of an AAE must follow its hypothesized cause. For example, causal theories of sleep disturbance, hypnosis-related experiences, temporal-lobe lability, or alien technology each lead to their own unique predictions about the characteristics of an experient's psychophysiological state. In the absence of controlled conditions for generating or observing an AAE, such speculation will remain untestable, although antecedent conditions may be amenable to experimental manipulation.

INDIVIDUAL DIFFERENCES

A number of theorists have suggested that certain special personality syndromes or propensities predispose individuals to incorporate information about alien abductions into their imaginative productions and to accept these productions as veridical experiences of historical events. Before we discuss individual differences, it is important to note that cultural beliefs have been implicated as the "ground" from which the abduction scenario emerges and form the core around which certain predispositions shape the abduction narrative. Indeed, the idea that cultural beliefs shape AAEs is close to the heart of many theoretical accounts of how UFO scenarios develop (e.g., Baker, 1992a, 1992b; Lynn, Pintar, Stafford, Marmelstein, & Lock, 1998; Spanos, Burgess, & Burgess, 1994).

Cultural Factors

A recent Time/CNN poll (1997) revealed that 22% of the American public believes that the earth has been visited by space aliens. Several researchers have examined the availability of imaginative narratives and the culturally derived beliefs associated with UFO narratives. Lawson (1980) hypnotized volunteers and told them to imagine an encounter with aliens. Although Lawson's hypothesis was that such reports could be easily distinguished from the reports of persons who claimed they had genuine contact experiences, he concluded that the hypnotically suggested reports were not, in fact, substantively different. Unfortunately, Lawson provided his hypnotized participants with specific suggestions to report information pertinent to what abductees claim, such as to imagine that they were examined by the aliens. So it is not surprising that the reports he obtained with hypnotic suggestion would have much in common with AAE reports coming from the general population. This makes it difficult to conclude that the participants' fantasies stemmed from culturally derived beliefs.

In a study designed to give participants more of an opportunity to interpret and describe a mysterious or ambiguous event, Lynn and Pezzo (1994) departed from Lawson's (1980) study by asking participants to role-play (simulate) the performance of excellent hypnotic subjects in response to hypnotic induction and suggestion scripts. Participants were read a script explaining that they would be hypnotized and made to recall a puzzling event that involved (a) driving in the country, (b) leaving the car to witness mysterious moving lights in the sky, and (c) afterward, having no clear recall of being in the car and noticing that there were 2 hr of time for which they could not account.

After a brief hypnotic induction script was read, an age regression script was presented instructing participants to "age regress" to the time they witnessed the lights in the sky and the 2-hr period, and they were asked to describe what they could see, feel, and hear. A structured interview followed, which began with open-ended questions and then became increasingly specific and direct.

Lynn and Pezzo's (1994) experiment was also designed to examine the effects of priming or cuing participants to construe the mysterious experience in terms of a UFO encounter. One group of participants (Group a) was given a questionnaire at the beginning of the experiment that was devised by *OMNI Magazine* with the assistance of Budd Hopkins and that was intended to serve as a "prime" insofar as it queried respondents about their beliefs in UFOs, if they had sighted what they believe to be a UFO, memory gaps associated with these sightings, and so on.

A second group (Group b) not only received the questionnaire at the beginning of the experiment but were also provided with an even more specific cue by the provision of an instruction to role-play a "close encounter of the third kind" in which they have contact with aliens on a spacecraft. A third group of participants (i.e., Group c) received no priming information prior to the interview. All three groups of participants received the *OMNI* questionnaire at the end of the experiment.

Lynn and Pezzo (1994) found that 19% of the participants in Group c identified what they had seen as a UFO in response to an initial opened-ended question. When asked more direct questions in the interview, 52% identified the lights as UFOs, 24% indicated that they had interacted with aliens, and 14% reported they boarded a UFO. When participants received the *OMNI* questionnaire before the interview (Group a), 62% of the participants reported they had witnessed a UFO, and all but one of the participants, or 95%, reported witnessing a UFO in response to a direct question. In addition, 62% reported that they interacted with aliens, and 33% reported that they boarded the spacecraft.

In Group b, composed of individuals specifically instructed to role-play an encounter with the aliens, 95% of the participants identified the lights as a UFO, and 91% stated that they interacted with aliens and boarded the spacecraft. As Lynn and Pezzo (1994) hypothesized, participants endorsed items more frequently as they received more cues to report experiences consistent with culture-based UFO narratives.

Finally, the simulated reports of many of the participants contained many of the features (e.g., telepathic contact, small bodies, large eyes and heads of occupants, forced or compelled actions, sexual contact with aliens, and operations) reported by individuals who claim that they have actually made contact with or were abducted by UFO occupants.

Randles (1994a) noted a number of inconsistencies between the prototypical AAE as told by American abduction experients and the stories made up by 20 British participants asked to imagine a close encounter. Nevertheless, as was the case for their American counterparts, the made-up British stories were consistent with the abduction reports from British abduction experients.

Taken together, these studies imply that certain elements of alien contact narratives are widely known (see Dean, 1998 for extensive coverage of the alien motif in American culture). However, because many individuals who endorse the belief that aliens have abducted humans do not believe they have been abducted personally, cultural beliefs cannot constitute a sufficient explanation for AAEs. Cultural beliefs may, however, be associated with the geographical distribution of abduction reports and variations in their content. Bullard (1987) noted that 47% of the abduction reports he studied came from the United States. Argentina, Brazil, Australia, and the United Kingdom also provided a large number of reports, collectively accounting for about 33% of abduction reports on file. Africa, Asia, continental Europe, and the Middle East were only barely represented, although the Associated Press (1996) news service reported "a flurry of media reports on . . . abductions by extraterrestrials" in Israel. It is unknown whether this geographical variation reflects differences in the prevalence of AAEs or only differences in reporting and investigating them. In either case, cultural factors would seem to be relevant.

Similarly, the typical content of the AAE varies with geographical origin. In particular, Bullard (1994) reported that compared with North American accounts, British and Australian reports differ both in terms of narrative descriptions and the experients' reactions to the reported events. Moura (1994), a Brazilian psychologist, found that compared to American recipients, those in her country are far more likely to view their experiences as friendly and for the benefit of mankind. However, many of the content elements remain constant across cultures, and one prominent abduction therapist maintains that his comparison of accounts from England, Mexico, Brazil, Chile, and Australia revealed "the same kinds of creatures, [space] crafts, procedures, . . . emotional reactions, and psychological responses" (Carpenter, 1997, p. 18). Although systematic, comprehensive, and large-scale cross-cultural content analyses of cases are lacking, culture remains an interesting variable in regard to the abduction experience. Its role in both its occurrence and reporting deserves additional attention.

Fantasy Proneness

One possible explanation for AAEs is that cultural beliefs about alien visitations are transformed into deeply felt personal experiences by a relatively small number of individuals who exhibit a propensity for making imaginative experiences seem "as real as real," thereby confusing fantasy with reality. Indeed, such a group of highly fantasy-prone individuals, also known as *fantasizers*, has been identified by S. C. Wilson and Barber (1981, 1983a).

Fantasy proneness is theoretically relevant to the AAE not only as a source of imaginative experience, but because of similarities between the experiences of fantasy-prone persons and those of abduction experients. For example, fantasizers report a high incidence of false pregnancies, paranormal and out-of-body experiences, the appearance of apparitions, and vivid sleep imagery that feels "as if they are seeing something that really exists out there or that they are looking into another dimension" (S. C. Wilson & Barber, 1981, p. 365). Each of these experiences has parallels with those reported by abduction experients (Bullard, 1987, 1994), suggesting that fantasizers and AAE reporters may belong to the same population. However, the empirical support for this hypothesis is mixed at best.

Ring and Rosing (1990) used a battery of tests to compare a group of abduction experients and others reporting UFO encounters with a group of control participants who expressed only an interest in UFOS. Although encounter participants were significantly more likely to report childhood experiences of paranormal phenomena, "nonphysical beings," and to "see into other realities that others didn't seem to be aware of" (p. 70; factors consistent with fantasy-prone characteristics originally reported by S. C. Wilson & Barber, 1981), they were not fantasy prone in any general sense.

Bartholomew, Basterfield, and Howard (1991) studied over 100 abduction experients and concluded that the vast majority (87%) had histories consistent with one or more of the major characteristics associated with the fantasy-prone profile. However, they assessed fantasy proneness by retrospective analysis of biographical data rather than by an independent test for fantasy proneness. And, contrary to the authors' conclusion, of all the fantasy-prone characteristics they examined, only the frequency of reported paranormal phenomena even approached the frequency found by S. C. Wilson and Barber (1981) in their fantasy-prone population.

In another study, Rodeghier, Goodpaster, and Blatterbauer (1991) assessed fantasy proneness with the Inventory of Childhood Memories and Imaginings (ICMI; S. C. Wilson & Barber, 1983b), an instrument adapted from one used by S. C. Wilson and Barber (1981) in their seminal study of fantasy-prone persons. Rodeghier et al. found no difference between the ICMI scores for their AAE group and those of a random sample of the population.

Similarly, Spanos, Cross, Dickinson, and Dubreuil (1993) found no statistical difference across or between AAE and non-AAE groups on fantasy proneness as measured by the ICMI. They did, however, find a correlation between ICMI scores and an Intensity-of-Experience scale. Nevertheless, even for the group of persons who reported "intense experiences" (e.g., missing time and communication with aliens), the mean ICMI score was only 22.4, a score that is at the mid-range of the distribution of the general population (Lynn & Rhue, 1988), leading Spanos et al. (1993) to conclude that their "findings clearly contradict the hypotheses that UFO reports . . . occur primarily in individuals who are highly fantasy prone" (p. 629).

However, it is premature to conclude that fantasy proneness is not associated with AAEs. First, the studies in this area have methodological limitations (e.g., nonvalidated, ad hoc measures and small sample sizes) that preclude drawing strong conclusions. Second, it is questionable whether any of the participants in Spanos et al.'s (1993) research claimed to have classic abduction experiences, limiting the potential relevance of this research to fantasy proneness and AAEs. Third, respondents in such studies are undoubtedly aware that many of the markers of fantasy proneness could indicate deviance or psychopathology (see Lynn & Rhue, 1988). Therefore, characteristics or experiences associated with fantasy proneness might not be reported in situations that trigger socially desirable responding, resulting in an underestimation of the correlation between fantasy proneness and AAEs (Newman & Baumeister, 1996a). Hence, the fantasy-proneness hypothesis deserves further attention in the context of more rigorous studies that take into consideration the methodological limitations of previous investigations, including the possible operation of response sets that moderate the relation between fantasy proneness and AAEs. In conclusion, the idea that fantasy proneness is linked with reports of alien abductions remains a plausible yet not well-tested hypothesis.

Boundary-Deficit Personality

Hartmann (1984) found that individuals with a history of frequent nightmares share a constellation of traits characterized by weak discrimination between basic cognitive categories such as self and nonself, fantasy and reality, and dream and waking experiences. These thin "boundaries" are said to result in individuals who are sensitive, artistic, empathetic, vulnerable, imaginative, have a weak sense of sexual or personal identity, have difficulty distinguishing periods of time, or who are perceived by others as "different."

On the basis of Hartmann's (1984) construct of thin boundaries, Kottmeyer (1988) argued that the characteristics of what he termed the *boundary-deficit personality* also describe the abduction experient. Spanos et al. (1993) administered a number of scales relevant to Kottmeyer's hypothesis and found that compared with the scores for control participants, Spanos et al.'s close encounter/UFO experient groups showed higher self-esteem, lower schizophrenia, higher well-being, lower perceptual aberration, lower perception of an unfriendly world, lower aggression, and no difference in social potency. Moreover, Spanos et al. found no difference between control and close-encounter participants on measures of absorption, fantasy proneness, and imaginal propensity, all of which should be elevated according to the thin-boundary or boundary-deficit hypothesis.

Each of these findings is either inconsistent with or clearly opposite to those the thin-boundary explanation predicts. However, other studies have found characteristics of AAE experients consistent with the boundary-deficit personality. These include a weak sense of personal or sexual identity (Slater, 1985), schizoid tendencies (Parnell & Sprinkle, 1990), greater sensitivity to nonordinary realities (Ring & Rosing, 1990), and a high rate of reported suicide attempts (Stone-Carmen, 1994). Hence, the link between boundary deficits and abduction reports warrants continued attention.

Escape-From-Self and Masochistic Fantasy

Newman and Baumeister (1996a, 1996b) detailed the many similarities between the UFO abduction experience and what might seem at first to be a very different kind of phenomenon: ritualized masochism. The main features of masochism, both actual activities and fantasies, are pain, helplessness, loss of control, and humiliation. All of these themes dominate abduction accounts, and Newman and Baumeister (1996b) hypothesized that abduction accounts might grow from the same motivational roots that attract some people to masochism. This is why (they argued) the demographic profile of the typical masochist (e.g., a person of reasonably high socioeconomic status from a Westernized individualistic society) is similar to that of the typical abductee. The underlying motive, according to Newman and Baumeister, is the wish of some individuals to "escape the self." The "threats, stresses, and other burdens of modern egotism" create a need in some individuals to "escape from self-awareness and identity" (p. 112); in other words, people sometimes seek relief from constant pressures to be independent, fulfilled, esteemed, and in control. Strategies that thwart self-esteem and control may accomplish this, and Newman and Baumeister (1996b) argued that masochism is an extreme but effective example (see Baumeister, 1989). Masochism can help people escape the self because the pain that is inflicted on masochists captures their attention and makes reflection and self-evaluation difficult. Restraint and immobilization nullifies the usual pressure to assert control over one's situation and paradoxically, the humiliation involved can liberate people from trying to meet their usual standards of esteem and dignity.

Newman and Baumeister (1996b) suggested that, among individuals inclined to escape the self, the influences of abduction investigators, media, and popular culture create the raw material for masochistic fantasy to manifest itself as an AAE (especially those aspects of the AAE dealing with sexual or gynecological procedures). Newman and Baumeister examined the abduction accounts presented in Bullard's (1987) compendium of AAEs for specific references to humiliating displays (e.g., "being stretched out on a table naked with lots of people watching"), a feature of masochistic fantasy more prevalent among female than male masochistic fantasizers (see Baumeister, 1988). Their analysis of Bullard's data showed that such features were present in the narratives of 50% of the men and 80% of the women, a statistically significant difference that supports their claim. Although Newman and Baumeister's hypothesis remains viable, there have been no other empirical tests of their theory. Further work on this hypothesis is clearly warranted.

"Psychically Sensitive" Personality

Abduction experients often mention having increased paranormal abilities as an aftereffect of the AAE (Bullard, 1994; Ring, 1992), and many report long histories of ostensibly paranormal events preceding their AAEs (Basterfield, 1994; Bullard, 1987, Randles, 1988; Ring, 1992). On several measures, abduction experients share personality characteristics with nonexperients who consider themselves to be psychically sensitive. For example, Ring (1992) found a constellation of traits in common among abduction experients and individuals who claim to be "electrically sensitive" (i.e., to have anomalous effects on electrical devices). On the basis of a comparison of the personality characteristics of 20 abduction experients and those of highly successful ESP participants, Johnson (1994) found that at least some experients share traits with participants who appear to have performed well in "remote viewing" experiments (see Targ, Schlitz, & Irwin, this volume, chap. 7).

A number of investigators have considered these psychic histories as a possible cause of the AAE. Ring (1992) suggested a connection between psychically sensitive personality traits and his model of an "encounter-prone personality." Randles (1988) described the paranormal histories of abduction experients as "the key to the entire [abduction] mystery" (p. 208). Of course, self-reports of paranormal experience are evidence of neither actual paranormal events nor paranormal performance. The data tell us only that individuals who report abductions tend to report paranormal experiences as well. This fact alone is worthy of further scrutiny, because abduction experients typically report telepathic communication with their alien abductors (Bullard, 1994).

Experiential Sleep Anomalies

Susceptibility to certain subjective and physiological concomitants of natural sleep or sleep disorders has been proposed as an explanation for the AAE (e.g., Baker, 1992a; Spanos et al., 1993). The reasons for this are numerous. AAEs are commonly reported as having occurred at bedtime or during the course of sleep. They are frequently first remembered as the content of an apparent (albeit "unusual") dream or as otherwise having a dreamlike subjective quality. Furthermore, they are often accompanied by the experience of paralysis, a condition that occurs during that part of the sleep period when motor tonus is lost.

The content of AAEs and sleep can also be compared. For example, Baker (1990) characterized the content of AAEs as "a classic, textbook description" (p. 251) of hypnagogic hallucinations. Part and parcel of hypnagogic states is the experience of unusual perceptual distortions and anomalies (e.g., round objects swell to gigantic size; at times the objects rush toward the observer), a sensation of pressure and heaviness on the body or, alternately, sensations of weightlessness and floating, and feelings of disorientation and fearfulness that extend to panic because the dreamer is unable to move (Baker, 1992a, 1992b, 1995). Hufford (1982) drew attention to the similarities of AAEs and a variety of sleep experiences across a wide range of cultures.

Despite these analogies, there have been no direct tests of a link between sleep anomalies and AAEs, and the prevalence of sleep disorders in the abduction experient population remains unknown. However, Gotlib (1996) provided a single case study of a client with both a sleep disorder and AAEs. Spanos et al. (1993) reported that, compared with participants with less involved UFO experiences, participants who report intense alien encounters have them more often in association with sleep-related experiences (e.g., sudden awakenings). In addition, Rodeghier (1994) reported a somewhat greater incidence of hypnagogic imagery in a subset of abduction experients, although he presented no evidence that the content of this imagery ever takes the form of an AAE. The relation between certain sleep anomalies and AAEs clearly warrants further study.

Hypnosis and Hypnotizability

AAEs do not arise in a contextual vacuum. Often their detail emerges during hypnosis sessions intended to recover presumably hidden aspects of a partially remembered experience. Bullard (1987) examined published AAE accounts prior to 1987 and determined that hypnosis had been used

31% of the time overall. However, for those reports that Bullard rated high in both reliability and information content, hypnosis was involved about 70% of the time (Bullard, 1989). Finally, a survey he conducted of active abduction investigators (Bullard, 1994) suggested that hypnosis is now being used in about 70% of all contemporary abduction investigations.

If hypnosis were, in fact, able to assist in the recovery of memories, it would lend credibility to AAEs that emerge during hypnosis. However, the empirical literature provides no support for the idea that hypnosis selectively increases accurate memories. The typical finding is that while hypnosis may produce a slight increase in accurate memories, this slim advantage, if present at all, comes at the expense of a trade-off of increased errors and an increased tendency to respond to misleading information (see Lynn, Lock, Myers, & Payne, 1997). In fact, the elaboration of confidently held spurious memories has been widely recognized as a by-product of hypnosis (see Lynn & Nash, 1994). Hence, hypnotic procedures may thus be *creating* rather than *uncovering* UFO abduction memories. That is, once the person has the glimmerings of a memory or the impression that an abduction occurred, hypnosis can facilitate the addition of many details to elaborate the episode.

Given the unreliability of hypnotic recall, hypnosis should have a greater potential to create false AAEs than to retrieve veridical ones. If so, it could be argued that the emergence of AAEs should vary with their hypnotic susceptibility. However, this contention has not been supported in the literature. For example, Rodeghier et al. (1991) used the Creative Imagination Scale (S. C. Wilson & Barber, 1978) to assess hypnotic responsiveness in a group of abduction experients. The authors found that, as a group, the abduction experients were no more responsive to hypnotic suggestion than were the general population. Spanos et al. (1993) used the Carleton University Responsiveness to Suggestion Scale (Spanos, Radtke, Hodgins, Stam, & Bertrand, 1983) to measure hypnotizability. The researchers found that their experient population was no different from control individuals on subjective and behavioral measures of hypnotizability.

Despite the fact that abduction experients are not particularly hypnotizable in formal testing situations, in clinical situations most abduction hypnotists regard them as easy to hypnotize. One interesting possibility is that there is something about the AAE that makes it particularly malleable in response to suggestive procedures. Alternatively, there may be little or no relation between hypnotizability and the response to certain hypnotic suggestions, an observation consistent with the possibility that the hypnotic context itself may be an influential source of AAEs, independent of the person's hypnotizability level.

Although no link between hypnotizability and AAEs has been established, this does not disqualify the hypnotic context as an influential determinant of AAEs. Whereas the available evidence does indicate a relation between hypnotizability and responsiveness to false-memory suggestions, it is not necessarily a linear relationship. Across studies, it is the high and medium hypnotizable participants who report more pseudo-memories than do low hypnotic particpants (see Lynn et al., 1997). The fact that many medium hypnotizable persons, who represent the modal participants in the general population, report pseudomemories indicates that the effect may be quite pervasive. Moreover, even low hypnotizable participants can be vulnerable to false memories in hypnotic conditions (Orne, Whitehouse, Dinges, & Orne, 1996). In short, it is possible that even low hypnotizable persons can be influenced by hypnotic suggestions that engender or reinforce beliefs in AAEs. If this were true, it would explain why there is not a high degree of association between AAEs and hypnotizability level.

In any case, if hypnosis is indeed responsible for false AAEs, its influence may be related more to recall quantity than to content. Bullard (1989, 1994) compared AAEs that emerged during hypnosis with those that were obtained without hypnotic assistance. On the basis of his findings, he concluded that "the form and content of abduction stories seems independent of hypnosis" (Bullard, 1989, p. 3). In his more recent examination, Bullard (1994) concluded that hypnosis is a significant factor with regard to the quantity of material reported, but not in any direct way to the content. These findings are consistent with the literature, which indicates that hypnosis often increases the productivity or sheer volume of responses, regardless of the accuracy of the responses obtained (see Lynn et al., 1997). If cultural factors or suggestions from a therapist or other authority figure shape the content of abduction narratives, it should not matter whether these narratives develop in hypnotic or nonhypnotic contexts.

Because as many as one third of AAEs do not seem to stem from hypnotic interventions, hypnosis is not a necessary condition for the emergence of abduction accounts. Lynn and Kirsch (1996) proposed the following account of how a UFO abduction narrative might unfold in the context of psychotherapy, regardless of whether hypnotic procedures are used:

(a) A person is predisposed to accept the idea that certain puzzling or "inexplicable" experiences (e.g., hypnagogic hallucinations, missing time) may be telltale signs of a UFO abduction.
(b) The person seeks out a therapist, whom he or she views as an authority and who is, at the very least, receptive to this explanation and is familiar with UFO abduction reports.
(c) The therapist frames the puzzling experiences in terms of an abduction narrative.
(d) Alternative explanations of the experiences are not explored.
(e) There is increasing commitment to the "abduction " explanation

and anxiety reduction in the patient, associated with ambiguity reduction.

(f) The therapist legitimates or ratifies the "abductee's" experience, which constitutes additional positive reinforcement. The therapist may use suggestive techniques such as hypnosis to fill in the details of the account.

(g) The client adopts the role of the "victim" or "abductee," which becomes integrated into the psychotherapy and the client's view of self. Adopting this new role may have powerful attendant reinforcements.

This account, while plausible, remains speculative and awaits empirical proof. Also, it does not address how AAEs arise independently of any contact with a psychotherapist, for instance, as the by-product of a variety of psychopathological conditions.

PSYCHOPATHOLOGY

Psychological disorders that might account for AAEs include the following: psychosis (including hallucinations and delusions), folie-à-deux (shared psychotic symptoms brought about by a close relationship between the percipients), conversion reactions (e.g., motor paralysis not explained by a medical condition and associated with psychological factors), physiological manifestations of a psychosomatic nature (e.g., marks, blotches, and discolorations of the skin), dissociative disorders (amnesia, fugue, and other conditions resulting in time loss, time distortion, and disorientation), dissociative identity disorder (which, in addition to "missing time," may be characterized by messages from and/or "dual identities"), and Munchausen's syndrome (self-inflicted injury or false claims of physical symptomatology). However, while psychopathology is indicated in some isolated AAE cases, assessment by both clinical examination and standardized tests has shown that, as a group, abduction experients are not different from the general population in terms of psychopathology prevalence.

Bloecher, Clamar, and Hopkins (1985) discussed the findings of Slater (1985), who did a "blind" evaluation of 9 abduction experients. Using the Rorschach and the Thematic Apperception Test, Slater found no evidence by which the reported AAEs could be accounted for on the basis of mental disorder. Similarly, Jacobson and Bruno (1994) examined AAE narratives from 12 individuals and found no narrative elements that would suggest "any currently recognized psychiatric syndrome" (p. 306). Nonetheless, hospital records showed that 2 participants had a major psychiatric illness around the time of their AAE, illustrating the danger in using indirect assessment methods.

Parnell and Sprinkle (1990) used the Minnesota Multiphasic Personality Inventory (MMPI) to test over 200 participants who reported UFO experiences. Although the authors concluded that "no overt psychopathology was indicated" (p. 45), a closer examination of their data suggests that among those participants who described communication with entities, some had scores on certain MMPI scales (e.g., Scale 8, which assesses schizophrenic tendencies) that could be considered in the abnormal range. However, because Scale 8 includes some items that could define the abduction experience, this finding is difficult to interpret. In a similar study, Rodeghier et al. (1991) used the MMPI-2 to evaluate 27 abduction experients. Again, no overt pathology was indicated for the group as a whole, but the findings were suggestive for several individuals in the sample.

Mack (1994) studied 76 abduction experients, and provided detailed case studies of 13. Mack concluded that their accounts could not be explained in terms of psychopathology. Spanos et al. (1993) compared a control group with 49 people who had reported UFO-related experiences. The UFO reporters were divided into those who merely saw unidentified lights and those who had more elaborate close encounters. The authors found that their encounter group scored no lower than the control group on any of the multiple measures of psychological health that were administered. They concluded that their findings "provide no support whatsoever for the hypothesis that UFO reporters are psychologically disturbed" (p. 628) and "the onus is on those who favor the psychopathology hypothesis to provide support for it" (p. 629).

Despite these findings, the implication of general normality can be misleading. "Normal" can be understood in the clinical sense as "not pathological" or in the statistical sense as "not significantly different from average." From a clinical perspective, the data so far are unambiguous: Most AAEs cannot be accounted for in terms of known psychological disorder as measured on standardized psychometric tests or as interpreted by means of the experient's personal and therapeutic history.

However, a number of studies have shown that abduction experients are not representative of the general population. For example, Parnell and Sprinkle (1990) found that participants claiming communication with aliens had a propensity for unusual feelings, thoughts, and attitudes; were suspicious, distrustful, and imaginative; and had schizoid tendencies. Ring and Rosing (1990) found that their participants reported more sensitivity to "nonordinary realities" as children. Rodeghier et al. (1991) found more loneliness, less happiness, and poorer sleep patterns in AAE reporters. Mack (1994) reported being "struck by how many abductees came from broken homes or had one or more alcoholic parents" (p. 17). Perhaps most troubling, Stone-Carmen (1994) found that 57% of her participants had reported suicide attempts. This compares with 1.28% in the general population (U.S. Department of Commerce, 1990).

CLINICAL ISSUES AND RISKS

It is not uncommon for abduction experients to present to mental health professionals with symptoms associated with a believed or suspected AAE. The issue of treatment for presenting symptoms is therefore an important consideration (Gotlib, 1996). As alluded to above, one concern is that abduction accounts represent false memories created by suggestive psychotherapeutic procedures (see Gotlib, 1993). Given that the spontaneous emergence during therapy of an AAE completely unsuspected by the client is apparently quite rare (based on the general lack of references to such cases in the clinical literature; see, however, Gotlib, 1996), suggestive influences could enrich an existing AAE or a fragmentary AAE memory or create whole new experiences beyond those initially presented by the client, as well as harden conviction regarding the validity of the experience.

The concern about such influences is sufficiently great that a number of professional organizations in the mental health field (e.g., American Psychiatric Association Board of Trustees, 1993; American Psychological Association, 1994; American Society of Clinical Hypnosis, 1995) have formally cautioned their members against practices that might produce false memories. An ethics committee comprising individuals interested in the AAE (Gotlib et al., 1994) has taken a similar position with regard to investigators and mental health professionals working with abduction experients.

Despite such cautions, a number of mental health practitioners continue to use aggressive techniques (e.g., frequent hypnosis sessions, support and discussion groups) to explore for AAEs and to provide (in the absence of independent corroborating evidence) validation of the experience as indicative of an actual alien abduction. These practices are often rationalized in terms of the emotional sincerity of the client or the apparent improvement in presenting symptoms that occur during the course of treatment. However, Nash (1994) noted that "clinical utility may have little or nothing to do with uncovering the truth about the patient's past. . . . What patients think they have found out about their past may be helpful, but that does not necessarily mean that it is accurate" (p. 351).

As prudent as these cautions may be, the ability of laboratory-based experiments to document the creation of complex false memories in real-life situations has been questioned (Pope, 1996), and the scope of the problem of the creation of false memories has been the subject of considerable debate (Hovdestad & Kristiansen, 1996). Nevertheless, clinicians should consider the potential hazards and avoid implicitly or explicitly suggesting an AAE or using suggestive memory recovery procedures with anyone who claims to have experiences consistent with an AAE or its potential antecedents (e.g., sleep paralysis and hypnagogic images).

While providing therapy has its risks, so does the withholding of treatment. Mental health practitioners must feel free to exercise their professional responsibilities to experients who are in need of their services, lest they exacerbate a client's feelings of rejection and helplessness and perpetuate the social and professional sanctions against the experience. With this in mind, the risks of providing therapy can be minimized, and positive outcomes best assured, when the focus of treatment deals with educating clients about possible explanations for the AAE, encouraging them to understand the AAE in terms of its meaning in their life, and otherwise working on coping strategies that transcend the inevitable inconclusiveness about the AAE's objective reality. Of course, any treatment should include thorough assessment for possible antecedent conditions stemming from psychological or organic abnormality.

THEORIES

In our discussion of potential predisposing factors to AAEs, we have presented a number of theories and explanations. However, a number of other theories have been proposed that merit discussion.

Hoaxes

The hoax explanation suggests that reports of alien abduction are not honest descriptions of experiences but are stories made up to deliberately deceive. It is generally assumed that the motivation for such deception lies in the opportunity for monetary or psychosocial reward (e.g., support groups, talk shows, and conferences) afforded by such stories. However, to take advantage of such opportunities, the abduction experient must go public with the experience, and the experient who goes public is a rarity. Much more commonly, an assurance of anonymity is desired.

On the other hand, deliberate misrepresentation can occur in the absence of normal incentives for deception. The term *factitious disorder* applies to individuals who feign physical or psychological illness in which "the motivation for the behavior is to assume the sick role" (*Diagnostic and Statistical Manual of Mental Disorders*, 4th ed.; American Psychiatric Association, 1994, p. 474). That is, the psychological need to be a patient is itself symptomatic of a disorder.

Despite some parallels with abduction accounts, there are a number of characteristics of factitious disorder that make it an unlikely source of abduction hoaxes. Individuals with factitious disorders are likely to have an extensive history of hospitalizations or treatment interventions; be extremely resistant to giving up the role as patient; and are reluctant, vague, and inconsistent when asked to provide information in detail. These and other differential diagnoses are not characteristic of the vast majority of abduction experients.

Psychoanalytic and Psychodynamic Theories

It has been suggested (Sagan, 1995; Vallee, 1969) that similar themes appear in both historical folklore (e.g., in tales of encounters with fairies, elves, angels) and contemporary abduction accounts. Some have argued that this indicates a common origin in the human unconscious (for a discussion of the folkloric dimensions of abduction accounts, see Bullard, 1991). A number of psychoanalytic theories have been proposed to explain the manifestation of such processes in the AAE.

One theory is based on a correlation between reported AAEs and reported childhood abuse (e.g., Laibow & Laue, 1993; Powers, 1994a, 1994b; Ring & Rosing, 1990; Rodeghier et al., 1991). Some theorists have suggested that this correlation reflects actual childhood abuse manifesting as screen (false) memories of alien abduction. Powers (1994a) suggested the AAE serves this role because abduction by aliens "is less stressful than confronting the trauma of childhood abuse perpetrated by relatives or family friends" (p. 49), and "recasting the experience [of early childhood abuse] as a selection with such a grand purpose [i.e., for the aliens' cosmic objectives] might restore meaning to lives threatened by traumatic memories" (Powers, 1994b, p. 46).

Alternative theories have been presented. Lawson (1984, 1985) argued that the AAE is the unconscious representation of the birth experience; Stacy (1992) suggested the AAE is "a reliving of the abortion experience"; and Grosso (1985) extended to AAEs the position of Carl Jung (1959) that some "flying saucer" sightings might be a manifestation of archetypal imagery associated with the collective unconscious. None of these theories have been tested adequately.

Finally, Evans (1989) suggested that some unique altered state may allow unconscious material to emerge into consciousness in the form of an AAE. In this regard, Bullard (1987) described 11 cases (out of the 270 he evaluated) that might reflect such an occurrence. He referred to these cases as "psychic abductions" during which the altered state "may trigger awareness . . . underway in the unconscious. . . . The witness slips into this [altered state] unprepared to believe that [this is] responsible for the vivid, weird pseudo-reality of the experience" (p. 361). However valid the altered-state explanation may be for some AAEs, Bullard's cases represent just 4% of the sample. It is unlikely that altered states account for a significant proportion of abduction reports.

Electromagnetic Effects

Anomalous responses to electromagnetic fields have been suggested as a cause of the AAE. Budden (1994) regarded such responses as a consequence of allergic reactions to ambient electrical fields from power lines and electronic equipment. Persinger (1990) regarded them as a manifestation of especially labile temporal-lobe activity in response to the effects of tectonic stress (a condition he argued propagates electromagnetic fields). However, the presence of such fields during AAEs has not been demonstrated, nor has the prevalence of temporal-lobe lability among abduction experients been established. Spanos et al. (1993) assessed temporal-lobe lability with the 52-item temporal-lobe subscale of the Personal Philosophy Inventory, an instrument designed by Persinger and Makarec (1987) specifically to measure this trait. Using Persinger and Makerec's own instrument, Spanos et al. found no differences between control participants and abduction experients.

Extraterrestrial (ET) Hypothesis

Perhaps the most provocative explanation of AAEs is that at least some of them are essentially veridical reports of actual abductions by ET entities. Critics of this hypothesis have argued that in the absence of tangible proof (e.g., indisputable physical evidence of alien contact, artifacts from an alien civilization, and direct contact of an alien civilization with authorities), parsimony requires that the ET hypothesis be dismissed. Its proponents take the position that a veridical interpretation of the AAE is consistent with its reported characteristics. Furthermore, they point to a number of features of the AAE as supporting the ET hypothesis, including the consistency of the accounts, down to very specific details. For example, Jacobs (1992) regarded "the strongest evidence presented [to be] . . . the congruence of narrative and the richness of exact detail" (p. 239). In a similar vein, on the basis of an exhaustive analysis of AAE content, Bullard (1987) concluded that "no accident, random hoax, or purely personal fantasy could reasonably explain so much consistency throughout this sizable body of reports" (p. 353). In his more recent analysis, Bullard (1994) noted that both prominent and obscure elements of the AAE are consistently reported by investigators: "The range of differences among major features and main patterns is quite narrow. . . . Abduction reports seem to converge toward a unity of content irrespective of the investigator" (p. 615).

Although consistency is well documented, the source of this consistency is still a subject of debate. For example, Kottmeyer (1989) argued that fantasy production could easily draw upon material readily available in the media and popular culture. Previously, we cited data implying that narratives widely circulating in the culture could account for many similarities in abduction reports. Other arguments that have been raised in support of a veridical interpretation of AAEs include corroborating testimony from very young children (Hopkins, 1994) and from multiple experients describing their participation in the same abduction event (Haines, 1994). However, Ceci, Loftus, Leichtman, and Bruck (1994) cited a body of evidence showing that children may be particularly susceptible to misattributing information coming from others as their own experience, and the issue of multiple participants in a common abduction may be as much a matter to be resolved by the methodology of the detective as by those of the scientist or clinician. In any case, the debate surrounding the veridicality of these experiences is not as simplistic as may be imagined and is beyond the scope of this chapter. Those interested in examining this controversy in greater depth are referred to Appelle (1996).

METHODOLOGICAL ISSUES

The AAE phenomenon does not suffer from a lack of hypotheses but from a lack of persuasive research. Many theories that seem both parsimonious and reasonable have been advanced to explain the AAE. But these theories have either not been supported by the literature or are yet to be adequately studied. Indeed, the methodological problems in this research area are legion. As we noted earlier, many of the studies reviewed rely on very small samples and retrospective analysis of biographical data. They do not use standardized interview or test procedures with established psychometric properties and are therefore vulnerable to potential experimenter bias. They also do not carefully establish the existence of psychological disorders or psychological diagnoses by way of reliable procedures. Furthermore, it is not always clear whether persons who are included in a particular study have a classic abduction experience or merely have had the experience of witnessing a UFO or an alien.

Apart from a few studies on the prevalence of AAEs done by investigators in the field, as well as surveys conducted with little or no methodological rigor, very little is known about the number and nature of persons who present with AAEs in the general psychological community and in the population more generally. Virtually nothing is known about whether the persons who present to their therapists with experiences consistent with AAEs or who report full-blown AAE narratives are representative of the population of persons who have AAEs in the larger community.

Questions can be raised about the validity of AAE reporters' responses to measures relevant to different explanations of the abduction experience. Once they profess to have experienced AAEs, abduction experients may be defensive or highly committed to their beliefs and status as "abductees," which may well engender response biases that distort their scores on measures of psychopathology, fantasy proneness, and hypnotizability scales. It may be as important to study the unique circumstances and self-presentational concerns of AAE reporters who are faced with measures that could potentially discredit or invalidate their self-presentation as it is to study the nature of their experiences.

Unfortunately, as yet there are no studies that manipulate the perceived characteristics of the experimental setting and the way that experimental scales and procedures are presented to AAE reporters. If self-presentational concerns were paramount in abduction experients' reports to investigators, then responses to measures such as fantasy proneness would be expected to vary as a function of what participants were told the scale was measuring (e.g., psychopathology vs. imagination). It is clear that scales with established and subtle validity indexes that can detect specific response sets, such as a tendency to deny or minimize symptoms, would be worth including in studies of abduction experients.

Various theorists have emphasized the role of therapy and therapists in the production of AAE reports. However, we know little about how therapists actually manage such reports and abduction experients in therapeutic situations. Because the use of hypnosis is often superimposed on the broader dynamics of psychotherapy, the specific role of hypnosis in treatment has not been isolated. Research conducted in this area must consider both the perceptions and behaviors of the client and the therapist in any complete account of what transpires in psychotherapy. This is a complex and challenging endeavor.

CONCLUSION

In a review of the literature on the AAE, it often appears that parsimony is given too much credit as the criterion against which explanations of the AAE should be compared. Parsimony is of value in developing and weighing hypotheses, but it is not, as some AAE theorists would have it, the definitive defense for a hypothesis. That must be established through a process of hypothesis testing. As such, the AAE literature has yet to establish the validity or falseness of any hypothesis so far advanced.

It may be argued that no single explanation has yet accounted for the AAE because the phenomenon is multicausal, and the AAE as a whole can be explained only by considering all prosaic explanations in their entirety. For example, if only some abduction reports are hoaxes, and only some are the result of pathology, fantasy, sleep anomalies, and so forth, perhaps in total, these disparate explanations can constitute a complete explanation (i.e., account for all of the variance in the data). However, the extant data suggest that each explanation, by itself, can account for a limited proportion of all cases, and that even in the aggregate they fall short as a complete explanation.

The notion that the AAE is multicausal leads to an additional possibility: namely, that it requires a constellation of factors to be present in an individual (e.g., that a person must be both fantasy prone and have a sleep disorder). Although this approach may also fail to provide a complete explanation, there is still much to be learned by studying the interaction of variables. This synergistic approach would examine what combinations of variables or measures, and in what specific circumstances, are most effective in predicting AAE reports. Fantasy proneness, for example, might not be a relevant variable unless it is combined with high suggestibility in the context of a person who believes aliens regularly abduct humans, has anomalous sleep experiences, and seeks out a therapist who reinforces the belief that such experiences can be accounted for in terms of an abduction scenario.

The available theories of AAEs should be regarded as provisional and necessarily incomplete. It may be asking too much for any theory or even any combination of variables identified to date to account for the detail, richness, and idiosyncratic aspects of any individual's AAE. At the same time, not all hypotheses remain as viable as others, or as strongly supported by empirical evidence. For example, our review finds only minimal support for certain hypotheses such as the boundary-deficit personality and the link between AAEs and psychopathology. On the other hand, the hypothesis that AAEs are associated with media influences, cultural scripts, expectancies, and the shaping influence of suggestive procedures deserves attention because of the considerable database documenting the influential role of these variables in the broader psychological literature.

If the hypotheses tendered so far cannot completely explain the AAE in prosaic terms, more esoteric explanations may be required. The most prominent among these is that the AAE is veridical. But here again, there is no solid evidence to support this explanation. And in the absence of such evidence, the argument strains credulity on many fronts. This notwithstanding, we might do well to keep in mind Meacham's definition of "wisdom" (cited in Seppa, 1997, p. 9) and "hold the attitude that knowledge is fallible and strive for a balance between knowing and doubting." In this respect, the study of AAEs might make us all a little wiser.

REFERENCES

American Psychiatric Association. (1994). *Diagnostic and statistical manual of mental disorders* (4th ed.). Washington, DC: Author.

American Psychiatric Association Board of Trustees. (1993). *Statement on memories of sexual abuse*. Washington, DC: American Psychiatric Association.

American Psychological Association. (1994). *American Psychological Association's interim report on adult memories of childhood sexual abuse.* Washington, DC: Author.

American Society of Clinical Hypnosis. (1995). *Clinical hypnosis and memory: Guidelines for clinicians and for forensic hypnosis.* Des Plaines, IL: Author.

Appelle, S. (1996). The abduction experience: A critical evaluation of theory and evidence. *Journal of UFO Studies, 6,* 29–79.

Associated Press. (1996, September 22). *UFO hysteria invades Holyland: Israeli media join craze of sightings, alien abductions.*

Baker, R. A. (1990). *They call it hypnosis.* Buffalo, NY: Prometheus Books.

Baker, R. A. (1992a). *Alien abductions or alien productions? Some not so unusual personal experiences.* Unpublished manuscript, Lexington, KY.

Baker, R. A. (1992b). *Hidden memories: Voices and visions from within.* Buffalo, NY: Prometheus Books.

Baker, R. A. (1995). Alien dreamtime. *The Anomalist, 2,* 94–137.

Bartholomew, R. E., Basterfield, K., & Howard, G. S. (1991). UFO abductees and contactees. *Professional Psychology, 22,* 215–222.

Basterfield, K. (1994). Abductions: The paranormal connection. In A. Pritchard, D. E. Pritchard, J. E. Mack, P. Kasey, & C. Yapp (Eds.), *Alien discussions: Proceedings of the Abduction Study Conference held at MIT* (pp. 149–150). Cambridge, MA: North Cambridge Press.

Baumeister, R. F. (1988). Gender differences in masochistic scripts. *Journal of Sex Research, 25,* 478–499.

Baumeister, R. F. (1989). *Masochism and the self.* Hillsdale, NJ: Erlbaum.

Bloecher, T., Clamar, A., & Hopkins, B. (1985). Summary report on the psychological testing of nine individuals reporting UFO abduction experiences. Mount Rainier, MD: Fund for UFO Research.

Budden, A. (1994). *Allergies and aliens—The visitation experience: An environmental health issue.* Trowbridge, England: Discovery Times Press.

Bullard, T. E. (1987). *UFO abductions: The measure of a mystery.* Mount Rainier, MD: Fund for UFO Research.

Bullard, T. E. (1989). Hypnosis and UFO abductions: A troubled relationship. *Journal of UFO Studies, 1,* 3–42.

Bullard, T. E. (1991). Folkloric dimensions of the UFO phenomenon. *Journal of UFO Studies, 3,* 1–58.

Bullard, T. E. (1994). The influence of investigators on UFO abduction reports: Results of a survey. In A. Pritchard, D. E. Pritchard, J. E. Mack, P. Kasey, & C. Yapp (Eds.), *Alien discussions: Proceedings of the Abduction Study Conference held at MIT* (pp. 571–619). Cambridge, MA: North Cambridge Press.

Carpenter, J. S. (1997). Encounters: Now and then. *MUFON UFO Journal, 353,* 18.

Ceci, S. J., Loftus, E. F., Leichtman, M. D., & Bruck, M. (1994). The possible role of source misattributions in the creation of false beliefs among preschoolers. *International Journal of Clinical and Experimental Hypnosis, 42,* 304–320.

Dean, J. (1998). *Aliens in America: Conspiracy cultures from outer space to cyber space.* Ithaca, NY: Cornell University Press.

Evans, H. (1989). *Altered states of consciousness: Unself, otherself, and superself.* Wellingborough, England: Aquarian Press.

Gotlib, D. (1993). FMS update. *Bulletin of Anomalous Experience, 4,* 11.

Gotlib, D. (1996). Psychotherapy for the UFO abduction experience. *Journal of UFO Studies, 6,* 1–23.

Gotlib, D., Appelle, S., Rodeghier, M., & Flamburis, G. (1994). Ethics code for investigation and treatment of the abduction experience. *Journal of UFO Studies, 5,* 55–82.

Grosso, M. (1985). *The final choice: Playing the survival game.* Walpole, NH: Stillpoint.

Haines, R. F. (1994). Multiple abduction evidence—What's really needed? In A. Pritchard, D. E. Pritchard, J. E. Mack, P. Kasey, & C. Yapp (Eds.), *Alien discussions: Proceedings of the Abduction Study Conference held at MIT* (pp. 240–244). Cambridge, MA: North Cambridge Press.

Hartmann, E. (1984). *The nightmare: The psychology and biology of terrifying dreams.* New York: Basic Books.

Hopkins, B. (1994). The Hopkins image recognition test (HIRT) for children. In A. Pritchard, D. E. Pritchard, J. E. Mack, P. Kasey, & C. Yapp (Eds.), *Alien discussions: Proceedings of the Abduction Study Conference held at MIT* (pp. 127–133). Cambridge, MA: North Cambridge Press.

Hopkins, B., Jacobs, D. M., & Westrum, R. (1992). *Unusual personal experiences: An analysis of the data from three national surveys conducted by the Roper organization.* Las Vegas: Bigelow Holding.

Hovdestad, M. A., & Kristiansen, C. M. (1996, Summer). A field study of "false memory syndrome": Construct validity and incidence. *Journal of Psychiatry and Law,* 299–338.

Hufford, D. J. (1982). *The terror that comes in the night.* Philadelphia: University of Pennsylvania Press.

Jacobs, D. M. (1992). *Secret life: First-hand accounts of UFO abductions.* New York: Simon & Schuster.

Jacobs, D. M. (1998). *The threat.* New York: Simon & Schuster.

Jacobson, E., & Bruno, J. (1994). Narrative variants and major psychiatric illnesses in close encounter and abduction narrators. In A. Pritchard, D. E. Pritchard, J. E. Mack, P. Kasey, & C. Yapp (Eds.), *Alien discussions: Proceedings of the Abduction Study Conference held at MIT* (pp. 304–309). Cambridge, MA: North Cambridge Press.

Johnson, D. A. (1994). Personality characteristics of UFO abductees. In A. Pritchard, D. E. Pritchard, J. E. Mack, P. Kasey, & C. Yapp (Eds.), *Alien discussions: Proceedings of the Abduction Study Conference held at MIT* (pp. 316–319). Cambridge, MA: North Cambridge Press.

Jung, C. G. (1959). *Flying saucers.* New York: Signet.

Klass, P. J. (1993). Additional comments about the "Unusual Personal Experiences" survey. *Skeptical Inquirer, 17,* 145–146.

Kottmeyer, M. (1988). *Abduction: The boundary deficit hypothesis.* Magonia, 37, 3–7.

Kottmeyer, M. (1989). *Gauche encounters: Bad films and the UFO mythos.* Unpublished manuscript.

Laibow, R. L., & Laue, S. (1993). Posttraumatic stress disorder in experienced anomalous trauma. In J. P. Wilson & B. Raphael (Eds.), *International handbook of traumatic stress syndromes* (pp. 93–103). New York: Plenum.

Lawson, A. H. (1980). Hypnosis of imaginary abductees. In C. Fuller (Ed.), *Proceedings of the First UFO Congress* (pp. 195–238), NY: Warner Books.

Lawson, A. H. (1984). Perinatal imagery in UFO abduction reports. *Journal of Psychohistory, 12,* 211–239.

Lawson, A. H. (1985). UFO abductions or birth memories. *Fate, 38,* 68–80.

Lynn, S. J., & Kirsch, I. (1996). False memories, hypnosis, and fantasy proneness: Their role in alleged alien abductions. *Psychological Inquiry, 7,* 151–155.

Lynn, S. J., Lock, T., & Myers, B., & Payne, D. (1997). Recalling the unrecallable: Should hypnosis be used for memory recovery in psychotherapy? *Current Directions in Psychological Science, 6,* 79–83.

Lynn, S. J., & Nash, M. R. (1994). Truth in memory: Ramifications for psychotherapy and hypnotherapy. *American Journal of Clinical Hypnosis, 36,* 194–208.

Lynn, S. J., & Pezzo, M. (1994, August). *Close encounters of a third kind: Simulated hypnotic interviews of alien contacts.* Paper presented at the 102nd Annual Convention of the American Psychological Association, Los Angeles.

Lynn, S. J., Pintar, J., Stafford, J., Marmelstein, L., & Lock, T. (1998). Rendering the implausible plausible: Narrative construction, suggestion, and memory. In J. Rivera & T. Sarbin (Eds.), *Believed-in-imaginings: The narrative construction of reality* (pp. 123–144). Washington, DC: American Psychological Association.

Lynn, S. J., & Rhue, J. W., (1988). Fantasy proneness: Hypnosis, developmental antecedents, and psychopathology. *American Psychologist, 43,* 35–44.

Mack, J. E. (1994). *Abduction: Human encounters with aliens.* New York: Scribner's.

Moura, G. (1994). The abduction phenomenon in Brazil. In A. Pritchard, D. E. Pritchard, J. E. Mack, P. Kasey, & C. Yapp (Eds.), *Alien abductions: Proceedings of the Abduction Study Conference held at MIT* (pp. 186–190). Cambridge, MA: North Cambridge Press.

Nash, M. R. (1994). Memory distortion and sexual trauma. *International Journal of Clinical and Experimental Hypnosis, 42,* 346–362.

Newman, L. S., & Baumeister, R. F. (1996a). Not just another false memory: Further thoughts on UFO abduction narratives. *Psychological Inquiry, 7*, 185–197.

Newman, L. S., & Baumeister, R. F. (1996b). Toward an explanation of the UFO abduction phenomenon: Hypnotic elaboration, extraterrestrial sadomasochism, and spurious memories. *Psychological Inquiry, 7*, 99–126.

Orne, E. C., Whitehouse, W. G., Dinges, D. F., & Orne, M. T. (1996). Memory liabilities associated with hypnosis: Does low hypnotizability confer immunity? *International Journal of Clinical and Experimental Hypnosis, 44*, 354–369.

Parnell, J. O., & Sprinkle, R. L. (1990). Personality characteristics of persons who claim UFO experiences. *Journal of UFO Studies, 2*, 45–58.

Persinger, M. A. (1990). The tectonic strain theory as an explanation for UFO phenomena: A non-technical review of the research, 1970–1990. *Journal of UFO Studies, 2*, 105–137.

Persinger, M. A., & Makarec, K. (1987). Temporal lobe signs and correlative behaviors displayed by normal populations. *Journal of General Psychology, 114*, 179–195.

Pope, K. (1996). Memory, abuse, and science: Questioning claims about the false memory syndrome epidemic. *American Psychologist, 51*, 957–974.

Powers, S. M. (1994a). Dissociation in alleged extraterrestrial abductees. *Dissociation, 12*, 44–50.

Powers, S. M. (1994b). Thematic content analysis of the reports of UFO abductees and close encounter witnesses: Indications of repressed sexual abuse. *Journal of UFO Studies, 5*, 35–54.

Pritchard, A., Pritchard, D. E., Mack, J. E., Kasey, P., & Yapp, C. (Eds.). (1994). *Alien discussions: Proceedings of the Abduction Study Conference held at MIT*. Cambridge, MA: North Cambridge Press.

Randles, J. (1988). *Abduction*. London: Robert Hale.

Randles, J. (1994a). An analysis of British abduction cases. In A. Pritchard, D. E. Pritchard, J. E. Mack, P. Kasey, & C. Yapp (Eds.), *Alien discussions: Proceedings of the Abduction Study Conference held at MIT* (pp. 174–176). Cambridge, MA: North Cambridge Press.

Randles, J. (1994b). An experiment to test imaginary versus real abductions. In A. Pritchard, D. E. Pritchard, J. E. Mack, P. Kasey, & C. Yapp (Eds.), *Alien discussions: Proceedings of the Abduction Study Conference held at MIT* (pp. 394–395). Cambridge, MA: North Cambridge Press.

Ring, K. (1992). *The Omega Project: Near-death experiences, UFO encounters, and mind at large*. New York: Morrow.

Ring, K., & Rosing, C. J. (1990). The Omega project: A psychological survey of persons reporting abductions and other encounters. *Journal of UFO Studies, 2*, 59–98.

Rodeghier, M. (1994). Psychosocial characteristics of abductees. In A. Pritchard,

D. E. Pritchard, J. E. Mack, P. Kasey, & C. Yapp (Eds.), *Alien discussions: Proceedings of the Abduction Study Conference held at MIT* (pp. 296–303). Cambridge, MA: North Cambridge Press.

Rodeghier, M., Goodpaster, J., & Blatterbauer, S. (1991). Psychosocial characteristics of abductees: Results from the CUFOS abduction project. *Journal of UFO Studies, 3,* 59–90.

Sagan, C. (1995). *The demon-haunted world: Science as a candle in the dark.* New York: Random House.

Seppa, N. (1997). Wisdom: A quality that may defy age. *The APA Monitor, 28*(2), 1–9.

Slater, E. (1985). Conclusions on nine psychologicals. In *Final report on the psychological testing of UFO "abductees."* Mount Rainier, MD: Fund for UFO Research.

Spanos, N. P., Burgess, C. A., & Burgess, M. F. (1994). Past life identities, UFO abductions, and satanic ritual abuse. *International Journal of Clinical and Experimental Hypnosis, 42,* 433–446.

Spanos, N. P., Cross, P. A., Dickson, K., & Dubreuil, S. C. (1993). Close encounters: An examination of UFO experiences. *Journal of Abnormal Psychology, 102,* 624–632.

Spanos, N. P., Radtke, H. L., Hodgins, D. C., Stam, H. J., & Bertrand, L. D. (1983). The Carleton University Responsiveness to Suggestion Scale: Normative data and psychometric properties. *Psychological Reports, 53,* 523–535.

Stacy, D. (1992). Abductions and abortions. *Bulletin of Anomalous Experiences, 3,* 3–5.

Stone-Carmen, J. (1994). A descriptive study of people reporting abduction by unidentified flying objects (UFOs). In A. Pritchard, D. E. Pritchard, J. E. Mack, P. Kasey, & C. Yapp (Eds.), *Alien discussions: Proceedings of the Abduction Study Conference held at MIT* (pp. 309–315). Cambridge, MA: North Cambridge Press.

Strieber, W. (1998). *Confirmation: The hard evidence of the aliens among us.* New York: St. Martin's Press.

Time/CNN (June 15, 1997). *Poll: U.S. hiding knowledge of aliens* [CNN Interactive poll posted on the World Wide Web]. Retrieved September 26, 1999 from the World Wide Web: http://www.cnn.com/us/9706/15/ufo.poll/index.html.

U.S. Department of Commerce, Bureau of Consensus (1990). *Statistical abstracts of the United States.* Washington, DC: Author.

Vallee, J. F. (1969). *Passport to Magonia.* Chicago: Henry Regnery.

Wilson, J. (1990). Posttraumatic stress disorder (PTSD) and experienced anomalous trauma (EAT): Similarities in reported UFO abductions and exposure to invisible toxic contaminants. *Journal of UFO Studies, 2,* 1–18.

Wilson, S. C., & Barber, T. X. (1978). The Creative Imagination Scale as a measure of hypnotic responsiveness: Applications to experimental and clinical hypnosis. *American Journal of Clinical Hypnosis, 20,* 235–249.

Wilson, S. C., & Barber, T. X. (1981). Vivid fantasy and hallucinatory abilities in the life histories of excellent hypnotic subjects ("somnambules"). In E. Klinger (Ed.), *Preliminary report with female subjects: Vol. 2. Imagery* (pp. 133–149). Concepts, results, and applications. New York: Plenum Press.

Wilson, S. C., & Barber, T. X. (1983a). The fantasy-prone personality: Implications for understanding imagery, hypnosis, and parapsychological phenomena. In A. A. Sheikh (Ed.), *Imagery: Current theory, research, and application* (pp. 340–387). New York: Wiley.

Wilson, S. C., & Barber, T. X. (1983b). *Inventory of Childhood Memories and Imaginings*. Framingham, MA: Cushing Hospital.

9

PAST-LIFE EXPERIENCES

ANTONIA MILLS AND STEVEN JAY LYNN

The case of Ajendra Singh Chauhan of northern India illuminates some of the fascinating and puzzling aspects of reported past-life experiences (PLEs). This previously unpublished case is rare insofar as a written record and a tape recording of the child's statements were obtained before the case was "solved." *Solving* a case is defined as matching an individual's PLEs with those that occurred in the life of a person who lived previously. In this case, the previous personality's family was unknown to Ajendra's family. Note that *previous personality* is the term used in this chapter for the person the experient claims, or is claimed by someone else, to have been in a previous life. The term is useful insofar as it is neutral with respect to whether the claim is accurate or not.

The case of Ajendra was first identified by G. S. Gaur, who recorded Ajendra's statements, as described by his father in 1992, when Ajendra was 13 years old. Ajendra made the statements between the ages of 36 and 60 months. In 1992, Gaur traveled the 75 kilometers to the town the experient claimed to have been from and found a corresponding previous personality. A few months later, the first author investigated the case with Gaur and took Ajendra and his family, for the first time, to the previous personality's village. It was evident that the families did not recognize each other initially and had not met before. Below is a summary of the account

Ajendra's father gave of the case before it was solved, from the notes Gaur wrote in Hindi, as translated by a University of Virginia Hindi instructor.

According to Ajendra's father, when Ajendra was about 3 years old he said, "Two water buffaloes used to give milk. I used to drink a bucket of milk." (He said this when he was offered only a glass at his aunt's home.) "One time a pundit [Brahmin] widow of fair complexion tried to mix poison in the food. Then I beat her a lot. Ashok Kumar Sharma lived in a village nearby. . . . Daddy, don't go in the garden in the dark. Dacoits [gangsters] live there." Then, one hot summer night when Ajendra was lying on his father's chest on the roof of their dwelling, Ajendra said, "Papa, the dacoit came. He started shooting from the wall, and I got hit." Ajendra mimed how he had crouched behind his father and shot at the dacoits.

In response to his father's questioning, the child then told his father, "I am from Fariha. There is a police office there. There are paved roads. One street goes into the town. On the corner of that street is the store of a merchant named Lala. Our groceries used to come from that store. There was a pundit widow who has a 6–7-year-old daughter. She used to cook our food." He also said, "One pair of pants is hanging in the room on a peg with some rupees in the back pocket. There is a gun in the wardrobe. The bolts of the rifle are pushed [he mimed the action to cock the gun]. Brass cartridges are used in the gun."

Ajendra's parents assumed that he was referring to a previous life but did not pursue the case, fearing "that it might affect the brain of the child." They were not sure where Fariha was, never having been there, and originally assumed he was referring to Faridha, a town near Ajendra's father's natal village. After Gaur recorded the statements in 1992, he discovered that there was a town named Fariha 75 kilometers away and went there to see if a person with a life that matched the child's statements could be found.

In Fariha, Gaur was able to find a man named Ashok Kumar Sharma (actually called Tiwari, another Brahmin name) who had been a close friend of one Naresh Chandra Gupta who was shot dead by dacoits on December 30, 1977, while taking position to shoot at them behind his father on the roof of their home. According to Naresh's father, they were in close physical contact as they crouched to fire at the dacoits.

The Gupta family had water buffaloes, and Naresh drank a considerable amount of milk. He was 20 years of age at the time of his death. They had owned a mare when Naresh was young. We were shown the gun Naresh was using at the time of his death, a Greener made in Birmingham, and the brass cartridges it used. Indeed it was bolted or cocked, as Ajendra had mimed when young by pushing down on a shaft that bent out and then bringing it up again. Streets are indeed paved in Fariha (as in many Indian towns, including the one in which Ajendra lived), and there is a police station (with records of the murder of Naresh), but at least at the time of investigation, the Guptas' shop, where most of the family's food comes from, was not located on a corner.

Regarding the fair-complexioned widow of a pundit who prepared the food and then poisoned it, some of Ajendra's statements are correct, some incorrect. Naresh's food was prepared by his elder brother's wife, who had a fair complexion and, like him, was of the merchant caste. Her daughter was about 3 or 4 years old at the time of Naresh's death. There was a great deal of animosity between Naresh and this woman and, according to Naresh's mother, Naresh apparently did suspect her of trying to poison him after he beat her (this sister-in-law stayed around long enough for me to see her light complexion but refused to be questioned). Perhaps Ajendra referred to the poisoner/food preparer as a widow of a pundit (*punditine* is the term in Hindi) because, at the time that Ajendra originally made these statements, his family rented their quarters from a fair-complexioned pundit widow who lived on the premises and also sometimes fed him.

It is difficult to assess the combined probability of randomly finding a Naresh Chandra Gupta, who (a) lived in a town named Fariha (very uncommon name), (b) shot at dacoits while on a roof close to his father, (c) used a gun cocked in a certain way, (d) was shot (the frequency of dacoit battles is difficult to ascertain for the area, but they are certainly not rare), and (e) was allegedly being poisoned by a fair-complexion woman, who was a Brahmin widow. Ultimately, we may never know whether the past-life narrative that unfolded in this instance reflected actual memories of a past life, a coincidental combination of stories that (largely) matched actual events, or an unknown cause. To what degree is this, or any, PLE shaped by the culture-based expectations regarding past lives, as well as by the suggestive, subtle factors that influence the reactions of those involved in studying and documenting current and historical events? These questions and others pertaining to the assessment and explanation of perplexing PLEs are the focus of this chapter. To address these questions, we first define PLEs with greater precision.

DEFINITION

Past-life experiences, or PLEs, can be defined as reported experiences or impressions of oneself as a particular person (other than one's current life identity) in a previous time or life. This spontaneous overlay of identity may be recurrent and persistent for children between the ages of 24 to 60 months but does not deny their current identity. This chapter summarizes much of the available evidence on PLEs. Data from persons who spontaneously report PLEs in childhood, as well as experimentally induced PLEs in adults, are examined. Although the focus of this chapter is on Ian Stevenson's research on spontaneous PLEs, which constitutes the most thorough and systematic database available on the correspondence of historical facts to apparent memories, nonspontaneous PLEs are also accorded attention.

Frequency of Experience

PLEs are reported most often among people with cultural beliefs in reincarnation, such as Hindus, Buddhists, a few subgroups of Muslims (e.g., the Alevi of Turkey, the Druse of Lebanon), and many tribal or indigenous peoples (Stevenson, 1986, 1987). A much smaller number of cases occur spontaneously among people who do not believe in or endorse the concept of reincarnation (Mills, 1994c; Stevenson, 1975, 1977a, 1983a, 1987). However, even in societies that do believe in reincarnation, spontaneous cases are not very common. A study in northern India of the incidence of such cases indicated that only 1 in 500 individuals had reported a spontaneous PLE (Barker & Pasricha, 1979); however, cases among the Native peoples of northwest British Columbia may exceed this rate (Matlock, 1990a; Matlock & Mills, 1994; Mills, 1988a, 1988b, 1994a, 1994e).

Spontaneous Versus Hypnotic and Other PLEs

Spontaneous PLEs may be contrasted with those induced during hypnosis or that are diagnosed or identified by a medium or psychic. In cases resulting from hypnotic induction in which it is implicitly or explicitly suggested that a person experienced a past life, it is not uncommon for reports of PLEs to emerge. The case of Virginia Tighe (Bernstein, 1956) is one of the best-known examples of an American who reported a compelling PLE during hypnosis. After repeated hypnotic inductions, Virginia came to believe she had lived a "past life" as a woman named Bridey Murphy, who had been born in Ireland in 1798. Although many people were convinced that her story was true, a search of records failed to corroborate the existence of a person named Bridey Murphy during the reported period. Some of Virginia's accounts of Irish life as Bridey were inaccurate, although she also made some accurate statements that are difficult to trace to sources proposed at the time, such as general knowledge; Virginia's childhood neighbor, Bridie Corkell; or her "Irish" aunt. (Virginia had an aunt of Scotch-Irish descent who came to live with the family when Virginia was 18.) Various authors have concluded that, under hypnosis, Virginia may have unconsciously woven early experiences into superficially convincing stories of her life as Bridey Murphy (Spanos, 1996; but see Ducasse, 1960, for a different evaluation of the case).

Hypnosis is similarly the basis of most past-life regression therapies. According to Spanos (1996), the premise of such therapies is that traumas that occurred in previous lives influence the patient's current psychological and physical symptoms (e.g., Woolger, 1988). Weiss (1988), for example, published a series of cases centering on his patients who were hypnotized and age regressed to "go back to" the source or origin of a particular present-day problem. When the patients were "regressed," they reported events that Weiss and his patients interpreted as having their source in a previous life. Just how prevalent such past-life therapies are is unknown. However, it is notable that the *Journal of Regression Therapy* is devoted to such interventions, and features case reports of hypnotic "past-life thera-pies." Lucas's book *Regression Therapy* (1993) also presents reports of re-putedly therapeutic PLEs, but the efficacy of such interventions is not nec-essarily documented.

It seems to be relatively easy for clients to respond to suggestions to experience a past life. Kampman (1976), for example, reported that when highly suggestible participants received suggestions to regress to a period before their birth and become a different person, 41% of them exhibited signs of a new identity and called themselves by different names.

Because hypnotic experiences and evoked memories are often vivid, affect-laden, and compelling fantasy-based constructions, they can easily be mistaken for historically accurate events. The client's or hypnotist's con-viction that a particular PLE is authentic by no means constitutes evidence that the experience is based on valid present or previous life events (Baker, 1982; Stevenson, 1990b, 1994). Indeed, there are many cases of hypnoti-cally elicited PLEs that include demonstrably inaccurate details of historical events (Spanos, Menary, Gabora, Dubreuil, & Dewhirst, 1991; Venn, 1986).

On the other hand, Tarazi (1990) presented an unsolved case in which a patient during a hypnotic age regression procedure cited over 100 facts that proved to be accurate for 16th century Spain, with no false information. One possible explanation is cryptomnesia or the forgetting of the source of information learned normally but attributed to PLE. Another possible explanation is that in such instances historical information is, at some level, available, but individuals consciously or unconsciously "hold back" reporting until they are hypnotized so that they can have a com-pelling experience of regression to a past life. Such a hold-back effect has been demonstrated with respect to a variety of hypnotic phenomena (Lynn & Rhue, 1991).

Spanos (1994, 1996) reviewed and conducted studies indicating that adults' experiences of a past-life identity were related to degree of hypno-tizability, hypnotist-transmitted expectations, and the credibility that they assigned to their PLE, which itself depended on whether the hypnotist defined such experiences as real or imagined.

Spanos's (1996) sociocognitive view holds that hypnotically induced PLEs are socially constructed accounts, the details of which can often be traced to widely available sources such as books, television, and other me-dia (Rogo, 1985; Spanos, 1996). The common phenomenon of cryptomnesia (i.e., amnesia for the source of learned information) is one explanation for how hypnotized, and perhaps nonhypnotized, individuals may come to hold strong beliefs in the reality of their PLEs. The individual may forget the source of a particular piece of information (the media, a book, or an aunt's tales) and instead come to believe that the information was derived from an actual PLE.

Stevenson's (1974b, 1976, 1983b) accounts detail several very rare and unusual cases of *xenoglossy*, in which participants during hypnosis spoke a language to which they had not apparently been exposed previously and recounted a previous identity. Stevenson argued that these cases support the hypothesis that in rare instances knowledge can be retained from a previous life (see also Andrade, 1988; Stevenson, 1974b; 1983b).

A third source of reports of PLEs are self-styled mediums or psychics, who claim to obtain information from deceased individuals. Such cases are subject to the same difficulties as past-life regression cases in terms of evidence of veridicality. Because these individuals do not claim to have been the deceased individuals, they are not discussed here. Matlock (1990b) provided a brief synopsis of the literature on the topic.

Spontaneous Cases

Spontaneous cases can easily be distinguished from those that are hypnotically induced or reported by mediums or psychics. Although a number of spontaneous cases were published before 1960 (Stevenson, 1960), the pioneer and chief proponent of the scientific study of PLEs, Ian Stevenson, did not begin investigating them until 1961. Since then, he has documented and evaluated more than 2,500 cases from a variety of countries, including India, Sri Lanka (formerly Ceylon), Thailand, Myanmar (formerly Burma), Turkey, Lebanon, and to a lesser extent the United States (Stevenson, 1974a, 1977a, 1980, 1983b, 1997). In this chapter, we focus on spontaneous PLEs, which have been more thoroughly studied than nonspontaneous PLEs, although the latter are mentioned in the Clinical Issues and Risks and the Theories sections. To our knowledge, no systematic studies on the relationship, if any, of nonspontaneous PLEs to psychopathology or mental health have been conducted.

Spontaneous PLEs occur most often in childhood and can be manifested from the time the child first begins to speak and becomes fluent until the time the child is between 5 and 7 to 8 years old. It is worth noting that this age range coincides with the ages when children report playing with so-called imaginary playmates (Mills, 1992; Singer & Singer, 1990; Taylor, Cartwright, & Carlson, 1993). Even in cultures that wholeheartedly embrace the concept of reincarnation and refer to children as a particular person reborn, children themselves gradually cease to experience themselves as reincarnated individuals. As they approach the age of approximately 80 months, children eventually forget or stop having the experiences that made them and others think they were remembering a previous life (Cook, Pasricha, Samararatne, Win Maung, & Stevenson, 1983), although they may be aware that they are credited with having such experiences.

In spontaneous childhood cases, PLEs are sometimes induced by apparent memory cues, such as travel to an area where the child says he or she previously lived or the sight of someone associated with the apparent previous life. However, some cases occur in the absence of obvious external memory triggers, such as when the child engages in reflective thought or contrasts current experiences with experiences he or she says were typical of a past life.

In contrast to those of children, the less frequent spontaneous adult PLEs are more often triggered by memory cues (Matlock, 1989). Such PLEs resemble unusually strong *déjà vu* experiences that, in some instances, are accompanied by the apparent ability to describe the topography of the surrounding area before the experient has had an opportunity to see it. When such experiences have not been reported before and are about knowledge limited to a specific area, they may be interpreted as the residue of experience from another life, regardless of whether the individual's memories permit the identification of an actual deceased person who knew the area (Cook et al., 1983). The interpretation of such experiences as rooted in a past life is, to at least some degree, a culture-based construction (Mills, 1989, 1992) shaped by religious views and the influence of agents of socialization such as parents.

Diagnostic Markers

In the sample of over 2,500 childhood spontaneous PLEs, Stevenson (1987) identified the following signals or accompaniments to the recall of a previous life: (a) verbal memories, or statements about events, others, or oneself that are consistent with a previous person and life and have no referent in the current life (e.g., people and places known to the experient in the present life); (b) behavioral memories, which include phobias and philias that are uncharacteristic of the person's current life but are meaningful in the context of a past-life identity; (c) special skills that are related to a deceased person's experience and not to a child's present life; and (d) birthmarks or birth defects that are not apparently genetically induced and that the child says, or others deduce, relate to accident, trauma, or intentionally made incisions or markings experienced by the previous personality. The cultural explanation for the birthmarks and birth defects is that an insult or trauma to a particular body part and markings on a previous body can impact the future body. That is, the mark can be manifested on the future body via the agency of the previous personality's will, concern with the trauma, or a mark in the previous life.

In addition, in cultures in which the concept of reincarnation is integral to the cultural world view, some PLEs are identified after a person declares that she or he will "come back" as a particular individual. Such predictions are most often made in cultures in which the expectation is that an individual will be reincarnated as a relative of the previous personality. This occurs more frequently in tribal and indigenous societies than in the larger Hindu and Buddhist societies (Stevenson, 1986). In some instances, such "premortem wishes" are accompanied by statements about how the baby will be recognized, which can include descriptions of birthmarks or distinctive behaviors (Mills, 1994e).

Before the birth, and in Myanmar before the conception of a baby, the mother of the child or one of the relatives of a deceased person may have a dream heralding the previous personality's "return." Such "announcing dreams" are particularly common in Sri Lanka and among the Native Tlingit and Gitxsan of North America (Stevenson, 1986). However, Keil (1996) noted that attribution of a past-life identity to a child on the basis of announcing dreams and/or birthmarks does not necessarily result in the child making statements from the point of view of the socially legitimized past-life personality.

Differentiation of Types

Spontaneous PLEs are differentiated on the basis of whether they are "solved" or "unsolved." Recall that cases are said to be solved when evidence of a person that corresponds to the experient's statements concerning a past life is found. In contrast, cases in which a search for a corresponding person is not successful are said to be unsolved cases (Cook et al., 1983). In terms of personal experience, unsolved cases can be very poignant for a child and his or her family; however, such cases are not useful in terms of providing evidence that the child's statements and the family's interpretation are veridical.

Interestingly, an analysis of solved and unsolved cases demonstrates that the two types share many of the same characteristics (Cook et al., 1983). There is more mention in unsolved cases than in solved cases of the violent death of a previous personality. Also, perhaps because of the absence of confirmatory data, children in unsolved cases cease talking about the PLE at an earlier age (70 months) than in solved cases (90 months). In unsolved cases, children mention the previous personalities' names less often. Children involved in both solved and unsolved cases mention their PLEs about the same number of times, making anywhere from zero to as many as 30 statements regarding the previous identity.

Solved cases differ in terms of whether the previous personality was known to the experient's family or not. In cases among the native peoples of North America, Australia, and Africa, for example, a second personality is almost always said to be someone from the same community and, in those societies with clans, the same clan as the first (Mills, 1988a; Mills & Champion, 1996; Stevenson, 1986). In the more populous Hindu and Buddhist societies, the expectation is that a remembered past life may refer to someone totally unrelated to the child. Indeed, in 41% of the cases reported from India, the previous personality was not known to the family at the time the child first began making statements interpreted as referring to a previous life (Cook et al., 1983). In cases in which the previous personality is known to the child's family, the child may be intentionally or unintentionally prompted by family members with suggestive information that is consistent with the belief that the child had a past life.

Stevenson (1987, 1997) has stated that cases like Ajendra's, in which a written record is made before the case is solved and a person whose life history corresponds to the child's statements is then identified, constitute the best evidence that a child's statements have not been contaminated by the expectations of the child's family. However, the presence of written records before the case is solved is relatively rare (Haraldsson, 1991; Stevenson & Samararatne, 1988), and social construction of the past-life narrative necessarily takes place whether or not written records are available (Mills, 1990).

Schouten and Stevenson (1998) analyzed a series of cases from Sri Lanka and India that were judged to be solved before they were formally investigated (Type A cases) or had a written record before they were solved (Type B cases). They found that the percentage of correct statements for both types of cases was very similar (78.4% for Type A, 76.7% for Type B), with Type A experients making 18.5 statements and Type B experients making 25.5 statements. In Type A cases, the number of total statements and the percentage of correct statements were similar whether or not a child's family had some knowledge of the previous personality (i.e., with some knowledge the number of correct statements was 21 [79%], without previous knowledge, 16.6 [76%]). The authors interpreted the lack of apparent influence of family members on reports of PLEs as inconsistent with the sociopsychological hypothesis, which emphasizes the shaping influence of agents of socialization, and which we examine in some detail below.

Varying Features and Cultural Expectations

From the evidence reviewed so far, it is evident that culture affects both beliefs about reincarnation and the nature of PLE reports. The ways in which cases vary in terms of cultural expectations, beliefs, and features are discussed next.

Interval Between Death and Rebirth

Some groups, such as the Druse of Lebanon, believe that the soul of a person will be reborn at the instant of death; accordingly, PLEs reported among the Druse tend to conform to this expectation (Stevenson, 1986). In contrast, Witsuwit'en (the Western Carrier Indians of British Columbia, Canada), who do not hold that belief, have the longest mean interval between a soul's death and its rebirth, about 180 months (Mills, 1988a).

Gender

Samples of cases analyzed by Stevenson (1986) and Mills (1994b) indicate that males report more PLEs than females (63% male vs. 37% female in the 1986 count), and that the ratio of male-to-female experients varies across cultures. The Igbo of Nigeria report the highest incidence of male experients (77%), in contrast to 50% among the Witsuwit'en experients of Canada, and 49% in a Sri Lankan sample.

Gender Change of Experients

In some cultures, such as the Alevi of Turkey, the Druse of Lebanon, the Tlingit, and Haida Natives of North America, there are virtually no instances in which the individuals and the previous personalities are of the opposite gender (Stevenson, 1986). In contrast, 50% of the Kutchin Native Canadian PLE cases (Mills, 1994e) and 33% of the Igbo cases are cross-gender (Mills, 1994b). Differences in the incidence of opposite-gender past-life personalities are associated with cultural beliefs about the possibility of being reborn as a member of the opposite gender.

AFTEREFFECTS

Short Term

Some childhood spontaneous PLE cases propel the affected children into a certain amount of notoriety. When publicity is generated, it may have both welcome and unwelcome consequences for the children and their families (Stevenson & Chadha, 1990). The PLE can be troubling for all those affected, particularly if the experient insists on being taken to the home of the previous personality or denies that his or her parents are the actual parents (Mills, 1989). Unfortunately, the sequelae to publicity and personal and familial reactions to past-life reports have not been investigated in a systematic manner.

PLEs can also help explain puzzling behaviors and experiences. For example, behaviors such as phobias of no apparent origin can, in the context of reincarnation, be understood in terms of a carryover of PLEs to the present day. One study (Stevenson, 1990a) found that 36% of phobias in a sample of 387 childhood spontaneous PLE cases waned in intensity as the memories of the previous life faded with age, although identification of the origin of the phobia as due to a previous life experience did not necessarily assuage the fear in childhood (Stevenson, 1990a). An alternative explanation is that the phobias waned in intensity not because the memories of the previous life faded, but because childhood phobias (especially animal phobias) are often transitory (*Diagnostic and Statistical Manual of Mental Disorders* [DSM–IV]; American Psychiatric Association, 1994, p. 408). Hence, Stevenson's findings are difficult to interpret. Nevertheless, it may be the case that the ability to explain current behaviors in terms of past-life events can be personally comforting for the child's family, thus reinforcing cultural beliefs in reincarnation.

Long Term

Children, like Ajendra, who report spontaneous PLEs appear to grow up and live normal lives without obvious signs of psychological impairment or dissociation (Mills, 1989, 1990; Stevenson, 1987). However, this observation must be tentative insofar as few thorough assessments of the psychological profile of such children after they reach adulthood have been undertaken. Follow-up interviews indicate that older children and adults are generally amnestic of the "past-life events" they reported as children, implying that the imprint of apparent PLEs is not permanent and that past-life remembrances play a small role or no role in the adult activities of the experient.

In cases of gender change, in which a child reports that he or she was a member of the opposite gender in the previous life, the child typically adjusts to the biological body by puberty (Mills, 1994e). Stevenson (1977c), however, did report one case of gender dysphoria in which the experient did not accept her biological identity and maintained a masculine identity into adulthood. Whether this individual would have experienced gender dysphoria in the absence of a PLE cannot be determined. Because much of the research on the sequelae of PLEs has not been conducted in the West, cross-cultural studies are an obvious priority.

BIOLOGICAL MARKERS

There is some indication (Stevenson, 1997) that the anatomy and physiology (e.g., facial features and body type) of children who are assumed to have been reborn may correspond to the features of the genetically unrelated identified previous personalities. Indeed, for Stevenson (1997) and others (Pasricha, 1998), the most compelling physiological evidence for the "reality" of PLEs is the frequency of birthmarks and birth defects that appear to correspond to trauma-related or intentional markings on the body of the previous personality. In about 35% of reincarnation cases, experients or their families attribute birthmarks or birth defects to wounds or intentional markings acquired in a previous life (Stevenson, 1993, 1997). In 43 cases, a medical document, such as a postmortem report, indicated the location of the wound on the deceased, which sometimes appeared to be strikingly close to the location of the birthmark or birth defect in the child. Sometimes multiple birthmarks or birth defects appear to correspond to wounds on the previous personality (Mills, 1989; Pasricha, 1998; Stevenson, 1993, 1997). There is no reason to believe that birthmarks have been fraudulently contrived to promote investigated cases (Stevenson, Pasricha, & Samararatne, 1988). Difficulties in interpreting findings related to birthmarks and body markings are discussed later in the chapter.

INDIVIDUAL DIFFERENCES

Studies designed to assess the motivations and psychological profiles of children in spontaneous PLE cases have only recently been initiated. Wilson (1982) proposed that people reporting PLEs are motivated by a desire to identify with a higher social class. Two thirds of respondents in a subsequent India study (Stevenson, 1987) claimed to remember lives in better circumstances (i.e., they were "demoted"), whereas in Sri Lanka, few cases showed a disparity (Matlock, 1990b). However, in societies that have no class or caste distinctions, promotion or demotion in social standing provides a less-than-compelling motivational account for the genesis of spontaneous PLEs (Matlock, 1990b; Mills, 1988a).

PSYCHOPATHOLOGY

To discern the psychological profile of children who report PLEs (or to see "how it affects the brain," as Ajendra's father put it), Haraldsson (1995, 1997) conducted a series of tests in Sri Lanka on such children and on matched comparison respondents who did not report PLEs. He was able to identify a number of differences across the samples studied. In contrast, Mills (1992) administered a similar series of tests in India to experients and a matched sample and failed to find significant differences across the samples studied. The intent of both studies was to determine if children who are said to remember a previous life share the psychological profile of Western children who have imaginary playmates (Singer & Singer, 1990) or are more suggestible, fantasy prone, or hypnotizable. These variables were included because J. Hilgard (1970) found that Western university students who remembered the details of their imaginary playmates were more susceptible to hypnosis, and therefore more suggestible, than those who did not report details of imaginary playmates.

In Haraldsson's (1997) study, 30 Sri Lankan children and a sample of children matched by age, gender, and community were administered the Colored Progressive Matrices (Raven, 1963), the Peabody Picture Vocabulary Test—Revised (Dunn & Dunn, 1981), and the Gudjonsson Suggestibility Scale (Gudjonsson, 1984, 1987), whereas children's parents responded to the Child Behavior Checklist (CBCL–Parent's Form; Achenbach & Edelbrock, 1983), and their teachers completed the CBCL–Teacher's Form (Achenbach & Edelbrock, 1986). These tests were translated into Sinhalese, adapted for Sri Lankan children, and administered by a Sri Lankan psychologist. The children ranged in age from 7 to 13 years.

Haraldsson (1997) found that, relative to a comparison sample, children identified as having PLEs exhibited a greater knowledge of words and understanding of language, demonstrated a better memory for recent events, and scored higher on Raven's (1963) Colored Progressive Matrices. These children also received higher grades in school than the control group. Children who claimed memories of a previous life were no more suggestible than the comparison group. Suggestibility scores were significantly lower among the children involved in "solved" cases than among the sample of "unsolved" cases; the control sample tended to be more suggestible than both the solved and unsolved samples (Haraldsson, 1997, p. 331). Both parents and the teachers reported that the school performance of the children who reported PLEs was superior to the performance of the matched control children. These observations were confirmed by school records.

On the basis of parental reports, children who reported PLEs conducted their social activities better than comparison children, and their teachers rated them higher than the control children on adaptive functioning, for example "they learn more, behave better in school, and work harder" (Haraldsson, 1995, p. 447). Teachers reported that the children with PLEs were, as a rule, well adapted to the school environment and differed from their matched counterparts in the following ways: They "feel they have to be perfect, get along better than other children, skip school much less often, are less disobedient, are more highly motivated, and are less explosive and unpredictable in behavior than the control group" (p. 448–449). The degree to which these observations are influenced by a cultural norm that is favorably disposed to those who have PLEs is unclear.

However, parents of the children with reported PLEs indicated that their children had more behavioral problems in comparison with parents of control participants, and they noted that their children were more argumentative, talkative, easily hurt, stubborn, and concerned with neatness and cleanliness. Furthermore, the parents of experients reported that their children preferred to be alone, tended to "show off" or "clown" less than other children, and did less than other children to get involved with others. Haraldsson (1995) noted that the past-life reporters tended to be "nervous, high strung, or tense, and feel that they have to be perfect and are sometimes confused. Some of them get teased, tend to cry more, and have more fears, which seem in many cases to be related to their claimed memories of a previous life" (p. 448). It is interesting to note that the fears expressed were often phobias related to the cause of death in the presumed previous life.

Haraldsson (1995, 1997) noted that the hypotheses that children who report past lives are more suggestible, confabulate more, and are more socially isolated were not supported, according to the results on the Gudjonsson Scale of Suggestibility, the Parent and Teacher's Form of the CBCL, and to the number of siblings of past-life experients. To date, Haraldsson's and Mills's data do not support the hypothesis that children who are said to remember past lives are more susceptible to suggestion.

Stevenson (1974a) reported a case in which an experient claimed to be an uncle who had murdered his wife; he was repeatedly admitted to mental hospitals in adulthood. Pasricha, Murthy, and Murthy (1978) described a case in which an adult began speaking of a PLE during a mental breakdown. However, cases in which the person who reported a markedly negative PLE also exhibited major psychopathology are the exception rather than the rule in the PLE literature (Stevenson, 1987). It is notable that children with PLEs rarely, if ever, develop dissociative identity disorder (formerly multiple personality disorder), or the cultural equivalent of this disorder, in adulthood.

CLINICAL ISSUES AND RISKS

Cultures that have a strong belief in reincarnation do not generally recommend seeking to learn about previous lives, for therapeutic reasons or otherwise. As Swami Sri Yuteswar counseled (see Yogananda, 1946/ 1993, p. 138), "The vanished lives of all men [and women] are dark with many shames." This noteworthy Hindu savant (Evans-Wentz, 1958) was making the point that knowledge about past lives should not be sought, unless these lives are recalled spontaneously. Hindu, Buddhist, and tribal cultures often attempt to suppress a child's apparent previous life memories, in the interest of having the child focus on his or her current life (Mills, 1994b), but do not often succeed (Stevenson & Chadha, 1990). Those peoples who believe in reincarnation (both Amerindian and other indigenous peoples, as well as Hindu and Buddhist peoples) generally attribute mental health or illness, at least in part, to the accumulated experience of previous lives (Krippner, 1986; Mills, 1994a).

As already noted, the spontaneous recall of memories attributed to a past life does not appear to be related to significant clinical problems, either during childhood or adulthood. Even phobias apparently related to memories of violent death dissipate, for the most part, after childhood (Stevenson, 1990a).

Whereas therapists who evoke memories during hypnosis (see Lucas, 1993) report that such procedures are beneficial in treating phobias, negative emotional reactions, habits, and other problems, to date there has been no systematic documentation or follow-up of these claims. In addition, there may well be considerable risk associated with using special procedures, such as hypnosis, to uncover past-life memories. By encouraging imagination and a heightened tolerance for logical incongruity, hypnotic procedures can facilitate the elaboration of imaginative scenarios and narratives that may have little or no relation to actual historical circumstances (Lynn, Lock, Myers, & Payne, 1997). The directive, highly leading procedures used by most past-life regression therapists have the potential to instantiate false memories that may not only come to be embraced with confidence by the patient but may also deter the patient from grappling with the true causes and factors that maintain vexing present-day concerns (Stevenson, 1990a, 1994; but see Hastings, 1990). There is no reason to believe that recalling past lives has any salutary effect on present-day problems, although this issue has not been systematically investigated. In fact, it could be argued that the person's best interests are not served if he or she is treated with past-life regression therapy when there is an empirically validated treatment for that particular problem. In keeping with this line of reasoning, Stevenson (1994) advised against the use of hypnotic regression either as a therapy or as a means of detecting past lives.

THEORIES

Several explanations of spontaneous childhood PLEs have been offered. They may represent (a) veridical PLEs (the reincarnation hypothesis: Mills, 1988a, 1989; Stevenson, 1960, 1987, 1997); (b) examples of telepathically transmitted information and affect (the extrasensory perception, or ESP, hypothesis: Chari, 1978); (c) cultural construction and interpretations of behavior, in whole or in part (the sociocognitive hypothesis: Brody, 1979a, 1979b; Chari, 1962, 1967, 1986; Mills, 1988a, 1989, 1990; Spanos, 1996); or (d) deliberately fraudulent or unconsciously motivated self-deceptions driven by a need for notoriety, self-aggrandizement, or confirmation of a belief in previous lives (Stevenson et al., 1988; Wilson, 1982). As stated earlier, fraud is neither a satisfactory nor plausible explanation for many of the most impressive and thoroughly investigated cases of spontaneous childhood PLE (see Brody, 1979a, 1979b; Matlock, 1990b).

Reincarnation Hypothesis

Stevenson (1960, 1977b) and Shweder (1986) noted the explanatory value of the reincarnation hypothesis. Shweder did not intend to advance the reincarnation hypothesis per se, but rather wanted to show that apparently nonrational or religious beliefs from other cultures may express "divergent rationalities," that is, rational theories about the world that are consistent with various observations. As he put it, reincarnation would explain why "identical twins reared together not infrequently display marked differences in personality; why the personalities of siblings who grow up in the same family are no more similar than random pairs of people drawn from different families; why some young children have unusual abilities, particularly in music or math, that their socializers do not; why some children have fears and phobias with no apparent cause; why some people have a strong *déjà vu* experience upon first coming to a new area; and why some people are born with, and some without, good health, status, or position" (Shweder, 1986, pp. 181–182). Shweder also believed the reincarnation hypothesis can provide an explanation for children's statements about having lived in another family and for the close correspondence of the descriptive statements to families with which the children are not familiar. To this list, Stevenson (1997) added the explanatory value of the reincarnation hypothesis in accounting for birthmarks and birth defects that apparently are not genetically explicable, and that are found in nearly a third of the cases of children who are said to remember a previous life.

Shweder (1986) and Stevenson (1960, 1977b) identified a number of observations consistent with the reincarnation hypothesis, but there are alternative explanations to many, if not all, of these observations. For instance, many fears and phobias are determined by a complex interaction of genetic and physiological vulnerabilities and subtle conditioning events and situational triggers (see Oltmanns & Emery, 1998). *Déjà vu* experiences have been ascribed to temporal-lobe lability and deficits that are by no means readily apparent or easily detectable (Sivec & Lynn, 1995). And contrary to some of Shweder's earlier claims, research on identical twins has not confirmed that identical twins reared together generally exhibit marked differences in personality or that the personalities of siblings differ as much as those of a pair of people chosen randomly (see Loehlin, 1992). The question of the genesis of birthmarks and experients' statements that are purportedly related to previous lives are considered below with reference to the sociocognitive hypothesis, which takes into account a variety of sociocultural influences on PLEs.

ESP Hypothesis

Chari (1978) advanced the position that ESP in conjunction with cryptomnesia and paramnesia, explains the features of spontaneous cases. However, the hypothesis that past-life memory is based on ESP such as the telepathic or clairvoyant discernment of the nature of a deceased person, does not imply that memory continues after death, if the information the experient states is known to the relatives of the deceased person. Also, this explanation does not answer the question of why a child would receive information from people related to a particular deceased person and not show other telepathic abilities. If one presumes that the child is receiving the information from the deceased, then this explanation conflates with the reincarnation hypothesis.

Sociocognitive Hypothesis

This hypothesis is based on the idea that cultural and social forces shape both parental interpretations of children's utterances and children's constructions of their past-life reports. According to this hypothesis, cultural construction explains not only the genesis of past-life reports but also their variability across disparate cultures. For example, parents predisposed to believe in reincarnation may believe that their child's behaviors, thoughts, feelings, and fantasies are indicative of a PLE. Much as a child elaborates the existence of an imaginary playmate in fantasy, a child may construct the details of a PLE based on cultural scripts, information conveyed by a variety of sources, and expectancies generated by parents or other significant persons who believe in reincarnation and interpret the child's experiences as representing the infiltration of past-life perceptions and memories (Mills, 1992). Communications from parents or other significant persons that imply that the child who reports a PLE is special, along with procedures, such as hypnosis in many Western cases, that focus attention on the child, may constitute powerful social rewards that establish, reinforce, or flesh out the details of the PLEs, thereby making them increasingly compelling. Once the parents and child are convinced of the reality of a PLE, the parents or an investigator may locate a person who once existed whose personal characteristics and life circumstances match to some degree the past life reported by the child.

Implicit in this hypothesis is the assumption that ideas circulating in the culture about the reality and nature of reincarnation are of central importance in the construction of PLEs. As we have seen, cultural expectations are usually responsible for whether or not a case is diagnosed as a "past-life" experience or, alternately, as fantasy. Furthermore, in societies in which PLEs are viewed as legitimate interpretations of current behaviors, differences in cultural expectations are associated with variations in pertinent demographic features, such as the total population of PLE cases in a society, the ratio of male-to-female cases, the percentage of gender-change cases, and the average interval between the death of a previous personality and the birth of an affected child (Mills & Champion, 1996). Matlock (1990b) observed that gender-change cases are not found or are extremely rare in cultures in which gender change between lives is thought to be impossible.

However, in stark contrast to the sociocognitive account of these findings, Matlock (1990b) proposed that "the dying person has some (albeit usually unconscious) control over the characteristics of his or her new incarnation. If one believed firmly that one could not change sex between lives, one might not be inclined to try" (p. 238). Unfortunately, there is no current way to test this hypothesis, because it does not seem to be falsifiable. It remains a speculative proposition that credits human will with the ability to survive bodily death.

Some of the variables relevant to PLEs, particularly in past-life regression cases, have been examined in the laboratory. Research has shown that it is possible to elicit and manipulate past-life reports by structuring participants' expectations about PLEs. In one study (Spanos et al., 1991, Experiment 2) in which participants were "regressed" to a past-life, some participants were informed at the outset of the experiment that past-life identities were likely to be of a different gender and race from that of the present personality and also likely be of a different culture. In contrast, other participants received no prehypnotic information about the characteristics of their past life identities. Spanos and his colleagues found that participants' PLEs were not only quite elaborate but that they also tended to vary in conformance with induced expectancies about the nature of past-life identities. In another experiment, Spanos and his associates (Spanos et al., 1991, Experiment 3) showed that participants' past-life reports during hypnotic age regression varied in terms of the prehypnotic information they received about whether children were frequently abused during past historical periods.

Spanos et al. (1991) found that past-life reports in hypnosis experiments were associated with participants' prior beliefs in reincarnation, as well as with measures of fantasy proneness and hypnotizability. In summary, participants' reports of a past life were consistent with their beliefs about reincarnation and with situational cues conveyed by the hypnotic suggestions they received to experience a past-life identity.

It is important to note that even though certain past-life reports were apparently experienced with great emotional intensity and may have appeared compelling to an observer, Spanos et al. (1991) determined that the information participants gave about specific time periods during their age regression enactments was almost "invariably incorrect" (p. 137). Spanos (1996) concluded that hypnotically induced PLEs are rule-governed, goal-directed fantasies that are context generated and sensitive to the demands of the hypnotic regression situation. Furthermore, he found such imaginative scenarios to be constructed from available cultural narratives about past lives and known or surmised details and facts regarding specific historical periods.

The laboratory studies reviewed are clearly germane to past-life therapy cases. In both hypnotically induced experimental studies on PLEs and in past-life therapies, there are explicit demands to report PLEs, hypnosis is used to uncover presumed, past-life memories, and suggestions or induced expectancies provide a framework for construing fantasy-based productions as PLEs.

However, the extent to which findings in the laboratory generalize to spontaneous PLE cases is questionable. For instance, in the laboratory studies reviewed above, situational demands for reporting PLEs are highly salient and may well differ from the conditions conducive to reporting such experiences in non-Western countries. This is not to say that similar sociocultural expectancies and variables (e.g., suggestive communications, cryptomnesia) are not antecedents of PLEs in both laboratory and naturalistic settings, but rather that the influence of such determining factors in spontaneous PLE cases has yet to be demonstrated.

Of course, all social experiences pass at least to some degree through the filter of social construction. The term *spontaneous childhood cases* in some sense cloaks the interactive construction of the experience, particularly for children. Skeptics of the sociocognitive hypothesis argue that whereas certain aspects of PLEs are shaped by contemporary cultural narratives, other aspects of present-day life experiences represent genuine vestiges of experiences from a prior life (Haraldsson, 1997; Stevenson, 1997).

The sociocultural hypothesis may overemphasize the specific link between cultural beliefs and manifestations of PLEs and thereby provide an incomplete account of all of the data. For instance, as Matlock (1990b) pointed out, "Although case characteristics do as a general rule follow the beliefs of their culture, not all cases in a given culture conform to the beliefs" (p. 236). For instance, certain widely held beliefs about reincarnation, such as that humans can have previous lives as nonhuman animals, are only rarely, if at all, reflected in spontaneous childhood PLE cases. Conversely, despite important cultural differences in beliefs about reincarnation, there appear to be consistent findings and themes that characterize past-life reports across disparate cultures (e.g., the younger the individual, the greater the likelihood that memories will arise without apparent stimulation, and violent deaths in past-life reports exceed the rate of those types of deaths in the culture). Nevertheless, if fantasy and wish fulfillment play a role in shaping past-life reports, it is plausible that individual cases may deviate from cultural norms in certain respects. For example, it may be the case that few people would fantasize being lowly animals in a previous life and would prefer to elaborate a more dramatic or "violent" scenario as the crux of a PLE. Merely because a particular case does not seem to be explicable in terms of social construction, it does not follow that the PLE reported is a genuine residue of a past life.

METHODOLOGICAL ISSUES

Need for Independent Replication

One striking feature of the research base on spontaneous PLE cases is that it has, for the most part, been secured by a single researcher, Stevenson, and his associates. He has emphasized detailed recording of the information about a case before checking the experient's statements (and birthmarks and birth defects) against the life of an identified alleged previous personality. A variety of questions have been raised about the methods used by Stevenson and his colleagues, including concerns about (a) the researchers' objectivity and bias (Wilson, 1982), (b) the degree to which the researchers could have been fooled or tricked by their informants (Wilson, 1982), (c) whether leading interview procedures were used (Rogo, 1985), (d) whether the investigators interpreted memories in such a way as to increase their conformance with the "previous person" identified (Rogo, 1985) and, finally, (e) whether the methods used were able to rule out imaginative storytelling.

Although Matlock (1990b) marshaled an ardent defense of many of Stevenson and his associates' methods, he acknowledged the benefits of replicating observations in past-life cases, with two or more researchers working independently. Unfortunately, there have been few such replication attempts. One of the few studies (Pasricha & Stevenson, 1987) in which findings were compared across investigators indicated that researcher agreement was far from perfect, with differences found on 12 of 56 (21%) variables compared over two generations.

Investigators who have conducted replication studies of Stevenson's work (Haraldsson, 1991; Keil, 1991; Mills, 1989; Mills, Haraldsson, & Keil, 1994) have sought to study further the details of construction and interpretation of cases by (a) video-recording children (some as young as 30 months) who visit the village and home of a previous personality for the first time (Mills, 1992); (b) systematically revisiting children assumed to have had a previous life who do or do not make verbal recognition of "familiar" surroundings or persons (Keil, 1996), to ascertain if promptings are sufficient to cause a child to speak in terms of a PLE; and (c) assessing the psychological characteristics of children who appear to remember and act on the basis of experiences purported to originate in previous lives (Haraldsson, 1995, 1997; Mills, 1992).

Interviewer Effects

Interviewer effects seem to be an important issue in PLE research. Bruck, Ceci, and Helmbrooke (1998) claimed that "interviewer bias is the central driving force in the creation of suggestive interviews" (p. 75) with children. That is, interviewers' expectancies and hypotheses about whether a particular event occurred can affect their interview behavior and the memory reports they elicit from interviewees. Interviewer bias occurs when the interviewer's sole focus is on gathering confirmatory evidence (e.g., leading questions or direct suggestions to support a particular hypothesis for PLEs). In particular, Bruck, Ceci, and Helmbrooke (1998) noted that in experiments with 3- and 4-year-olds, when the children are misinformed about their own experience over a period of time, they incorporate the misinformation and reiterate it as actual experience. The phenomenon of interviewer bias raises the possibility that socializers' and researchers' expectancies, communications, and suggestions might shape children's past-life reports.

Most spontaneous past-life cases occur in non-Western cultures that believe in reincarnation. Their investigation typically involves use of a translator familiar with the native language and typically imbued with the cultural expectation that past-life recall is a valid phenomenon. How potential biases and suggestive procedures affect interviews with children and their families is difficult for the nonfluent investigator to assess and is a source of potential methodological variance.

This discussion implies that it would be worthwhile to examine the role of investigator effects (see Johnson & Foley, 1984) in studies of children's past-life memory reports. It is essential that investigators be well trained, that interview protocols minimize potential sources of interviewer bias, that interviews be carefully scrutinized for potential sources of contamination, and that future research compares the findings of credulous and skeptical interviewers.

Fantasy, Suggestibility, and Hypnosis

It would be worthwhile to examine the extent to which suggestive procedures (particularly hypnosis, but also waking expectations transmitted about a past life) influence children to interpret imaginary playmate experiences as having their roots in a past life. Conducting such experiments in cultures that endorse reincarnation is problematic, insofar as parents are concerned about the impact of external suggestions and suggestive procedures on the child's psyche. However, studies of Western children can more successfully address the question of whether and by what means children of various ages can be induced to interpret present-day experiences as the result of past-life events. Of course it is essential that researchers address the ethical concerns in research on PLEs with children, which includes securing the informed consent of participants and their parents and appropriate debriefing.

Stevenson found that it was generally unproductive to use hypnosis to acquire verifiable information from children in spontaneous cases (see Matlock, 1990b). However, the use of hypnosis in this area has received little systematic attention to date, because the reliability and validity of hypnotizability tests for children under the age of 7 is questionable (Morgan, Johnson, & Hilgard, 1974).

Indeed, obtaining a psychological profile of children at the age they initially report a PLE does pose a number of challenges. As implied above, many of the tests (e.g., hypnotizability and fantasy proneness) that are used with adults are not designed to be used with young children at the age when they typically first manifest what appears to be a past-life or secondary identity. Research findings across studies of childhood PLE cases may also diverge because children's characteristics vary across the span of development. For example, Haraldsson (1995, 1997) compared children who had and had not reported a PLE some years after the reports were initially made. He found interesting differences between the two samples, which incidentally did not support the fantasy-proneness hypothesis. In contrast, Mills (1992) tested considerably younger children and found no differences between children who had and had not reported a PLE.

Additional studies of the psychological profiles of children who report PLEs and of the profiles of adults who as children were said to remember previous lives are in order. The following questions warrant attention: Do children who speak in terms of a past-life identity, and those who do not but are identified by their families as a particular person reborn, differ in terms of hypnotizability, fantasy proneness, and imaginative involvement? Are the children in Stevenson's sample of unsolved PLE cases more fantasy prone, suggestible, or prone to confabulation than the children in those cases that are eventually solved? That is, are the cases unsolved because the reports represent so-called false memories? Is Keil's (1996) sample of children who are identified as being reborn individuals (on the basis of birthmarks or announcing dreams), yet never make any statements indicating that they share this identification, any more or less suggestible, fantasy prone, or hypnotizable than a sample of children who claim they are reborn or children who are never identified as a specific person reborn?

Difficulties With Probability Assessments

As the case of Ajendra Singh Chauhan demonstrates, it is difficult to assess the likelihood that various statements that children express regarding past lives exceed chance probability. Each spontaneous PLE case is unique and requires its own assessment of probabilities, which is difficult, if not impossible, to do. For instance, with respect to Ajendra's example, how should one calculate the number of people who had two water buffaloes in Fariha when Naresh was small? What weight should incorrect or invalid statements be given, such as the statements that indicated that the person who cooked Naresh's food was a widow and a Brahmin? The difficulties in probability assessment are compounded when the investigator is not from the child's culture and requisite data are difficult to obtain. As in the assessment of evidence provided by children in sexual assault and criminal cases, in general, it is questionable whether all testimony should be discredited if a small proportion of the testimony proves to be untrue (Terr, 1990).

In terms of assessing the probability of having one or more birthmarks on the same part of the body, Stevenson (1997) devised a way of dividing the human body into a grid and of determining the probability of two birthmarks (e.g., corresponding to bullet entry and exit wounds) being in the same quadrant in both a child and the body of his or her previous personality. Stevenson calculated this probability to be 1 in 416,025 (Stevenson, 1997, p. 1135; see also Mills, 1989, for such a case). However, Stevenson's assessment of the probability of finding a correspondence between multiple birthmarks on a child and a reputed previous personality needs to be verified by evaluating the coincidence of birthmarks in particular body areas (and matching them) with wounds recorded in autopsies of persons in the general population who are not linked by a purported PLE. Until such studies are done, it is impossible to determine whether the seemingly impressive findings of correspondence between birthmarks across present and "past lives" exceed base-rate levels of correspondence in the general population.

Stevenson (1993, 1997), Pasricha (1998), and Mills (1994d, 1996) have continued to study cases featuring birthmarks and birth defects that correspond to accidental or intentional markings on the bodies of previous personalities. The data are complex, and coinvestigation with a geneticist would be useful to assess, for instance, whether the set of cases of Native Gitxsan and Witsuwit'en children born with pierced-ear birthmarks (Mills, 1994a, 1996), a phenomenon rich with cultural meaning, has a genetic component. In cases in which the child and the previous personality are unrelated, the correspondence requires further stochastic assessment.

It is worth noting that if a case is solved because a person who lived at one time is identified as a previous personality on the basis of a correspondence of bodily markings with a child who reports past-life memories, it is not surprising to find that a high degree of correspondence exists between these individuals in terms of shared bodily markings. The accuracy of the child's statements (if there are any) in a case such as this again needs to be evaluated, noting whether socializers imparted knowledge to the child consistent with their interpretation of the child as the reincarnation of a previous personality. Consideration of the cultural aspects of ascribing meaning to behavior, birthmarks, birth defects, or any of the other characteristics associated with the rebirth cases reviewed is paramount insofar as in the absence of cultural beliefs in reincarnation, the behavior or physical features shared by living and dead persons is typically not interpreted in terms of PLE.

Finally, a fruitful research endeavor would be to randomly generate scripts to conform to a prototypic PLE and to determine whether "masked" investigators are able to solve the case (i.e., match the child's descriptive statements with the characteristics of a deceased person's life). The comparison of such fabricated cases with cases in which children spontaneously report subjectively compelling PLEs could be a useful starting point in addressing whether base rates of correspondence between events thought to be associated with PLEs differ significantly from chance.

Need for Valid and Reliable Rating Systems

The development of valid and reliable multivariate scoring systems to codify PLEs and determine whether a PLE case can be considered solved or unsolved is a priority. For example, scoring systems can be devised to determine the extent to which cases can be accounted for by a variety of variables, including expectancies, mundane means of information transfer, reinterpretation of behavior, interviewer contamination and bias, fantasy proneness, the extent to which PLE reports match characteristics of the person thought to have been reincarnated, and the degree of confidence that a particular case is correctly solved. Assessing the degree of certainty about the presence or absence of contact between and among study participants is essential to evaluating whether normal means of data transmission combine with cultural construction to create a plausible case of reincarnation. Whether a case is solved or not is only one of an array of meaningful criteria that have figured prominently in past and current research on PLE.

CONCLUSION

The study of PLEs poses numerous methodological, inferential, and conceptual challenges. It is undeniable that inquiry into and evaluation of the existing data in this area have suffered from, if not been stifled by, negative attitudes about the topic that range from benign neglect to derision. Yet these challenges and negative attitudes have not deterred investigators from expanding our understanding of how cultural beliefs, values, and theories about human life and the proposed afterlife are propagated and affect individuals across very different cultures. It is evident that there are many indigenous theories of PLE, as exemplified by the Native peoples of North America, Australia, Siberia, and West Africa, who believe that their ancestors return again and again in their same locale and form, and by Hindus and Buddhists who theorize that one reincarnates until he or she attains enlightenment, or release from rebirth (Obeyesekere, 1980, 1994).

Empirical studies reveal that spontaneous PLE cases unfold in similar ways across cultures but also reflect, among other things, cultural expectations. Additional empirical studies of PLEs may expand the variables found to differ from culture to culture, as well as confirm the fundamental commonalities that exist across cultures. This cross-cultural research will further enhance our understanding of the development of children's experience and sense of identity and how it relates to the internalization of cultural expectations. Such research can also expand the understanding of humanity's deepest needs, wishes, and yearnings, and it can probe, if not answer, the question of survival after bodily death.

As this review has indicated, hypnotically induced past-life regression experiences are not completely trustworthy or comparable with spontaneous PLEs. The question that remains to be further assessed in spontaneous cases is whether the statements about PLEs made by experients that are demonstrably correct, particularly in cases in which a written record exists before the identification of a previous personality, can be explained in terms of chance coincidence and cultural construction, or represent veridical "memories" consistent with a reincarnation hypothesis. At the very least, the pursuit of such questions represents a viable way of exploring the depth of sociocultural construction of both veridical and false memories in Western culture and the culture of the "other."

REFERENCES

Achenbach, T. M., & Edelbrock, C. (1983). *Manual of the Child Behavior Checklist and revised Child Behavior Profile*. Burlington: University of Vermont, Department of Psychiatry.

Achenbach, T. M., & Edelbrock, C. (1986). *Manual of the Teacher's Report Form and Teacher Version of the Child Behavior Profile*. Burlington: University of Vermont, Department of Psychiatry.

American Psychiatric Association. (1994). *Diagnostic and statistical manual of mental disorders* (4th ed.). Washington, DC: Author.

Andrade, H. G. (1988). *Reencarnacão no Brasil: Oito casos que sugerem renascimento* [Reincarnation in Brazil: Eight cases of rebirth]. Matão, Brazil: Case Editora O Clarim.

Baker, R. A. (1982). The effect of suggestion on past-life regression. *American Journal of Hypnosis, 25*, 71–76.

Barker, D., & Pasricha, S. K. (1979). Reincarnation cases in Fatehabad: A systematic survey in north India. *Journal of Asian and African Studies, 14*, 231–240.

Bernstein, M. (1956). *The search for Bridey Murphy*. Garden City, NY: Doubleday.

Brody, E. B. (1979a). Review of the book *Cases of the Reincarnation Type: Vol. II. Ten cases in Sri Lanka. Journal of Nervous and Mental Disease, 167*, 769–774.

Brody, E. B. (1979b). Review of the book *Cases of the Reincarnation Type: Vol. II. Ten cases in Sri Lanka. Journal of the American Society for Psychical Research, 73*, 71–81.

Bruck, M., Ceci, S. J., & Helmbrooke, H. (1998). Reliability and credibility of young children's reports. *American Psychologist, 53*, 71–81.

Chari, C. T. K. (1962). Paramnesia and reincarnation. *Proceedings of the Society for Psychical Research, 53*, 264–286.

Chari, C. T. K. (1967). Reincarnation: New light on an old doctrine. *International Journal of Parapsychology, 9*, 217–222.

Chari, C. T. K. (1978). Reincarnation research: Method and interpretation. In M. Ebon (Ed.), *Signet handbook of parapsychology* (pp. 313–324). New York: NAL Books.

Chari, C. T. K. (1986). Letter to the editor. *Journal of the Society for Psychical Research, 53*, 474.

Cook, E. W., Pasricha, S., Samararatne, G., U Win Maung, & Stevenson, I. (1983). A review and analysis of "unsolved" cases of the reincarnation type: II. Comparison of features of solved and unsolved cases. *Journal of the American Society for Psychical Research, 77*, 115–135.

Ducasse, C. J. (1960). How the case of the search for Bridey Murphy stands today. *Journal of the American Society for Psychical Research, 54*, 3–22.

Dunn, L. M., & Dunn, L. M. (1981). *Peabody Picture Vocabulary Test—Revised: Manual for Forms M and L*. Circle Pines, MN: American Guidance Service.

Evans-Wentz, W. Y. (1958). *Tibetan yoga and secret doctrines*. London: Oxford University Press.

Gudjonsson, G. H. (1984). A new scale of interrogative suggestibility. *Personality and Individual Differences, 5*, 303–314.

Gudjonsson, G. H. (1987). A parallel form of the Gudjonsson Suggestibility Scale. *British Journal of Clinical Psychology, 26*, 215–221.

Haraldsson, E. (1991). Children claiming previous-life memories: Four cases in Sri Lanka. *Journal of Scientific Exploration, 5*, 233–261.

Haraldsson, E. (1995). Personality and abilities of children claiming previous-life memories. *Journal of Nervous and Mental Disease, 183*, 445–451.

Haraldsson, E. (1997). A psychological comparison between ordinary children and those who claim previous-life memories. *Journal of Scientific Exploration, 11*, 323–335.

Hastings, A. (1990). Review of "Other Lives, Other Selves." *Journal of Near-Death Studies, 9*, 58–64.

Hilgard, J. (1970). *Personality and hypnosis*. Chicago: University of Chicago Press.

Johnson, M. K., & Foley, M. A. (1984). Differentiating fact from fantasy: The reliability of children's memory. *Journal of Social Issues, 40*, 33–50.

Kampman, R. (1976). Hypnotically induced multiple personality: An experimental study. *International Journal of Clinical and Experimental Hypnosis, 24*, 215–227.

Keil, H. H. J. (1991). New cases in Burma, Thailand, and Turkey: A limited field study replication of some aspects of Ian Stevenson's research. *Journal of Scientific Exploration, 5*, 27–59.

Keil, H. H. J. (1996). Cases of the reincarnation type: An evaluation of some indirect evidence with examples of "silent" cases. *Journal of Scientific Exploration, 10*, 467–485.

Krippner, S. (1986). Cross-cultural approaches to multiple personality disorder: Therapeutic practices in Brazilian spiritism. *Humanistic Psychologist, 14*, 177–193.

Loehlin, J. (1992). *Genes and environment in personality development.* Newbury Park, CA: Sage.

Lucas, W. B. (1993). *Regression therapy: A handbook for professionals.* Crest Park, CA: Deep Forest Press.

Lynn, S. J., Lock, T. G., Myers, B., & Payne, D. G. (1997). Recalling the unrecallable: Should hypnosis be used to recover memories in psychotherapy? *Current Directions in Psychological Science, 6*, 79–83.

Lynn, S. J., & Rhue, J.W. (1991). *Theories of hypnosis.* New York: Guilford Press.

Matlock, J. G. (1989). Age and stimulus in past life memory cases: A study of published cases. *Journal of the American Society for Psychical Research, 83*, 303–316.

Matlock, J. G. (1990a). Of names and signs: Reincarnation, inheritance, and social structure on the Northwest coast. *Anthropology of Consciousness, 1*, 9–18.

Matlock, J. G. (1990b). Past life memory case studies. In S. Krippner (Ed.), *Advances in parapsychological research* (Vol. 6, pp. 187–267). Jefferson, NC: McFarland.

Matlock, J. G., & Mills, A. (1994). A trait index to North American Indian and Inuit reincarnation. In A. Mills & R. Slobodin (Eds.), *Amerindian rebirth: Reincarnation belief among North American Indians and Inuit* (pp. 299–356). Toronto, Ontario, Canada: University of Toronto Press.

Mills, A. (1988a). A comparison of Witsuwit'en cases of the reincarnation type with Gitxsan and Beaver. *Journal of Anthropological Research, 44*, 385–415.

Mills, A. (1988b). A preliminary investigation of reincarnation among the Beaver and Gitxsan Indians. *Anthropologica, 30*, 23–59.

Mills, A. (1989). A replication study: Three cases of children in north India who are said to remember a previous life. *Journal of Scientific Exploration, 3*, 133–184.

Mills, A. (1990). Moslem cases of the reincarnation type in Northern India: A test of the hypothesis of imposed identification. Part I: Analysis of 26 cases. Part II: Reports of three cases. *Journal of Scientific Exploration, 4*, 171–202.

Mills, A. (1992, December). *Childhood alternate identities: A comparison of children said to remember previous lives and children with imaginary playmates.* Paper presented at the annual meeting of the American Anthropological Association, San Francisco.

Mills, A. (1994a). *Eagle down is our law: Witsuwit'en laws, feasts and land claims.* Vancouver, British Columbia, Canada: University of British Columbia Press.

Mills, A. (1994b). Making a scientific investigation of ethnographic cases suggestive of reincarnation. In D. Young & J. -G. Goulet (Eds.), *Being changed: The anthropological experience* (pp. 237–269). Peterborough, Ontario, Canada: Broadview Press.

Mills A. (1994c). Nightmares in Western children: An alternative interpretation suggested by data in three cases. *Journal of the American Society for Psychical Research, 88,* 309–326.

Mills, A. (1994d). Rebirth and identity: Three cases of pierced ear birthmarks among the Gitxsan. In A. Mills & R. Slobodin (Eds.), *Amerindian rebirth: Reincarnation belief among North American Indians and Inuit* (pp. 211–241), Toronto, Ontario, Canada: University of Toronto Press.

Mills A. (1994e). Reincarnation belief among North American Indians and Inuit: Context, distribution and variation. In A. Mills & R. Slobodin (Eds.), *Amerindian rebirth: Reincarnation belief among North American Indians and Inuit* (pp. 15–38). Toronto, Ontario, Canada: University of Toronto Press.

Mills, A. (1996, October). *Three new Gitxsan cases of children born with pierced ear birthmarks.* Paper presented at the European Convention of the Society for Scientific Exploration, Freiburg, Germany.

Mills, A., & Champion, L. (1996). Come-backs/reincarnation as integration; adoption-out as disassociation: Examples from First Nations of northwest British Columbia. *Anthropology of Consciousness, 7,* 30–43.

Mills, A., Haraldsson, E., & Keil, H. H. J. (1994). Replication studies of cases suggestive of reincarnation by three independent investigators. *Journal of the American Society for Psychical Research, 88,* 207–219.

Morgan, A. H., Johnson, D. L., & Hilgard, E. R. (1974). The stability of hypnotic susceptibility: A longitudinal study. *International Journal of Clinical and Experimental Hypnosis, 22,* 249–357.

Obeyesekere, G. (1980). The rebirth eschatology and its transformations: A contribution to the sociology of early Buddhism. In W. O'Flaherty (Ed.), *Karma and rebirth in classical Indian traditions* (pp. 137–164). Berkeley: University of California Press.

Obeyesekere, G. (1994). Reincarnation eschatologies and the comparative study of religions. In A. Mills & R. Slobodin (Eds.), *Amerindian rebirth: Reincarnation belief among North American Indians and Inuit* (pp. xi-xxiv). Toronto, Ontario, Canada: University of Toronto Press.

Oltmanns, T., & Emery, R. (1998). *Abnormal psychology* (2nd ed.). Englewood Cliffs, NJ: Prentice Hall.

Pasricha, S. K. (1998). Cases of the reincarnation type in northern India with birthmarks and birth defects. *Journal of Scientific Exploration, 12,* 259–293.

Pasricha, S. K., Murthy, H. N., & Murthy, V. N. (1978). Examination of the claims of reincarnation in a psychotic condition. *Indian Journal of Clinical Psychology, 5,* 197–202.

Pasricha, S. K., & Stevenson, I. (1987). Indian cases of the reincarnation type: Two generations apart. *Journal of the Society for Psychical Research, 54,* 239–246.

Raven, J. C. (1963). *Guide to using the Coloured Progressive Matrices, Sets A, Ab, B.* Dumfries, Scotland: Crichton Royal.

Rogo, D. S. (1985). *The search for yesterday.* Englewood Cliffs, NJ: Prentice Hall.

Schouten, S., & Stevenson, I. (1998). Does the socio-psychological hypothesis explain cases of the reincarnation type? *Journal of Nervous and Mental Disease, 186,* 504–506.

Shweder, R. (1986). Divergent rationalities. In D. Fiske & R. Shweder (Eds.), *Metatheory in social science: Pluralisms and subjectivities* (pp. 163–196). Chicago: University of Chicago Press.

Singer, D. G., & Singer, J. L. (1990). *The house of make-believe.* Cambridge, MA: Harvard University Press.

Sivec, H., & Lynn, S. J. (1995). Dissociative and neuropsychological symptoms: The question of differential diagnosis. *Clinical Psychology Review, 15,* 297–316.

Spanos, N. P. (1994). Multiple identity enactments and multiple personality disorder: A sociocognitive perspective. *Psychological Bulletin, 116,* 143–165.

Spanos, N. P. (1996). *Multiple identities and false memories.* Washington, DC: American Psychological Association.

Spanos, N. P., Menary, E., Gabora, N. J., Dubreuil, S. C., & Dewhirst, B. (1991). Secondary identity enactments during hypnotic past-life regression: A sociocognitive perspective. *Journal of Personality and Social Psychology, 61,* 308–320.

Stevenson, I. (1960). The evidence of survival from claimed memories of former incarnations. *Journal of the American Society for Psychical Research, 54,* 51–71, 95–117.

Stevenson, I. (1974a). *Twenty cases suggestive of reincarnation* (2nd rev. ed.). Charlottesville: University Press of Virginia.

Stevenson, I. (1974b). *Xenoglossy: A review and report of a case.* Charlottesville: University Press of Virginia.

Stevenson, I. (1975). *Cases of the reincarnation type: Vol. 1, Ten cases in India.* Charlottesville: University Press of Virginia.

Stevenson, I. (1976). A preliminary report of a new case of responsive xenoglossy: The case of Gretchen. *Journal of the American Society for Psychical Research, 70,* 65–77.

Stevenson, I. (1977a). *Cases of the reincarnation type: Vol. 2, Ten cases in Sri Lanka.* Charlottesville: University Press of Virginia.

Stevenson, I. (1977b). The explanatory value of the idea of reincarnation. *Journal of Nervous and Mental Disease, 164,* 305–326.

Stevenson, I. (1977c). The southeast Asian interpretation of gender dysphoria: An illustrative case report. *Journal of Nervous and Mental Disease, 165,* 201–208.

Stevenson, I. (1980). A preliminary report on an unusual case of the reincarnation type with xenoglossy. *Journal of the American Society for Psychical Research, 74,* 331–348.

Stevenson, I. (1983a). American children who claim to remember previous lives. *Journal of Nervous and Mental Disease, 171,* 742–748.

Stevenson, I. (1983b). *Unlearned language: New studies in xenoglossy.* Charlottesville: University Press of Virginia.

Stevenson, I. (1986). Characteristics of cases of the reincarnation type among the Igbo of Nigeria. *Journal of Asian and African Studies, 21,* 204–216.

Stevenson, I. (1987). *Children who remember previous lives: A question of reincarnation.* Charlottesville: University Press of Virginia.

Stevenson, I. (1990a). Phobias in children who claim to remember previous lives. *Journal of Scientific Exploration, 4,* 243–254.

Stevenson, I. (1990b). Review of "Other Lives, Other Selves." *Journal of Near-Death Studies, 9,* 55–57.

Stevenson, I. (1993). Birthmarks and birth defects corresponding to wounds on deceased persons. *Journal of Scientific Exploration, 7,* 403–410.

Stevenson, I. (1994). A case of the psychotherapist's fallacy: Hypnotic regression to "previous lives." *American Journal of Clinical Hypnosis, 36,* 188–193.

Stevenson, I. (1997). *Biology and reincarnation: A contribution to the etiology of birthmarks and birth defects.* Westport, CT: Praeger.

Stevenson, I. & Chadha, N. K. (1990). Can children be stopped from speaking about previous lives? Some further analyses of features in cases of the reincarnation type. *Journal of the Society for Psychical Research, 56,* 82–90.

Stevenson, I., Pasricha, S., & Samararatne, G. (1988). Deception and self-deception in cases of the reincarnation type: Seven illustrative cases in Asia. *Journal of the American Society for Psychical Research, 82,* 1–31.

Stevenson, I., & Samararatne, G. (1988). Three new cases of the reincarnation type in Sri Lanka with written records made before verification. *Journal of Scientific Exploration, 2,* 217–238.

Tarazi, K. (1990). An unusual case of hypnotic regression with some unexplained contents. *Journal of the American Society for Psychical Research, 84,* 309–344.

Taylor, M., Cartwright, B. S., & Carlson, S. M. (1993). A developmental investigation of children's imaginary companions. *Developmental Psychology, 29,* 276–283.

Terr, L. (1990). *Too scared to cry.* New York: Harper & Row.

Venn, J. (1986). Hypnosis and the reincarnation hypothesis: A critical review and intensive case study. *Journal of the American Society for Psychical Research, 80,* 409–425.

Weiss, B. L. (1988). *Many lives, many masters*. New York: Simon & Schuster.

Wilson, I. (1982). *All in the mind: Reincarnation, hypnotic regression, stigmata, multiple personality, and other little understood powers of the mind*. Garden City, NY: Doubleday.

Woolger, R. J. (1988). *Other lives, other selves: A Jungian psychotherapist discovers past lives*. New York: Bantam Books.

Yogananda, P. (1993). *Autobiography of a yogi*. Los Angeles: Self-Realization Fellowship. (Original work published 1946)

10

NEAR-DEATH EXPERIENCES

BRUCE GREYSON

A 55-year-old married White truck driver was admitted to the hospital with irregular heartbeat, and during diagnostic angiography suffered a coronary occlusion. He then underwent emergency quadruple bypass surgery, following which he reported having had a clear sensation of leaving his body and observing the operating room from above. He reported accurately certain idiosyncratic behaviors of the cardio-vascular surgeon, pinpointing when they had occurred during the op-eration. He also described being distracted from the operating room scene by a brilliant light and following it through a tunnel to a region of warmth, love, and peace, where he experienced an apparent en-counter with his deceased mother and brother-in-law, who communi-cated to him, without speaking, that he should return to his body. He awoke with an intense passion for helping others and a desire to talk about his experience, much to the dismay of his embarrassed wife.

DEFINITION

Near-death experiences (NDEs) are profound psychological events with transcendental and mystical elements, typically occurring to individuals close to death or in situations of intense physical or emotional danger. These elements include ineffability, a sense that the experience transcends personal ego, and an experience of union with a divine or higher principle. NDEs, once regarded as meaningless hallucinations, have become the subject of serious study by medical and other researchers in recent years. Once thought to be rare, the NDE has been estimated to be reported by at least a third of people who come close to death (Ring, 1984; Sabom, 1982) or about 5% of the U.S. population (Gallup & Proctor, 1982); however, a recent reassessment has suggested that that estimate may be inflated (Greyson, 1998). Although the term *near-death experience* and its acronym, *NDE*, were not coined until 1975, accounts of similar events can be found in the folklore and writings of European, Middle Eastern, African, Indian, East Asian, Pacific, and Native American peoples. The phenomenon was first described as a clinical syndrome in 1892, when Heim published a collection (translated into English by Noyes & Kletti, 1972) of the subjective experiences of mountain climbers who had fallen in the Alps (as he himself had done), soldiers wounded in war, workers who had fallen from scaffolds, and individuals who had nearly died in accidents or near-drownings.

Moody, who coined the term *near-death experience* in 1975, first defined it in 1977 as "any conscious perceptual experience which takes place during . . . an event in which a person could very easily die or be killed (and may even be so close as to be believed or pronounced clinically dead) but nonetheless survives, and continues physical life" (p. 124). Moody later redefined NDEs as "profound spiritual events that happen, uninvited, to some individuals at the point of death" (Moody & Perry, 1991, p. 11).

The Dictionary of Modern Medicine has offered a more specific definition:

> A phenomenon of unclear nature that may occur in patients who have been clinically dead and then resuscitated; the patients report a continuity of subjective experience, remembering visitors and other hospital events despite virtually complete suppression of cortical activity; near-death experiences are considered curiosities with no valid explanation in the context of an acceptable biomedical paradigm; the trivial synonym, Lazarus complex refers to the biblical Lazarus who was raised from the dead by Jesus of Nazareth. (Segen, 1992, p. 483)

NDEs are reported by individuals who had been pronounced clinically dead but then resuscitated; by individuals who actually died but were able to describe their experiences in their final moments ("deathbed visions"); and by individuals who, in the course of accidents or illnesses, feared that they were near death. Although initial studies suggested that how one came close to death, or how close one actually came to death, does not influence the occurrence or type of NDE (Ring, 1980, 1984), more recent research has indicated that physiological details of the close brush with death may play a minor role.

It appears, for example, that NDEs dominated by cognitive features, such as temporal distortions, accelerated thoughts, and a life review, are more common in near-death events that are sudden and unexpected than in those in which the demise may have been anticipated (Greyson, 1985). NDEs associated with cardiac arrest resemble out-of-body experiences (OBEs; see Alvarado, this volume, chap. 6), whereas those without it are more similar to depersonalization, in which one feels oneself or one's body to be unreal; and NDEs occurring to intoxicated persons tend to be bizarre and confused, like hallucinations (Twemlow, Gabbard, & Coyne, 1982). Furthermore, although all elements of the NDE can be reported by individuals who merely perceive themselves to be near death, certain features such as an encounter with a brilliant light, enhanced cognitive function, and positive emotions are more common among individuals whose closeness to death can be corroborated by medical records (Owens, Cook, & Stevenson, 1990). Closeness to death may be an even more significant factor in determining NDEs among children: In one study, although NDEs were recounted by up to half of the children who survived critical illnesses, they were not recounted by children who suffered serious illnesses that were not potentially fatal (Morse, Castillo, Venecia, Milstein, & Tyler, 1986).

PHENOMENOLOGY

In coining the term *near-death experience*, Moody (1975) identified 15 elements that seemed to recur in NDE reports, to which he later added four additional features (Moody, 1977). These phenomenological elements are listed in Exhibit 10.1. The sense of surviving one's own death and the enhancement of mental functioning at a time when the brain is physiologically impaired, as well as the paranormal and otherworldly experiences, render NDEs anomalous. Moody (1975) noted that no two NDE accounts were precisely the same, that no experience in his collection included more than 12 of these original 15 elements, that no one element appeared in every narrative, and that the order in which elements appeared varied from one experience to another. He cautioned against taking his description of NDEs as prescription, warning that his list was intended as a rough theoretical model rather than a fixed definition (Moody, 1977). Children's NDEs are similar to those of adults, except that they tend not to include a life review or meetings with deceased friends and relatives, two differences that could be expected because of children's brief experience with life (Bush, 1983; Morse et al., 1986).

Several investigators have attempted to classify the common features of the NDE into discrete phenomenological categories. Noyes and Slymen (1978–1979) factor analyzed the features reported by near-death experients

EXHIBIT 10.1
Common Elements Recurring in Adult Near-Death
Experiences (Moody, 1975, 1977)

Elements occurring during near-death experiences:
  Ineffability
  Hearing oneself pronounced dead
  Feelings of peace and quiet
  Hearing unusual noises
  Seeing a dark tunnel
  Being "out of the body"
  Meeting "spiritual beings"
  Experiencing a bright light as a "being of light"
  Panoramic life review
  Experiencing a realm in which all knowledge exists
  Experiencing cities of light
  Experiencing a realm of bewildered spirits
  Experiencing a "supernatural rescue"
  Sensing a border or limit
  Coming back "into the body"
Elements occurring as aftereffects:
  Frustration relating the experience to others
  Subtle "broadening and deepening" of life
  Elimination of fear of death
  Corroboration of events witnessed while "out of the body"

and classified them into (a) mystical elements, such as a feeling of great understanding, vivid images, and revival of memories; (b) depersonalization elements, which may include loss of emotion, separation from the body, and feelings of strangeness or unreality; and (c) hyperalertness elements, such as vivid and rapid thoughts and sharper vision and hearing. Greyson (1985), on the basis of a cluster analysis of reported elements, classified them into (a) cognitive features (time distortion, thought acceleration, a life review, and revelation), (b) affective features (peace, joy, cosmic unity, and an encounter with light), (c) paranormal features (vivid sensory events, apparent extrasensory perception and precognitive visions, and OBEs), and (d) transcendental features (otherworldly encounters with mystical beings, visible spirits, and an uncrossable border).

Other classifications of the NDE have assumed that the experience unfolds in a consistent temporal pattern. Noyes (1972) described the following developmental stages of NDE: (a) resistance, terminated by surrender and tranquility; (b) review, including out-of-body and panoramic memory experiences; and (c) transcendence, involving a nontemporal dimension of existence. Ring (1980) classified the unfolding stages of the NDE into (a) peace and well-being, (b) separation from the physical body, (c) entrance into a transitional region of darkness, (d) seeing a brilliant light, and (e) entering, through the light, another realm of existence. Although Ring acknowledged that these stages do not always unfold in that strict sequence, he and other researchers have used this model to measure the "depth" of an NDE, such that, for example, an experience with the light might be considered "deeper" than one of separation from the body. Ring (1984) later described the progression of what he called the *core NDE*, a particularly deep experience: speed and acceleration as one approaches a light that, despite its brilliance, does not hurt the eyes; pure love, total acceptance, forgiveness, and a sense of homecoming in the presence of the light; instantaneous, nonverbal communication with the light, which imparts knowledge, helping the experient through a life review to identify what really matters in life; transcendental music, paradisiacal environments, and cities of light; and a yearning to remain with the light forever.

Still other classifications of NDEs have assumed that there are discrete phenomenological types of experience. Sabom (1982) classified NDEs into (a) autoscopic experiences involving self-visualization from a position of height, (b) transcendental experiences involving apparent passage into a foreign realm or dimension, and (c) a combination of experiences with both autoscopic and transcendental features. Greyson (1985) classified NDEs according to the specific dominance of his previously identified phenomenological components as (a) cognitive, (b) affective, and (c) transcendental types. Twemlow et al. (1982), on the basis of a multivariate cluster analysis of phenomenological features, suggested a classification of experiences into those associated with preexisting conditions of (a) low stress, (b) emotional stress, (c) intoxication, (d) cardiac arrest, or (e) anesthesia.

Greyson and Bush (1992) classified the rarer, distressing type of NDE into (a) experiences phenomenologically like the blissful type but interpreted as terrifying, (b) experiences of nonexistence or eternal void, and (c) experiences with blatant hellish imagery. Despite the richness of the data covered by these various classifications, to date none of them has been tested in terms of its clinical usefulness or validity in predicting NDE aftereffects.

AFTEREFFECTS

Regardless of their cause, transcendent NDEs can permanently and dramatically alter the individual experient's attitudes, beliefs, and values. The growing literature on the aftereffects of NDEs has focused on the beneficial personal transformations that often follow them. The most common aftereffects include increases in spirituality, concern for others, and appreciation of life and decreases in fear of death, materialism, and competitiveness (Flynn, 1986; Grey, 1985; Sabom, 1982). Near-death experients tend to see themselves as integral parts of a benevolent and purposeful universe in which personal gain, particularly at others' expense, is no longer relevant. In studies comparing the experients' attitudes before and after their experiences, Noyes (1980) found that they reported a reduced fear of death, a sense of relative invulnerability, a feeling of special importance or destiny, and a strengthened belief in postmortem existence. Ring (1980, 1984) found that near-death experients reported a greater appreciation for life, a renewed sense of purpose, greater confidence and flexibility in coping with life's vicissitudes, increased value of love and service and decreased concern with personal status and material possessions, greater compassion for others, a heightened sense of spiritual purpose, and a greatly reduced fear of death.

Flynn (1982) found that near-death experients reported a greatly increased concern for others, decreased fear of death, increased belief in an afterlife, increased religious interest and feeling, and lessened desire for material success and approval of others. Bauer (1985), using an instrument based on Frankl's (1969) logotherapy, found that NDEs led to significant positive changes in the purpose and meaning of life and in death acceptance. In studies comparing the attitudes of near-death experients with those of other groups, including persons who had come close to death but had not had NDEs, Greyson found that experients placed significantly lower value on social status, professional and material success, and fame (Greyson, 1983a) and found death less threatening (Greyson, 1992). Although a less fearful attitude toward death has been associated with an increase in suicidal thoughts (Shneidman, 1971), near-death experients paradoxically express stronger objections to suicide than do comparison samples, primarily on the basis of increased transpersonal or transcendental beliefs (Greyson, 1992–1993). These profound changes in attitudes and in behavior have been corroborated in long-term studies of near-death experients and in interviews with their significant others (Ring, 1984).

INDIVIDUAL DIFFERENCES

Researchers have identified very few personal traits or variables that can predict who will have an NDE or what kind of NDE a person may have. Retrospective studies of near-death experients have shown them collectively to be psychologically healthy individuals who do not differ from comparison groups in age, gender, race, religion, religiosity, or mental health (Gabbard & Twemlow, 1984; Greyson, 1991; Irwin, 1985; Ring, 1980; Sabom, 1982). Locke and Shontz (1983) found near-death experients to be indistinguishable from nonexperients in intelligence, neuroticism, extroversion, trait and state anxiety, or in relevant Rorschach measures. However, some studies have suggested that the experients tend to be better hypnotic subjects, remember their dreams more often, are more adept at using mental imagery (Council & Greyson, 1985; Irwin, 1985), and tend to acknowledge significantly more childhood trauma and resultant dissociative tendencies (Ring, 1992) than their nonexperient counterparts. It is not clear, however, whether these traits and recall of prior experiences are the results of having had an NDE or whether people who already have those characteristics are more prone to have NDEs when they come close to death.

Comparisons of NDE accounts from different cultures suggest that prior beliefs have some influence on the kind of experience a person will report following a close brush with death. Whereas features such as encounters with other beings and realms are cross-cultural elements, the life review and tunnel sensation, for example, are primarily reported in NDEs from Christian and Buddhist cultures but are rare among native populations in North America, Australia, and the Pacific islands (Kellehear, 1993). Cultural influences have led some scholars to interpret NDEs as nothing more than emotional reactions to the threat of imminent death (Ehrenwald, 1974; Lukianowicz, 1958; Noyes, Hoenk, Kuperman, & Slymen, 1977; Noyes & Kletti, 1976), but they may reflect not so much the experience itself as the experients' ability to process and express an event that is largely ineffable.

PSYCHOPATHOLOGY

As noted above, retrospective studies of near-death experients have shown most of them to be psychologically healthy individuals who do not differ from nonexperient comparison groups on measures of mental health (Gabbard & Twemlow, 1984; Greyson, 1991; Irwin, 1985; Locke & Shontz, 1983). However, NDEs have been speculatively linked to several psychopathological conditions.

Dissociation

Although clinical descriptions of NDEs can be found in 19th-century medical journals, the psychological analysis of the phenomenon was rare until Pfister's 1930 article, translated into English a half-century later (Kletti & Noyes, 1981). Pfister proposed that persons faced with potentially inescapable danger attempt to exclude this unpleasant reality from perception by replacing it with pleasurable fantasies that protect the individual from being paralyzed by emotional shock. Pfister's interpretation of the NDE as a defense against the threat of death was elaborated by Noyes and Kletti (1976, 1977), who conceived of the NDE as a type of depersonalization, consisting of feelings of strangeness or unreality. To the extent that a state of depersonalization mimics a state of death, this mechanism could be interpreted as a sacrifice of a part of the self to avoid actual death.

However, as Noyes and his colleagues have indicated, this model can accommodate only some of the phenomena common to NDEs. Noyes and Kletti (1977) found that survivors of life-threatening danger reported depersonalization and a sense of detachment from their own bodies, derealization (a feeling of detachment from, or unreality of, the environment), time distortion, and lack of emotion. However, as noted above, in a factor analysis of responses to life-threatening danger, Noyes and Slymen (1978–1979) identified, in addition to depersonalization, a "hyperalertness" factor diametrically opposed to depersonalization, and a "mystical consciousness" factor not addressed by the depersonalization model. Gabbard and Twemlow (1984) differentiated between depersonalization and NDEs on a number of parameters. They pointed out that depersonalization usually does not include a sense of being "out of the body"; is experienced as "dreamlike"; is typically unpleasant; is characterized affectively by anxiety, panic, and emptiness; is experienced as pathological and strange; typically occurs in persons between 15 and 30 years of age and rarely in those over 40; and occurs twice as often to women as to men. NDEs, by contrast, often include a sense of being "out of the body"; are not experienced as dreamlike; are typically pleasant; are characterized affectively by joy, ecstasy, and feelings of calm, peace, and quiet; are experienced as religious, spiritual, and noetic; have no characteristic age group; and have an even gender distribution.

Irwin (1993) argued against viewing the NDE as a type of depersonalization, in that the NDE experient's sense of identity is not altered but is in fact unusually lucid; what is altered is one's identity's association with bodily sensations. Thus, he argued that the NDE is not an example of depersonalization but rather of dissociation of the self-identity from bodily sensation and emotions. The concepts of dissociation include a lack of integration between psychological processes that should ordinarily be integrated, an alteration of consciousness characterized by disconnection from or disengagement with the environment, and a defense mechanism to ward off anxiety or pain (Cardeña, 1994). Dissociation may describe the separation of emotions from ideas or situations, so that experiencing some emotional impact can be deferred or delayed. NDEs do not appear to be related to dissociative disorders, which are characterized by persistent, recurrent, or chronic dissociation that entails distress or maladjustment.

Irwin (1993) found no significant difference in dissociative coping style between near-death experients and a comparison sample, but did find a significantly higher rate of childhood trauma among the experients. Thus, despite reporting a greater number of episodic and unpredictable traumatic events in childhood, near-death experients did not develop a proneness to dissociation. Irwin speculated that near-death experients may develop a tendency to dissociate in response to very stressful unforeseen events but do not develop a general dissociative defense style to cope with everyday stressors.

Ring (1992) suggested that dissociation might account for what he called near-death experients' "sensitivity to alternate realities" (p. 115). By "alternate realties," Ring meant dimensions or realms of existence distinct from, but objectively as real as, the world of ordinary waking consciousness. As a reason for suspecting dissociation to be part of the experients' psychological profile, he cited evidence from his research that near-death experients are more likely than others to have suffered childhood abuse and trauma. Ring found the dissociative tendencies of near-death experients to be significantly greater than those of a comparison sample, and he argued that the experients may have dissociative tendencies even though they do not manifest dissociative disorders. He proposed a developmental theory of sensitivity to extraordinary experiences such as NDEs, in which childhood abuse or trauma stimulates the development of a dissociative response style as a means of psychological defense. As dissociating allows the child to "tune out" threatening aspects of the physical and social environment by splitting him- or herself off from the sources of those threats, it also allows the child to "tune into" alternate realities in which, by virtue of the dissociated state, he or she can feel safe regardless of what is happening to the body.

Absorption and Fantasy Proneness

Ring (1992) argued, however, that attunement to alternate realities is not a result of dissociation itself, which only allows it, but of psychological absorption, or the propensity to focus one's attention on imaginative or selected sensory experiences to the exclusion of other events in the external environment (Tellegen & Atkinson, 1974). According to this model, to register and recall alternate realities, one must transcend the sensory world (dissociation) and attend to internal states (absorption). Ring summarized the development of what he called the *encounter-prone* personality, that is, an individual who, coming from a history of childhood abuse and trauma, has developed dissociative tendencies as well as a capacity to become deeply absorbed in alternate realities. Such an individual, Ring argued, would be well accustomed to such unusual states of consciousness by virtue of this kind of psychological conditioning in childhood and would, because of familiarity with these alternate realities, be more likely than others in a near-death state to "flip" into that mode of consciousness and thereby "see" what other persons may not perceive. Ring (1992) concluded that certain persons experience the NDE as "a kind of compensatory gift in return for the wounds they have incurred in growing up" (p. 146). He also noted that childhood abuse and trauma are only one of the routes to the propensity to undergo extraordinary encounters such as NDEs. Some people have an inborn predisposition to these experiences, whereas others may be nurtured through positive means, such as by having imaginative involvement encouraged in childhood, to cultivate sensitivity or nonordinary realities.

Related to Tellegen and Atkinson's (1974) concept of absorption and Ring's (1992) encounter-prone personality is the construct of the fantasy-prone personality. In an intensive interview study of excellent hypnotic subjects, Wilson and Barber (1981, 1983) discovered a trait they labeled *fantasy proneness*, characterized by a strong investment in fantasy life, vivid hallucinatory ability, intense sensory experience, and excellent eidetic memory. They hypothesized that fantasizers' intense involvement in imagination represents the adaptive extreme end of a continuum and a central dimension of hypnotic responsiveness, and they estimated that as much as 4% of the U.S. population comprised a previously unrecognized unitary entity, the "fantasy-prone personality." Wilson and Barber (1983) suggested that fantasizers may be more likely than the rest of the population to report NDEs, as well as other paranormal phenomena such as OBEs, religious visions, apparitions, and psychic abilities. They postulated that fantasy-prone personalities may develop either as a means of coping with childhood trauma or neglect, or as a result of early encouragement of fantasy by significant adults, just as Ring (1992) later hypothesized for the origin of the encounter-prone personality.

In a series of studies investigating fantasy proneness in a sample larger than that of Wilson and Barber (1983), and one including a wider range of fantasy proneness, Lynn and Rhue (1986, 1988) corroborated that fantasizers report more frequent and severe childhood physical punishment and loneliness than do nonfantasizers, and they found that fantasizers outperformed less-fantasy-prone participants on measures of hypnotizability, absorption, vividness of mental imagery, response to waking suggestion, and creativity. They also confirmed Wilson and Barber's observations as to the adaptive nature of fantasy proneness. In Lynn and Rhue's studies, overall, fantasizers showed adequate reality testing, had a rich affective and cognitive life, were in touch with social norms, were cognitively and affectively versatile and well-adjusted, and had many close friends and positive self-concepts, although a subset of fantasizers was more disturbed than the comparison sample. However, their studies raised questions about the discriminability of the constructs of fantasy proneness, imaginative involvement, and absorption and found the association of these traits with hypnotizability to be less robust than did Wilson and Barber. Most significantly, they concluded that, because of the diversity inherent in the fantasy-prone population, it is misleading to think of individuals at the extreme end of the fantasy-proneness continuum as conforming to a unitary personality type. Contrary to Wilson and Barber's observations, Lynn and Rhue's sample of fantasizers did not hallucinate "as real as real," but reported incomplete and imperfect hallucinatory experiences that were not lifelike, stable, or detailed.

Empirical data regarding absorption and fantasy proneness among near-death experients have been suggestive but not compelling. Irwin (1985) documented that OBEs are in fact related to absorption abilities, whereas Council and Greyson (1985) found greater tendencies toward both absorption and fantasy proneness among near-death experients than among comparison groups, and small positive correlations between the "depth" of NDEs and both absorption and fantasy proneness. However, the experients' scores on the measure of fantasy proneness were substantially lower than those of Wilson and Barber's fantasizers. Ring (1992) found that near-death experients and a comparison sample of persons interested in NDEs did not differ in fantasy proneness, although the experients did report a higher incidence of childhood abuse and trauma and greater sensitivity to nonordinary realities in childhood than the comparison group. However, Ring assessed fantasy proneness with a 10-item questionnaire, whereas other investigators have reported that differences between fantasizers and comparison samples may be more apparent when intensive interviews are used to evaluate fantasy proneness (Lynn & Rhue, 1988).

In the context of hypnosis, Barber (1999) recently proposed that there are three types of individuals who may exhibit alterations in behavior and experience: fantasy-prone individuals, those who tend to experience amnesia and other forms of dissociation, and highly motivated and eager individuals. This proposal seems to have cross-cultural validity (Cardeña, 1996) and supports the notion that there are various routes to having unusual experiences.

Posttraumatic Stress Disorder

The differential diagnosis of NDE-related problems includes posttraumatic stress disorder (PTSD), as both conditions may involve distress following exposure to a threat of death or serious injury. Near-death experients, like people with PTSD, may report recurrent, intrusive recollections of the event, and at times a feeling of reliving the experience. Near-death experients who have difficulty coping with their experience and its aftereffects may also report the PTSD symptoms of recurrent distressing dreams of the event, psychological distress, and physiological reactivity to exposure to cues that symbolize the event. In addition to these common intrusive symptoms, some near-death experients also report avoidance symptoms, such as diminished interest in activities, estrangement from others, restricted range of affect, and a sense of a foreshortened future. Occasionally, they may report efforts to avoid reminders of the experience or difficulty recalling part of the experience. Nonetheless, the majority of people who have experienced an NDE do not exhibit the diagnostic criteria for PTSD or other mental pathologies.

Religious or Spiritual Problem

The *Diagnostic and Statistical Manual of Mental Disorders* (4th ed., *DSM–IV*) distinguishes a category of problems labeled "other conditions that may be a focus of clinical attention" (American Psychiatric Association, 1994, pp. 675–686). These conditions may occur in individuals who have no mental disorder, in individuals who have a mental disorder to which the "other condition" is unrelated, or associated with a mental disorder but sufficiently severe by themselves to warrant individual attention. Lukoff, Lu, and Turner (1992) proposed that this category include a diagnosis of *religious or spiritual problem* to offset the tendency of mental health professionals to ignore or pathologize religious and spiritual issues, creating iatrogenic harm; the *DSM–IV* in fact warns against misinterpreting as mental disorders "certain religious practices or beliefs (e.g., hearing or seeing a deceased relative during bereavement)" (American Psychiatric Association, 1994, p. xxiv).

Turner, Lukoff, Barnhouse, and Lu (1995) compared the triggering of religious or spiritual problems by an extremely stressful event, such as an NDE, with uncomplicated bereavement. Just as the diagnosis of a major depressive episode should not be given when depressive symptoms result from a normal reaction to a death, so the characteristic sequelae of an NDE should not be viewed as evidence of a mental disorder, but rather as a normal reaction to a life-threatening stressor. This new category in *DSM–IV* acknowledges that psychological problems of a religious and spiritual nature are not necessarily attributable to a mental disorder or reducible to biological explanation and treatment (Turner et al., 1995).

Whereas Lukoff et al. (1992) had included in their definition of "religious or spiritual problem" two specific examples, mystical experiences and NDEs, the DSM–IV replaced these examples by the less specific phrase "questioning of other spiritual values which may not necessarily be related to an organized church or religious institution" (American Psychiatric Association, 1994, p. 685). Turner et al. (1995) noted that this may involve questioning one's whole way of life, purpose for living, and source for meaning. They argued that scientific research over the past decade has established the NDE as an identifiable psychological phenomenon that, although not attributable to a mental disorder, often precipitates significant intrapsychic and interpersonal difficulties such as anger, depression, and isolation. Regarding NDE-related distress as a religious or spiritual problem may decrease inappropriate diagnoses and interventions and lead to more focused treatment strategies (Greyson, 1997).

Other Psychopathological Phenomena

NDEs bear some resemblance to the symptom of autoscopy, which has been documented in association with a variety of brain lesions. However, NDEs differ from autoscopic phenomena in that the observing self or point of perception is experienced as outside the physical body, from which perspective the individual sees his or her own inactive physical body, in contrast with autoscopy, which involves seeing an active apparitional "double" (Gabbard & Twemlow, 1984).

NDEs also have superficial similarities to psychoactive substance-induced hallucinations, such as sensations of movement through dark tunnels and seeing bright lights, but are more complex than most of the mental imagery induced by drugs, are more often endowed with personal meaning (Bates & Stanley, 1985), and often occur in the absence of psychoactive substances.

Spiritual experiences such as NDEs can be differentiated from at least some brief psychotic disorders by their acute onset following a stressful precipitant and by the experients' good premorbid functioning and positive exploratory attitude toward the experience (Lukoff, 1985). The *DSM–IV* cautions against confusing symptoms of brief psychotic disorder with religious experiences that are not perceived as being pathological (American Psychiatric Association, 1994, p. 303). While schizotypal personality disorder can include cognitive and perceptual distortions, it also involves a pervasive pattern of interpersonal deficits that are not seen in near-death experients (Gabbard & Twemlow, 1984; Irwin, 1985; Locke & Shontz, 1983). Again, the *DSM–IV* warns that religious beliefs can appear schizotypal to uninformed observers (American Psychiatric Association, 1994, p. 643).

A diagnosis of adjustment disorder is not appropriate for cases of NDE-related problems in that it requires emotional or behavioral symptoms in excess of normal reactions to a stressor. The anger, depression, and interpersonal difficulties that may follow an NDE are appropriately considered to be expected responses to a tumultuous situation and should not be regarded as adjustment disorders any more than is normal bereavement (Lukoff et al., 1992). Finally, the occurrence of NDEs at virtually any point in the life cycle from childhood to old age argues against its diagnosis as a phase-of-life problem.

Thus, although near-death and related experiences bear some similarity to some symptoms of mental illness, NDEs and their sequelae are readily distinguished from mental illnesses in their phenomenology, antecedents, and aftereffects. It is plausible then to assume that they may also be distinct in their etiology and response to various treatments. Awareness of the new diagnostic label of religious or spiritual problem can guide the clinician to the relevant diagnostic and treatment literature (Turner et al.,

1995) and minimize or prevent unnecessary suffering as a result of misdiagnosis and inappropriate care (Bowers, 1974; Greyson, 1996; Greyson & Harris, 1987). The *DSM–IV* allows the option to diagnose religious or spiritual problems even when they appear related to a mental disorder, provided they are sufficiently severe to warrant independent clinical attention. Such cases raise questions not only of differential diagnosis of the comorbid conditions but also of the causal relationship between them: that is, whether NDEs may predispose toward certain mental disorders or whether certain mental disorders may predispose toward spiritual problems in near-death experients. Further research is needed to refine diagnostic guidelines, but the lack of definitive differential diagnostic criteria at the present time should not preclude recognizing NDEs as conditions distinct from mental disorders (Greyson, 1997).

CLINICAL ISSUES AND RISKS

The NDE is usually regarded as a positive experience, and when it does lead to distress, most near-death experients gradually adjust on their own, without any help. However, that adjustment often requires them to adopt new values, attitudes, and interests. Family and friends may then find it difficult to understand the experient's new beliefs and behavior. On the one hand, significant others may avoid the experient, who they feel has come under some unwelcomed influence. On the other hand, friends and family influenced by the popular publicity about the positive effects of NDEs may place the experient on a pedestal and expect unrealistic changes. Sometimes, friends expect superhuman patience and forgiveness from the experient or miraculous healing and prophetic powers and may become bitter and reject the experient who does not live up to these unrealistic expectations.

The way a psychotherapist responds to a near-death experient can have a tremendous influence on whether the NDE is accepted and becomes a stimulus for psychospiritual growth or whether it is regarded as a bizarre experience that must not be shared, for fear of being labeled as mentally ill. Despite the prevalence of NDEs and considerable research into their positive aftereffects, little has been written about the psychosocial and psychospiritual problems that often follow NDEs. Although near-death experients sometimes feel distress if the NDE conflicts with their previously held beliefs and attitudes, the emphasis in the popular media on the positive benefits of NDEs may inhibit those who are having problems from seeking help. Sometimes people who have had a totally unexpected NDE may doubt their sanity but are often afraid of rejection or ridicule if they discuss this fear with friends or professionals. Too often, near-death experients do receive negative reactions from professionals when they describe their experiences, which discourages them even further from seeking help in understanding the experience (Hoffman, 1995a, 1995b).

Emotional problems following NDEs include anger and depression at having been "returned," perhaps unwillingly. The experients may have problems fitting the experience into their traditional religious beliefs, values, or lifestyles. Because the experience seems so central to the experients' sense of self and seems to set them apart from other people around them, the experients may come to define themselves exclusively in those terms. Because many of their new attitudes and beliefs are so different from those around them, near-death experients can overcome the worry that they are somehow abnormal by redefining for themselves what is normal. They may feel a sense of distance or separation from people who have not had similar experiences and may fear being ridiculed or rejected by others, sometimes with good reason. Difficulty reconciling the new attitudes and beliefs with the expectations of family and friends can interfere with maintaining old roles and lifestyles that no longer have the same meaning. Near-death experients may find it impossible to communicate to others the meaning and impact of the NDE on their lives. Frequently, having experienced a sense of unconditional love in the NDE, the experient cannot accept afterward the conditions and limitations of human relationships (Greyson, 1996, 1997; Greyson & Harris, 1987). Above and beyond these problems, which all near-death experients may face to one degree or another, people who have had frightening NDEs have additional concerns about why they had that kind of experience and may be troubled by terrifying flashbacks of the experience itself. Additional problems may follow NDEs in young children or in those arising out of a suicide attempt.

Several researchers have noted that the value incongruities between near-death experients and their families lead to a relatively high divorce rate among experients (Bush, 1991), although no study has reported comparison with appropriately matched groups of nonexperients. Although many divorces among nonexperients occur because of arguments over not having enough money, the experients' marital breakdowns seem to take place because they no longer share materialistic values with their spouses (Flynn, 1986). The "social death" that occurs when the familiar personality of a near-death experient changes can be as disruptive to a family as the physical death of that person (Insinger, 1991). Bush (1991) concluded that the price of an NDE "may include long-term depression, broken relationships, disrupted career, feelings of severe alienation, an inability to function in the world, long years of struggling with the keen sense of altered reality" (p. 7). She quoted a divorce rate among experients as high as 75%, although she acknowledged the unreliability of that estimate. She also noted that although the most disabling aftereffects of the NDE seem to affect only a minority of experients, their impact is severe, and effective interventions are hard to find.

TREATMENT OF NDE-RELATED PROBLEMS

Although there have been no controlled outcome studies of therapeutic approaches to NDE-related problems, the following strategies for use in individual psychotherapy were developed by a consensus conference of 32 clinicians who have worked extensively with near-death experients (Greyson, 1996; Greyson & Harris, 1987). It is usually valuable to let patients who have had NDEs verbalize their confusion and distress, even when they seem difficult to put into words. Unlike delirious patients, who may become more agitated if allowed uncontrolled speech, near-death experients usually become more frustrated if told not to talk about their experience. Reflection and clarification of patients' perceptions and emotions are usually more helpful than interpretations, which are often regarded by patients as misinterpretations, and objective information about the frequency and common effects of NDEs often alleviates concern about their implications and consequences, both for patients and for their families.

Regarding the near-death experient as a victim is often countertherapeutic, whereas helping patients appreciate their active role in generating the specific details of their experience may help them resolve problems arising from it. A therapeutic aspect resulting from many NDEs is what Rosen (1976) called *egocide* or *symbolic suicide*, the sacrifice of conflicted parts of the personality that had been a source of suffering for the individual. In such cases, grieving for the loss of those conflicted parts may be appropriate. The induction of controlled alterations in experience through hypnosis or guided imagery and the use of nonverbal media such as art may help patients express conflicts that they deem to be ineffable. A sense of having been "returned" to life for a reason or of having chosen to "return" is a common source of conflict; regrets, ambivalence, and frustration over the "return" should be explored (Greyson, 1996; Greyson & Harris, 1987).

Changes in values, beliefs, and attitudes may require changes in familial interactions, which in turn can lead to secondary problems. A here-and-now focus in therapy may help individuals who have difficulty appreciating temporal constraints after an apparently "timeless" experience. Unlike patients with PTSD, near-death experients rarely want to eliminate intrusive reminders of their experience. More commonly, they request help integrating the experience and its lessons into their daily lives.

With an experience as foreign to mundane life as the NDE, exploring problems and solutions with fellow experients can reduce the sense of bizarreness associated with the phenomenon. Some may find it easier to explore issues in a psychotherapy group with patients who have had NDEs or similar experiences than with a single therapist who, even if he or she has had an NDE, may legitimately be unwilling to share it with patients to avoid influencing their recollections and interpretations. Some patients will benefit from referral to the near-death experient support groups that exist in many cities. (A list of support groups is available from the International Association for Near-Death Studies, P. O. Box 502, East Windsor Hill, CT 06028–0502.) Talking with other near-death experients in such a setting can help normalize the experience, although identifying and associating only with persons who have shared similar experiences may reinforce the experient's sense of alienation from nonexperients.

There is no evidence that psychotropic medications can help with problems following an NDE, unless patients meet criteria for comorbid depressive disorder or PTSD (Greyson, 1997). In fact, some writers have cautioned against medicating individuals in the midst of spontaneous spiritual awakening, as that may freeze the process in mid-course and prevent any further reparative developments (Grof, 1975; Wilber, 1984). As an alternative to medication, consciously engaging the reparative process by taking up a contemplative discipline such as meditation or prayer may help the individual in spiritual crisis. However, if a spiritual awakening involves psychoticlike features, contemplative disciplines, which require a sturdier ego than psychotic or borderline individuals possess, are contraindicated. Not only is meditation unhelpful for such patients, it can also dismantle what little structure they have, even though they are often drawn to meditation as a rationalization for their "nonego" states (Engler, 1983; Wilber, 1984). Patients should be helped to integrate spiritual practice into daily life and work, rather than to withdraw, because the path of ascetic withdrawal confuses suppression of earthly life with transcendence of earthly life (Wilber, 1984).

Some form of psychosocial rehabilitation may be helpful when experients have difficulty adapting to the daily demands of mundane life that no longer seem relevant to them but are still necessary. At times, the near-death experient may need to alter external reality to reflect the internal changes brought about by the experience. Individuals who find old careers or relationships irreconcilable with new attitudes and values may need counseling to address the dissolution of the previous lifestyle or the reconstruction of a new, compatible one. Couples or family therapy may be indicated when changes in the experient demand changes in close relationships. Greyson (1997) described three clinical cases in which career changes based on NDE-related attitude shifts were critical therapeutic strategies.

Psychological Hypotheses

Since Pfister's (1930) original interpretation of NDEs as a defense against the threat of death, several psychological hypotheses have been proposed to explain them and their consistent features (Greyson, 1983c). The most comprehensive psychodynamic models of NDEs have been based on the concepts of dissociation, absorption, and fantasy proneness, described earlier. As noted, there is indirect empirical support for these models, although direct evidence has been difficult to obtain.

Along the lines of Pfister's (1930) explanation, the expectancy model suggests that NDEs are products of imagination, constructed from one's personal and cultural expectations, to protect oneself from facing the threat of death. Empirical data do not support this hypothesis. Although there are some cross-cultural variations in NDE content, individuals often report experiences that conflict with their specific religious and personal expectations of death (Abramovitch, 1988; Ring, 1984). Furthermore, people who had never heard or read of NDEs describe the same kinds of experiences as do people who are quite familiar with the phenomenon, and the knowledge individuals had about NDEs previously does not seem to influence the details of their own experiences (Greyson, 1991; Greyson & Stevenson, 1980; Ring, 1980; Sabom, 1982). Another problem for the expectancy model of NDEs is that children too young to have received substantial cultural and religious conditioning about death report the same kinds of events as do adults. There are also reports of NDEs occurring before the child could have acquired any language skills, but described by the child years later (Herzog & Herrin, 1985; Serdahely & Walker, 1990). Of course, retrospective narratives by adults of their childhood NDEs may be subject to the same cultural influences as NDEs of adults, but several researchers have now published collections of NDEs described by children who are still quite young (Bush, 1983; Gabbard & Twemlow, 1984; Morse et al., 1986). Serdahely (1991) compared retrospective accounts of childhood NDEs with contemporary accounts given by children and found no evidence that the retrospective accounts were embellished or distorted.

The view of NDEs as recollections of the birth experience, popularized by Sagan (1979), has been plausibly refuted both by theoretical argument and by empirical evidence. Becker (1982) summarized the preponderance of evidence that newborns lack the visual acuity, spatial stability of visual images, mental alertness, and cortical coding capacity to register memories of the birth experience. He also described the lack of meaningful correspondence between the birth experience and important features of NDEs. Blackmore (1983) surveyed reports of OBEs given by persons born by cesarean section and those born by normal vaginal delivery: Claims of such experiences and of passing through a tunnel to another realm were equally common in both groups, contradicting the prediction of the birth-memory model that such experiences should be rare following cesarean births. Grof (1975) avoided that prediction, as well as the reductionistic implications of a literal birth-memory model, by conceptualizing NDEs as representations of a Jungian archetype of a birth experience rather than as memories of actual birth events. Grosso (1983) described what he called "the archetype of death and enlightenment" (p. 15), a psychic template of rebirth experience that he saw reflected in NDEs as well as in dreams, mythology, ancient mystery rites, and psychedelic experiences. Although the framework espoused by Grof and Grosso places NDEs within a larger context, its proponents have not described how it leads either to testable hypotheses or to therapeutic interventions.

Hypoxia Hypothesis

A common assumption has been that anoxia or hypoxia, as a common final pathway to brain death, must be implicated in NDEs. However, the only published report in which an investigator has been able to measure blood levels of oxygen and carbon dioxide during NDEs found no effects of either anoxia or hypercapnia on the experience (Sabom, 1982). Whinnery (1997) developed a hypoxia model of NDEs based on the brief periods of unconsciousness induced in fighter pilots by rapid acceleration, which reduces blood flow to the head. He argued that many features of NDEs are consistent with these hypoxic unconsciousness episodes, which are characterized by incapacitation, myoclonic convulsions, memory alterations, and visual effects. Whinnery proposed that as distal circulation within the retina is compromised, the visual field is contracted concentrically, leading to tunnel vision and eventually to complete loss of vision, or blackout. The incorporation of tunnel vision into a "dreamlet" (brief, fragmented images pilots report when they lose consciousness as a result of high acceleration) might be interpreted as passing through a tunnel into bright light. Myoclonic jerks are also frequently incorporated into the dreamlets as purposeful, rhythmic activity of the limbs. Memory, which is usually lost during acceleration-induced unconsciousness, usually returns before sensory awareness; thus, physiological input such as myoclonic convulsions could also be incorporated into memories of the dreamlets. Additional symptoms of acceleration-induced unconsciousness include tingling in extremities and around the mouth, confusion and disorientation upon awakening, and periawakening paralysis. A sense of floating, autoscopy, automatic movement, paralysis, dissociation, and pleasurable sensations have also been reported. Although not common, OBEs are reported with increasingly severe ischemic insults. The loss of motor output to the peripheral nervous system produces a sensation of being out of or disconnected from the body.

The major features that acceleration-induced loss of consciousness shares with NDEs are tunnel vision and bright lights, floating sensations, automatic movement, OBEs, not wanting to be disturbed, paralysis, vivid dreamlets of beautiful places that frequently include family members and close friends, pleasurable sensations, euphoria, and some pleasurable memories. No life review or panoramic memory has been reported in acceleration-induced loss of consciousness. It would be odd if the symptoms of loss of consciousness were not associated with NDEs. Whinnery cautioned that his model does not explain all near-death phenomena but may be used to differentiate those components of the phenomena that occur as a result of unconsciousness from those that are beyond the scope of the hypoxic experience and are unique to the NDE.

Other Physiological Hypotheses

Because near-death experients report events that others around them cannot see or experience, it is plausible to hypothesize that NDEs are elaborate hallucinations produced either by medications given to dying patients or by metabolic disturbances or brain malfunctions as a person approaches death. However, many NDEs are recounted by individuals who had no metabolic or organic malfunctions that might have caused hallucinations. Furthermore, organic brain malfunctions generally produce clouded thinking, irritability, fear, belligerence, and idiosyncratic visions, quite unlike the exceptionally clear thinking, peacefulness, calmness, and predictable content that typifies the NDE. Visions in patients with delirium are generally of living persons, whereas those of patients with a clear sensorium as they approached death are almost invariably of deceased persons (Osis & Haraldsson, 1977). Patients who have experienced both hallucinations and NDEs generally discount the superficial similarities between the two and describe the world of the NDE as being "more real" than ordinary reality which, in turn, is described as "more real" than the world of waking hallucinations. Surveys have documented that patients who are febrile, anoxic, or given drugs when near death report fewer NDEs and less elaborate experiences than do patients who remain drug-free and are neither febrile nor anoxic (Osis & Haraldsson, 1977; Ring, 1980; Sabom, 1982). Such findings suggest either that drug- or metabolically induced delirium, rather than causing NDEs, in fact inhibits them from occurring or that delirious patients tend not to recall their experiences upon recovery.

Several neurobiological models have been proposed to explain the NDE, invoking the role of endorphins or other endogenous opioid peptides (Carr, 1982; Saavedra-Aguilar & Gómez-Jeria, 1989), serotonin (Morse, Venecia, & Milstein, 1989), glutamate or endopsychosins acting on N-methyl-D-aspartate (NMDA)-phencyclidine receptors (Jansen, 1997a, 1997b), and to an interaction between muscarinic, NMDA, adrenocorticotropic hormone, and enkephalin systems (Persinger, 1994). NDEs have been hypothetically localized in the limbic lobe (Saavedra-Aguilar & Gómez-Jeria, 1989), primarily the hippocampus (Carr, 1982; Jourdan, 1994); in a locus along the Sylvian fissure on the right temporal lobe (Morse et al., 1989); and in Reissner's fiber in the central canal of the spinal cord (Wile, 1994). At this point, such models are speculative and have not been tested.

Persinger (1994) proposed a vectorial hemisphericity hypothesis to explain mystic experiences in terms of intrusion of the right hemispheric equivalent of the sense of self into left hemispheric awareness. He claimed (Persinger, 1989) that major components of NDEs, including OBEs, floating sensations, feeling pulled toward a light, hearing strange music, and having profound meaning, can be provoked experimentally by inducing electrical currents in the temporal region through exogenous spike-and-wave magnetic field sources. He also noted (Persinger, 1994) that the most common experiences reported by his participants were dizziness and tingling, which are not characteristic near-death phenomena, and that these induced experiences were fragmented and variable, unlike the integrated and temporally focused sensations of NDEs. Participants in his experimental protocol were able to converse with the experimenter and to report their sensations as they occurred. Unlike near-death experients, they remained subjectively in the mundane reality and did not experience a subjective shift to a supramundane world during the experience.

A comprehensive neurobiological model of NDEs was proposed by Saavedra-Aguilar and Gómez-Jeria (1989), invoking temporal-lobe dysfunction, hypoxia, psychological stress, and neurotransmitter changes, as modulated by the individual's memory and language systems. They proposed that following a traumatic event, brain stress leads to release of endogenous neuropeptides, neurotransmitters, or both, producing analgesia, euphoria, and detachment, while oxygen tension decreases in the brain, primarily in limbic structures. Those two effects combine to excite epileptiform discharges in the hippocampus and amygdala, producing complex visual hallucinations and a life review. After-discharges propagating through the limbic connections to other brain structures produce further hallucinations and a sensation of a brilliant light. Following recovery, the linguistic system reconstructs out of these sensations an experience consistent with the individual's cultural beliefs. Like other physiological models of NDEs, this model assumes physical trauma and hypoxia and thus does not explain those NDEs that occur in the absence of physiological injury. Furthermore, it ascribes to temporal-lobe malfunction key features of NDEs that have not in fact been reported either in clinical seizures or in electrical stimulation of those brain structures, such as feelings of peace or bliss and sensations of being out of the body (Rodin, 1989). This model is based on numerous unsupported assumptions and speculations derived from neurochemical research with nonhuman animals, and its key elements—"brain stress" and unspecified neurotransmitters and neuroanatomical sites—are vague. That is not to say that the model is incorrect, rather that its neurophysiology is too ambiguous; it is a plausible model, but not a testable one.

Jansen (1997a) proposed that NDEs are produced by blockade of NMDA receptors in the brain. He argued that some conditions that precipitate NDEs, such as hypoxia, release a flood of the excitatory neurotransmitter glutamate, which kills neurons by overactivating NMDA receptors. This neurotoxicity can be blocked if the NMDA receptors are bound by the dissociative anesthetic ketamine, whose psychoactive properties can induce NDE-like alterations of consciousness. Jansen speculated that, in individuals not under the influence of ketamine, unidentified neuroprotective "endopsychosins" bind to the NMDA receptors to prevent this neurotoxicity, and that these endopsychosins also alter consciousness just as ketamine does. Jansen argued that ketamine can induce experiences of tunnels, lights, and sensations of telepathic communication with what appear to be mystical entities, and he proposed that his NMDA receptor model could be a final common pathway for near-death phenomena precipitated by depersonalization, regression in the service of the ego, reactivation of birth memories, sensory deprivation, temporal-lobe epilepsy, endorphin release, and hypoxia.

Although Jansen's (1997a) ketamine model of NDEs is appealing, it hinges on speculation about the existence of "endopsychosins" as yet unidentified. Unlike NDEs, ketamine experiences are frequently fearful (Strassman, 1997) and rarely regarded by experients as "real" (Fenwick, 1997). Furthermore, the clarity present during NDEs and clear memory for them afterward are inconsistent with a model based on compromised cerebral function, as is the fact that NDEs may occur in the absence of upset cerebral physiology.

Jourdan (1994) proposed a similar model implicating blockade of hippocampal NMDA receptors by endopsychosins, adding that alteration of the hippocampal theta rhythm during meditative states could produce similar physiological events to NDEs. He hypothesized that NMDA receptor blockade in the hippocampus prevents "long-term potentiation," a longlasting enhancement of hippocampal synaptic efficacy secondary to repeated neural input, which would close access to sensory information, a common stimulus to mystical experience.

To the extent that these psychological and physiological hypotheses succeed in explaining NDEs, they do so by focusing selectively on certain features of the experience and by declaring other features they do not explain to be peripheral to the phenomenon. No theory has yet been proposed that can account satisfactorily for all of the common elements of NDEs. There is no logical reason, however, to demand that one comprehensive theory explain the entire phenomenon. It may well be that the out-of-body component of NDEs, for example, is best understood as a dissociative defense, whereas the sense of peace and well-being is a function of endorphins, and the life review is related to NMDA receptor blockade.

Blackmore (1993) proposed such a multifaceted model of NDEs in which various components of the experience were explained by different psychological or physiological mechanisms. She attributed noises heard by near-death experients either to stimulation of the cochlea or to the temporal lobe by cerebral anoxia; the tunnel and the light to neuronal disinhibition in the visual cortex, again activated by anoxia; feelings of peace and well-being to the release of endorphins; and frightening experiences to morphine antagonists. Blackmore ascribed the sense of being out of the body to the brain's retrospective reconstruction of a plausible reality after the normal body image is broken down by lack of sensory input, and the life review to temporal-limbic seizures induced by endorphins and to hippocampal stimulation by certain neurotransmitters.

Although many of these neurophysiological mechanisms are plausible, none have been demonstrated to occur in a near-death state, and some, such as those based on cerebral anoxia, have been contradicted by empirical data. Likewise, in denying the possibility that anything can separate from the physical body at death and survive, Blackmore (1993) was required also to discount empirical data on the paranormal aspects of NDEs that her model does not accommodate (e.g., pp. 169, 262). Unlike some other theoreticians who ignore the paranormal facet of the experience, Blackmore acknowledged the challenge it poses for psychological and physiological models, conceding that "If . . . truly convincing paranormal events are documented then certainly the theory I have proposed will have to be overthrown" (p. 262).

Ultimately, even when these physiological models for the NDE have some supporting data, they leave us in a philosophically ambiguous situation: Correlating a brain state with an experience does not necessarily imply that brain states cause the experience; the brain state may alternatively allow access to or simply reflect the experience. In fact, this latter possibility has been defended by some researchers who have championed neurophysiological studies of NDEs. Persinger (1989, pp. 237–238) wrote that transient changes in the brain during an NDE might allow perception of paranormal information; Jansen (1997b, p. 94) described his postulated NMDA receptor changes as creating "a door to a place we cannot normally get to; it is definitely not evidence that such a place does not exist"; and Jourdan (1994, p. 198) wrote that, despite his proposal of a neurochemical model of NDEs, the evidence for paranormal aspects of the NDE "rules out any hypothesis that these experiences are hallucinations or purely neurological phenomena." As Strassman (1997, p. 38) expressed it, "understanding how the television set works does not yield any information regarding from where the images and sounds arise."

This dichotomy between brain states as the origin of NDEs and brain states as the mediator of NDEs has been illustrated by two contrasting analogies. In one model, Siegel (1980, pp. 926–927) applied Jackson's (1931) perceptual-release theory of hallucinations to NDEs: If awareness persists while sensory input is reduced, images originating in the brain are perceived as if they originated from the senses. In Siegel's analogy, a person looks out a window at a garden. In the daylight, the person sees the garden and not the interior of the room. As dusk approaches, however, the images of objects in the illuminated room are dimly reflected in the window, and the observer can focus either on the garden outside or on the reflection of the room's interior. As night falls, the interior of the illuminated room is vividly reflected in the window and appears to be outside. Ring (1997, p. 118) offered an alternative model of NDEs based on James's (1902/1958, pp. 378–379) concept of different forms of consciousness: As sensory input is reduced, another reality, usually masked by sensory input, is revealed. In Ring's counteranalogy, a person looking up at the sky in the daylight sees only the bright sun; only at night, when sunlight is absent, can the observer see the stars and other heavenly bodies.

Mind–Body Separation and Afterlife Hypothesis

The explanatory hypothesis endorsed by most near-death experients is that during the NDE some part of them separated from their physical bodies and experienced an introduction to the afterlife. While research into NDEs has proliferated in recent years, with rare exceptions, investigators have ignored the question of survival of consciousness beyond death of the body, despite the fact that popular interest in NDEs seems largely due to their implication that death is a transition rather than an end. Some of the cross-cultural similarities among NDEs, however, are difficult to explain in terms of universal psychological or physiological processes. For example, experients often report that during the NDEs they seemed to view their bodies as if from a different point in space. Several researchers have collected cases in which individuals were later able to describe with uncanny accuracy what was going on around them while they were ostensibly unconscious (Hampe, 1979; Kübler-Ross, cited in Ebon, 1977; Moody, 1977; Sabom, 1982). Some of those descriptions may be attributable to high base-rate guesses about events likely to have occurred or to retrospective reconstruction of a scenario based on objects and events glimpsed prior to or after the period of unconsciousness. However, when Sabom (1982) asked resuscitated patients to describe what they thought their resuscitation scenarios might have looked like, some near-death experients were able to relate accurate details of idiosyncratic and unexpected events during their resuscitations, but comparable patients who did not report NDEs were unable to do so. Some experients report additionally that, while ostensibly "out of the body," they became aware of events they could not have perceived normally even if they had been conscious, events occurring at a distance outside the range of their sense organs. Ring and Lawrence (1993) published details of three cases for which they obtained independent corroboration of unconscious patients' accurate out-of-body perceptions from physicians and nurses present during the NDEs. Some of those accurate perceptions included highly unlikely objects, such as the plaid shoelaces of a nurse who was present only during the patient's resuscitation and not before or after, and unexpected objects in locations to which the patient did not have access. Ring and Cooper (1997, 1999) reported 31 cases of blind individuals, some blind from birth, who experienced accurate visual perceptions of objects and events during their NDEs.

Sabom (1998) described in great detail the anomalous NDE of a woman with a giant basilar artery aneurysm, the rupture of which would be immediately fatal. Because the size and location of the aneurysm precluded its safe removal by standard neurosurgical techniques, she was referred for hypothermic cardiac arrest, a procedure during which her body temperature was lowered to 60°F, her heartbeat and breathing stopped, her brain waves flattened, and the blood drained from her head. During this procedure, she met all the accepted criteria for brain death: Her electroencephalogram (EEG) was totally flat, indicating no cerebral electrical activity; auditory-evoked potentials ceased, indicating cessation of brainstem function; and blood was completely drained from the brain, effecting absence of any brain function. Unlike most NDE accounts, in which there is little documentation of the experient's physiological state, this case provided continuous documentation of blood pressure, cardiac output, heart rate and rhythm, oxygenation of the blood, core body and brain temperatures, cerebral cortical brain activity, and evoked potentials in the brainstem.

Repairing this type of aneurysm requires that the blood flow through the cerebral arteries be diverted for the duration of the procedure, generally around 45 minutes. The brain at normal body temperature cannot withstand the disruption of its oxygen supply for more than a few minutes. However, when patients' bodies are cooled to 60°F, metabolic demands are reduced and most can tolerate complete cessation of cerebral blood flow for at least 45 minutes (Weiss et al., 1998). This extraordinary neurosurgical procedure involves diverting the body's blood supply to a cardiopulmonary bypass machine so that the blood can be completely drained from the brain and cooled to 60°F before being returned to the body. The following is a brief description of Sabom's patient's experience.

The patient's eyes were taped shut and molded speakers were inserted into her ears to emit 100-decibel clicks and block out any other auditory stimulation. After she was fully anesthetized, the neurosurgeon opened her scalp, cut the skull open with a special pneumatic saw, and opened the dura mater to expose the brain. Meanwhile, a cardiac surgeon located the femoral vessels in the patient's groin for the cardiopulmonary bypass but found the artery too small and had to switch to the opposite leg, in which blood was diverted from the artery into the bypass machine, where it was chilled and then returned to her vein. When her body temperature had fallen 25°, she went into ventricular fibrillation and her heart stopped, after which her brain waves flattened. Twenty minutes later, her body temperature now 60°F, the clicks from her ear speakers stopped eliciting a response from the brainstem, indicating total shutdown of her entire brain. At that point, the head of the operating table was tilted up, the cardiopulmonary bypass machine was turned off, and the blood was drained out of her body, collapsing the aneurysm sac so that it could safely be clipped and excised. Once the aneurysm was repaired, the bypass machine was turned on again, and warmed blood was infused back into her body, which was followed by return of the brainstem-evoked potentials and then electrical activity on the EEG. As that was happening, however, her heart went back into ventricular fibrillation, and she had to be shocked twice to restore a regular heart rhythm.

The patient reported subsequently that she was awakened out of anesthesia by the sound of the pneumatic saw, felt herself pulled out of the top of her head, and viewed the operating room from above the neurosurgeon's shoulder. She accurately described the 20 doctors, nurses, and technicians in the room, most of whom she had never met, and several peculiar details of the unique pneumatic saw used to cut open her skull, the cardiac surgeon's surprise at finding the initial femoral artery too small to use, and the music playing in the operating room when she returned to her body but was still unconscious. She reported that after her heart had stopped and the blood was drained from her body, she went through a tunnel into a brilliant light, where she met many people, including several deceased relatives, who warned her that if she did not turn back she would not survive the operation. Sabom (1998) noted that while this woman was dead, as defined by silent EEG, absence of brainstem response, and lack of blood in the brain, she had the deepest NDE of any patient in his study; her NDE scored 27 points on the NDE Scale, almost 2 standard deviations above the mean for near-death experients.

The meticulous monitoring of this patient allows common physiological explanatory hypotheses to be addressed. This case cannot be explained by temporal-lobe seizure activity, because brain waves were continuously monitored and showed no such activity. It cannot be explained by reconstruction based on overheard conversations during the operation, because the molded speakers in her ears blocked out any possible hearing, and her brainstem responses showed absolutely no response to auditory stimulation. It cannot be explained by reconstruction based on observations before and after she was anesthetized, because she accurately described people, equipment, and events that were not observable to her either before or after the procedure.

Individuals who have these veridical out-of-body perceptions usually claim that their mental processes were remarkably clear when they seemed to be separated from their physical bodies, and become convinced by this experience that they will survive the death of their bodies. However, because near-death experients in fact are still alive, they have not existed independently of their physical bodies; even though consciousness may seem to be detached from the body, it may still remain dependent on it for continued existence (Ducasse, 1961). Thus, although veridical extrasensory experiences or OBEs near death may bear on the relationship between the mind and the body while it is alive, they do not necessarily tell us anything about postmortem conditions. However, if minds are capable of functioning outside the body while it is alive, then it is conceivable that they are capable of functioning after the body dies (Osis & Mitchell, 1977).

Some people who approach death and recover report that, during the time they seemed to be dying, they met deceased relatives and friends. Some of these cases may be hallucinatory reflections of the dying individual's expectations or may represent defensive attempts to reduce fear of impending death by imagining reunion with familiar persons. This explanation is less plausible for children, who have not acquired a concept of death as permanent and who would more naturally hallucinate their living parents or other protectors in times of stress. In fact, however, children virtually never see their living parents during NDEs (Kübler-Ross, cited in Badham & Badham, 1982). In some cases, child near-death experients purportedly describe meeting persons, whom they did not know, in sufficient detail to allow their parents to recognize those persons as deceased relatives, or the child may later identify the person from the NDE in a family portrait he or she had never seen before (Badham & Badham, 1982).

Another type of near-death vision that may provide evidence for survival is the so-called "Peak in Darien" type (Cobbe, 1882), in which experients on their deathbeds see a recently deceased person of whose death they had no knowledge, excluding the possibility that the vision was a hallucination related to the experients' expectations. Such cases have been reported by several investigators (Badham & Badham, 1982; Barrett, 1926; Callanan & Kelley, 1993; Hyslop, 1908; Kübler-Ross, 1983; Moody, 1975; Moody & Perry, 1988; Ring, 1980; Sabom, 1982; Spraggett, 1974). As Blackmore (1993) acknowledged, these aspects of NDEs present us with data that cannot be accounted for by physiological or psychological variables or by cultural or religious expectations. Although these data are not compelling proof of survival, they provide convergent evidence that, when combined with data from other sources, may be considered suggestive of it.

METHODOLOGICAL ISSUES

A basic methodological problem in near-death research has been lack of consensus among researchers as to the definition of the phenomenon. Various investigators have used the term *near-death experience* to refer to any experience of clinically dead persons who return to life, any experiences undergone by individuals who are judged to be near death, and any similar experience that leads to personal transformation whether or not the individual was near death when it occurred (Smith, 1991). In some instances, the term has been used so broadly as to include any close brush with death, whether or not the survivor can recall any experience associated with it. The lack of consensus on a definition of NDE has made it difficult to compare research findings of different investigators and has hampered the precision and credibility of near-death research. Although most investigators seem to have in mind comparable definitions of the NDE, few have specified criteria for identifying a case as an NDE. Likewise, criteria for coming "close to death" have been inconsistent among studies, so that differences in experience based on precise proximity to death or cause of the near-death event may have been obscured.

Beyond some criteria for identifying whether an NDE has occurred, there are no universally accepted measures of the depth or intensity of the experience. Rating scales such as Ring's (1980) Weighted Core Experience Index and Greyson's (1983b) NDE Scale are broad-based, not only because the NDE has numerous features but also because none of those features have been definitively established as defining the NDE. Such broad-based scales are useful in comparing individuals with very different experiences, with the assumption that some underlying core experience is common to them all. However, there are problems with summing characteristic elements to achieve a numerical score of "depth." First, the elements might not be equally representative of depth; some features may be seen only in extreme cases and may therefore be good measures of intensity, whereas others may be seen in both extreme and mild cases. For example, encounters with deceased persons are reported only rarely in NDEs and thus may be sensitive indicators of depth, whereas feelings of peace are reported by the large majority of near-death experients and thus are not sensitive indicators of depth. Second, each item on the scale may not be equally related to the phenomenon being measured. Some features, such as the life review, are unusual outside of the NDE and thus are specific indicators of an NDE, whereas other items, such as time distortion or the tunnel phenomenon, are common to other phenomena (e.g., Cardeña, 1996) and thus are not specific indicators of an NDE. Third, specific items may have different sensitivities and specificities in different populations, so that features that may be good indicators of depth in one group of people may not be good indicators of depth in another group. For example, persons who have given considerable thought to their imminent death or even planned it are less likely to report a life review in the NDE than persons who come close to death unexpectedly (Greyson, 1985).

Research into the etiology of NDEs remains hampered by the difficulty of obtaining direct evidence bearing on the plausible hypotheses, in part due to the unpredictable occurrence of the experience. Psychological hypotheses can be tested indirectly by examining personality traits and cognitive styles of experients; but no matter how detailed, such psychological profiles cannot reveal what defenses may have operated at the time of the experience. The neurophysiological hypotheses that have been proposed so far cannot be tested in terms of the current methodological sophistication. They do, however, offer the hope of one day bridging the gap between mystical experience and physiological events. While correlating NDEs with specific brain structures or neurotransmitters would not necessarily tell us what causes NDEs, it would potentially open up new tools and techniques for investigating the mechanisms and aftereffects of these experiences. While it is debatable whether direct evidence of postmortem survival is even logically possible, investigation of near-death experients' mental functioning during ostensible unconsciousness can provide indirect evidence of the separability of "mind" and "body."

Studies of the purportedly accurate out-of-body vision that has sometimes been reported by near-death experients have been compromised by their reliance on random observations of experients while allegedly out of their bodies, which may be difficult to verify or to assess retrospectively. There have been at least two unsuccessful attempts to correct that deficiency by placing unusual "targets" in locations likely to be seen by persons having NDEs. In the first, Holden and Joesten (1990) placed visual stimuli in the corners of hospital rooms so as to be visible only by looking down from the ceiling. Cardboard "targets" differing in color and content were randomly selected and placed blindly on specially constructed holders in the corner of rooms in the emergency department, the coronary care unit, and the intensive care unit at a general hospital. Patients who underwent cardiac arrest in any of the targeted rooms were interviewed about their experiences, both with open-ended questions and with specific questions about the target card. After 1 year, only one resuscitation was reported to have occurred in any of the targeted rooms, and that patient did not speak English well enough to participate in the interview. Subsequent review of the study protocol suggested that the vast majority of cardiac arrests in the hospital did not occur in the targeted rooms, and that most patients in monitored beds had their potential cardiac arrests anticipated and prevented.

In the second attempt, Lawrence (Madelaine Lawrence, personal communication, May 12, 1995) used as a target a light-emitting diode display that was programmed by someone outside the hospital to display a different nonsense phrase each day. This target was placed near the ceiling, facing upward, in the electrophysiology clinic at a teaching hospital. In that unpublished study, no patient reported an NDE during a 6-month period, after which Lawrence's position as director of nursing research was eliminated for fiscal reasons, and the study was terminated. Despite the researchers' original intentions, the two studies failed to secure NDE reports, so the original hypotheses could not be tested.

The most promising aspect of NDEs for future research is their role in personal transformation, as this is certainly the most easily measured and, arguably, the most important feature of the experience. However, many of the studies conducted so far have been limited by the unrepresentative nature of their participant populations, the lack of a suitable comparison group, and the lack of a structured interview protocol and standardized, objective scales.

Many researchers have relied on fairly small participant samples, and even those larger samples that have been studied are rarely unbiased or intact cohorts. Some investigators have relied on experients who responded voluntarily to research announcements in newspapers or newsletters of various organizations and who may differ in unknown ways from experients who chose not to respond. Other researchers have relied on survivors referred to them by medical personnel, who may have been selective in the type of survivor they recalled or chose to refer. Some of the studies that surveyed entire cohorts of survivors have had high rates of refusal to participate, in one case, 80%, which may have left a biased respondent sample. Some researchers, in an effort to enlarge their samples, have retrospectively surveyed persons who had come close to death many years ago. That strategy may have introduced biases resulting from memory distortion over time or from differential survival rates among persons with different types of experience (Greyson, 1998).

An additional problem is what Rosenthal (1979) called the *file-drawer problem*, the suspicion that studies that are published are a biased sample of the studies that are actually conducted. In a field as small as near-death research, if only a few studies are relegated to the file drawer rather than submitted for publication, the resulting picture of NDEs may be distorted. It is plausible that those studies that found more elaborate NDEs, or more sensational aftereffects, may have been more likely to be submitted for publication than studies with less dramatic findings.

Because many near-death experients are reluctant to discuss their experiences, some researchers have gone to great lengths to appease their fears, sometimes compromising scientific protocol and objective instruments to foster rapport with participants. In some cases, researchers' personal involvement with participants and casual study protocols may have influenced the participants' reports in unknown ways.

A further problem in some near-death research has been the lack of appropriate comparison samples with which to contrast the apparent aftereffects of NDEs. Because coming close to death in itself, even without an NDE, may plausibly produce profound changes in attitudes and behavior, it is important to include such persons in studies of NDE aftereffects for purposes of comparison. In addition, the quality of near-death outcome research would be enhanced by the use of objective measurements and the corroboration of apparent aftereffects by independent witnesses to complement the first-hand reports of the experients themselves.

CONCLUSION

Transcendental or mystical NDEs have occurred throughout history in many diverse cultures and continue to be reported today by a number of patients who come close to death. Although cultural expectations and parameters of the close brush with death may influence the content of some NDEs, there is a core phenomenon that has been invariant through the centuries and around the globe. Controversy persists over whether that invariance is a reflection of universal psychological defenses, specieswide neurophysiological imperatives, or actual experience of a transcendent or mystical domain. Research into these alternative explanations has been hampered by the spontaneous and unpredictable occurrence of NDEs, and has provided indirect evidence supporting all three paradigms of NDE etiology (i.e., psychological, neurophysiological, and transcendent), but no direct evidence so far for any of them. Whereas much of the public's fascination with NDEs resides in their implication that humans can survive the death of the body, their significance to the experients themselves and to health care professionals rests largely on the aftereffects of NDEs on the individuals' attitudes, beliefs, and values and on their power to effect profound personal transformation.

REFERENCES

Abramovitch, H. (1988). An Israeli account of a near-death experience: A case study of cultural dissonance. *Journal of Near-Death Studies*, 6, 175–184.

American Psychiatric Association. (1994). *Diagnostic and statistical manual of mental disorders* (4th ed.). Washington, DC: Author.

Badham, P., & Badham, L. (1982). *Immortality or extinction?* Totowa, NJ: Barnes & Noble.

Barber, T. X. (1999). A comprehensive three-dimensional theory of hypnosis. In I. Kirsch, A. Capafons, E. Cardeña, & S. Amigó (Eds.), *Clinical hypnosis and self-regulation therapy: A cognitive–behavioral perspective* (pp. 3–48). Washington, DC: American Psychological Association.

Barrett, W. (1926). *Death-bed visions*. London: Methuen.

Bates, B. C., & Stanley, A. (1985). The epidemiology and differential diagnosis of near-death experience. *American Journal of Orthopsychiatry, 55,* 542–549.

Bauer, M. (1985). Near-death experiences and attitude change. *Anabiosis: The Journal of Near-Death Studies, 5,* 39–47.

Becker, C. B. (1982). The failure of Saganomics: Why birth models cannot explain near-death phenomena. *Anabiosis: The Journal of Near-Death Studies, 2,* 102–109.

Blackmore, S. (1983). Birth and the OBE: An unhelpful analogy. *Journal of the American Society for Psychical Research, 77,* 229–238.

Blackmore, S. (1993). *Dying to live: Near-death experiences*. Buffalo, NY: Prometheus.

Bowers, M. (1974). *Retreat from sanity: The structure of emerging psychosis*. New York: Human Sciences Press.

Bush, N. E. (1983). The near-death experience in children: Shades of the prison-house reopening. *Anabiosis: The Journal of Near-Death Studies, 3,* 177–193.

Bush, N. E. (1991). Is ten years a life review? *Journal of Near-Death Studies, 10,* 5–9.

Callanan, M., & Kelley, P. (1993). *Final gifts: Understanding the special needs, awareness, and communications of the dying*. New York: Poseidon.

Cardeña, E. (1994). The domain of dissociation. In S. J. Lynn & J. W. Rhue (Eds.), *Dissociation: Clinical, theoretical, and research perspectives* (pp. 15–31). New York: Guilford Press.

Cardeña, E. (1996). "Just floating in the sky": A comparison of shamanic and hypnotic phenomenology. In R. Quekelbherge & D. Eigner (Eds.), *6th jahrbuch für transkulturelle medizin und psychotherapie* [6th yearbook of cross-cultural medicine and psychotherapy] (pp. 367–380). Berlin: Verlag für Wissenschaft und Bildung.

Carr, D. (1982). Pathophysiology of stress-induced limbic lobe dysfunction: A hypothesis for NDEs. *Anabiosis: The Journal of Near-Death Studies, 2,* 75–89.

Cobbe, F. P. (1882). *Peak in Darien: With some enquiries touching concerns of the soul and body*. London: Williams & Norgate.

Council, J. R., & Greyson, B. (1985, August). *Near-death experiences and the "fantasy-prone" personality: Preliminary findings*. Paper presented at the 93rd Annual Convention of the American Psychological Association, Los Angeles.

Ducasse, C. J. (1961). *A critical examination of the belief in a life after death.* Springfield, IL: Charles C Thomas.

Ebon, M. (1977). *The evidence for life after death.* New York: Signet.

Ehrenwald, J. (1974). Out-of-the-body experiences and the denial of death. *Journal of Nervous and Mental Disease, 159,* 227–233.

Engler, J. (1983). Vicissitudes of the self according to psychoanalysis and Buddhism: A spectrum model of object relations development. *Psychoanalysis and Contemporary Thought, 6,* 29–72.

Fenwick, P. (1997). Is the near-death experience only N-methyl-D-aspartate blocking? *Journal of Near-Death Studies, 16,* 43–53.

Flynn, C. P. (1982). Meanings and implications of NDEr transformations: Some preliminary findings and implications. *Anabiosis: The Journal of Near-Death Studies, 2,* 3–13.

Flynn, C. P. (1986). *After the beyond: Human transformation and the near-death experience.* Englewood Cliffs, NJ: Prentice Hall.

Frankl, V. E. (1969). *The will to meaning: Foundations and applications of logotherapy.* New York: World Publishing.

Gabbard, G. O., & Twemlow, S. W. (1984). *With the eyes of the mind: An empirical analysis of out-of-body states.* New York: Praeger.

Gallup, G., & Proctor, W. (1982). *Adventures in immortality: A look beyond the threshold of death.* New York: McGraw-Hill.

Grey, M. (1985). *Return from death: An exploration of the near-death experience.* London: Arkana.

Greyson, B. (1983a). Near-death experiences and personal values. *American Journal of Psychiatry, 140,* 618–620.

Greyson, B. (1983b). The Near-Death Experience Scale: Construction, reliability, and validity. *Journal of Nervous and Mental Disease, 171,* 369–375.

Greyson, B. (1983c). The psychodynamics of near-death experiences. *Journal of Nervous and Mental Disease, 171,* 376–381.

Greyson, B. (1985). A typology of near-death experiences. *American Journal of Psychiatry, 142,* 967–969.

Greyson, B. (1991). Near-death experiences precipitated by suicide attempt: Lack of influence of psychopathology, religion, and expectations. *Journal of Near-Death Studies, 9,* 183–188.

Greyson, B. (1992). Reduced death threat in near-death experiencers. *Death Studies, 16,* 533–546.

Greyson, B. (1992–1993). Near-death experiences and antisuicidal attitudes. *Omega, 26,* 81–89.

Greyson, B. (1996). The near-death experience as transpersonal crisis. In B. W. Scotton, A. Chinen, & J. R. Battista (Eds.), *Textbook of transpersonal psychiatry and psychology* (pp. 302–315). New York: Basic Books.

Greyson, B. (1997). The near-death experience as a focus of clinical attention. *Journal of Nervous and Mental Disease, 185,* 327–334.

Greyson, B. (1998). The incidence of near-death experiences. *Medicine & Psychiatry*, *1*, 92–99.

Greyson, B., & Bush, N. E. (1992). Distressing near-death experiences. *Psychiatry*, *55*, 95–110.

Greyson, B., & Harris, B. (1987). Clinical approaches to the near-death experiencer. *Journal of Near-Death Studies*, *6*, 41–52.

Greyson, B., & Stevenson, I. (1980). The phenomenology of near-death experiences. *American Journal of Psychiatry*, *137*, 1193–1196.

Grof, S. (1975). *Realms of the human unconscious: Observations from LSD psychotherapy*. New York: Viking.

Grosso, M. (1983). Jung, parapsychology, and the near-death experience: Toward a transpersonal paradigm. *Anabiosis: The Journal of Near-Death Studies*, *3*, 3–38.

Hampe, J. C. (1979). *To die is gain*. Atlanta, GA: John Knox.

Heim, A. v. St. G. (1892). Notizen über den Tod durch absturz [Remarks on fatal falls]. *Jahrbuch des Schweitzer Alpenclub*, *27*, 327–337.

Herzog, D. B., & Herrin, J. T. (1985). Near-death experiences in the very young. *Critical Care Medicine*, *13*, 1074–1075.

Hoffman, R. M. (1995a). Disclosure habits after near-death experiences: Influences, obstacles, and listener selection. *Journal of Near-Death Studies*, *14*, 29–48.

Hoffman, R. M. (1995b). Disclosure needs and motives after a near-death experience. *Journal of Near-Death Studies*, *13*, 237–266.

Holden, J. M., & Joesten, L. (1990). Near-death veridicality research in the hospital setting: Problems and promise. *Journal of Near-Death Studies*, *9*, 45–54.

Hyslop, J. H. (1908). *Psychical research and the resurrection*. Boston: Small, Maynard.

Insinger, M. (1991). The impact of a near-death experience on family relationships. *Journal of Near-Death Studies*, *9*, 141–181.

Irwin, H. J. (1985). *Flight of mind: A psychological study of the out-of-body experience*. Metuchen, NJ: Scarecrow Press.

Irwin, H. J. (1993). The near-death experience as a dissociative phenomenon: An empirical assessment. *Journal of Near-Death Studies*, *12*, 95–103.

Jackson, J. H. (1931). *Selected writings of John Hughlings Jackson* (J. Taylor, Ed.). London: Hodder & Stoughton.

James, W. (1958). *The varieties of religious experience: A study in human nature*. New York: Modern Library. (Originial work published 1902)

Jansen, K. L. R. (1997a). The ketamine model of the near-death experience: A central role for the N-methyl-D-aspartate receptor. *Journal of Near-Death Studies*, *16*, 5–26.

Jansen, K. L. R. (1997b). Response to commentaries on "The ketamine model of the near-death experience . . ." *Journal of Near-Death Studies*, *16*, 79–95.

Jourdan, J.-P. (1994). Near-death and transcendental experiences: Neurophysiological correlates of mystical traditions. *Journal of Near-Death Studies*, *12*, 177–200.

Kellehear, A. (1993). Culture, biology, and the near-death experience: A reappraisal. *Journal of Nervous and Mental Disease, 181*, 148–156.

Kletti, R., & Noyes, R. (1981). Mental states in mortal danger. *Essence, 5*, 5–20.

Kübler-Ross, E. (1983). *On children and death*. New York: Macmillan.

Locke, T. P., & Shontz, F. C. (1983). Personality correlates of the near-death experience: A preliminary study. *Journal of the American Society for Psychical Research, 77*, 311–318.

Lukianowicz, N. (1958). Autoscopic phenomena. AMA *Archives of Neurology and Psychiatry, 80*, 199–220.

Lukoff, D. (1985). Diagnosis of mystical experiences with psychotic features. *Journal of Transpersonal Psychology, 17*, 155–181.

Lukoff, D., Lu, F., & Turner, R. (1992). Toward a more culturally sensitive *DSM–IV*: Psychoreligious and psychospiritual problems. *Journal of Nervous and Mental Disease, 180*, 673–682.

Lynn, S. J., & Rhue, J. W. (1986). The fantasy-prone person: Hypnosis, imagination, and creativity. *Journal of Personality and Social Psychology, 51*, 404–408.

Lynn, S. J., & Rhue, J. W. (1988). Fantasy proneness: Hypnosis, developmental antecedents, and psychopathology. *American Psychologist, 43*, 35–44.

Moody, R. A. (1975). *Life after life*. Covington, GA: Mockingbird Books.

Moody, R. A. (1977). *Reflections on life after life*. St. Simon's Island, GA: Mockingbird Books.

Moody, R. A., & Perry, P. (1988). *The light beyond*. New York: Bantam.

Moody, R. A., & Perry, P. (1991). *Coming back: A psychiatrist explores past-life journeys*. New York: Bantam.

Morse, M., Castillo, P., Venecia, D., Milstein, J., & Tyler, D. C. (1986). Childhood near-death experiences. *American Journal of Diseases of Children, 140*, 1110–1114.

Morse, M. L., Venecia, D., & Milstein, J. (1989). Near-death experiences: A neurophysiological explanatory model. *Journal of Near-Death Studies, 8*, 45–53.

Noyes, R. (1972). The experience of dying. *Psychiatry, 35*, 174–184.

Noyes, R. (1980). Attitude change following near-death experience. *Psychiatry, 43*, 234–242.

Noyes, R., Hoenk, P. R., Kuperman, S., & Slymen, D. J. (1977). Depersonalization on accident victims and psychiatric patients. *Journal of Nervous and Mental Disease, 164*, 401–407.

Noyes, R., & Kletti, R. (1972). The experience of dying from falls. *Omega, 3*, 45–52.

Noyes, R., & Kletti, R. (1976). Depersonalization in the face of life-threatening danger: An interpretation. *Omega, 7*, 103–114.

Noyes, R., & Kletti, R. (1977). Depersonalization in response to life-threatening danger. *Comprehensive Psychiatry, 18*, 375–384.

Noyes, R., & Slymen, D. (1978–1979). The subjective response to life-threatening danger. *Omega, 9,* 313–321.

Osis, K., & Haraldsson, E. (1977). *At the hour of death.* New York: Avon.

Osis, K., & Mitchell, J. L. (1977). Physiological correlates of reported out-of-the-body experiences. *Journal of the Society for Psychical Research, 49,* 525.

Owens, J. E., Cook, E. W., & Stevenson, I. (1990). Features of "near-death experience" in relation to whether or not patients were near death. *Lancet, 336,* 1175–1177.

Persinger, M. A. (1989). Modern neuroscience and near-death experiences: Expectancies and implications. Comments on "A neurobiological model for near-death experiences." *Journal of Near-Death Studies, 7,* 233–239.

Persinger, M. A. (1994). Near-death experiences: Determining the neuroanatomical pathways by experiential patterns and simulation in experimental settings. In L. Bessette (Ed.), *Healing: Beyond suffering or death* (pp. 277–286). Chabanel, Québec, Canada: MNH.

Pfister, O. (1930). Shockdenken und shockphantasien bei höchster todesgefahr [Shock thoughts and fantasies in extreme mortal danger]. *Zeitschrift für Psychoanalyse, 16,* 430–455.

Ring, K. (1980). *Life at death: A scientific investigation of the near-death experience.* New York: Coward, McCann & Geoghegan.

Ring, K. (1984). *Heading toward omega: In search of the meaning of the near-death experience.* New York: Morrow.

Ring, K. (1992). *The Omega Project: Near-death experiences, UFO encounters, and mind at large.* New York: Morrow.

Ring, K. (1997). Dialogue with Kenneth Ring. In E. E. Valarino (Ed.), *On the other side of life: Exploring the phenomenon of the near-death experience* (pp. 85–160). New York: Insight/Plenum.

Ring, K., & Cooper, S. (1997). Near-death and out-of-body experiences in the blind: A study of apparent eyeless vision. *Journal of Near-Death Studies, 16,* 101–147.

Ring, K., & Cooper, S. (1999). *Mindsight: Near-death and out-of-body experiences in the blind.* Palo Alto, CA: William James Center/Institute of Transpersonal Psychology.

Ring, K., & Lawrence, M. (1993). Further evidence for veridical perception during near-death experiences. *Journal of Near-Death Studies, 11,* 223–229.

Rodin, E. (1989). Comments on "A neurobiological model for near-death experiences." *Journal of Near-Death Studies, 7,* 255–259.

Rosen, D. H. (1976). Suicide survivors: Psychotherapeutic implications of egocide. *Suicide and Life-Threatening Behavior, 6,* 209–215.

Rosenthal, R. (1979). The "file drawer problem" and tolerance for null results. *Psychological Bulletin, 86,* 638–641.

Saavedra-Aguilar, J. C., & Gómez-Jeria, J. S. (1989). A neurobiological model for near-death experiences. *Journal of Near-Death Studies, 7,* 205–222.

Sabom, M. (1982). *Recollections of death: A medical investigation.* New York: Harper & Row.

Sabom, M. (1998). *Light and death: One doctor's fascinating account of near-death experiences.* Grand Rapids, MI: Zondervan.

Sagan, C. (1979). *Broca's brain: Reflections on the romance of science.* New York: Random House.

Segen, J. C. (Ed.). (1992). *The dictionary of modern medicine.* Carnforth, England: Parthenon.

Serdahely, W. J. (1991). A comparison of retrospective accounts of childhood near-death experiences with contemporary pediatric near-death experience accounts. *Journal of Near-Death Studies, 9,* 219–224.

Serdahely, W. J., & Walker, B. A. (1990). A near-death experience at birth. *Death Studies, 14,* 177–183.

Shneidman, E. S. (1971). On the deromanticization of death. *American Journal of Psychotherapy, 25,* 4–17.

Siegel, R. K. (1980). The psychology of life after death. *American Psychologist, 35,* 911–931.

Smith, R. P. (1991). The examination of labels—A beginning. *Journal of Near-Death Studies, 9,* 205–209.

Spraggett, A. (1974). *The case for immortality.* New York: Signet.

Strassman, R. (1997). Endogenous ketamine-like compounds and the NDE: If so, so what? *Journal of Near-Death Studies, 16,* 27–41.

Tellegen, A., & Atkinson, G. (1974). Openness to absorbing and self-altering experiences ("absorption"), a trait related to hypnotic susceptibility. *Journal of Abnormal Psychology, 83,* 268–277.

Turner, R. P., Lukoff, D., Barnhouse, R. T., & Lu, F. G. (1995). Religious or spiritual problem: A culturally sensitive diagnostic category in the DSM–IV. *Journal of Nervous and Mental Disease, 183,* 435–444.

Twemlow, S. W., Gabbard, G. O., & Coyne, L. (1982). A multivariate method for the classification of preexisting near-death conditions. *Anabiosis: The Journal of Near-Death Studies, 2,* 132–139.

Weiss, L., Grocott, H. P., Rosanaia, R. A., Friedman, A., Newman, M. F., & Werner, D. S. (1998). Case 4–1998. Cardiopulmonary bypass and hypothermic circulatory arrest for basilar artery aneurysm clipping. *Journal of Cardiothoracic and Vascular Anesthesia, 12,* 473–479.

Whinnery, J. E. (1997). Psychophysiologic correlates of unconsciousness and near-death experiences. *Journal of Near-Death Studies, 15,* 231–258.

Wilber, K. (1984). The developmental spectrum and psychopathology: Part II. Treatment modalities. *Journal of Transpersonal Psychology, 16,* 137–166.

Wile, L. (1994). Near-death experiences: A speculative neural model. *Journal of Near-Death Studies, 12,* 133–142.

Wilson, S. C., & Barber, T. X. (1981). Vivid fantasy and hallucinatory abilities in the life histories of excellent hypnotic subjects ("somnambules"): Preliminary report with female subjects. In E. Klinger (Ed.), *Imagery: Vol. 2. Concepts, results, and applications* (pp. 133–149). New York: Plenum.

Wilson, S. C., & Barber, T. X. (1983). The fantasy-prone personality: Implications for understanding imagery, hypnosis, and parapsychological phenomena. In A. A. Sheikh (Ed.), *Imagery: Current theory, research, and application* (pp. 340–390). New York: Wiley.

11

ANOMALOUS HEALING EXPERIENCES

STANLEY KRIPPNER AND JEANNE ACHTERBERG

After receiving his MD degree from Stanford University, Lewis Mehl-Madrona studied with various Native American medicine men and women and shamans. One of these shamans, Paul, invited Mehl-Madrona to accompany him to a ceremony to be held on a Sioux reservation in North Dakota. Mehl-Madrona helped Paul build a *tipi*, or ceremonial structure, that would hold about 20 people who knew a young woman whose health was dwindling away. Before entering the *tipi*, the group participated in an afternoon sweat lodge experience, except for the patient, who was too frail for the intense heat and whose brother "stood in" for her. That night, Paul brought the young woman, as well as a singer, a drummer, a fire maker, and several community members and friends into the *tipi*. As the singing commenced, Mehl-Madrona recalls, "A host of other voices seemed to be joining . . . the solitary singer . . . , until there was an enormous crash. The *tipi* was shaking as Paul's main spirit helper arrived. A strange grinding noise came from somewhere underground. Blue lights flashed on and off everywhere. . . . I felt something furry walking over my hand. A long tail brushed against me. . . . An icy tentacle of uneasiness wrapped around me. . . . I found myself walking unsteadily down a long, grand corridor. People stood grouped on either side, laughing and chattering. . . . In the small room under the stairs, I saw someone being raped. It was the girl who was sick." Suddenly, Paul shouted, "I know what is wrong." Pointing his finger at the girl's uncle, Paul said, "The spirits have told me. Confess or you will die." The uncle trembled and acknowledged the rape of his niece, then collapsed on the ground. Paul put his mouth to the young woman's abdomen; making a loud, sucking sound, he pulled something out and threw it in the fire. "She is well," he proclaimed. Over the next few days, the young woman improved remarkably; Paul stayed to counsel the family, to prevent this taboo from being broken again and to mend the broken pieces of the lives affected (Mehl-Madrona, 1997, pp. 32–33). This and similar experiences prompted Mehl-Madrona to return to his Native American background to obtain insights that he integrated into his medical practice. This is an example of healing experiences that Western biomedicine would consider "anomalous" and that have been widely reported over millennia.

Frank and Frank (1991) described how most ailments were once attributed to possession by an evil spirit, loss of one's soul, or a sorcerer's curse. Suitable treatment was administered by shamans or other magico–religious practitioners (p. 3). These belief systems are still maintained by some groups of people, and indigenous medical practitioners still service about three fourths of the world's population (Mahler, 1977). Yet, in the West and other parts of the world under Western influence, allopathic biomedicine has become the dominant curative paradigm, bolstered by political, economic, and legal institutions. As a result, reported healing behaviors and experiences that deviate from this paradigm are regarded as *anomalous*, that is, at variance with biomedical diagnosis, prognosis, and treatment. Indeed, the word *healing* is rarely mentioned within the context of the biomedical model.

Western perspectives of health emanated principally from the Age of Enlightenment and the philosophy of elementalism, which divided the human being into body (*soma*), mind (*psyche*), and spirit (*pneuma*). Elementalism's assumption that sickness within one component could be treated without regard to the other components laid the groundwork for allopathic biomedicine, and the elevation of rationality, reductionism, and materialism in 18th-century Western Europe made spiritual concerns irrational and irrelevant (Westgate, 1996). What is anomalous from the Western biomedical perspective might not be anomalous from an indigenous perspective (e.g., shamanism), from a religious perspective (e.g., Christian Science), or from the standpoint of other medical systems (e.g., Ayurvedic medicine or Chinese medicine) that include spiritual dimensions (O'Connor et al., 1997). However, Kleinman (1995) reminded us that biomedicine has attained such a degree of primacy throughout the world that the adjective *Western* is unsatisfactory (p. 25).

Anomalous healing experiences are often reported by people who have undergone nothing but conventional medical treatment. Another body of reports has been elicited from Westerners who have engaged in procedures labeled as *complementary* (i.e., treatments used to complement biomedicine) and *alternative* (i.e., treatments used as an alternative to biomedicine). Such descriptors indicate that these treatments do not adhere to the mainstream political, economic, and legal structure of a particular society in a given historical period. Gerber (1988) used the term *vibrational medicine* and Srinivasan (1988) used the term *energy medicine* to refer to such alternative and complementary practices as acupuncture, electrotherapy, and homeopathy. (Barrett and Jarvis, 1993, referred to the same practices as "quackery.") In a 1993 study, these and other "unconventional" therapies were being used by two out of three U.S. patients (Eisenberg et al., 1993). Because the premises underlying these treatments (e.g., "like cures like" and "*qi* energy balance") depart from biomedicine, any ailments successfully treated by these practices (in the absence of other treatments) could be regarded as anomalous. (These practitioners also report anomalous healings that are not circumscribed by the paradigms of Chinese medicine, chiropractic, and so on, suggesting that one practitioner's conventional cure may be another practitioner's anomaly.)

Some writers have attempted to recast aspects of complementary and alternative practices in conventional biomedical or psychophysiological terms (e.g., Chaves & Barber, 1975), whereas others have accused practitioners of vibrational and energy medicines (as well as the even more exotic indigenous treatments) of "attempting to undermine the very concept of rational science" (Stalker & Glymour, 1985, p. 124). In any case, the study of experiential reports of healing, whether given by respondents treated by conventional physicians, by complementary or alternative practitioners, or by indigenous or "folk" practitioners, is well within the purview of psychology.

In 1995, a panel convened by the Office of Alternative Medicine, U.S. National Institutes of Health, identified 13 parameters needed to evaluate the theoretical infrastructure of systems of complementary and alternative medicine (CAM) and to design appropriate research protocols (O'Connor et al., 1997). The parameters include the following: the lexicon and taxonomy of the system, epistemology, theories, goals for interventions, outcome measures, the context of the social organization surrounding the system, specific activities and *materia medica*, the scope of the system, an analysis of the benefits and costs, views of suffering and death, comparison and interaction with the dominant medical system in the culture, and responsibilities of the patient, practitioner, and others. The panel also provided a useful definition:

> *Complementary and alternative medicine* (CAM) is a broad domain of healing resources that encompasses all health systems, modalities, and practices and their accompanying theories and beliefs, other than those intrinsic to the politically dominant health system of a particular

society or culture in a given historical period. CAM includes all such practices and ideas self-defined by their users as preventing or treating illness or promoting health and well-being. Boundaries within CAM and between the CAM domain and the domain of the dominant system are not always sharp and fixed. . . . In the United States in the 20th century, the dominant healthcare system is, for want of a better term, biomedicine. (O'Connor et al., 1997, pp. 50–51; emphasis added)

Many of the world's societies do not accept that the causal categories of Western biomedicine (e.g., accidents, infections, and organic deterioration) provide important explanations for illness; indeed, Murdock's (1980) survey found alternatives to Western biomedicine's explanations of disease in a majority of the 139 societies he reviewed.

The goals of biomedicine might differ from the goals of an alternative or complementary treatment. For example, biomedical investigators rarely ask such questions as, Is there a recovery-prone personality? Cardeña (1996) added that there is no current diagnosis in psychology or psychiatry for the underdevelopment of a person's capacities for achieving an enjoyable quality of life (p. 94); nor is disregard for the environment looked upon as a disorder by biomedical practitioners, although it would be a sign of imbalance and dysfunction by most indigenous practitioners. It can be seen that the investigation of complementary and alternative procedures needs to focus on the experience as well as the event of healing if these systems are to be adequately fathomed and appropriately evaluated.

DEFINITION

Because health care systems are socially constructed, they are most usefully studied in relationship to their cultural and historical contexts (Kleinman, 1980, pp. 33–35). There are numerous accounts of unexpected recoveries from serious sickness that, if veridical, have little or no explanatory basis in the context of biomedicine. To merely describe (much less explain) these events, Western researchers sometimes take nomenclature with which they are conversant and superimpose it on situations with which they are unfamiliar (Gergen, 1985, p. 266). Examples of terminology with an obvious bias are "witch doctor," "voodoo treatment," and "magical thinking." Shweder (1990) made the point that such Western terminology represents a reductionistic cultural imperialism that assumes a "psychic unity" among humankind, disregarding the different ways that people function (and malfunction) in different times and places. There are many versions of reality a society can live by, and these "divergent rationalities" demonstrate that not every rational process is universal (Shweder, 1986, p. 191).

Glik (1993) differentiated *healing events* (i.e., treatment outcomes) from *healing experiences* (i.e., the subjective aspects of treatment, including its attributed meanings, its ritual context, and the client's feelings). This chapter summarizes the literature that focuses on what Glick called anomalous healing experiences but it also cites pertinent anomalous healing events; the latter have been reviewed and evaluated in several penetrating chapters and books, even though the authors have not always reached the same conclusions (e.g., Benor, 1992, 1994; French, 1996; Schouten, 1993; Solfvin, 1984; Stalker & Glymour, 1985). The study of anomalous healing reports is in the tradition of first eminent psychologist in the United States, William James (1904), who called for a *radical empiricism* that would study any human experience, no matter how unusual it might seem at first glance. These reports may be either in the form of events (an outcome or result) or experiences (James's ongoing "stream of consciousness" during an "event"; see Glik, 1993).

The literature contains three descriptive terms that we consider near-synonyms of anomalous healing events: changes in unchangeable bodily processes (Barber, 1984), remarkable recoveries (Hirshberg & Barasch, 1995), and spontaneous remissions (O'Regan & Hirshberg, 1993; van Baalen & DeVries, 1987). There is an additional group of terms that refer to the procedures held to be responsible for the alleged anomalies:

- absent healing (Edwards, 1953)
- bioenergotherapy (Adamenko, 1970; Benor, 1992, p. 44)
- directed prayer (Dossey, 1993a, pp. 105–106)
- faith healing (Haynes, 1977)
- healing at a distance (Remen, 1996)
- intercessory prayer (LeShan, 1976)
- laying-on of hands (Grad, 1967)
- magnetic healing (Bendit, 1958, pp. 54–56; Edwards, 1953)
- mental healing (Solfvin, 1984)
- metaphysical healing (Bird & Reimer, 1982)
- noncontact therapeutic touch (Krieger, 1979; Schouten, 1993)
- nonlocal healing (Levin, 1996)
- occult medicine (Shealy, 1975)
- paranormal healing (Worrall, 1970)
- psi healing (Benor, 1992, pp. 11–12; Stetler, 1976)
- psychic healing (St. Clair, 1974; Wallace & Henkin, 1978)
- psychic surgery (Benor, 1994, p. 53)
- shamanic healing (Harner, 1980, p. 44)
- spiritual healing (Edwards, 1953; Weston, 1991, p. 38).

Only a few of these terms are interchangeable, and most of them are idiosyncratic. For example, Edwards (1953) proposed that (a) magnetic healing is an innate capacity of most people and involves a laying-on of hands, (b) spiritual healing uses the assistance of discarnate entities, and (c) absent healing is directed toward someone at a distance. Benor (1992, p. 13) used spiritual healing as a synonym for psi healing, whereas Haynes (1977) differentiated psychic healing from faith healing on the basis of the purported spiritual factors that operate in the latter phenomenon.

LeShan (1974) differentiated between Type 1 healing, during which healers enter an altered state of awareness in which they view themselves and the client as one entity, and Type 2 healing, during which healers describe sensing a "healing energy" (which they define in various ways), usually during a laying-on of hands. Type 1 healers simply "unite" with their clients; Type 2 healers deliberately try to heal their clients using a variety of procedures. There are several other groups of healers in LeShan's typology, but he offered them simply as descriptions of what the healers claim to do. Type 3 healers purport to work with discarnate entities or "spirits"; Type 4 healers perform psychic surgery, in which the healer supposedly enters a client's body with a simple instrument or with bare hands; and Type 5 healers contend that they produce major biological changes in a few minutes, changes beyond the capacities of their client's self-repair mechanisms, often in a religious shrine or natural setting. From an experiential standpoint, most of the healers interviewed by LeShan fall into the Type 1 category, the second largest group into Type 3, and the third largest group into Type 2.

When the term *spontaneous remission* is used, it is with the implicit understanding that no cure is spontaneous in the sense that it lacks a causal agent but, rather, that the putative cause is unknown. Indeed, relatively little is known about the absolute course of any disease, and the rates of remission for untreated conditions are uncertain. One can never be certain what might constitute active interventions, especially when a variety of treatments are used simultaneously. Simonton, Matthews-Simonton, and Creighton (1978) sardonically commented that when a malady does not proceed in ways that can be easily explained, the result is called *spontaneous* in much the same way as the term *spontaneous generation* covered medical ignorance during the late Middle Ages. At that time, there was no easy explanation for why maggots could grow out of nonliving matter, such as rotten food, and so it was said that they were spontaneously generated. Spontaneous remission is held to result from mechanisms that are not yet understood (Simonton et al., 1978, p. 21).

Other terms are equally problematic. What parameters separate the normal from the paranormal, the physical from the paraphysical, the nonmiraculous and nonremarkable from the miraculous and the remarkable? By definition, a *miracle* is an event that can be perceived by the senses but operates outside the ordinary laws of nature and is brought about by some power outside those laws (e.g., Broderick, 1956, p. 240). If such events occur, there is a limit to the extent that they can be studied scientifically because science, in Popper's (1959) opinion, demands that assertions made by investigators of these phenomena be, in principle, falsifiable.

From our point of view, the term *anomalous* carries less ideological baggage than its alternatives. In anomalous healing *events*, people claim to have recovered from serious conditions even though these purported recoveries do not seem to be the result of any obvious process, especially a treatment regimen prescribed by biomedical practitioners. Examples of what biomedicine would consider anomalous healing events include the documented growth of sizable pieces of new bone following healing sessions in Great Britain (FitzHerbert, 1971), the removal of bone spurs in Brazil (Maki, 1998, pp. 176–177), and the remission from lupus nephritis following treatment by a native Filipino healer (Kirkpatrick, 1981). In the last example, a young Filipino American woman was diagnosed with lupus, a disease notably resistant to treatment, and conventional biomedical procedures were unsuccessful. In desperation, she went to the remote Philippine village of her birth, returning with a "normal" diagnosis 3 weeks later. She reported that the village healer had removed a curse placed on her by a disgruntled suitor; 23 months later she gave birth to a healthy baby girl.

Anomalous healing *experiences* are individuals' descriptive reports of their sensations, feelings, thoughts, and imagery before, during, or after an anomalous healing event. The experiences described in this chapter are delimited to those falling outside the parameters of biomedicine, although examples could also be given from cases directly associated with hypnosis, suggestion, visualization, and other procedures that have found a place in the repertoire of many biomedical practitioners.

Dossey (1993b) contrasted anomalous healing experiences and events with "normal" healing experiences and events, noting that the mechanisms of the latter are proposed and accepted by biomedicine. What constitutes an appropriate treatment is culturally and historically driven. For example, a cancer patient given Coley's toxins, believed to be a quack nonallopathic remedy a few decades ago, and who recovered would have likely been classified as a case of spontaneous remission by allopathic physicians. Since then, these toxins have been tested in clinical trials and found to be responsible for enhancing immune response and have demonstrated effectiveness against certain forms of the disease (DeVita, Hellman, & Rosenberg, 1991).

Many alternative and complementary practitioners, as well as indigenous healers, differentiate *healing* from *curing*, maintaining that a healing can even occur in the event of death (Dossey, 1995, p. 6). Many indigenous practitioners consider the concept of healing to refer to the restoration of the client's physical, mental, emotional, or spiritual capacities, as contrasted with curing, which refers to surmounting a disease or dysfunction that is primarily biologically based. If a client dies, curing has failed, but if that person has been spiritually restored before death, healing has been successful (Krippner & Welch, 1992, p. 25).

Another contrast can be made between *illness* and *disease*, the latter term referring to a pathological or dysfunctional bodily process resulting from injury, infection, or an ecological disequilibrium (as in environmental diseases). In contrast, illness describes how people experience their health and well-being, that is, how they have constructed their beliefs, behaviors, moods, and feelings. Illness can accompany an injury, infection, or imbalance, or can exist without them (French, 1996, p. 599; Kleinman, 1995, pp. 31–32; Krippner & Welch, 1992, p. 26). Following a healing service, many ardent worshippers may no longer feel ill but may still have a disease.

In both the popular and the academic literature, the term *healer* is variously applied to practitioners, such as shamans and other spiritual practitioners, folk and native functionaries, and mediums and channelers, who have reputations for restoring health, balance, and well-being to an indisposed client. The use of the term *healer* does not necessarily imply that clients actually respond favorably to the practitioner's ministrations. Nor is the term reserved for indigenous or alternative practitioners; some physicians and psychotherapists are informally referred to as healers by their satisfied patients and clients. Such terms as *healer* and *healing* are extremely subjective, and their demonstrated effectiveness depends on the criteria used for one's restoration to *health*, yet another elusive concept. Pelletier (1994), for example, defined health as an orientation of confidence in one's ability to control life and circumstances in such a way that meaning or purpose is created, rather than taking the customary biomedical stance that health is merely the absence of disease.

PHENOMENOLOGY

The phenomenology of anomalous healing experiences for both the client and the healer has been investigated. Despite the limitations inherent in small, retrospective studies of people's experiences, these findings bear consideration. At the same time, one must always ask if similar subjective reports could have been elicited from individuals who did not survive their disease. Some studies have taken this group into consideration, but others have not.

Client Descriptions

Several investigators have produced data bearing on the phenomenology of anomalous healing experiences. Important factors to consider in these studies include (a) the individuals' poor track record in making causal attributions—their preferred attributions are more likely the reflection of their causal schemata and "personal myths" rather than consensual reality (Krippner & Winkler, 1996), and (b) the typical lack of control or comparison groups in most of these studies.

Knight (1994) asked 3 people who recovered unexpectedly from serious medical conditions to describe the "experience of hope in your illness" (p. 57), and then used Giorgi's (1970) method of phenomenological analysis to identify the description's general structure of meaning. This structure consisted of "immediate rupture" (e.g., a break with one's former concepts about the illness), a reactive phase in which this rupture was pondered and conceptualized, an engagement of alternatives (in which the polarity between old and new concepts was engaged), and the realization and embodiment of such new concepts as hope, transformation, and integration.

Berland (1995) conducted semistructured, in-depth interviews with 33 long-term survivors who had been given less than a 15% chance of 5-year life expectancy and yet had lived long after this limit. He also administered the Health Attribution Test (Achterberg & Lawlis, 1989), which taps belief about one's responsibility for the control over health and illness, and the Pie Chart (Achterberg & Lawlis, 1989), an informal measure in which the participants divided circles into "pie slices" that represented factors to which they attributed their recovery. When asked what they personally believed accounted for their longevity, the participants cited psychosocial factors (attitudes, behaviors, spiritual beliefs and practices, social support) twice as often as medical treatment. Berland found that they did not attribute their longevity to chance or to any spontaneous events, but rather to causal events about which they had clear and steadfast opinions (even though these opinions may not have been shared by medical practitioners).

Hawley (1989) also conducted in-depth interviews with 16 cancer survivors whose recovery was considered unlikely, finding that almost all had paradoxical responses to their diagnoses. They did not deny that they had cancer and that it is often a fatal disease, but they did not accept that it was fatal for them. Nor were most of them "good patients" who lacked initiative or were just obedient. Instead, they assumed appropriate control, feeling that they were active participants in their own health care team. In general, they regarded their diagnosis as a challenge to be overcome and their conditions as signals that they had to take charge of serious and very challenging life events.

Psychosocial and spiritual experiences were investigated in some 45 individuals who were deemed to have made remarkable recoveries (Hirshberg & Barasch, 1995). Activities practiced by more than 50% of the group were prayer, meditation, exercise, guided imagery, walking, music, and stress reduction (p. 332). Other items cited most frequently as important in recovery were believing in a positive outcome, having a fighting spirit, accepting the disease, seeing the disease as a challenge, having the will to live, taking responsibility, displaying positive emotions, retaining faith, renewing a sense of purpose, making changes in lifestyle and behavior, eliciting a sense of control, nurturing oneself, and seeking social support (p. 333).

Greenfield (1997) interviewed 32 clients of Mauricio Magalhães, a Brazilian practitioner of Spiritist religious persuasion who claimed to "incorporate" the spirit of a deceased German physician, who allegedly directed Magalhães's hands while he performed minor and major surgery. Only 14% of these patients claimed to have experienced pain during the intervention, despite the lack of anesthetics, even though all but one said they had been subjected to the insertion of needles or cutting with a scalpel. Only one of the respondents reported complications; 88% claimed to have been helped by the treatment, and 64% pronounced that they had been "cured." Of the clients, 95% said that they preferred Magalhães's treatment to conventional medical treatment. When asked if their experience had influenced their point of view about religion, 56% answered that they were more positively inclined toward Spiritism after treatment.

Westerbeke and Krippner (1980) obtained data from 88 tourists who visited one or more Filipino healers and completed standardized forms immediately after their healing session and 6 and 12 months later. Degree of confidence in mental healing both before and after seeing the healer and perceived amount of energy and vitality change were significantly correlated with reported long-term physical, mental, and spiritual improvements. Willingness to change one's behavior was significantly correlated with positive long-term mental and spiritual, but not physical, improvement. Because not all of the tourists completed the questionnaires, self-selection must be considered when evaluating the results.

The same questionnaire was used by Krippner (1990) in a study of 25 North Americans visiting a Brazilian healer. He found that willingness to change behavior was positively correlated with spiritual improvement, whereas energy and vitality were positively related to mental improvement. Responses to the open-ended questions in both studies confirmed the importance for recovery of the clients' attitudinal shifts.

The results of these studies reflect, of course, the perceived causal association of the participants. In this regard, Gilovich (1991) described various ways in which everyday reasoning can be attenuated by cognitive errors and personal heuristics. Krippner and Winkler (1996) described how the need to believe affects rational judgment, critical thinking, and evidence assessment.

In the Netherlands, van Baalen and collaborators compared interview data from 6 people whose recovery from cancer had been attributed to spontaneous remission, with that from 6 patients with advanced progressive cancer collaborators (van Baalen, DeVries, & Gondrie, 1987). The investigators found that members of the former group were more likely to report enhanced sensory acuity, with life events being more vivid, detailed, and magnified. In addition, they were more likely to report profound fluctuations in mood around the time of the remission, shifting from experiencing depression and hopelessness to experiencing a profound sense of autonomy. One of these individuals was transported to a hospice while in a coma. On awakening, she was angry to discover that she was expected to die, pulled out her urinary catheter, and cursed continuously and sang filthy songs for 3 weeks. After a few weeks, the fluid from her belly disappeared; her liver, which had grown into her pelvis, returned to a normal size. She was still in remission a year later (van Baalen, et al., 1987).

Numerous case reports indicate that during the time the anomalous healing takes place, it is not unusual to see religious figures or balls of great white light, to have special dreams or visions, and to feel heat and tingling in the location of the problem (e.g., Gowan, 1980; McClenon, 1997). In this regard, LeShan (1974) observed that the sensation of "heat" is simply the expected response when someone's hands are held on someone else's body (pp. 112–113); there is a phenomenological difference between the perception of "heat" and heat as measured in degrees. Instrumentation has not shown a difference in degrees, even when both healer and healee strongly reported such a perception.

Poloma and Hoelter (1998) obtained questionnaire data from 918 individuals in the United States, most of whom identified themselves as "charismatic, Pentecostal, or full gospel" (p. 264); all had experienced the same structured healing ritual at two international conferences held in 1995. Prayer during these rituals was significantly related to bodily manifestations such as deep weeping, uncontrolled shaking, rolling and thrashing on the floor, dancing or jumping, glossolalia, "holy laughter," or "roaring like a lion." These experiences were significantly related to positive affect. Positive affect, prayer during the ritual, and bodily manifestations were in turn significantly related to purported spiritual healings.

The phenomenological experiences of those exposed to both "official" and "unofficial" cures at the shrine at Lourdes, France, include mention of a sense of unawareness, of being absorbed in thought, dazed, transported beyond themselves, and exhibiting such physical sensations as "red hot heat" permeating the body (Cranston, 1955/1957).

There are few research studies that have attempted to identify the degree to which psychological processes contribute to anomalous healing experiences, but one of the most ingenious is that of McClenon (1997). He supervised an ethnographic research study in which anthropology students at a North Carolina college obtained reports of over 1,000 anomalous experiences from their relatives, friends, neighbors, and acquaintances. Of these transcribed narratives, 85 pertained to folk-healing practices. To determine the role that suggestion and placebo processes played in the reported experiences, two independent judges coded the narratives on 11 dimensions, for example, "Does the person being healed report an instantaneous reduction of pain attributed to the healing activity?" "Is belief mentioned as a factor influencing either behavior or the outcome of treatment?" and "Is there a person . . . regarded as able to perform healing?"

Belief was cited as a factor in healing in 13% of the narratives, supporting the hypothesis that hypnotic and placebo processes are shaped and enhanced by a person's beliefs. In addition, 39% of healings by preachers and healers, 25% of church healings, and 26% of prayer healings included anomalous perceptions, sensations, or bodily movements (e.g., unusual heat or "energy"). The frequency of unusual experience motifs in the narratives supported McClenon's hypothesis that folk healing and hypnotically facilitated therapy use parallel methods, involving a special person who provides therapeutic suggestions through ritual procedures. However, the experimenters were students with a minimum degree of training, and the questions asked admitted variable interpretations; thus, these results can be best considered as suggestive and as a stimulus for future research.

Irwin (1994) summarized the anomalous healing experiences of clients from several studies in a number of Western cultures, noting that many clients are at a low ebb when they first visit an alternative practitioner. The practitioner attempts to encourage rapport, expectation, and relaxation. During the treatment session, such physical sensations as heat and increased vitality are typically reported; following the session, conviction in the treatment's efficacy is usually stronger, and a commitment is made to take a greater sense of responsibility for one's life (pp. 40–41). However, the clients' improvement after a low ebb can be interpreted as a regression-to-the-mean effect. Over time, one would expect a sizable percentage of clients using conventional or nonconventional treatment to show improvement as their health status returns to average status. Irwin emphasized that research efforts would be facilitated if care were taken to ensure that the healer's language and concepts were understood by clients, who often represent a wide range of occupations, ages, and cultural backgrounds (see Harvey, 1983).

Practitioner Descriptions

A major contribution to standardizing the terminology of healing practitioners has been made by Winkelman (1992), who studied the records of spiritual practices in 47 societies, past and present. He found documentary evidence identifying several categories of practitioners. Their healing practices include access to spiritual entities (e.g., deities, ghosts, and spirits), direction of their society's healing activities (e.g., prayer and sacred ceremonies), and employment of special powers (e.g., casting spells, bestowing blessings, and exorcising demons).

Winkelman (1992) found that practitioners' roles changed as societies became more complex. For example, shamans (i.e., practitioners who claim to access and interact with the "spirit world" by deliberately changing their ordinary modes of perceiving, thinking, and feeling through drumming, dancing, ingesting psychoactive drugs, etc.) were typically found in groups with no formal social classes, such as hunting-and-gathering tribes and fishing societies. Once a society began to practice agriculture, social and economic stratification accelerated. Concomitant with this development, priests and priestesses emerged who controlled a society's religious rituals; the political power and social status of shamans were reduced, and they became "shaman/healers" (or "shamanic" healers) because healing became their major function. The shamanic healer typically engaged in more self-regulatory activities, such as changed states of awareness, than did priests and priestesses.

Social and economic differentiation became even more complex with the appearance of separate judicial, military, and legislative institutions. As the competition between (and within) these groups took place, the role of the malevolent practitioner (e.g., sorcerer or witch) appeared. Both shamans and sorcerers claimed to enter changed states of awareness, as did another type of healing practitioner, diviners or mediums, who claimed to "incorporate" spirits, allowing them to speak and act through their voices and bodies. The shamans' remaining functions included such specialized healing capacities as the performing of healing songs and dances, dispensing herbal medicines, diagnosis, bone setting, midwifery, and surgery. Winkelman (1992) referred to these practitioners as healers (i.e., shamanistic healers), for whom a changed states of awareness was no longer a defining characteristic.

Winkelman's (1992) classification system was remarkably accurate when cross-societal comparisons were made; with only two exceptions, shamans never were found in tribal groups displaying an administrative political organization beyond the local level, and no shamans were found in sedentary agricultural societies in which the nomadic way of life was absent. These distinctions have important research implications; Rouget (1980/1985) pointed out that shamanism and mediumship "are products of two quite different ideologies of trance" (p. 25; see also Cardeña, 1996). The role played by social context and personal intention in constructing experience requires research methodologies that do justice to the complexity of the phenomena they hope to describe and understand.

The experiences of contemporary healing practitioners have been the topic of several investigations. Cooperstein (1992) read 10 first-person accounts by well-known healers and interviewed an additional 10 healers who had participated in laboratory experiments. An analysis of their cognitive styles indicated that their attention tended to become diffuse, neither exclusively focused externally or internally, but simultaneously encompassing both the outer and inner environment. There was a tendency for healers to use mental imagery and become absorbed in the process, often to the point of feeling that they were "merging" with the client. The types of imagery reported by the healers included mythic symbols that supported the healers' belief systems, diagnostic information, and treatment process.

Appelbaum (1993) conducted a participant/observation research study, combined with psychological testing, involving 26 self-described healers who claimed to heal their clients through touch. There were many individual differences among the healers: 3 demonstrated psychiatric disturbances, 12 were "psychologically sound," and 11 were inclined to "shape reality according to their wishes." In general, Appelbaum's test results indicated "expansiveness, grandiosity, and a belief in limitless possibilities" (p. 37) among the healers. They enjoyed "being the center of attention" (p. 37) and had great confidence in their capacities. Appelbaum concluded that "the typical healer basically tests reality accurately, but is open to self-delusion through being less interested in checking ideas with reality than in having wishes supported by like-minded people" (p. 37). Although professing humility, the healer resents rules and structure and is committed to finding his or her own path. "Healers are aided in this pursuit by sublime self-confidence . . . , and are drawn, in fact or in fantasy, to center stage" (p. 38).

Appelbaum (1993) conjectured that people who benefit most from such healing may have similar or complementary personalities. They, too, may be people who tend to suspend disbelief, who submit easily to awe and admiration of others, who are oriented toward having their needs met by others, and who are confident that others have the power to help them. Some of the healers Appelbaum worked with told him they experienced conducting "God's healing power," whereas others experienced transferring "energy" from their bodies to those of their clients.

McClelland (1989) personally tested his hypothesis that healers were most successful when they elicited what he thought of as "affective trust." Feeling a horrible cold coming on, McClelland decided to visit a charismatic Boston healer who called himself Karmu, known for his utilization of herbal concoctions, massage, and humor. When McClelland arrived, Karmu took one look at him, realized his condition, and sent his other clients away. Much to McClelland's surprise, Karmu held him like a baby for 30 minutes; his cold was gone the following day. McClelland then conducted a study with university student volunteers, finding that those who felt the symptoms of a cold were more likely, at statistically significant levels, to demonstrate an abatement of cold symptoms and an increase in IgA antibodies after a session with Karmu. For McClelland, these results were largely a function of the establishment of feelings of trust between client and caregiver (see Borysenko, 1985). There are research data suggesting that such variables as hypnotizability and absorption might have played a crucial role as well (e.g., Wickramasekera, 1989).

BIOLOGICAL MARKERS

Biological markers of anomalous healing have been inadequately investigated, in part because of the prevailing skepticism about anomalous healing, the difficulty in determining what is anomalous and what is not, and the difficulty of studying a person's psychophysiology in nonlaboratory settings. The most thorough collection of unusual recoveries from cancer was drawn from a medical database of 3,500 references collected from 800 journals (O'Regan & Hirshberg, 1993). This collection also includes accounts of unusual recoveries from other conditions, predominantly infectious, parasitic, endocrine, nutritional, and metabolic diseases. This worthy effort, the largest of its kind in the world, contains little information on the patients themselves, and we know nothing of their experience or the related biological correlates.

Medical anthropologists have identified unusual recoveries from depression, anxiety, and addictive behavior as the apparent result of tribal ceremony and dance (Achterberg, 1985). A few studies (e.g., Jilek, 1982) have proposed that shamanic drumming has an *acoustic driving* effect on brainwaves, in which the rhythm of drumming "drives" brainwaves into the low-frequency, high-amplitude theta range. However, Rouget (1980/ 1985, pp. 172–176) noted that native drumming rituals use a wide variety of rhythms, producing stimuli that constantly vary. In addition, the concept of *photic driving* by means of light stimulation is backed up by a considerable experimental and clinical literature; both are lacking in the case of so-called acoustic driving.

An investigation of a therapeutic-touch practitioner showed electro-encephalographic (EEG) changes in the healer (Krieger, 1979, pp. 153–163), with a preponderance of rapid EEG activity, suggesting what Krieger called "an attentive meditation style." This report needs to be replicated to ascertain its generalizability and validity.

Benson (1996) attempted to translate the spiritual factors of anomalous healing experiences into psychological and psychophysiological terms. He found that patients who report the intimate presence of a "higher power" have more rapid recoveries than those who do not. Benson proposed that prayer and the relaxation response affect epinephrine and other corticosteroid messengers (i.e., stress hormones), leading to lower blood pressure and a more relaxed heart rate and respiration. He suggested that spirituality may be "hard-wired" into humanity's genetic makeup and that the power of belief may have had survival value previously. Tessman and Tessman (1997), although tolerant of Benson's reconceptualization of the placebo effect, claimed to have discovered exaggerations and simplifications in his review of the pertinent research in this area.

In this literature review on the biological correlates of anomalous healing experiences, it is apparent that this inquiry has barely been initiated. The few research studies that exist are fragmentary, and the variety of healers and clients in different parts of the world prevent generalizations from being made on the basis of research that ignores cross-cultural considerations.

INDIVIDUAL DIFFERENCES

Are there predisposing factors to anomalous healing experiences and events? Given the problems noted earlier in determining what qualifies as an anomalous healing, it is not surprising that little research has been conducted on this important question, especially in the case of healing practitioners. The exceptions are case studies and autobiographies (e.g., Cardeña, 1991; Somé, 1994).

There is a body of investigative data on exceptional survivors of usually catastrophic fatal diseases. Psychological testing on cancer patients who survived significantly longer than predicted, as compared with those who died within the median life expectancy, indicates they were more creative, flexible, had greater ego strength, and were more argumentative, even ornery (Achterberg, Simonton, & Simonton, 1976). A 10-year follow-up study of women with breast cancer showed that those whose test responses paradoxically showed either a fighting spirit or denial toward the disease had a more favorable outcome than did those who were either stoic or who exhibited helplessness/hopelessness (Greer, Morris, Pettingale, & Haybittle, 1990; Pettingale, Greer, Morris, & Haybittle, 1985).

Hirshberg and Barasch (1995) enlisted the aid of several research psychologists and psychiatrists to determine the psychosocial characteristics of the individuals whom they considered to have made remarkable recoveries. Although the research was not systematic, the results provide clues that can be useful to future investigators. For example, 77% of the 43 individuals studied tended to prefer, at least consciously, "to confront their problems directly, rather than avoiding them" (p. 331), and 80% were deemed to be capable of positive mood states. However, there were many individual differences, and on some of the tests the group fell within the range of scores characterizing the general population (pp. 326–330).

Berland (1995), in his study of long-term survivors, used his interview data to classify the participants, finding 5 who were "determined fighters" who attributed their recovery to their determination to get well; 10 who were "attitudinally and behaviorally focused" who took an active role in promoting change in their attitudes toward themselves and their life situations; and 18 who were "spiritually and existentially oriented." Berland concluded that "people approach their illness in distinct ways and must be helped to achieve their own specific goals" (p. 15).

Solomon and his associates (Solomon, Kemeny, & Temoshok, 1991; Solomon, Temoshok, O'Leary, & Zich, 1987) studied long-term survivors of AIDS, finding that they were more likely than nonsurvivors to view their physicians as partners, accept the diagnosis and take some degree of personal responsibility for their disease, feel they had unfinished goals or business to which they needed to attend, and find new meaning and purpose in life as a result of their diagnosis.

Glik (1993) compared 93 members of charismatic Christian healing groups with 83 members of metaphysical New Age healing groups on several standardized health status protocols. Glik found that the former tended to attribute their condition to sin, weakness, lack of belief, and loss of faith, whereas the latter tended to associate their condition to imbalances and blockages between soma and psyche, self and society, or conscious and unconscious material. Neither rejected biomedical explanations of causation and cure but framed them within broader definitions of health and sickness. Recovery was often phrased symbolically, for example, in terms of *surrender* by the charismatic group and *inner peace* by the metaphysical group; changed states of awareness were associated with recovery by members of both groups. Glik proposed that Fischer's (1971) model of cortical hyperarousal (common among charismatics) typified the former group, whereas cortical hypoarousal (common among meditators) was more typical of the latter group. People in both of Glik's groups who reframed or redefined their health problems "had significantly higher levels of reported healing experiences . . . than those who did not" (p. 211).

The role of fantasy proneness in spontaneous healing experiences has been explored by a few investigators. Noll (1986), for example, suggested that shamans might demonstrate this proclivity. Barber (1984; Wilson & Barber, 1978) proposed that fantasy-prone individuals are characterized by a psychosomatic plasticity that facilitates extraordinary bodily changes. For example, the most fantasy-prone individuals had a profound imagination ranging from daydreaming to out-of-body experiences (OBEs) to sexual orgasm produced purely through fantasy. In addition, Cardeña, (1996), in dispelling the notion that hypnosis is a unitary state of awareness, found that highly hypnotizable people can fantasize without dissociating, can dissociate without fantasizing, can display during hypnosis only mild to moderate losses in rationality, or can report considerable loss of rationality and memory (pp. 88–89). According to him, the characteristics of some highly hypnotizable individuals (high imagery, traumatic history, talent for the arts) parallel those of some traditional healers.

Irwin's (1994) summary of practitioner experiences indicates several commonalities: a period of preparation; a period of initial absorption in the process; a period of engagement with the client; and a concluding period in which practitioners may or may not feel depleted, depending on their efforts and their belief as to the source of their healing power (e.g., Harvey, 1983, p. 114). Some of the accounts cited by Irwin describe individual differences in these factors (e.g., Krippner & Villoldo, 1986).

In reviewing research studies in this area, one must consider the limitations of the research methodology. For example, Hirshberg and Barasch (1995) admitted that the at-risk personality features that marked their remarkable-recovery group probably existed before their cancers developed. These traits may have contributed to the disease process and, if reversed, might have contributed to the healing process. Because no before-and-after tests were given, it is impossible to assess the reported scores. In the same study, there were several traits (e.g., social extraversion and positive coping) that seemed to be associated with recovery; yet if these qualities were present before the cancer occurred, why did they not play a preventive role?

PSYCHOPATHOLOGY

There is very little direct research on whether healers or patients who have anomalous healing experiences also have a predisposition to some forms of psychopathology (see also the section on Clinical Issues and Risks below). For many decades, Western social scientists observed the links between shamanic experiences and changed states of awareness, concluding that shamanism involved some type of psychopathology. J. Silverman (1967) postulated that shamanism is a form of acute schizophrenia because the two conditions have in common "grossly non-reality-oriented ideation, abnormal perceptual experiences, profound emotional upheavals, and bizarre mannerisms" (p. 22). Indeed, Silverman reported that the only difference between shamanic states and contemporary schizophrenia in Western industrialized cultures was "the degree of cultural acceptance of the individual's psychological resolution of a life crisis" (p. 23). Silverman claimed that the social supports available to the shaman are "often completely unavailable to the schizophrenic in our culture" (p. 29). Devereux (1961) described shamans as neurotics and hysterics, whereas Radin (1937) equated them with epileptics and hysterics (p. 108).

Boyer, Klopfer, Brawer, and Kawai (1964) gathered data on this issue by administering Rorschach inkblots to 12 male Apache shamans, 52 nonshamans, and 7 "pseudoshamans" who claimed to possess special powers but who had not been accorded shamanic status by members of their tribe. Rorschach analysis demonstrated that the shamans showed as high a degree of reality-testing potential as did members of the nonshamanic group. Pseudoshamans, however, were more variable on this dimension and demonstrated "impoverished personalities" (p. 179). The shamanic group approached ambiguous stimuli similarly to nonshamans but showed a higher degree of ability to "regress in the service of the ego," a keener awareness of peculiarities, more theoretical interests, and more "hysterical" tendencies (p. 179). The shamans were distinguished by the high frequency of anatomical and sexual responses to the Rorschach inkblots as well as the mention of color. Even so, Boyer et al. (1964) stated, "in their mental approach, the shamans appear less hysterical than the other groups" (p. 176). The study concluded that the shamans were "healthier than their societal co-members. . . . This finding argues against [the] stand that the shaman is severely neurotic or psychotic, at least insofar as the Apaches are concerned" (p. 179).

Noll (1983) compared the experiential reports of both people with schizophrenia and shamans to the criteria for schizophrenia of the third edition of the *Diagnostic and Statistical Manual of Mental Disorders* (American Psychiatric Association, 1980). He concluded that important phenomenological differences exist between the two groups and that the "schizophrenic metaphor" of shamanism is untenable (p. 455). In fact, Murphy (1976) noted that indigenous people generally differentiate between shamans and those who Westerners would consider as having schizophrenia, adding that similar kinds of disturbed behavior are identified as aberrant in diverse cultures.

In fact, some social scientists (e.g., Peters & Price-Williams, 1983) have claimed that such altered states as spirit possession and OBE can be therapeutic. Indeed, there is an anthropological literature indicating that these altered states can be socially adaptive and empowering, especially in the case of female healers, who have few other means in many cultures for asserting their capabilities (Krippner, 1994, p. 358).

As mentioned above, Appelbaum (1993) found that only a small proportion of self-described Western healers showed psychiatric disturbances. This finding is consistent with cross-cultural studies but requires replication. Heber, Fleisher, Ross, and Stanwick (1989) studied 12 alternative healers in a Canadian city and reported that although, as compared with a control group, they expressed a number of unusual experiences; these experiences were not indicative of psychopathology.

OUTCOMES

Several writers (e.g., Achterberg, Simonton, & Simonton, 1976; Cunningham, 1984) have described the outcomes of anomalous healing experiences and unexpected responses to particular diagnoses and treatments. In his literature review, Schouten (1993) found no evidence that patients' contacts with complementary and alternative medical systems had any strong negative effects; indeed, there were several indications that these experiences were associated with positive effects. However, psychological variables had "a much stronger effect than the effect of the method itself" (p. 394), and many methodological shortcomings of the studies were noted (e.g., lack of comparison groups and absence of normative data). For example, Kleijnen, ter Riet, and Knipschild's (1991) overview of the effect of acupuncture on asthma reported a positive effect of the method but found that the rate of success decreased as the quality of the investigation increased. Even so, "There is not much to be gained by calling the results of complementary treatment just 'placebo' or 'suggestion.' This would merely mean replacing one term with another and would contribute little to the explanation of the phenomenon" (Schouten, 1993, p. 397).

Appelbaum (1993) observed that most of the favorable outcomes from healers rest on anecdotal reports and are subject to considerable error.

> Healers may report only seemingly successful cases, patients are often loathe to report that the healing was ineffective, something other than the laying on of hands could have brought about the cure, and—given the fallibility of some medical diagnoses, the person may not have had the alleged ailment in the first place. (p. 33)

French (1996) added that many ailments are self-limiting, and others show a natural variability (pp. 598–599). Furthermore, in discussing healing outcome research, even briefly, one must distinguish between an effect (e.g., a decrease in gastric secretion) and effectiveness (e.g., cessation of pain and other symptoms). Few studies of alternative medical treatments have made this differentiation (Ernst & White, 1997). For example, in a study of 21 therapeutic-touch practitioners (Rosa, Rosa, Sarner, & Barrett, 1998), the practitioners were unable, under masked conditions, to perceive a "human energy field" (i.e., an effect); on this basis, Rosa et al. claimed that "no well-designed study demonstrates any health benefit from [therapeutic touch]. These facts, together with our experimental findings, suggest that . . . further use of [therapeutic touch] by health professionals is unjustified" (p. 1010). Rosa et al. reached this conclusion even though they themselves had not collected data regarding therapeutic touch's possible effectiveness, and despite the fact that their literature review unearthed no harmful effects of the procedure (see also Leskowitz, 1998).

THERAPEUTIC POTENTIALS AND EFFICACY

Various instances of the reputed efficacy of complementary and alternative techniques have been described in previous sections. A literature review conducted by McClenon (1997) found evidence that indigenous treatments "have a high degree of efficacy, particularly for disorders with a psychological basis" (p. 61). For example, Kleinman (1980) observed that Taiwanese shamans were regarded as more successful when dealing with acute, self-limited sicknesses, secondary somatic manifestations of psychological disorders, and chronic ailments that were not life-threatening. Finkler (1985) observed that diarrhea, simple gynecological disorders, somatic manifestations of distress, and psychological disorders were most amenable to treatment by Mexican spiritists. Thong (1993) surveyed clients of traditional Balinese healers, reporting that most of those with self-limiting ailments improved over time. Also, according to self-reports, 58% of the clients with chronic physical conditions and 60% of those with psychiatric problems claimed to have improved or to have been cured. Those not claiming improvement were those with mental retardation, severe psychoses, or repetitive antisocial behavior. The latter findings suggest that the efficacy of indigenous treatments may reflect therapeutic rapport, other psychological variables, and a regression-to-the-mean effect and that the term *anomalous* is inappropriate in these cases unless conventional healing variables can be explained away.

In regard to controlled research, Schouten (1993) concluded that "few experimental studies on the effect of psychic healing . . . are available which fulfill basic requirements such as matched groups and a double-blind design" (p. 389); as for case histories in which alternative practices are successful, "there hardly exists a case which is well-documented" (p. 378). However, after examining the same body of evidence, Benor (1992) concluded that "there is highly significant evidence for healing effects on enzymes, cells in the laboratory, bacteria, yeast, plants, animals and humans" (p. 11). An intermediate conclusion has been offered by Solfvin (1984):

> The studies reviewed here show a rather high rate of success for observing, with varying degrees of control, apparent influences on living matter in mental healing contexts. This is very encouraging in that it represents a solid first step toward building a science of mental healing, or mental intention to heal. It is clear, too, that it is only a first step. (p. 63)

Intriguing, but controversial, results reported by Grossarth-Matticek, Bastiaans, and Kanazir (1985) suggest that therapy that emphasizes such issues as a healthy lifestyle, relaxation, positive self-suggestions, hope, trust, problem-solving, "natural piety," and an examination of one's beliefs and expectations results in extended survival rates from cancer, heart disease, and strokes as compared with comparison groups treated with standard procedures. In addition, a prospective, randomized study of 86 women with metastatic breast cancer by Spiegel, Bloom, Kraemer, and Gottheil (1989) indicated that women who received group therapy with an emphasis on social support survived about twice as long as those who were not in the therapy groups. Fawzy et al. (1993) reported similar results with persons diagnosed with melanoma, who underwent an intervention that included education, stress management, enhancement of coping skills, and psychosocial support.

Various elements of rituals and ceremonies, such as drumming, dancing, chanting, expressive arts, and practices such as fasting and sensory deprivation, have been associated with reports of healing in various cultural contexts (Achterberg, 1985; Krippner, 1996; Lawlis, 1996; Rebman et al., 1995). To the extent that they can be integrated into a belief system (without violating the cultural underpinning of the traditions), these elements may link anomalous healing experiences with clinical and research interventions. Indeed, Fuller (1989) regarded unorthodox medical treatment as an initiatory rite for many Americans for whom a secularized culture has led to a desacralization of life (pp. 120–121).

These studies indicate that there may be substantial health benefits associated with relatively simple interventions. The use of behavioral and relaxation approaches in the treatment of chronic pain and insomnia was advocated by a U.S. National Institutes of Health (NIH) panel (Richmond et al., 1996), and another NIH panel supported the utility of mind–body interventions in the treatment of various health problems (Achterberg et al., 1994). Social support may be a contributing factor to the reported healings that take place in shamanic societies, indigenous cultures, and even religious settings that emphasize family and community nurturance (Kleinman, 1995). Social support and a concomitant reduction in loneliness and anxiety have been associated with significant hormonal changes that could facilitate healing (Melnechuk, 1988). The associations among health and hope, optimism, and relief from distress (Knight, 1994; Peterson, Seligman, & Vaillant, 1988) suggest that psychosocial clinical interventions, if appropriately selected and wisely applied, can be safe, cost-effective, and efficacious in healing.

CLINICAL ISSUES AND RISKS

Writers have disagreed on the risk factors involved in anomalous healing. Critics have identified what they consider to be serious fallacies in the decision-making processes of people who invest their time and money searching for an anomalous healing rather than accepting conventional medical care. Wikler (1985) saw a pernicious danger in the behavior of health practitioners who claim that individuals should "be accountable" for their own health and that "health care is a matter of individual responsibility" (e.g., Pelletier, 1977, p. 302). For Wikler, the debate is not over the concept of accountability itself, but over what actions lead to what consequences and how clients' responsibility can be most effectively discharged. Practitioners can hardly be faulted if they encourage and assist clients to adopt healthy lifestyles and attitudes. The danger arises when a practitioner suggests that it is one's unconscious resistances, lack of faith, or self-destructive tendencies that prevent recovery.

Various observers have linked the behavior of some groups devoted to anomalous healing with such factors as psychopathology and irrational risk-taking. Brenneman (1990) observed that the doctrine of Christian Science holds that its practitioners cannot treat anyone undergoing medical care, unless the patient is a Christian Scientist undergoing involuntary medical care (e.g., the unconscious victim of an automobile accident). He documented several cases in which patients, including children, have died as a result of this harsh dictum. This type of world view is not limited to Christian Science; at least 22 other religions have been implicated in religion-motivated medical neglect and about 140 instances of U.S. fatalities have been documented in which treatment by religious rituals was implemented instead of medical care in which the expected survival rate exceeds 90% (Asser & Swan, 1998).

Radner and Radner (1985) warned against accepting an irrational cognitive style that would place one at risk and identified several examples of such styles. These include (a) anachronistic thinking (e.g., dependency on ancient modes of treatment); (b) argument from spurious similarity (e.g., attempts to gain scientific status for a controversial mode of treatment on the grounds of its alleged resemblance to a recognized scientific theory); (c) a grab-bag approach to evidence (e.g., dependence on anecdotes about anomalous healing rather than rigorously conducted studies); and (d) refusal to correct in light of criticism (e.g., finding excuses when accounts of anomalous healing do not measure up to standard criteria of verification). Many investigators who are sympathetic to the consideration of healing anomalies agree that critical thinking is important to evaluating them (e.g., LeShan, 1982, p. 130).

There is the constant risk of gullible people spending time and money with so-called healers of questionable ethics and dubious effectiveness instead of seeking prompt medical attention. The responsible advocates of alternative approaches recognize this danger. St. Clair (1974), for example, in his attempts to identify exceptional healers around the world, found several practitioners whom he considered fraudulent and who "know that ill people are easy targets" (p. 321). Even at their best, psychic healers "cannot take care of a ruptured appendix, do not handle emergency cases like drowning, shootings and automobile accidents," and "are not infallible" (p. 321). The magician James Randi (1987) investigated several contemporary faith healers, concluding that they were performing sleight of hand disguised as healing miracles. Randi's debunking activities have triggered controversy, but an editorial in the *American Society for Psychical Research Newsletter* remarked, "We are united on this front and should work together to help protect the desperate and the credulous against those who would exploit their deepest needs" (McCormick, 1986, p. 23).

For any model of healing to be taken seriously, it must take the placebo effect into account in the evaluation of healing events in conventional biomedical practices. At its best, this effect is a simple nontoxic, nonmutilating, and often effective method of stimulating and facilitating the client's own intrinsic healing process. Technically speaking, a biomedically inert substance given in such a manner to produce relief is known as a *placebo*, and the resulting patient effect is called the *placebo effect*. In other words, the effect is a response to the act of being treated, not to the administered treatment itself (Dodes, 1997).

Frank and Frank (1991) reviewed data indicating that the placebo effect is often so strong that it has produced salutary effects even when patients are told that the substance they are taking is a sugar pill (pp. 144–154). They concluded that the patient's state of mind is a critical variable. This point is underscored by Rehder (1955), who asked a celebrated faith healer to perform three at-a-distance healings with three seriously ill patients who were not told about his intervention; no change was noted in their condition. Later, the patients were told about the healer and for several days they prepared for his distant treatment, but the healer was told to do something else at the time. Nevertheless, one patient was cured permanently, and the other two made dramatic improvements.

However, a placebo can actually increase the recipient's discomfort if he or she has been led to expect such results (French, 1996, p. 600). Dodes (1997) noted ways in which placebos can be harmful: Various allergic reactions have resulted from placebo therapy; patients can be led to believe that their sickness is only amenable to treatment from a specific practitioner; and placebo effects can mask serious disorders, resolving subjective symptoms while allowing the objective ones to remain. Finally, the use of placebos can undermine the practitioner–patient relationship by requiring deception on the part of a caregiver (pp. 44–45).

Psychotherapists and other professional practitioners may be called upon to counsel people about their purported anomalous experiences; obviously, these cases may reflect patients' needs and motives. Irwin (1999, pp. 295–300) divided them into the hoaxers, the seekers of reassurance, and those in need of psychotherapy. The hoaxers frequently seek attention and will magnify or fabricate extravagant tales of anomalous healing to serve their purposes. This behavior calls for a noncommittal and nonevaluative stance, at least in the first stages of counseling. The reassurance-seekers may report healing experiences that are so uncanny that they dare not confide in friends or family for fear of ridicule or because they suspect they are suffering from a delusion. Again, a nonevaluative approach is appropriate until more information is forthcoming. If the account seems plausible, reference may be made to the fact that many other people report similar experiences. The psychotherapist may also help the client work through the experience to establish its personal significance, leaving its veridicality open unless medical records are available for verification. There are some cases in which clients will confide experiences that appear to be part of an ongoing pathological condition, often frankly delusional in nature. A client might claim to have God-given healing powers, to have been healed by a "spiritual implant," or to have been chosen to "suffer for humanity's benefit." In these cases, the psychotherapist should determine the needs being satisfied by the delusion and to place the experiential report in the broader context of the client's presenting problem, diagnosis, and treatment plan.

THEORIES

Theories and explanatory models attempt to provide verbal or pictorial representations of reality. They often serve as heuristic devices, as tools for thinking, investigating, and constructing testable hypotheses. Weston (1991), in his book on so-called healing miracles, stated that "both religion and science describe reality" (pp. 37–38). We suggest that the former yields models that are closed-ended, whereas the latter (at its best) provides open-ended models that build on accumulated data and search for ways in which new data can be added.

Psychophysiological Models

There are any number of possible psychophysiological explanations that might underlie anomalous healing experiences. In offering an explanation for his collection of instances of "changes in unchangeable bodily processes," Barber (1984, p. 104–105) identified several possible contributing factors. He began with the example of how cognition, imagination, and emotions affect blood supply to the genital areas during sexual fantasizing. If these thoughts, images, and feelings can produce variations in blood supply, it is likely that the blood flow to other parts of the body is continually affected by what people are thinking, imagining, and experiencing (p. 105). By being deeply absorbed in imagining a physiological change, some individuals can evoke the same thoughts and feelings that are present when an actual physiological change occurs, hence stimulating the cells to produce the desired physiological change (p. 118).

For instance, during the spontaneous disappearance of warts, some investigators (e.g., Samek, 1931) have reported an inflammatory reaction in the dermis consisting of dilation of blood vessels, hyperemia (increased blood supply), edema, and perivascular infiltration of white blood cells.

Hypnotic treatment of "fish-skin" diseases may involve stimulation of the affected area's vascular bed, countering the disturbed metabolism (Kidd, 1966). Changes in blood supply have also been implicated in rapid recovery from burns (Barber, 1984, pp. 87–93). In addition, there is an extensive literature on individuals who can shift more blood to a specific area of the skin through biofeedback or other forms of self-regulation (e.g., A. J. Silverman & McGough, 1971; Snyder & Noble, 1968).

There are also some studies showing that body temperature can be controlled through psychological mechanisms. Under controlled conditions, an Indian swami was able to produce a significant difference in skin temperature between the two sides of his palm (Green & Green, 1977, pp. 197–199). Through biofeedback, volunteers can attain a remarkable amount of finger temperature control (Taub & Emurian, 1976). In gTum-mo meditation, some Tibetan lamas were able to produce extraordinary amounts of body heat and showed no reaction to the cold sheets draped around their bodies during this feat (Benson, 1982). Tessman and Tessman (1997) replicated this effect on themselves at nearly identical temperatures and experienced no serious discomfort.

Barber (1984, p. 106) called for additional research to determine if local changes in blood supply are related to alterations in immunological functions. He suspected that the ability to alter bodily processes thought to be unchangeable is related to the practitioner–client relationship and to individual differences. Barber also proposed that the capacity to alter bodily processes may be related to the degree of fantasy proneness a culture manifests.

For Barber (1984), the meanings and ideas embedded in words spoken by one person and deeply accepted by another can be communicated to the cells of the body and to the chemicals within these cells; the cells then can change their activities to conform to the meaning or ideas that have been communicated. This type of change is especially possible when practitioners and clients have a close personal relationship; when the clients' maximum cooperation has been elicited; when the clients' expectations have been enhanced; and when distracting thoughts and extraneous concerns have been reduced, allowing them to be absorbed in the suggestions to think, imagine, and feel along with the practitioner (p. 117). Barber did not limit his explanatory model to hypnotic suggestion; unusual changes can occur under informal circumstances when someone is talked to in an especially meaningful way (p. 117).

The most widely promulgated psychophysiological model to account for anomalous healings is the placebo effect. The power of the placebo has been demonstrated by Roberts, Kewman, Mercier, and Hovell (1993), who analyzed data for treatments that had been abandoned as ineffective but in which there were strong positive reports by two or more groups of investigators. Kewman et al. concluded that treatment outcome is always due to some interactive combination of specific and nonspecific effects. Dodes (1997) surmised that belief in a treatment explains only a portion of its effect; operant conditioning and suggestibility also may play important roles.

Wickramasekera (1980) asserted that the Pavlovian conditioning theory of the placebo response best accounts for the empirical data, but transference and attribution represent competing theories. In transference, placebo effects are seen as regressive behaviors that harken back to child–parent interactions. The attribution explanation asserts that clients pay more attention to subtle changes in their internal state while undergoing treatment and attributed these changes to the placebo.

McClenon (1997) pointed out that the placebo effect and hypnotic induction may use different psychological mechanisms and that response to placebos is not correlated with hypnotizability. Kirsch (1990) added that hypnosis and placebos both can be used in alleviating pain, tension, and various somatic conditions; perhaps their common link is a response expectancy (p. 145). The need to posit a psychological link suggests the value of psychological contributions to treatment outcomes.

Parapsychological Models

Parapsychologists study reported interactions between organisms and their environment (including other organisms) that appear to be inconsistent with Western science's concepts of time, space, and energy. Although the origins of parapsychology lie in spontaneous anomalous experiences and in the activities of mediums and healers, parapsychology has developed into an experimental field of research (Schouten, 1993, p. 375). The research studies on mediums and healers have focused on the outcomes of their ministrations rather than on their inner experiences. Attevelt (1988) reported that 80% of asthma patients treated by psychic healers reported some degree of improvement. Strauch (1963), who followed up 650 patients treated by a psychic healer, reported that 61% of patients felt their conditions had improved, whereas an 11% improvement rate was acknowledged by their physicians. Of great importance is the lack of a control group in both studies. Important questions that have been neglected include how effective healers operate, what they experience during their attempted healings, and what these data suggest as to the most promising explanations of their successes when they occur.

An example of an investigation of prayer and *distant intentionality* is Byrd's (1988) 10-month study with 393 patients. Byrd asked volunteers, who described themselves as "born-again Christians," to attempt intercessory prayer for half of the coronary patients (representing several Christian denominations) who had been randomly assigned to a prayer or no-prayer group. The "praying people" were asked to pray every day but were not given instructions on how to pray except that they should ask for a rapid recovery with no complications. Each patient in the prayer group had 3 to 7 people praying for him or her; the patients were known to the praying people only by their first names and medical diagnoses. Neither the physicians nor the nurses knew who was being prayed for. Members of the prayer group did significantly better on several indexes: They were less likely to develop pulmonary edema, none required endotracheal intubation, and they were less likely to require antibiotics. Mortality differences did not attain significance.

Although generally well-designed, this study is not immune from criticisms. There was no standardization of prayer technique, quality of prayer, or quantity of prayer. No attempt was made to determine if the number of praying people per patient made a difference. In addition, other studies (e.g., Joyce & Weldon, 1965) have failed to demonstrate positive effects of intercessory prayer. Byrd's (1988) study, like most parapsychological studies of anomalous healing effects (e.g., de Carvalho, 1996), was a single attempt, but programmatic series of experiments have been occasionally carried out, such as Grad's (e.g., 1967) work with animals and plants, and Schlitz and Braud's (e.g., 1997) work with organisms ranging from bacteria to humans. O'Laoire's (1997) review of the literature identified some three dozen studies, including his own, on the effects of prayer on humans; only 9 of the studies investigated psychological parameters such as anxiety and self-esteem.

Levin (1996) maintained that hypotheses that invoke such concepts as "nonlocal healing" are no less naturalistic than the mechanisms proposed by biomedicine. He proposed that transcending space and time, as it is currently understood by conventional science, is not the same as transcending nature. Here rests the major difficulty with parapsychological models. If they are in accord with natural laws, rather than in violation of them, they need to propose mechanisms and outcomes that can be examined, replicated, and confirmed or falsified. The literature reveals a paucity of such proposals.

Systems Models

General systems theory has been defined by Miller (1978, p. 9) as a set of related definitions, assumptions, and propositions that deal with reality as an integrated hierarchy of organizations of matter and energy. Krippner and Villoldo (1986) observed that a *system* is an indivisible whole, one that loses its coherence when taken apart (p. 167), and they proposed that anomalous healing can best be understood if it is cast within a multidimensional model (p. 152). Cross-cultural studies may be beneficial in understanding systemic issues in health and sickness; Kleinman (1995) reminded us that no medicine is independent of its historical context (p.

23). Many indigenous peoples take a systems orientation in which human functioning is conceived as a synthesized whole, with each component inextricably interrelated with other components (Kleinman, 1980; Westgate, 1996). Western systems theorists propose that the sum of a system's components is larger than the sum of the individual measurements of its units (Miller, 1978, p. 16).

Torrey (1986) proposed a systems model of treatment after surveying both Western and non-Western healing practices, concluding that both are about equally effective. For him, the nature of effective treatment inevitably contains one or more of four fundamental factors: (a) a shared world view by healer and patient, which makes the diagnosis or naming process possible; (b) certain personal qualities of the practitioner that appear to facilitate the client's recovery; (c) positive client expectations that assist progress; and (d) a sense of mastery that empowers the client. None of these elements is necessarily anomalous in nature, but anomalous experiences can be analyzed within this framework. An example of this proposed interaction is the study by León (1975), a Colombian psychiatrist, who undertook a 7-year study of spirit possession. Leon interviewed all members of the 12 families involved and gave psychological and polygraph tests to the "possessed" individuals, concluding that the afflicted men and women presented symptoms compatible with physical or mental disorders or both. Leon did not rule out the possibility that parapsychological factors were involved, especially in those cases in which there were reports (not observed by Leon) of unusual events. Families claimed that treatment by local spiritistic practitioners were more effective than exorcisms by Roman Catholic priests; some clients claimed that the offending spirits could not understand Latin!

For Rosen (1991), lower order information-based systems play a central role in regulating an organism's physiology because organisms, including humans, are self-regulating systems whose stability depends on the information they generate. These information systems contribute to an organism's stability by anticipating and regulating changes in metabolic states. There is a spectrum of complexity in the information that an organism is capable of generating. An individual may respond positively to self-suggestion, to suggestion from an authoritative practitioner, or to suggestion from a congenial group. This capacity may allow an individual or groups of individuals to shape or influence the information they experience in ways that are physiologically beneficial. In Rosen's model, there is a feedback from mental models that can lead to changes in physiologic states. Sickness, then, is more than a cellular process; the mental world a person experiences has physiological consequences, and therapies need to be directed toward the models of reality held by patients (Staiger, 1995).

Another systemic model was proposed by O'Regan and Hirschberg

(1993), who pointed out that the fact that healing takes place at all implies the existence of a tripartite healing system involving some degree of self-diagnosis, self-repair, and self-regeneration. One can assume that any healing ministration, anomalous or not, triggers the activities of this healing system.

Perhaps the emerging field of psychoneuroimmunology (PNI) provides the best example of a systems model that explores the relationship between psychological and physiological factors in the onset of sickness, the maintenance of health, and anomalous healing. Since the 1950s, there has been growing evidence that the central nervous system, the endocrine system, the immune system, and virtually every other bodily system function not as separate but as overlapping subsystems (Ader, 1981; Solomon, 1990). Simply put, the systems are "hard-wired" (i.e., neurally connected) to work together, and they are also "soft-wired" via hormones, neuropeptides, and other neurotransmitters (e.g., Rossi, 1993).

Some of the most relevant work testing this model is that of Pert and her associates (e.g., Pert, Ruff, Weber, & Herkenham, 1985), who have identified the receptor sites for neuropeptides and hypothesized that they serve as "messengers," or bridges to link emotions and thoughts with bodily processes, to the extent that it makes more sense to speak of a "bodymind" rather than of body and mind as separate entities. Rossi's (1993) psychobiological hypothesis also holds that there is no gap between mind and body and that neuropeptides may be the psychobiological basis of many poorly understood forms of healing. As Levin (1996) stated, "both psychophysiology and . . . psychoneuroimmunology have demonstrated the impact of feelings and emotions on the physical body" (p. 68).

Rotenberg, Sirota, and Elizur (1996) took the position that PNI's theoretical basis is still "vague and ambiguous" (p. 331); even so, they pointed out that the research literature indicates that behaviors that initiate search activity (i.e., those oriented to change a situation or the participant's attitude toward it in the absence of the precise prediction of the final outcome of such activity) prevent autoimmune disorders; ending search activities predisposes the organism to health problems. To describe this latter predisposition, Solomon (1993) coined the term "immunodysregulation-prone personality pattern" (p. 355). Because positive emotional changes facilitate biological events associated with healing (e.g., enhanced DNA repair, increases in natural killer cells and T cells, and a decrease in stress hormones), PNI represents an important landmark in understanding the psychophysiological characteristics of anomalous healing experiences. However, as is the case with other landmarks, PNI and similar system approaches have proposed structures that still need to be fully understood, reliably applied, and comfortably "lived in" to demonstrate their worth.

METHODOLOGICAL ISSUES

Anomalous Healing Experiences

The topic of methodological issues in understanding anomalous healing experiences is crucial. Theoretically, it should be possible for longitudinal studies to be made of anomalous healing experiences and for these experiences to be studied with a variety of scientific methods.

After reviewing the available literature, Irwin (1994) concluded that "notwithstanding the admirable efforts of a handful of investigators, considerably more phenomenological research into the healing experience should be undertaken because the present research literature is relatively meager and much of it is unsystematic" (p. 41). Particular attention needs to be given to the interactions among the experience of anomalous healing, the setting in which the experience takes place, and the beliefs and personalities of the experients.

Research methods used to study anomalous healing experiences have mostly included autobiographical accounts, semistructured interviews, unstructured interviews, questionnaires, personality measures, participant–observation reports, and case studies (see Pekala & Cardeña, this volume, chap. 2). Additional research strategies should be included to permit both greater qualitative and quantitative depth (e.g., Wickramasekera, 1986, 1995). Highly sophisticated phenomenological analytic methods (e.g., Colaizzi, 1989; Giorgi, 1970) can be used to determine the similar and dissimilar themes of the experiences. The Phenomenology of Consciousness Questionnaire developed by Pekala (1991) and similar instruments allow for valid and reliable assessment of various dimensions of the anomalous healing experience (e.g., arousal, affect, imagery, and volitional control). The contextual mediation categories developed by Lange, Houran, Harte, and Havens (1996) illustrate important variables that are rarely assessed or compared, such as state of arousal, cultural beliefs or expectations, demand characteristics of the situation, embedded cues in the environment, metaphorical or symbolic references, time of day, and climactic conditions. Past research on anomalous healing has been primarily ethnographic, clinical, or experimental, thus somewhat proscribed in regard to the analysis and description of the social characteristics of healing groups and their members. Prospective interview data that include sociological information (especially the symbolic and metaphorical nature of participation in group rituals) are needed to redress that imbalance and help formulate a more comprehensive analysis of these complex behaviors and experiences (Glik, 1993).

In reflecting on his own investigation, Berland (1995) stated that "a primary concern of scientists regarding research is that subjects may not accurately remember events, emotions, or representations of self at an earlier time. Moreover, their remembrances may be filtered through the screen of more recent events" (p. 5). He asked, "How can psychosocial researchers know whether their subjects, often diagnosed many years earlier, are distorting their narratives about their recoveries in what amounts to a form of self-deception?" (p. 5). To guard against the possibility that the participants are unknowingly distorting their stories because of their own belief systems or the beliefs that they attribute to the researcher, they can be tested using tools that measure denial and social desirability. Berland concluded that

> How can we know whether a psychosocial change described by a survivor has anything to do with his or her survival? We cannot know with certainty.... But we can use cross-sectional longitudinal, and prospective studies to investigate coping styles, personality traits, and mental states. (p. 6)

Anomalous Healing Events

The question of methodology is no less critical in the investigation of anomalous healing events. Archival methodology was used by Bourguignon (1976) in her survey of the anthropological literature on the success of spiritually oriented healing practices. She concluded that its success "is greatest where there is a great psychological involvement in the illness, [and] where the disorder is primarily of a psychosomatic or hysterical nature" (p. 18). This statement would have carried more weight had it resulted from quantitative content analysis.

Experimental research has the disadvantage of isolating experients from typical healing contexts, but it has the advantage of controlling respondents' activities and meticulously recording their verbal statements (Schouten, 1993, p. 378). Drawing on the biofeedback literature, Young (1985) listed several considerations that should govern the evaluation of a technique's therapeutic potential: (a) the degree of clinical meaningfulness of the changes reported; (b) the quality of the experimental design used in gathering and reporting the data; (c) the extent of follow-up obtained or reported; (d) the proportion of the treated patient sample that improved significantly; (e) the degree of replicability of the results; and (f) the degree to which changes obtained in the clinic or laboratory transferred to the patient's ordinary environment (p. 355). In following these guidelines, one must discriminate the efficacy of the various alternative and complementary medicines because different mechanisms may be at work. McClenon (1997) and Schouten (1993) wrote commendable evaluative reviews that keep the distinctions in mind.

After reviewing the available research on the topics of psychic healing and complementary medicine, Schouten (1993) proposed that the effect of a treatment is mainly associated with the difference in the state of health between onset and completion of treatment. The difference between experimental and control or placebo groups is the effect of the method. Improvement means that the feeling of well-being and the ability to function have been enhanced. Marnham (1980/1981, p. 185) reported an analysis in which the alleged cures at Lourdes were examined over five time periods; from the period 1862 to 1979, the number of cures went from 4 to 29, to 2, to 20, to 2. He attributed this uneven distribution to a difference in the standards used by the commissioners who, of course, changed over the years. Hence, even though the stated standards for an anomalous "cure" are the same from one year to the next, human judgment may differ.

Zusne and Jones (1989) described several ways in which legerdemain can be used in cases of so-called psychic surgery, whereas Krippner and Villoldo (1986) emphasized the importance of including a sleight-of-hand specialist on a research team whenever this phenomenon is investigated in a field setting. This procedure was adopted in a 1974 excursion to the Philippines when the magician David Hoy joined a group of physicians and therapists who observed a variety of sessions in which the healers' hands seemed to enter their clients' bodies, purportedly extracting a number of organic and nonorganic materials. At the end of the trip, Hoy wrote that in every case he witnessed, he detected techniques, moves, and the use of props that "are reproducible by talented professional magicians. . . . I was able to reproduce several of the effects with the very simplest materials which I procured from a Manila drugstore and an art supply store" (Meek & Hoy, 1977, p. 110).

Schlitz (1995) proposed that individuals' intentions interact with their body's self-healing capacities, but the associated methodological issues are serious and complex. For example, how can a subjective experience that is intimate and personal be understood and communicated in experimental language while still honoring the deeply individual nature of the experience? What are appropriate ways to evaluate outcomes in laboratory and clinical studies? How do alternative and complementary treatment modalities interact with intentionality to promote health? Many of the investigations summarized in this chapter represent initial attempts to answer these questions.

CONCLUSION

The most characteristic term used by biomedicine to refer to anomalous healings is *spontaneous remission*. However, such terms as *remarkable recoveries* and *changes in unchangeable bodily processes* imply paradoxes that biomedicine sometimes ignores. The U.S. Office of Alternative Medicine has seen its budget grow from $2 million in 1992 to $12 million in 1997

(OAM Budget Update, 1997), but its research projects are principally outcome studies that focus on events rather than experiences.

Research in anomalous healing would do well to avoid such simplistic terms as *mind–body healing* and other concepts that reify either psychological or bioenergetic causation. Turkheimer (1998) deconstructed many of these unsophisticated terms, wisely commenting that "all human behavior that varies among individuals is partially heritable and correlated with measurable aspects of brains, but the very ubiquity of these findings makes them a poor basis for reformulating scientists' concepts of human behavior" (p. 782).

A joint committee of the British Medical Association and Anglican Archbishops' healing commission called for a wider scope of inquiry into unusual healing, noting that "there are multiple factors—whether of body or mind—which . . . conduce to the restoration of health" (cited in Bendit, 1958, pp. 90–91). The commission added that because the human being "is a unity and health a condition of full functioning, we cannot afford, especially in critical illnesses, to disregard any means at our disposal which may lead to the restoration of . . . health, since all the functions of the personality react upon one another" (pp. 90–91). It is precisely these "means at our disposal" that are deserving of attention in the study of the experiential aspects of anomalous healing.

REFERENCES

Achterberg, J. (1985). *Imagery and healing*. Boston: Shambhala.

Achterberg, J., Dossey, L., Gordon, J. S., Hegedis, C., Herrmann, M. W., & Nelson, R. (1994). Mind–body interventions. In *Alternative medicine: Expanding medical horizons* (pp. 3–45). Washington, DC: U.S. Government Printing Office.

Achterberg, J., & Lawlis, G. F. (1989). *Health Attribution Test*. Champaign, IL: Institute for Personality and Ability Testing.

Achterberg, J., Simonton, O. C., & Simonton, S. (1976). *Stress, psychological factors, and cancer*. Ft. Worth, TX: New Medicine Press.

Adamenko, V. (1970). Electrodynamic systems. *Journal of Paraphysics, 4*, 113–121.

Ader, R. (Ed.). (1981). *Psychoneuroimmunology*. New York: Academic Press.

American Psychiatric Association. (1980). *Diagnostic and statistical manual of mental disorders* (3rd ed.). Washington, DC: Author.

Appelbaum, S. A. (1993, Winter). The laying on of healing: Personality patterns of psychic healers. *Bulletin of the Menninger Clinic*, pp. 33–40.

Asser, S. M., & Swan, R. (1998). Child fatalities from religion-motivated medical neglect. *Pediatrics, 101*, 625–629.

Attevelt, J. T. M. (1988). *Research into paranormal healing*. Unpublished doctoral dissertation. University of Utrecht, Utrecht, The Netherlands.

Barber, T. X. (1984). Changing "unchangeable" bodily processes by (hypnotic) suggestions: A new look at hypnosis, cognitions, imagining, and the mind–body problem. In A. A. Sheikh (Ed.), *Imagination and healing* (pp. 69–127). Farmingdale, NY: Baywood.

Barrett, S., & Jarvis, W. T. (Eds.). (1993). *The health robbers: A close look at quakery in America*. Amherst, NY: Prometheus Books.

Bendit, L. J. (Ed.). (1958). *The mystery of healing*. Wheaton, IL: Quest.

Benor, D. J. (1992). *Healing research: Vol. 1. Research in healing*. Munich, Germany: Helix.

Benor, D. J. (1994). *Healing research: Vol. 2. Holistic energy medicine and spirituality*. Munich, Germany: Helix.

Benson, H. (1982). Body temperature changes during the practice of gTum-mo yoga. *Nature, 298,* 402.

Benson, H. (with Stark, M.). (1996). *Timeless healing: The power and biology of belief*. New York: Simon & Schuster.

Berland, W. (1995). Unexpected cancer recovery: Why patients believe they survive. *Advances: The Journal of Mind–Body Health, 11,* 5–19.

Bird, F., & Reimer, B. (1982). Participation rates in new religions and para-religious movements. *Journal for the Scientific Study of Religion, 21,* 1–14.

Borysenko, J. Z. (1985). Healing motives: An interview with David C. McClelland. *Advances: The Journal of Mind–Body Health, 2,* 29–41.

Bourguignon, E. (1976). The effectiveness of religious healing movements: A review of the literature. *Transcultural Psychiatric Research, 13,* 5–21.

Boyer, L. B., Klopfer, B., Brawer, F. B., & Kawai, H. (1964). Comparisons of the shamans and pseudoshamans of the Apaches of the Mescalero Indian reservation: A Rorschach study. *Journal of Projective Techniques, 28,* 173–180.

Brenneman, R. J. (1990). *Deadly blessings: Faith healing on trial*. Buffalo, NY: Prometheus Books.

Broderick, R. C. (1956). *The Catholic concise encyclopedia*. New York: Catechetical Guild Educational Society/Simon & Schuster.

Byrd, R. C. (1988). Positive therapeutic effects of intercessory prayer in a coronary care unit population. *Southern Medical Journal, 81,* 826–829.

Cardeña, E. (1991). Max Beauvoir: An island in an ocean of spirits. In R. -I. Heinze (Ed.), *Shamans of the 20th century* (pp. 27–32). New York: Irvington.

Cardeña, E. (1996). "Just floating on the sky": A comparison of hypnotic and shamanic phenomena. In R. van Quekelberghe & D. Eigner (Eds.), *Yearbook of cross-cultural medicine and psychotherapy 1994* (pp. 85–98). Berlin: Verlag für Wissenchaft und Bildung.

Chaves, J., & Barber, T. X. (1975). Acupuncture analgesia: A six-factor theory. In S. Krippner & D. Rubin (Eds.), *The energies of consciousness* (pp. 181–197). New York: Interface/Gordon & Breech.

Colaizzi, P. F. (1989). Psychological research as the phenomenologist views it. In

R. S. Valle & S. Halling (Eds.), *Existential–phenomenological alternatives for psychology* (pp. 48–71). New York: Oxford University Press.

Cooperstein, M. A. (1992). The myths of healing: A summary of research into transpersonal healing experiences. *Journal of the American Society for Psychical Research, 86,* 99–133.

Cranston, R. (1957). *The miracle of Lourdes.* New York: Popular Library. (Original work published 1955)

Cunningham, A. (1984). Psychotherapy and cancer: A review. *Advances: The Journal of Mind–Body Health, 9,* 8–14.

de Carvalho, M. M. (1996). An eclectic approach to group healing in São Paulo, Brazil: A pilot study. *Journal of the Society for Psychical Research, 61,* 243–250.

Devereux, G. (1961). Shamans as neurotics. *American Anthropologist, 63,* 1088–1090.

DeVita, V. T., Hellman, S., & Rosenberg, S. A. (1991). *Biologic therapy of cancer.* Philadelphia: Lippincott.

Dodes, J. E. (1997, January/February). The mysterious placebo. *Skeptical Inquirer,* pp. 44–45.

Dossey, L. (1993a). *Healing words: The power of prayer and the practice of medicine.* San Francisco: HarperSanFrancisco.

Dossey, L. (1993b). The integration of healing and modern medicine. *American Society for Psychical Research Newsletter, 18*(2), 1–4.

Dossey, L. (1995). Whatever happened to healers? *Alternative Therapies, 1,* 6–13.

Edwards, H. (1953). *The evidence for spirit healing.* London: Spiritualist Press.

Eisenberg, D. M., Kessler, R. C., Foster, C., Norlock, F. E., Calkins, D. R., & Delbanco, T. L. (1993). Unconventional medicine in the United States: Prevalence, costs, and patterns of use. *New England Journal of Medicine, 328,* 246–252.

Ernst, E., & White, E. R. (1997). A review of problems in clinical acupuncture research. *American Journal of Chinese Medicine, 25,* 3–11.

Fawzy, F., Fawzy, N. W., Hyun, C. S., Elashoff, R., Guthrie, D., Fahey, J., & Morton, D. L. (1993). Malignant melanoma: Effects of an early structured psychiatric intervention, coping, and affective state on recurrence and survival 6 years later. *Archives of General Psychiatry, 50,* 681–689.

Finkler, K. (1985). *Spiritualist healers in Mexico: Successes and failures of alternative therapies.* New York: Bergin & Garvey.

Fischer, R. (1971). A cartography of the ecstatic and meditative states. *Science, 174,* 897–904.

FitzHerbert, J. (1971). The nature of hypnosis and paranormal healing. *Journal of the Society for Psychical Research, 46,* 1–14.

Frank, J. D., & Frank, J. B. (1991). *Persuasion and healing: A comparative study of psychotherapy* (3rd ed.). Baltimore: Johns Hopkins University Press.

French, C. (1996). Psychic healing. In G. Stein (Ed.), *The encyclopedia of the paranormal* (pp. 597–604). Amherst, NY: Prometheus Books.

Fuller, R. C. (1989). *Alternative medicine and American religious life*. New York: Oxford University Press.

Gerber, R. (1988). *Vibrational medicine: New choices for healing ourselves*. Santa Fe, NM: Bear.

Gergen, K. J. (1985). The social constructionist movement in modern psychology. *American Psychologist, 40,* 266–275.

Gilovich, T. (1991). *How we know what isn't so: The fallibility of human reason in everyday life*. New York: Free Press.

Giorgi, A. (1970). *Psychology as a human science: A phenomenologically based approach*. New York: Harper & Row.

Glik, D. C. (1993). Beliefs, practices, and experiences of spiritual healing adherents in an American industrial city. In W. Andritsky (Ed.), *Yearbook of cross-cultural medicine and psychotherapy, 1992* (pp. 199–223). Berlin: Verlag für Wissenchaft und Bildung.

Gowan, J. C. (1980). *Operations of increasing order*. Westlake Village, CA: Author.

Grad, B. (1967). The "laying on of hands": Implications for psychotherapy, gentling, and the placebo effect. *Journal of the American Society for Psychical Research, 61,* 286–305.

Green, E., & Green, A. (1977). *Beyond biofeedback*. New York: Delacorte/Seymour Lawrence.

Greenfield, S. M. (1997). The patients of Dr. Fritz: Assessments of treatment by a Brazilian spiritist healer. *Journal of the Society for Psychical Research, 61,* 372–383.

Greer, S., Morris, T., Pettingale, K. W., & Haybittle, J. (1990). Psychological response to breast cancer and fifteen-year outcome. *The Lancet, 335,* 49–50.

Grossarth-Maticek, R., Bastiaans, J., & Kanazir, D. T. (1985). Psychosocial factors as strong predictors of mortality from cancer, ischaemic heart disease, and stroke: The Yugoslav prospective study. *Journal of Psychosomatic Research, 29,* 167–176.

Harner, M. (1980). *The way of the shaman: A guide to power and healing*. San Francisco: Harper & Row.

Harvey, D. (1983). *The power to heal: An investigation of healing and the healing experience*. Wellingborough, England: Aquarian Press.

Hawley, G. (1989). *The role of holistic variables in the attribution of cancer survival*. Unpublished doctoral dissertation, Saybrook Institute, San Francisco.

Haynes, R. (1977, July–August). Faith healing and psychic healing: Are they the same? *Parapsychology Review,* pp. 1–3.

Heber, A. S., Fleisher, W. P., Ross, C. A., & Stanwick, R. S. (1989). Dissociation in alternative healers and traditional therapists: A comparative study. *American Journal of Psychotherapy, 43,* 562–574.

Hirschberg, C., & Barasch, M. I. (1995). *Remarkable recovery*. New York: Riverhead.

Irwin, H. J. (1994). The phenomenology of parapsychological experience. In S.

Krippner (Ed.), *Advances in parapsychological research* (Vol. 7, pp. 10–76). Jefferson, NC: McFarland.

Irwin, H. J. (1999). *An introduction to parapsychology* (3rd ed.). Jefferson, NC: McFarland.

James, W. (1904). A world of pure experience. *Journal of Philosophy, Psychology, and Scientific Methods, 1,* 533–543.

Jilek, W. G. (1982). Altered states of consciousness in North American Indian ceremonials. *Ethos, 10,* 326–343.

Joyce, C. R., & Weldon, R. M. (1965). The objective efficacy of prayer: A double-blind study. *Journal of Chronic Diseases, 18,* 367–377.

Kidd, C. B. (1966). Congenial ichthyosiform erythrodermia treated by hypnosis. *British Journal of Dermatology, 78,* 101–105.

Kirkpatrick, R. A. (1981). Witchcraft and lupus rythematosus. *Journal of the American Medical Association, 245,* 1937.

Kirsch, I. (1990). *Changing expectations.* Pacific Grove, CA: Brooks/Cole.

Kleijnen, J., ter Riet, G., & Knipschild, P. (1991). Acupuncture and asthma: A review of controlled trials. *Thorax, 46,* 799–802.

Kleinman, A. (1980). *Patients and healers in the context of culture: An exploration of the borderland between anthropology, medicine, and psychiatry.* Berkeley: University of California Press.

Kleinman, A. (1995). *Writing at the margin.* Berkeley: University of California Press.

Knight, K. L. (1994). *The lived experience of hope in seriously ill persons: A psychological phenomenological analysis.* Unpublished doctoral dissertation, Saybrook Institute, San Francisco.

Krieger, D. (1979). *The therapeutic touch.* Englewood Cliffs, NJ: Prentice Hall.

Krippner, S. (1990). A questionnaire study of experiential reactions to a Brazilian healer. *Journal of the Society for Psychical Research, 56,* 208–215.

Krippner, S. (1994). Cross-cultural treatment perspectives on dissociative disorders. In S. J. Lynn & J. W. Rhue (Eds.), *Dissociation: Clinical and theoretical perspectives* (pp. 338–361). New York: Guilford Press.

Krippner, S. (1996). The use of altered conscious states in North and South American Indian shamanic healing rituals. In R. van Quekelberghe & D. Eigner (Eds.), *Yearbook of cross-cultural medicine and psychotherapy 1994* (pp. 181–202). Berlin, Germany: Verlag für Wissenchaft und Bildung.

Krippner, S., & Villoldo, A. (1986). *The realms of healing.* Berkeley, CA: Celestial Arts.

Krippner, S., & Welch, P. (1992). *Spiritual dimensions of healing.* New York: Irvington.

Krippner, S., & Winkler, M. (1996). The "need to believe." In G. Stein (Ed.), *The encyclopedia of the paranormal* (pp. 441–454). Amherst, NY: Prometheus Books.

Lange, R., Houran, J., Harte, T. M., & Havens, R. A. (1996). Contextual mediation of perceptions in hauntings and poltergeist-like experiences. *Perceptual and Motor Skills, 82,* 755–762.

Lawlis, G. F. (1996). *Transpersonal medicine.* Boston: Shambhala.

León, C. A. (1975). *El duende* and other incubi. *Archives of General Psychiatry, 32,* 155–162.

LeShan, L. (1974). *The medium, the mystic, and the physicist: Toward a general theory of the paranormal.* New York: Viking Press.

LeShan, L. (1976). *Alternate realities.* New York: Lippincott.

LeShan, L. (1982). *The mechanic and the gardener: Making the most of the holistic revolution in medicine.* New York: Holt, Rinehart & Winston.

Leskowitz, E. (1998). Un-debunking therapeutic touch. *Alternative Therapies, 4,* 101–102.

Levin, J. S. (1996). How prayer heals: A theoretical model. *Alternative Therapies, 2,* 66–73.

Mahler, H. (1977, November). The staff of Aesculapius. *World Health,* p. 3.

Maki, M. (1998). *In search of Brazil's quantum surgeon.* San Francisco: Cadence.

Marnham, P. (1981). *Lourdes: A modern pilgrimage.* New York: Coward, McCann & Geoghegan. (Original work published 1980)

McClelland, D. C. (1989). Motivational factors in health and disease. *American Psychologist, 44,* 675–683.

McClenon, J. (1997). Spiritual healing and folklore research: Evaluating the hypnosis/placebo theory. *Alternative Therapies in Health and Medicine, 3,* 61–66.

McCormick, D. (1986, July). Faith healer exposed. *American Society for Psychical Research Newsletter,* p. 23.

Meek, G., & Hoy, D. (1977). Deception and slight-of-hand. In G. W. Meek (Ed.), *Healers and the healing process* (pp. 97–114). Wheaton, IL: Theosophical Publishing.

Mehl-Madrona, L. (1997, March/May). Lessons in coyote medicine. *Shaman's Drum,* pp. 27–33.

Melnechuk, T. (1988). Emotion, brain, immunity, and health: A review. In M. Clynes & J. Panksepp (Eds.), *Emotions in psychopathology* (pp. 181–247). New York: Plenum.

Miller, J. G. (1978). *Living systems.* New York: McGraw-Hill.

Murdock, G. P. (1980). *Theories of illness: A world survey.* Pittsburgh, PA: University of Pittsburgh Press.

Murphy, J. M. (1976). Psychiatric labeling in cross-cultural perspective. *Science, 191,* 1019–1028.

Noll, R. (1983). Shamanism and schizophrenia. *American Ethnologist, 10,* 443–459.

Noll, R. (1986). Mental imagery cultivation as a cultural phenomenon: The role of visions in shamanism (with commentaries). *Current Anthropology, 27,* 443–461.

OAM budget update. (1997, January). *Complementary and Alternative Medicine at the NIH*, p. 3.

O'Connor, B., Calabrese, C., Cardeña, E., Eisenberg, D., Fincher, J., Hufford, D. J., Jonas, W. B., Kaptchuck, T., Martin, S. C., Scott, A. W., & Zhang, X. (1997). Defining and describing complementary and alternative medicine. *Alternative Therapies, 3*, 49–57.

O'Laoire, S. (1997). An experimental study of the effects of intercessory prayer-at-a-distance on self-esteem, anxiety, and depression. *Alternative Therapies, 3*, 38–53.

O'Regan, B., & Hirshberg, C. (1993). *Spontaneous remission: An annotated bibliography*. Sausalito, CA: Institute for Noetic Sciences.

Pekala, R. J. (1991). *Quantifying consciousness: An empirical approach*. New York: Plenum.

Pelletier, K. (1977). *Mind as healer, mind as slayer*. New York: Dell.

Pelletier, K. (1994). *Sound mind, sound body: A new model for lifelong health*. New York: Simon & Schuster.

Pert, C., Ruff, M., Weber, R., & Herkenham, M. (1985). Neuropeptides and their receptors: A psychosomatic network. *Journal of Immunology, 135*, 820–826.

Peters, L. G., & Price-Williams, D. (1983). A phenomenological overview of trance. *Transcultural Psychiatric Research Review, 29*, 5–39.

Peterson, C., Seligman, M. E. P., & Vaillant, G. E. (1988). Pessimistic explanatory style is a risk factor for physical illness. *Journal of Personality and Social Psychology, 55*, 23–27.

Pettingale, K. W., Greer, S., Morris, T., & Haybittle, J. (1985). Mental attitudes to cancer: An additional prognostic factor. *The Lancet, 330*, 750.

Poloma, M. M., & Hoelter, L. F. (1998). The "Toronto blessing": A holistic model of healing. *Journal for the Scientific Study of Religion, 37*, 257–272.

Popper, K. R. (1959). *The logic of scientific discovery*. New York: Basic Books.

Radin, P. (1937). *Primitive religion*. New York: Viking Press.

Radner, D., & Radner, M. (1985). Holistic methodology and pseudoscience. In D. Stalker & C. Glymour (Eds.), *Examining holistic medicine* (pp. 149–159). Buffalo, NY: Prometheus Books.

Randi, J. (1987). *The faith-healers*. Buffalo, NY: Prometheus Books.

Rebman, J. M., Wezelman, R., Radin, D. I., Stevens, P., Hapke, R., & Haughan, K. Z. (1995). Remote influences of human physiology by a ritual healing technique. *Subtle Energies, 6*, 111–134.

Rehder, H. (1955). Wunderheilungen, ein Experiment [Wonderhealing, an experiment]. *Hippokrates, 26*, 577–580.

Remen, R. N. (1996). *Kitchen table wisdom: Stories that heal*. New York: Riverhead Books.

Richmond, K., Berman, B. M., Docherty, J. P., Holdstein, L. B., Kaplan, G., Keil, J. E., Krippner, S., Lyne, S., Mosteller, F., O'Connor, B. B., Rudy, E. B., &

Schatzberg, A. F. (1996). Integration of behavioral and relaxation approaches into the treatment of chronic pain and insomnia. *Journal of the American Medical Association, 276,* 313–318.

Roberts, A. H., Kewman, D. G., Mercier, L., & Hovell, M. (1993). The power of nonspecific effects in healing. *Clinical Psychology Review, 13,* 375–391.

Rosa, L., Rosa, E., Sarner, L., & Barrett, S. (1998). A close look at therapeutic touch. *Journal of the American Medical Association, 279,* 1005–1010.

Rosen, R. (1991). *Life itself.* New York: Columbia University Press.

Rossi, E. L. (1993). *The psychobiology of mind–body healing: New concepts of therapeutic hypnosis* (Rev. ed.). New York: Norton.

Rotenberg, V. S., Sirota, P., & Elizur, A. (1996). PNI: Searching for the main deteriorating psychobehavioral factor. *Genetic, Social, and General Psychology Monographs, 122,* 329–346.

Rouget, G. (1985). *Music and trance: A theory of the relations between music and possession* (B. Bieboyck & G. Rouget, Trans). Chicago: University of Chicago Press. (Original French ed. published 1980)

Samek, J. (1931). Zum wesen der Suggestiven Warzenheilund [The effects of suggestion on healing warts]. *Dermatologische Wochenschrift, 93,* 1853–1857.

Schlitz, M. (1995). Intentionality in healing: Mapping the integration of body, mind, and spirit. *Alternative Therapies, 1,* 119–120.

Schlitz, M., & Braud, W. (1997). Distant intentionality and healing: Assessing the evidence. *Alternative Therapies, 3,* 62–73.

Schouten, S. A. (1993). Applied parapsychology studies of psychics and healers. *Journal of Scientific Exploration, 7,* 375–401.

Shealy, C. N. (with Freese, A. S.). (1975). *Occult medicine can save your life.* New York: Dial Press.

Shweder, R. A. (1986). Divergent rationalities. In D. W. Fiske & R. A. Shweder (Eds.), *Metatheory in social science: Pluralisms and subjectivities* (pp. 163–196). Chicago: University of Chicago Press.

Shweder, R. A. (1990). Cultural psychology—What is it? In J. W. Stigler, R. A. Schweder, & G. Herdt (Eds.), *Cultural psychology: Essays on comparative human development* (pp. 1–43). New York: Cambridge University Press.

Silverman, A. J., & McGough, W. E. (1971). Personality, stress and venous flow rates. *Journal of Psychosomatic Research, 15,* 315.

Silverman, J. (1967). Shamans and acute schizophrenia. *American Anthropologist, 69,* 21–31.

Simonton, O. C., Matthews-Simonton, S., & Creighton, J. (1978). *Getting well again.* Los Angeles: Jeremy P. Tarcher/St. Martin's Press.

Snyder, C., & Noble, M. (1968). Operant conditioning of vasoconstriction. *Journal of Experimental Psychology, 77,* 263–268.

Solfvin, J. (1984). Mental healing. In S. Krippner (Ed.), *Advances in parapsychological research* (Vol. 4, pp. 31–63). Jefferson, NC: McFarland.

Solomon, G. F. (1990). Emotions, stress, and immunity. In R. Ornstein & C.

Swencionis (Eds.), *The healing brain: A scientific reader* (pp. 174–181). New York: Guilford Press.

Solomon, G. F., Kemeny, M. E., & Temoshok, L. (1991). Psychoneuroimmunologic aspects of human immunodeficiency virus infection. In R. Adler, D. L. Fenton, & N. Cohen (Eds.), *Psychoneuroimmunology II* (pp. 1081–1113). New York: Academic Press.

Solomon, G. F., Temoshok, L., O'Leary, A., & Zich, J. (1987). An intensive psychoimmunologic study of long-surviving persons with AIDS. *Annals of the New York Academy of Sciences, 496*, 647–655.

Solomon, G. F. (1993). Whither psychoneuroimmunology? A new era of immunology, of psychosomatic medicine, and of neuroscience. *Brain, Behavior, and Immunity, 7*, 352–366.

Somé, M. P. (1994). *Of water and the spirit.* New York: Jeremy P. Tarcher/Putnam.

Spiegel, D., Bloom, J. R., Kraemer, H. C., & Gottheil, E. (1989, October 14). Effect of psychosocial treatment on survival of patients with metastatic breast cancer. *The Lancet,* pp. 888–890.

Srinivasan, T. M. (Ed.). (1988). *Energy medicine around the world.* Phoenix, AZ: Gabriel Press.

St. Clair, D. (1974). *Psychic healers.* Garden City, NY: Doubleday.

Staiger, T. (1995). A new biological model of physiology and mental processes: An examination of Robert Rosen's Life itself. *Advances: The Journal of Mind-Body Health, 11*, 52–56.

Stalker, D., & Glymour, C. (1985). Quantum medicine. In D. Stalker & C. Glymour (Eds.), *Examining holistic medicine* (pp. 107–125). Buffalo, NY: Prometheus Books.

Stetler, A. (1976). *Psi-healing.* New York: Bantam Books.

Strauch, I. (1963). Medical aspects of "mental" healing. *International Journal of Parapsychology, 5*, 136–166.

Taub, E., & Emurian, C. S. (1976). Feedback aided self-regulation of skin temperature with a single feedback locus: I. Acquisition and reversal training. *Biofeedback and Self-Regulation, 1*, 147–148.

Tessman, I., & Tessman, J. (1997). Mind and body. *Science, 276*, 369–370.

Thong, D. (with Carpenter, B., & Krippner, S.). (1993). *A psychiatrist in paradise: Treating mental illness in Bali.* Bangkok, Thailand: White Lotus Press.

Torrey, E. F. (1986). *Witchdoctors and psychiatrists: The common roots of psychotherapy and its future.* New York: Harper & Row.

Turkheimer, E. (1998). Heritability and biological explanation. *Psychological Review, 105*, 782–891.

van Baalen, D. C., & DeVries, M. J. (1987, April). "Spontaneous" regression of cancer. *Humane Medicine,* pp. 15–25.

van Baalen, D. C., DeVries, M. J., & Gondrie, M. T. (1987, April). Psychosocial correlates of "spontaneous" regression of cancer. *Humane Medicine,* pp. 1–14.

Wallace, A., & Henkin, B. (1978). *The psychic healing book.* New York: Delacorte.

Weil, A. (1995). *Spontaneous healing*. New York: Knopf.

Westgate, C. E. (1996). Spiritual wellness and depression. *Journal of Counseling Psychology, 75*, 26–35.

Weston, W. L. (1991). *Healing, reason and miracles*. Pickerinton, OH: Advocate.

Westerbeke, P., & Krippner, S. (1980). Subjective reactions to the Filipino "healers." *International Journal of Paraphysics, 14*, 9–17.

Wickramasekera, I. (1980). A conditioned response model of the placebo effect: Predictions from the model. *Biofeedback and Self-Regulation, 5*, 5–18.

Wickramasekera, I. (1986). A model of people at high risk to develop chronic stress related symptoms: Some predictions. *Professional Psychology: Research and Practice, 17*, 437–447.

Wickramasekera, I. (1989). Risk factors for parapsychological verbal reports, hypnotizability and somatic complaints. In B. Shapin & L. Coly (Eds.), *Parapsychology and human nature* [Proceedings of an international conference held in Washington, DC, November 1–2, 1986] (pp. 19–28). New York: Parapsychology Foundation.

Wickramasekera, I. (1995). Somatization: Concepts, data, and predictions from the high risk model of threat perception. *Journal of Nervous and Mental Disease, 183*, 15–23.

Wikler, D. (1985). Holistic medicine: Concepts of personal responsibility for health. In D. Stalker & C. Glymour (Eds.), *Examining holistic medicine* (pp. 137–146). Buffalo, NY: Prometheus Books.

Wilson, S. C., & Barber, T. X. (1978). The Creative Imagination Scale as a measure of hypnotic responsiveness: Applications to experimental and clinical hypnosis. *American Journal of Clinical Hypnosis, 20*, 235–249.

Winkelman, M. (1992). *Shamans, priests and witches: A cross-cultural study of magico-religious practitioners*. Tempe: University of Arizona Press.

Worrall, O. N. (1970). *Explore your psychic world*. New York: Harper & Row.

Young, L. D. (1985). Holistic medicine's use of biofeedback. In D. Stalker & C. Glymour (Eds.), *Examining holistic medicine* (pp. 341–359). Buffalo, NY: Prometheus Books.

Zusne, L., & Jones, W. H. (1989). *Anomalistic psychology: A study of magical thinking* (2nd ed.). Hillsdale, NJ: Erlbaum.

12

MYSTICAL EXPERIENCE

DAVID M. WULFF

Falling by definition outside the realm of ordinary discourse, mystical experience eludes any precise description or characterization. Furthermore, as relatively recent constructions that serve diverse and even opposing purposes, the terms *mystical* and *mysticism* are themselves hard to pin down. *Mystic* and its variants derive from the Latin *mysticus*, of mysteries, and from the Greek *mystikos*, from *mystes*, initiate. The 26 definitions of mysticism that Inge (1899) assembled a century ago illustrate how loosely the word was used then, often in disparaging or contemptuous ways. Scholars today (e.g., Forman, 1990) continue to remark on how variable the definitions of this term are. Most commentators agree, however, that any experience qualified as mystical diverges in fundamental ways from ordinary conscious awareness and leaves a strong impression of having encountered a reality different from—and, in some crucial sense, higher than—the reality of everyday experience.[1] Rare and fleeting though they usually are,

---

[1]If one considered these criteria as sufficient for identifying an experience as mystical, near-death experiences (NDEs) would easily qualify. However, the accent on individual identity (e.g., in the form of a life review and encounters with deceased relatives), the relative clarity of events, and the absence of the experience of union distinguish most NDEs from classic mystical experiences. The two are usually discussed separately, as in this book. *Peak experiences*, Maslow's (1964, 1968) preferred phrase, is still looser in meaning than *mystical experiences*, emphasizing the individual's experience over, if not to the exclusion of, the reality that is

397

such experiences often stand out as defining moments in the lives of those who have them.

THREE EXAMPLES

Given the extraordinary range of experiences that are described as mystical, a few examples cannot possibly represent the whole. Yet a sampling of first-hand reports is essential to ground us in the lived reality of these compelling experiences. The first of these describes an experience of author Sophy Burnham (1997), who at the time was a freelance writer on assignment in Central and South America. A spiritual seeker and meditator whose mother had died a few months earlier, she had been deeply stirred by the discussions of God she had had with a group of three extraordinary men she met in Costa Rica. Still in a state of transport when she arrived in Peru, Burnham joined a tour group visiting the ancient sacred site of Machu Picchu. Suddenly assailed by a hollow roaring in her ears and the sense that she was there for some purpose, she separated herself from the group, climbed the hillside, and threw herself to the ground.

> I felt a pressure on my neck, as if a dark hand were pressing me down. Terrible and majestic it was. . . . From the midst of black roaring, came a voice: *You belong to me* or *You are mine.* Not in words, but rather as a form of knowledge, resounding in blackness. . . . For a moment I fought it, terrified. Then: "If you are God, yes," I surrendered with my last coherent thoughts. "I belong only to God." . . . With that I was immersed in a sweetness words cannot express. I could hear the singing of the planets, and wave after wave of light washed over me. But this is wrong, because I *was* the light as well, without distinction of self or of being washed. It is hard to speak of what happened at this stage. At one level I ceased to exist, was swallowed into light. How long that lasted I do not know. At another level, although I no longer existed as a separate "I," nonetheless I saw things, thus indicating the duality of "I" and "other." In that state I knew things that today I haven't even the wit to ask questions about. Some I do not remember, but I know that I saw into the structure of the universe. I had the impression of knowing beyond knowledge and being given glimpses into ALL. . . . It was knowledge untranslatable, and it filled me with joy. (Burnham, 1997, pp. 78–79)

In the next example, taken from a collection of documents solicited by zoologist Alister Hardy (1979) as the founding director of the Religious

---

encountered. *Flow experiences*, which are said to share many features with peak experiences, including self-forgetfulness, only occasionally include the transcendent, ecstatic, or visionary element of "deep flow," which seems to occur mainly in nature settings (Csikszentmihalyi, 1982).

Experience Research Unit at Oxford University, an officer recalled an experience he had during World War I:

> I walked eastward for about two miles along the towpath and then turned about. The nearer I drew to the village, the more alive my surroundings seemed to become. It was as if something which had been dormant when I was in the wood were coming to life. I must have drifted into an exalted state. The moon, when I look up at it, seemed to have become personalised and observant, as if it were aware of my presence on the tow-path [sic]. A sweet scent pervaded the air. . . . The slowly moving waters of the canal, which was winding its unhurried way from the battlefields to the sea, acquired a "numen" which endorsed the intimations of the burgeoning trees. . . . A feeling that I was being absorbed into the living surroundings gained in intensity and was working up to a climax. Something was going to happen. Then it happened. The experience lasted, I should say, about thirty seconds and seemed to come out of the sky in which were resounding harmonies. The thought: "That is the music of the spheres" was immediately followed by a glimpse of luminous bodies—meteors or stars—circulating in predestined courses emitting both light and music. I stood still on the tow-path and wondered if I was going to fall down. I dropped on to one knee and thought: "How wonderful to die at this moment!" (p. 41)

Our third example, cited by William James (1902/1985), comes from the English writer and poet John Addington Symonds (1840–1893), who described a trancelike[2] mood that recurred, with diminishing frequency, until he was 28.

> Suddenly, at church, or in company, or when I was reading . . . I felt the approach of the mood. Irresistibly it took possession of my mind and will, lasted what seemed an eternity, and disappeared in a series of rapid sensations, which resembled the awakening from anaesthetic influence. One reason why I disliked this kind of trance was that I could not describe it to myself. I cannot even now find words to render it intelligible. It consisted in a gradual but swiftly progressive obliteration of space, time, sensation, and the multitudinous factors of experience which seem to qualify what we are pleased to call our self. In proportion, as these conditions of ordinary consciousness were subtracted, the sense of an underlying or essential consciousness acquired

---

[2]*Trance* should be understood to refer to a state of profound absorption or lack of mental content during which the individual is experientially cut off from the outside world; it is frequently accompanied by vocal and motor automatisms, lack of reflective awareness, and amnesia. *Ecstasy*, as the title of Arbman's (1963–1970) three-volume work, *Ecstasy, or Religious Trance*, suggests, is a specifically religious or mystical state distinguished by the profound emotionality that accompanies the narrowing of awareness to the contemplative object. In contrast to trance, ecstasy is marked by little or no movement and may be accompanied by vivid imagery. Rouget (1980/1985) suggests several further distinctions, noting that states of trance are often the product of over-stimulation in a group setting, whereas states of ecstasy more often occur in solitary settings marked by sensory reduction (see also Cardeña, 1996).

intensity. At last nothing remained but a pure, absolute, abstract self. The universe became without form and void of content. But self persisted, formidable in its vivid keenness, feeling the most poignant doubt about reality. . . . The return to ordinary conditions of sentient existence began by my first recovering the power of touch, and then by the gradual though rapid influx of familiar impressions and diurnal interests. At last I felt myself once more a human being; and though the riddle of what is meant by life remained unsolved, I was thankful for this return from the abyss—this deliverance from so awful an initiation into the mysteries of scepticism. (James, 1902/1985, p. 306)

Symonds also supplied James with an example of mystical ecstasy induced by chloroform—in this instance, a deeply intimate sense of God's presence, the fading of which, as Symonds regained consciousness following surgery, left him feeling devastated (James, 1902/1985, p. 310).

CHARACTERISTICS AND TYPES OF MYSTICAL EXPERIENCE

From such variable descriptions as well as the more traditional mystical literatures, various commentators have abstracted a common core of essential traits that remains invariant from one context to the next. Perhaps the most famous and perdurable characterization of mystical experience is the one offered by James (1902/1958), who identified two essential traits, one negative and the other positive. Such experience is marked, first of all, by *ineffability*, the quality of eluding any adequate account in words. Thus, like feeling states, the experience can be truly comprehended only by those who have known it at first hand. Second, it possesses a *noetic quality*: It is experienced as a state of deep, authoritative knowledge or insight unknown to the discursive intellect. These two qualities are often accompanied by two less-distinctive characteristics: *transiency*, a tendency for the experience to fade within an hour or two, leaving behind an imperfect recollection though an enduring sense of its importance, and *passivity*, the feeling that, after the experience sets in, one is no longer in control and is perhaps even in the grasp of a superior power (pp. 302–303).

A more elaborate and serviceable set of characteristics defining a universal core of a mystical experience was subsequently put forward by Stace (1960) from his study of Christian, Islamic, Judaic, Hindu, Buddhist, and Taoist mystical sources. Of the seven characteristics Stace identified, the first stands out as the "very inner essence of all mystical experience" (p. 132): (a) the disappearance of all the physical and mental objects of ordinary consciousness and, in their place, the emergence of a unitary, undifferentiated, or pure consciousness. Accordingly, (b) the experience is located neither in space nor in time. Furthermore, it is marked by (c) a sense of objectivity or reality; (d) feelings of peace, bliss, joy, and blessedness; (e) the feeling, in varying degrees, of having encountered the holy, the sacred, or the divine (sometimes identified as "God"); (f) paradoxicality, apparent violations of the usual laws of logic as illustrated by a consciousness that has no object; and (g) alleged ineffability—"alleged" because Stace is less certain than James what this common claim of the mystics means.

Together, these seven characteristics constitute what Stace (1960) called *introvertive* mystical experience. The first and third examples cited at the beginning of the chapter mentioned illustrate such experience, Symonds's (the third example) most explicitly when he wrote of a pure self and a universe beyond space and time and without form or content. As Stace pointed out, however, Symonds's experience is rather unusual in its lack of peace and joy or the conviction of objective reality. These qualities, along with the others, are unmistakable in Burnham's (1997) account.

In the case of *extrovertive* mystical experience, illustrated by our second example, the objects of the material world do not vanish but are directly and mysteriously perceived as possessing an underlying unity. This unity is understood as basic to the universe, and thus extrovertive mystical experience differs from the introvertive type on the second characteristic as well: In place of a nontemporal and nonspatial experience is a perceived "inner subjectivity, or life, in all things" (Stace, 1960, p. 131). The two types have in common, then, the remaining five characteristics. In Stace's view, the extrovertive mystical experience is both inferior to and less significant than the introvertive type, which is far more common in the literature on mysticism. In contrast, Forman (1998b) concluded that introvertive mystical experience, which he relabeled a *pure consciousness event* to emphasize the absence of any experienced object, is the more elemental form. Two further states develop from this—the dualistic mystical state, which combines a heightened awareness-of-one's-own-awareness with consciousness of thoughts and objects, and the unitive mystical state, in which one's awareness and its objects become one, which is Stace's extrovertive experience. Forman rejected the label *extrovertive* because it seems to suggest that one is having the experience "out in the world" (p. 186).

A further typological distinction will be helpful here. Critical to any right understanding of mysticism, according to Pratt (1920), is the differentiation of two forms of mystical experience: the mild and the extreme. The latter type is featured by James (1902/1985), who maintained that only by examining extreme cases will one see the essential characteristics of a mystical experience and be able to judge their consequences. In contrast, Pratt argued that most of mysticism's positive fruits have come from the less noticeable, but more common, milder type.

In either case, according to Pratt (1920), the individual experiences the presence of a greater reality without the evident participation of ordinary perceptual processes but with the same compelling sense of objectivity that sensory experience provides. The extreme type adds a number of distinctive elements, including dramatic swings from painful suffering and profound feelings of unworthiness at one pole to joyful ecstasy and bliss at the other. Typical of the extreme type, too, is the use of various ascetic practices—including fasting, flagellation, isolation, and other forms of abstinence and austerity—as a means of spiritual training, and the occurrence of such exceptional phenomena as visions, inner voices, the feeling of levitation, and abnormal bodily changes.

Erotic language and images are common among these extreme mystics as well. Perhaps the most famous example, immortalized by Bernini's well-known sculpture of the scene, is the description by Saint Teresa of Avila (1515–1582) of her encounter with a handsome angel, whose repeated plunging of his fiery spear into her "entrails" caused her to moan from the intense but deliciously sweet pain (Moller, 1965, p. 263). Some commentators (e.g., Montmorand, 1920) have argued that the mystics resorted to erotic language because no other came as close to expressing their mystical ecstasies. Other observers (e.g., Pratt, 1920; Leuba, 1925), however, have pointed out that in various religious traditions the intensity and literalness of the mystic's imagery leave little doubt that sexual impulses are to some degree implicated. Flournoy's (1915) modern mystic was frank about the sexual influences in her own mystical experience just as Mallory's (1977) comtemplatives were candid about the erotic elements in theirs.

Taken together, the various features of the extreme form of mysticism have suggested to many psychologists that mystical experience is symptomatic of mental disorder. While defending the extreme type from any sweeping comparisons to mental illness, Pratt (1920) acknowledged that pathology may color the experience of some of the great ecstatics and even take over the lives of some of the minor ones. But he noted that the mystics themselves often resist these tendencies and discount their importance. Moreover, their disciplined dedication to a higher purpose sets them apart from the pathologically disturbed. Pratt was nevertheless convinced that ecstasy is in some sense dangerous, and thus he was anxious to dissociate the mild form of mystical experience from any judgments of the extreme type. The possible connections between pathology and mystical experience are addressed below.

AFTEREFFECTS

The aftereffects of mystical experience have been explored mainly by case studies and anecdotes, techniques that, while unserviceable for empirical generalizations, can be very useful in phenomenological research (see van Manen, 1990). Anecdotes bring home how individual and striking the aftereffects of mystical experience can be at the same time that they make apparent—in some cases, at least—the intimate connection between the particular content of the experience and its effects. Although a profound sense of fatigue may immediately follow a mystical experience, and the knowledge or insight that defines it often proves frustratingly difficult to recapture and articulate, there remains the joyful impression of having encountered a higher reality and discovered new truths. Ordinary concerns recede in importance or appear in a new light, and new beliefs and values take the place of old ones. Some experients report feeling an intensified love and compassion for others, and many say that life as a whole has taken on new meaning.

Writing many years after her own experience of a compelling luminous presence that remained with her for 5 days, even in the midst of ordinary activities and relationships, Foster (1985) said that her life was permanently altered and that the values she became aware of during those days became ascendant over all others. Moreover, the vision itself did not entirely fade: From that time forward, she wrote, she had "an intuitive awareness of being 'companioned,'" and any work she did was an offering to "that Other whom I now recognized" (pp. 47, 48). A theologian who experienced an ecstatic vision of unity while swinging in Houston and Masters's (1972) Altered States of Consciousness Induction Device found a long-standing writing block suddenly dissolved, and he reported improved family relations and teaching as well as a sense of continuing growth.

The most systematic empirical study of the aftereffects of mystical experience was undertaken by Pahnke (1966) and extended years later by Doblin (1991). With 20 Protestant seminarians serving as his participants, Pahnke set about to establish that psilocybin, the primary psychoactive substance contained in "sacred mushrooms," can precipitate experiences similar to those reported by the classic mystics. Carefully controlling for all other variables including set or expectation, Pahnke randomly gave psilocybin to half of his participants (who thereby became the experimental group) and nicotinic acid, a B vitamin that causes flushing sensations, to the other half (the control group). Together, the two groups of participants then listened to a 2.5-hr broadcast of a nearby Good Friday service. Statistical analysis of coded interviews and written descriptions of the experience along with responses to a 147-item questionnaire based mainly on Stace's (1960) phenomenology allowed Pahnke to conclude that the experiences reported by those who ingested psilocybin were significantly closer to the classic mystical experience than those reported by the participants receiving the B vitamin.

Six months later, all 20 of Pahnke's (1966) volunteers completed a lengthy questionnaire designed to reassess the experience and to measure any enduring changes that may have resulted. Members of the experimental group, beyond confirming their initial reports of having had mysticlike experiences under the influence of psilocybin, reported significantly more enduring positive changes in their attitudes and behavior—toward themselves, others, life, and the psilocybin experience itself—than those in the control group. After a quarter of a century, the 7 participants from the experimental group who were interviewed by Doblin (1991) and retook the follow-up questionnaire unanimously agreed that their experience had had genuinely mystical elements and, despite the frightening or painful moments that most experienced, was one of the high points in their spiritual lives. Their questionnaire replies once again showed a much higher rate of persisting positive changes than those of the 9 control individuals who participated in the follow-up study. In particular, the individuals in the experimental group reported that the experience had helped them to settle on a career (a majority had become ministers); deepened their faith and their understanding of elements of the Christian tradition; increased their identification with minorities, women, and the environment; reduced their fear of death; and heightened their experience of beauty and joy (Doblin, 1991, p. 12).

As seminary students, Pahnke's (1966) participants were likely disposed not only to have religious experiences under psilocybin but also to integrate them into their lives later on. When experiences facilitated by psilocybin and other such entheogens[3] occur outside a religious context or tradition, however, they may be expected to have less "staying power" than Pahnke and Doblin documented (Smith, 1967, p. 144; see also Deikman, 1966). A study by S. R. Wilson and Spencer (1990) supports such a conclusion. Two groups of participants—one of undergraduate sociology students, the other of members of a yogi ashram who were similar in age and gender composition—were asked to describe their most positive experiences and then to rate them on a series of indexes. Those of the nonashram respondents who had used mind-altering substances were asked to describe experiences both under and apart from the influence of these substances. Ratings of the substance-facilitated experiences yielded a profile similar in many respects to the profile of the ashram members, but the yogi practitioners were dramatically higher on mystical interpretation, felt personality change, and perceived life changes resulting from the experience.

American participants in Asia-derived spiritual practices often have a history of having used plant or chemical psychoactives first. Certainly that was the case for the majority of the students whom Tart (1991) queried at a Tibetan Buddhist retreat. Furthermore, although most said that such experience was important in their spiritual lives, the overwhelming majority reported that they no longer used such substances. Like Jordan (1971),

---

[3] The terms *entheogen* and *entheogenic*, derived from the Greek *entheos*, "god within," have been proposed by Ruck, Bigwood, Staples, Otto, and Wassen (1979) and adopted by others as more accurate and more devoid of misleading connotations than *hallucinogen*, *psychotomemetic*, or *psychedelic* for referring to the substances and effects associated with shamanic and related altered states of consciousness.

they may have found that more traditional spiritual practices carried out in sustained association with others yielded experiences more profound, meaningful, and consequential than those they had under the entheogens.

Altogether, these findings suggest that healthy, highly educated persons who are open to mystical experiences and have them in supportive contexts may enjoy long-enduring positive aftereffects, especially when the experiences are dramatic. Yet such conditions do not always hold, and mystical experiences come in a great many varieties, including what James (1902/1985, p. 337) called *diabolical mysticism*. The experience of John Symonds described above was certainly a dramatic one, but he neither welcomed it nor recorded, apparently, any long-term effects. In his own analysis of the aftereffects (i.e., the "fruits") of religious experience, James (1902/1985) suggested that mystical impulses yield admirable lives only in combination with a high degree of intelligence and imagination. Although struck by the superficiality and pettiness of many of the mystics he examined, James concluded that the greatest of them possess qualities "indispensable to the world's welfare" (p. 299).

Pratt (1920), on the other hand, inferred from his exceptionally heterogeneous collection of documents that positive aftereffects come mainly out of the more common and less definite mild forms of mystical experience. One of Pratt's (1920) respondents wrote: "I have experienced God's presence so that I felt the lack of nothing and feared nothing. It is hard to describe the feeling, but everything seems bright and clear ahead, and I feel as if I had the support of some great unimpeachable authority behind me for everything I may do then. It feels as though I were not standing alone" (pp. 341–342). Such undramatic experiences, Pratt concluded, are of supreme value to those who have them, making possible a religious outlook even for the skeptic and providing the self-transcending aspiration and insight that are necessary, he said, for continued inner growth.

BIOLOGICAL MARKERS

Whether mild or extreme, mystical experiences are increasingly thought to be correlates of certain forms of activity in the brain's temporal lobes. Unfortunately, however, few data directly support this speculation. There are numerous electroencephalographic (EEG) studies of meditation (Murphy & Donovan, 1996), a traditional precursor of mystical experience, but because mystical states are so difficult to generate, they are most unlikely to appear during these studies, even among highly proficient meditators. Lower still is the probability of a laboratory occurrence of the more common and spontaneous, mild forms of mystical experience. Furthermore, those who are trying to construct models of meditative and mystical consciousness tend to distrust the meditative research that does exist, given that it has been carried out largely by partisan groups of investigators (d'Aquili, 1993, p. 260).

The first clues to the possible neural origins of mystical experience came from research on epilepsy, which has long been associated with religious preoccupations and sometimes with remarkable religious experiences. More recent investigations of epilepsy suggest that religiousness in general and trance states in particular are associated with activity in the temporal lobes (Bear & Fedio, 1977; Geschwind, 1983; Mandel, 1980). Persinger (1983, 1987) postulated a continuum of temporal-lobe lability representing the varying degrees to which individuals are predisposed to experience "temporal-lobe transients" (TLTs), momentary foci of electrical activity or microseizures, which are said to yield mystical and related experiences and in time produce alterations in the synaptic organization of limbic regions. Contributing to the occurrence of these TLTs is a variety of culturally conditioned factors, including the various techniques and procedures traditionally used for the induction of trance states (Winkelman, 1986). Persinger found indirect support for his hypothesis in a series of studies, including one in which the number of EEG spikes in the temporal lobe in response to exotic rhythmic sounds and pulsating light correlated significantly with measures of religious belief, paranormal or mystical experience, and a sense of presence, whereas measures of spike activity in the occipital lobe did not (Makarec & Persinger, 1985). More encompassing explanatory theories based on such evidence are considered below.

PREVALENCE AND PREDISPOSING FACTORS

National surveys using single-item scales suggest that mystical experiences, at least of Pratt's (1920) mild type, are surprisingly widespread. The best known of these studies was carried out by Greeley (1975, p. 58) and his associates, who asked a national sample of 1,460 Americans, "Have you ever felt as though you were very close to a powerful, spiritual force that seemed to lift you out of yourself?" An accompanying checklist of descriptors allowed for a closer analysis of affirmative responses. Among the respondents, 35% reported having felt such a spiritual force at least once or twice in their lives; 12% claimed that they had had the experience several times, and 5% said that it happened often. In a British national sample of 1,865 persons polled at about the same time, 30.4% answered Greeley's question affirmatively and 36.4% reported being "aware of or influenced by a presence or power, whether referred to as God or not, which was different from their everyday selves" (Hay & Morisy, 1978, p. 257). In surveys in the United States since then, Greeley's question has drawn affirmative answers from between 30.9% and 39.3% of respondents. To Back and Bourque's (1970) question, which asked respondents if they had had "a 'religious or mystical experience'—that is, a moment of sudden religious awakening or insight," between 21% and 41% responded affirmatively in national polls in the 1960s and a robust 53% in each of two Gallup polls in 1990 (Levin, 1993; Yamane & Polzer, 1994).

Thus, a substantial minority of Americans and British nationals would seem to have had at least one mystical experience, though it is apparently uncommon, as Laski (1961) also concluded, to have them more than a few times. The actual prevalence of mystical experience, however, may be lower than these figures suggest. In a random sample of 30 nonpsychiatric hospital patients, Hufford (1985) found that 8 of the 14 who responded affirmatively to Greeley's (1975) question proved to be false positives when their descriptions of the experience were closely analyzed. Six respondents, for example, took the expression "lift out" simply to mean feeling uplifted in a metaphoric sense, and they equated feeling "close to a powerful, spiritual force" with the belief that God is always near. And whereas 34% of Thomas and Cooper's (1980) sample of 305 adults endorsed Greeley's question—a nearly perfect replication of the original finding—analysis of their written statements showed that the experiences they referred to varied enormously. As many as 10% of the sample wrote replies that were uncodable, and only 2 respondents described experiences that were deemed to be genuinely mystical. The largest proportion, 16% of the total sample, fell into the category "faith and consolation," which consisted of intense spiritual experiences.

In both Greeley's (1975) and the Hay and Morisy's (1978) studies, there was a slight but significant tendency for the occurrence of mystical experience to increase with age, education, and income; sex differences were inconsistent between the two studies. Whereas a century ago, Bucke (1901/1923) noted that his rare exemplars of "cosmic consciousness" were mainly in their 30s, in Greeley's study mystical experience was most often reported by persons in their 40s and 50s—a roughly comparable point in the life span, perhaps, given the increase in life expectancy in the 20th century. In the 1988 General Social Survey analyzed by Levin (1993), on the other hand, no significant age trends were found among the responses to Greeley's question.

Children, who are not represented in these national samples, have been thought by some to be peculiarly subject to mystical experience. In a study of children's religious drawings, Bindl (1965) reported that spontaneous experiences of the *numinous* (Otto's [1917/1950] now-famous term for "the holy") are common among children under 7, but then gradually fade as naive credulity declines. Among those who responded to an advertisement placed by the Religious Experience Research Unit at Oxford University, only 15% referred back to childhood experiences (Armstrong, 1984), whereas in the grammar-school sample queried by Paffard (1973) at about the same time, 40% of the boys and 61% of the girls affirmed that they had had experiences akin to those celebrated by the poet Wordsworth. Although Laski (1961) likewise made note of many recollections of ecstatic experiences in essays written by 12- to 15-year-old girls, she concluded that the Wordsworthian notion that childhood is normally "a Golden Age of ecstasy," a time of almost continuous ecstasy, is insupportable (p. 137).

Any estimate of the prevalence of mystical experience in the general population clearly depends on how one defines the term. Even in its mild forms, however, it is uncommon enough to invite consideration of predisposing factors, perhaps something akin to a "mystical trait." James (1902/ 1985) proposed that mystical experience originates in a region lying outside of normal awareness, a region that he called the "subliminal" or "subconscious self," a notion he borrowed from Myers (1892). According to Myers, the limen, or threshold, below which this subliminal self is found marks the boundary of the ordinary self, which is that selection of conscious sensations and thoughts that best serves us in everyday life. Differences in the character and accessibility of the subliminal self are reflected in differences in religious or mystical experience. In persons prone to mystical experience, this self is relatively large and active, and the margin of the conscious field relatively leaky or pervious (James, 1902/1985, p. 197).

Contemporary correlational research suggests in various ways the continuing aptness of James's metaphors (at least for those who grant metaphor a significant role in scientific thought; see Leary, 1990). Persons who tend to score high on mysticism scales tend also to score high on such variables as complexity, openness to new experience, breadth of interests, innovation, tolerance of ambiguity, and creative personality (Cowling, 1985; Hood, Hall, Watson, & Biderman, 1979; Thalbourne & Delin, 1994; Thomas & Cooper, 1980). Furthermore, they are likely to score high on measures of hypnotizability, absorption,[4] and fantasy proneness,[5] suggesting a capacity to suspend the judging process that distinguishes imaginings and real events and to commit their mental resources to representing the imaginal object as vividly as possible (Nelson, 1992; Spanos & Moretti, 1988; Thalbourne, Bartemucci, Delin, Fox, & Nofi, 1997). Individuals high

---

[4]Whereas in Albrecht's (1951) work, the term *absorption* (*die Versunkenheit*) refers to the unique and relatively rare psychological state out of which full-scale mystical experiences emerge, here it refers to a disposition to have episodes of "total" attention that fully engage perceptual, imaginative, and ideational resources. Possessing both cognitive and motivational–affective components, this capacity is said to be associated with hypnosis, artistic creativity, and mystical experience (Tellegen & Atkinson, 1974). Kumar and Pekala (1988) found that persons who are high in absorption capacity report experiences of greater intensity than lower-scoring participants. Absorption has been found to be positively correlated with an intrinsic religious orientation (Levin, Wickramasekera, & Hirshberg, 1998), which in turn has been associated with more frequent reports of experiences akin to Stace's (1960) introvertive mysticism (Hood, 1973).
[5]In their originating study of the fantasy-prone personality, S. C. Wilson and Barber (1983) reported that 6 of the 27 women in their fantasy-prone group—who were initially identified by their excellence as hypnotic subjects—but none of the 25 in the comparison group, reported intense, life-changing religious experiences that were marked by visions and voices and described as deeply moving, overwhelming, and awesome.

on hypnotic susceptibility are also more likely to report having undergone religious conversion, which for them is primarily an experiential rather than a cognitive phenomenon—that is, one marked by notable alterations in perceptual, affective, and ideomotor response patterns (Gibbons & De Jarnette, 1972). Although religious conversion can be distinguished from mystical experience both phenomenologically and dynamically, some of the perceptual and affective changes in question here represent points of commonality.

The correlates of reported mystical experience also include other variables: belief in paranormal phenomena, such as extrasensory perception and psychokinesis, magical ideation, and manic and depressive experiences. Noting a consistent interrelationship among these variables and a creative personality scale, Australian researchers Thalbourne and Delin (1994) subjected student data on all of these dimensions to a principal-components analysis. A single factor emerged, accounting for 52.8% of the variance in the initial study and 54.2% in a replication (Thalbourne et al., 1997). The common thread among these disparate experiences, Thalbourne and Delin concluded, is a high degree of accessibility to subliminal consciousness. Thus they proposed calling the factor *transliminality*. Although Thalbourne and Delin (1994) have not proposed how to operationalize the "barrier or gating" mechanisms between the subliminal and conscious regions, they found that those who are high in transliminality, because the barrier or gating mechanism between the subliminal and supraliminal (conscious) regions operates relatively freely, will be highly susceptible to incursions of large amounts of ideational and affective input from subliminal regions (p. 22).

In additional research, Thalbourne and Delin (1994) found that persons who score high in transliminality tend to agree that they have "received a communication from the Divinity"; that, "in some *symbolic* sense," they have "gone through the process of being martyred, of dying, and of being spiritually reborn"; and that they have had "the experience in which life appeared to be simply a play, or like a dream in the mind of the Creator" (pp. 27, 29). In a follow-up study, Thalbourne and Delin (1999) found that transliminality scores correlated .67 with a modified version of Hood's (1975) 25-item Mysticism Scale, which is based on Stace's (1960) analysis, and .57 with their own Mystical Experience Ratings, an adaptation of Hood's (1970) earlier Religious Experience Episodes Measure, which consists of 15 examples from James's (1902/1985) *Varieties*. High scorers in transliminality also tended to rate themselves as more religious, to identify with some religious group, and to report reading about Eastern religious traditions (Bible reading, in contrast, did not correlate with transliminality).

Whatever one calls it, a certain predisposition evidently plays a major role in mystical experience. But set and setting are also significant factors, as research with psychedelic drugs has made apparent. On the basis of observations carried out mainly in the United States, researchers estimate that, in general, at least 25% to 33% of persons taking such drugs will have intense mystical experiences, but if such persons have a religious background and the context in which they take the drug is explicitly designed to facilitate a religious response, as in the case of Pahnke's (1966) experiment, up to 90% will have such experiences (Wulff, 1997, p. 92). The specific "triggers" that often play a role in spontaneous cases include, in addition to religious services, such stimuli as impressive natural settings, flowers, scents, fine (or sometimes violent) weather, sunrise or sunset, breezes, light patterns, music, poetry, art, beautiful cities, sacred places, swift movement, creative work, sex, childbirth, watching children, illness, depression, the prospect of death, personal crisis, and so on (Greeley, 1975; Hardy, 1979; Laski, 1961).

RELATIONSHIP TO PSYCHOPATHOLOGY

The unusual experiences of the classic mystics, combined as they so often were with self-deprivation and self-torture, extraordinary bodily maladies, tidal swings in mood, and claims of erotic trysts with divinity, led many early psychiatrists and psychologists to conclude that mysticism is fundamentally a pathological process. Janet (1926–1928), for example, after observing parallels among the sufferings and ecstasies of a patient he studied for years and those reported by the great Christian mystics, concluded that all ecstatics suffer from *psychasthenia*, a term he coined for a group of neuroses marked by extreme anxiety, obsessions, and phobias. On the basis of his own study of the Christian mystics, Leuba (1925) was convinced that mystical experience can be entirely accounted for by various psychological and physiological processes, especially the disorders of hysteria (a group of neuroses marked by hallucinations, anesthesias, paralyses, and somnambulism) and neurasthenia (a disease characterized by such symptoms as chronic physical and mental exhaustion, hypersensitivity, sleeplessness, and loss of appetite; see Ellenberger [1970] on these now-dated diagnostic categories).

Pratt's (1920) more favorable view—according to which, even though pathology may indeed mark some mystics' lives, mystical experience per se is not pathological but a factor for growth—finds substantial support in the contemporary empirical and transpersonal literatures. There are, first of all, several studies suggesting that measures of mystical experience tend not to be correlated with measures of pathology. In a study of 38 female outpatients, for example, Kroll, Fiszdon, and Crosby (1996) found that the tendency to experience pathological, or dissociative, altered states of consciousness was not correlated with a disposition to have positive mystical experiences. Among female undergraduates in Canada, Spanos and Moretti (1988) found Hood's Mysticism Scale to be correlated with hypnotizability and absorption, consistent with a trend I noted earlier, but not with measures of neuroticism, self-esteem, depressive affect, or psychosomatic symptoms. On the other hand, their Diabolical Experiences Scale, which assesses the felt reality of the Devil, Satan, and evil spirits, correlated significantly with neuroticism and psychosomatic symptoms as well as hypnotizability and absorption. Finally, Oxman, Rosenberg, Schnurr, Tucker, and Gala (1988) found that autobiographical accounts of mystical ecstasy, hallucinogenic drug-induced states, and schizophrenia are more different than similar when assessed in terms of patterns of lexical choice.

That mystical experience may be a positive factor in people's lives is suggested by Greeley's (1975) finding that, in his national U.S. sample, the reported occurrence of mystical experience correlated .34 with the Positive Affect Scale developed by Bradburn (1969) as a measure of psychological well-being, and −.31 with the Negative Affect Scale, an indicator of poor mental health. The correlation with positive affect was still higher, .52, with a "'twice-born' mysticism" factor on which four classic criteria had loaded: ineffability, passivity, a sense of new life, and the experience of light. Greeley concluded, "Mystics are happier. Ecstasy is good for you" (p. 77). In Hay and Morisy's (1978) parallel study in Great Britain, reported mystical experience again proved to be significantly related to the Positive Affect Scale, but at a greatly reduced level (.05). At about the same time, Hood (1974) found a negative correlation between his Religious Experience Episodes Measure and Stark's Index of Psychic Inadequacy, and in a group of 54 members of the contemplative Discalced Carmelite Order, Mallory (1977) found mystical experience to be positively correlated with happy emotionality and negatively correlated to neuroticism and unhappy emotionality.

In yet another study of peak experiences among persons living in the San Francisco Bay area, Wuthnow (1978) found a significant relationship between "deep and lasting" peak experiences and several measures of positive mental health. He established, once again, that such experiences are not uncommon: 50% reported an experience of contact with "something holy or sacred," 82% recalled having felt deeply moved by the beauty of nature, and 39% said they had had a feeling of harmony with the universe. Wuthnow also demonstrated that the more recent and lasting such experiences were, the more likely the respondents would report that they found life meaningful, thought about life's purpose, meditated about their lives, and felt self-assured.

Yet we also have the finding of Thalbourne and Delin (1994) alluded to above: In a student population, their Mystical Experience Scale, which correlates .72 with Hood's Mysticism Scale, was significantly related (.37 to .53) to measures of manic and depressive experience. Furthermore, two clinical samples recruited from self-help groups, one of people diagnosed as manic depressives and another of individuals with schizophrenia (most of whom were well at the time), scored significantly higher than the students on their mysticism scale. Thalbourne and Delin, as noted earlier, proposed that the common factor in the correlations they found is transliminality, a susceptibility to incursions from subliminal regions. If mystical experience and psychotic disposition are linked in sharing this susceptibility, as these data suggest, it bears emphasizing that individual clinical variables account at most for a quarter of the variance in mystical-experience scores (Thalbourne, 1991, p. 181).

In their systematic comparisons of mystical and schizophrenic experience, Arbman (1963–1970) and Austin (1998) noted that the former is distinguished in numerous ways: by its transience, the absence of coercive impulses, evident conscious striving, ongoing orderly development, conditioning by training within some tradition, the diminution of self-reference and sense of unity with the environment, the retention of social attachments, the recognition of the demands of logic and collective knowledge, positive visual hallucinations rather than negative auditory ones, and so on. Arbman allowed that, in rare cases, genuine religious ecstatics have suffered from schizophrenia, and he noted that "religious insanity" is not infrequently a concomitant of this serious disorder. But in general he considered the dementia of schizophrenia to constitute "a practically insurmountable obstacle to the provocation of any religious transports of the trance-like kind" (Arbman, 1970, p. 385). Both Arbman and Austin concluded that mysticism and psychosis have little, if anything, in common. Noll (1983) reached much the same conclusion from a comparison of shamanic states of consciousness and activities with the diagnostic criteria for schizophrenia.

THERAPEUTIC POTENTIAL

According to various commentators, the therapeutic possibilities of mystical experience are intrinsic to its very nature. At the heart of the "mystic way," Underhill (1911/1930) wrote in her classic study, is a process of profound psychological transformation. In a series of five stages, she suggested, the aspirant's center of interest is shifted to a higher plane, false and inharmonious elements of the self are systematically stripped away, a deeper apprehension of the nature of things emerges, and—with the establishment of the long-sought-for higher state of consciousness—the self undergoes a final transformation that brings to light the "deepest, richest levels of human personality" (p. 416). The religious traditions share a common message, according to James (1902/1985): There is something wrong about human beings in their natural condition, but deliverance from this wrongness is available through connection with "the higher powers," that is, through mystical experience.

The potential healing power of mystical experience per se, apart from any systematic spiritual quest, is illustrated by Horton (1973) in a series of three case studies of severely depressed adolescents who suffered schizophrenic reactions in the process of separating themselves from their nuclear families. The 18-year-old participant in one of these cases, for example, had a history of self-injury from childhood, when his parents nearly divorced and were able to show him little affection. His father, a poorly integrated obsessive–compulsive man who sought to relive his own, deeply disappointing life through his son, strove to keep the boy in a symbiotic union. When that effort failed, the disturbed father harassed his son by every means possible, including anonymous phone calls and efforts to drive his son's friends away. Feeling an uncanny sense of being followed by "someone," the son suffered overwhelming nightmares of being completely annihilated. Lonely and afraid, he experimented with prayer and meditation. One night, far from home and feeling defeated and disconsolate, he had a union mystical experience, "like a fountain bursting forth." The profound changes he felt, including "limitless courage and strength" and the inspiration to make his life "a continuous celebration" of what he had found within himself, was validated weeks later by a visiting friend, who was astonished by his changed demeanor. Able at last to resist his father's efforts and less inclined to engage in reckless behavior, the young man entered psychotherapy. Recurrence of mystical experiences, he said, gave him the "courage and strength to go on" (Horton, 1973, p. 295).

The therapeutic potential of mainly spontaneous mystical experiences has been noted in relationship to threats to life (Noyes & Slymen, 1979), solitary ordeals (Logan, 1985), unresolved grief (Aberbach, 1987), and posttraumatic stress disorder (Decker, 1993). The possible therapeutic value of actively inducing mystical experience in receptive clients has been explored by numerous investigators. Sacerdote (1977), for example, sought to treat physical and emotional pain—apparently with some success—by hypnotically altering space and time perceptions in his patients, and thus inducing mystical-like states, much as Aaronson (1967, 1969, 1970) had done. Although Cardeña's (1996) study of the experience of neutral "deep hypnosis" among hypnotic virtuosos was not intended to be therapeutic, 4 months afterward the participants claimed positive aftereffects of their experiences during the experiment. The original experiences included spontaneous reports of timelessness, bright light, a sense of oneness with the world, and profound peace.

The most extensive exploration of the therapeutic possibilities of mysticlike experiences is represented by Grof's (1980, 1985, 1993) work on LSD psychotherapy and, since the legal ban on hallucinogens, his "holotropic breathwork." Grof (1980) reported that volunteers in LSD therapy pass through a series of more or less predictable stages, full of highly dramatic imagery and deep emotion, and representing both personal and transpersonal levels of the psyche. Ordinarily encountered over a series of sessions using lower doses of the drug in combination with dynamic psychotherapy ("psycholytic therapy"), this sequence of phenomena can also take place in a single session with a dosage high enough to trigger the egoless and usually contentless psychedelic peak experience ("psychedelic therapy"). Transformation can be sudden and dramatic, Grof claimed, bringing about radical changes in outlook and ways of being. Intense interest in mysticism, spiritual disciplines, and mythology commonly result, along with a new transcendental ethic. The replication of Grof's observations and evaluation of his claims by independent investigators are clearly warranted, as is a thorough examination of the possible role of demand characteristics and expectancy effects in shaping the experience of "holotropic" breathwork and LSD psychotherapy.

According to Grinspoon and Bakalar (1979), between 1950 and the mid-1960s, the heyday of psychedelic drug therapy, six international conferences were held on this topic, several dozen books were published, and more than 1,000 clinical papers presented results from work with 40,000 patients. LSD and related substances were given to patients presenting psychosomatic and neurotic symptoms, to children with schizophrenia or autism, to chronic criminal offenders, to alcoholics, and to persons who were dying. Extravagant therapeutic claims were sometimes made and important methodological issues, including the problem of obtaining informed consent without suggesting particular experiences, were insufficiently addressed; but there was a general consensus among researchers that there was enough positive evidence to justify continued research. Nonetheless, the religious fervor of casual users and their calls for social revolution evoked a backlash that transformed LSD into a pariah substance and triggered the laws that made its use in any context illegal.[6] That therapy using LSD and similar substances continues underground gives testimony to the promise that some think it still holds (Grinspoon & Bakalar, 1979).

CLINICAL ISSUES AND RISKS

The use of LSD will most likely remain controversial for the foreseeable future. Recent, dispassionate reviews of research findings conclude, contrary to earlier claims, that LSD "appears to pose few if any risks to

---

[6]Potential users should be aware of the severe penalties that apply under the current laws (Henderson & Glass, 1994). The Multidisciplinary Association for Psychedelic Studies, founded by Rick Doblin in 1986, is working to reverse the legal suppression of research on entheogens and to raise funds to support whatever research the increasingly open Food and Drug Administration may allow.

physical health" and that prolonged psychiatric illness is a rare complication (Henderson & Glass, 1994, pp. 64, 70). Furthermore, as a nonaddictive substance that rapidly loses its novelty, LSD is rarely abused. Yet casual use of LSD by unstable personalities and in negative, nonsupportive settings can be dangerous. Its use in clinical settings, where its purity can be assured, vulnerable individuals can be screened out, and both setting and supervision, including the management of negative sequelae, can be carefully optimized, is generally considered safe. The chief adverse effects of LSD are "bad trips"; acute anxiety or panic reactions that usually yield to simple reassurance; and "flashbacks," or recurrences of the LSD-induced perceptual and emotional experiences that are often triggered by the use of other drugs (Grinspoon & Bakalar, 1979; Henderson & Glass, 1994).

Can acute adverse reactions likewise be triggered by traditional approaches to mystical experience? Greenberg, Witztum, and Buchbinder (1992) considered this question in their presentation of four cases of young men who became severely disordered after becoming ultraorthodox and undertaking the study of Jewish mysticism. All of the participants suffered from unresolved grief reactions in conjunction with the death of close friends or family members, and they chose mystical texts and practices that offered the possibility of atonement for the guilt they felt. If the mystical teachings regarding supernatural forces and creatures of evil did not help to precipitate their subsequent hallucinatory and delusional experiences, they appear at least to have justified these experiences and given them traditional form. The congruence between their psychotic experiences and the mystical teachings also encouraged these patients' wives, fellow students, and rabbis to ascribe to them a measure of sanctity, even in the face of severe deterioration and subsequent psychiatric treatment.

In interviews with members of a mystical cult in India, Kakar (1991) likewise found that loss was the outstanding factor impelling involvement. Yet whatever issues or predispositions people may bring to the "mystic journey," it is widely understood to be inherently marked by a variety of problems and pitfalls. In the Christian tradition, the chief psychological crisis is the "dark night of the soul," Underhill's (1911/1930) fourth stage of the mystic way, the painful interval when the joyous illumination of the third stage fades away and a state of emptiness, misery, and chaos takes its place. There are parallels in the Eastern traditions, including the agonizing pain and powerful recollections that come with "the surfacing of the deep patterns of blocks and bound energies" (Kornfield, 1989, p. 142) that is common in the course of Buddhist meditation. Such complications represent what are today called *spiritual emergencies*, crises occasioned by the revolution in values and the sense of identity that mystical experiences can bring about. Long familiar to traditional spiritual directors, such chaotic and overwhelming experiences are today being addressed by psychologists and psychiatrists who view them as transformational crises in the evolution of consciousness (Grof & Grof, 1989).

EXPLAINING MYSTICAL EXPERIENCE

In this section, six groups of explanations or interpretations of mystical experience are considered: neuropsychological, psychoanalytic, analytical (Jungian), humanistic–transpersonal, perceptual–cognitive, and contextual. These approaches differ not only in the constructs they use but also in the degree to which they explicitly position mystical experience in the framework of an underlying process and take into account social–historical factors. They vary, too, in the degree to which they attend to the specific contents of mystical experiences and take seriously the mystic's claims to a higher knowing. Their amenability to systematic empirical testing also varies enormously.

Neuropsychological Explanations

The association of mystical experience with epilepsy, noted earlier, as well as with systematic bodily stimulation or manipulation and the taking of plant or chemical substances, has prompted some researchers to look for a biological explanation. From the 19th century to the present, some scientists have assumed that, if mystical experience can be linked to neurophysiological processes, especially pathological ones, it will have to forfeit any claims to epistemological significance (e.g., Leuba, 1925; Rose, 1989). Others have reached the opposite conclusion: If there are brain structures that mediate mystical experience such experience must in some fundamental way accord with the nature of things.

The "split-brain" research of the 1960s offered evidence that the two hemispheres of the brain tend to specialize in separate functions, the left one showing greater development of linguistic, rational, mathematical, and logical abilities and the right one exhibiting superiority in visuospatial and musical capacities, emotional response, and synthetic or holistic perception. Some researchers proposed that the right hemisphere might be the primary source of mystical experiences, given especially their reported ineffability (Fenwick, 1996). Intrigued by Penfield and Perot's (1963) report that mild electric stimulation of the right temporal lobes of surgical patients would frequently produce hazy, unknown voices emanating from mysterious places, Jaynes (1976) proposed that such voices were commonplace several thousand years ago, when, according to his controversial reconstructions, the two hemispheres operated relatively independently. In times of crisis, according to Jaynes, when the left hemisphere could think of no solution, the right hemisphere's more astute problem solving would be experienced as the helpful voice of a god. Jaynes speculated that although consciousness eventually inhibited the right temporal lobe areas and thus quieted the intimate voice of divinity, a vestigial neurological structure survives in each person, making possible still today a variety of exceptional phenomena, including oracles, possession states, speaking in tongues, and mystical experiences.

Most of the speculation today regarding mysticism's neurophysiological conditions is grounded in Gellhorn's (1967, 1969) concept of the "tuning" of the body's two activation systems: the *ergotropic*, which is marked by increased activity of the sympathetic nervous system, muscle tension, and diffuse cortical excitation, and the *trophotropic*, which consists of increased parasympathetic discharges, reduced cortical activity, and thus hypoarousal. The two systems often act reciprocally, the one tending to suppress the other; furthermore, the somatic and cerebral components usually exhibit congruence as a result of being activated in concert. Under stress or other circumstances triggering high levels of activation, however, both reciprocity and congruence break down. It is this failure in the systems' ordinary tuning, Gellhorn thought, that underlies altered states of consciousness and various forms of psychopathology (Davidson, 1976, p. 359).

On the basis of Gellhorn's (1967, 1969) leads and his own research on psilocybin, Fischer (1971, 1975) developed a circular "cartography of ecstatic and meditative states." Clockwise movement in the diagram represents increasing trophotropic arousal, characteristic of various forms of meditation; counterclockwise movement indicates a preponderance of ergotropic arousal, associated with creative, psychotic, and ecstatic states. In either case, the arousal is subcortical, producing diffuse emotional states that are interpreted in diverse ways at the cortical level. Although these movements represent physiological processes that are ordinarily opposites, they are alleged to have a common starting point, the rational "I" that experiences itself in an objective time–space world, and a common end point, the ecstatic "Self," which represents the mystical experience of oneness with the universe. Observing that the syntactical structure of language becomes increasingly simplified as the level of drug-induced arousal increases, Fischer (1972) suggested that the movement from the I to the Self corresponds to a gradual shift from rational, left-hemispheric functioning to intuitive, right-hemispheric activity.

A similar neuropsychological model of mystical states, but reflective of the more complicated picture that has come with the recent shift in interest from hemispheric to regional brain function (Liddon, 1989), has been developed by d'Aquili and Newberg (1993, 1999). Their theoretical model is not easily summarized, but a brief overview of the events postulated to occur during "passive meditation" will at least give a flavor of it. They posited a reverberating circuit that originates with impulses in the right prefrontal cortex representing the intent to eliminate thoughts from the mind. These impulses pass to the right posterior-superior parietal lob-ule, a structure implicated in the analysis and integration of higher order information. From there they pass to the right hippocampus, which mod-ulates emotional response; to the right amygdala, part of the ancient, emotion-mediating limbic system; to the ventromedial structures of the hypothalamus, which are an extension of the trophotropic system into the brain stem; then back to the right amygdala, the right hippocampus, and finally the right prefrontal cortex.

As meditation continues, perhaps after months or even years of prac-tice, neural activity may finally build to a maximum level in the tropho-tropic system. At that critical moment, the resulting "spillover" triggers a maximal arousal of the ergotropic system, culminating in intense stimula-tion of the lateral hypothalamus and the median forebrain bundle, which is experienced as an ecstatic and blissful state. The immediate consequence of this stimulation is the total cutting off of input to both posterior-superior parietal lobules, resulting, in the right one, in a sensation of pure space that is subjectively experienced as absolute unity or wholeness and, in the left one, the obliteration of the self–other dichotomy (d'Aquili & New-berg, 1993, pp. 187–190).

This model integrates what is now known about brain activity during various mystical or religious states, but it also expands on these findings to explain the phenomenology of such experiences. According to d'Aquili and Newburg (1993), new technologies for the study of brain activity may assist in testing this model, but the unpredictability of these experiences will in any case make such research exceedingly difficult. Whether or not their model proves to be basically accurate, the authors warn against any facile reduction of the experiences in question to neurochemical flux. It is not obvious that the "objective reality" of ordinary consciousness has a higher ontological status than the "hyperlucid" and "highly integrated and *inte-grating* visions" of mystical experience (p. 197).

Psychoanalytic Interpretations

In spite of Freud's deep and sustained interest in applying psychoan-alytic theory to religion, he had little to say about mystical experience. His few published remarks on the subject were written in response to a friend, writer and mystic Romain Rolland, who expressed regret over Freud's ne-glect of the "oceanic feeling"—the sense of being one with the surrounding world—which Rolland took to be the fountainhead of the religious sen-timent and hence the religious traditions. Acknowledging the elusiveness of this phenomenon, Freud (1930/1961) speculated that it constitutes a revival of feelings belonging to the earliest stages of the ego, before it has separated itself from the external world. Whereas Freud allowed that this restoration of limitless primary narcissism, the earliest form of self-love, may serve as a religious consolation, he declined to consider it the source of religious needs, which he insisted on tracing to later feelings of helplessness.

Other psychoanalytic interpreters, writing both before and after Freud published his remarks, were less reticent about declaring mystical experience to be a sign of severe regression and a loss of reality orientation. Morel (1918), for example, attributed to the mystics a universal tendency toward regression, a nostalgic longing for the mother if not for the womb itself, compelled in part by sexual anxieties that the mystic suppresses through ascetic renunciation. The outcome, he said, may be either megalomania or an autistic system centering on erotic relations with imaginary objects or persons. According to Alexander (1923/1931), Buddhist meditative practices set in motion a systematically regressive process that culminates in a schizophreniclike state equivalent to the experience of intrauterine life. Likewise pathologizing the mystic life by equating it with narcissistic regression, the Group for the Advancement of Psychiatry, Committee on Psychiatry and Religion (1976) concluded that it is a response to overwhelming demands or disappointments in the outer world. Confession, abstinence, purification, and other such preparations for mystical experience are interpreted as ways of warding off depression, by inviting the forgiveness and love of a parental figure.

Some psychoanalysts, however, came to see mystical regression as a potentially constructive process—a form of "regression in the service of the ego" akin to the rejuvenating state of sleep, certain creative experiences, and some forms of psychotherapy (Prince & Savage, 1966). The viewpoint of this *adaptive school* of interpretation, as Parsons (1999) called it, has been most fully developed by ego psychologists and object-relations theorists. Horton (1974, p. 379), for example, argued that, as quintessentially "an upsurgence of residual primary narcissism," mystical experience may serve as a transitional phenomenon and hence as a potentially adaptive ego mechanism of defense. For a 20-year-old patient, it offered a last refuge from overwhelming anxiety and loneliness while also providing resources for more adaptive individuation and integration. In his book-length study of Ignatius of Loyola, the founder of the Society of Jesus, Meissner (1992) likewise used Winnicott's (1953) notion of transitional experience as a way of drawing meaningful connections between Ignatius's mystical ecstasy and grandiose hallucinatory visions and the complex of needs that were traceable in part to his mother's death when he was an infant and to the severe narcissistic insult of a crippling accident. Like Kakar (1991), whom Parsons also associated with the adaptive school, Meissner took care to place his subject's mystical experience in its social and cultural context and to avoid reductionistic claims about its content.

Parsons (1999) identified a third cluster of psychoanalytic interpretations of mystical experience, in addition to the classic and adaptive ones, which he called the *transformative school*. Like the adaptive school, it recognizes both regressive, pathological elements and ego-adaptive ones; but in addition, those associated with it "tend to be mystical, or are receptive to mysticism, or make use of mystical experience as intuitive models for psychoanalytic experience" (Eigen, 1995, p. 371). Both Parsons and Eigen located Bion (1970) here for characterizing psychoanalytic processes with such expressions as "O," "void," and "formlessness" while interweaving Western and Asian mystical images throughout his writing. The potential complementarity of psychoanalysis and the mystical traditions is illustrated in the work of Engler (1984), who combined object-relations theory with Buddhist psychology to map out a sequence of developmental stages and their corresponding pathologies. In the initial, personal stages, addressed by object-relations theory, the deepest pathological problem is the *lack* of a sense of self; in the subsequent transpersonal stages, delineated by Buddhist psychology, it is the *presence* of a self. Thus, self-transcending mystical states that would be appropriate in the later stages may be considered pathological if they occur in earlier ones.

To empirical psychologists who take seriously in psychoanalysis only what finds support in rigorous scientific assessment, the addition of Buddhist psychology can only make matters worse. But for hermeneutically oriented psychologists who view psychoanalysis as a heuristic of considerable explanatory power, Engler's (1984) construction effectively counters what Wilber (1996) called the *pre/trans fallacy*, the simple equating of prepersonal states of consciousness, those existing before the emergence of self-conscious awareness, with later transpersonal, or ego-transcendent, ones. Whereas the ontogenetic source of the numinous may indeed lie in the infant–mother relationship, as Erikson (1977) claimed, and some mystics' experiences may hark back on some level to infantile experience, it seems highly doubtful that the mystical absorption that Albrecht (1951) characterized as the most orderly state known in human experience is simply a regression to the vague and shifting pre-egoic states of awareness. Regressive explanations, argued Hood (1976), confuse what is analogical in mystical expression with the mystical experience itself.

Analytical Interpretations

Whereas Freud viewed mystical experience as a personal phenomenon, the product of a regressive turn in individual development, Jung saw it as a collective one, a manifestation of a positive, universal process. Jung's analytical psychology is distinguished foremost by the positing of a collective unconscious, a deep layer of the psyche hypothesized to contain a reservoir of universal archetypes, an indeterminate number of interpenetrating forms or templates that dispose individuals to experience the typical persons, situations, and processes that have structured human experience since time immemorial. The gradual differentiation and integration of these archetypes, and of both conscious and unconscious attitudes, is said to lie at the heart of individuation, the life-long process of self-realization that was traditionally facilitated, Jung said, by the mysterious and often dramatic images and rituals of the religious traditions.

In this framework, mystics are persons who vividly experience the processes of the collective unconscious. "Mystical experience," Jung (1935/ 1976, p. 98) once remarked in a discussion, "is experience of archetypes." Encounter with manifestations of the archetypes is always numinous, Jung said in an allusion to Otto's (1917/1950) phenomenological work on the experience of the holy, and its intensity is in proportion to the clarity of the representations. Given the power of these factors and their apparent independence of individual will and understanding, they are almost inevitably experienced as originating from outside the person.

The classic exposition of mystical experience from the perspective of analytical psychology is an essay by Neumann (1948/1968), who considered the mystical to be a fundamental category of human experience. According to Neumann, mystical experience appears wherever consciousness is not centered around the ego, beginning with the earliest stage of original unity. During the long, difficult struggle into a differentiated and responsible awareness, the ego battles for supremacy over the forces of the unconscious, or nonego, by appropriating and assimilating its content. But to encounter the nonego, the ego must temporarily renounce conscious reality and suspend the polarization of world and self. The result is a numinous experience, a mystical encounter of ego and nonego, during which, Neumann claimed, both are transformed.

Although the content of such experience will reflect prevailing teachings, an underlying uniformity can be expected, given that such experiences are grounded in the universal archetypes. The various forms and levels of mystical experience correspond to different life phases, the highest of them signaling the achievement of personality integration, the attainment of the formless Self, the archetype of wholeness. The human being, Neumann (1948/1968) declared, is by nature a *homo mysticus*. Whether or not people are aware of it, he said, the inner development of each person has a mystical stamp, the result of recurring archetypal encounters. A contemporary reworking of such themes, especially in relation to American Indian and Australian aboriginal spirituality, can be found in Broadribb (1995).

Support of a kind for Jung's controversial claims regarding the collective unconscious and the healing power of encounter with the archetypes has been offered by therapist-researchers using entheogens. Naranjo (1973) reported that he was dramatically surprised by the recurring mythical themes and images that harmaline, a nonhallucinatory entheogen, precipitated in a group of 30 volunteers, and no less by the observation that

10 of them (60% of those with obvious neurotic symptoms) showed "remarkable improvement or symptomatic change comparable only to that which might be expected from intensive psychotherapy" (p. 126). Naranjo interpreted this outcome as evidence in support of the Jungian hypothesis —one he had not intended to test—that elicitation of archetypal experience will facilitate personality integration.

Grof (1985, p. 190) remarked that his own extensive observations from LSD psychotherapy have repeatedly confirmed most of Jung's fundamental ideas, including the collective unconscious, the dynamics of the archetypes, the distinction between ego and Self, and the concept of the individuation process. Given the extraordinary character of both Grof's and Naranjo's findings and the understandable skepticism they tend to arouse in other scientific investigators, independent replications under well-controlled conditions would be extremely helpful, especially to evaluate the role of expectancy in these experiences, the durability of the treatment effects, and the generalizability of the overall findings. Under current laws, however, such replications are essentially ruled out.

Regrettably, there is little research evidence of a more conventional type that addresses the validity of Jung's theories. But then it is exceedingly difficult if not impossible to subject major aspects of these theories, and of the psychoanalysts' theories as well, to the typical empirical verification. Whereas many empiricists thus reject such theories out of hand, other scholars have proposed that psychoanalysis and analytical psychology may best be evaluated from an interpretive, or hermeneutical, perspective. Rigorously empirical in its own way, such an approach begins with reflections on the very nature of understanding and proceeds, then, to a critique of a psychology's metatheoretical assumptions, its guiding metaphors, its rhetoric style, its use of data, and so on, and finally to an evaluation of its adequacy as a system of interpretation, using such criteria as coherence, comprehensiveness, and productivity (Packer & Addison, 1989; Strenger, 1991). The direction that a hermeneutical critique of the Jungian interpretation of mysticism might take is briefly suggested by McGinn (1991, p. 333), who noted its lack of attention to historical particularities and its deviation from traditional mystical models. In Jungian hands, said McGinn, the mystical has become too general.

Humanistic–Transpersonal Perspectives

Among humanistic perspectives on mystical experience, no others are as well known as Maslow's (1964, 1968). In the course of his famous studies of self-actualizing persons, Maslow noticed that it was common for these exceptional individuals to report having had mystical experiences. Wishing to dissociate such experiences from their traditional religious contexts and to make them available for scientific investigation, Maslow called them *peak experiences*, a term that other psychologists have adopted as well. In describing peak experiences, Maslow reiterated the ecstatic feelings of ego-less fusion with the world, of wholeness and integration, and of effortless existence in the here and now. James's (1902/1985) noetic quality becomes for Maslow a "Cognition of Being," or *B-cognition*, a receptive and holistic perceiving of "B-values," including truth, beauty, goodness, justice, play-fulness, and perfection. As the moments when a person is most fully alive, peak experiences are profoundly satisfying, Maslow noted, and they have the potential for revolutionizing the lives in which they occur.

Eager to make such experiences and their putative benefits widely available in an increasingly secular world, Maslow argued (1964) that the traditional religious contextualizations of this intrinsic core of experience serve not only to distort and suppress it but also to create divisiveness where otherwise there might be profound accord. According to Maslow, by studying and promoting this core outside of its traditional contexts, hu-manistic psychology could revolutionize human existence by making the peak experience and its values the ultimate goals of education, if not of every other social institution as well.

Maslow has been faulted for his uncritical embracing of the peren-nialist[7] view of mystical experience and his triumphant sense of having reached a breakthrough in understanding this phenomenon (Hufford, 1985); for sanitizing an experience that is far more ambivalent in its po-tential than he represented it (Blanchard, 1969); and for his unsupportable reconstructions of religious history (Bregman, 1976). Yet his hierarchy-of-needs model does offer a testable hypothesis for why the higher reaches of human potential are seldom attained, and his rhetoric of peak experiences has helped to foster discussion of mystical experience in various psycho-logical contexts while providing a model for interpreting related phenom-ena (e.g., Csikszentmihalyi, 1982).

The apparent association of peak experiences with exceptional psy-chological well-being suggested what Maslow claimed was a still higher form of psychological science, transpersonal psychology, of which he be-came the philosophical father. *Transpersonal psychology*, one of a cluster of related transpersonal disciplines, takes seriously a wide range of self-transcending phenomena, including mystical experiences, while declining any interpretations that reduce them to something else. Hanegraaff (1996, p. 51) distinguished two branches of transpersonal psychology, an empirical one, which has been chiefly preoccupied with research on altered states of

---

[7]The adjective *perennialist* derives from *philosophia perennis*, perennial philosophy, a term coined by the German philosopher Gottfried Wilhem Leibniz and still used today to refer to a putative common core in the world's religious traditions, ranging from practice and morality to metaphysical truths. Huxley's (1945) anthology with commentary helped to give currency to this term in the 20th century, although Smith (1976) more recently championed the phrase *the primordial tradition* to avoid the suggestion that the core consists of an articulate formal philosophy.

consciousness and the techniques associated with them, and a theoretical one, which has been working on cartographies or hierarchical models of consciousness, according to which the world's great mystics represent the upper reaches of human development (Wilber, 1996). The latter branch especially has sought to develop new paradigms of scientific understanding and, taking the perennial philosophy as axiomatic, to appropriate insights from the spiritual traditions, especially those of the East (see Walsh & Vaughan, 1993).

Like analytical psychology, with which it bears an obvious kinship, transpersonal psychology entails a general framework and underlying assumptions that diverge from the reigning models in psychology and resist empirical assessment and analysis. Unlike Jungian psychology, however, transpersonal psychology is committed to using the best of modern empirical methods to carry out its own research (see, e.g., Shapiro & Walsh, 1984) at the same time that it explores current revolutionary changes in scientific thinking and strives to develop new models of humankind's evolution (Washburn, 1995; Wilber, 1977/1993, 1995). But with the perennial philosophy explicitly posited as its foundation, transpersonal psychology has become "an openly religious psychology" (Hanegraaff, 1996, p. 51), bringing it into fundamental conflict with strictly scientific views.

Perceptual–Cognitive Explanations

Given the singular perceptual and cognitive changes that lie at the heart of mystical experience—including dramatic modifications in bodily sensations and in the appearance of the world and the accompanying conviction of new knowledge and understanding—it is surprising that few efforts have been made to explain such experience in terms of perceptual–cognitive principles. The best known of these efforts is Deikman's (1963, 1966) widely cited theory of *deautomatization*. Deikman suggested that the mystic's basic techniques of contemplation and renunciation inhibit ordinary cognitive processes and thus serve to undo the psychological structures responsible for selecting, organizing, and interpreting perceptual stimuli. A receptive and more inclusive perceptual mode takes over.

In an "experiment" designed to explore this process, Deikman (1963) asked a dozen or so observers to meditate on a blue vase for about 30 min three times a week for as many weeks as they were willing to continue. Those who persisted the longest (1 observer completed 106 sessions) reported a series of striking changes in perceptual experience: increased vividness and richness, animation, merging, a fusing of perceptual modes and, when looking out a window afterward, dedifferentiation of the landscape. Such changes were suggestive of the perceptual and cognitive functioning of young children, but they were also reminiscent of the main features of mystical experience, including intense realness, unusual sensations, the feeling of unity, and the quality of ineffability. Rather than considering deautomatization as merely regressive, Deikman proposed that the suspension of the usual organization of consciousness may allow the mobilizing of undeveloped or unused perceptual capacities, as suggested by mystics' reports of sensate phenomena that do not fit ordinary sensory categories. It correspondingly enhances "the observing self," the transparent center of awareness, the development of which Deikman (1982) placed at the heart of psychotherapy.

A more elaborate cognitive psychology of mystical experience has been put forward by Hunt (1984, 1985, 1995), who drew on holistic–phenomenological cognitive theories and took as his model of mystical experience Otto's (1917/1950) classic description of the numinous consciousness. Hunt sought to demonstrate through his analysis that, in contrast to those who view mystical and related altered states of consciousness as products of regression or perceptual breakdown, these states represent an emergent cognitive capacity, a separate line of development of higher mental abilities. Because of the close-up view that these states offer of certain fundamental processes, Hunt (1985) argued that their study is vital for any general cognitive theory.

According to Hunt (1985), mystical experiences represent a recombination, condensation, and intensification of the earliest, ultrarapid, and normally masked constructions—the microgenesis—of perceptual and affective meaning structures. Citing remarkable impressions that first emerge in response to tachistoscopic images, Hunt noted that these microgenetic schemas are typically synesthetic (i.e., they simultaneously engage two or more sensory modalities), thus facilitating, when they are prolonged and stabilized, the process of cross-modal translations (see Marks, this volume, chap. 4). The appearance of white light that is a major feature of classic mystical experiences (see Wulff, 1997, pp. 147–152) testifies to light's being "the most primitive quale of the visual system" (Hunt, 1984, p. 486) and thus, when reused metaphorically, the most open and encompassing.

The line of cognitive development represented here, which signals the growth of the capacity to use abstract, presentational symbols and which eventually culminates in mystical and other altered states, ordinarily takes second place to more literal and practical intelligence, if it is not masked entirely. As Hunt (1984) suggested, his explanation of mystical experiences "has the immense theoretical advantage of reconciling the clearly primitive aspects of these phenomena with their symbolic and highly abstract features" (p. 497). His analysis has the additional virtue of encompassing major elements from other interpretive perspectives already considered here, including Jungian geometric symbolism and Grof's transpersonal imagery.

Contextual Explanations

All of the perspectives considered so far give primacy to the role of internal factors in the shaping of mystical experience, whether they be neuropsychological, psychodynamic, transpersonal, or cognitive–perceptual. Although they allow for individual differences, these viewpoints nevertheless posit a core of experiences reflecting universal features of the structure and dynamics of the brain on one level, and of the human personality on another. In the past two decades, however, this essentialist or perennialist perspective has been challenged by a number of scholars (see Katz, 1978, 1983) who together put forward a contextualist view, according to which the contexts of tradition, discipline, and culture do not simply add an interpretation to an autonomous core experience but shape experience through and through (Gimello, 1983; Hollenback, 1996).

To explain mystical experience, then, one must attend to the conditions of experience in general, and to the specific concepts, images, symbols, cultural–social beliefs, and ritual practices that define in advance what the mystic's experience will be (Katz, 1978, p. 34). The Jewish "pre-experiential" or "conditioning pattern," Katz pointed out in illustration, includes the teaching that experiences of unity with the divine do not happen, given the Jewish conception of God as radically Other and the principles traditionally recommended for reaching the mystic goal. The result is that ecstatic, self-forgetting moments of unity, of absorption into God, are rare among Jewish mystics, who are far more likely to experience "the Divine Throne, or the angel Metatron, or aspects of the *Sefiroth* [Divine Emanations], or the heavenly court and palaces, or the Hidden Torah, or God's secret Names" (Katz, 1978, p. 34). The complex Buddhist preconditioning, in contrast, prepares the Buddhist mystic for a rather different experience, *nirvana*, a state not of relationship but apparently of selfless tranquillity. One major implication is that lists of phenomenological characteristics such as James and Stace have to offer are too general to delineate what mystical experience actually is (Katz, 1978, p. 51).

In the psychology of religion, the contextual perspective has been most systematically developed by Sundén (1959/1966, 1970), who argued that religious experience is the result of shifts in the perceptual field brought about by the taking on of roles learned from religious texts. "Without a religious reference system, without religious tradition, without myth and ritual," Sundén (1959/1966, p. 27) wrote, "religious experiences are unthinkable." In an experiment designed to test out Sundén's theory, Lans (1987) found that half of his 14 participants with strong religious frames of reference reported religious experiences during a 4-week course of Zen meditation, whereas none of the 21 without such frameworks reported such experiences.

What Sundén's (1959/1966) theory fails to address is how these traditions were established in the first place. It is likewise challenged by Grof's (1980) observation that LSD experiences sometimes occur in the framework of a religious tradition other than the experient's own. The contemporary essentialist–contextualist debate centers mainly on whether there is a tradition-independent core experience and, in particular, an experience of pure consciousness (see Forman, 1990, 1998a; Janz, 1995), and on the role that tradition plays in shaping individual experience. As in the case of the hoary nature–nurture debate in psychology, which it resembles to a certain degree, a reasonable resolution to this debate would seem to lie in an intermediate position (see King, 1988; Parsons, 1999). Thus one would recognize that mystical experiences frequently occur apart from any formal preconditioning, suggesting some fundamental internal mechanism, but also that such conditioning doubtless plays a major role in shaping the experiences of those who are grounded in a mystical tradition.

METHODOLOGICAL ISSUES

Perhaps more than any other subjective phenomenon, mystical experience continues in essential respects to elude rigorous scientific investigation. Relatively rare and unpredictable, it has proved difficult if not impossible to study in the laboratory. Even in Pahnke's (1966) famous double-blind experiment, conducted before the legal ban on the hallucinogens, the variable of expectation ultimately proved impossible to control, leaving its relative contribution to the final results in question (see Wulff, 1997, pp. 191). Correlational research has been facilitated by the development of mysticism scales with respectable psychometric properties (e.g., Hood, Morris, & Watson, 1993), but many of the scales with which they are correlated have items sufficiently similar to their own to raise doubts about whether these various scales represent truly discrete variables. There is also the serious problem uncovered by Hufford (1985) and Thomas and Cooper (1980) that the rather abstract statements found on mysticism questionnaires are subject to widely varying interpretations, leaving in doubt what the scores really mean and how well they represent the individual's experience. Demand characteristics of either the questionnaires or the situations in which they are given may distort scores as well.

But such technical problems pale in significance in the face of a much larger issue. Mysticism not only eludes empirical study but by its very nature also calls into question the assumptions, methods, and modes of thought of modern Western scientific investigation. As Stace (1960, p. 65) remarked, "Any writer who is honest about mysticism, as well as familiar with it, will know that it is utterly irreconcilable with all the ordinary rules of human thinking, that it blatantly breaches the laws of logic at every turn." Thus it is essential, argued Deikman (1977), that those who wish to understand mystical experience must participate in it to some degree themselves. James shared the same view, but as a professed outsider, he held out the possibility of understanding others' mystical experience empathically, through the use of personal documents, and subsequently shedding new light on it. Albrecht (1951), in carrying out his subtle phenomenology of mystical consciousness, drew on his own meditative experience and that of his patients, some of whom were able to make verbal reports while deep in the state of absorption.

Even if one is able to approach mystical experience from the inside, however, there remains the problem of how to translate it into the language of the outsider and to subject it, then, to scientific analysis in a way that does not violate the original apprehension. Tart (1972) proposed the possibility of state-specific sciences, according to which one would carry out observations, data reduction, and theorizing all while in a specific altered state. Among the many difficulties raised by such a proposal, especially in conjunction with mystical states, is the question of how one is to maintain a posture of disinterested agnosticism in the face of the overwhelming impressions of reality that are characteristic of such experiences.

Even the empathic outsider may find such impressions difficult to resist. It is not uncommon for investigators, originally neutral about the exceptional psychological phenomena they are studying, to become convinced that the phenomena genuinely do reflect reality and to shift, then, to a world view that is harmonious with them. Morse (1990), for example, who began his studies of near-death experiences as a strictly empirical physician-researcher, 8 years later found his life thoroughly transformed by the accumulation of stories he was told and especially by the seemingly inexplicable descriptions of light. Grof's (1993) transformation was more dramatic, starting off as it did with the thunderbolt of a first LSD experience, which Grof said moved him to the core. During the years of research he subsequently conducted on the therapeutic potential of LSD, "the unrelenting influx of incontrovertible evidence" (p. 16) gradually shifted his outlook on the world from an atheistic posture to a mystical one. Inevitably, it seems, one has but two choices in the study of mystical experience: working as an outsider whose pronouncements are likely to be viewed by insiders as uncomprehending and thus irrelevant, or becoming an insider oneself, thereby risking the loss not only of the minimal critical distance that disinterested scholarly analysis requires but also of one's credibility— one's "objectivity"—in the eyes of many outsiders.

As in the case of meditation researchers, who are almost always themselves dedicated practitioners, it may be that, with few exceptions, only insiders have sufficient interest and motivation to pursue research on the difficult subject of mysticism. They are also likely, then, to share West's (1987, p. 193) frustration over the great gulf between the fruitfulness of their own compelling experience and what they are able to establish and say about it as scientists. Many will continue to seek a compromise between the two approaches, grounding themselves in their own experience but relying as fully as they can on accepted empirical methods and well-established interpretive frameworks. Others may join the transpersonalists in seeking out a new paradigm sufficient to embrace both personal experience and scientific investigation. The rest may abandon the quest altogether, content to let the mystic way provide its own interpretations.

SUMMARY AND RECOMMENDATIONS

Although full-scale, classic mystical experiences are relatively rare, a third to half of the populations in the United States and Great Britain report having had at least one experience that minimally qualifies as mystical. Whereas many early investigators were inclined to consider such experiences as pathological, evidence today suggests that, in general, those who report them show signs of more adequate adjustment, not less. Even in the lives of distressed individuals, mystical experiences can serve a positive function. There is no doubt, however, that mystical elements do sometimes appear in the symptomatology of seriously disturbed persons and that mystical teachings and practices can either exacerbate existing psychological disturbance, even precipitating psychotic episodes, or disguise them by giving them an acceptable form. It appears that some of the great mystics were themselves troubled, but there are no grounds for interpreting their exceptional experiences as psychotic reactions. Rather, for some of them at least, the experience seems to have helped them to live lives of exceptional dedication and productivity.

The disposition to have mystical experiences varies considerably from person to person and is related to such traits as absorption, hypnotizability, and fantasy proneness as well as complexity, openness to experience, and tolerance for ambiguity. Entheogens seem to override such differences, however, if administered in a supportive setting designed to encourage mystical responses. When mystical experiences have occurred in research settings, whether facilitated by psychoactive substances (Grof, 1980; Pahnke, 1966), hypnosis (Cardeña, 1996), meditation (Gifford-May & Thompson, 1994), or sensory modification (Masters & Houston, 1973), there has been a high degree of consistency in the general contours of such experience, reminiscent of classic reports but not explainable in terms of expectations or induction procedures, suggesting a common core that is likely a reflection of structures and processes in the human brain. There does seem indeed to be an innate capacity for such experiences (Buckley, 1981; Forman, 1998a).

Some of the classic interpreters of mystical experience were inclined to reduce mystical experience to pathological processes or to interpret them as regressive modes of defense. The trend more recently has been to view them either as constructive reactions to crisis or as evidence of healthy growth toward higher stages of awareness. Yet even those who are most positive about mystical experience acknowledge that it entails risks, about which psychotherapists in particular should be knowledgeable. It can be added that the valorizing of mystical experience is also risky for the field of psychology, for to take mysticism seriously—to view it as in some sense a healthy and veridical response to the world—is to open oneself to a world view that fundamentally challenges the assumptions, theories, and procedures of modern empirical psychology.

In the midst of the growing postmodern critique of psychology (e.g., Kvale, 1992), taking this risk may serve as further impetus for change and growth, just as mystical experience can in the lives of individuals. In the place of today's sheer plurality of interpretive frameworks and research methods, we may look forward to a genuinely pluralistic mode of inquiry —what Roth (1987) called *methodological pluralism*—according to which no point of view is finally privileged over any other, but each is entertained as a potential source of insight. Rather than anchoring ourselves in a particular theory or method, then, we would take our grounding in the phenomena themselves, which are far more likely to yield their secrets to a pluralistic approach.

In the study of mystical experience, the initial, great challenge is accessing such experiences as fully and openly as possible. Disciplined phenomenological study—direct where possible but otherwise vicarious (Spiegelberg, 1975)—that builds on work already completed is the crucial first step as well as the final court of appeal for any subsequent interpretation. Yet the Sirens of mystical experience are highly seductive, and like Odysseus, investigators have to find some way to stay on course. A model of a sort is offered by Flournoy's (1915) gifted 20th-century mystic, Mlle Vé, who serves as Höffding's (1918/1923) example of the historically emerging capacity to separate interpretation from experience, to the degree that that is possible. But Mlle Vé's achievement did not come easily. Here, if anywhere, the *discipline* of scholarly inquiry will be engaged to its fullest.

REFERENCES

Aaronson, B. S. (1967). Mystic and schizophreniform states and the experience of depth. *Journal for the Scientific Study of Religion, 6,* 246–252.

Aaronson, B. S. (1969, March). *The hypnotic induction of the void.* Paper presented at the annual meeting of the American Society of Clinical Hypnosis, San Francisco.

Aaronson, B. S. (1970). Some hypnotic analogues to the psychedelic state. In B. S. Aaronson & H. Osmond (Eds.), *Psychedelics: The uses and implications for hallucinogenic drugs* (pp. 279–295). Garden City, NY: Anchor Books.

Aberbach, D. (1987). Grief and mysticism. *International Review of Psycho-Analysis*, *14*, 509–526.

Albrecht, C. (1951). *Psychologie des mystischen Bewußtseins* [Psychology of mystical consciousness]. Bremen, Germany: Carl Schünemann.

Alexander, F. (1931). Buddhistic training as an artificial catatonia (The biological meaning of psychic occurrences). *Psychoanalytic Review*, *18*, 129–145. (Original work published 1923)

Arbman, E. (1963–1970). *Ecstasy, or religious trance, in the experience of the ecstatics and from the psychological point of view* (3 vols.). Norstedts, Sweden: Svenska Bokförlaget.

Armstrong, T. (1984). Transpersonal experience in childhood. *Journal of Transpersonal Psychology*, *16*, 207–230.

Austin, J. H. (1998). *Zen and the brain: Toward an understanding of meditation and consciousness*. Cambridge, MA: MIT Press.

Back, K., & Bourque, L. (1970). Can feelings be enumerated? *Behavioral Science*, *15*, 487–496.

Bear, D., & Fedio, P. (1977). Quantitative analysis of interictal behavior in temporal lobe epilepsy. *Archives of Neurology*, *34*, 454–467.

Bindl, M. F. (1965). *Das religiöse Erleben im Spiegel der Bildgestaltung: Eine entwicklungs-psychologische Untersuchung* [Religious experience in the mirror of picture drawing: A study in development psychology]. Freiburg, Germany: Herder.

Bion, W. R. (1970). *Attention and interpretation: A scientific approach to insight in psycho-analysis and groups*. New York: Basic Books.

Blanchard, W. H. (1969). Psychodynamic aspects of the peak experience. *Psychoanalytic Review*, *56*, 87–112.

Bradburn, N. M. (1969). *The structure of psychological well-being*. Chicago: Aldine.

Bregman, L. (1976). Maslow as theorist of religion: Reflections on his popularity and plausibility. *Soundings*, *59*, 139–163.

Broadribb, D. (with Holly, M., & Lyons, N.). (1995). *The mystical chorus: Jung and the religious dimension*. Alexandria, Australia: Millennium Books.

Bucke, R. M. (1923). *Cosmic consciousness: A study in the evolution of the human mind*. New York: Dutton. (Original work published 1901)

Buckley, P. (1981). Mystical experience and schizophrenia. *Schizophrenia Bulletin*, *7*, 516–521.

Burnham, S. (1997). *The ecstatic journey: The transforming power of mystical experience*. New York: Ballantine Books.

Cardeña, E. (1996). "Just floating in the sky": A comparison of hypnotic and shamanic phenomena. In R. van Quekelberghe & D. Eigner (Eds.), *Yearbook of cross-cultural medicine and psychotherapy 1994* (pp. 85–112). Berlin: Verlag für Wissenschaft und Bildung.

Cowling, W. R. (1985). Relationship of mystical experience, differentiation, and creativity. *Perceptual and Motor Skills*, *61*, 451–456.

Csikszentmihalyi, M. (1982). *Beyond boredom and anxiety: The experience of play in work and games.* San Francisco: Jossey-Bass.

d'Aquili, E. G. (1993). Apologia pro scriptura sua, or maybe we got it right after all. *Zygon, 28,* 251–266.

d'Aquili, E. G., & Newberg, A. B. (1993). Religious and mystical states: A neuropsychological model. *Zygon, 28,* 177–200.

d'Aquili, E. G., & Newberg, A. B. (1999). *The mystical mind: Probing the biology of religious experience.* Minneapolis, MN: Fortress Press.

Davidson, J. M. (1976). The physiology of meditation and mystical states of consciousness. *Perspectives in Biology and Medicine, 19,* 345–379.

Decker, L. R. (1993). Beliefs, post-traumatic stress disorder, and mysticism. *Journal of Humanistic Psychology, 33,* 15–32.

Deikman, A. J. (1963). Experimental meditation. *Journal of Nervous and Mental Disease, 136,* 329–343.

Deikman, A. J. (1966). Deautomatization and the mystic experience. *Psychiatry, 29,* 324–338.

Deikman, A. J. (1977). Comments on the GAP report on mysticism. *Journal of Nervous and Mental Disease, 165,* 213–217.

Deikman, A. J. (1982). *The observing self: Mysticism and psychotherapy.* Boston: Beacon Press.

Doblin, R. (1991). Pahnke's "Good Friday experiment": A long-term follow-up and methodological critique. *Journal of Transpersonal Psychology, 23,* 1–28.

Eigen, M. (1995). Stones in a stream. *Psychoanalytic Review, 82,* 371–390.

Ellenberger, H. F. (1970). *The discovery of the unconscious: The history and evolution of dynamic psychiatry.* New York: Basic Books.

Engler, J. (1984). Therapeutic aims in psychotherapy and meditation: Developmental stages in the representation of self. *Journal of Transpersonal Psychology, 16,* 25–61.

Erikson, E. H. (1977). *Toys and reasons: Stages in the ritualization of experience.* New York: Norton.

Fenwick, P. (1996). The neurophysiology of religious experiences. In D. Bhugra (Ed.), *Psychiatry and religion: Context, consensus, and controversies* (pp. 167–177). London: Routledge.

Fischer, R. (1971). A cartography of ecstatic and meditative states. *Science, 174,* 897–904.

Fischer, R. (1972). Letter to Raymond Prince. *R. M. Bucke Memorial Society Newsletter-Review, 5,* 42–45.

Fischer, R. (1975). Transformations of consciousness. A cartography: I. The perception–hallucination continuum. *Confinia Psychiatrica, 18,* 221–244.

Flournoy, T. (1915). Une mystique moderne (Documents pour la psychologie religieuse) [A modern mystic (Documents for the psychology of religion)]. *Archives de Psychologie, 15,* 1–224.

Forman, R. K. C. (1990). (Ed.). *The problem of pure consciousness: Mysticism and philosophy.* New York: Oxford University Press.

Forman, R. K. C. (1998a). (Ed.). *The innate capacity: Mysticism, psychology, and philosophy.* New York: Oxford University Press.

Forman, R. K. C. (1998b). What does mysticism have to teach us about consciousness? *Journal of Consciousness Studies, 5,* 185–201.

Foster, G. W. (1985). *The world was flooded with light: A mystical experience remembered.* Pittsburgh, PA: University of Pittsburgh Press.

Freud, S. (1961). Civilization and its discontents. In J. Strachey (Ed. and Trans.), *The standard edition of the complete psychological works of Sigmund Freud* (Vol. 21, pp. 59–145). London: Hogarth Press. (Original work published 1930)

Gellhorn, E. (1967). *Principles of autonomic–somatic integrations: Physiological basis and psychological and clinical implications.* Minneapolis: University of Minnesota Press.

Gellhorn, E. (1969). Emotions and the ergotropic–trophotropic systems. *Psychologische Forschung, 34,* 48–94.

Geschwind, N. (1983). Interictal behavior changes in epilepsy. *Epilepsia, 24*(Suppl. 1), S23–S30.

Gibbons, D., & De Jarnette, J. (1972). Hypnotic susceptibility and religious experience. *Journal for the Scientific Study of Religion, 11,* 152–156.

Gifford-May, D., & Thompson, N. L. (1994). "Deep states" of meditation: Phenomenological reports of experience. *Journal of Transpersonal Psychology, 26,* 117–138.

Gimello, R. M. (1983). Mysticism in its contexts. In S. T. Katz (Ed.), *Mysticism and religious traditions* (pp. 61–88). Oxford, England: Oxford University Press.

Greeley, A. M. (1975). *The sociology of the paranormal: A reconnaissance* (Sage Research Papers in the Social Sciences, Vol. 3, Series No. 90-023). Beverly Hills, CA: Sage.

Greenberg, D., Witztum, E., & Buchbinder, J. T. (1992). Mysticism and psychosis: The fate of Ben Zoma. *British Journal of Medical Psychology, 65,* 223–235.

Grinspoon, L., & Bakalar, J. B. (1979). *Psychedelic drugs reconsidered.* New York: Basic Books.

Grof, S. (1980). *LSD psychotherapy.* Pomona, CA: Hunter House.

Grof, S. (1985). *Beyond the brain: Birth, death, and transcendence in psychotherapy.* Albany: State University of New York Press.

Grof, S. (1993). *The holotropic mind: The three levels of human consciousness and how they shape our lives.* San Francisco: HarperSanFrancisco.

Grof, S., & Grof, C. (Eds.). (1989). *Spiritual emergency: When personal transformation becomes a crisis.* New York: Putnam's.

Group for the Advancement of Psychiatry, Committee on Psychiatry and Religion. (1976). *Mysticism: Spiritual quest or psychic disorder?* (GAP Publication No. 97). New York: Author.

Hanegraaff, W. J. (1996). *New age religion and Western culture: Esotericism in the mirror of secular thought*. Leiden, The Netherlands: Brill.

Hardy, A. (1979). *The spiritual nature of man: A study of contemporary religious experience*. Oxford, England: Oxford University Press.

Hay, D., & Morisy, A. (1978). Reports of ecstatic, paranormal, or religious experience in Great Britain and the United States—A comparison of trends. *Journal for the Scientific Study of Religion, 17*, 255–268.

Henderson, L. A., & Glass, W. J. (Eds.). (1994). *LSD: Still with us after all these years*. San Francisco: Jossey-Bass.

Höffding, H. (1923). *Erlebnis und Deutung. Eine vergleichende Studie zur Religionspsychologie* [Experience and interpretation: A comparative study in the psychology of religion] (E. Magnus, Trans.). Stuttgart, Germany: Frommanns Verlag (H. Kurtz). (Original Danish edition published 1918)

Hollenback, J. B. (1996). *Mysticism: Experience, response, and empowerment*. University Park: Pennsylvania State University Press.

Hood, R. W., Jr. (1970). Religious orientation and the report of religious experience. *Journal for the Scientific Study of Religion, 9*, 285–291.

Hood, R. W., Jr. (1973). Religious orientation and the experience of transcendence. *Journal for the Scientific Study of Religion, 12*, 441–448.

Hood, R. W., Jr. (1974). Psychological strength and the report of intense religious experience. *Journal for the Scientific Study of Religion, 13*, 65–71.

Hood, R. W., Jr. (1975). The construction and preliminary validation of a measure of reported mystical experience. *Journal for the Scientific Study of Religion, 14*, 29–41.

Hood, R. W., Jr. (1976). Conceptual criticisms of regressive explanations of mysticism. *Review of Religious Research, 17*, 179–188.

Hood, R. W., Jr., Hall, J. R., Watson, P. J., & Biderman, M. (1979). Personality correlates of the report of mystical experience. *Psychological Reports, 44*, 804–806.

Hood, R. W., Jr., Morris, R. J., & Watson, P. J. (1993). Further factor analysis of Hood's mysticism scale. *Psychological Reports, 3*, 1176–1178.

Horton, P. C. (1973). The mystical experience as a suicide preventive. *American Journal of Psychiatry, 130*, 294–296.

Horton, P. C. (1974). The mystical experience: Substance of an illusion. *Journal of the American Psychoanalytic Association, 22*, 364–380.

Houston, J., & Masters, R. E. L. (1972). The experimental induction of religious-type experiences. In J. White (Ed.), *The highest state of consciousness* (pp. 303–321). Garden City, NY: Doubleday Anchor.

Hufford, D. J. (1985). Commentary: Mystical experience in the modern world. In G. W. Foster, *The world was flooded with light: A mystical experience remembered* (pp. 87–183). Pittsburgh, PA: University of Pittsburgh Press.

Hunt, H. T. (1984). A cognitive psychology of mystical and altered-state experience. *Perceptual and Motor Skills, 58*, 467–513.

Hunt, H. T. (1985). Relations between the phenomena of religious mysticism (altered states of consciousness) and the psychology of thought: A cognitive psychology of states of consciousness and the necessity of subjective states for cognitive theory. *Perceptual and Motor Skills, 61,* 911–961.

Hunt, H. T. (1995). *On the nature of consciousness: Cognitive, phenomenological, and transpersonal perspectives.* New Haven, CT: Yale University Press.

Huxley, A. (1945). *The perennial philosophy.* New York: Harper.

Inge, W. R. (1899). *Christian mysticism.* New York: Scribner's.

James, W. (1958). *The varieties of religious experience: A study in human nature.* Cambridge, MA: Harvard University Press. (Original work published 1902)

Janet, P. (1926–1928). *De l'angoisse a l'extase, études sur les croyances et les sentiments* [From anguish to ecstasy: Studies of beliefs and sentiments] (2 vols.). Paris: Félix Alcan.

Janz, B. (1995). Mysticism and understanding: Steven Katz and his critics. *Studies in Religion, 24,* 77–94.

Jaynes, J. (1976). *The origin of consciousness in the breakdown of the bicameral mind.* Boston: Houghton Mifflin.

Jordan, G. R., Jr. (1971). Psychedelics and zen: Some reflections. *The Eastern Buddhist, 4,* 138–140.

Jung, C. G. (1976). The Tavistock lectures on the theory and practice of analytical psychology. In H. Read, M. Fordham, & G. Adler (Eds.), W. McGuire (Exec. Ed.), & R. F. C. Hull (Trans.), *The collected works of C. G. Jung* (Vol. 18, pp. 1–182). Princeton, NJ: Princeton University Press. (Originally delivered 1935)

Kakar, S. (1991). *The analyst and the mystic: Psychoanalytic reflections on religion and mysticism.* Chicago: University of Chicago Press.

Katz, S. T. (Ed.). (1978). *Mysticism and philosophical analysis.* New York: Oxford University Press.

Katz, S. T. (Ed.). (1983). *Mysticism and religious traditions.* Oxford, England: Oxford University Press.

King, S. (1988). Two epistemological models for the interpretation of mysticism. *Journal of the American Academy of Religion, 56,* 257–279.

Kornfield, J. (1989). Obstacles and vicissitudes in spiritual practice. In S. Grof & C. Grof (Eds.), *Spiritual emergency: When personal transformation becomes a crisis* (pp. 137–169). New York: Putnam's.

Kroll, J., Fiszdon, J., & Crosby, R. (1996). Childhood abuse and three measures of altered states of consciousness (dissociation, absorption and mysticism) in a female outpatient sample. *Journal of Personality Disorders, 10,* 345–354.

Kumar, V. K., & Pekala, R. J. (1988). Hypnotizability, absorption, and individual differences in phenomenological experience. *International Journal of Clinical and Experimental Hypnosis, 36,* 80–88.

Kvale, S. (Ed.). (1992). *Psychology and postmodernism.* London: Sage.

Lans, J. M. van der. (1987). The value of Sundén's role-theory demonstrated and tested with respect to religious experiences in meditation. *Journal for the Scientific Study of Religion, 26*, 401–412.

Laski, M. (1961). *Ecstasy: A study of some secular and religious experiences.* London: Cresset Press.

Leary, D. E. (1990). (Ed.). *Metaphors in the history of psychology.* Cambridge, England: Cambridge University Press.

Leuba, J. H. (1925). *The psychology of religious mysticism.* New York: Harcourt, Brace.

Levin, J. S. (1993). Age differences in mystical experience. *The Gerontologist, 33*, 507–513. [see also Errata in 33(5), Table of Contents]

Levin, J. S., Wickramasekera, I. E., & Hirshberg, C. (1998). Is religiousness a correlate of absorption? Implications for psychophysiology, coping, and morbidity. *Alternate Therapies in Health and Medicine, 4*, 72–76.

Liddon, S. C. (1989). *The dual brain, religion, and the unconscious.* Buffalo, NY: Prometheus Books.

Logan, R. D. (1985). The "flow experience" in solitary ordeals. *Journal of Humanistic Psychology, 25*, 79–89.

Makarec, K., & Persinger, M. A. (1985). Temporal lobe signs: Electroencephalographic validity and enhanced scores in special populations. *Perceptual and Motor Skills, 60*, 831–842.

Mallory, M. M. (1977). *Christian mysticism: Transcending techniques.* Amsterdam: Van Gorcum.

Mandel, A. (1980). Toward a psychobiology of transcendence: God in the brain. In J. Davidson & R. Davidson (Eds.), *The psychobiology of consciousness* (pp. 379–464). New York: Plenum.

Maslow, A. H. (1964). *Religions, values, and peak-experiences.* Columbus: Ohio State University Press.

Maslow, A. H. (1968). *Toward a psychology of being* (2nd ed.). New York: Van Nostrand Reinhold.

Masters, R. E. L., & Houston, J. (1973). Subjective realities. In B. Schwartz (Ed.), *Human connection and the new media* (pp. 88–106). Englewood Cliffs, NJ: Prentice Hall.

McGinn, B. (1991). *The foundations of mysticism.* New York: Crossroad.

Meissner, W. W. (1992). *Ignatius of Loyola: The psychology of a saint.* New Haven, CT: Yale University Press.

Moller, H. (1965). Affective mysticism in western civilization. *Psychoanalytic Review, 52*, 259–274.

Montmorand, M. de. (1920). *Psychologie des mystiques catholiques orthodoxes* [Psychology of orthodox Catholic mystics]. Paris: Félix Alcan.

Morel, F. (1918). *Essai sur l'introversion mystique: Étude psychologique de Pseudo-Denys l'Areopagite et de quelques autres cas de mysticisme* [Essays on mystical introversion: A psychological study of Pseudo-Dionysius, the Areopagite, and of some other cases of mysticism]. Geneva: Albert Kundig.

Morse, M. (1990). *Closer to the light: Learning from the near-death experiences of children.* New York: Villard Books.

Murphy, M., & Donovan, S. (1996). *The physical and psychological effects of meditation: A review of contemporary research with a comprehensive bibliography, 1931–1996* (2nd ed.). (E. I. Taylor, Ed.). Sausalito, CA: Institute of Noetic Sciences.

Myers, F. W. H. (1892). The subliminal consciousness. Chapter I. General characteristics of subliminal messages. *Proceedings of the Society for Psychical Research, 7,* 298–327.

Naranjo, C. (1973). *The healing journey: New approaches to consciousness.* New York: Pantheon.

Nelson, P. L. (1992). Personality attributes as discriminating factors in distinguishing religio-mystical from paranormal experients. *Imagination, Cognition, and Personality, 11,* 389–406.

Neumann, E. (1968). Mystical man. In J. Campbell (Ed.) & R. Manheim (Trans.), *The mystic vision: Papers from the eranos yearbooks* (pp. 375–415). Princeton, NJ: Princeton University Press. (Originally delivered 1948)

Noll, R. (1983). Shamanism and schizophrenia: A state-specific approach to the "schizophrenia metaphor" of shamanic states. *American Ethnologist, 10,* 443–459.

Noyes, R., & Slymen, D. J. (1979). The subjective response to life-threatening danger. *Omega: Journal of Death and Dying, 9,* 313–321.

Otto, R. (1950). *The idea of the holy: An inquiry into the non-rational factor in the idea of the divine and in relation to the rational* (2nd ed.). (J. W. Harvey, Trans.). London: Oxford University Press. (Original German edition published 1917)

Oxman, T. E., Rosenberg, S. D., Schnurr, P. P., Tucker, G. J., & Gala, G. (1988). The language of altered states. *Journal of Nervous and Mental Disease, 176,* 401–408.

Packer, M. J., & Addison, R. B. (Eds.). (1989). *Entering the circle: Hermeneutic investigation in psychology.* Albany: State University of New York Press.

Paffard, M. (1973). *Inglorious Wordsworths: A study of some transcendental experiences in childhood and adolescence.* London: Hodder & Stoughton.

Pahnke, W. N. (1966). Drugs and mysticism. *International Journal of Parapsychology, 8,* 295–314.

Parsons, W. B. (1999). *The enigma of the oceanic feeling: Revisioning the psychoanalytic theory of mysticism.* New York: Oxford University Press.

Penfield, W., & Perot, P. (1963). The brain's record of auditory and visual experience: A final summary and discussion. *Brain, 86,* 595–702.

Persinger, M. A. (1983). Religious and mystical experiences as artifacts of temporal lobe function: A general hypothesis. *Perceptual and Motor Skills, 57,* 1255–1262.

Persinger, M. A. (1987). *Neuropsychological bases of god beliefs.* New York: Praeger.

Pratt, J. B. (1920). *The religious consciousness: A psychological study*. New York: Macmillan.

Prince, R., & Savage, C. (1966). Mystical states and the concept of regression. *Psychedelic Review*, No. 8, 59–75.

Rose, S. (1989). *The conscious brain* (Rev. ed.). New York: Paragon House.

Roth, P. A. (1987). *Meaning and method in the social sciences: A case for methodological pluralism*. Ithaca, NJ: Cornell University Press.

Rouget, G. (1985). *Music and trance: A theory of the relations between music and possession* (B. Biebuyck & G. Rouget, Trans.). Chicago: University of Chicago Press. (Original French edition published 1980)

Ruck, C. A. P., Bigwood, J., Staples, D., Otto, J., & Wassen, R. G. (1979). Entheogens. *Journal of Psychedelic Drugs, 11*, 145–146.

Sacerdote, P. (1977). Applications of hypnotically elicited mystical states to the treatment of physical and emotional pain. *International Journal of Clinical and Experimental Hypnosis, 25*, 309–324.

Shapiro, D. H., Jr., & Walsh, R. N. (Eds.). (1984). *Meditation: Classic and contemporary perspectives*. New York: Aldine.

Smith, H. (1967). Psychedelic theophanies and the religious life. *Christianity and Crisis, 27*, 144–147.

Smith, H. (1976). *Forgotten truth: The primordial tradition*. New York: Harper & Row.

Spanos, N. P., & Moretti, P. (1988). Correlates of mystical and diabolical experiences in a sample of female university students. *Journal for the Scientific Study of Religion, 27*, 105–116.

Spiegelberg, H. (1975). Phenomenology through vicarious experience. In *Doing phenomenology: Essays on and in phenomenology* (pp. 35–53). The Hague, The Netherlands: Martinus Nijhoff.

Stace, W. T. (1960). *Mysticism and philosophy*. Philadelphia: Lippincott.

Strenger, C. (1991). *Between hermeneutics and science: An essay on the epistemology of psychoanalysis*. Madison, CT: International Universities Press.

Sundén, H. (1966). *Die Religion und die Rollen. Eine psychologische Untersuchung der Frömmigkeit* [Religion and roles: A psychological investigation of piety]. Berlin: Alfred Töpelmann. (Original Swedish edition published 1959)

Sundén, H. (1970). Meditation and perception: Some notes on the psychology of religious mysticism. In S. S. Hartman & C. M. Edsman (Eds.), *Mysticism* (pp. 34–46). Stockholm: Almqvist & Wiksell.

Tart, C. T. (1972). States of consciousness and state-specific sciences. *Science, 176*, 1203–1210.

Tart, C. T. (1991). Influences of previous psychedelic drug experiences on students of Tibetan Buddhism: A preliminary exploration. *Journal of Transpersonal Psychology, 23*, 139–173.

Tellegen, A., & Atkinson, G. (1974). Openness to absorbing and self-altering experiences ("absorption"), a trait related to hypnotic susceptibility. *Journal of Abnormal Psychology, 43,* 111–122.

Thalbourne, M. A. (1991). The psychology of mystical experience. *Exceptional Human Experience, 9,* 168–186.

Thalbourne, M. A., Bartemucci, L., Delin, P. S., Fox, B., & Nofi, O. (1997). Transliminality: Its nature and correlates. *Journal of the American Society for Psychical Research, 91,* 305–331.

Thalbourne, M. A., & Delin, P. S. (1994). A common thread underlying belief in the paranormal, creative personality, mystical experience and psychopathology. *Journal of Parapsychology, 58,* 3–38.

Thalbourne, M. A., & Delin, P. S. (1999). Transliminality: Its relation to dream life, religiosity, and mystical experience. *International Journal for the Psychology of Religion, 9,* 35–43.

Thomas, L. E., & Cooper, P. E. (1980). Incidence and psychological correlates of intense spiritual experience. *Journal of Transpersonal Psychology, 12,* 75–85.

Underhill, E. (1930). *Mysticism: A study in the nature and development of man's spiritual consciousness* (Rev. ed.). London: Methuen. (Original work published 1911)

van Manen, M. (1990). *Researching lived experience; Human science for an action sensitive pedagogy.* Albany: State University of New York Press.

Walsh, R., & Vaughan, F. (Eds.). (1993). *Paths beyond ego: The transpersonal vision.* Los Angeles: Tarcher.

Washburn, M. (1995). *The ego and the dynamic ground: A transpersonal theory of human development.* Albany: State University of New York Press.

West, M. A. (Ed.). (1987). *The psychology of meditation.* Oxford, England: Oxford University Press.

Wilber, K. (1993). *The spectrum of consciousness* (2nd ed). Wheaton, IL: Quest. (Original work published 1977)

Wilber, K. (1995). *Sex, ecology, spirituality: The spirit of evolution.* Boston: Shambhala.

Wilber, K. (1996). *Eye to eye: The quest for the new paradigm* (3rd ed.). Boston: Shambhala.

Wilson, S. C., & Barber, T. X. (1983). The fantasy-prone personality: Implications for understanding imagery, hypnosis, and parapsychological phenomena. In A. A. Sheikh (Ed.), *Imagery: Current theory, research, and application* (pp. 340–387). New York: Wiley.

Wilson, S. R., & Spencer, R. C. (1990). Intense personal experiences: Subjective effects, interpretations, and after-effects. *Journal of Clinical Psychology, 46,* 565–573.

Winkelman, M. (1986). Trance states: A theoretical model and cross-cultural analysis. *Ethos, 14,* 174–203.

Winnicott, D. W. (1953). Transitional objects and transitional phenomena. *International Journal of Psychoanalysis, 34,* 89–97.

Wulff, D. M. (1997). *Psychology of religion: Classic and contemporary* (2nd ed.) New York: Wiley.

Wuthnow, R. (1978). Peak experiences: Some empirical tests. *Journal of Humanistic Psychology, 18*(3), 59–75.

Yamane, D., & Polzer, M. (1994). Ways of seeing ecstasy in modern society: Experimental–expressive and cultural–linguistic views. *Sociology of Religion, 55*, 1–25.

AUTHOR INDEX

Numbers in italics refer to listings in the reference sections.

441

442   AUTHOR INDEX

Lucescu, M. L., 160, *181*
Ludwig, A. H., 48, 58, *77*
Lukianowicz, N., 321, *349*
Lukoff, D., 226, 248, 326, 327, *349, 351*
Luria, A. R., 63, *77*, 100, *117*, 121, *147*
Lyne, S., *392*
Lynn, S. J., 16, *20*, 196, 206, *215*, 258,
    259, 262, 266, 267, *279*, 287,
    297, 298, *309*, *311*, 324, 325,
    349

MacDonald, D. A., 63, *77*
MacDonald, W. L., 5, *20*
Machado, F. R., 185, *218*, 222, 226, *251*
Mack, J. E., 256, 269, *279*, 280
Mackinnon, A., 87, *113*
MacMillan, F., 109, *114*
MacMillan, J. F., 93, *116*
Macquarrie, J., 71, *78*
Madow, L., 99, *113*
Mahéo, P., 201, 208, *214*
Maher, B. A., 35, 36, *45*
Mahler, H., 354, *391*
Mahling, F., 122, *147*
Maitz, E. A., 66, *78*, 206, *214*
Makarec, K., 197, *216*, 273, 280, 406,
    436
Maki, M., 359, *391*
Malcolm, N., 157, 158, *181*
Mallory, M. M., 402, 411, *436*
Mandel, A., 406, *436*
Mandler, G., 49, *78*
Marcano, G., 58, *79*, 185, *216*, 228, *248*
Marean, M., *177*
Margaro, P. A., 102, *116*
Margo, A., 97, *117*
Mark, M., 99, *119*
Marks, D. F., 239, *248*
Marks, I., 109, *118*
Marks, L. E., 122, 124, 128, 129, 135,
    137, 138–143, *145, 147, 148*
Marean, M., *178*
Marmelstein, L., 258, *279*
Marnham, P., 385, *391*
Marsh, C. A., 49, *78*
Marston, A., 165, *182*
Martin, J. L., 40, *45*
Martindale, C., 62, *78*
Martino, G., 141, *147*
Maslow, A. H., 397, 422, 423, *436*

Mason, L. I., 171, *181*
Massimo, L., *178*
Mastel, J., *178*
Masters, R. E. L., 403, 429, 434, *436*
Matlock, J. G., 238, *248*, 286, 288, 289,
    294, 298, 300, 301, 304, *309*
Matthews-Simonton, S., 358, *393*
Mattison, A., 123, *147*
Maurer, D., 132, 135, 136, *147*
Maurer, R. L., 66, *78*
May, E. C., 235, *250*
Mayan, M., *178*
McCarthy, E., *119*
McClelland, D. C., 366, *391*
McClelland, J. L., 49, *78*
McClenon, J., 5, 6, *20*, 185, *214*, 222,
    227, *247, 248*, 363, 372, 379,
    384, *390*
McConkey, K. M., 57, 61, *78, 80*
McCormick, D., 200, 204, 208, *215*, 376,
    391
McCreery, C., 190, 191, 193, 194, 197,
    198, 203, 204, 206, *213, 214*,
    215
McGinn, B., 422, *436*
McGough, W. E., 378, *393*
McGowan, K., 158, *181*
McGuffin, P., 41, *45*
McGuigan, F. J., 100, *117*
McGuire, P. K., 91, 101, 111, *117*
McKane, J. P., 134, *148*
McKellar, P., 94, *117*, 124, 134, *148*
McKenna, P. J., 39, 44, *119*
McNally, D., 96, *117*
McNichol, D., 105, *117*
McPhilips, M., *120*
Meehl, P. E., 43, *46*
Meek, G., 385, *391*
Mehl-Madrona, L., 353, *391*
Meier, P., 40, *45*
Meissner, W. W., 419, *436*
Melara, R. D., 140, 141, *148*
Melnechuk, T., 374, *391*
Menary, E., 287, *311*
Mercier, L., 378, *393*
Merleau-Ponty, M., 59, *78*
Mezzich, J., 93, *114*
Michelson, L., 16, *20*
Miller, F., 50, *80*
Miller, J. G., 380, 381
Miller, L. C., 194, *215*
Miller, L. J., 89, *117*

456   AUTHOR INDEX

SUBJECT INDEX

in out-of-body experience, 189, 190,
197, 333–335
in psi-related experiences, 229
psychoneuroimmunological model, 382
in synesthesia, 131–133, 140, 143–144
vectoral hemisphericity hypothesis, 335
Buddhism, 426
lucid dreaming and, 174–175

Case studies, 63
Charles Bonnet syndrome, 29
Childhood. *See also* Childhood trauma;
Development
Childhood trauma, 231
alien abduction experience and, 272
among fantasy prone individuals, 324
among near-death experients, 320–323
in anomalous experience and psychopathology, 39–40
out-of-body experience and, 196
Children
with imaginary playmates, 294–295
mystical experiences of, 407–408
near-death experiences of, 317, 332,
341
out-of-body experiences of, 196
past-life reports of, 288–289, 292–296,
303–304
Chlorpromazine, 107–108
Christian Science, 375
Clairvoyance
See also Psi-related experiences
definition, 220
prevalence, 222
Classification of anomalous experiences,
29–31
alien abduction experience, 255
ESP experience, 223
mystical experiences, 401–402
near-death experiences, 317–319
reality characteristics, 89–90
synesthesia, 122
Cognitive processes
of anomalous healers, 365–366
associated with out-of-body experience,
193–194
deautomatization, 424–425
evolution of psychology research, 47–
50
explanations of mystical experience,
424–425

healing effects of information processing systems, 381
hypnotizability and, 69
limits of introspective observation, 50–
57
in lucid dreaming, 154–155
mediation of synesthesia, 136–137
in near-death experience, 318
patterns common to psychopathology
and anomalous experience, 38–
39
predictors of out-of-body experience,
208
predisposing to alternative healing, 375
predisposing to psi-related experiences,
228
source monitoring, 101–102
supporting belief in unusual events, 8,
9
Collective unconscious, 420–422
Colored hearing, 123, 136, 144
Complementary and alternative medicine, 354–355
anomalous healing in, 354–355
clinical risks associated with, 374–377
concepts of healing and curing, 359–
360
definition, 355–356
efficacy, 371–374
experience vs. events, 355–356
frauds, 375–376
goals, 356
healer characteristics, 364–367
placebo effects, 376
research, 355
Confabulation, 52–53
Consciousness
See also Altered states of consciousness
assessment techniques, 50
characteristics of mystical experience,
400–401
clinical conceptualization, 47–50
individual differences in anomalous experiences, 68–69
in lucid dreaming, 152–153, 156–158,
170, 171
psychophenomenological assessment,
64–68
reliability–validity of introspection, 49,
50–51, 71–72
in sleep, 156
subliminal consciousness, 409

psychoanalytic theory of mystical experience, 418–419, 420

schizophrenia model, 110–111

synesthesia, 135–139

Diabolical mysticism, 405, 411

Diagnostic and Statistical Manual of Mental Disorders, 26, 27

Diaries, 62

Dimensions of Attention Questionnaire, 65–68

Dissociation–dissociative tendencies, 5–6, 16, 35

 alien abduction report and, 268

 among near-death experients, 320–323

 clinical meaning, 322

 early research, 7–8

 hypnotizability and, 69

 out-of-body experience and, 192–193

 as predictor of anomalous experience, 69

 psi-related experiences and, 228

Distractibility, 133

Dopaminergic system, 108

Dreaming

 See also Lucid dreaming

 alien abduction experience and, 265

 ESP experience in, 223–224

 out-of-body experience and, 194, 202–203

Drumming, 367

Ecstasy, 399, 408

Eidetic imagery, synesthesia and, 131–132

Electromagnetic effects, 273

Encounter-prone personality, 323, 324

Endopsychosins, 334–336

Endorphins, 334–335

Energy medicine, 355

Enkephalin system, 334–335

Entheogens, 404–405

Epidemiology

 alien abduction experience, 255–256

 fantasy proneness, 324

 hallucinations, 94–96

 lucid dreaming, 153

 mystical experience, 406–407

 near-death experience, 316

 out-of-body experiences, 184–186

 past-life experiences, 286

 psi-related phenomenon, 222–224

 synesthesia, 123

Epilepsy, 406

 mystical experience and, 416–418

 out-of-body experience and, 197

 psi-related experiences and, 229

Ergotropic arousal, 417

ESP. *See* Extrasensory perception

Event recording, 60

Expectation effects

 in anomalous healing, 376

 in near-death experience, 332

 in past-life experiences, 300

Experiential analysis technique, 57

Extrasensory perception (ESP)

 See also Psi-related experiences

 circumstances of, 224–225

 content, 224

 experient's belief in truth of, 224

 forms of, 223–224

 out-of-body experience and, 194–195, 199

 past-life reports related to, 299

 phenomenology, 223–225

 prevalence, 224

Factitious disorders, 271–272

False memories, 266–267, 270–271. *See also* Confabulation

Fantasy proneness, 5–6

 alien abduction experience and, 261–262

 among near-death experients, 324–325

 anomalous healing and, 369

 causes of, 324

 characteristics, 324

 hallucinatory experiences, 324–325

 mystical experience proneness and, 408

 out-of-body experiences and, 185, 192

 past-life reports and, 304

 prevalence, 324

 psi-related experiences and, 228

Fear of anomalous experience, 226–227

Firewalking, 66–67

Folie-à-deux, 268

Functional impairment, 34–35

Gender differences

 female healers, 371

 in lucid dreaming, 165

 past-life experiences and, 292

Gender differences (*continued*)
  psi-related experiences and, 228–229
Glutamate, 334–336
Grieving, hallucinations and, 99

Hallucination(s)
  See also Auditory hallucinations; Visual
    hallucinations
  among fantasy prone individuals, 324–
    325
  assessment, 87–88
  associated medical conditions, 93
  autoscopic, 197
  biological markers, 91, 100–101, 107
  classification by reality characteristics,
    89–90
  clinical conceptualizations, 85, 86, 99
  content, 97
  continuum model, 90–91
  coping responses, 92
  definition, 27, 86
  developmental course in schizophrenia,
    110–111
  environmental stimulation, 97–98
  epidemiology, 94–96
  ESP experience as, 223
  grieving and, 99
  near-death experience(s) and, 327, 334
  out-of-body experience(s) and, 194
  outcomes, 91–92
  in peculiarity continuum, 27
  pharmacotherapy, 107–108
  phenomenology, 88–91, 95–96
  psychopathology and, 4, 93–96
  psychotherapy, 108–110
  recognizing nonveridicality of, 28–29
  research needs, 110, 111
  sensory deprivation experiments, 97–
    98
  signal detection sensitivity, 105–106
  sociocultural mediators, 96–97, 102
  source monitoring judgments in, 101–
    107
  stress as mediator of, 98–99
  substance-induced, 37, 93
  without associated pathology, 94
Harmaline, 421–422
Hashish, 127
Headaches, 197
Healing experiences and events, 5, 14–15
  acoustic driving effects, 367

in alternative medicine, 354–356
attributions of disease cause, 369
biological markers, 367–368
characteristics of disease survivors,
  368–369
clinical risk in, 374–377
common features of, 381
concepts of illness and disease, 360
conceptual basis, 354
counseling of experients of, 376–377
cultural context, 354, 359, 364–365
curing and, 359–360
efficacy, 371–374, 379–380, 384–385
fantasy proneness and, 369
female healers, 371
forms of, 357–359
healer characteristics, 364–367, 369–
  370
healer types, 358, 364–365
individual differences, 368–370
laying-on of hands, 357–358, 363, 367
in mystical experiences, 413
Native American practice, 353–354
parapsychological research, 379–380
patient characteristics, 360–364
phenomenology, 360, 383
placebo effects, 376, 378–379
prayer interventions, 379–380
process, 369–370
psychopathology and, 370–371
psychophysiological models, 377–379
recommendations for research, 385–
  386
religious doctrines and medical neglect,
  375
in religious settings, 362–368
research methodology, 355, 370, 372,
  383–385
rituals and ceremonies as, 374
Spiritist surgeon, 362
as spontaneous remission, 358, 362–
  363
systems models, 380–382
terminology, 356–360
theories of, 377–382
therapeutic relationship in, 366–367
Western approach, 354
Hearing loss, 36
Help seeking
  anomalous healing experients, 376
  factitious disorders, 271–272
  psi-related experiences, 233

Hoaxes and frauds
  alien abduction experience, 271–272
  anomalous healing experients, 376
  past-life reports, 297–298
  psychic healers, 375–376, 385
Hypnagogic imagery, 193, 202
  alien abduction experience and, 265
Hypnopompic imagery, 193
Hypnosis, 4
  depth ratings, 61
  emergence of alien abduction experience in, 254, 265–267
  for examining past-life reports, 304
  firewalking and, 67
  individual differences in, 68–69
  lucid dreaming and, 169
  out-of-body experience in, 192
  past-life experiences elicited in, 286–288, 300–301
  psychophenomenological assessment, 66
  recall effects, 266
  visualizers, 69
Hypnotizability, 5–6
  alien abduction experience and, 266–267
  imaginal ability and, 369
  mystical experience proneness and, 408, 409
  of near-death experients, 320
  out-of-body experience and, 185, 192, 204
  past-life reports and, 304
  placebo effect and, 379
  predictive of anomalous experience, 69–71
  psi-related experiences and, 228
  of traditional healers, 369

Imaginal ability
  of anomalous healers, 365–366
  lucid dreaming and, 164
  mystical experience proneness and, 408
  of near-death experients, 320
  out-of-body experience and, 193, 202
Immune function, 382
Individual differences
  alien abduction experience, 258–268
  anomalous healing experiences and events, 368–370
  assessment, 72–73

auditory hallucinations, 88–89
common to psychopathology and anomalous experience, 38–40
disease survivors, 368–369
in hypnosis, 68–69
lucid dreaming, 163–166
mystical experience, 429
near-death experiences, 320–321
out-of-body experiences, 190–196
past-life experiences, 294
as peculiarity, 27
psi-related experiences, 227–229
states of consciousness in anomalous experiences, 68–69
in synesthesia, 134–136
Inner speech, hallucinations and, 99–101
Intelligence
  lucid dreaming and, 164–165
  near-death experients, 320
Interpersonal relations
  aftereffects of near-death experience, 328–330
  healing effects of social support, 374
  psi-related experiences and, 231, 237
  response to reported anomalous experience, 36
Interviews, 62
Intraception, 191
Introspection
  clinical conceptualizations, 49
  concurrent reporting methodologies, 60–61
  dissembling in, 55–56
  distortion through observation, 53–54
  experimenter expectancy effects, 56
  limitations of, 52–57
  lucid dreaming research, 171–172
  memory effects, 52–53
  out-of-body experience research, 205
  reliability–validity, 50–51, 71–72
  research approach, 59–60
  retrospective reporting methodologies, 61–64
  self-censorship, 54
  state-specific memory, 56–57
  synesthesia research, 139
  verbal description, 53
Introversion–extroversion
  lucid dreaming and, 165–166
  near-death experients, 320
  out-of-body experience and, 191

Masochism
in alien abduction experience, 263–263
as escape-from-self, 263
Meaning making
benefits of anomalous experience, 37
in definition of experience, 28
Meditation, 15, 169, 417
brain function in, 417–418
Mediums, 288
early research, 7
Memory
confabulation, 52–53
cultural determinants, 52
in defining lucid dreaming, 152
false, 266–267, 270–271
limitations of introspective reports, 52–53
reliability over time, 383–384
retrieval in hypnosis, 265–266
self-reports of psi-related experiences, 241
source monitoring, 101–102
state-specific, 56–57
Mental Health Research Institute Unusual Perceptions Schedule, 87–88
Methodological issues, 10–11
alien abduction experience research, 274–275
altered states of consciousness research, 58–68
anomalous healing research, 370, 372, 383–385
case collections, 240–241
experient's recall of events, 241
experimenter effects, 53, 56
investigator bias, 242, 303
longitudinal research, 42
lucid dreaming research, 171–173
meta-analysis, 235–236
mystical experiences research, 427–429
near-death experience research, 342–345
out-of-body experience research, 205–206
past-life experience research, 302–306
phenomenological research methods, 59–63
psi-related experience research, 235–237
psychophenomenological research methods, 64–68

reliability–validity of self-reports about cognition, 50–57, 71–72
subjectivity of scientific method, 71
synesthesia research, 139–142
technical integration, 63–64
Migraines, 197
Miracle, 358
Mood disorders, 137
Motivation
in support of questionable beliefs, 9
Munchausen's syndrome, 268
Myoclonic convulsions, 333
Mystical experience
adverse reactions, 415
aftereffects, 402–405
assessment, 427–428
biological markers, 405–406
brain dysfunction as source of, 335
case examples, 398–400
in children, 407–408
contextual explanations, 426–427
current conceptualization, 429–430
diabolical, 405, 411
erotic content, 402
explanations, 416–427
extrovertive, 401
features of, 397–398, 400–401
hallucinogenic drugs and, 403–404, 410
humanistic perspectives, 422–423
individual differences, 429
induced, 402
introvertive, 401
Jungian interpretation, 420–422
light in, 425
limits of verbal description, 53
near-death experiences as, 315–316, 318
neuropsychological models, 416–418
opportunities for research, 430
out-of-body experience and, 195–196
perceptual–cognitive explanations, 424–425
personality correlates, 408–409
personality traits associated with, 39
prevalence, 406–407
psi-related phenomenon as, 237–238
psychoanalytic interpretation, 418–420
psychopathology and, 402, 410–412, 415, 429
religious conversion experience and, 409

Perceptual processes (*continued*)
in near-death experience, 338
observational errors as basis for false
belief, 8
out-of-body experiences and distortions
of, 194
sensitivity measures, 105–106
signal detection theory, 105–106
synesthesia, 11–12, 125–127
Personality
alien abduction experients, 262–267
anomalous healers, 366
boundary deficit, 262–263
characteristics of disease survivors,
368–369
of children with past-life experiences,
295–296
correlates of out-of-body experience,
191, 198
encounter prone, 323, 324
individual peculiarity, 31–32
lucid dreaming correlates, 165–166
near-death experients, 320–321
predisposition to mystical experiences,
408–409
predisposition to psi-related experiences, 228
psychically sensitive persons, 264–265
synesthesia correlates, 133–134
traits associated with encounter experiences, 71
traits common to psychopathology and
anomalous experience, 38–39
Pharmacotherapy
for hallucinating persons, 107–108
near-death experience related to delirium induced by, 334
for problems related to near-death experience, 331
Phenomenology
altered states of consciousness research,
59–64
of anomalous experience, 29, 30–31
anomalous healing experiences and
events, 360–367, 383
concurrent reporting, 60–61
diagnosis of psychopathology and, 34
hallucinations, 88–91, 95–96
lucid dreaming, 151, 153, 154–156
near-death experiences, 317–319
out-of-body experience, 183–184, 186–
187, 206–207

psi-related experiences, 223–225
retrospective reporting, 61–64
synesthesia, 121–122, 124–127
Phenomenology of Consciousness Inventory, 65–68
Physical component of anomalous experience
aftereffects of alien abduction experience, 256–257
anomalous healing outcomes, 371–374,
379–380, 384–385
biological markers of anomalous healing, 367–368
biological markers of hallucination, 91
classification of experiences, 30–31
explanations of anomalous healing,
377–382
lucid dreaming, 157–162, 170, 172
medical conditions associated with hallucinations, 93
mystical experience, 405–406, 416–
418
near-death experience hypotheses,
333–338
out-of-body experience, 189–190, 197
past-life experience, 293–294
Placebo effect, 376, 378–379
Pleasant anomalous experience, 30
auditory hallucinations, 89
diagnosis of psychopathology and, 34
positive experience, 36–37
Positive and Negative Syndrome Schedule, 87
Postmodern approach, 3, 430
Posttraumatic stress disorder
near-death experience and, 325–326
Prayer, 379–380
Precognition
See also Psi-related experiences
definition, 220
Present State Examination, 87
Psi-related experiences, 12–13
aftereffects, 225–227
assessment, 220, 221, 233, 243
benefits of, 227, 231
case collections, 223, 240–241
case example, 219–220
circumstances of, 224–225
clinical approach, 233–235, 242–243
cultural context, 221, 222, 226, 232–
233
definition, 220–221

Sleep
anomalies among alien abduction experients, 265
forms of consciousness in, 156
lucid dreaming physiology, 153, 158–161, 170, 172
paradoxical, 173
physiological correlates of out-of-body experience, 189–190
REM cycle, 158–162, 170, 172
transition states, 193, 202
Society for Psychical Research, 6
Sorcerers, 365
Source monitoring, 101–107
Spiritism, 362
Spiritual healing, 358
Spontaneous remission, 358, 362–363
Stroop effect, 139–142
Subjective paranormal experience psychosis, 230–231
Subliminal self, 408, 409
Substance use
See also specific drug; specific type of drug
contributions to anomalous experiencing, 37
hallucinations associated with, 37, 93, 327
out-of-body experience and, 185, 196
Synesthesia, 4, 11–12, 17
among artists, 127, 133–135
awareness and, 30
brain function in, 39, 131–133, 140, 143–144
color temperature, 128
as colored hearing, 123, 136, 144
common features, 139
conscious mediation, 136–137
consistency, 124, 137
constitutional, 124
continuum model, 131
definition, 11, 121
developmental course, 135–139
etiology, 35
frequency, 123
individual differences, 134–136
intermodal relations, 127–131, 140
learning theory, 125, 128, 144–145
lexical, 123, 125–126, 132
neural encoding in, 143–144
out-of-body experience and, 203
perceptual, 125–127
personality traits associated with, 39, 133–134

phenomenology, 121–122, 124–127
psychopathology and, 133–134
research methodologies, 139–142
response times, 140–141
sensory, 125
strong form, 123–124, 131, 136–137
Stroop effect, 139–140
theories, 131–133, 142–143
visual hearing, 127, 128–131
weak form, 122–123, 131, 136–137
Systems theory, 380–382

Telepathy, 229
See also Psi-related experiences
definition, 220
prevalence, 222
Therapeutic relationship
psychophysiological interactions, 378
significance of psi-related experiences, 232
Thinking out loud, 60
Thought sampling, 61
Time travel, 31
Trait negative affectivity, 38
Trances, 399
Transcendent experience, 318, 319
Transference–countertransference issues
placebo effects, 379
significance of psi-related experiences, 232
Transforming experiences, 31. *See also* Life-changing events
Transliminality, 409
Transpersonal psychology, 423–424
lucid dreaming, theories of, 170–171
Trauma
See also Childhood trauma
in anomalous experience and psychopathology, 39–40
neurobiological response, 335–336
Trophotropic arousal, 417

Unconscious
collective, 420–422
sensory processing in out-of-body experience, 202, 203
as source of alien abduction experiences, 272

Veridicality
  of alien abduction experience, 273–
    274
  assessment of anomalous experiences,
    73
  of introspective reports, 54–55
  out-of-body experience, 187, 199–
    200
  of psi phenomena, 4, 211
  peculiarity and, 27–28
  recognizing nonveridical sensory per-
    ception, 28–29
  of research data, 55
Vibrational medicine, 355
Visual hallucinations
  cultural correlates, 97

epidemiology, 94, 95
Visual hearing, 127
Volition
  in classification of anomalous experi-
    ence, 30
  diagnosis of psychopathology and, 34
  individual differences in hypnosis, 69

Wishful thinking, 8
Witnessing dreaming, 156

Xenoglossy, 288

Yogic states, 174–175

ABOUT THE EDITORS

Etzel Cardeña, PhD, is a native of México. He received his doctorate in psychology from the University of California, Davis, and is a former post-doctoral fellow at Stanford University. He is currently a fellow and president elect of Division 30 (Psychological Hypnosis) of American Psychological Association (APA) and of the Society for Clinical and Experimental Hypnosis (SCEH), editor of *Psychological Hypnosis*, and associate editor of the *American Journal of Clinical Hypnosis*, and *Trauma and Dissociation*. He is coeditor of *Clinical Hypnosis and Self-Regulation* and has published more than 70 articles and chapters on hypnotic, dissociative, and related phenomena and acute reactions to trauma. From his empirical and theoretical work, he has received, among others, the Ernest R. Hilgard and Morton Prince awards, and the Early Career Achievement Award from APA Division 30.

Steven Jay Lynn, PhD, is a professor of psychology at the State University of New York at Binghamton. He is a former president of the APA's Division 30 (Psychological Hypnosis) and a diplomate of the American Board of Professional Psychology and of the American Board of Psychological Hypnosis. He has received awards for the Best Books Published in 1991, 1992, and 1993 from the Society for Clinical and Experimental Hypnosis and is an advisory editor to many professional journals, including the *Journal of Abnormal Psychology*. Dr. Lynn has published more than 170 books, articles, and chapters on hypnosis, memory, victimization, and psychotherapy.

Stanley Krippner, PhD, is a professor of psychology at the Saybrook Graduate School and Research Center in San Francisco, CA. He is the former Director of the Dream Laboratory, Maimonides Medical Center, Brooklyn, and the former director of the Child Study Center, Kent State University.

He is a charter member of both the International Society for the Study of Dissociation and the American Creativity Association and is past president of APA Divisions 30 and 32, the Association for the Study of Dreams, the Parapsychological Association, and the Association for Humanistic Psychology. He is coeditor of several books, including *Broken Images, Broken Selves: Dissociative Narratives in Clinical Practice*, and is editor of *Dreamtime and Dreamwork*. During his career, he has received numerous awards, including the Pathfinder Award from the Association for Humanistic Psychology in 1998, the Charlotte and Karl Buhler Award from APA Division 32 in 1992, the Bicentennial Medal from the University of Georgia in 1985, and the Membership Service Award from the National Association for Gifted Children in 1981.